Wesley's Notes on the Bible
The Old Testament: Genesis - Ruth
by John Wesley
Edited by Anthony Uyl

Woodstock, Ontario, 2017

Wesley's Notes on the Bible - The Old Testament: Genesis - Ruth
by John Wesley
Edited by Anthony Uyl

The text of Wesley's Notes on the Bible - The Old Testament: Genesis - Ruth is all in the Public Domain. This edition is published by Devoted Publishing a division of 2165467 Ontario Inc.

**What kind of philosophies do you have?
Let us know!**

Contact us at: devotedpub@hotmail.com
Visit our shop on Facebook: @DevotedPublishing

Published in Woodstock, Ontario, Canada 2017

For bulk educational rates, please contact us at the above email address.

ISBN: 978-1-77356-067-0

John Wesley

Table of Contents

PREFACE 4
NOTES ON THE FIRST BOOK OF MOSES CALLED GENESIS 8
NOTES ON THE SECOND BOOK OF MOSES CALLED EXODUS 87
NOTES ON THE THIRD BOOK OF MOSES CALLED LEVITICUS 140
NOTES ON THE FOURTH BOOK OF MOSES CALLED NUMBERS 174
NOTES ON THE FIFTH BOOK OF MOSES CALLED DEUTERONOMY 212
NOTES ON THE BOOK OF JOSHUA 248
NOTES ON THE BOOK OF JUDGES 280
NOTES ON THE BOOK OF RUTH 309

PREFACE

ABOUT ten years ago I was prevailed upon to publish Explanatory Notes upon the New Testament. When that work was begun, and indeed when it was finished, I had no design to attempt anything farther of the kind. Nay, I had a full determination, Not to do it, being throughly fatigued with the immense labour (had it been only this; tho' this indeed was but a small part of it,) of writing twice over a Quarto book containing seven or eight hundred pages.

2. But this was scarce published before I was importuned to write Explanatory Notes upon the Old Testament. This importunity I have withstood for many years. Over and above the deep conviction I had, of my insufficiency for such a work, of my want of learning, of understanding, of spiritual experience, for an undertaking more difficult by many degrees, than even writing on the New Testament, I objected, That there were many passages in the Old, which I did not understand myself, and consequently could not explain to others, either to their satisfaction, or my own. Above all, I objected the want of time: Not only as I have a thousand other employments, but as my Day is near spent, as I am declined into the vale of years. And to this day it appears to me as a dream, a thing almost incredible, that I should be entering upon a work of this kind, when I am entering into the sixty-third year of my age.

3. Indeed these considerations, the last particular, still appear to me of such weight, that I cannot entertain a thought of composing a body of Notes on the whole Old Testament. All the question remaining was, "Is there extant any Exposition which is worth abridging?" Abundantly less time will suffice for this and less abilities of every kind. In considering this question, I soon turned my thought on the well-known Mark Henry. He is allowed by all competent Judges, to have been a person of strong understanding, of various learning, of solid piety, and much experience in the ways of God. And his exposition is generally clear and intelligible, the thoughts being expressed in plain words: It is also found, agreeable to the tenor of scripture, and to the analogy of faith. It is frequently full, giving a sufficient explication of the passages which require explaining. It is in many parts deep, penetrating farther into the inspired writings than most other comments do. It does not entertain us with vain speculations, but is practical throughout: and usually spiritual too teaching us how to worship God, not in form only, but in spirit and in truth.

4. But it may be reasonably inquired, "If Mark Henry's exposition be not only plain, sound, full, and deep, but practical, yea and spiritual too, what need is there of any other? Or how is it possible to mend This? to alter it for the better?" I answer, very many who have This, have no need of any other: particularly those who believe (what runs thro' the whole work and will much recommend it to them) the doctrine of absolution, irrespective, unconditional Predestination. I do not advise these, much to trouble themselves about any other exposition than Mark Henry's: this is sufficient, thro' the assistance of the Blessed Spirit, to make private Christians wise unto salvation, and (the Lord applying his word) throughly furnished unto every good work.

5. But then it is manifest on the other hand, every one cannot have this exposition. It is too large a purchase: there are thousands who would rejoice to have it; but it bears too high a price. They have not Six Guineas (the London price) in the world, perhaps from one year's end to another. And if they sometimes have, yet they have it not to spare; they need it for other occasions. How much soever therefore they desire so valuable a work, they must content themselves to go without it.

6. But suppose they have money enough to purchase, yet they have not time enough to read it: the size is as unsurmountable an objection as the price itself. It is not possible for men who have their daily bread to earn by the sweat of their brows, who generally are confined to their work, from six in the morning 'till six in the evening, to find leisure for reading over six folios, each containing seven or eight hundred pages. These therefore have need of some other exposition than Mark Henry's. As excellent as it is in its kind, it is not for their purpose; seeing they have neither money to make the purchase, nor time to read it over.

7. It is very possible then to mend this work valuable as it is, at least by shortening it. As the grand objection to it is the size, that objection may be removed: and they who at present have no possibility of profiting by it, while it is of so great a bulk and so high a price, may then enjoy part at least of the same advantage with those who have more money and more leisure. Few I presume that have the whole and leisure to read it, will concern themselves with an extract. But those who cannot have all, will (for the

present at least) be glad to have a part. And they who complain it is too short, may yet serve themselves of it, 'till they can procure the long work.

8. But I apprehend this valuable work may be made more valuable still, by making it plainer as well as shorter. Accordingly what is here extracted from it, (which indeed makes but a small part of the following volumes) is considerably plainer than the original. In order to this not only all the Latin sentences occasionally interspersed are omitted, but whatever phrases or words are not so intelligible to persons of no education. Those only who frequently and familiarly converse with men that are wholly uneducated, can conceive how many expressions are mere Greek to them, which are quite natural to those who have any share of learning. It is not by reading, much less by musing alone, that we are enabled to suit our discourse to common capacities. It is only by actually talking with the vulgar, that we learn to talk in a manner they can understand. And unless we do this, what do we profit them? Do we not lose all our labour? Should we speak as angels, we should be of no more use to them, than sounding brass or a tinkling cymbal.

9. Nay I apprehend what is extracted from Mark Henry's work, may in some sense be more sound than the original. Understand me right: I mean more conformable to that glorious declaration, God willeth all men to be saved, and to come to the knowledge of his truth. And let it not be objected, That the making any alteration with regard to a point of doctrine, is a misrepresentation of the author's sense, and consequently an injury done to him. It would so, if an alteration were made of his words, so as to make them bear a different meaning; or if any words were recited as His, which he did not write. But neither of these is the case. Nothing is recited here as written by him which he did not write. Neither is any construction put upon his words, different from his own. But what he wrote in favour of Particular Redemption, is totally left out. And of this I here give express notice to the reader once for all.

10. Again. It certainly possible that a work abundantly shorter than Mark Henry's may nevertheless be considerably fuller, in some particulars. There are many words which he passes over without any explanation at all; as taking it for granted that the reader already knows the meaning of them. But this is a supposition not to be made; it is an entire mistake. For instance: What does a common man know of an Omer, or a Hin? "Why Moses explains his own meaning: "An Omer is the tenth part of an ephah." True; but what does the honest man know of an ephah? Just as much as of an Omer. I suppose that which led Mark Henry into these omissions, which otherwise are unaccountable, was the desire of not saying what others had said before, Mark Pool in particular. This is easily gathered from his own words, "Mark Pool's English Annotations are of admirable use; especially for "the explaining of scripture phrases, opening the sense and clearing "of difficulties. I have industriously declined as much as I could what "is to be found there." I wish he had not. Or at least that he had given us the same sense in other words. Indeed he adds, "Those "and other annotations are most easy to be consulted upon occasion." Yes by those that have them: but that is not the case with the generality of Mark Henry's readers. And besides they may justly expect that so large a comment will leave them no occasion to consult others.

11. It is possible likewise to penetrate deeper into the meaning of some scriptures than Mark Henry has done. Altho' in general he is far from being a superficial writer, yet he is not always the same. Indeed if he had, he must have been more than man, considering the vastness of his work. It was scarce possible for any human understanding, to furnish out such a number of folios, without sinking sometimes into trite reflections and observations, rather lively than deep. A stream that runs wide and covers a large tract of land, will be shallow in some places. If it had been confined within a moderate channel, it might have flowed deep all along.

12. Nay, it cannot be denied, that there may be an exposition of scripture more closely practical, than some parts of Mark Henry's are, as well as more spiritual. Even his exposition of the twentieth chapter of Exodus, where one would naturally have expected to find a compleat scheme of Christian practice, does not answer that expectation. Nor do I remember that he has any where given us, a satisfactory account of Spiritual Religion, of the kingdom of God within us, the fruit of Christ dwelling and reigning in the heart. This I hoped to have found particularly in the exposition of our Lord's Sermon upon the mount. But I was quite disappointed of my hope. It was not by any means what I expected.

13. I do not therefore intend the following Notes for a bare abridgment of Mark Henry's exposition. Far from it: I not only omit much more than nineteen parts out of twenty of what he has written, but make many alterations and many additions, well nigh from the beginning to the end. In particular, I everywhere omit the far greater part of his inferences from and improvement of the chapter. They who think these the most valuable part of the work, may have recourse to the author himself. I likewise omit great part of almost every note, the sum of which is retained: as it seems to be his aim, to say as much, whereas it is mine to say as little as possible. And I omit abundance of quaint sayings and lively antitheses; as, "God feeds his birds. Shall he not feed his babes!" "Pharaoh's princes: his pimps rather." Indeed every thing of this kind which occurred I have left quite untouched: altho' I am sensible these are the very flowers which numberless readers admire; nay which many, I doubt not, apprehend to be the chief beauties of the book. For that very reason I cannot but wish, they had never had a place

therein; for this is a blemish, which is exceeding catching: he that admires it, will quickly imitate it. I used once to wonder, whence some whom I greatly esteem, had so many pretty turns in preaching. But when I read Mark Henry, my wonder ceased. I saw, they were only copying after him: altho' many of them probably without designing or even adverting to it. They generally consulted his exposition of their text, and frequently just before preaching. And hence little witticisms and a kind of archness insensibly stole upon them, and took place of that strong, manly eloquence, which they would otherwise have learned from the inspired writers.

14. With regard to alterations, in what I take from Mark Henry, I continually alter hard words into easy, and long sentences into short. But I do not knowingly alter the sense of any thing I extract from him, I only endeavour in several places, to make it more clear and determinate. I have here and there taken the liberty of altering a word in the text. But this I have done very sparingly, being afraid of venturing too far; as being conscious of my very imperfect acquaintance with the Hebrew tongue. I have added very largely from Mark Pool, as much as seemed necessary for common readers, in order to their understanding those words or passages, which Mark Henry does not explain. Nay, from the time that I had more maturely considered Mark Pool's annotations on the Bible, (which was soon after I had gone thro' the book of Genesis) I have extracted far more from him than from Mark Henry: it having been my constant method, after reading the text, first to read and weigh what Mark Pool observed upon every verse, and afterwards to consult Mark Henry's exposition of the whole paragraph. In consequence of this, instead of short additions from Mark Pool to supply what was wanting in Mark Henry, (which was my first design) I now only make extracts from Mark Henry, to supply so far as they are capable, what was wanting in Mark Pool. I say, so far as they are capable: for I still found in needful to add to both such farther observations, as have from time to time occurred to my own mind in reading or thinking on the scriptures, together with such as I have occasionally extracted from other authors.

15. Every thinking man will now easily discern my design in the following sheets. It is not, to write sermons, essays or set discourses, upon any part of scripture. It is not to draw inferences from the text, or to shew what doctrines may be proved thereby. It is this: To give the direct, literal meaning, of every verse, of every sentence, and as far as I am able, of every word in the oracles of God. I design only, like the hand of a dial, to point every man to This: not to take up his mind with something else, how excellent soever: but to keep his eye fixt upon the naked Bible, that he may read and hear it with understanding. I say again, (and desire it may be well observed, that none may expect what they will not find) It is not my design to write a book, which a man may read separate from the Bible: but barely to assist those who fear God, in hearing and reading the bible itself, by shewing the natural sense of every part, in as few and plain words as I can.

16. And I am not without hopes, that the following notes may in some measure answer this end, not barely to unlettered and ignorant men, but also to men of education and, learning: (altho' it is true, neither these nor the Notes on the New Testament were principally designed for Them.) Sure I am, that tracts wrote in the most plain and simple manner, are of infinitely more service to me, than those which are elabourated with the utmost skill, and set off with the greatest pomp of erudition.

17. But it is no part of my design, to save either learned or unlearned men from the trouble of thinking. If so, I might perhaps write Folios too, which usually overlay, rather than help the thought. On the contrary, my intention is, to make them think, and assist them in thinking. This is the way to understand the things of God; Meditate thereon day and night; So shall you attain the best knowledge; even to know the only true God and Jesus Christ whom He hath sent. And this knowledge will lead you, to love Him, because he hath first loved us: yea, to love the Lord your God with all your heart, and with all your soul, and with all your mind, and with all your strength. Will there not then be all that mind in you, which was also in Christ Jesus? And in consequence of this, while you joyfully experience all the holy tempers described in this book, you will likewise be outwardly holy as He that hath called you is holy, in all manner of conversation.

18. If you desire to read the scripture in such a manner as may most effectually answer this end, would it not be advisable,

1. To set apart a little time, if you can, every morning and evening for that purpose?

2. At each time if you have leisure, to read a chapter out of the Old, and one out of the New Testament: is you cannot do this, to take a single chapter, or a part of one?

3. To read this with a single eye, to know the whole will of God, and a fixt resolution to do it? In order to know his will, you should,

4. Have a constant eye to the analogy of faith; the connection and harmony there is between those grand, fundamental doctrines, Original Sin, Justification by Faith, the New Birth, Inward and Outward Holiness.

5. Serious and earnest prayer should be constantly used, before we consult the oracles of God, seeing "scripture can only be understood thro' the same Spirit whereby "it was given." Our reading should likewise be closed with prayer, that what we read may be written on our hearts.

6. It might also be of use, if while we read, we were frequently to pause, and examine ourselves by

John Wesley

what we read, both with regard to our hearts, and lives. This would furnish us with matter of praise, where we found God had enabled us to conform to his blessed will, and matter of humiliation and prayer, where we were conscious of having fallen short. And whatever light you then receive, should be used to the uttermost, and that immediately. Let there be no delay. Whatever you resolve, begin to execute the first moment you can. So shall you find this word to be indeed the power of God unto present and eternal salvation. EDINBURGH, April 25, 1765.

NOTES ON THE FIRST BOOK OF MOSES CALLED GENESIS

THE Holy Bible, or Book, is so called by way of eminency, as it is the best book that ever was written. The great things of God's law and gospel are here written, that they might be reduced to a greater certainty, might spread farther, remain longer, and be transmitted to distant places and ages, more pure and entire than possibly they could be by tradition. That part of the Bible which we call the Old Testament, contains the acts and monuments of the church from the creation, almost to the coming of Christ in the flesh, which was about four thousand years: the truths then revealed, the laws enacted, the prophecies given, and the chief events that concerned the church. This is called a testament or covenant, because it was a declaration of the will of God concerning man in a federal way, and had its force from the designed death of the great testator, the Lamb slain from the foundation of the world, Rev. xiii, 8 - 'Tis called the Old Testament with relation to the New, which doth not cancel, but crown and perfect it, by bringing in that better hope which was typified and foretold in it. This part of the Old Testament we call the Pentateuch, or five books of Moses. These books were, probably, the first that ever were written; for we have no mention of any writing in all the book of Genesis, nor 'till God bid Moses write, Exod. xvii, 14. and set him his copy in the writing of the ten commandments upon the tables of stone. However, we are sure these books are the most ancient writings now extant. The first of these, which we call Genesis, Moses probably wrote in the wilderness, after he had been in the mount with God. And as he framed the tabernacle, so he did the more excellent and durable fabric of this book, according to the pattern shewed him in the mount: into which it is better to resolve the certainty of the things herein contained, than into any tradition which possibly might be handed down to the family of Jacob.-Genesis is a name borrowed from the Greek: it signifies the original or generation: fitly is this book so called, for it is a history of originals; the creation of the world, the entrance of sin and death into it, the invention of arts, the rise of nations, and especially the planting of the church, and the state of it in its early days. 'Tis also a history of generations, the generations of Adam, Noah, Abraham, &c. - The beginning of the New Testament is called Genesis too, Matt. i, 1, the book of the Genesis, or generation of Jesus Christ. Lord, open our eyes, that we may see the wondrous things both of thy law and gospel!

I

The holy scripture, being designed to maintain and improve natural religion, to repair the decays of it. and supply the defects of it, since the fall, lays down at first this principle of the unclouded light of nature: That this world was, in the beginning of time, created by a Being of infinite wisdom and power, who was himself before all time, and all worlds. And the first verse of the Bible gives us a surer and better, a more satisfying and useful knowledge of the origin of the universe, than all the volumes of the philosophers. We have three things in this chapter.

I. A general idea of the work of creation, ver. 1, 2.

II. A particular account of the several days work, distinctly and in order. The creation of light, the first day, ver. 3-5. Of the firmament, the second day, ver. 6-8. Of the sea, the earth and its fruits, the third day, ver. 9-13. Of the lights of heaven, the fourth day, ver. 14-19. Of the fish and fowl, the fifth day, ver. 20-23. Of the beasts, ver. 24, 25. Of man, ver. 26-28. And food for both, the sixth day, ver. 29, 30.

III. The review and approbation of the whole work, ver. 31.
    1. Observe here.
    1. The effect produced, The heaven and the earth - That is, the world, including the whole frame and furniture of the universe. But 'tis only the visible part of the creation that Moses designs to give an account of. Yet even in this there are secrets which cannot be fathomed, nor accounted for. But from what we see of heaven and earth, we may infer the eternal power and godhead of the great Creator. And let our make and place, as men, mind us of our duty, as Christians, which is always to keep heaven in our eye, and the earth under our feet. Observe

2. The author and cause of this great work, God. The Hebrew word is Elohim; which (1.) seems to mean The Covenant God, being derived from a word that signifies to swear. (2.) The plurality of persons in the Godhead, Father, Son, and Holy Ghost. The plural name of God in Hebrew, which speaks of him as many, tho' he be but one, was to the Gentiles perhaps a favour of death unto death, hardening them in their idolatry; but it is to us a favour of life unto life, confirming our faith in the doctrine of the Trinity, which, tho' but darkly intimated in the Old Testament, is clearly revealed in the New. Observe

3. The manner how this work was effected; God created, that is, made it out of nothing. There was not any pre-existent matter out of which the world was produced. The fish and fowl were indeed produced out of the waters, and the beasts and man out of the earth; but that earth and those waters were made out of nothing. Observe

4. When this work was produced; In the beginning - That is, in the beginning of time. Time began with the production of those beings that are measured by time. Before the beginning of time there was none but that Infinite Being that inhabits eternity. Should we ask why God made the world no sooner, we should but darken counsel by words without knowledge; for how could there be sooner or later in eternity?

2. Where we have an account of the first matter, and the first Mover.

1. A chaos was the first matter. 'Tis here called the earth, (tho' the earth, properly taken, was not made 'till the third day, ver. 10) because it did most resemble that which was afterwards called earth, a heavy unwieldy mass. 'Tis also called the deep, both for its vastness, and because the waters which were afterwards separated from the earth were now mixed with it. This mighty bulk of matter was it, out of which all bodies were afterwards produced. The Creator could have made his work perfect at first, but by this gradual proceeding he would shew what is ordinarily the method of his providence, and grace. This chaos, was without form and void. Tohu and Bohu, confusion and emptiness, so those words are rendered, Isaiah xxxiv, 11. 'Twas shapeless, 'twas useless, 'twas without inhabitants, without ornaments; the shadow or rough draught of things to come. To those who have their hearts in heaven, this lower world, in comparison of the upper, still appears to be confusion and emptiness. And darkness was upon the face of the deep-God did not create this darkness, (as he is said to create the darkness of affliction, Isaiah xlv, 7.) for it was only the want of light.

2. The Spirit of God was the first Mover; He moved upon the face of the waters - He moved upon the face of the deep, as the hen gathereth her chicken under her wings, and hovers over them, to warm and cherish them, Matt. xxiii, 37 as the eagle stirs up her nest, and fluttereth over her young, ('tis the same word that is here used) Deut. xxxii, 11.

3, 4, 5. We have here a farther account of the first day's work. In which observe,

1. That the first of all visible beings which God created was light, the great beauty and blessing of the universe: like the first-born, it doth, of all visible beings, most resemble its great parent in purity and power, brightness and beneficence.

2. That the light was made by the word of God's power; He said, Let there be light - He willed it, and it was done; there was light - Such a copy as exactly answered the original idea in the eternal mind.

3. That the light which God willed, he approved of. God saw the light, that it was good - 'Twas exactly as he designed it; and it was fit to answer the end for which he designed it.

4. That God divided the light from the darkness - So put them asunder as they could never be joined together: and yet he divided time between them, the day for light, and the night for darkness, in a constant succession. Tho' the darkness was now scattered by the light, yet it has its place, because it has its use; for as the light of the morning befriends the business of the day, so the shadows of the evening befriend the repose of the night. God has thus divided between light and darkness, because he would daily mind us that this is a world of mixtures and changes. In heaven there is perpetual light, and no darkness; in hell utter darkness, and no light: but in this world they are counter-changed, and we pass daily from one to another; that we may learn to expect the like vicissitudes in the providence of God.

5. That God divided them from each other by distinguishing names. He called the light Day, and the darkness he called night - He gave them names as Lord of both. He is the Lord of time, and will be so 'till day and night shall come to an end, and the stream of time be swallowed up in the ocean of eternity.

6. That this was the first day's work, The evening and the morning were the first day - The darkness of the evening was before the light of the morning, that it might set it off, and make it shine the brighter. See note at "ver. 3"

6, 7, 8. We have here an account of the second day's work, the creation of the firmament. In which observe,

1. The command of God: Let there be a firmament - An expansion; so the Hebrew word signifies, like a sheet spread, or a curtain drawn out. This includes all that is visible above the earth, between it and the third heavens, the air, its higher, middle, and lower region, the celestial globe, and all the orbs of light above; it reaches as high as the place where the stars are fixed, for that is called here the firmament

of heaven, ver. 14, 15, and as low as the place where the birds fly for that also is called the firmament of heaven, ver. 20.

2. The creation of it: and God made the firmament.

3. The design of it; to divide the waters from the waters-That is, to distinguish between the waters that are wrapt up in the clouds, and those that cover the sea; the waters in the air, and those in the earth.

4. The naming it: He called the firmament Heaven - 'Tis the visible heaven, the pavement of the holy city. The height of the heavens should mind us of God's supremacy, and the infinite distance that is between us and him; the brightness of the heavens, and their purity, should mind us of his majesty, and perfect holiness; the vastness of the heavens, and their encompassing the earth, and influence upon it, should mind us of his immensity and universal providence. See note at "ver. 6"

9, 10, 11, 12, 13. The third day's work is related in these verses; the forming the sea and the dry land, and making the earth fruitful. Hitherto the power of the Creator had been employed about the upper part of the visible world; now he descends to this lower world, designed for the children of men, both for their habitation, and their maintenance. And here we have an account of the fitting of it for both; the building of their house, and the spreading of their table. Observe,

1. How the earth was prepared to be a habitation for man by the gathering of the waters together, and making the dry land appear. Thus, instead of that confusion which was, when earth and water were mixed in one great mass; now there is order, by such a separation as rendered them both useful. (1.) The waters which covered the earth were ordered to retire, and to gather into one place, viz. those hollows which were fitted for their reception. The waters thus lodged in their proper place, he called Seas; for though they are many, in distant regions, yet either above ground or under ground, they have communication with each other, and so they are one, and the common receptacle of waters, into which all the rivers run. (2.) The dry land was made to appear, and emerge out of the waters, and was called Earth. Observe,

2. How the earth was furnished for the support of man, ver. 11, 12. Present provision was made, by the immediate products of the earth, which, in obedience to God's command, was no sooner made but it became fruitful. Provision was likewise made for time to come, by the perpetuating of the several species of vegetables, every one having its seed in itself after its kind, that during the continuance of man upon the earth, food might be fetched out of the earth, for his use and benefit. See note at "ver. 9"

14, 15, 16, 17, 18, 19. This is the history of the fourth day's work, the creating the sun, moon and stars. Of this we have an account,

1. In general, verse 14, 15. where we have, (1.) The command given concerning them. Let there be lights in the firmament of heaven - God had said, ver. 3 Let there be light, and there was light; but that was, as it were, a chaos of light, scattered and confused; now it was collected and made into several luminaries, and so rendered both more glorious and more serviceable. (2.) The use they were intended to be of to this earth. [1.] They must be for the distinction of times, of day and night, summer and winter. [2.] They must be for the direction of actions: they are for signs of the change of weather, that the husbandman may order his affairs with discretion. They do also give light upon the earth - That we may walk John xi, 9 and work John ix, 4 according as the duty of every day requires. The lights of heaven do not shine for themselves, nor for the world of spirits above, they need them not; but they shine for us, and for our pleasure and advantage. Lord, what is man that he should be thus regarded, Psalm viii, 3, 4.

2. In particular, ver. 16, 17, 18, The lights of heaven are the sun, moon and stars, and these all are the work of God's hands. (1.) The sun is the greatest light of all, and the most glorious and useful of all the lamps of heaven; a noble instance of the Creator's wisdom, power and goodness, and an invaluable blessing to the creatures of this lower world. (2.) The moon is a lesser light, and yet is here reckoned one of the greater lights, because, though in regard of its magnitude, it is inferior to many of the stars, yet in respect of its usefulness to the earth, it is more excellent than they. (3.) He made the stars also - Which are here spoken of only in general; for the scriptures were written not to gratify our curiosity, but to lead us to God. Now, these lights are said to rule, ver. 16, 18; not that they have a supreme dominion as God has, but they are rulers under him. Here the lesser light, the moon, is said to rule the night; but Psalm lxxxvi, 9 the stars are mentioned as sharers in that government, the moon and stars to rule by night. No more is meant, but that they give light, Jer. xxxi, 35. The best and most honourable way of ruling is, by giving light, and doing good. See note at "ver. 14"

20, 21, 22, 23. Each day hitherto hath produced very excellent beings, but we do not read of the creation of any living creature till the fifth day. The work of creation not only proceeded gradually from one thing to another, but advanced gradually from that which was less excellent, to that which was more so. 'Twas on the fifth day that the fish and fowl were created, and both out of the waters. Observe,

1. The making of the fish and fowl at first. ver. 20, 21 God commanded them to be produced, he said, Let the waters bring forth abundantly - The fish in the waters, and the fowl out of them. This command he himself executed, God created great whales, &c.-Insects which are as various as any species of animals, and their structure as curious, were part of this day's work, some of them being allied to the fish, and others to the fowl. Notice is here taken of the various species of fish and fowl,

each after their kind; and of the great numbers of both that were produced, for the waters brought forth abundantly; and in particular of great whales the largest of fishes, whose bulk and strength, are remarkable proofs of the power and greatness of the Creator. Observe, 2, The blessing of them in order to their continuance. Life is a wasting thing, its strength is not the strength of stones; therefore the wise Creator not only made the individuals, but provided for the propagating of the several species, ver. 22. God blessed them, saying, Be fruitful, and multiply - Fruitfulness is the effect of God's blessing, and must be ascribed to it; the multiplying of the fish and fowl from year to year, is still the fruit of this blessing here. See note at "ver. 20"

24, 25. We have here the first part of the sixth day's work. The sea was the day before replenished with fish, and the air with fowl; and this day are made the beasts of the earth, cattle, and the creeping things that pertain to the earth. Here, as before,

1. The Lord gave the word: he said, Let The earth bring forth - Let these creatures come into being upon the earth, and out of it, in their respective kinds.

2. He also did the work; he made them all after their kind - Not only of divers shapes, but of divers natures, manners, food, and fashions: In all which appears the manifold wisdom of the Creator. See note at "ver. 2".

26, 27, 28. We have here the second part of the sixth day's work, the creation of man, which we are in a special manner concerned to take notice of. Observe,

1. That man was made last of all the creatures, which was both an honour and a favour to him: an honour, for the creation was to advance from that which was less perfect, to that which was more so and a favour, for it was not fit he should be lodged in the palace designed for him, till it was completely fitted and furnished for his reception. Man, as soon as he was made, had the whole visible creation before him, both to contemplate, and to take the comfort of.

2. That man's creation was a mere signal act of divine wisdom and power, than that of the other creatures. The narrative of it is introduced with solemnity, and a manifest distinction from the rest. Hitherto it had been said, Let there be light, and Let there be a firmament: but now the word of command is turned into a word of consultation, Let us make man - For whose sake the rest of the creatures were made. Man was to be a creature different from all that had been hitherto made. Flesh and spirit, heaven and earth must be put together in him, and he must be allied to both worlds. And therefore God himself not only undertakes to make, but is pleased so to express himself, as if he called a council to consider of the making of him; Let us make man - The three persons of the Trinity, Father, Son, and Holy Ghost, consult about it, and concur in it; because man, when he was made, was to be dedicated and devoted to Father, Son, and Holy Ghost.

3. That man was made in God's image, and after his likeness; two words to express the same thing. God's image upon man, consists,

1. In his nature, not that of his body, for God has not a body, but that of his soul. The soul is a spirit, an intelligent, immortal spirit, an active spirit, herein resembling God, the Father of spirits, and the soul of the world.

2. In his place and authority. Let us make man in our image, and let him have dominion. As he has the government of the inferior creatures, he is as it were God's representative on earth. Yet his government of himself by the freedom of his will, has in it more of God's image, than his government of the creatures.

3. And chiefly in his purity and rectitude. God's image upon man consists in knowledge, righteousness, and true holiness, Eph. iv, 24; Colossians iii, 10. He was upright, Eccl. vii, 29. He had an habitual conformity of all his natural powers to the whole will of God. His understanding saw divine things clearly, and there were no errors in his knowledge: his will complied readily and universally with the will of God; without reluctancy: his affections were all regular, and he had no inordinate appetites or passions: his thoughts were easily fixed to the best subjects, and there was no vanity or ungovernableness in them. And all the inferior powers were subject to the dictates of the superior. Thus holy, thus happy, were our first parents, in having the image of God upon them. But how art thou fallen, O son of the morning? How is this image of God upon man defaced! How small are the remains of it, and how great the ruins of it! The Lord renew it upon our souls by his sanctifying grace!

4. That man was made male and female, and blessed with fruitfulness. He created him male and female, Adam and Eve: Adam first out of earth, and Eve out of his side. God made but one male and one female, that all the nations of men might know themselves to be made of one blood, descendants, from one common stock, and might thereby be induced to love one another. God having made them capable of transmitting the nature they had received, said to them, Be fruitful, and multiply, and replenish the earth - Here he gave them,

1. A large inheritance; replenish the earth, in which God has set man to be the servant of his providence, in the government of the inferior creatures, and as it were the intelligence of this orb; to be likewise the collector of his praises in this lower world, and lastly, to be a probationer for a better state.

2. A numerous lasting family to enjoy this inheritance; pronouncing a blessing upon them, in the

virtue of which, their posterity should extend to the utmost corners of the earth, and continue to the utmost period of time.

5. That God gave to man a dominion over the inferior creatures, over fish of the sea, and over the fowl of the air - Though man provides for neither, he has power over both, much more over every living thing that moveth upon the earth - God designed hereby to put an honour upon man, that he might find himself the more strongly obliged to bring honour to his Maker. See note at "ver. 26"

29, 30. We have here the third part of the sixth day's work, which was not any new creation, but a gracious provision of food for all flesh, Psalm lxxxvi, 25.-Here is,

1. Food provided for man, ver. 29. herbs and fruits must be his meat, including corn, and all the products of the earth. And before the earth was deluged, much more before it was cursed for man's sake, its fruits no doubt, were more pleasing to the taste, and more strengthening and nourishing to the body.

2. Food provided for the beasts, ver. 30. Doth God take care of oxen? Yes, certainly, he provides food convenient for them; and not for oxen only that were used in his sacrifices, and man's service, but even the young lions and the young ravens are the care of his providence, they ask and have their meat from God. See note at "ver. 29"

31. We have here the approbation and conclusion of the whole work of creation. Observe,

1. The review God took of his work, he saw every thing that he had made - So he doth still; all the works of his hands are under his eye; he that made all sees all.

2. The complacency God took in his work. When we come to review our works we find to our shame, that much has been very bad; but when God reviewed his, all was very good.

1. It was good. Good, for it is all agreeable to the mind of the creator. Good, for it answers the end of its creation. Good, for it is serviceable to man, whom God had appointed Lord of the visible creation. Good, for it is all for God's glory; there is that in the whole visible creation which is a demonstration of God's being and perfections, and which tends to beget in the soul of man a religious regard to him.

2. It was very good - Of each day's work (except the second) it was said that it was good, but now it is very good. For,

1. Now man was made, who was the chief of the ways of God, the visible image of the Creator's glory,

2. Now All was made, every part was good, but all together very good. The glory and goodness, the beauty and harmony of God's works both of providence and grace, as this of creation, will best appear when they are perfected.

3. The time when this work was concluded. The evening and the morning were the sixth day - So that in six days God made the world. We are not to think but that God could have made the world in an instant: but he did it in six days, that he might shew himself a free agent, doing his own work, both in his own way, and in his own time; that his wisdom, power and goodness, might appear to us, and be meditated upon by us, the more distinctly; and that he might set us an example of working six days, and resting the seventh. And now as God reviewed his work, let us review our meditations upon it; let us stir up ourselves, and all that is within us, to worship him that made the, heaven, earth, and sea, and the fountains of waters. All his works in all places of his dominion bless him, and therefore bless thou the Lord, O my soul.

II

This chapter is an appendix to the history of the creation, explaining, and enlarging on that part of it, which relates immediately to man. We have in it,

I. The institution of the sabbath, which was made for man, to further his holiness and comfort, ver. 1-3.

II. A more particular account of man's creation, as the summary of the whole work, ver. 4-7.

III. A description of the garden of Eden, and the placing of man in it under the obligations of a law and covenant, ver. 8-17.

IV. The creation of the woman, her marriage to the man, and the institution of the ordinance of marriage, ver. 18-25.

1, 2, 3. We have here, (1.) The settlement of the kingdom of nature, in God's resting from the work of creation, ver. 1, 2. Where observe,

1. That the creatures made both in heaven and earth, are the hosts or armies of them, which speaks them numerous, but marshalled, disciplined, and under command. God useth them as his hosts for the defense of his people, and the destruction of his enemies.

2. That the heavens and the earth are finished pieces, and so are all the creatures in them. So

perfect is God's work that nothing can be added to it or taken from it, Eccl iii, 14.

3. That after the end of the first six days, God ceased from all work of creation. He hath so ended his work, as that though in his providence he worketh hitherto, John v, 17. preserving and governing all the creatures, yet he doth not make any new species of creatures.

4. That the eternal God, tho' infinitely happy in himself, yet took a satisfaction in the work of his own hands. He did not rest as one weary, but as one well-pleased with the instances of his own goodness. (2.) The commencement of the kingdom of grace, in the sanctification of the sabbath day, ver. 3. He rested on that day, and took a complacency in his creatures, and then sanctified it, and appointed us on that day to rest and take a complacency in the Creator; and his rest is in the fourth commandment made a reason for ours after six days labour. Observe,

1. That the solemn observation of one day in seven as a day of holy rest, and holy work, is the indispensible duty of all those to whom God has revealed his holy sabbaths.

2. That sabbaths are as ancient as the world.

3. That the sabbath of the Lord is truly honourable, and we have reason to honour it; honour it for the sake of its antiquity, its great author, and the sanctification of the first sabbath by the holy God himself, and in obedience to him, by our first parents in innocency. See note at "ver. 1"

4, 5, 6, 7. In these verses,

1. Here is a name given to the Creator, which we have not yet met with, Jehovah. The LORD in capital letters, is constantly used in our English translation, for Jehovah. This is that great and incommunicable name of God, which speaks his having his being of himself, and his giving being to all things. It properly means, He that was, and that is, and that is to come.

2. Further notice taken of the production of plants and herbs, because they were made to be food for man.

3. A more particular account of the creation of man, ver. 7. Man is a little world, consisting of heaven and earth, soul and body. Here we have all account of the original of both, and the putting of both together: The Lord God, the great fountain of being and power, formed man. Of the other creatures it is said, they were created and made; but of man, that he was formed, which notes a gradual process in the work with great accuracy and exactness. To express the creation of this new thing, he takes a new word: a word (some think) borrowed from the potter's forming his vessel upon the wheel. The body of man is curiously wrought. And the soul takes its rise from the breath of heaven. It came immediately from God; he gave it to be put into the body, Eccl xii, 7 as afterwards he gave the tables of stone of his own writing to be put into the ark. 'Tis by it that man is a living soul, that is, a living man. The body would be a worthless, useless carcase, if the soul did not animate it. See note at "ver. 4"

8, 9, 10, 11, 12, 13, 14, 15. Man consisting of body and soul, a body made out of the earth, and a rational immortal soul, we have in these verses the provision that was made for the happiness of both. That part of man, which is allied to the world of sense, was made happy, for he was put in the paradise of God; that part which is allied to the world of spirits was well provided for, for he was taken into covenant with God. Here we have,

1. A description of the garden of Eden, which was intended for the palace of this prince. The inspired penman in this history writing for the Jews first, and calculating his narratives from the infant state of the church, describes things by their outward sensible appearances, and leaves us, by farther discoveries of the divine light, to be led into the understanding of the mysteries couched under them. Therefore he doth not so much insist upon the happiness of Adam's mind, as upon that of his outward estate. The Mosaic history, as well as the Mosaic law, has rather the patterns of heavenly things, than the heavenly things themselves, Heb. ix, 23. Observe, (1.) The place appointed for Adam's residence was a garden; not an ivory house. As clothes came in with sin, so did houses. The heaven was the roof of Adam's house, and never was any roof so curiously cieled and painted: the earth was his floor, and never was any floor so richly inlaid: the shadow of the trees was his retirement, and never were any rooms so finely hung: Solomon's in all their glory were not arrayed like them. (2.) The contrivance and furniture of this garden was the immediate work of God's wisdom and power. The Lord God planted this garden, that is, he had planted it, upon the third day when the fruits of the earth were made. We may well suppose it to be the most accomplished place that ever the sun saw, when the All-sufficient God himself designed it to be the present happiness of his beloved creature. (3.) The situation of this garden was extremely sweet; it was in Eden, which signifies delight and pleasure. The place is here particularly pointed out by such marks and bounds as were sufficient when Moses wrote, to specify the place to those who knew that country; but now it seems the curious cannot satisfy themselves concerning it. Let it be our care to make sure a place in the heavenly paradise, and then we need not perplex ourselves with a search after the place of the earthly paradise. (4.) The trees wherewith this garden was planted. [1.] It had all the best and choicest trees in common with the rest of the ground. It was beautified with every tree that was pleasant to the sight - It was enriched with every tree that yielded fruit grateful to the taste, and useful to the body. But, [2.] It had two extraordinary trees peculiar to itself, on earth there were not their like.

Wesley's Notes on the Bible - The Old Testament: Genesis - Ruth

1. There was the tree of life in the midst of the garden - Which was not so much a natural means to preserve or prolong life; but was chiefly intended to be a sign to Adam, assuring him of the continuance of life and happiness upon condition of his perseverance in innocency and obedience.

2. There was the tree of the knowledge of good and evil - So called, not because it had any virtue to beget useful knowledge, but because there was an express Revelation of the will of God concerning this tree, so that by it he might know good and evil. What is good? It is good not to eat of this tree: what is evil? To eat of this tree. The distinction between all other moral good and evil was written in the heart of man; but this, which resulted from a positive law, was written upon this tree. And in the event it proved to give Adam an experimental knowledge of good by the loss of it, and of evil by the sense of it. (5.) The rivers wherewith this garden was watered, ver. 10-14. These four rivers, (or one river branched into four streams) contributed much both to the pleasantness and the fruitfulness of this garden. Hiddekel and Euphrates are rivers of Babylon. Havilah had gold and spices and precious stones; but Eden had that which was infinitely better, the tree of life, and communion with God.

2. The command which God gave to man in innocency, and the covenant he than took him into. Hither we have seen God; man's powerful Creator, and his bountiful benefactor; now he appears as his ruler and lawgiver. See note at "ver. 8"

16, 17. Thou shall die - That is, thou shalt lose all the happiness thou hast either in possession or prospect; and thou shalt become liable to death, and all the miseries that preface and attend it. This was threatened as the immediate consequence of sin. In the day thou eatest, thou shalt die - Not only thou shalt become mortal, but spiritual death and the forerunners of temporal death shall immediately seize thee. See note at "ver. 17"

18, 19, 20. It is not good that man - This man, should be alone - Though there was an upper world of angels, and a lower world of brutes, yet there being none of the same rank of beings with himself, he might be truly said to be alone. And every beast of the field, and every fowl of the air God brought to Adam-Either by the ministry of angels, or by a special instinct that he might name them, and so might give a proof of his knowledge, the names he gave them being expressive of their inmost natures. See note at "ver. 18"

21, 22. This was done upon the sixth day, as was also the placing of Adam in paradise, though it be here mentioned after an account of the seventh day's rest: but what was said in general, chap. i, 27, that God made man male and female is more distinctly related here, God caused the sleep to fall on Adam, and made it a deep sleep, that so the opening of his side might be no grievance to him: while he knows no sin, God will take care he shall feel no pain. See note at "ver. 21"

23. And Adam said, this is now bone of my bones - Probably it was revealed to Adam in a vision, when he was asleep, that this lovely creature, now presented to him, was a piece of himself and was to be his companion, and the wife of his covenant - In token of his acceptance of her, he gave her a name, not peculiar to her, but common to her sex; she shall be called woman, Isha, a She- man, differing from man in sex only, not in nature; made of man, and joined to man.

24. The sabbath and marriage were two ordinances instituted in innocency, the former for the preservation of the church, the latter for the preservation of mankind. It appears by Matt. xix, 4, 5, that it was God himself who said here, a man must leave all his relations to cleave to his wife; but whether he spake it by Moses or by Adam who spake, ver. 23 is uncertain: It should seem they are the words of Adam in God's name, laying down this law to all his posterity. The virtue of a divine ordinance, and the bonds of it, are stronger even than those of nature. See how necessary it is that children should take their parents consent with them in their marriage; and how unjust they are to their parents, as well as undutiful, if they marry without it; for they rob them of their right to them, and interest in them, and alienate it to another fraudulently and unnaturally.

25. They were both naked, they needed no cloaths for defense against cold or heat, for neither could be injurious to them: they needed none for ornament. Solomon in all his glory was not arrayed like one of these. Nay, they needed none for decency, they were naked, and had no reason to be ashamed. They knew not what shame was, so the Chaldee reads it. Blushing is now the colour of virtue, but it was not the colour of innocency.

III

The general contents of this chapter we have Rom. v, 12. By one man sin entered into the world, and death by sin, and so death passed upon all men, for that all have sinned. More particularly, we have here,

I. The innocent tempted, ver. 1-5.

II. The tempted transgressing, ver. 6, 7, 8.

III. The transgressors arraigned, ver. 9, 10.

IV. Upon their arraignment convicted, ver. 11-13.

V. Upon their conviction sentenced, ver. 14-19.

VI. After sentence, reprieved, ver. 20, 21.

VII. Notwithstanding their reprieve, execution in part done, ver. 22-24, and were it not for the gracious intimations of redemption, they and all their race had been left to despair.

1, 2, 3, 4, 5. We have here an account of the temptation wherewith Satan assaulted our first parents, and which proved fatal to them. And here observe, (1.) The tempter, the devil in the shape of a serpent. Multitudes of them fell; but this that attacked our first parents, was surely the prince of the devils. Whether it was only the appearance of a serpent, or a real serpent, acted and possessed by the devil, is not certain. The devil chose to act his part in a serpent, because it is a subtle creature. It is not improbable, that reason and speech were then the known properties of the serpent. And therefore Eve was not surprised at his reasoning and speaking, which otherwise she must have been. (2.) That which the devil aimed at, was to persuade Eve to eat forbidden fruit; and to do this, he took the same method that he doth still.

1. He questions whether it were a sin or no, ver. 1,
2. He denies that there was any danger in it, ver. 4.
3. He suggests much advantage by it, ver. 5. And these are his common topics. As to the advantage, he suits the temptation to the pure state they were now in, proposing to them not any carnal pleasure, but intellectual delights.

1. Your eyes shall be opened - You shall have much more of the power and pleasure of contemplation than now you have; you shall fetch a larger compass in your intellectual views, and see farther into things than now you do.

2. You shall be as gods - As Elohim, mighty gods, not only omniscient but omnipotent too:

3. You shall know good and evil - That is, everything that is desirable to be known. To support this part of the temptation, he abuseth the name given to this tree. 'Twas intended to teach the practical knowledge of good and evil, that is, of duty and disobedience, and it would prove the experimental knowledge of good and evil, that is, of happiness and misery. But he perverts the sense of it, and wrests it to their destruction, as if this tree would give them a speculative notional knowledge of the natures, kinds, and originals of good and evil. And,

4. All this presently, In the day you eat thereof - You will find a sudden and immediate change for the better. See note at "ver. 1"

6, 7, 8. Here we see what Eve's parley with the tempter ended in: Satan at length gains his point. God tried the obedience of our first parents by forbidding them the tree of knowledge, and Satan doth as it were join issue with God, and in that very thing undertakes to seduce them into a transgression; and here we find how he prevailed, God permitting it for wise and holy ends. (1.) We have here the inducements that moved them to transgress. The woman being deceived, was ring-leader in the transgression, 1 Tim. ii, 14

1. She saw that the tree was - It was said of all the rest of the fruit trees wherewith the garden of Eden was planted, that they were pleasant to the sight, and good for food.

2. She imagined a greater benefit by this tree than by any of the rest, that it was a tree not only not to be dreaded, but to be desired to make one wise, and therein excelling all the rest of the trees. This she saw, that is, she perceived and understood it by what the devil had said to her. She gave also to her husband with her - 'Tis likely he was not with her when she was tempted; surely if he had, he would have interposed to prevent the sin; but he came to her when she had eaten, and was prevailed with by her to eat likewise. She gave it to him; persuading him with the same arguements that the serpent had used with her; adding this to the rest, that she herself had eaten of it, and found it so far from being

deadly that it was extremely pleasant and grateful. And he did eat - This implied the unbelief of God's word, and confidence in the devil's; discontent with his present state, and an ambition of the honour which comes not from God. He would be both his own carver, and his own master, would have what he pleased, and do what he pleased; his sin was in one word disobedience, Rom. v, 19, disobedience to a plain, easy and express command, which he knew to be a command of trial. He sins against light and love, the clearest light and the dearest love that ever sinner sinned against. But the greatest aggravation of his sin was, that he involved all his posterity in sin and ruin by it. He could not but know that he stood as a public person, and that his disobedience would be fatal to all his seed; and if so, it was certainly both the greatest treachery and the greatest cruelty that ever was. Shame and fear seized the criminals, these came into the world along with sin, and still attend it. The Eyes of them both were opened - The eyes of their consciences; their hearts smote them for what they had done Now, when it was too late, they saw the happiness they were fallen from, and the misery they were fallen into. They saw God provoked, his favour forfeited, his image lost; they felt a disorder in their own spirits, which they had never before been conscious of; they saw a law in their members warring against the law of their minds, and captivating them both to sin and wrath; they saw that they were naked, that is, that they were stripped, deprived of all the honours and joys of their paradise state, and exposed to all the miseries that might justly be expected from an angry God; laid open to the contempt and reproach of heaven and earth, and their own consciences. And they sewed or platted fig leaves together, and, to cover, at least, part of their shame one from another, made themselves aprons. See here what is commonly the folly of those that have sinned: they are more solicitous to save their credit before men, than to obtain their pardon from God. And they heard the voice of the Lord God walking in the garden in the cool of the day - Tis supposed he came in a human shape; in no other similitude than that wherein they had seen him when he put them into paradise; for he came to convince and humble them, not to amaze and terrify them. He came not immediately from heaven in their view as afterwards on Mount Sinai, but he came in the garden, as one that was still willing to be familiar with them. He came walking, not riding upon the wings of the wind, but walking deliberately, as one slow to anger. He came in the cool of the day, not in the night, when all fears are doubly fearful; nor did he come suddenly upon them, but they heard his voice at some distance, giving them notice of his coming; and probably it was a still small voice, like that in which he came to inquire after Elijah. And they hid themselves from the presence of the Lord God - A sad change! Before they had sinned, if they heard the voice of the Lord God coming towards them, they would have run to meet him, but now God was become a terror to them, and then no marvel they were become a terror to themselves. See note at "ver. 6"

9. Where art thou? - This enquiry after Adam may be looked upon as a gracious pursuit in order to his recovery. If God had not called to him to reduce him, his condition had been as desperate as that of fallen angels.

10. I heard thy voice in the garden: and I was afraid - Adam was afraid because he was naked; not only unarmed, and therefore afraid to contend with God, but unclothed and therefore afraid so much as to appear before him.

11. Who told thee that thou wast naked? - That is, how camest thou to be sensible of thy nakedness as thy shame? Hast thou eaten of the tree? - Tho' God knows all our sins, yet he will know them from us, and requires from us an ingenuous confession of them, not that he may be informed, but that we may be humbled. Whereof I commanded thee not to eat of it, I thy maker, I thy master, I thy benefactor, I commanded thee to the contrary. Sin appears most plain and most sinful in the glass of the commandment.

13. What is this that thou hast done? - Wilt thou own thy fault? Neither of them does this fully. Adam lays all the blame upon his wife: She gave me of the tree - Nay, he not only lays the blame upon his wife, but tacitly on God himself. The woman thou gavest me, and gavest to be with me as my companion, she gave me of the tree. Eve lays all the blame upon the serpent; the serpent beguiled me. The prisoners being found guilty by their own confession, besides the infallible knowledge of the Judge, and nothing material being offered in arrest of judgment, God immediately proceeds to pass sentence, and in these verses he begins (where the sin began) with the serpent. God did not examine the serpent, nor ask him what he had done, but immediately sentenced him, (1.) Because he was already convicted of rebellion against God. (2.) Because he was to be forever excluded from pardon; and why should any thing be said to convince and humble him, who was to find no place for repentance?

14. To testify a displeasure against sin, God fastens a curse upon the serpent, Thou art cursed above all cattle - Even the creeping things, when God made them, were blessed of him, chap. i, 22, but sin turned the blessing into a curse. Upon thy belly shalt thou go - No longer upon feet, or half erect, but thou shalt crawl along, thy belly cleaving to the earth. Dust thou shalt eat - Which signifies a base and despicable condition.

15. And I will put enmity between thee and the woman - The inferior creatures being made for man, it was a curse upon any of them to be turned against man, and man against them. And this is part of the serpent's curse.

John Wesley

1. A perpetual reproach is fastened upon him. Under the cover of the serpent he is here sentenced to be, (1.) Degraded and accursed of God. It is supposed, pride was the sin that turned angels into devils, which is here justly punished by a great variety of mortifications couched under the mean circumstances of a serpent, crawling on his belly, and licking the dust. (2.) Detested and abhorred of all mankind: even those that are really seduced into his interest, yet profess a hatred of him. (3.) Destroyed and ruined at last by the great Redeemer, signified by the bruising of his head; his subtle politics shall be all baffled, his usurped power entirely crushed.

2. A perpetual quarrel is here commenced between the kingdom of God, and the kingdom of the devil among men; war proclaimed between the seed of the woman, and the seed of the serpent, Rev. xii, 7. It is the fruit of this enmity, (1.) That there is a continual conflict between God's people and him. Heaven and hell can never be reconciled, no more can Satan and a sanctified soul. (2.) That there is likewise a continual struggle between the wicked and the good. And all the malice of persecutors against the people of God is the fruit of this enmity, which will continue while there is a godly man on this side heaven, and a wicked man on this side hell.

3. A gracious promise is here made of Christ as the deliverer of fallen man from the power of Satan. By faith in this promise, our first parents, and the patriarchs before the flood, were justified and saved; and to this promise, and the benefit of it, instantly serving God day and night they hoped to come. Notice is here given them of three things concerning Christ. (1.) His incarnation, that he should be the seed of the woman. (2.) His sufferings and death, pointed at in Satan's bruising his heel, that is, his human nature. (3.) His victory over Satan thereby. Satan had now trampled upon the woman, and insulted over her; but the seed of the woman should be raised up in the fulness of time to avenge her quarrel, and to trample upon him, to spoil him, to lead him captive, and to triumph over him, Colossians ii, 15.

16. We have here the sentence past upon the woman; she is condemned to a state of sorrow and a state of subjection: proper punishments of a sin in which she had gratified her pleasure and her pride. (1.) She is here put into a state of sorrow; one particular of which only is instanced in, that in bringing forth children, but it includes all those impressions of grief and fear which the mind of that tender sex is most apt to receive, and all the common calamities which they are liable to. It is God that multiplies our sorrows, I will do it: God, as a righteous Judge, doth it, which ought to silence us under all our sorrows; as many as they are we have deserved them all, and more: nay, God as a tender Father doth it for our necessary correction, that we may be humbled for sin, and weaned from it. (2.) She is here put into a state of subjection: the whole sex, which by creation was equal with man, is for sin made inferior.

17. Because thou hast hearkened to the voice of thy wife - He excused the fault, by laying it on his wife, but God doth not admit the excuse; tho' it was her fault to persuade him to eat it, it was his fault to hearken to her. Cursed is the ground for thy sake - And the effect of that curse is, Thorns and thistles shall it bring forth unto thee - The ground or earth, by the sin of man, is made subject to vanity, the several parts of it being not so serviceable to man's comfort and happiness, as they were when they were made. Fruitfulness was its blessing for man's service, chap. i, 11-29, and now barrenness was its curse for man's punishment.

19. In the sweat of thy face shalt thou eat bread - His business before he sinned was a constant pleasure to him; but now his labour shall be a weariness. Unto dust shalt thou return - Thy body shall be forsaken by thy soul, and become itself a lump of dust, and then it shall be lodged in the grave, and mingle with the dust of the earth.

20. God having named the man, and called him Adam, which signifies red earth, he in farther token of dominion named the woman, and called her Eve - That is, life. Adam bears the name of the dying body, Eve of the living soul. The reason of the name is here given, some think by Moses the historian, others by Adam himself, because she was - That is, was to be the mother of all living. He had called her Isha, woman, before, as a wife; here he calls her Evah, life, as a mother. Now,

1. If this was done by divine direction, it was an instance of God's favour, and, like the new naming of Abraham and Sarah, it was a seal of the covenant, and an assurance to them, that notwithstanding their sin, he had not reversed that blessing wherewith he had blessed them, Be fruitful and multiply: it was likewise a confirmation of the promise now made, that the seed of the woman, of this woman, should break the serpent's head.

2. If Adam did of himself, it was an instance of his faith in the word of God.

21. These coats of skin had a significancy. The beasts whose skins they were, must be slain; slain before their eyes to shew them what death is. And probably 'tis supposed they were slain for sacrifice, to typify the great sacrifice which in the latter end of the world should be offered once for all. Thus the first thing that died was a sacrifice, or Christ in a figure.

22. Behold, the man is become as one of us, to know good and evil - See what he has got, what advantages, by eating forbidden fruit! This is said to humble them, and to bring them to a sense of their sin and folly, that seeing themselves thus wretchedly deceived by following the devil's counsel, they might henceforth pursue the happiness God offers, in the way he prescribes.

23. *He sent him forth* - Bid him go out, told him he should no longer occupy and enjoy that garden; but he was not willing to part with it.

24. *God drove him out* - This signified the exclusion of him and his guilty race from that communion with God which was the bliss and glory of paradise. But whether did he send him when he turned him out of Eden? He might justly have chased him out of the world, Job xviii, 18, but he only chased him out of the garden: he might justly have cast him down to hell, as the angels that sinned were, when they were shut out from the heavenly paradise, 2 Pet. ii, 4, but man was only sent to till the ground out of which he was taken. He was only sent to a place of toil, not to a place of torment. He was sent to the ground, not to the grave; to the work-house, not to the dungeon, not to the prison-house; to hold the plough, not to drag the chain: his tilling the ground would be recompensed by his eating its fruits; and his converse with the earth, whence he was taken, was improveable to good purposes, to keep him humble, and to mind him of his latter end. Observe then, That though our first parents were excluded from the privileges of their state of innocency, yet they were not abandoned to despair; God's thoughts of love designing them for a second state of probation upon new terms. And he placed at the east of the garden of Eden, a detachment of cherubim, armed with a dreadful and irresistible power, represented by flaming swords which turned every way, on that side the garden which lay next to the place whither Adam was sent, to keep the way that led to the tree of life.

IV

In this chapter we have both the world and the church in Adam's family, and a specimen of the character and state of both in all ages. As all mankind were represented in Adam, so that great distinction of mankind into the children of God and the children of the wicked one, was here represented in Cain and Abel; and an early instance of the enmity between the seed of the woman and the seed of the serpent. We have here,

I. The birth, names, and callings of Cain and Abel, ver. 1, 2.

II. Their religion, and different success in it, ver. 3, 4, and part of ver. 5.

III. Cain's anger at God, and the reproof of him for that anger, ver. 5, 6, 7.

IV. Cain's murder of his brother, and the process against him for that murder. The murder committed, ver. 8. The proceedings against him. (1.) His arraignment, ver. 9, former part. (2.) His plea, ver. 9. latter part. (3.) His conviction, ver. 10. (4.) The sentence passed upon him, ver. 11, 12. (5.) His complaint against the sentence, ver. 13, 14. (6.) The ratification of the sentence, ver. 15. (7.) The execution of the sentence, ver. 15, 16.

V. The family and posterity of Cain, ver. 17-24.

VI. The birth of another son and grandson of Adam, ver. 25, 26.

1. Adam and Eve had many sons and daughters, chap. v, 4. But Cain and Abel seem to have been the two eldest. Cain signifies possession; for Eve when she bare him said with joy and thankfulness, and great expectation, I have gotten a man from the Lord.

2. Abel signifies vanity. The name given to this son is put upon the whole race, Psalm xxxix, 5. Every man is at his best estate vanity; Abel, vanity. He chose that employment which did most befriend contemplation and devotion, for that hath been looked upon as the advantage of a pastoral life. Moses and David kept sheep, and in their solitudes conversed with God.

3. *In process of time* - At the end of days, either at the end of the year when they kept their feast of in-gathering, or at the end of the days of the week, the seventh day; at some set time Cain and Abel brought to Adam, as the priest of the family, each of them an offering to the Lord; for which we have reason to think there was a divine appointment given to Adam, as a token of God's favour notwithstanding their apostacy.

4. *And the Lord God had respect to Abel and to his offering, and shewed his acceptance of it,* probably by fire from heaven but to Cain and to his offering he had not respect. We are sure there was a good reason for this difference: that Governor of the world, though an absolute sovereign, doth not act arbitrarily in dispensing his smiles and frowns.

1. There was a difference in the characters of the persons offering: Cain was a wicked man, but Abel was a righteous man, Matt. xxiii, 35.

2. There was a difference in the offerings they brought. Abel's was a more excellent sacrifice than Cain's; Cain's was only a sacrifice of acknowledgment offered to the Creator; the meat-offerings of the

fruit of the ground were no more: but Abel brought a sacrifice of atonement, the blood whereof was shed in order to remission, thereby owning himself a sinner, deprecating God's wrath, and imploring his favour in a Mediator. But the great difference was, Abel offered in faith, and Cain did not. Abel offered with an eye to God's will as his rule, and in dependence upon the promise of a Redeemer. But Cain did not offer in faith, and so it turned into sin to him.

    5. And Cain was wroth, and his countenance fell - Not so much out of grief as malice and rage. His sullen churlish countenance, and down-look, betrayed his passionate resentment.

    7. If thou dost well, shalt thou not be accepted? - Either,

    1. If thou hadst done well, as thy brother did, thou shouldest have been accepted as he was. God is no respecter of persons; so that if we come short of acceptance with him, the fault is wholly our own. This will justify God in the destruction of sinners, and will aggravate their ruin. There is not a damned sinner in hell, but if he had done well, as he might have done, had been a glorified saint in heaven. Every mouth will shortly be stopt with this. Or,

    2. If now thou do well: if thou repent of thy sin, reform thy heart and life, and bring thy sacrifice in a better manner; thou shalt yet be accepted. See how early the gospel was preached, and the benefit of it here offered even to one of the chief of sinners. He sets before him death and a curse; but, if not well - Seeing thou didst not do well, not offer in faith, and in a right manner, sin lieth at the door - That is, sin only hinders thy acceptance. All this considered, Cain had no reason to be angry with his brother, but at himself only. Unto thee shall be his desire - He shall continue in respect to thee as an elder brother, and thou, as the first-born, shall rule over him as much as ever. God's acceptance of Abel's offering did not transfer the birth-right to him, (which Cain was jealous of) nor put upon him that dignity, and power, which is said to belong to it, chap. xlix, 3.

    8. And Cain talked with Abel his brother - The Chaldee paraphrast adds, that Cain, when they were in discourse, maintained there was no judgment to come, and that when Abel spoke in defense of the truth, Cain took that occasion to fall upon him. The scripture tells us the reason wherefore he slew him, because his own works were evil, and his brother's righteous; so that herein he shewed himself to be a child of the devil, as being an enemy to all righteousness. Observe, the first that dies is a saint, the first that went to the grave, went to heaven. God would secure to himself the first fruits, the first born to the dead, that first opened the womb into another world.

    9. And the Lord said unto Cain, Where is Abel thy brother? - God knew him to be guilty; yet he asks him, that he might draw from him a confession of his crime; for those who would be justified before God, must accuse themselves. And he said, I know not - Thus in Cain the devil was both a murderer, and a liar from the beginning. Am I my Brother's keeper? - Sure he is old enough to take care of himself, nor did I ever take charge of him. Art not thou his keeper? If he be missing, on thee be the blame, and not on me, who never undertook to keep him.

    10. And he said, What hast thou done? - Thou thinkest to conceal it, but the evidence against thee is clear and uncontestable, the voice of thy brother's blood crieth - He speaks as if the blood itself were both witness and prosecutor, because God's own knowledge testified against him, and God's own justice demanded satisfaction. The blood is said to cry from the ground, the earth, which is said, ver. 11, to open her mouth to receive his brother's blood from his hand. The earth did as it were blush to see her own face stained with such blood; and therefore opened her mouth to hide that which she could not hinder.

    11. And now art thou cursed from the earth -

    1. He is cursed, separated to all evil, laid under the wrath of God, as it is revealed from heaven against all ungodliness and unrighteousness of men.

    2. He is cursed from the earth. Thence the cry came up to God, thence the curse came up to Cain. God could have taken vengeance by an immediate stroke from heaven: but he chose to make the earth the avenger of blood; to continue him upon the earth, and not presently to cut him off; and yet to make even that his curse. That part of it which fell to his share, and which he had the occupation of, was made unfruitful, by the blood of Abel. Besides, A fugitive and a vagabond shalt thou be in the earth. By this he was here condemned, to perpetual disgrace and reproach, and to perpetual disquietment and horror in his own mind. His own guilty conscience should haunt him where ever he went. Now to justify his complaint, Observe his descants upon the sentence.

    1. He sees himself excluded by it from the favour of his God; and concludes, that being cursed, he was hid from God's face, and that is indeed the true nature of God's curse; damned sinners find it so, to whom it is said, Depart from me ye cursed. Those are cursed indeed that are forever shut out from God's love and care, and from all hopes of his grace.

    2. He sees himself expelled from all the comforts of this life; and concludes, ver. 14. Thou hast driven me out this day from the face of the earth - As good have no place on earth as not have a settled place. Better rest in the grave than not rest at all. And from thy face shall I be hid - Shut out of the church, not admitted to come with the sons of God to present himself before the Lord. And it shall come to pass that every one that finds me shall slay me - Wherever he wanders he goes in peril of his life.

There were none alive but his near relations, yet even of them he is justly afraid, who had himself been so barbarous to his own brother.

15. Whosoever slayeth Cain vengeance shall be taken on him seven-fold - God having said in Cain's case Vengeance is mine, I will repay; it had been a daring usurpation for any man to take the sword out of God's hand. And the Lord set a mark upon Cain - To distinguish him from the rest of mankind. What the mark was, God has not told us: therefore the conjectures of men are vain.

16. And Cain went out from the presence of the Lord, and dwelt on the east of Eden - Somewhere distant from the place were Adam and his religious family resided: distinguishing himself and his accursed generation from the holy seed; in the land of Nod - That is, of shaking or trembling, because of the continual restlessness of his spirit. Those that depart from God cannot find rest any where else. When Cain went out from the presence of the Lord, he never rested after.

17. And he builded a city - In token of a settled separation from the church of God. And here is an account of his posterity, at least the heirs of his family, for seven generations. His son was Enoch, of the same name, but not of the same character with that holy man that walked with God. The names of more of his posterity are mentioned, and but just mentioned, as those of the holy seed, chap. v, 1-32. They are numbered in haste, as not valued or delighted in, in comparison with God's children.

19. And Lamech took two wives - It was one of the degenerate race of Cain who first transgressed that original law of marriage, that two only should be one flesh.

1. Jabal was a famous shepherd; he delighted much in keeping cattle, and was so happy in devising methods of doing it to the best advantage, and instructing others in them, that the shepherds of those times, nay, the shepherds of after-times, called him Father; or perhaps his children after him, being brought up to the same employment: the family was a family of shepherds.

2. Jubal was a famous musician, and particularly an organist, and the first that gave rules for that noble art or science of music. When Jabal had set them in a way to be rich, Jubal put them in a way to be merry. From Jubal probably the Jubilee trumpet was so called; for the best music was that which proclaimed liberty and redemption.

22. From Tubal-Cain, probably the Heathen Vulcan came. Why Naamah is particularly named, we know not: probably they did, who lived when Moses wrote.

23. This passage is extremely obscure. We know not whom he slew, or on what occasion: neither what ground he had to be so confident of the Divine protection.

25. This is the first mention of Adam in the story of this chapter. No question the murder of Abel, and the impenitency and apostacy of Cain, were a very great grief to him and Eve, and the more because their own wickedness did now correct them, and their backsliding did reprove them. Their folly had given sin and death entrance into the world, and now they smarted by it, being by means thereof deprived of both their sons in one day, chap. xxvii, 45. When parents are grieved by their children's wickedness, they should take occasion from thence to lament that corruption of nature which was derived from them, and which is the root of bitterness. But here we have that which was a relief to our first parents in their affliction, namely, God gave them to see the rebuilding of their family which was sorely shaken and weakened by that sad event. For, they saw their seed, another instead of Abel. And Adam called his name Seth - That is, Set, settled or placed, because in his seed mankind should continue to the end of time.

26. And to Seth was born a son called Enos, which is the general name for all men, and speaks the weakness, frailty, and misery of man's state. Then began men to call upon the name of the Lord - Doubtless God's name was called upon before, but now,

1. The worshippers of God began to stir up themselves to do more in religion than they had done; perhaps not more than had been done at first, but more than had been done since the defection of Cain. Now men began to worship God, not only in their closets and families, but in public and solemn assemblies.

2. The worshippers of God began to distinguish themselves: so the margin reads it. Then began men to be called by the name of the Lord, or, to call themselves by it. Now Cain and those that had deserted religion had built a city, and begun to declare for irreligion, and called themselves the sons of men. Those that adhered to God began to declare for him and his worship, and called themselves the sons of God.

John Wesley

V

This chapter is the only authentic history extant of the first age of the world from the creation to the flood, containing (according to the Hebrew text) 1656 years. The genealogy here recorded is inserted briefly in the pedigree of our saviour, Luke iii, 36, 37. and is of great use to shew that Christ was the seed of the woman, that was promised. We have here an account,

I. Concerning Adam, ver. 1-5.

II. Seth, ver. 6-8.

III. Enos, ver. 9-11.

IV. Cainan, ver. 12-14.

V. Mahalaleel, ver. 15-17.

VI. Jared, ver. 18-20.

VII. Enoch, ver. 21-24.

VIII. Mathuselah, ver. 25-27.

IX. Lamech and his son Noah, ver. 28-32.
    1. The first words of the chapter are the title of argument of the whole chapter; it is the book of the generations of Adam - It is the list or catalogue of the posterity of Adam, not of all, but only of the holy seed, and of whom as concerning the flesh Christ came; the names, ages, and deaths of those that were the successors of the first Adam in the custody of the promise, and the ancestors of the second Adam.

    1, 2. Where we have a brief rehearsal of what was before at large related concerning the creation of man. This is what we have need frequently to hear of, and carefully to acquaint ourselves with. Observe here.
    1. That God created man. Man is not his own maker, therefore he must not be his own master; but the author of his being must be the director of his motions, and the center of them.
    2. That there was a day in which God created man, he was not from eternity, but of yesterday; he was not the first-born, but the junior of the creation.
    3. That God made him in his own likeness, righteous and holy, and therefore undoubtedly happy; man's nature resembled the divine nature more than that of any of the creatures of this lower world.
    4. That God created them male and female, ver. 2, for their mutual comfort, as well as for the preservation and increase of their kind. Adam and Eve were both made immediately by the hand of God, both made in God's likeness; and therefore between the sexes there is not that great difference and inequality which some imagine.
    5. That God blessed them. It is usual for parents to bless their children, so God the common Father blessed his; but earthly parents can only beg a blessing, it is God's prerogative to command it. It refers chiefly to the blessing of increase, not excluding other blessings.
    2. He called their name Adam - He gave this name both to the man and the woman. Being at first one by nature, and afterwards one by marriage; it was fit they should both have the same name, in token of their union. See note - part two at - "ver. 1"
    3. Seth was born in the 130th year of Adam's life, and probably the murder of Abel was not long before. Many other sons and daughters were born to Adam besides Cain and Abel before this; but no notice is taken of them, because an honourable mention must be made of his name only, in whose loins Christ and the church were. But that which is most observable here concerning Seth, is, that Adam begat him in his own likeness after his image - Adam was made in the image of God; but when he was fallen and corrupted, he begat a son in his own image, sinful and defiled, frail and mortal, and miserable like himself; not only a man like himself, consisting of body and soul; but a sinner like himself, guilty and obnoxious, degenerate and corrupt. He was conceived and born in sin, Psalm li, 5. This was Adam's own likeness, the reverse of that Divine likeness in which Adam was made; but having lost it himself he could not convey it to his seed.
    5. In the day Adam ate forbidden fruit, he became mortal, he began to die; his whole life after was but a forfeited condemned life, nay it was a wasting dying life; he was not only like a criminal sentenced, but as one already crucified, that dies slowly and by degrees. 6-19. We have here all that the Holy Ghost thought fit to leave upon record concerning five of the patriarchs before the flood, Seth,

Enos, Cainan, Mahalaleel, and Jared. There is nothing observable concerning any of those particularly, tho' we have reason to think they were men of eminency, both for prudence and piety: But in general, observe how largely and expressly their generations are recorded. We are told how long they lived that lived in God's fear, and when they died, that died in his favour; but as for others it is no matter: the memory of the just is blessed, but the name of the wicked shall rot. That which is especially observable, is, that they all lived very long; not one of them died 'till he had seen the revolution of almost eight hundred years, and some of them much longer; a great while for an immortal soul to be imprisoned in an house of clay. The present life surely was not to them such a burden as commonly it is now, else they would have been weary of it; nor was the future life so clearly revealed then, as it is now under the gospel, else they would have been impatient to remove it. Some natural causes may be assigned for their long life in those first ages. It is very probable that the earth was more fruitful, the products of it more strengthening, the air more healthful, and the influences of the heavenly bodies more benign before the flood than they were after. Though man was driven out of paradise, yet the earth itself was then paradisaical; a garden in comparison with its present state: and some think, that their knowledge of the creatures and their usefulness both, for their food and medicine, together with their sobriety and temperance, contributed much to it; yet we do not find that those who were intemperate, as many were, Luke xvii, 27, as short-lived as temperate men generally are now. It must therefore chiefly be resolved into the power and providence of God; he prolonged their lives, both for the more speedy replenishing of the earth, and for the more effectual preservation of the knowledge of God and religion, then when there was no written word, but tradition was the channel of its conveyance. All the patriarchs here (except Noah) were born before Adam died, so that from him they might receive a full account of the creation, paradise, the fall, the promise, and those divine precepts which concerned religious worship and a religious life: and if any mistake arose, they might have recourse to him while he lived, as to an oracle, for the rectifying of it, and after his death to Methuselah, and others that had conversed with him; so great was the care of Almighty God to preserve in his church the knowledge of his will, and the purity of his worship. See note at "ver. 6"

22. And Enoch walked with God after he begat Methuselah - To walk with God, is to set God always before us, and to act as those that are always under his eye. It is to live a life of communion with God, both in ordinances and providences; it is to make God's word our rule, and his glory our end, in all our actions; it is to make it our constant care and endeavour in every thing to please God, and in nothing to offend him; it is to comply with his will, to concur with his designs, and to be workers together with him. He walked with God after he begat Methuselah, which intimates, that he did not begin to be eminent for piety 'till about that time.

24. He was not, for God took him - That is, as it is explained, Heb. xi, 5, he was translated that he should not see death; and was not found, because God had translated him. But why did God take him so soon? Surely because the world, which was now grown corrupt, was not worthy of him. Because his work was done, and done the sooner for his minding it so closely. He was not, for God took him - He was not any longer in this world: it was not the period of his being, but of his being here. He was not found; so the apostle explains it from the seventy; not found by his friends, who sought him, as the sons of the prophets sought Elijah, 2 Kings ii, 17. God took him body and soul to himself in the heavenly paradise, by the ministry of angels, as afterwards he took Elijah. He was changed, as those saints shall be that will be found alive at Christ's second coming.

25. Methuselah signifies, He dies, there is a sending forth, viz. of the deluge, which came the very year that Methuselah died. If his name was so intended, it was a fair warning to a careless world long before the judgment came. However, this is observable, that the longest liver that ever was, carried death in his name, that he might be minded of its coming surely, tho' it came slowly. He lived nine hundred sixty and nine years, the longest we read of that ever any man lived on earth, and yet he died: the longest liver must die at last. Neither youth nor age will discharge from that war, for that is the end of all men: none can challenge life by long prescription, nor make that a plea against the arrests of death. 'Tis commonly supposed, that Methuselah died a little before the flood; the Jewish writers say, seven days before, referring to chap. vii, 10, and that he was taken away from the evil to come.

29. This same shall comfort us concerning our work and toil of our hands, because of the ground which the Lord hath cursed - Very probably there were some prophecies that went before of him, as a person that should be wonderfully serviceable to his generation.

32. And Noah begat Shem, Ham, and Japheth - These Noah begat (the eldest of these) when he was six hundred years old. It should seem that Japheth was the eldest, chap. x, 21, but Shem is put first, because on him the covenant was entailed, as appears by chap. ix, 26, where God is called the Lord God of Shem. To him 'tis probable the birthright was given, and from him 'tis certain both Christ the head, and the church the body, were to descend; therefore he is called Shem, which signifies a name, because in his posterity the name of God should always remain, 'till He should come out of his loins, whose name is above every name; so that in putting Shem first, Christ was in effect put first, who in all things must have the pre-eminence. For the glory of God's justice, and for warning to a wicked world, before

the history of the ruin of the old world we have a full account of its degeneracy, its apostacy from God, and rebellion against him. The destroying of it was an act not of absolute sovereignty, but of necessary justice for the maintaining of the honour of God's government.

VI

In this chapter we have,

I. The abounding iniquity of that wicked world, ver. 1-5. and ver. 11, 12.

II. God's just resentment of that iniquity, and his holy resolution to punish it, ver. 6, 7.

III. The special favour of God to his servant Noah. (1.) In the character given of him, ver. 8, 9, 10. (2.) In the communication of God's purpose to him, ver. 13-17. (3.) In the directions he gave him to make an ark for his own safety, ver. 14, 15, 16. (4.) In the employing of him for the preservation of the rest of the creatures, ver. 18, 19, 20, 21. Lastly, Noah's obedience to the instructions given him, ver. 22.

1. Men began to multiply upon the face of the earth - This was the effect of the blessing, chap. i, 28, and yet man's corruption so abused this blessing, that it turned into a curse.

2. The sons of God - Those who were called by the name of the Lord, and called upon that name, married the daughters of men - Those that were profane, and strangers to God. The posterity of Seth did not keep to themselves as they ought, but intermingled with the race of Cain: they took them wives of all that they chose - They chose only by the eye: They saw that they were fair - Which was all they looked at.

3. My spirit shall not always strive with man - The spirit then strove by Noah's preaching, 1 Pet. iii, 19, and by inward checks, but 'twas in vain with the most of men; therefore saith God, he shall not always strive, for that he also is flesh - Incurably corrupt and sensual, so that 'tis labour lost to strive with him. He also, that is, all, one as well as another; they are all sunk into the mire of flesh. Yet his days shall be an hundred and twenty years - So long will I defer the judgment they deserve, and give them space to prevent it by their repentance and reformation. Justice said, cut them down; but mercy interceded, Lord, let them alone this year also; and so far mercy prevailed, that a reprieve was obtained for six score years.

4. There were giants, and men of renown - They carried all before them,

1. With their great bulk, as the sons of Anak, Num. xiii, 33, and,

2. With their great name, as the king of Assyria, Isaiah xxxvii, 11. Thus armed, they daringly insulted the rights of all their neighbours, and trampled upon all that is just and sacred.

5. And God saw that the wickedness of man was great in the earth - Abundance of sin was committed in all places, by all sorts of people: and those sins in their own nature most gross and heinous, and provoking: and committed daringly, with a defiance of heaven. And that every imagination of the thoughts of his heart was only evil continually - A sad sight, and very offensive to God's holy eye. This was the bitter root, the corrupt spring: all the violence and oppression, all the luxury and wantonness that was in the world, proceeded from the corruption of nature; lust conceives them, James i, 15, see Matt. xv, 19. The heart was evil, deceitful and desperately wicked; the principles were corrupt, and the habits and dispositions evil. The thoughts of the heart were so. Thought is sometimes taken for the settled judgment, and that was biased and misled; sometimes for the workings of the fancy, and those were always either vain or vile. The imagination of the thought of the heart was so, that is, their designs and devices were wicked. They did not do evil only through carelessness, but deliberately and designedly, contriving how to do mischief. 'Twas bad indeed, for it was only evil, continually evil, and every imagination was so. There was no good to be found among them, no not at any time: the stream of sin was full and strong, and constant; and God saw it. Here is God's resentment of man's wickedness. He did not see it as an unconcerned spectator, but as one injured and affronted by it; he saw it as a tender father sees the folly and stubbornness of a rebellious and disobedient child, which not only angers but grieves him, and makes him wish he had been written childless.

6. And it repented the Lord that he had made man upon the earth - That he had made a creature of such noble powers, and had put him on this earth, which he built and furnished on purpose to be a comfortable habitation for him; and it grieved him at his heart - These are expressions after the manner of men, and must be understood so as not to reflect upon God's immutability or felicity. It doth not speak any passion or uneasiness in God, nothing can create disturbance to the eternal mind; but it speaks his just and holy displeasure against sin and sinners: neither doth it speak any change of God's mind; for with him there is no variableness; but it speaks a change of his way. When God had made man upright, he rested and was refreshed, Exod. xxxi, 17. and his way towards him was such as shewed him well pleased with the work of his own hands; but now man was apostatized, he could not do otherwise, but

shew himself displeased; so that the change was in man, not in God.

7. *I will destroy man* - The original word is very significant. I will wipe off man from off the earth; as dirt is wiped off from a place which should be clean, and thrown to the dunghill. Or, I will blot out man from the earth, as those lines are blotted out of a book which displease the author, or as the name of a citizen is blotted out of the rolls of the freemen when he is disfranchised. *Both man and beast the creeping thing, and the fowls of the air* - These were made for man, and therefore must be destroyed with man. *It repenteth me that I have made them* - For the end of their creation also was frustrated: they were made that man might serve and honour God with them and therefore were destroyed, because he had served his lusts with them, and made them subject to vanity.

8. *But Noah found grace in the eyes of the Lord* - This vindicates God's justice in his displeasure against the world, and shews that he had examined the character of every person in it, before he pronounced it universally corrupt; for there being one good man he smiled upon him.

9. *Noah was a just man* - Justified before God by faith in the promised seed; for he was an heir of the righteousness which is by faith, Heb. xi, 7. He was sanctified, and had right principles and dispositions implanted in him: and he was righteous in his conversation, one that made conscience of rendering to all their due, to God his due, and to men theirs. And he walked with God as Enoch had done before him: in his generation, even in that corrupt degenerate age. It is easy to be religious when religion is in fashion; but it is an evidence of strong faith to swim against the stream, and to appear for God, when no one else appears for him: so Noah did, and it is upon record to his immortal honour.

11. *The earth also was corrupt before God* - That is, in the matters of God's worship; either they had other gods before him, or worshipped him by images: or, they were corrupt and wicked in despite of God. The earth was also filled with violence, and injustice towards men; there was no order nor regular government, no man was safe in the possession of that which he had the most clear right to, there was nothing but murders, rapes and rapines.

12. *God looked upon the earth* - And was himself an eye-witness of the corruption that was in it, *for all flesh had corrupted his way* - It was not some particular nations that were thus wicked, but the whole world so; there was none good beside Noah.

13. *The end of all flesh is come before me; I will destroy them* - The ruin of this wicked world is decreed; it is come, that is, it will come surely, and come quickly.

14. *I will destroy them with the earth, but make thee an ark* - I will take care to preserve thee alive. This ark was like the hulk of a ship, fitted not to sail upon the waters, but to float waiting for their fall. God could have secured Noah, by the ministration of angels without putting him to any care or pains, but he chose to employ him in making that which was to be the means of his preservation, both for the trial of his faith and obedience, and to teach us that none shall be saved by Christ, but those only that work out their salvation; we cannot do it without God, and he will not without us: both the providence of God and the grace of God crown the endeavours of the obedient and diligent. God gave him particular instructions concerning this building.

1. It must be made of Gopher-wood; Noah, doubtless, knew what sort of wood that was, though now we do not.

2. He must make it three stories high within: and,

3. He must divide it into cabins with partitions, places fitted for the several sorts of creatures, so as to lose no room.

4. Exact dimensions are given him, that he might make it proportionable, and might have room enough in it to answer the intention, and no more.

5. He must pitch it within and without: without, to shed off the rain, and to prevent the water from soaking in; within, to take away the ill smell of the beasts when kept close.

6. He must make a little window towards the top to let in light.

7. He must make a door in the side of it by which to go in and out.

17. *And behold, I, even I, do bring a flood of waters upon the earth* - I that am infinite in power, and therefore can do it; infinite in justice, and therefore will do it.

18. *But with thee will I establish my covenant* - (1.) The covenant of Providence, that the course of nature shall be continued to the end of time, not withstanding the interruption which the flood would give to it: this promise was immediately made to Noah and his sons, chap. ix, 8, &c. they were as trustees for all this part of the creation, and a great honour was thereby put upon him and his. God would be to him a God, and that out of his seed God would take to himself a people.

VII

We have in this chapter,

I. God's gracious call to Noah to come into the ark, ver. 1. and to bring the creatures that were to be preserved alive, with him, ver. 2, 3. in consideration of the deluge at hand, ver. 4.

II. Noah's obedience, ver. 5. he came with his family into the ark, ver. 6, 7. and brought the creatures with him, ver. 8, 9. An account of which is repeated, ver. 13, 14, 15, 16. to which is added God's tender care to shut him in.

III. The coming of the threatened deluge, ver. 10. the causes of it, ver. 11, 12. the prevalency of it, ver. 17, 18, 19, 20.

IV. The dreadful desolations that were made by it, in the death of every living creature upon earth, except what were in the ark, ver. 21, 22,23.

V. The continuance of it in full sea, before it began to ebb, 150 days, ver. 24.

    1. Here is a gracious invitation of Noah and his family into a place of safety, now the flood of waters was coming. For thee have I seen righteous before me in this generation - Those are righteous indeed that are righteous before God; that have not only the form of godliness by which they appear righteous before men, who may easily be imposed upon; but the power of it, by which they approve themselves to God, who searcheth the heart.
    2. Here are necessary orders given concerning the brute creatures that they were to be preserved alive with Noah in the ark. He must carefully preserve every species, that no tribe, no, not the least considerable, might entirely perish out of the creation. Observe in this: (1.) God's care for man. Doth God take care for oxen? 1 Cor. ix, 9, or was it not rather for man's sake that this care was taken? (2.) Even the unclean beasts were preserved alive in the ark, that were least valuable. For God's tender mercies are over all his works, and not only over those that are of most use. (3.) Yet more of the clean were preserved than of the unclean.
    1. Because the clean were most for the service of man; and therefore in favour to him, more of them were preserved and are still propagated. Thanks be to God there are not herds of lions as there are of oxen, nor flocks of tigers as there are of sheep.
    2. Because the clean were for sacrifice to God; and therefore, in honour to him, more of them were preserved, three couple for breed, and the odd seventh for sacrifice, chap. viii, 20.
    4. Yet seven days and I will cause it to rain - It shall be seven days yet before I do it, After the 120 years were expired, God grants them a reprieve of seven days longer, both to shew how slow he is to anger, and to give them some farther space for repentance. But all in vain; these seven days were trifled away after all the rest, they continued secure until the day that the flood came. While Noah told them of the judgment at a distance, they were tempted to put off their repentance: but now he is ordered to tell them that it is at the door; that they have but one week more to turn them in, to see if that will now at last awaken them to consider the things that belong to their peace. But it is common for those that have been careless for their souls during the years of their health, when they have looked upon death at a distance, to be as careless during the days, the seven days of their sickness, when they see it approaching, their hearts being hardened by the deceitfulness of sin.
    7. And Noah went in with his sons, and his wife, and his sons wives - And the brute creatures readily went in with him. The same hand that at first brought them to Adam to be named, now brought them to Noah to be preserved.
    11. The six hundredth year of Noah's life, was 1656 years from the creation. In the second month, the seventeenth day of the month - Which is reckoned to be about the beginning of November; so that Noah had had a harvest just before, from which to victual his ark. The same day the fountains of the great deep were broken up - There needed no new creation of waters; God has laid up the deep in storehouses, Psalm xxxiii, 7, and now he broke up those stores. God had, in the creation, set bars and doors to the waters of the sea, that they might not return to cover the earth, Psalm civ; Job xxxviii, 9-11, and now he only removed these ancient mounds and fences, and the waters of the sea returned to cover the earth, as they had done at first, chap. i, 9. And the windows of heaven were opened - And the waters which were above the firmament were poured out upon the world; those treasures which God has reserved against the time of trouble, the day of battle and war, Job xxxviii, 22, 23. The rain, which ordinarily descends in drops, then came down in streams. We read, Job xxvi, 8. That God binds up the waters in his thick clouds, and the cloud is not rent under them; but now the bond was loosed, the cloud was rent, and such rains descended as were never known before or since.

12. It rained without intermission or abatement, forty days and forty nights - And that upon the whole earth at once.

14. And every beast after his kind - According to the phrase used in the history of the creation, chap. i, 21, 24, 25, to intimate, that just as many species as were created at first were saved now, and no more.

20. The mountains were covered - Therefore there were mountains before the flood.

21. All flesh died, all in whose nostrils was the breath of life, of all that was on the dry land, every living substance - And why so? Man only had done wickedly, and justly is God's hand against him, but these sheep what have they done? I answer,

1. We are sure God did them no wrong. He is the sovereign Lord of all life, for he is the sole fountain and author of it. He that made them as he pleased, might unmake them when he pleased, and who shall say unto him, What dost thou?

2. God did admirably serve the purposes of his own glory by their destruction, as well as by their creation. Herein his holiness and justice were greatly magnified: by this it appears that he hates sin, and is highly displeased with sinners, when even the inferior creatures, because they are the servants of man, and part of his possession, and because they have been abused to be the servants of sin, are destroyed with him. It was likewise an instance of God's wisdom. As the creatures were made for man when he was made, so they were multiplied for him when he was multiplied; and therefore, now mankind was reduced to so small a number, it was fit that the beasts should proportionable be reduced, otherwise they would have had the dominion, and would have replenished the earth, and the remnant of mankind that was left would have been overpowered by them.

VIII

We have here,

I. The earth made anew, by the recess of waters, and the appearing of the dry land a second time. (1.) The increase of the waters is stayed, ver. 1, 2. (2.) They begin sensibly to abate, ver. 3. (3.) After fifteen days ebbing the ark rests, ver. 4. (4.) After sixty days ebbing the tops of the mountains appear, ver.5. (5.) After forty days ebbing, and twenty days before the mountains appeared, Noah begins to send out his spies, a raven and a dove to gain intelligence, ver. 6-12. (6.) Two months after the appearing of the tops of the mountains the waters were gone, and the face of the earth was dry, ver. 13. tho' not dried so as to be fit for man 'till almost two months after, ver. 14.

II. Man placed anew upon the earth. In which,
 1. Noah's discharge and departure out of the ark, ver. 15-19.
 2. His sacrifice of praise which he offered to God upon his enlargement, ver. 20.

III. God's acceptance of his sacrifice; and the promise he made thereupon not to drown the world again, ver. 21, 22. And thus at length mercy rejoiceth against judgment.

1. And God remembered Noah and every living thing - This is an expression after the manner of men, for not any of his creatures, much less any of his people are forgotten of God. But the whole race of mankind, except Noah and his family, was now extinguished, and gone into the land of forgetfulness, so that God's remembering Noah was the return of his mercy to mankind, of whom he would not make a full end. Noah himself, tho' one that had found grace in the eyes of the Lord, yet seemed to be forgotten in the ark; but at length God returned in mercy to him, and that is expressed by his remembering him.

3. The waters returned from off the earth continually - Hebrew. they were going and returning; a gradual departure. The heat of the sun exhaled much, and perhaps the subterraneous caverns soaked in more.

4. And the ark rested - upon the mountains of Ararat - Or, Armenia, whether it was directed, not by Noah's prudence, but the wise providence of God.

5. The tops of the mountains were seen - Like little islands appearing above water. They felt ground above forty days before they saw it, according to Dr. Lightfoots's computation, whence he infers that if the waters decreased proportionably, the ark drew eleven cubits in water.

7. Noah sent forth a raven through the window of the ark, which went forth, as the Hebrew phrase is, going forth and returning, that is, flying about, but returning to the ark for rest; probably not in it, but upon it. This gave Noah little satisfaction: therefore,

8. He sent forth a dove - Which returned the first time with no good news, but probably wet and dirty; but the second time she brought an olive leaf in her bill, which appeared to be fresh plucked off; a plain indication that now the trees began to appear above water. Note here, that Noah set forth the dove the second time, seven days after the first time, and the third time was after seven days too: and

probably the first sending of her out was seven days after the sending forth of the raven. The olive branch is an emblem of peace.

13. Noah removed the covering of the ark - Not the whole covering, but so much as would suffice to give him a prospect of the earth about it: and behold the face of the ground was dry.

14. The earth was dried - So as to be a fit habitation for Noah.

20. And Noah built an altar - Hitherto he had done nothing without particular instructions and commands from God but altars and sacrifices being already of Divine institution, he did not stay for a particular command thus to express his thankfulness. And he offered on the altar, of every clean beast and of every clean fowl - One, the odd seventh that we read of, ver. 2, 3.

21. And God smelled a sweet savour - Or a savour of rest from it, as it is in the Hebrew. He was well pleased with Noah's pious zeal, and these hopeful beginnings of the new world, as men are with fragrant and agreeable smells. I will not again curse the ground, Hebrew. I will not add to curse the ground any more - God had cursed the ground upon the first entrance of sin, chap. iii, 17, when he drowned it he added to that curse: but now he determines not to add to it any more. Neither will I again smite any more every living thing - That is, it was determined that whatever ruin God might bring upon particular persons, families or countries, he would never again destroy the whole world, 'till the day when time shall be no more. But the reason of this resolve is surprising; for it seems the same with the reason given for the destruction of the world, chap. vi, 5. Because the imagination of man's heart is evil from his youth. But there is this difference: there it is said, the imagination of man's heart is evil continually, that is, his actual transgressions continually cry against him; here it is said, that it is evil from his youth or childhood; he brought it into the world with him, he was shapen and conceived in it. Now one would think it should follow, therefore that guilty race shall be wholly extinguished: No; therefore I will no more take this severe method; for he is rather to be pitied: and it is but what might be expected from such a degenerate race. So that if he be dealt with according to his deserts, one flood must succeed another 'till all be destroyed. God also promises, that the course of nature should never be discontinued. While the earth remaineth, and man upon it, there shall be summer and winter, not all winter, as had been this last year; day and night, not all night, as probably it was while the rain was descending. Here it is plainly intimated that this earth is not to remain always; it and all the works therein must shortly be burnt up. But as long as it doth remain, God's providence will carefully preserve the regular succession of times and seasons. To this we owe it, that the world stands, and the wheel of nature keeps its tack. See here how changeable the times are, and yet how unchangeable!

1. The course of nature always changing. As it is with the times, so it is with the events of time, they are subject to vicissitudes, day and night, summer and winter counterchanged. In heaven and hell it is not so; but on earth God hath set the one over against the other.

2. Yet never changed; it is constant in this inconstancy; these seasons have never ceased, nor shall cease while the sun continues such a steady measurer of time, and the moon such a faithful witness in heaven. This is God's covenant of the day and of the night, the stability of which is mentioned for the confirming our faith in the covenant of grace, which is no less inviolable, Jer. xxxiii, 20. We see God's promises to the creatures made good, and thence may infer that his promises to believers shall be so.

IX

In this chapter is,

I. The covenant of providence settled with Noah and his sons, ver. 1-11. In this covenant, (1.) God promiseth them to take care of their lives; so that,

1. They should replenish the earth, ver. 1-7.

2. They should be safe from the insults of the brute creatures, which should stand in awe of them, ver. 2.

3. They should be allowed to eat flesh for the support of their lives, only they must not eat blood, ver. 3, 4.

4. The world should never be drowned again, ver. 8-11. (2.) God requires of them to take care of one another's lives, and of their own, ver. 5, 6.

II. The seal of that covenant, viz. the rainbow, ver. 12-17.

III. A particular passage concerning Noah and his sons, which occasioned some prophecies that related to after-times. (1.) Noah's sin and shame, ver. 20-21. (2.) Ham's impudence and impiety, ver. 22. (3.) The pious modesty of Shem and Japheth, ver. 23. (4.) The curse of Canaan and the blessing of Shem and Japheth, ver. 24-27.

IV. The age and death of Noah, ver. 28, 29.

Wesley's Notes on the Bible - The Old Testament: Genesis - Ruth

1. And God blessed Noah and his sons - He assured them of his goodwill to them, and his gracious intentions concerning them. The first blessing is here renewed, Be fruitful, and multiply, and replenish the earth, and repeated, ver. 7; for the race of mankind was as it were to begin again. By virtue of this blessing mankind was to be both multiplied and perpetuated upon earth; so that in a little time all the habitable parts of the earth should be more or less inhabited; and tho' one generation should pass away, yet another generation should come, so that the stream of the human race should be supplied with a constant succession, and run parallel with the current of time, 'till both be swallowed up in the ocean of eternity.

2. He grants them power over the inferior creatures. He grants, 1. A title to them; into your hands they are delivered - For your use and benefit. 2. A dominion over them, without which the title would avail little; The fear of you and the dread of you shall be upon every beast - This revives a former grant, chap. i, 28, only with this difference, that man in innocency ruled by love, fallen man rules by fear. And thus far we have still the benefit of it,

1. That those creatures which are any way useful to us are reclaimed, and we use them either for service or food, or both, as they are capable.

2. Those creatures that are any way hurtful to us are restrained; so that tho' now and then man may be hurt by some of them, yet they do not combine together to rise up in rebellion against man.

3. Every moving thing that liveth shall be meat for you - Hitherto man had been confined to feed only upon the products of the earth, fruits, herbs and roots, and all sorts of corn and milk; so was the first grant, chap. i, 29. But the flood having perhaps washed away much of the virtue of the earth, and so rendered its fruits less pleasing, and less nourishing, God now enlarged the grant, and allowed man to eat flesh, which perhaps man himself never thought of 'till now. The precepts and provisos of this charter are no less kind and gracious, and instances of God's goodwill to man. The Jewish doctors speak so often of the seven precepts of Noah, or of the sons of Noah, which they say were to be observed by all nations, that it may not be amiss to set them down. The first against the worship of idols. The second against blasphemy, and requiring to bless the name of God. The third against murder. The fourth against incest and all uncleanness. The fifth against theft and rapine. The sixth requiring the administration of justice. The seventh against eating flesh with the life. These the Jews required the observation of, from the proselytes of the gate. But the precepts here given, all concern the life of man. Man must not prejudice his own life by eating that food which is unwholsome, and prejudicial to his health.

4. But flesh with the life thereof, which is the blood thereof, shall ye not eat - Blood made atonement for the soul, Lev. xvii, 11. The life of the sacrifice was accepted for the life of the sinner. Blood must not be looked upon as a common thing, but must be poured out before the Lord, 2 Sam. xxiii, 16. Mark Henry indeed has a strange conceit, That this is only a prohibition to eat flesh. This does such apparent violence to the text, that to mention it, is sufficient.

5. And surely your blood of your lives will I require - Our own lives are not so our own, that we may quit them at our own pleasure; but they are God's, and we must resign them at his pleasure. If we any way hasten our own deaths, we are accountable to God for it. Yea, At the hand of every beast will I require it - To shew how tender God was of the life of man, he will have the beast put to death that kills a man. This was confirmed by the law of Moses, Exod. xxi, 28, and it would not be unsafe to observe it still. And at the hand of every man's brother will I require the life of a man - I will avenge the blood of the murdered upon the murderer. When God requires the life of a man at the hand of him that took it away unjustly, he cannot render that, and therefore must render his own in lieu of it, which is the only way left of making restitution.

6. Whoso sheddeth man's blood - Whether upon a sudden provocation, or premeditated, (for rash anger is heart-murder as well as malice prepense, Matt. v, 21, 22), by man shall his blood be shed - That is, by the magistrate, or whoever is appointed to be the avenger of blood. Before the flood, as it should seem by the story of Cain, God took the punishment of murder into his own hands; but now he committed this judgment to men, to masters of families at first, and afterwards to the heads of countries. For in the image of God made he man - Man is a creature dear to his Creator, and therefore ought to be so to us; God put honour upon him, let us not then put contempt upon him. Such remains of God's image are still even upon fallen man, that he who unjustly kills a man, defaceth the image of God, and doth dishonour to him.

9. We have here the general establishment of God's covenant with this new world, and the extent of that covenant.

11. There shall not any more be a flood - God had drowned the world once, and still it is as provoking as ever; yet he will never drown it any more, for he deals not with us according to our sins. This promise of God keeps the sea and clouds in their decreed place, and sets them gates and bars, Hitherto they shall come, Job xxxviii, 10, 11. If the sea should flow but for a few days, as it doth twice every day for a few hours, what desolations would it make? So would the clouds, if such showers as we have sometimes seen, were continued long. But God by flowing seas, and sweeping rains, shews what he could do in wrath; and yet by preserving the earth from being deluged between both, shews what he

can do in mercy, and will do in truth.

13. I set my bow in the clouds - The rainbow, 'tis likely was seen in the clouds before, but was never was a seal of the covenant 'till now. Now, concerning this seal of the covenant, observe, (1.) This seal is affixed with repeated assurances of the truth of that promise, which it was designed to be the ratification of; I do set my bow in the cloud, ver. 13. It shall be seen in the cloud, ver. 14. and it shall be a token of the covenant, ver. 12, 13. And I will remember my covenant, that the waters shall no more become a flood, ver. 15. Nay, as if the eternal Mind needed a memorandum, I will look upon it that I may remember the everlasting covenant, ver. 16. (2.) The rainbow appears when the clouds are most disposed to wet; when we have most reason to fear the rain prevailing, God shews this seal of the promise that it shall not prevail. (3.) The rainbow appears when one part of the sky is clear, which imitates mercy remembered in the midst of wrath, and the clouds are hemmed as it were with the rainbow, that it may not overspread the heavens, for the bow is coloured rain, or the edges of a cloud gilded. As God looks upon the bow that he may remember the covenant, so should we, that we also may be ever mindful of the covenant with faith and thankfulness.

20. And Noah began to be an husbandman - Hebrew. a man of the earth, a man dealing in the earth, that kept ground in his hand and occupied it. Sometime after his departure out of the ark he returned to his old employment, from which he had been diverted by the building of the ark first, and probably after by the building an house for himself and family. And he planted a vineyard - And when he had gathered his vintage, probably he appointed a day of mirth and feasting in his family, and had his sons and their children with him, to rejoice with him in the increase of his house, as well as in the increase of his vineyard; and we may suppose he prefaced his feast with a sacrifice to the honour of God. If that was omitted, 'twas just with God to leave him to himself, to end with the beasts that did not begin with God: but we charitably hope he did. And perhaps he appointed this feast with design in the close of it to bless his sons, as Isaac, chap. xxvii, 3, 4. That I may eat, and that my soul may bless thee.

21. And he drank of the wine and was drunk - 'Tis highly probable, he did not know the effect of it before. And he was uncovered in his tent - Made naked to his shame.

22. And Ham saw the nakedness of his father, and told his two brethren -- to have seen it accidentally and involuntarily would not have been a crime. But he pleased himself with the sight. And he told his two brethren without - In the street, as the word is, in a scornful deriding manner.

23. And Shem and Japheth took a garment, and went backward, and covered the nakedness of their father - They not only would not see it themselves, but provided that no one else might see it; herein setting an example of charity, with reference to other men's sin and shame.

25. A servant of servants - That is, the meanest and most despicable servant shall he be, even to his brethren. Those who by birth were his equals, should by conquest be his lords. This certainly points at the victories obtained by Israel over the Canaanites, by which they were all either put to the sword, or put under tribute. Josh. ix, 23; Jude i, 28, 30,

33, 35, which happened not 'till about eight hundred years after this. God often visits the iniquity of the fathers upon the children, especially when the children inherit the fathers wicked dispositions, and imitate the father's wicked practices.

26. The God of Shem - All blessings are included in this. This was the blessing conferred on Abraham and his seed, the God of heaven was not ashamed to be called their God, Heb. xi, 16. Shem is sufficiently recompensed for his respect to his father by this, that the Lord himself puts this honour upon him to be his God; which is a sufficient recompense for all our services and all our sufferings for his name.

27. God shall enlarge Japheth, and he shall dwell in the tents of Shem - His seed shall be so numerous and so victorious, that they shall be masters of the tents of Shem, which was fulfilled when the people of the Jews, the most eminent of Shem's race, were tributaries to the Grecians first, and after to the Romans, both of Japhet's seed. This also speaks the conversion of the Gentiles, and the bringing of them into the church; and then we should read it, God shall persuade Japheth; (for so the word signifies) and being so persuaded, he shall dwell in the tents of Shem - That is, Jews and Gentiles shall be united together in the gospel-fold: after many of the Gentiles shall have been proselyted to the Jewish religion, both shall be one in Christ, Eph. ii, 14, 15. When Japheth joins with Shem, Canaan falls before them both: when strangers become friends, enemies become servants.

X

This chapter contains, the only certain account extant of the original of nations; and yet, perhaps, there is no nation, but that of the Jews, that can be confident from which of these seventy fountains (for many there are here) it derived its streams. Through the want of early records, the mixtures of people, the revolutions of nations, and distance of time, the knowledge of the lineal descent of the present inhabitants of the earth is lost: nor were any genealogies preserved but those of the Jews, for the sake of the Messiah. Only, in this chapter, we have a brief account,

I. Of the posterity of Japheth, ver. 2-5.

II. The posterity of Ham, ver. 6-20. and, in that particular notice taken of Nimrod, ver. 8-9.

III. The posterity of Shem, ver. 23-31.

2. Moses begins with Japhet's family, either because he was the eldest, or because that lay remotest from Israel, and had least concern with them, at that time when Moses wrote; and therefore he mentions that race very briefly; hastening to give account of the posterity of Ham, who were Israel's enemies, and of Shem, who were Israel's ancestors: for it is the church that the scripture designed to be the history of, and of the nations of the world only as they were some way or other interested in the affairs of Israel.

5. The posterity of Japheth were allotted to the isles of the Gentiles, which were solemnly, by lot, after a survey, divided among them, and probably this island of ours among the rest. All places beyond the sea, from Judea, are called isles, Jer. xxv, 22, and this directs us to understand that promise, Isaiah xlii, 4, the isles shall wait for his law, of the conversion of the Gentiles to the faith of Christ.

8. Began to be mighty on the earth - That is, whereas those that went before him were content to stand upon the same level with their neighbours, Nimrod could not rest in this parity, but he would top his neighbours, and Lord over them. The same spirit that the giants before the flood were acted by, chap. vi, 4, now revived in him; so soon was that tremendous judgment, which the pride and tyranny of those mighty men brought upon the world, forgotten.

9. Nimrod was a mighty hunter - This he began with, and for this became famous to a proverb. Some think he did good with his hunting, served his country by ridding it of wild beasts, and so insinuated himself into the affections of his neighbours, and got to be their prince. And perhaps, under pretense of hunting, he gathered men under his command, to make himself master of the country. Thus he became a mighty hunter, a violent invader of his neighbour's rights and properties. And that, before the Lord - Carrying all before him, and endeavouring to make all his own by force and violence. He thought himself a mighty prince; but before the Lord, that is, in God's account, he was but a mighty hunter. Note, Great conquerers are but great hunters. Alexander and Caesar would not make such a figure in scripture history as they do in common history. The former is represented in prophecy but as a he-goat pushing, Dan. viii, 5. Nimrod was a mighty hunter against the Lord, so the seventy; that is, he set up idolatry, as Jeroboam did, for the confirming of his usurped dominion; that he might set up a new government, he set up a new religion upon the ruin of the primitive constitution of both.

10. The beginning of his kingdom was Babel - Some way or other, he got into power: and so laid the foundations of a monarchy which was afterwards a head of gold. It doth not appear that he had any right to rule by birth; but either his fitness for government recommended him, or by power and policy he gradually advanced into the throne. See the antiquity of civil government, and particularly that form of it which lodges the sovereignty in a single person.

15. The account of the posterity of Canaan, and the land they possessed is more particular than of any other in this chapter, because these were the nations that were to be subdued before Israel, and their land was to become Immanuel's land. And by this account, it appears that the posterity of Canaan was both numerous and rich, and very pleasantly seated, and yet Canaan was under a curse. Canaan here has a better land than either Shem or Japheth and yet they have a better lot, for they inherit the blessing.

21. Two things especially are observable in this account of the posterity of Shem. The description of Shem, ver. 21, we have not only his name, Shem, which signifies a name; but two titles to distinguish him by.

1. He was the father of all the children of Eber. Eber was his great grandson, but why should he be called the father of all his children, rather than of all Arphaxad's or Salah's? Probably because Abraham and his seed, not only descended from Hebser, but from him were called Hebrews. Eber himself, we may suppose, was a man eminent for religion in a time of general apostasy; and the holy tongue being commonly called from him the Hebrew, it is probable he retained it in his family in the confusion of Babel, as a special token of God's favour to him.

2. He was the brother of Japheth the elder; by which it appears, that though Shem be commonly

put first, yet he was not Noah's first-born, but Japheth was elder. But why should this also be put as part of Shem's description, that he was the brother of Japheth, since that had been said before? Probably this is intended to signify the union of the Gentiles with the Jews in the church. He had mentioned it as Shem's honour, that he was the father of the Hebrews; but lest Japheth's seed should therefore be looked upon as shut out from the church, he here minds us, that he was the brother of Japheth, not in birth only, but in blessing, for Japheth was to dwell in the tents of Shem. The reason of the name of Peleg, ver. 25, because, in his days, (that is, about the time of his birth) was the earth divided among the children of men that were to inhabit it; either when Noah divided it, by an orderly distribution of it, as Joshua divided the land of Canaan by lot, or when, upon their refusal to comply with that division, God, in justice, divided them by the confusion of tongues.

XI

The distinction between the sons of God and the sons of men, now appeared again, when men began to multiply. According to this distinction, we have in this chapter,

I. The dispersion of the sons of men at Babel, ver. 1-9. where we have (1.) Their presumptuous design, to build a city and a tower, ver. 1- 4. (2.) The righteous judgment of God upon them in disappointing the design, by confounding their language, and so scattering them, ver. 5-9.

II. The pedigree of the sons of God down to Abraham, ver. 10-26. with a general account of his family, and remove out of his native country, ver. 27-32.

1. And the whole earth was of one language - Now while they all understood one another, they would be the more capable of helping one another, and the less inclinable to separate.
2. And they found a plain in the land of Shinar - A spacious plain, able to contain them all.
3. Go to, let us make brick, let us build us a city - The country being a plain, yielded neither stone nor morter, yet that did not discourage them, but they made brick to serve instead of stone, and slime, or pitch, instead of morter. Some think they intended hereby to secure themselves against the waters of another flood, but if they had, they would have chosen to build upon a mountain rather than upon a plain. But two things it seems they aimed at in building.
1. To make them a name: they would do something to be talked of by posterity. But they could not gain this point; for we do not find in any history the name of so much as one of these Babel - builders. Philo Judeus saith they engraved every one his name upon a brick; yet neither did that serve their purpose.
2. They did it to prevent their dispersion; lest we be scattered abroad upon the face of the earth - It was done (saith Josephus) in disobedience to that command, chap. ix, 1, replenish the earth. God orders them to scatter. No, say they, we will live and die together. In order hereunto they engage themselves and one another in this vast undertaking. That they might unite in one glorious empire, they resolve to build this city and tower, to be the metropolis of their kingdom, and the center of their unity.
5. And the Lord came down to see the city - 'Tis an expression after the manner of men, he knew it as clearly as men know that which they come upon the place to view. And the tower which the children of men builded - Which speaks, (1.) Their weakness and frailty, it was a foolish thing for the children of men, worms of the earth, to defy heaven. (2.) Their sinfulness, they were the sons of Adam, so it is in the Hebrew; nay, of that Adam, that sinful disobedient Adam, whose children are by nature children of disobedience. (3.) Their distinction from the children of God, from whom those daring builders had separated themselves, and built this tower to support and perpetuate the separation.
6. And the Lord said, Behold the people is one, and they have all one language - And if they continue one, much of the earth will be left uninhabited, and these children of men, if thus incorporated, will swallow up the little remnant of God's children, therefore it is decreed they must not be one. And now nothing will be restrained from them - And this is a reason why they must be crossed, in their design.
7. Go to, let us go down and there confound their language - This was not spoken to the angels, as if God needed either their advice or their assistance, but God speaks it to himself, or the Father to the Son and Holy Ghost. That they may not understand one another's speech - Nor could they well join hands when their tongues were divided: so that this was a proper means, both to take them off from their building, for if they could not understand one another, they could not help one another; and to dispose them to scatter, for when they could not understand one another, they could not enjoy one another. Accordingly three things were done,
1. Their language was confounded. God, who when he made man taught him to speak, now made those builders to forget their former language; and to speak a new one, which yet was the same to those of the same tribe or family, but not to others: those of one colony could converse together, but not with

those of another. We all suffer hereby to this day: in all the inconveniences we sustain by the diversity of languages, and all the trouble we are at to learn the languages we have occasion for, we smart for the rebellion of our ancestors at Babel; nay, and those unhappy controversies, which are strifes of words, and arise from our misunderstanding of one another's languages, for ought I know, are owing to this confusion of tongues. The project of some to frame an universal character in order to an universal language, how desirable soever it may seem, yet I think is but a vain thing for it is to strive against a divine sentence, by which the languages of the nations will be divided while the world stands. We may here lament the loss of the universal use of the Hebrew tongue, which from henceforth was the vulgar language of the Hebrews only, and continued so till the captivity in Babylon, where, even among them, it was exchanged for the Syriac. As the confounding of tongues divided the children of men, and scattered them abroad, so the gift of tongues bestowed upon the Apostles, Acts ii, 4-11, contributed greatly to the gathering together of the children of God, which were scattered abroad, and the uniting of them in Christ, that with one mind and mouth they might glorify God, Rom. xv, 6.

1. The imagination of a late writer, that God did not confound their tongues, but their religious worship, is grounded on criticisms concerning the meaning of the Hebrew word, which are absolutely false. Beside, would God confound their religious worship? Surely, He is a God of order, and not of confusion.

2. Their building was stopped, they left off to build the city - This was the effect of the confusion of their tongue's; for it not only disabled them from helping one another, but probably struck a damp upon their spirits, since they saw the hand of the Lord gone out against them.

3. The builders were scattered abroad from thence upon the face of the whole earth - They departed in companies after their families and after their tongues, chap. x, 5, 20, 31, to the several countries and places allotted to them in the division that had been made, which they knew before, but would not go to take possession of, 'till now they were forced to it. Observe

1. The very thing which they feared came upon them; that dispersion which they thought to evade.

2. That it was God's work; the Lord scattered them; God's hand is to be acknowledged in all scattering providences; if the family be scattered, relations scattered, churches scattered, it is the Lord's doing.

3. That they left behind them a perpetual memorandum of their reproach in the name given to the place; it was called Babel, confusion.

4. The children of men were now finally scattered, and never will come all together again 'till the great day. when the Son of Man shall sit upon the throne of his glory, and all nations shall be gathered before him, Matt. xxv, 31, 32.

10. Observe here,

1. That nothing is left upon record concerning those of this line, but their names and ages; the Holy Ghost seeming to hasten thro' them to the story of Abraham. How little do we know of those that are gone before us in this world, even those that lived in the same places where we live! Or indeed of those who are our contemporaries, but in distant places.

2. That there was an observable gradual decrease in the years of their lives. Shem reached to 600 years, which yet fell short of the age of the patriarchs before the flood; the three next came short of 500, the three next did not reach to 300, and after them we read not of any that attained to 200 but Terah; and not many ages after this, Moses reckoned 70 or 80 to be the utmost men ordinarily arrive at. When the earth began to be replenished, mens lives began to shorten so that the decrease is to be imputed to the wise disposal of providence, rather than to any decay of nature.

3. That Eber, from whom the Hebrews were denominated, was the longest lived of any that were born after the flood; which perhaps was the reward of his strict adherence to the ways of God.

27. Here begins the story of Abram. We have here,

1. His country: Ur of the Chaldee's - An idolatrous country, where even the children of Eber themselves degenerated.

2. His relations, mentioned for his sake, and because of their interest in he following story.

1. His father was Terah, of whom it is said, Josh. xxiv, 2, that he served other gods on the other side the flood; so early did idolatry gain footing in the world. Enough it is said, ver. 26, that when Terah was seventy years old he begat Abram, Nabor and Haran, which seems to tell us that Abram was the eldest son of Terah, and born in the 70th year; yet by comparing ver. 32, which makes Terah to die in his 205th year, with Acts vii, 4, where it is said that Abram removed from Haran when his father was dead, and chap. xii, 4, where it is said that he was but 75 years old when he removed from Haran, it appears that he was born in the 130th year of Terah, and probably was his youngest son. We have,

2. Some account of his brethren (1.) Nahor, out of whole family both Isaac and Jacob had their wives. (2.) Haran, the father of Lot, of whom it is here said, ver. 28, that he died before his father Terah. 'Tis likewise said that he died in Ur of the Chaldees, before that happy remove of the family out of that idolatrous country. (3.) His wife was Sarai, who, tho' some think was the same with Iscah the daughter of Haran. Abram himself saith, she was the daughter of his father, but not the daughter of his mother,

chap. xx, 12. She was ten years younger than Abram.

3. His departure out of Ur of the Chaldees, with his father Terah, and his nephew Lot, and the rest of his family, in obedience to the call of God. This chapter leaves them in Haran or Charran, a place about the mid-way between Ur and Canaan, where they dwelt 'till Terah's head was laid; probably because the old man was unable, through the infirmities of age, to proceed in his journey.

XII

From henceforward Abram and his seed are almost the only subject of the sacred history. In this chapter we have,

I. God's call of Abram to the land of Canaan ver. 1, 2, 3.

II. Abram's obedience to this call, ver. 4, 5.

III. His welcome to the land of Canaan, ver. 6-9.

IV. His occasional remove into Egypt, with an account of what happened to him there. Abram's flight and fault, ver. 10-13. Sarai's danger and deliverance, ver. 14-20.

1. We have here the call by which Abram was removed out of the land of his nativity into the land of promise, which was designed both to try his faith and obedience, and also to set him apart for God. The circumstances of this call we may be somewhat helped to the knowledge of, from Stephen's speech, Acts vii, 2, where we are told, 1. That the God of glory appeared to him to give him this call, appeared in such displays of his glory as left Abram no room to doubt. God spake to him after in divers manners: but this first time, when the correspondence was to be settled, he appeared to him as the God of glory, and spake to him. 2. That this call was given him in Mesopotamia, before he dwelt in Charran, and in obedience to this call, he came out of the land of the Chaldeans, and dwelt in Charran or Haran about five years, and from thence, when his father was dead, by a fresh command, he removed him into the land of Canaan. Some think Haran was in Chaldea, and so was still a part of Abram's country; or he having staid there five years, began to call it his country, and to take root there, till God let him know this was not the place he was intended for. Get thee out of thy country - Now, (1.) By this precept he was tried whether he loved God better than he loved his native soil, and dearest friends, and whether he could willingly leave all to go along with God. His country was become idolatrous, his kindred and his father's house were a constant temptation to him, and he could not continue with them without danger of being infected by them; therefore get thee out, (Hebrew.) vade tibi, get thee gone with all speed, escape for thy life, look not behind thee. (2.) By this precept he was tried whether he could trust God farther than he saw him, for he must leave his own country to go to a land that God would shew him; he doth not say, 'tis a land that I will give thee nor doth he tell him what land it was, or what kind of land; but he must follow God with an implicit faith, and take God's word for it in the general, though he had no particular securities given him, that he should be no loser by leaving his country to follow God.

2. Here is added an encouraging promise, nay a complication of promises,

1. I will make of thee a great nation - When God took him from his own people, he promised to make him the head of another people. This promise was.

1. A great relief to Abram's burden, for he had now no child.

2. A great trial to Abram's faith, for his wife had been long barren, so that if he believe, it must be against hope, and his faith must build purely upon that power which can out of stones raise up children unto Abraham.

2. I will bless thee - Either particularly with the blessing of fruitfulness, as he had blessed Adam and Noah; or in general, I will bless thee with all manner of blessings, both of the upper and nether springs: leave thy father's house, and I will give thee a father's blessing, better than that of thy progenitors.

3. I will make thy name great - By deserting his country he lost his name there: care not for that, (saith God) but trust me, and I will make thee a greater name than ever thou couldst have had there.

4. Thou shalt be a blessing - That is, thy life shall be a blessing to the places where thou shalt sojourn.

5. I will bless them that bless thee, and curse him that curseth thee - This made it a kind of league offensive and defensive between God and Abram. Abram heartily espoused God's cause, and here God promiseth to interest himself in his.

6. In thee shall all the families of the earth be blessed - This was the promise that crowned all the rest, for it points at the Messiah, in whom all the promises are yea and amen.

4. So Abram departed - He was not disobedient to the heavenly vision. His obedience was speedy

and without delay, submissive and without dispute.

5. *They took with them the souls that they had gotten* - That is, the proselytes they had made, and persuaded to worship the true God, and to go with them to Canaan; the souls which (as one of the Rabbins expresseth it) they had gathered under the wings of the divine Majesty.

6. *The Canaanite was then in the land* - He found the country possessed by Canaanites, who were likely to be but bad neighbours; and for ought appears he could not have ground to pitch his tent on but by their permission.

7. *And the Lord appeared to Abram* - Probably in a vision, and spoke to him comfortable words; *Unto thy seed will I give this land* - No place or condition can shut us out from God's gracious visits. Abram is a sojourner, unsettled, among Canaanites, and yet here also he meets with him that lives, and sees him. Enemies may part us and our tents, us and our altars, but not us and our God.

8. *And there he built an altar unto the Lord who appeared to him, and called on the name of the Lord* - Now consider this, (1.) As done upon a special occasion when God appeared to him, then and there he built an altar, with an eye to the God that appeared to him: thus he acknowledged with thankfulness God's kindness to him in making him that gracious visit and promise: and thus he testified his confidence in, and dependence upon the word which God had spoken. (2.) As his constant practice, whithersoever he removed. As soon as Abram was got to Canaan, though he was but a stranger and sojourner there, yet he set up, and kept up, the worship of God in his family; and wherever he had a tent, God had an altar and that an altar sanctified by prayer.

10. *And there was a famine in the land* - Not only to punish the iniquity of the Canaanites, but to exercise the faith of Abram. Now he was tried whether he could trust the God that brought him to Canaan, to maintain him there, and rejoice in him as the God of his salvation, when the fig-tree did not blossom. *And Abram went down into Egypt* - See how wisely God provides, that there should be plenty in one place, when there was scarcity in another; that, as members of the great body, we may not say to one another, I have no need of you.

13. *Say thou art my sister* - The grace Abram was most eminent for was faith, and yet he thus fell through unbelief and distrust of the divine Providence, even after God had appeared to him twice. Alas, What will become of the willows, when the cedars are thus shaken

17. *And the Lord plagued Pharaoh and his house* - Probably, those princes especially that had commended Sarai to Pharaoh. We are not told, particularly, what these plagues were; but, doubtless, there was something in the plagues themselves, or some explication added to them, sufficient to convince them that it was for Sarai's sake they were thus plagued.

18. *What is this that thou hast done?* - What an ill thing; how unbecoming a wife and good man! *Why didst thou not tell me that she was thy wife?* - Intimating, that if he had known that, he would not have taken her. It is a fault, too common among good people, to entertain suspicions of others beyond what there is cause for. We have often found more of virtue, honour, and conscience in some people, than we thought there was; and it ought to be a pleasure to us to be thus disappointed, as Abram was here, who found Pharaoh to be a better man than he expected.

20. *And Pharaoh commanded his men concerning him* - That is, he charged them not to injure him in any thing. And he appointed them, when Abram was disposed to return home, after the famine, to conduct him safe out of the country, as his convoy.

XIII

In this chapter we have a farther account of Abram;

I. In general, of his condition and behaviour in the land of promise, which was, now, the land of his pilgrimage. (1.) His removes, ver. 1,3, 4, 18. (2.) His riches, ver. 2. (3.) His devotion, ver. 4, 18.

II. A particular account of a quarrel that happened between him and Lot. (1.) The occasion of their strife, ver. 5, 6. (2.) The parties concerned in the strife, with the aggravation of it, ver. 7. (3.) The stopping of it by the prudence of Abram, ver. 8, 9.

III. Lot's departure from Abram to the plain of Sodom, ver. 10-14.

IV. God's appearance to Abram, to confirm the promise of the land of Canaan to him, ver. 14-17.

3. *He went on to Bethel* - Thither he went, not only because he was willing to go among his old acquaintance; but because there he had formerly had his altar. and though the altar was gone, probably he himself having taking it down when he left the place, lest it should be polluted by the idolatrous Canaanites; yet he came to the place of the altar, either to revive the remembrance of the sweet communion he had had with God at that place, or, perhaps, to pay the vows he had there made to God

when he undertook his journey into Egypt.

6. The land was not able to bear them - The place was too strait for them, and they had not room for their flocks.

7. And the Canaanite and the Perizzite dwelled in the land - This made the quarrel,

1. Very dangerous; if Abram and Lot cannot agree to feed their flocks together, it is well if the common enemy do not come upon them and plunder them both.

2. Very scandalous: No doubt the eyes of all the neighbours were upon them, because of the singularity of their religion, and the extraordinary sanctity they professed; and notice would soon be taken of this quarrel, and improvement made of it to their reproach by the Canaanites and Perizzites.

10. The garden of the Lord - That is, paradise.

13. Sinners before the Lord - That is, impudent daring sinners.

16. I will make thy seed as the dust of the earth - That is, they shall increase incredibly, and take them altogether; they shall be such a great multitude as no man can number. They were so in Solomon's time, 1 Kings iv, 20. Judah and Israel were many as the land which is by the sea in multitude. This God here gives him the promise of.

17. Arise, walk through the land - Enter and take possession, survey the parcels, and it will appear better than upon a distant prospect.

18. Then Abram removed his tent - God bid him walk through the land, that is, Do not think of fixing in it, but expect to be always unsettled, and walking through it to a better Canaan; in compliance with God's will herein, he removed his tent, conforming himself to the condition of a pilgrim. And he built there an altar - in token of his thankfulness to God for the kind visit he had made him.

XIV

We have in this chapter,

I. A war with the king of Sodom and his allies, ver. 1-12.

II. Abram's rescue of Lot from captivity, ver. 13-16.

III. Abram's return from that expedition, ver. 17. with an account of what passed, (1.) Between him and the king of Salem, ver. 18-20. (2.) Between him and the king of Sodom, ver. 21-24. In part fulfilled, that God would make his name great.

1. We have here an account of the first war that ever we read of in scripture, in which we may observe. [1.] The parties engaged in it. The invaders were four kings; two of them no less than kings of Shinar and Elam - That is, Chaldea and Persia; yet probably not the sovereign princes of those great kingdoms, but rather the heads of some colonies which came out thence, and settled themselves near Sodom, but retained the names of the countries from which they had their origin. The invaded were the kings of five cities that lay near together in the plain of Jordan, Sodom and Gomorrah, Admah, Zeboiim, and Zoar. [2.] The occasion of this war was, the revolt of the five kings from under the government of Chedorlaomer.

4. Twelve years they served him - The Sodomites were the posterity of Canaan, whom Noah had pronounced a servant to Shem, from whom Elam descended. Thus soon did that prophecy begin to be fulfilled. In the thirteenth year, beginning to be weary of their subjection, they rebelled - Denied their tribute, and attempted to shake off the yoke.

5. In the fourteenth year - After some pause and preparation, Chedorlaomer, in conjunction with his allies, set himself to reduce the revolters. See note at "ver. 1" (For [1.], [2.]) [3.] The progress of the war. The four kings laid the neighbouring countries waste, and enriched themselves with the spoil of them, ver. 5, 6, 7. Upon the alarm of which, the king of Sodom and his allies went out and were routed.

13. We have here an account of the only military action we ever find Abram engaged in; and this he was not prompted to by avarice or ambition, but purely by a principle of charity.

14. He armed his trained servants, born in his house - To the number of three hundred and eighteen: a great family, but a small army; about as many as Gideon's that routed the Midianites, Jude vii, 7. He drew out his trained servants, or his catechized servants; not only instructed in the art of war, but instructed in the principles of religion; for Abram commanded his household to keep the way of the Lord.

16. His brother Lot - That is, his kinsman.

18. The Rabbins say, that Melchizedek was Shem the son of Noah, who was king and priest to those that descended from him, according to the patriarchal model. Many Christian writers have thought that this was an appearance of the Son of God himself, our Lord Jesus, known to Abram at this time by this name. But as nothing is expressly revealed concerning it, we can determine nothing. He brought

forth bread and wine - For the refreshment of Abram and his soldiers, and in congratulation of their victory. This he did as a king. As priest of the most high God he blessed Abram, which we may suppose a greater refreshment to Abram than his bread and wine were.

19. Blessed be Abram, of the most high God - Observe the titles he here gives to God, which are very glorious.

1. The most high God, which speaks his absolute perfections in himself, and his sovereign dominion over all the creatures.

2. Possessor of heaven and earth - That is, rightful owner and sovereign Lord of all the creatures; because he made them.

20. And blessed be the most high God - Note,

1. In all our prayers we must praise God, and join hallelujahs with all our hosannas. These are the spiritual sacrifices we must offer up daily, and upon particular occasions.

2. God as the most high God must have the glory of all our victories. In them he shews himself higher than our enemies, and higher than we, for without him we could do nothing. And he gave him tithes of all - That is, of the spoils, Heb. vii, 4. This may be looked upon, (1.) As a gratuity presented to Melchizedek, by way of return for his respects. (2.) As an offering dedicated to the most high God, and therefore put into the hands of Melchizedek his priest. Jesus Christ, our great Melchizedek, is to be humbly acknowledged by every one of us as our king and priest, and not only the tithe of all, but all we have, must be given up to him.

21. Give me the souls, and take thou the substance - So the Hebrew reads it. Here he fairly begs the persons, but as freely bestows the goods on Abram. Gratitude teaches us to recompense to the utmost of our power those that have undergone fatigues, or been at expence for our service.

22. I have lift up mine hand to the Lord that I will not take anything - Here Observe, (1.) The titles he gives to God, the most high God, the possessor of heaven and earth - The same that Melchizedek had just now used. It is good to learn of others how to order our speech concerning God, and to imitate those who speak well in divine things. (2.) The ceremony used in this oath; I have lift up my hand - In religious swearing we appeal to God's knowledge of our truth and sincerity, and imprecate his wrath if we swear falsely; and the lifting up of the hands is expressive of both. Lest thou shouldst say, I have made Abram rich - Probably, Abram knew the king of Sodom to be a proud and scornful man, and one that would be apt to turn such a thing as this to his reproach afterwards, and when we have to do with such men, we have need to act with particular caution.

23. From a thread to a shoe-latchet - Not the least thing that had ever belonged to the king of Sodom.

XV

In this chapter we have a solemn treaty between God and Abram,

I. A general assurance of God's kindness and goodwill to Abram, ver. 1.

II. A particular declaration of the purposes of his love concerning him, in two things. (1.) That he would give him a numerous issue, ver. 2-7. (2.) That he would give him Canaan for an inheritance, ver. 7-16.

1. After these things - (1.) After that act of generous charity which Abram had done, in rescuing his neighbours, God made him this gracious visit. (2.) After that victory which he had obtained over four kings; lest Abram should be too much elevated with that, God comes to tell him he had better things in store for him. The word of the Lord came unto Abram - That is, God manifested himself to Abram, in a vision - Which supposeth Abram awake, and some sensible token of the presence of the divine glory, saying, Fear not Abram - Abram might fear lest the four kings he had routed, should rally and fall upon him. No, saith God, fear not: fear not their revenge, nor thy neighbour's envy; I will take care of thee. I am thy shield - Or, emphatically, I am a shield to thee, present with thee, actually defending thee. The consideration of this, that God himself is, a shield to his people, to secure them from all destructive evils, a shield ready to them, and a shield round about them, should silence all perplexing fears. And thy exceeding great reward - Not only thy rewarder, but thy reward. God himself is the felicity of holy souls; He is the portion of their inheritance, and their cup.

3. Behold to me thou hast given no seed - Not only no son, but no seed. If he had had a daughter, from her the promised Messias might have come, who was to be the Seed of the Woman; but he had neither son nor daughter.

5. And he brought him forth - It seems, early in the morning, and said, look now toward heaven, and tell the stars: so shall thy seed be -

1. So innumerable, for so the stars seem to a common eye. Abram feared he should have no child at all, but God tells him his descendents should be so many as not to be numbered.

John Wesley

2. So illustrious, as the stars of heaven for splendour; for to them pertained the glory, Rom. ix, 4. Abram's seed according to the flesh were like the dust of the earth, Chap. xiii, 16, but his spiritual seed are like the stars of heaven.

6. And he believed in the Lord - That is, believed the truth of that promise which God had now made him, resting upon the power, and faithfulness of him that made it: see how the apostle magnifies this faith of Abram, and makes it a standing example, Rom. iv, 19-21. He was not weak in faith; he staggered not at the promise: he was strong in faith; he was fully persuaded. The Lord work such a faith in every one of us. And he counted it to him for righteousness - That is, upon the score of this he was accepted of God, and, by faith he obtained witness that he was righteous, Heb. xi, 4. This is urged in the New Testament to prove, that we are justified by faith without the works of the law, Rom. iv, 3,Gal. iii, 6, forABram was so justified, while he was yet uncircumcised. If Abram, that was so rich in good works, was not justified by them, but by his faith, much less can we. This faith, which was imputed to Abram for righteousness, had newly struggled with unbelief, ver. 2, and coming off, conqueror, it was thus crowned, thus honoured.

7. I am the Lord that brought thee out of Ur of the Chaldees - Out of the fire of the Chaldees, so some: that is, from their idolatries; for the Chaldeans worshipped the fire. Or, from their persecutions. The Jewish writers have a tradition, that Abram was cast into a fiery furnace for refusing to worship idols, and was miraculously delivered. It is rather a place of that name. Thence God brought him by an effectual call, brought him by a gracious violence; snatched him as a brand out of the burning. Observe how God speaks of it as that which he gloried in. I am the Lord that brought thee out - He glories in it as an act both of power and grace. To give thee this land to inherit it - Not only to possess it, but to possess it as an inheritance, which is the surest title. The providence of God hath secret, but gracious designs in all its various dispensations: we cannot conceive the projects of providence, 'till the event shews what it was driving at.

8. Whereby shall I know that I shall inherit it? - This did not proceed from distrust of God's power or promise, but he desired this,

1. For the strengthening of his own faith. He believed, ver. 6, but here he prays, Lord help me against my unbelief, Now, he believed, but he desired a sign, to be treasured up against an hour of temptation.

2. For the ratifying of the promise to his posterity, that they also might believe it.

9. Take me an heifer - Perhaps Abram expected some sign from heaven, but God gives him a sign upon a sacrifice. Those that would receive the assurances of God's favour, must attend instituted ordinances, and expect to meet with God in them. Observe,

1. God appointed that each of the beasts used for his service should be three years old, because then they were at their full growth and strength. God must be served with the best we have.

2. We do not read that God gave Abram particular directions how to manage these, knowing that he was well versed in the custom of sacrifices.

3. Abram took as God appointed him, though as yet he knew not how these things should become a sign to him. He divided the beasts in the midst, according to the ceremony used in continuing covenants, Jer. xxxiv, 18, 19, where it is said, they cut the calf in twain, and passed between the parts.

4. Abram, having prepared according to God's appointment, set himself to expect what sign God would give him by these.

12. And when the sun was going down - About the time of the evening oblation. Early in the morning, while the stars were yet to be seen, God had given him orders concerning the sacrifices, ver. 5, and we may suppose it was at least his morning's work to prepare them, and set them in order; which when he had done, he abode by them praying and waiting 'till towards evening. A deep sleep fell upon Abram - Not a common sleep through weariness or carelessness, but a divine extasy, that being wholly taken off from things sensible, he might be wholly taken up with the contemplation of things spiritual. The doors of the body were locked up, that the soul might be private and retired, and might act the more freely. And lo, a horror of great darkness fell upon him - This was designed to strike an awe upon the spirit of Abram, and to possess him with a holy reverence. Holy fear prepares the soul for holy joy; God humbles first, and then lifts up.

13. Thy seed shall be strangers - So they were in Canaan first, Psalm cv, 11, 12, and afterwards in Egypt: before they were lords of their own land, they were strangers in a strange land. The inconveniences of an unsettled state make a happy settlement the more welcome. Thus the heirs of heaven are first strangers on earth. And them they shall serve - So they did the Egyptians, Exod. i, 13. See how that which was the doom of the Canaanites, chap. ix, 25, proves the distress of Abram's seed: they are made to serve; but with this difference, the Canaanites serve under a curse, the Hebrews under a blessing. And they shall afflict them - See Exod. i, 11. Those that are blessed and beloved of God are often afflicted by wicked men. This persecution began with mocking, when Ishmael the son of an Egyptian, persecuted Isaac, chap. xxi, 9, and it came at last to murder, the basest of murders, that of their new born children; so that more or less it continued 400 years.

14. That nation whom they shall serve, even the Egyptians, will I judge - This points at the plagues of Egypt, by which God not only constrained the Egyptians to release Israel, but punished them for all the hardships they had put upon them. The punishing of persecutors is the judging of them; it is a righteous thing with God, and a particular act of justice, to recompense tribulation to those that trouble his people. 3. The deliverance of Abram's seed out of Egypt. And afterwards shall they come out with great substance - Either after they have been afflicted 400 years, or, after the Egyptians are judged and plagued.

15. Thou shalt go to thy fathers - At death we go to our fathers, to all our fathers that are gone before us to the state of the dead, to our godly fathers that are gone before us to the state of the blessed. The former helps to take off the terror of death, the latter puts comfort into it. Thou shalt be buried in a good old age - Perhaps mention is made of his burial here, where the land of Canaan is promised him, because a burying-place was the first possession he had in it. Old age is a blessing, if it be a good old age: theirs may be called a good old age,

1. That are old and healthful, not loaded with such distempers as make them weary of life:

2. That are old and holy, whose hoary head is found in the way of righteousness, old and useful, old and exemplary for godliness, that is indeed a good old age.

16. They shall come hither again - Hither to the land of Canaan, wherein thou now art. The reason why they must not have the land of promise in possession till the fourth generation, is because the iniquity of the Amorites was not yet full. The righteous God has determined, that they shall not be cut off till they are arrived to such a pitch of wickedness; and therefore till it come to that, the seed of Abram must be kept out of possession.

17. When the sun was gone down the sign was given - The smoking furnace signified the affliction of his seed in Egypt: they were there in the furnace of affliction, and labouring in the very fire. They were there in the smoke, their eyes darkened that they could not see to the end of their troubles. 2. The burning lamp speaks comfort in this affliction; and this God shewed Abram at the same time with the smoking furnace. The lamp notes direction in the smoke; God's word was their lamp, a light shining in a dark place. Perhaps too this burning lamp prefigured the pillar of a cloud and fire which led them out of Egypt. 3. The passing of these between the pieces was the confirming of the covenant God now made with him. It is probable this furnace and lamp, which passed between the pieces, burned and consumed them, and so compleated the sacrifice, and testified God's acceptance of it, as of Gideon's, Jude vi, 21, Manoah's, Jude xiii, 19, 20, and Solomon's, 2 Chron. vii, 1. So it intimates,

1. That God's covenants with man are made by sacrifice, Psalm l, 5, by Christ, the great sacrifice.

2. God's acceptance of our spiritual sacrifices is a token for good, and an earnest of farther favours.

18. In that same day, the Lord made a covenant with Abram, saying, Unto thy seed have I given this land - He had said before, To thy seed will I give this land, but here he saith, I have given it; that is,

1. I have given the promise, the charter is sealed and delivered, and cannot be disanulled.

2. The possession is as sure in due time, as if it were now actually delivered to them. In David's time and Solomon's their jurisdiction extended to the utmost of these limits, 2 Chron. ix, 26. And it was their own fault that they were not sooner and longer in possession of all these territories. They forfeited their right by their sins, and by their own sloth and cowardice kept themselves out of possession. The present occupants are named, because their number and strength and long prescription, should be no hindrance to the accomplishment of this promise in its season; and to magnify God's love to Abram and his seed, in giving to that one nation the possession of many nations.

XVI

Hagar probably was one of those maid-servants which the king of Egypt (among other gifts) bestowed upon Abram, chap. xii. 16. Concerning her we have four things in this chapter,

I. Her marriage to Abram her master, ver. 1-3.

II. Her misbehaviour towards Sarai her mistress, ver. 4-6.

III. Her discourse with an angel that met her in her flight, ver. 7- 14.

IV. Her delivery of a son, ver. 15, 16.

1. We have here the marriage of Abram to Hagar, who was his secondary wife. Herein, though he may be excused, he cannot be justified; for from the beginning it was not so: and when it was so, it seems to have proceeded from an irregular desire to build up their families, for the speedier peopling of the world. But now we must not do so? Christ has reduced this matter to the first institution, and makes

John Wesley

the marriage union to be between one man and one woman only.

4. We have here the ill consequences of Abram's marriage to Hagar: a deal of mischief it made presently. Hagar no sooner perceives herself with child, but she looks scornfully upon her mistress; upbraids her perhaps with her barrenness, and insults over her. Sarai falls upon Abram, and very unjustly charges him with the injury, suspecting that he countenanced Hagar's insolence: and as one not willing to hear what Abram had to say she rashly appeals to God. The Lord judge between me and thee, as if Abram had refused to right her. When passion is upon the throne, reason is out of doors, and is neither heard nor spoken. Those are not always in the right that are most forward in appealing to God. Rash and bold imprecations are commonly evidences of guilt and a bad cause.

6. Thy maid is in thy hand - Though she was his wife, he would not countenance her in any thing disrespectful to Sarai. Those who would keep up peace and love, must return first answers to hard accusations; husbands and wives particularly should endeavour not to be both angry together. And when Sarai dealt hardly with her - Making her to serve with rigor; she fled from her face - She not only avoided her wrath for the present, but totally deserted her service.

7. Here is the first mention we have in scripture of an angel's appearance, who arrested her in her flight. It should seem she was making towards her own country, for she was in the way to Shur, which lay towards Egypt. 'Twere well if our afflictions would make us think of our home, the better county. But Hagar was now out of the way of her duty, and going farther astray, when the angel found her. It is a great mercy to be stopt in a sinful way, either by conscience or providence.

8. And he said, Hagar, Sarai's maid -

1. As a check to her pride. Though she was Abram's wife, yet he calls her Sarai's maid to humble her.

2. As a rebuke to her flight. Sarai's maid ought to be in Sarai's tent, and not wandering in the wilderness. Whence comest thou - Consider that thou art running away both from the duty thou wast bound to, and the privileges thou wast blest with, in Abram's tent. And Whither wilt thou go? - Thou art running thyself into sin in Egypt; if she return to that people, she will return to their gods. And she said, I flee from the face of my mistress - She acknowledges her fault in fleeing from her mistress; and yet, excuses it, that it was from the face, or displeasure, of her mistress.

9. And the angel said, Return to thy mistress, and submit thyself under her hand - Go home and humble thyself for what thou hast done amiss, and resolve for the future to behave thyself better.

10. I will multiply thy seed exceedingly - Hebrew. multiplying I will multiply it, that is, multiply it in every age, so as to perpetuate it. 'Tis supposed that the Turks at this day descended from Ishmael, and they are a great people.

11. Ishmael, that is, God will hear; and the reason is, because the Lord hath heard: he hath, and therefore he will. The experience we have had of God's seasonable kindness in distress should encourage us to hope for the like help in the like exigencies. Even there, where there is little cry of devotion, the God of pity hears the cry of affliction: tears speak as well as prayers.

12. He will be a wild man - A wild ass of a man, so the word is: rude, and bold and fearing no man; untamed, untractable, living at large, and impatient of service and restraint. His hand will be against every man - That is his sin, and every man's hand against him - That is his punishment. Note, Those that have turbulent spirits have commonly troublesome lives: they that are provoking, and injurious to others, must expect to be repaid in their own coin. And yet, he shall dwell in the presence of all his brethren -- though threatened and insulted by all his neighbours, yet he shall keep his ground, and, for Abram's sake more than his own, shall be able to make his part good with them. Accordingly we read, chap. xxv, 18, that he died, as he lived, in the presence of all his brethren.

13. And she called the name of the Lord that spake unto her - That is, thus she made confession of his name, Thou God seest me - This should be with her, his name forever, and this his memorial, by which she will know him, and remember him while she lives, Thou God seest me. Thou seest my sorrow and affliction. This Hagar especially refers to: when we have brought ourselves into distress by our own folly, yet God has not forsaken us. Thou seest the sincerity of my repentance. Thou seest me, if in any instance I depart from thee. This thought should always restrain us from sin, and excite us to duty, Thou God seest me. Have I here also looked after him that seeth me? - Probably she knew not who it was that talked with her till he was departing, and then looking after him, with a reflexion like that of the two disciples, Luke xxiv, 31, 32. Here also - Not only in Abram's tent, and at his altar, but here also, in this wilderness: here, where I never expected it, where I was out of the way of my duty?

14. The well was called Beer-lahai-roi - The well of him that lives and sees me. 'Tis likely Hagar put this name upon it, and it was retained long after. This was the place where the God of glory manifested the special care he took of a poor woman in distress. Those that are graciously admitted into communion with God, and receive seasonable comforts from him, should tell others what he has done for their souls, that they also may be encouraged to seek him and trust in him.

Wesley's Notes on the Bible - The Old Testament: Genesis - Ruth
XVII

This chapter contains articles of agreement betwixt the great Jehovah, the father of mercies, and pious Abram, the father of the faithful. Mention was made of this covenant, chap. xv, 18. but here it is particularly drawn up. Here are,

I. The circumstances of the making of this covenant, the time and manner, ver. 1. and the posture Abram was in, ver. 3.

II. The covenant itself, in the particular instances.
    1. That he should be the father of many nations, ver.4. 6. and in token of that his name was changed, ver. 5.
    2. That God would be a God to him and his seed, and would give them the land of Canaan, ver. 7, 8. and the seal of this part of the covenant was circumcision, ver. 9-14.
    3. That he should have a son by Sarai, and in token of that her name was changed, ver. 15, 16. This promise Abraham received, ver. 17. And his request for Ishmael, (ver. 18.) was answered abundantly to his satisfaction, ver. 19-22.

III. The circumcision of Abraham and his family, according to God's appointment, ver. 23-27.

    1. And when Abram was ninety nine years old - Full thirteen years after the birth of Ishmael. So long the promise of Isaac was deferred;
        1. Perhaps to correct Abram's over-hasty marrying of Hagar.
        2. That Abram and Sarai being so far striken in age, God's power in this matter might be the more magnified. The Lord appeared unto Abram - In some visible display of God's immediate glorious presence with him. And said, I am the Almighty God - By this name he chose to make himself known to Abram, rather than by his name Jehovah, Exod. vi, 3. He used it to Jacob, chap. xxxv, 11. They called him by this name, chap. xxviii, 5; xliii, 14; xlviii, 3. It is the name of God that is mostly used throughout the book of Job, at least 30 times in the discourses of that book, in which Jehovah is used but once. After Moses, Jehovah is more frequently used, and this very rarely. I am El-Shaddai. It speaks the almighty power of God, either
        1. As an avenger, from |wrv| he destroyed, or laid waste; so some: and they think God took this title from the destruction of the old world: Or,
        2. As a benefactor, |v| for |rva| who, and |yr| it sufficeth. Our old English translation reads it here, very significantly, I am God All- sufficient. The God with whom we have to do, is self-sufficient; he hath every thing, and he needs not any thing. And he is enough to us, if we be in covenant with him; we have all in him, and we have enough in him; enough to satisfy our most enlarged desires; enough to supply the defect of every thing else, and to secure us happiness for our immortal souls. But the covenant is mutual, walk before me, and be thou perfect - That is, upright and sincere. Observe,
        1. That to walk before God, is to set God always before us, and to think, and speak, and act, in every thing as those that are always under his eye. It is to have a constant regard to his word, as our rule, and to his glory, as our end, in all our actions. It is to be inward with him in all the duties of religious worship, and to be entire for him in all holy conversation.
        2. That upright walking with God is the condition of our interest in his all-sufficiency. If we neglect him, or dissemble with him, we forfeit the benefit of our relation to him.
        3. A continual regard to God's all-sufficiency will have a great influence upon our upright walking with him.
    3. And Abram fell on his face while God talked with him - Either,
        1. As one overcome by the brightness of the Divine glory: Daniel and John did so likewise. Or.
        2. As one ashamed of himself, and blushing to think of the honours done to one so unworthy. He looks upon himself with humility, and upon God with reverence, and, in token of both, falls on his face.
    4. The promise is here introduced with solemnity: As for me, saith the Great God, Behold, behold and admire it, behold and be assured of it, my covenant is with thee. And thou shalt be a father of many nations - This implies,
        1. That his seed after the flesh should be very numerous, both in Isaac and in Ishmael, and in the sons of Keturah. And the event answered, for there have been, and are, more of the children of men descended from Abraham, than from any one man at equal distance with him from Noah, the common root.
        2. That all believers, in every age, should be looked upon as his spiritual seed, as the father of the faithful. In this sense the apostle directs us to understand this promise, Rom. iv, 16, 17. He is the father of those, in every nation, that, by faith, enter into covenant with God, and (as the Jewish writers express it) are gathered under the wings of the divine majesty.

John Wesley

5. In token of this, his name was changed from Abram, a high father, to Abraham, the father of a multitude. This was to confirm the faith of Abraham, while he was childless; perhaps even his own name was sometimes an occasion of grief to him; Why should he be called a high father, who was not a father at all? But now God had promised him a numerous issue, and had given him a name which signified so much; that name was his joy.

7. And I will establish my covenant - Not to be altered or revoked; not with thee only, then it would die with thee but with thy seed after thee; and it is not only thy seed after the flesh, but thy spiritual seed. It is everlasting in the evangelical meaning of it. The covenant of grace is everlasting; it is from everlasting in the counsels of it, and to everlasting in the consequences of it; and the external administration of it is transmitted, with the seal of it, to the seed of believers, and the internal administration of it by the Spirit to Christ's seed in every age. This is a covenant of exceeding great and precious promises. Here are two which indeed are all-sufficient, that God would be their God. All the privileges of the covenant, all its joys, and all its hopes, are summed up in this. A man needs desire no more than this to make him happy. What God is himself, that he will be to his people: wisdom to guide and counsel them, power to protect and support them, goodness to supply and comfort them; what faithful worshippers can expect from the God they serve, believers shall find in God as theirs. This is enough, yet not all.

8. And I will give thee Canaan for an everlasting possession - God had before promised this land to Abraham and his seed, ver. 18. But here, it is promised for an everlasting possession, as a type of heaven, that everlasting rest which remains for the people of God. This is that better country to which Abraham had an eye, and the grant of which was that which answered the vast extent of that promise, that God would be to them a God; so that if God had not designed this, he would have been ashamed to be called their God, Heb. xi, 16. As the land of Canaan was secured to the seed of Abraham, according to the flesh; so heaven is secured to all his spiritual seed for a possession truly everlasting. The offer of this eternal life is made in the word, and confirmed by the sacraments, to all that are under the external administration of the covenant, and the earnest of it is given to all believers.

10. The token of the covenant, is circumcision, for the sake of which the covenant is itself called the covenant of circumcision, Acts vii, 8. It is here said to be the covenant which Abraham and his seed must keep, as a copy or counterpart, it is called a sign and seal, Rom. iv, 11, for it was.

1. A confirmation to Abraham and his seed of those promises which were God's part of the covenant, assuring them that, in due time, Canaan should be theirs: and the continuance of this ordinance, after Canaan was theirs, intimates, that that promise looked farther, to another Canaan.

2. An obligation upon Abraham and his seed to that duty which was their part of the covenant, not only to the duty of accepting the covenants and putting away the corruption of the flesh, which were primarily signified by circumcision, but in general to the observation of all God's commands. They who will have God to be to them a God, must consent to be to him a people. Now,

1. Circumcision was a bloody ordinance, for all things by the law were purged with blood, Heb. ix, 22. See Exod. xxiv, 8. But the blood of Christ being shed, all bloody ordinances are now abolished. Circumcision therefore gives way to baptism.

2. It was peculiar to the males, though the women also were included in the covenant.

3. Christ having not yet offered himself for us, God would have man to enter into covenant, by the offering of some part of his own body, and no part could be better spared.

4. The ordinance was to be administered to children when they were eight days old, that they might gather some strength to be able to undergo the pain of it.

5. The children of the strangers were to be circumcised, which looked favourable upon the Gentiles, who should, in due time be brought into the family of Abraham, by faith. Here is, (1.) The promise made to Abraham of a son by Sarai, that son in whom the promise made to him should be fulfilled, that he should be the father of many nations, for she also shall be a mother of nations, and kings of people shall be of her, ver. 16. Note,

1. God reveals the purposes of his goodwill to his people by degrees. God had told Abraham long before, that he should have a son, but never 'till now that he should have a son by Sarai.

2. The blessing of the Lord makes fruitful, and adds no sorrow with it; no such sorrow as was in Hagar's case. I will bless her, with the blessing of fruitfulness, and then thou shalt have a son of her.

3. Civil government and order is a great blessing to the church. It is promised not only that people, but kings of people should be of her; not a headless rout, but a well modelled, well governed society.

15. Sarah shall her name be - The same letter is added to her name that was to Abraham's. Sarai signifies my princess, as if her honour were confined to one family only: Sarah signifies a princess, viz. of multitudes.

17. Then Abraham fell on his face, and laughed - It was a laughter of delight, not of distrust. Now it was that Abraham rejoiced to see Christ's day, now he saw it and was glad, John viii, 56, for as he saw heaven in the promise of Canaan, so he saw Christ in the promise of Isaac, and said, Shall a child be born to him that is an hundred years old? - He doth not here speak of it, as at all doubtful, for we are

sure he staggered not at the promise, Rom. iv, 20, but as wonderful, and that which could not be effected but by the almighty power of God.

18. And Abraham said, O that Ishmael might live before thee! - This he speaks nor as desiring that Ishmael might be preferred before the son he should have by Sarah, but as dreading lest he should be forsaken of God, he puts up this petition on his behalf. The great thing we should desire of God, for our children, is, that they may live before him, that is, that they may be kept in covenant with him, and may have grace to walk before him in their uprightness. God's answer to this prayer, is an answer of peace. Abraham could not say he sought God's face in vain.

20. As for Ishmael, I have heard thee; I have blessed him - That is, I have many blessings in store for him.

1. His posterity shall be numerous; I will multiply him exceedingly;

2. They shall be considerable; twelve princes shall he beget. We may charitably hope that spiritual blessings also were bestowed upon him, though the visible church was not brought out of his loins.

21. He names that child, Isaac - Laughter, because Abraham rejoiced in spirit when this son was promised him.

XVIII

We have an account in this chapter of another interview between God and Abraham, probably within a few days after the former, as the reward of his chearful obedience to the law of circumcision. Here is,

I. The visit which God made him, ver. 1-8

II. The matters discoursed of between them,
 1. The purposes of God's love concerning Sarah, ver. 9-15.
 2. The purposes of God's wrath concerning Sodom. (1.) The discovery God made to Abraham of his design to destroy Sodom, ver. 16-22. (2.) The intercession Abraham made for Sodom, ver. 23-33.

1. This appearance of God to Abraham seems to have had in it more of freedom and familiarity, and less of grandeur and majesty, than those we have hitherto read of, and therefore more resembles that great visit which in the fulness of time the Son of God was to make to the world. He sat in the tent-door in the heat of the day - Not so much to repose himself, as to seek an opportunity of doing good, by giving entertainment to strangers.

2. And lo three men - These three men were three spiritual heavenly beings, now assuming human shapes, that they might be visible to Abraham, and conversable with him. Some think they were all three created angels; others, that one of them was the Son of God. He bowed himself towards the ground - Religion doth not destroy but improve good manners, and teaches us to honour all men.

9. Where is Sarah thy wife? - By naming her, they gave intimation to Abraham, that tho' they seemed strangers, yet they well knew him and his family: by enquiring after her, they shewed a kind concern for the family of one, whom they found respectful to them. And by speaking of her, she over-hearing it, they drew her to listen to what was farther to be said.

10. I will certainly return unto thee - And visit thee. God will return to those that bid him welcome.

12. Sarah laughed within herself - It was not a laughter of faith, like Abraham's, chap. xvii, 17, but a laughter of doubting and distrust. The great objection which Sarah could not get over was her age. I am waxed old, and past child-bearing in a course of nature, especially having been hitherto barren, and which magnifies the difficulty, My Lord is old also. Observe here, That Sarah calls Abraham her Lord, and the Holy Ghost takes notice of it to her honour, and recommends it to the imitation of all Christian wives, 1Pe iii, 6. Sarah obeyed Abraham calling him Lord, in token of respect and subjection.

17. Shall I hide from Abraham that thing which I do - Thus doth God in his councils express himself after the manner of men, with deliberation. The secret of the Lord is with them that fear him. Those that by faith live a life of communion with God, cannot but know more of his mind than other people. They have a better insight into what is present, and a better foresight of what is to come.

19. I know Abraham that he will command his children, and his household after him - This is a bright part of Abraham's character. He not only prayed with his family, but he taught them, as a man of knowledge; nay, he commanded them as a man in authority, and was prophet and king, as well as priest, in his own house. And he not only took care of his children, but of his household: his servants were catechized servants. Masters of families should instruct, and inspect the manners of all under their roof. And this is given as the reason why God would make known to him his purpose concerning Sodom; because he was communicative of his knowledge, and improved it for the benefit of those that were under his charge.

21. I will go down now and see - Not as if there were any thing concerning which God is in doubt; but he is pleased thus to express himself after the manner of men.

23. Abraham drew near - This expression intimates, A holy concern. A holy confidence; he drew near with an assurance of faith, drew near as a prince, Job xxxi, 37.

27. Behold now, I have taken upon me to speak unto the Lord, who am but dust and ashes - He speaks as one amazed at his own boldness, and the liberty God graciously allowed him, considering God's greatness, he is the Lord; and his own meanness, but dust and ashes. Whenever we draw near to God, it becomes us reverently to acknowledge the vast distance that there is between us and Him. He is the Lord of glory, we are worms of the earth.

30. Oh let not the Lord be angry - The importunity which believers use in their addresses to God is such, that if they were dealing with a man like themselves, they could not but fear that he would be angry with them. But he with whom we have to do is God and not man, and he is pleased when he is wrestled with. But why then did Abraham leave off asking when he had prevailed so far as to get the place spared if there were but ten righteous in it? Either,

1. Because he owned that it deserved to perish if there were not so many: as the dresser of the vineyard, who consented that the barren tree should be cut down if one year's trial more did not make it fruitful, Luke xiii, 9. Or,

2. Because God restrained his spirit from asking any further. When God hath determined the ruin of a place, he forbids it to be prayed for, Jer. vii, 16.

33. Abraham returned into his place - To wait what the event would be; and it proved that his prayer was heard, and yet Sodom not spared, because there were not ten righteous in it.

XIX

We read, chap. 18. of God's coming to take a view of the state of Sodom, what its wickedness was, and what righteous there were in it: here we have the result of that enquiry.

I. It was found upon trial that Lot was very good, ver. 1, 2, 3. and it did not appear that there were any more of the same character.

II. It was found that the Sodomites were very wicked, ver. 4-11.

III. Special care was therefore taken for the securing of Lot and his family, ver. 12-23.

IV. The ruin of Sodom, and of Lot's wife, ver. 24-26. with a general repetition of the story, ver. 27-29.

V. A foul sin that Lot was guilty of, in committing incest with his two daughters, ver. 30-38.

1. And there came two - Probably two of the three that had just before been with Abraham, the two created angels who were sent to execute God's purpose concerning Sodom.

3. And he pressed upon them greatly - Partly because he would by no means have them to expose themselves to the perils of lodging in the streets of Sodom, and partly because he was desirous of their converse.

4. Here were old and young all from every quarter - The old were not past it, and the young were soon come up to it. Either they had no magistrates to protect the peaceable, or their magistrates were themselves aiding and abetting.

8. I have two daughters - This was unadvisedly and unjustifiably offered. It is true, of two evils we must chose the less, but of two sins we must chose neither, nor ever do evil that good may come of it.

11. And they smote the men with blindness - This was designed to put an end to their attempt, and to be an earnest of their utter ruin the next day.

13. We will destroy this place - The holy angels are ministers of God's wrath for the destruction of sinners, as well as of his mercy for the preservation and deliverance of his people.

14. Up, get you out this place - The manner of expression is startling. It was not time to trifle, when the destruction was just at the door. But he seemed to them as one that mocked - They thought perhaps that the assault which the Sodomites had just now made upon his house had disturbed his head, and put him into such a fright that knew not what he said. They that made a jest of every thing, made a jest of that, and so perished in the overthrow. Thus many who are warned of the danger they are in by sin, make a light matter of it; such will perish with their blood upon their heads.

16. Tho' Lot did not make a jest of the warning as his sons-in-law, yet he lingered, he did not make so much haste as the case required. And it might have been fatal to him, if the angels had not laid hold on his hand, and brought him forth. Herein the Lord was merciful to him, otherwise he might justly have left him to perish, since he was loath to depart. If God had not been merciful to us, our lingering

had been our ruin.

17. *Look not behind thee* - He must not loiter by the way; stay not in all the plain - For it would all be made one dead sea: he must not take up short of the place of refuge appointed him; escape to the mountain - Such as these are the commands given to those who through grace are delivered out of a sinful state.

1. Return not to sin and Satan, for that's looking back to Sodom.
2. Rest not in the world, for that's staying in the plain. And,
3. Reach toward Christ and heaven, for that is escaping to the mountain, short of which we must not take up.

22. *I cannot do any thing till thou be come thither* - The very presence of good men in a place helps to keep off judgments. See what care God takes for the preservation of his people!

24. *Then the Lord rained - from the Lord* - God the Son, from God the Father, for the Father has committed all judgment to the Son. He that is the saviour will be the destroyer of those that reject the salvation.

25. *And he overthrew the cities, and all the inhabitants of them, the plain, and all that grew upon the ground* - It was an utter ruin, and irreparable; that fruitful valley remains to this day a great lake, or dead sea. Travelers say it is about thirty miles long, and ten miles broad. It has no living creature in it: it is not moved by the wind: the smell of it is offensive: things do not easily sink in it. The Greeks call it Asphaltis, from a sort of pitch which it casts up. Jordan falls into it, and is lost there. It was a punishment that answered their sin. Burning lusts against nature were justly punished with this preternatural burning.

26. *But his wife looked back from behind him* - Herein she disobeyed an express command. Probably she hankered after her house and goods in Sodom, and was loath to leave them. Christ intimates this to be her sin, Luke xvii, 31, 32, she too much regarded her stuff. And her looking back spoke an inclination to go back; and therefore our saviour uses it as a warning against apostasy from our Christian profession. And she became a pillar of salt - She was struck dead in the place, yet her body did not fall down, but stood fixed and erect like a pillar or monument, not liable to waste or decay, as human bodies exposed to the air are, but metamorphosed into a metallic substance, which would last perpetually. Our communion with God consists in our gracious regard to him, and his gracious regard to us. We have here therefore the communion that was between God and Abraham in the event concerning Sodom, as before in the consultation concerning It; for communion with God is to be kept up in providences as well as in ordinances.

27. *And Abraham gat up early* - And to see what was become of his prayers, he went to the very place were he had stood before the Lord.

28. *And he looked toward Sodom* - Not as Lot's wife did, tacitly reflecting upon the divine severity, but humbly adoring it, and acquiescing in it. Here is God's favourable regard to Abraham, ver. 29. As before when Abraham prayed for Ishmael, God heard him for Isaac, so now when he prayed for Sodom, he heard for Lot.

29. *God remembered Abraham, and for his sake sent Lot out of the overthrow* - God will certainly give an answer of peace to the prayer of faith in his own way and time.

30. *He feared to dwell in Zoar* - Here is the great trouble and distress that Lot was brought into after his deliverance, ver. 29. He was frightened out of Zoar, durst not dwell there, either because he was conscious to himself that it was a refuge of his own chusing, and that therein he had foolishly prescribed to God, and therefore could not but distrust his safety in it. Probably he found it as wicked as Sodom; and therefore concluded it could not long survive it; or perhaps he observed the rise and increase of those waters, which, after the conflagration, began to overflow the plain, and which, mixing with the ruins, by degrees made the dead sea; in those waters he concluded Zoar must needs perish, (though it had escaped the fire) because it stood upon the same flat. He was now glad to go to the mountain, the place which God had appointed for his shelter. See in Lot what those bring themselves to at last, that forsake the communion of saints for secular advantages.

XX

John Wesley

We have here,

I. Abraham's sin in denying his wife, and Abimelech's sin thereupon in taking her, ver. 1, 2.

II. God's discourse with Abimelech in a dream upon this occasion; wherein he shews him his error, ver. 3. accepts his plea, ver. 4, 5, 6. and directs him to make restitution, ver. 7.

III. Abimelech's discourse with Abraham; wherein he chides him for the cheat he had put upon him, ver. 8, 9, 10. and Abraham excuses it as well as he can, ver. 11, 12, 13.

IV. The good issue of the story; in which Abimelech restores Abraham his wife, ver. 14, 15, 16. and Abraham by prayer prevails with God for the removal of the judgment Abimelech was under, ver. 17, 18.

    1. And Abraham sojourned in Gerar - We are not told upon what occasion he removed, whether terrified by the destruction of Sodom, or, as some of the Jewish writers say, because he was grieved at Lot's incest with his daughters, and the reproach which the Canaanites cast upon him for his kinsman's sake. The king of Gerar sent and took her - To his house, in order to the taking of her to his bed.
    3. But God came to Abimelech in a dream - It appears by this that God revealed himself by dreams, which evidenced themselves to be divine and supernatural, not only to his servants the prophets, but even to those that were out of the pale of the church; but then usually it was with some regard to God's own people.
    4. Wilt thou slay also a righteous nation - Not such a nation as Sodom.
    6. I withheld thee from sinning against me - It is God that restrains men from doing the ill they would do; it is not from him that there is sin, but it is from him that there is not more sin, either by his influence on mens minds checking their inclination to sin, or by his providence taking away the opportunity. It is a great mercy to be hindered from committing sin, which God must have the glory of whoever is the instrument.
    9. Thou hast done deeds that ought not to be done - Equivocation and dissimulation, however they may be palliated, are very ill things, and by no means to be admitted in any case. He takes it as a very great injury to himself and his family, that Abraham had thus exposed them to sin, What have I offended thee? - If I had been thy worst enemy, thou couldst not have done me a worse turn, nor taken a more effectual course to be avenged on me. Note, We ought to reckon, that those do us the greatest dislikedness in the world, that any way tempt us or expose us to sin, though they may pretend friendship, and offer that which is grateful enough to the corrupt nature. He challenges him to assign any just cause he had to suspect them as a dangerous people for an honest man to live among.
    10. What sawest thou that thou hast done this thing - What reason hadst thou to think, that if we had known her to be thy wife, thou wouldst have been exposed to any danger by it?
    11. I thought surely the fear of God is not in this place, and they will slay me - There are many places and persons that have more of the fear of God in them than we think they have; perhaps they are not called by our name, they do not wear our badges, they do not tie themselves to that which we have an opinion of; and therefore we conclude they have not the fear of God in their hearts!
    13. When God caused me to wander from my father's house - Then we settled this matter. It may be, that God denied Abraham and Sarah the blessing of children so long to punish them for this sinful compact they had made to deny one another: if they will not own their marriage, why should God own it? But we may suppose, that after this reproof they agreed never to do so again, and then presently we read, chap. xxi, 1, 2, that Sarah conceived.
    16. Thy brother is to thee a covering of the eyes - Thou must look at no other, nor desire to be looked at by any other. Yoke-fellows must be to each other for a covering of the eyes. The marriage-covenant is a covenant with the eyes, like Job's, Job xxxi, 1.

XXI

In this chapter we have,

I. Isaac, the child of promise, born into Abraham's family, ver. 1- 8.

II. Ishmael, the son of the bond-woman, cast out of it, ver. 9-21.

III. Abraham's league with Abimelech, ver. 22-32.

IV. His devotion to God, ver. 33, 34.

2. *Sarah conceived* - Sarah by faith, received strength to conceive, Heb. xi, 11. God therefore, by promise, gave that strength. Abraham was old, and Sarah old, and both as good as dead, and then the word of God took place.

4. *He circumcised his son* - The covenant being established with him, the seal of the covenant was administered to him.

6. *And Sarah said, God has made me to laugh* - He hath given me both cause to rejoice, and a heart to rejoice. And it adds to the comfort of any mercy to have our friends rejoice with us in it, See Luke i, 58. *They that hear will laugh with me* - Others will rejoice in this instance of God's power and goodness, and be encouraged to trust in him.

9. *Sarah saw the son of the Egyptian mocking* - Mocking Isaac no doubt, for it is sad, with reference to this, Gal. iv, 29, that he that was born after the flesh, persecuted him that was born after the spirit. Ishmael is here called the son of the Egyptian, because (as some think) the four hundred years affliction of the seed of Abraham by the Egyptians began now, and was to be dated from hence.

10. *Cast out the bond-woman* - This was a type of the rejection of the unbelieving Jews, who, though they were the seed of Abraham, yet, because they submitted not to the gospel-covenant, were unchurched and disfranchised. And that, which above any thing provoked God to cast them off, was, their mocking and persecuting the gospel-church, God's Isaac, in his infancy.

11. *The thing was very grievous in Abraham's sight* - it grieved him that Ishmael had given such provocation. And still more that Sarah insisted upon such a punishment.

13. *The casting out of Ishmael was not his ruin. He shall be a nation because he is thy seed* - We are not sure that it was his eternal ruin. It is presumption to say, that all these who are left out of the external dispensation of God's covenant are excluded from all his mercies. Those may be saved who are not thus honoured.

14. *And Abraham rose up early in the morning* - We may suppose immediately after he had in the night-visions received orders to do this.

17. *God heard the voice of the lad* - We read not of a word be said; but his sighs and groans, cried loud in the ears of the God of mercy. An angel was sent to comfort Hagar, who assures her, God has heard the voice of the lad where he is - Though he be in the wilderness; for wherever we are, there is a way open heavenwards; therefore lift up the lad, and hold him in thy hand - God's readiness to help us when we are in trouble must not slacken, but quicken our endeavours to help ourselves. He repeats the promise concerning her son, that he should be a great nation, as a reason why she should bestir herself to help him.

31. *Beer-sheba* - That is, the well of the oath, in remembrance of the covenant that they swear to, that they might be ever mindful of it.

33. *And Abraham planted a grove* - For a shade to his tent, or perhaps an orchard of fruit trees; and there, though we cannot say he settled, for God would have him while he lived to be a stranger and a pilgrim, yet he sojourned many days. *And called there on the name of the Lord* - Probably in the grove he planted, which was his oratory, or house of prayer: he kept up publick worship, to which probably his neighbours resorted, and joined with him. Men should not only retain their goodness wherever they go, but do all they can to propagate it, and make others good. *The everlasting God* - Though God had made himself known to Abraham as his God in particular; yet he forgets not to give glory to him as the Lord of all, the everlasting God, who was before all worlds, and will be when time and days shall be no more.

XXII

We have here,

I. The strange command which God gave to Abraham, ver. 1, 2.

II. Abraham's strange obedience to this command, ver. 3-10.

III. The strange issue of this trial. (1.) The sacrificing of Isaac was countermanded, ver. 11, 12. (2.) Another sacrifice was provided, ver. 13, 14. (3.) The covenant was renewed with Abraham hereupon, ver. 15- 19.

IV. An account of some of Abraham's relations, ver. 20-24.

1. Here is the trial of Abraham's faith, whether it continued so strong, so vigourous, so victorious, after a long settlement in communion with God, as it was at first, when by it he left his country: then it appeared that he loved God better than his father; now, that he loved him better than his son. After these things - After all the other exercises he had had, all the difficulties he had gone through: now perhaps he was beginning to think the storms were blown over but after all, this encounter comes, which is stranger than any yet. God did tempt Abraham - Not to draw him to sin, so Satan tempts; but to discover his graces, how strong they were, that they might be found to praise and honour and glory. The trial itself: God appeared to him as he had formerly done, called him by name Abraham, that name which had been given him in ratification of the promise: Abraham, like a good servant, readily answered, Here am I; what saith my Lord unto his servant? Probably he expected some renewed promise, like those, chap. xv, 1; xvii, 1, but to his great amazement that which God hath to say to him is in short, Abraham, go kill thy son: and this command is given him in such aggravating language as makes the temptation abundantly more grievous. When God speaks, Abraham, no doubt, takes notice of every word, and listens attentively to it: and every word here is a sword in his bones; the trial is steel'd with trying phrases. Is it any pleasure to the Almighty that he should afflict? No, it is not; yet when Abraham's faith is to be tried, God seems to take pleasure in the aggravation of the trial.

2. And he said, take thy son - Not thy bullocks and thy lambs; how willingly would Abraham have parted with them by thousands to redeem Isaac! Not thy servant, no, not the steward of thine house. Thine only son - Thine only son by Sarah. Ishmael was lately cast out, to the grief of Abraham, and now Isaac only was left and must he go too? Yes: take Isaac, him by name, thy laughter, that son indeed. Yea, that son whom thou lovest - The trial was of Abraham's love to God, and therefore it must be in a beloved son: in the Hebrew 'tis expressed more emphatically, and I think might very well be read thus, Take now that son of thine, that only son of thine, whom thou lovest, that Isaac. And get thee into the land of Moriah - Three days journey off: so that he might have time to consider it, and if he do it, must do it deliberately. And offer him for a burnt offering - He must not only kill his son, but kill him as a sacrifice, with all that sedateness and composedness of mind, with which he used to offer his burnt-offering.

3. The several steps of this obedience, all help to magnify it, and to shew that he was guided by prudence, and governed by faith, in the whole transaction. (1.) He rises early - Probably the command was given in the visions of the night, and early the next morning he sets himself about it, did not delay, did not demur. Those that do the will of God heartily will do it speedily. (2.) He gets things ready for a sacrifice, and it should seem, with his own hands, cleaves the wood for the burnt-offering. (3.) He left his servants at some distance off, left they should have created him some disturbance in his strange oblation. Thus when Christ was entering upon his agony in the garden, he took only three of his disciples with him.

6. Isaac's carrying the wood was a type of Christ, who carried his own cross, while Abraham, with a steady and undaunted resolution, carried the fatal knife and fire.

7. Behold the fire and the wood, but where is the lamb? - This is,

1. A trying question to Abraham; how could he endure to think that Isaac is himself the lamb?

2. 'Tis a teaching question to us all, that when we are going to worship God, we should seriously consider whether we have every thing ready, especially the lamb for a burnt-offering. Behold, the fire is ready; that is, the Spirit's assistance, and God's acceptance: the wood is ready, the instituted ordinances designed to kindle our affections, which indeed, without the Spirit, are but like wood without fire, but the Spirit works by them. All things are now ready, but where is the lamb? Where is the heart? Is that ready to be offered up to God, to ascend to him as a burnt- offering?

8. My son, God will provide himself a lamb - This was the language either,

1. Of his obedience; we must offer the lamb which God has appointed now to be offered; thus giving him this general rule of submission to the divine will to prepare him for the application of it to

himself. Or,

2. Of his faith; whether he meant it so or no, this proved to be the meaning of it; a sacrifice was provided instead of Isaac. Thus,

1. Christ the great sacrifice of atonement was of God's providing: when none in heaven or earth could have found a lamb for that burnt-offering, God himself found the ransom.

2. All our sacrifices of acknowledgement are of God's providing too; 'tis he that prepares the heart. The broken and contrite spirit is a sacrifice of God, of his providing.

9. With the same resolution and composedness of mind, he applies himself to the compleating of this sacrifice. After many a weary step, and with a heavy heart, he arrives at length at the fatal place; builds the altar, an altar of earth, we may suppose, the saddest that ever be built; lays the wood in order for Isaac's funeral pile; and now tells him the amazing news. Isaac, for ought appears, is as willing as Abraham; we do not find that he made any objection against it. God commands it to be done, and Isaac has learned to submit. Yet it is necessary that a sacrifice be bound; the great Sacrifice, which, in the fulness of time, was to be offered up, must be bound, and therefore so must Isaac. Having bound him he lays him upon the altar, and his hand upon the head of the sacrifice. Be astonished, O heavens, at this, and wonder, O earth! here is an act of faith and obedience which deserves to be a spectacle to God, angels and men; Abraham's darling, the church's hope, the heir of promise, lies ready to bleed and die by his own father's hands! Now this obedience of Abraham in offering up Isaac is a lively representation,

1. Of the love of God to us, in delivering up his only begotten Son to suffer and die for us, as a sacrifice. Abraham was obliged both in duty and gratitude to part with Isaac and parted with him to a friend, but God was under no obligations to us, for we were enemies.

2. Of our duty to God in return of that love we must tread in the steps of this faith of Abraham. God, by his word, calls us to part with all for Christ, all our sins, tho' they have been as a right hand, or a right eye, or an Isaac; all those things that are rivals with Christ for the sovereignty of our heart; and we must cheerfully let them all go. God, by his providence, which is truly the voice of God, calls us to part with an Isaac sometimes, and we must do it by a chearful resignation and submission to his holy will.

11. The Angel of the Lord - That is, God himself, the eternal Word, the Angel of the covenant, who was to be the great Redeemer and Comforter.

12. Lay not thine hand upon the lad - God's time to help his people is, when they are brought to the greatest extremity: the more eminent the danger is, and the nearer to be put in execution, the more wonderful and the more welcome is the deliverance. Now know I that thou fearest God - God knew it before, but now Abraham had given a memorable evidence of it. He need do no more, what he had done was sufficient to prove the religious regard he had to God and his authority. The best evidence of our fearing God is our being willing to honour him with that which is dearest to us, and to part with all to him, or for him.

13. Behold a ram - Tho' that blessed Seed was now typified by Isaac, yet the offering of him up was suspended 'till the latter end of the world, and in the mean time the sacrifice of beasts was accepted, as a pledge of that expiation which should be made by that great sacrifice. And it is observable, that the temple, the place of sacrifice, was afterward built upon this mount Moriah, 2 Chron. iii, 1, and mount Calvary, where Christ was crucified, was not far off.

14. And Abraham called the place Jehovah-jireh - The Lord will provide. Probably alluding to what he had said, ver. 8. God will provide himself a lamb - This was purely the Lord's doing: let it be recorded for the generations to come; that the Lord will see; he will always have his eyes upon his people in their straits, that he may come in with seasonable succor in the critical juncture. And that he will be seen, be seen in the mount, in the greatest perplexities of his people; he will not only manifest but magnify his wisdom, power and goodness in their deliverance. Where God sees and provides, he should be seen and praised. And perhaps it may refer to God manifest in the flesh.

15. And the Angel - Christ. Called unto Abraham - Probably while the ram was yet burning. Very high expressions are here of God's favour to Abraham, above any he had yet been blessed with.

16. Because thou hast done this thing, and hast not with-held thy son, thine only son - He lays a mighty emphasis upon that, and ver. 18, praises it as an act of obedience, in it thou hast obeyed my voice. By myself have I sworn - For he could swear by no greater.

17. Multiplying I will multiply thee - Those that part with any thing for God, shall have it made up to them with unspeakable advantage. Abraham has but one son, and is willing to part with that one in obedience to God; well, saith God, thou shalt be recompensed with thousands and millions. Here is a promise,

1. Of the Spirit, In blessing I will bless thee - The Gift of the Holy Ghost; the promise of the Spirit was that blessing of Abraham which was to come upon the Gentiles through Jesus Christ, Gal. iii, 14.

2. Of the increase of the church; that believers, his spiritual seed, should be many as the stars of heaven.

3. Of spiritual victories; Thy seed shall possess the gate of his enemies - Believers by their faith overcome the world, and triumph over all the powers of darkness. Probably Zacharias refers to this part of the oath, Luke i, 74. That we being delivered out of the hand of our enemies might serve him without fear. But the crown of all is the last promise,

4. Of the incarnation of Christ; In thy seed (one particular person that shall descend from thee, for he speaks not of many but of one, as the apostle observes, Gal. iii, 16.) shall all the nations of the earth be blessed - Christ is the great blessing of the world. Abraham was ready to give up his son for a sacrifice to the honour of God, and on that occasion God promised to give his son a sacrifice for the salvation of man.

20. This is recorded here, 1. To show that tho' Abraham saw his own family highly dignified with peculiar privileges, yet he did not look with contempt upon his relations, but was glad to hear of the increase and prosperity of their families. 2. To make way for the following story of the marriage of Isaac to Rebekah, a daughter of this family.

XXIII

Here is,

I. Abraham a mourner, for the death of Sarah, ver. 1, 2.

II. Abraham a purchaser of a burying place for Sarah. (1.) The purchase proposed by Abraham, ver. 3, 4. (2.) Treated of and agreed, ver. 5-16. (3.) The purchase-money paid, ver. 16. (4.) The premises conveyed and secured to Abraham, ver. 17, 18, 20. (5.) Sarah's funeral, ver. 19.

2. Abraham came to mourn for Sarah and to weep - He did not only perform the ceremonies of mourning according to the custom of those times, but did sincerely lament the great loss he had, and gave proof of the constancy of his affection. Therefore these two words are used, he came both to mourn and to weep.

4. I am a stranger and a sojourner with you - Therefore I am unprovided, and must become a suiter to you for a burying-place. This was one occasion which Abraham took to confess that he was a stranger and a pilgrim upon earth. The death of our relations should effectually mind us that we are not at home in this world. That I may bury my dead out of my sight - Death will make those unpleasant to our sight, who while they lived were the desire of our eyes. The countenance that was fresh and lively becomes pale and ghastly, and fit to be removed into the land of darkness.

6. Thou art a prince of God among us - So the word is; not only great, but good. He called himself a stranger and a sojourner, they call him a great prince.

7. Abraham returns them thanks for their kind offer, with all possible decency and respect. Religion teaches good manners, and those abuse it that place it in rudeness and clownishness.

11. The field give I thee - Abraham thought he must be intreated to sell it, but upon the first mention, without intreaty, he freely gives it.

13. I will give thee money for the field - It was not in pride that Abraham refused the gift; but

1. In justice. Abraham was rich in silver and gold, and therefore would not take advantage of Ephron's generosity.

2. In prudence. He would pay for it, lest Ephron, when this good humour was over, should upbraid him with it.

15. The land is worth four hundred shekels of silver - About fifty pounds of our money, but what is that between me and thee? - He would rather oblige his friend than have so much money.

20. A burying place - 'Tis worth noting,

1. That a burying-place was the first spot of ground Abraham was possessed of in Canaan.

2. That it was the only piece of land he was ever possessed of, tho' it was all his own in reversion. Those that have least of this earth find a grave in it.

XXIV

The subjoining of Isaac's marriage to Sarah's funeral (with a particular reference to it, ver. 67.) shews us, that as one generation passeth away, another generation comes; and thus the entail of human nature is preserved. Here is,

I. Abraham's care about the marrying of his son, and the charge he gave to his servant about it, ver. 1-9.

II. The servant's journey into Abraham's country to seek a wife for his young master among his own relations, ver. 10-14.

III. The kind providence which brought him acquainted with Rebekah, whose father was Isaac's cousin german, ver. 15-28.

IV. The treaty of marriage with her relations, ver. 29-49.

V. Their consent obtained, ver. 50-60.

VI. The happy meeting and marriage between Isaac and Rebekah, ver. 61-67.

1. Abraham's pious care concerning his son was, that he should not marry with a daughter of Canaan, but with one of his kindred because he saw, the Canaanites were degenerating into great wickedness, and knew, that they were designed for ruin: would not marry his son among them, lest they should be either a snare to his soul, or, at least, a blot to his name. Yet he would not go himself among his kindred, lest he should be tempted to settle there: this caution is given, ver. 6, and repeated, ver. 8. Parents, in disposing of their children, should carefully consult their furtherance in the way to heaven.

2. His eldest servant - Probably Eliezer of Damascus, one whose conduct and affection he had had long experience of: he trusted him with this great affair, and not Isaac himself, because he would not have Isaac go at all into that country, but marry thither by proxy; and no proxy so fit as the steward of his house. This matter is settled between the master and the servant with a great deal of care and solemnity. The servant is bound by an oath to do his utmost to get a wife for Isaac among his relations, ver. 3, 4. Abraham swears him to it, both for his own satisfaction, and for the engagement of his servant to all possible care and diligence. Thus God swears his servants to their work, that, having sworn, they may perform it. Swearing being an ordinance, not peculiar to the church, but common to mankind, is to be performed by such signs as are the common usages of our country.

7. God's angels are ministering spirits, sent forth, not only for the protection, but guidance of the heirs of promise, Heb. i, 14. He shall send his angel before thee - And then thou shalt speed well.

11. He made his camels kneel down - Perhaps to unload them.

12. Send me good speed this day - We have leave to be particular in recommending our affairs to the care of Divine providence. Those that would have good speed must pray for it this day, in this affair. Thus we must, in all our ways acknowledge God.

14. Let it come to pass - He prays God, that he would please to make his way plain and clear before him, by the concurrence of minute circumstances in his favour. It is the comfort, as well as the belief, of a good man, that God's providence extends itself to the smallest occurrences, and admirably serves its own purposes by them. And it is our wisdom, in all our affairs, to follow providence. Yea, it is very desirable, and that which we may lawfully pray for, while, in the general, we set God's will before us as our rule, that he will, by hints of providence, direct us in the way of our duty, and give us indications what his mind is. Thus he guides his people with his eye, and leads them in a plain path.

15. And before he had done speaking, behold Rebekah came out - Who in all respects, answered the characters he wished for in the woman that was to be his master's wife, handsome and healthful, humble and industrious, courteous and obliging to a stranger. And providence so ordered it, that she did that which exactly answered his sign. She not only gave him drink, but, which was more than could have been expected, she offered her service to give his camels drink, which was the very sign he proposed. God, in his providence, doth sometimes wonderfully own the prayer of faith, and gratify the innocent desires of his praying people even in little things, that he may shew the extent of his care, and may encourage them at all times, to seek him, and trust in him; yet we must take heed of being over bold in prescribing to God, lest the event should weaken our faith rather than strengthen it. And the concurrence of providences, and their minute circumstances, for the furtherance of our success in any business, ought to be particularly observed with wonder and thankfulness to the glory of God. We have been wanting to ourselves both in duty and comfort, by neglecting to observe providence.

27. Blessed be the Lord God of my master Abraham - Observe here,

1. He had prayed for good speed, and now he had sped well, he gives thanks.

2. As yet, he was not certain what the issue might prove, yet he gives thanks. When God's favours are coming towards us; we must meet them with our praises. The Lord led me to the house of my master's brethren -- those of them that were come out of Ur of the Chaldees, though they were not come to Canaan, but staid in Haran. They were not idolaters, but worshippers of the true God, and inclinable to the religion of Abraham's family.

29. We have here the making up of the marriage between Isaac and Rebekah, related largely and particularly. Thus we are directed to take notice of God's providence in the little common occurrences of human life, and in them also to exercise our own prudence, and other graces: for the scripture was not intended only for the use of philosophers and statesmen, but to make us all wise and virtuous in the conduct of ourselves and families.

31. Come in thou blessed of the Lord - Perhaps, because they heard from Rebekah, of the gracious words which proceeded out of his mouth, they concluded him a good man, and therefore blessed of the Lord.

34. I am Abraham' servant - Abraham's name, no doubt, was well known among them, and respected; and we may suppose them not altogether ignorant of his state, for Abraham knew theirs, chap. xxii, 20.

45. Before I had done speaking in my heart - Which perhaps he mentions, lest it should be suspected that Rebekah had overheard his prayer, and designedly humoured it; no, saith he, I spake it in my heart, so that none heard it but God, to whom thoughts are words, and from him the answer came.

50. The thing proceedeth from the Lord - Providence smiles upon it, and we have nothing to say against it. A marriage is then likely to be comfortable when it appears to proceed from the Lord.

52. He worshipped the Lord - As his good success went on, he went on to bless God: those that pray without ceasing should in every thing give thanks, and own God in every step of mercy.

55. Let her abide a few days, at least ten - They had consented to the marriage, and yet were loth to part with her. It is an instance of the vanity of this world, that there is nothing in it so agreeable but has its allay. They were pleased that they had matched a daughter of their family so well, and yet it was with reluctancy that they sent her away.

57. Call the damsel, and inquire at her mouth - As children ought not to marry without their parents consent, so parents ought not to marry them without their own. Before the matter is resolved on, ask at the damsel's mouth, she is a party principally concerned; and therefore ought to be principally consulted.

61. And her damsels - It seems then, when she went to the well for water, it was not because she had no servants at command, but because she took pleasure in the instances of humanity and industry.

63. He went out to meditate (or pray) in the field at the even tide - Some think he expected his servants about this time, and went out on purpose to meet them. But it should seem he went out to take the advantage of a silent evening, and a solitary field, for mediation and prayer. Our walks in the field are then truly pleasant, when in them we apply ourselves to meditation and prayer, we there have a free and open prospect of the heavens above us, and the earth around us, and the hosts and riches of both, by the view of which we should be led to the contemplation of the Maker and Owner of all. Merciful providences are then doubly comfortable, when they find us in the way of our duty: some think Isaac was now praying for good success in this affair, and meditating upon that which was proper to encourage his hope in God concerning it; and now when he sets himself, as it were, upon his watch-tower, to see what God would answer him, he sees the camels coming.

64. She lighted off her camel, and took a vail and covered herself - In token of humility, modesty and subjection.

XXV

The sacred historian in this chapter,

I. Takes his leave of Abraham with an account, (1.) Of his children by another wife, ver. 1-4. (2.) Of his last will and testament, ver. 5, 6. (3.) Of his age, death and burial, ver. 7, 8, 9, 10.

II. He takes his leave of Ishmael, with a short account, (1.) Of his children, ver. 12-16. (2.) Of his age and death, ver. 17, 18.

III. He enters upon the history of Isaac; (1.) His posterity, ver. 11. (2.) The conception and birth of his two sons, with the oracle of God concerning them, ver. 19-26. (3.) Their different characters, ver. 27, 28. (4.) Esau's selling his birth-right to Jacob, ver. 29-34.

1. Five and thirty years Abraham lived after the marriage of Isaac, and all that is recorded concerning him during that time lies here in a very few verses: we hear no more of God's extraordinary

appearances to him, or trials of him; for all the days even of the greatest saints are not eminent days, some slide on silently, and neither come nor go with observation: such were these last days of Abraham. We have here an account of his children by Keturah, another wife, which he married after the death of Sarah. He had buried Sarah, and married Isaac, the two dear companions of his life, and was now solitary; his family wanted a governess and it was not good for him to be thus alone; he therefore marries Keturah, probably the chief of his maid servants, born in his house, or bought with money. By her he had six sons, in whom the promise made to Abraham concerning the great increase of his posterity was in part fulfilled. The strength he received by the promise still remained in him, to shew how much the virtue of the promise exceeds the power of nature.

5. And Abraham gave all that he had to Isaac - As he was bound to do in justice to Sarah his first wife, and to Rebekah who married Isaac upon the assurance of it.

6. He gave gifts - Or portions to the rest of his children, both to Ishmael, though at first he was sent empty away, and to his sons by Keturah. It was justice to provide for them; parents that do not that, are worse than infidels. It was prudence to settle them in places distant from Isaac, that they might not pretend to divide the inheritance with him. He did this while he yet lived, lest it should not have been done, or not so well done afterwards. In many cases it is wisdom for men to make their own hands their executors, and what they find to do, to do it while they live. These sons of the concubines were sent into the country that lay east from Canaan, and their posterity were called the children of the east, famous for their numbers. Their great increase was the fruit of the promise made to Abraham, that God would multiply his seed.

7. And these are the days of Abraham -- he lived one hundred and seventy-five years; just a hundred years after he came to Canaan; so long he was a sojourner in a strange country.

8. He died in a good old age, an old man - So God had promised him. His death was his discharge from the burdens of his age: it was also the crown of the glory of his old age. He was full of years - A good man, though he should not die old, dies full of days, satisfied with living here, and longing to live in a better place. And was gathered to his people - His body was gathered to the congregation of the dead, and his soul to the congregation of the blessed. Death gathers us to our people. Those that are our people while we live, whether the people of God, or the children of this world, to them death will gather us.

9. Here is nothing recorded of the pomp or ceremony of his funeral; only we are told, his sons Isaac and Ishmael buried him - It was the last office of respect they had to pay to their good father. Some distance there had formerly been between Isaac and Ishmael, but it seems either Abraham had himself brought them together while he lived, or at least his death reconciled them. They buried him, in his own burying-place which he had purchased and in which he had buried Sarah. Those that in life have been very dear to each other, may not only innocently, but laudably, desire to be buried together, that, in their deaths, they may not be divided, and in token of their hopes of rising together.

11. And God blessed Isaac - The blessing of Abraham did not die with him, but survived to all the children of the promise. But Moses presently digresseth from the story of Isaac, to give a short account of Ishmael, for as much as he also was a son of Abraham; and God had made some promises concerning him, which it was requisite we should know the accomplishment of. He had twelve sons, twelve princes they are called, ver. 16, heads of families, which, in process of time, became nations, numerous and very considerable. They peopled a very large continent that lay between Egypt and Assyria, called Arabia. The names of his twelve sons are recorded: Midian and Kedar we oft read of in scripture. And his posterity had not only tents in the fields wherein they grew rich in times of peace, but they had towns and castles, ver. 16, where in they fortified themselves in time of war. Their number and strength was the fruit of the promise made to Hagar concerning Ishmael, chap. xvi, 10. and to Abraham, chap. xvii, 20; xxi, 13.

17. He lived an hundred and thirty and seven years - Which is recorded to shew the efficacy of Abraham's prayer for him, chap. xvii, 18. O that Ishmael might live before thee! Then he also was gathered to his people. And he died in the presence of all his brethren - With his friends about him. Who would not wish so to do?

20. And Isaac was forty years old - Not much is related concerning Isaac, but what had reference to his father, while he lived, and to his sons afterward; for Isaac seems not to have been a man of action, nor much tried, but to have spent his day, in quietness and silence.

21. And Isaac intreated the Lord for his wife - Though God had promised to multiply his family, he prayed for it; for God's promises must not supersede but encourage our prayers, and be improved as the ground of our faith. Though he had prayed for this mercy many years, and it was not granted, yet he did not leave off praying for it.

22. The children struggled within her - The commotion was altogether extra-ordinary, and made her very uneasy: If it be so, or, since it is so, why am I thus? - Before the want of children was her trouble, now the struggle of the children is no less so. And she went to inquire of the Lord - Some think Melchizedek was now consulted as an oracle, or perhaps some Urim or Teraphim were now used to

inquire of God by, as afterwards in the breast-plate of judgment. The word and prayer, by which we now inquire of the Lord, give great relief to those that are upon any account perplexed: it is a mighty ease to spread our case before the Lord, and ask council at his mouth.

23. *Two nations are in thy womb* - She was now big not only with two children, but two nations, which should not only in their manners greatly differ from each other, but in their interest contend with each other, and the issue of the contest should be that the elder should serve the younger, which was fulfilled in the subjection of the Edomites for many ages to the house of David.

25. Esau when he was born was red and hairy, as if he had been already a grown man, whence he had his name Esau, made, reared already. This was an indication of a very strong constitution, and gave cause to expect that he would be a very robust, daring, active man. But Jacob was smooth and tender as other children.

26. *His hand took hold on Esau's heel* - This signified,

1. Jacob's pursuit of the birth-right and blessing; from the first he reached forth to have catched hold of it, and if possible to have prevented his brother.

2. His prevailing for it at last: that in process of time he should gain his point. This passage is referred to Hosea xii, 3, and from hence he had his name Jacob, a supplanter.

27. *Esau was an hunter* - And a man that knew how to live by his wits, for he was a cunning hunter. *A man of the field* - All for the game, and never so well but as when he was in pursuit of it. And Jacob was a plain man - An honest man, that dealt fairly. *And dwelt in tents* - Either,

1. As a shepherd, loving that safe and silent employment of keeping sheep, to which also he bred up his children, chap. xlvi, 34. Or,

2. As a student, he frequented the tents of Melchizedek or Heber, as some understand it, to be taught by them divine things.

28. *And Isaac loved Esau* - Isaac though he was not a stirring man himself, yet he loved to have his son active. Esau knew how to please him, and shewed a great respect for him, by treating him often with venison, which won upon him more than one would have thought. But Rebekah loved him whom God loved.

29. *Sod* - That is, boiled.

30. *Edom* - That is, red.

31. *Sell me this day thy birth-right* - He cannot be excused in taking advantage of Esau's necessity, yet neither can Esau be excused who is profane, Heb. xii, 16, because for one morsel of meat he sold his birth-right. The birth-right was typical of spiritual privileges, those of the church of the first-born: Esau was now tried how he would value those, and he shews himself sensible only of present grievances: may he but get relief against them, he cares not for his birth-right. If we look on Esau's birth-right as only a temporal advantage, what he said had something of truth in it, that our worldly enjoyments, even those we are most fond of, will stand us in no stead in a dying hour. They will not put by the stroke of death, nor ease the pangs, nor remove the sting. But being of a spiritual nature, his undervaluing it, was the greatest profaneness imaginable. It is egregious folly to part with our interest in God, and Christ, and heaven, for the riches, honours, and pleasures of this world.

34. *He did eat and drink, and rise up went his way* - Without any serious reflections upon the ill bargain he had made, or any shew of regret. *Thus Esau despised his birth-right* - He used no means to get the bargain revoked, made no appeal to his father about it but the bargain which his necessity had made, (supposing it were so) his profaneness confirmed, and by his subsequent neglect and contempt, he put the bargain past recall.

XXVI

In this chapter we have,

I. Isaac in adversity, by reason of a famine in the land; which, (1.) Obliges him to change his quarters, ver 1. but, (2.) God visits him with direction and comfort, ver. 2-5. (3.) He denies his wife, and is reproved for it by Abimelech, ver. 6-11.

II. Isaac in prosperity, by the blessing of God upon him, ver. 12- 14. (1.) The Philistines were envious at him, ver. 14-17. (2.) He continued industrious in his business, ver. 18-23. (3.) God appeared to him, and encouraged him, and he returned to his duty, ver. 24-25. (4.) The Philistines at length made court to him, and made a covenant with him, ver. 26-33.

III. The disagreeable marriage of his son Esau was an allay to his prosperity, ver. 34. 35.

2. *The Lord said, go not down into Egypt. Sojourn in this land* - There was a famine in Jacob's days, and God bid him go down into Egypt, chap. xlvi, 3, 4, a famine in Isaac's days, and God bid him

not go down: a famine in Abraham's days, and God left him to his liberty, directing him neither way, which (considering that Egypt was always a place of trial to God's people) some ground upon the different characters of these three patriarchs. Abraham was a man of very intimate communion with God, and to him all places and conditions were alike; Isaac a very good man, but not cut out for hardship, therefore he is forbidden to go to Egypt; Jacob inured to difficulties, strong and patient, and therefore he must go down into Egypt, that the trial of his faith might be to praise, and honour, and glory. Thus God proportions his people's trials to their strength.

5. *Abraham obeyed my voice* - Do thou do so too, and the promise shall be sure to thee. A great variety of words is here used to express the Divine Will to which Abraham was obedient, *my voice, my charge, my commandments, my statutes, and my laws* - Which may intimate, that Abraham's obedience was universal; he obeyed the original laws of nature, the revealed laws of divine worship, particularly that of circumcision, and all the extraordinary precepts God gave him, as that of quitting his country, and that (which some think is more especially referred to) the offering up of his son, which Isaac himself had reason enough to remember. Those only shall have the benefit of God's covenant with their parents, that tread the steps of their obedience.

7. *He said, she is my sister* - So Isaac enters into the same temptation that his father had been once and again surprised and overcome by, viz. to deny his wife, and to give out that she was his sister! It is an unaccountable thing, that both these great and good men should be guilty of so odd a piece of dissimulation, by which they so much exposed both their own and their wives reputation.

8. This Abimelech was not the same that was in Abraham's days, chap. xx, 2-18, for this was near an hundred years after, but that was the common name of the Philistine kings, as Caesar of the Roman emperors.

10. *Lightly* - Perhaps.

12. *Isaac received an hundred fold* - And there seems to be an emphasis laid upon the time; it was that same year when there was a famine in the land; while others scarce reaped at all, he reaped thus plentifully.

20. *Esek* - That is, contention.

21. *Sitnah* - That is, hatred.

22. *He digged a well, and for that they strove not* - Those that follow peace, sooner or later, shall find peace: those that study to be quiet seldom fail of being so. This well they called Rehoboth - Enlargements, room enough.

24. *Fear not, I am with thee, and will bless thee* - Those may remove with comfort that are sure of God's presence with them wherever they go.

28. *The Lord is with thee, and thou art the blessed of the Lord,* q.d. Be persuaded to overlook the injuries offered thee, for God has abundantly made up to thee the damage thou receivedst. Those whom God blesseth and favours, have reason enough to forgive those that hate them, since the worst enemy they have cannot do them any real hurt. *Let there be an oath betwixt us* - Whatever some of his envious subjects might mean, he and his prime ministers, whom he had now brought with him, designed no other but a cordial friendship. Perhaps Abimelech had received by tradition the warning God gave to his predecessor not to hurt Abraham, chap. xx, 7, and that made him stand in such awe of Isaac, who appeared to be as much the favourite of heaven as Abraham was.

34. *He took to wife* - Marrying Canaanites, who were strangers to the blessing of Abraham, and subject to the curse of Noah.

XXVII

We have here,

I. Isaac's purpose to entail the blessing upon Esau, ver. 1-4.

II. Rebekah's plot to procure it for Jacob, ver. 6-17.

III. Jacob's obtaining of the blessing, ver. 18-29.

IV. Esau's resentment of this. In which, (1.) His importunity with his father to obtain a blessing, ver. 30-40. (2.) His enmity to his brother for defrauding him, ver. 41-46.

1. Here is Isaac's design to declare Esau his heir. The promise of the Messiah and the land of Canaan was a great trust first committed to Abraham, inclusive and typical of spiritual and eternal blessings; this by divine direction he transmitted to Isaac. Isaac being now old, and either not knowing, or not duly considering the divine oracle concerning his two sons, that the elder should serve the younger, resolves to entail all the honour and power that was wrapt up in the promise upon Esau, his

eldest son. He called Esau - Tho' Esau, had greatly grieved his parents by his marriage, yet they had not expelled him, but it seems were pretty well reconciled to him.

2. I am old, and know not the day of my death - How soon I may die.

3. Take me some venison that I may; bless thee - Esau must go a hunting and bring some venison. In this he designed not so much the refreshment of his own spirits, as the receiving a fresh instance of his son's, filial duty and affection to him, before he bestowed this favour upon him. That my soul may bless thee before I die - Prayer is the work of the soul, and not of the lips only; as the soul must be employed in blessing God, Psalm ciii, 1, so it must be in blessing ourselves and others: the blessing will not go to the heart, if it do not come from the heart.

6. Rebekah is here contriving to procure the blessing for Jacob, which was designed for Esau. If the end was good, the means were bad, and no way justifiable. If it were not a wrong to Esau to deprive him of the blessing, he himself having forfeited it by selling the birth right, yet it was a wrong to Isaac, taking advantage of his infirmity, to impose upon him: it was a wrong to Jacob, whom she taught to deceive, by putting a lie in his mouth. If Rebekah, when she heard Isaac promise the blessing to Esau, had gone to him, and with humility and seriousness put him in remembrance of that which God had said concerning their sons; if she had farther shewed him how Esau had forfeited the blessing, both by selling his birth-right, and by marrying of strange wives; 'tis probable Isaac would have been prevailed with to confer the blessing upon Jacob, and needed not thus to have been cheated into it. This had been honourable and laudable, and would have looked well in history; but God left her to herself to take this indirect course, that he might have the glory of bringing good out of evil.

19. And Jacob said, I am Esau - Who would have thought this plain man could have played such a part? His mother having put him in the way of it, he applies himself to those methods which he had never accustomed himself to, but had always conceived an abhorrence of. But lying is soon learned. I wonder how honest Jacob could so readily turn his tongue to say, I am Esau thy first-born: and when his father asked him, ver. 24. Art thou my very son Esau? to reply I am. How could he say, I have done as thou badst me, when he had received no command from his father, but was doing as his mother bid him? How could he say, Eat of my venison, when he knew it came not from the field, but from the fold? But especially I wonder how he could have the forehead to father it upon God, and to use his name in the cheat.

20. The Lord thy God brought it to me - Is this Jacob? It is certainly written not for our imitation, but our admonition, Let him that, standeth, take heed lest he fall. Now let us see how Isaac gave Jacob his blessing. 27-1. He kissed him; in token of particular affection to him. Those that are blessed of God are kissed with the kisses of his mouth, and they do by love and loyalty kiss the son, Psalm ii, 12. 2. He praised him. Upon occasion of the sweet smell of his garments he said, See the smell of my son is as the smell of a field which the Lord hath blessed - That is, like that of the most fragrant flowers and spices. Three things Jacob is here blessed with, (1.) Plenty, ver. 28. Heaven and earth concurring to make him rich. (2.) Power, ver. 29. Particularly dominion over his brethren, viz. Esau and his posterity. (3.) Prevalency with God, and a great interest in heaven, Cursed be every one that curseth thee - Let God be a friend to all thy friends, and an enemy to all thine enemies. Now, certainly more is comprised in this blessing than appears at first; it must amount to an entail of the promise of the Messiah: that was in the patriarchal dialect the blessing; something spiritual doubtless is included in it. First, That from him should come the Messiah, that should have a sovereign dominion on earth. See Num. xxiv, 19. Out of Jacob shall come he that shall have dominion, the star and scepter, Num. xxiv, 17. Jacob's dominion over Esau was to be only typical of this, chap. xlix, 10. Secondly, That from him should come the church that should be particularly owned and favoured by Heaven. It was part of the blessing of Abraham when he was first called to be the father of the faithful, chap. xii, 3. I will bless them that bless thee; therefore when Isaac afterwards confirmed the blessing to Jacob, he called it the blessing of Abraham, chap. xxviii, 4.

33. Isaac trembled exceedingly - Those that follow the choice of their own affections rather than the dictates of the Divine will, involve themselves in such perplexities as these. But he soon recovers himself, and ratifies the blessing he had given to Jacob, I have blessed him, and he shall be blessed - He might have recalled it, but now at last he is sensible he was in an error when he designed it for Esau. Either recollecting the Divine oracle, or having found himself more than ordinarily filled with the Holy Ghost when he gave the blessing to Jacob, he perceived that God did as it were say Amen to it.

39. Esau likewise obtained a blessing: yet it was far short of Jacob's.

1. In Jacob's blessing the dew of heaven is put first, as that which he most valued and desired: in Esau's the fatness of the earth is put first, for that was it which he had the principal regard to.

2. Esau hath these, but Jacob hath them from God's hand. God give thee the dew of heaven, ver. 28. It was enough to have the possession, but Jacob desired it by promise.

3. Jacob shall have dominion over his brethren, for the Israelites often ruled over the Edomites. Esau shall have dominion, he shall gain some power, but shall never have dominion over his brother: we never find that the Jews were sold into the hands of the Edomites, or that they oppressed them. But

the great difference is, that there is nothing in Esau's blessing that points at Christ, nothing that brings either him or his into the church, and without that the fatness of the earth, and the plunder of the field, will stand him in little stead. Thus Isaac by faith blessed them both, according as their lot should be.

45. Why should I be deprived of you both? - Not only of the murdered, but of the murderer, who either by the magistrate, or by the immediate hand of God would be sacrificed to justice.

46. If Jacob take a wife of the daughters of Heth - As Esau has done. More artifice still. This was not the thing she was afraid of. But if we use guile once, we shall be very ready to use it again. It should be carefully observed, That altho' a blessing came on his posterity by Jacob's vile lying and dissimulation, yet it brought heavy affliction upon himself, and that for a long term of years. So severely did God punish him personally, for doing evil that good might come.

XXVIII

We have here,

I. Jacob's parting with his parents to go to Padan-aram: the charge his father gave him, ver. 1, 2. the blessing he sent him away with, ver. 3, 4. his obedience to the orders given him, ver. 5-10. and the influence this had upon Esau, ver. 6.

II. Jacob's meeting with God, and his communion with him by the way. And there, (1.) His vision of the ladder, ver. 11, 12. (2.) The gracious promise God made him, ver. 13, 14, 15. (3.) The impression this made upon him, ver. 16-19. (4.) The vow he made to God upon this occasion, ver. 20, 21, 22.

1. Isaac blessed him, and charged him - Those that have the blessing must keep the charge annexed to it, and not think to separate what God has joined.

3, 4. Two great promises Abraham was blessed with, and Isaac here entails them both upon Jacob. (1.) The promise of heirs, God make thee fruitful and multiply thee.

1. Through his loins that people should descend from Abraham which should be numerous as the stars of heaven.

2. Through his loins should descend from Abraham that person in whom all the families of the earth should be blessed. (2.) The promise of an inheritance for those heirs, ver. 4. That thou mayest inherit the land of thy sojournings - (So the Hebrew) Canaan was hereby entailed upon the seed of Jacob, exclusive of the seed of Esau. Isaac was now sending Jacob away into a distant country to settle there for some time; and lest this should look like disinheriting him, he here confirms the settlement of it upon him. This promise looks as high as heaven, of which Canaan was a type. That was the better country which Jacob, with the other patriarchs, had in his eye when he confessed himself a stranger and pilgrim on the earth, Heb. xi, 16. See note at "ver. 3"

5. Rebekah is here called Jacob's and Esau's mother - Jacob is named first, not only because he had always been his mother's darling, but because he was now made his father's heir, and Esau was postponed.

6. This passage comes in, in the midst of Jacob's story, to shew the influence of a good example. Esau now begins to think Jacob the better man, and disdains not to take him for his pattern in this particular instance of marrying with a daughter of Abraham.

11. The stones for his pillow, and the heavens for his canopy! Yet his comfort in the divine blessing, and his confidence in the divine protection, made him easy, even when he lay thus exposed: being sure that his God made him to dwell in safety, he could lie down and sleep upon a stone.

12. Behold a ladder set upon the earth, and the top of it reached heaven, the angels ascending and descending on it, and the Lord stood above it - This might represent

1. The providence of God, by which there is a constant correspondence kept up between heaven and earth. The counsels of heaven are executed on earth, and the affairs of this earth are all known in heaven. Providence doth his work gradually and by steps; angels are employed as ministering spirits to serve all the designs of providence, and the wisdom of God is at the upper end of the ladder, directing all the motions of second causes to his glory. The angels are active spirits, continually ascending and descending; they rest not day nor night. They ascend to give account of what they have done, and to receive orders; and desend to execute the orders they have received. This vision gave seasonable comfort to Jacob, letting him know that he had both a good guide and good guard; that though he was to wander from his father's house, yet he was the care of Providence, and the charge of the holy angels.

2. The mediation of Christ. He is this ladder: the foot on earth in his human nature, the top in heaven in his divine nature; or the former is his humiliation, the latter is his exaltation. All the intercourse between heaven and earth since the fall is by this ladder. Christ is the way: all God's favours come to us, and all our services come to him, by Christ. If God dwell with us, and we with him, it is by Christ: we have no way of getting to heaven but by this ladder; for the kind offices the angels do us, are

all owing to Christ, who hath reconciled things on earth and things in heaven, Colossians i, 20.

14. In thy seed shall all the families of the earth be blessed - Christ is the great blessing of the world: all that are blessed, whatever family they are of, are blessed in him, and none of any family are excluded from blessedness in him, but those that exclude themselves.

15. Behold I am with thee - Wherever we are, we are safe, if we have God's favourable presence with us. He knew not, but God foresaw what hardships he would meet with in his uncle's service, and therefore promiseth to preserve him in all places. God knows how to give his people graces and comforts accommodated to the events that shall be, as well as to those that are. He was now going as an exile into a place far distant, but God promiseth him to bring him again to this land. He seemed to be forsaken of all his friends, but God gives him this assurance, I will not leave thee.

16. Surely the Lord is in this place, and I knew it not - God's manifestations of himself to his people carry their own evidence along with them. God can give undeniable demonstrations of his presence, such as give abundant satisfaction to the souls of the faithful, that God is with them of a truth; satisfaction not communicable to others, but convincing to themselves. We sometimes meet with God there, where we little thought of meeting with him. He is there where we did not think he had been, is found there where we asked not for him.

17. He was afraid - So far was he from being puffed up. The more we see of God, the more cause we see for holy trembling and blushing before him. Those whom God is pleased to manifest himself to, are laid and kept very low in their own eyes, and see cause to fear even the Lord and his goodness, Hosea iii, 5. And said, How dreadful is this place! - That is, the appearance of God in this place is to be thought of, but with a holy awe and reverence; I shall have a respect for this place, and remember it by this token as long as I live. Not that he thought the place itself any nearer the divine visions than any other places; but what he saw there at this time was, as it were, the house of God, the residence of the Divine Majesty, and the gate of heaven, that is, the general rendezvous of the inhabitants of the upper world; as the meetings of a city were in their gates; or, the angels ascending and descending were like travelers passing and repassing through the gates of a city.

18. He set up the stone for a pillar - To mark the place again, if he came back, and erect a lasting monument of God's favour to him: and because he had not time now to build an altar here, as Abraham did in the places where God appeared to him, chap. xii, 7, he therefore poured oil on the top of this stone, which probably was the ceremony then used in dedicating their altars, as an earnest of his building an altar when he should have conveniencies for it, as afterwards he did, in gratitude to God, chap. xxxv, 7. Grants of mercy call for our returns of duty and the sweet communion we have with God ought ever to be remembered.

19. It had been called Luz, an almond-tree, but he will have it henceforth called Beth-el, the house of God. This gracious appearance of God to him made it more remarkable than all the almond-trees that flourished there.

20. And Jacob vowed a vow - By religious vows we give glory to God, and own our dependance upon him, and we lay a bond upon our own souls, to engage and quicken our obedience to him. Jacob was now in fear and distress, and in times of trouble it is seasonable to make vows, or when we are in pursuit of any special mercy, John i, 16 Psalm lxvi, 13, 14; 1 Sam. i, 11 Num. xxi, 1, 2, 3. Jacob had now had a gracious visit from heaven, God had renewed his covenant with him, and the covenant is mutual; when God ratifies his promises to us, it is proper for us to repeat our promises to him. If thou wilt be with me and keep me - We need desire no more to make us easy and happy wherever we are, but to have God's presence with us, and to be under his protection. It is comfortable in a journey to have a guide in an unknown way, a guard in a dangerous way, to be well carried, well provided for, and to have good company in any way; and they that have God with them, have all this in the best manner. Then shall the Lord be my God - Then I will rejoice in him as my God, then I will be the more strongly engaged to abide with him. And this pillar shall be God's house - That is, an altar shall be erected here to the honour of God. And of all that thou shalt give me I will surely give the tenth unto thee - To be spent either upon God's altar or upon his poor, which are both his receivers in the world. The tenth is a very fit proportion to be devoted to God, and employed for him; though as circumstances vary, it may be more or less, as God prospers us.

XXIX

This chapter gives us an account of God's providences concerning Jacob, pursuant to the promise made him in the foregoing chapter.

I. How he was brought in safety to his journey's end, and directed to his relations there, who bid him welcome, ver. 1-14.

II. How he was comfortably disposed of in marriage, ver. 15-30.

III. How his family was built up in the birth of four sons, ver. 31- 35.

2. Providence brought him to the very field where his uncle's flock's were to be watered, and there he met with Rachel that was to be his wife. The Divine Providence is to be acknowledged in all the little circumstances which concur to make a journey or other undertaking comfortable and successful. If, when we are at a loss, we meet with those seasonably that can direct us; if we meet with a disaster, and those are at hand that will help us; we must not say it was by chance, but it was by providence: our ways are ways of pleasantness, if we continually acknowledge God in them. The stone on the well's mouth was either to secure their property in it, for water was scarce, to save the well from receiving damage from the heat of the sun, or to prevent the lambs of the flock from being drowned in it.

9. She kept her father's sheep - She took the care of them, having servants under her that were employed about them when he understood that this was his kinswoman (probably he had heard of her name before) knowing what his errand was into that country, we may suppose it struck into his mind immediately, that this must be his wife, as one already smitten with an honest comely face (though it is likely, sun-burnt, and she in the homely dress of a shepherdess) he is wonderfully officious, and ready to serve her, ver. 10, and addresses himself to her with tears of joy, and kisses of love, ver. 11, she runs with all haste to tell her father, for she will by no means entertain her kinsman's address without her father's knowledge and approbation, ver. 12. These mutual respects at their first interview were good presages of their being a happy couple. Providence made that which seemed contingent and fortuitous to give a speedy satisfaction to Jacob's mind as soon as ever he came to the place he was bound for. Abraham's servant, when he came upon a like errand, met with the like encouragement. Thus God guides his people with his eye, Psalm xxxii, 8. It is a groundless conceit which some of the Jewish writers have, that Jacob when he kissed Rachel wept, because he had been set upon his journey by Eliphaz the eldest son of Esau, at the command of his father, and robbed him of all his money and jewels, which his mother had given him when she sent him away: it is plain it was his passion for Rachel, and the surprise of this happy meeting that drew these tears from his eyes. Laban, though none of the best humoured men, bid him welcome, was satisfied in the account he gave of himself, and of the reason of his coming in such poor circumstances. While we avoid the extreme on the one hand of being foolishly credulous, we must take heed of falling into the other extreme of being uncharitably jealous and suspicious. Laban owned him for his kinsman, ver. 14. Thou art my bone and my flesh. Note, Those are hard-hearted indeed that are unkind to their relations, and that hide themselves from their own flesh, Isaiah lviii, 7.

15. Because thou art my brother - That is, kinsman. Should thou therefore serve me for nought? - No, what reason for that? If Jacob be so respectful as to give him his service without demanding any consideration for it, yet Laban will not be so unjust as to take advantage either of his necessity, or of his good nature. It appears by computation that Jacob was now seventy years old when he bound himself apprentice for a wife; probably Rachel was young and scarce marriageable when Jacob came first, which made him the more willing to stay for her till his seven years were expired.

20. They seemed to him but a few days for the love he had to her - An age of work will be but as a few days to those that love God, and long for Christ's appearing.

25. Behold it was Leah - Jacob had cheated his own father when he pretended to be Esau, and now his father-in-law cheated him. Herein, how unrighteous soever Laban was, the Lord was righteous.

26. It must be so done in our country - We have reason to think there was no such custom in his country; but if there was, and that he resolved to observe it, he should have told Jacob so, when he undertook to serve him for his younger daughter.

27. We will give thee this also - Hereby he drew Jacob into the sin and snare, and disquiet of multiplying wives. Jacob did not design it, but to have kept as true to Rachel as his father had done to Rebekah; he that had lived without a wife to the eighty fourth year of his age could then have been very well content with one: but Laban to dispose of his two daughters without portions, and to get seven years service more out of Jacob, thus imposeth upon him, and draws him into such a strait, that he had some colourable reason for marrying them both.

31. When the Lord saw that Leah was hated - That is, loved less than Rachel, in which sense it is

required that we hate father and mother, in comparison with Christ, Luke xiv, 26, then the Lord granted her a child, which was a rebuke to Jacob for making so great a difference between those he was equally related to; a check to Rachel, who, perhaps insulted over her sister upon that account; and a comfort to Leah, that she might not be overwhelmed with the contempt put upon her.

32. She appears very ambitious of her husband's love; she reckoned the want of it her affliction, not upbraiding him with it as his fault, nor reproaching him for it; but laying it to heart as her grief, which she had reason to bear, because she was consenting to the fraud by which she became his wife. She called her first-born Reuben, see a son, with this pleasant thought, Now will my husband love me. And her third son Levi, joined, with this expectation, Now will my husband be joined unto me. The Lord hath heard, that is, taken notice of it, that I was hated, he hath therefore given me this son. Her fourth she called Judah, praise, saying, Now will I praise the Lord. And this was he, of whom, as concerning the flesh Christ came. Whatever is the matter of our rejoicing, ought to be the matter of our thanksgiving. And all our praises must center in Christ, both as the matter of them, and as the Mediator of them. He descended from him whose name was praise, for he is our praise. Is Christ formed in my heart? Now will I praise the Lord.

XXX

In this chapter we have an account of the increase,

I. Of Jacob's family; eight children more we find registered in this chapter; Daniel and Naphtali by Bilhah, Rachel's maid, ver. 1-8. Gad and Asher by Zilpah, Leah's maid, ver. 9-13. Issachar, Zebulon, and Dinah, by Leah, ver. 14-21. And last of all Joseph by Rachel, ver. 22-24.

II. Of Jacob's estate. He comes upon a new bargain with Laban, ver. 25-34. And in the six years further service he did to Laban, God wonderfully blessed him, so that his flock of all cattle became very considerable, ver. 35-43, And herein was fulfilled the blessing which Isaac dismissed him with, chap. xxviii. 3. God make thee fruitful and multiply thee.

1. Rachel envied her sister - Envy is grieving at the good of another, than which no sin is more injurious both to God, our neighbour, and ourselves. But this was not all, she said to Jacob, give me children or else I die - A child would not content her; but because Leah has more than one, she must have more too; Give me children: her heart is set upon it. Give them me, else I die, That is, I shall fret myself to death. The want of this satisfaction will shorten my days. Observe a difference between Rachel's asking for this mercy, and Hannah's, 1 Sam. i, 10, &c. Rachel envied, Hannah wept: Rachel must have children, and she died of the second; Hannah prayed for this child, and she had four more: Rachel is importunate and peremptory, Hannah is submissive and devout, If thou wilt give me a child, I will give him to the Lord. Let Hannah be imitated, and not Rachel; and let our desires be always under the conduct and check of reason and religion.

2. And Jacob's anger was kindled - He was angry, not at the person, but at the sin: he expressed himself so as to shew his displeasure. It was a grave and pious reply which Jacob gave to Rachel, Am I in God's stead? - Can I give thee that which God denies thee? He acknowledges the hand of God in the affliction: He hath withheld the fruit of the womb. Whatever we want, it is God that with-holds it, as sovereign Lord, most wise, holy, and just, that may do what he will with his own, and is debtor to no man: that never did, nor ever can do, any wrong to any of his creatures. The key of the clouds, of the heart, of the grave, and of the womb, are four keys which God has in his hand, and which (the Rabbins say) he intrusts neither with angel nor seraphin. He also acknowledges his own inability to alter what God appointed, Am I in God's stead? What, dost thou make a God of me? There is no creature that is, or can be, to us in God's stead. God may be to us, instead of any creature, as the sun instead of the moon and stars; but the moon and all the stars will not be to us instead of the sun. No creature's wisdom, power, and love will be to us instead of God's. It is therefore our sin and folly to place that confidence in any creature, which is to be placed in God only.

3. Behold my maid, Bilhah - At the persuasion of Rachel he took Bilhah her handmaid to wife, that, according to the usage of those times, his children by her might be adopted and owned as her mistresses children. She would rather have children by reputation than none at all; children that she might call her own, though they were not so. And as an early instance of her dominion over the children born in her apartment, she takes a pleasure in giving them names, that carry in them nothing but marks of emulation with her sister. As if she had overcome her,

1. At law, she calls the flrst son of her handmaid, Daniel, Judgment, saying, God hath Judged me - That is, given sentence in my favour.

2. In battle, she calls the next Naphtali, Wrestlings, saying, I have wrestled with my sister, and have prevailed - See what roots of bitterness envy and strife are, and what mischief they make among

relations!

9. Rachel had done that absurd and preposterous thing of putting her maid into her husband's bed, and now Leah (because she missed one year in bearing children) doth the same, to be even with her. See the power of rivalship, and admire the wisdom of the divine appointment, which joins together one man and one woman only. Two sons Zilpah bare to Jacob, whom Leah looked upon herself as intitled to, in token of which she called one Gad, promising herself a little troop of children. The other she called Asher, Happy, thinking herself happy in him, and promising herself that her neighbours would think so too.

14. Reuben, a little lad of five or six years old, playing in the field, found mandrakes. It is uncertain what they were; the critics are not agreed about them: we are sure they were some rarities, either fruits or flowers that were very pleasant to the smell, So vii, 13. Some think these mandrakes were Jessamin flowers. Whatever they were, Rachel, could not see them in Leah's hands, but she must covet them.

17. And God hearkened unto Leah - Perhaps the reason of this contest between Jacob's wives for his company, and their giving him their maids to be his wives, was the earnest desire they had to fulfil the promise made to Abraham (and now lately renewed to Jacob) that his seed should be as the stars of heaven for multitude, and that, in one seed of his, the Messiah, all the nations of the earth shall be blessed. Two sons Leah was now blessed with; the flrst she called Issachar, a hire, reckoning herself well repaid for her mandrakes; nay, (which is a strange construction of the providence) rewarded for giving her maid to her husband. The other she called Zebulun, dwelling, owning God's bounty to her, God has endowed me with a good dowry. Jacob had not endowed her when he married her; but she reckons a family of children, a good dowry.

21. Mention is made, of Dinah, because of the following story concerning her, chap. xxxiv, 1-16, &c. Perhaps Jacob had other daughters, though not registered.

22. God remembered Rachel, whom he seemed to have forgotten, and hearkened to her, whose prayers had been long denied, and then she bare a son. Rachael called her son Joseph, which, in Hebrew, is a-kin to two words of a contrary signification: Asaph, abstulit, he has taken away my reproach, as if the greatest mercy she had in this son were, that she had saved her credit: and Joseph, addidit, the Lord shall add to me another son: which may be looked upon as the language of her faith; she takes this mercy as an earnest of further mercy: hath God given me this grace? I may call it Joseph, and say, he shall add more grace.

34. Laban was willing to consent to this bargain, because he thought if those few he had that were now speckled and spotted were separated from the rest, which was to be done immediately, the body of the flock which Jacob was to tend, being of one colour, either all black or all white, would produce few or none of mixt colours, and so he should have Jacob's service for nothing, or next to nothing.
According to this bargain, those few that were party-coloured were separated, and put into the hands of Laban's sons, and sent three days journey off: so great was Laban's jealouly lest any of those should mix with the rest of the flock to the advantage of Jacob.

37. Here is Jacob's policy to make his bargain more advantageous to himself than it was likely to be: and if he had not taken some course to help himself, it would have been an ill bargain indeed; which he knew Laban would never have considered, who did not consult any one's interest but his own.

1. Now Jacob's contrivances were, He set pilled sticks before the cattle where they were watered, that looking much at those unusual party-coloured sticks, by the power of imagination, they might bring forth young ones in like manner party-coloured. Probably this custom was commonly used by the shepherds of Canaan, who coveted to have their cattle of this motly colour.

2. When he began to have a flock of ring-straked and brown, he contrived to set them first, and to put the faces of the rest towards them, with the same design as he did the former. Whether this was honest policy, or no, may admit of a question. Read chap. xxxi, 7- 16, and the question is resolved.

XXXI

John Wesley

Jacob was in general, a man of devotion and integrity; yet he had more trouble than any of the patriarchs. Here is,

I. His resolution to return, ver. 1-16.

II. His clandestine departure, ver. 17-21.

III. Laban's pursuit of him in displeasure, ver. 22-25.

IV. The hot words that passed between them, ver. 26-42.

V. Their amicable agreement at last, ver. 43-55.

    1. It should seem they said it in Jacob's hearing. The last chapter began with Rachel's envying Leah; this begins with Laban's sons envying Jacob. He has gotten all his glory - And what was this glory? It was a parcel of brown sheep and speckled goats, and some camels and asses. Jacob has taken away all that was our fathers - Not all, sure; what was become of those cattle which were committed to the custody of Laban's sons, and sent three days journey off?
    3. The Lord said unto Jacob, Return and I will be with thee - though Jacob had met with very hard usage, yet he would not quit his place 'till God bid him. He came thither by orders from heaven, and there he would slay 'till he was ordered back. The direction he had from heaven is more fully related in the account he gives of it to his wives, where he tells them of the dream he had about the cattle, and the wonderful increase of those of his colour; and how the angel of God in that dream instructed him that it was not by chance, nor by his own policy, that he obtained that great advantage but by the providence of God, who had taken notice of the hardships Laban had put upon him, and in performance of his promise.
    4. And Jacob sent for Rachel and Leah to the field - That he might discourse with them more privately.
    9. God hath taken away the cattle of your father and given them to me - Thus the righteous God paid Jacob for his hard service out of Laban's estate; as afterwards he paid the seed of Jacob for their service of the Egyptians with their spoils.
    16. Whereas Jacob looked upon the wealth which God had passed over from Laban to him as his wages, they look upon it as their portions; so that both ways God forced Laban to pay his debts, both to his servant and to his daughters.
    19. Laban went to shear his sheep - That part of his flock which was in the hands of his sons, three days journey off. Now, (1.) It is certain it was lawful for Jacob to leave his service suddenly: it was not only justified by the particular instructions God gave him, but warranted by the fundamental law of self-preservation which directs us, when we are in danger, to shift for our own safety, as far as we can do it without wronging our consciences. (2.) It was his prudence to steal away unawares to Laban, lest if Laban had known, he should have hindered him, or plundered him. (3.) It was honestly done to take no more than his own with him, the cattle of his getting. He took what providence gave him, and would not take the repair of his damages into his own hands. Yet Rachel was not so honest as her husband; she stole her father's images, and carried them away. The Hebrew calls them Teraphim. Some think they were only little representations of the ancestors of the family in statue or picture, which Rachel had a particular fondness for, and was desirous to have with her now she was going into another country. It should rather seem they were images for a religious use, penates, household gods, either worshipped, or consulted as oracles; and we are willing to hope, that she took them away, not out of covetousness much less for her own use, or out of any superstitious fear lest Laban, by consulting his teraphim, might know which way they were gone; (Jacob no doubt dwelt with his wives as a man of knowledge, and they were better taught than so) but with a design to convince her father of the folly of his regard to those as gods which could not secure themselves.
    23. He took his brethren -- that is, his relations, and pursues Jacob to bring him back into bondage, or, to strip him of what he had.
    24. Speak not, either good or bad - That is, say nothing against his going on with his journey, for the thing proceedeth from the Lord. The same Hebraism we have, chap. xxiv, 50. The safety of good men is very much owing to the hold God has of the consciences of bad men, and the access he has to them.
    27. I might have sent thee away with mirth and with songs, with tabret and with harp - Not as Rebekah was sent away out of the same family above one hundred and twenty years before, with prayers and blessings, but with sport and merriment; which was a sign that religion was much decayed

in the family.

29. *It is in the power of my hand to do you hurt* - He supposeth that he had both right on his side, and strength on his side, either to revenge the wrong, or recover the right. Yet he owns himself under the restraint of God's power; he durst not injure one of whom he saw to be the particular care of heaven.

30. *Wherefore hast thou stolen my gods?* - Foolish man! to call those his gods that could be stolen! Could he expect protection from them that could neither resist nor discover their invaders? Happy are they who have the Lord for their God. Enemies may steal our goods, but not our God.

31. Jacob clears himself by giving the true reason why he went away unknown to Laban; he feared lest Laban would by force take away his daughters and so oblige him to continue in his service. As to the charge of stealing Laban's gods, he pleads not guilty. He not only did not take them himself, but he did not know that they were taken.

42. Jacob speaks of God as the God of his father, intimating that he thought himself unworthy to be thus regarded, but was beloved for his father's sake. He calls him the God of Abraham and the fear of Isaac: for Abraham was dead, and gone to that world where there is no fear; but Isaac was yet alive, sanctifying the Lord in his heart as his fear and his dread.

43. *All his mine* - That is, came by me.

44. *Let us make a covenant* - It was made and ratified with great solemnity, according to the usages of those times.

1. A pillar was erected, and a heap of stones raised, to perpetuate the memory of the thing, writing being then not known.

2. A sacrifice was offered, a sacrifice of peace-offerings.

3. They did eat bread together, jointly partaking of the feast upon the sacrifice. This was in token of a hearty reconciliation. Covenants of friendship were anciently ratified by the parties eating and drinking together.

4. They solemnly appealed to God concerning their sincerity herein; (1.) As a witness, ver. 49. *The Lord watch between me and thee* - That is, the Lord take cognizance of every thing that shall be done on either side in violation of this league. (2.) As a judge, The God of Abraham, from whom Jacob was descended, and The God of Nahor, from whom Laban was descended, the God of their father, the common ancestor from whom they were both descended, judge betwixt us. God's relation to them is thus expressed, to intimate that they worshipped one and the same God, upon which consideration there ought to be no enmity betwixt them. Those that have one God should have one heart: God is judge between contending parties, and he will judge righteously, whoever doth wrong it is at their peril.

5. They gave a new name to the place, ver. 47, 48. Laban called it in Syriac, and Jacob in Hebrew, The heap of witness. And ver. 49, it was called Mizpah, a watch-tower. Posterity being included in the league, care was taken that thus the memory of it should be preserved. The name Jacob gave this heap stuck by it, Galeed, not the name Laban gave it.

54. *And Jacob swear by the fear of his father Isaac* - The God whom his father Isaac feared, who had never served other gods, as Abraham and Nahor had done.

XXXII

We have here Jacob still upon his journey towards Canaan. Never did so many memorable things occur in any march, as in this in Jacob's little family. By the way he meets,

I. With good tidings from his God, ver. 1, 2.

II. With bad tidings from his brother, to whom he sent a message to notify his return, ver. 2-7. In his distress,

1. He divides his company, ver. 8.
2. He makes his prayer to God, ver. 9-12.
3. He sends a present to his brother, ver. 13-23.
4. He wrestles with the angel, ver. 24-32.

1. *And the Angel of God met him* - In a visible appearance; whether in a vision by day, or in a dream by night, as when he saw them upon the ladder, is uncertain. They met him to bid him welcome to Canaan again; a more honourable reception than ever any prince had that was met by the magistrates of a city. They met him to congratulate his arrival, and his escape from Laban. They had invisibly attended him all along, but now they appeared, because he had greater dangers before him. When God designs his people for extraordinary trials, he prepares them by extraordinary comforts.

2. *This is God's house* - A good man may, with an eye of faith, see the same that Jacob saw with his bodily eyes. What need we dispute whether he has a guardian angel, when we are sure he has a guard of angels about him? To preserve the remembrance of this favour, Jacob gave a name to the place

from it, Mahanaim, two hosts, or two camps probably they appeared to him in two hosts, one on either side, or one in the front, and the other in the rear, to protect him from Laban behind, and Esau before, that they might be a compleat guard. Here was Jacob's family that made one army, representing the church militant and itinerant on earth; and the angels another army, representing the church triumphant, and at rest in heaven.

4. He calls Esau his Lord, himself his servant, to intimate that he did not insist upon the prerogatives of the birth-right and blessing he had obtained for himself, but left it to God to fulfil his own purpose in his seed. He gives him a short account of himself, that he was not a fugitive and a vagabond, but though long absent had dwelt with his own relations. I have sojourned with Laban, and staid there till now: and that he was not a beggar, nor likely to be a charge to his relations; no, I have oxen and asses - This he knew would (if any thing) recommend him to Esau's good affection. And, he courts his favour; I have sent that I may find grace in thy sight - It is no disparagement to those that have the better cause to become petitioners for reconciliation, and to sue for peace as well as right.

6. He cometh to meet thee, and four hundred men with him - He is now weary of waiting for the days of mourning for his father, and before those come resolves to slay his brother. Out he marches with four hundred men, probably such as used to hunt with him, armed no doubt, ready to execute the word of command.

7. Then Jacob was greatly afraid and distressed - A lively apprehension of danger, may very well consist with a humble confidence in God's power and promise.

9. He addresseth himself to God as the God of his fathers: such was the sense he had of his own unworthiness, that he did not call God his own God, but a God in covenant with his ancestors. O God of my father Abraham, and God of my father Isaac. And this he could better plead, because the covenant was entailed upon him. Thou saidst unto me, Return unto thy country - He did not rashly leave his place with Laban, out of a foolish fondness for his native country; but in obedience to God's command.

10. I am not worthy - It is a surprising plea. One would think he should have pleaded that what was now in danger was his own against all the world, and that he had earned it dear enough; no, he pleads, Lord, I am not worthy of it. Of the least of all the mercies - Here is mercies in the plural number, an inexhaustible spring, and innumerable streams; mercies and truth, past mercies given according to the promise and farther mercies secured by the promise. I am not worthy of the least of all the mercies, much less am I worthy of so great a favour as this I am now suing for. Those are best prepared for the greatest mercies that see themselves unworthy of the least. For with my staff I passed over this Jordan - Poor and desolate, like a forlorn and despised pilgrim: He had no guides, no companions, no attendants. And now I am become two bands - Now I am surrounded with a numerous retinue of children and servants. Those whose latter end doth greatly increase, ought with humility and thankfulness to remember how small their beginning was.

11. Lord, deliver me from Esau, for I fear him - The fear that quickens prayer is itself pleadable. It was not a robber, but a murderer that he was afraid of: nor was it his own life only that lay at stake, but the mothers, and the childrens.

12. Thou saidst, I will surely do thee good - The best we can say to God in prayer is, what he hath said to us. God's promises as they are the surest guide of our desires in prayer, and furnish us with the best petitions, so they are the firmest ground of our hopes, and furnish us with the best pleas. Thou saidst, I will do thee good - Lord, do me good in this matter. He pleads also a particular promise, that of the multiplying of his seed. Lord, what will become of that promise, if they be all cut off?

13. Jacob having piously made God his friend by a prayer, is here prudently endeavouring to make Esau his friend by a present. He had prayed to God to deliver him from the hand of Esau - His prayer did not make him presume upon God's mercy, without the use of means.

17. He sent him also a very humble message, which he ordered his servants to deliver in the best manner. They must call Esau their Lord, and Jacob his servant: they must tell him the cattle they had was a small present which Jacob had sent him. They must especially take care to tell him that Jacob was coming after, that he might not suspect him fled. A friendly confidence in mens goodness may help to prevent the mischief designed us by their badness.

24. Very early in the morning, a great while before day. Jacob had helped his wives and children over the river, and he desired to be private, and was left alone, that he might again spread his cares and fears before God in prayer. While Jacob was earnest in prayer, stirring up himself to take hold on God, an angel takes hold on him. Some think this was a created angel, one of those that always behold the face of our Father. Rather it was the angel of the covenant, who often appeared in a human shape, before he assumed the human nature. We are told by the prophet, Hosea xii, 4, how Jacob wrestled, he wept and made supplication; prayers and tears were his weapons. It was not only a corporal, but a spiritual wrestling by vigourous faith and holy desire.

25. The angel prevailed not against him - That is, this discouragement did not shake his faith, nor silence his prayer. It was not in his own strength that he wrestled, nor by his own strength that he prevails; but by strength derived from heaven. That of Job illustrates this, Job xxiii, 6. Will he plead

against me with his great power? No; had the angel done so, Jacob had been crushed; but he would put strength in me: and by that strength Jacob had power over the angel, Hosea xii, 3. The angel put out Jacob's thigh, to shew him what he could do, and that it was God he was wrestling with, for no man could disjoint his thigh with a touch. Some think that Jacob felt little or no pain from this hurt; it is probable be did not, for he did not so much as halt 'till the struggle was over, ver. 31, and if so, that was an evidence of a divine touch indeed, which wounded and healed at the same time.

26. Let me go - The angel, by an admirable condescension, speaks Jacob fair to let him go, as God said to Moses, Exod. xxxii, 10. Let me alone. Could not a mighty angel get clear of Jacob's grapples? He could; but thus he would put an honour upon Jacob's faith and prayer. The reason the angel gives why he would be gone is because the day breaks, and therefore he would not any longer detain Jacob, who had business to do, a journey to go, a family to look after. And he said, I will not let thee go except thou bless me - He resolves he will have a blessing, and rather shall all his bones be put out of joint, than he will go away without one. Those that would have the blessing of Christ must be in good earnest, and be importunate for it.

27. What is thy name? - Jacob (saith he) a supplanter, so Jacob signifies. Well, (faith the angel) be thou never so called any more: thou shalt be called Israel, a prince with God. He is a prince indeed, that is a prince with God; and those are truly honourable that are mighty, in prayer. Yet this was not all; having power with God, he shall have power with men too; having prevailed for a blessing from heaven, he shall, no doubt, prevail for Esau's favour. Whatever enemies we have, if we can but make God our friend, we are well enough; they that by faith have power in heaven, have thereby as much power on earth as they have occasion for.

29. Wherefore dost thou ask after my name? - What good will it do thee to know that? The discovery of that was reserved for his death-bed, upon which he was taught to call him Shiloh. But instead of telling him his name, he gave him his blessing, which was the thing he wrestled for; he blessed him there, repeated and ratified the blessing formerly given him. See how wonderfully God condescends to countenance and crown importunate prayer? Those that resolve though God slay them, yet to trust in him, will at length be more than conquerors.

30. Peniel - That is, the face of God, because there he had seen the appearance of God, and obtained the favour of God.

31. He halted on his thigh - And some think he continued to do so to his dying day. If he did, he had no reason to complain, for the honour and comfort he obtained by his struggle was abundantly sufficient to countervail the damage, though he went limping to his grave.

XXXIII

We read in the former chapter how Jacob had power with God, and prevailed; here we find what power he had with men too. Here is,

I. A friendly meeting between Jacob and Esau, ver. 1-4.

II. Their conference at their meeting. Their discourse is, (1.) About Jacob's family, ver. 5-7. (2.) About the present he had sent, ver. 8-11. (3.) About the progress of their journey, ver. 12-15.

III. Jacob's settlement in Canaan, his house-ground, and altar, ver. 16-20.

3. He bowed - Though he feared Esau as an enemy, yet he did obeisance to him as an elder brother.

4. And Esau ran to meet him - Not in passion but in love. Embraced him, fell on his neck and kissed him - God hath the hearts of all men in his hands, and can turn them when and how he pleases. He can of a sudden convert enemies into friends, as he did two Sauls, one by restraining grace, 1 Sam. xxvi, 21, 25, the other by renewing grace, Acts ix, 21. And they wept - Jacob wept for joy to be thus kindly received; Esau perhaps wept for grief and shame to think of the ill design he had conceived against his brother.

5. Eleven or twelve little ones followed Jacob, the eldest of them not fourteen years old: Who are these? saith Esau. Jacob had sent him an account of the increase of his estate, but made no mention of his children, perhaps because he would not expose them to his rage, if he should meet him as an enemy. Esau therefore had reason to ask who are those with thee? To which Jacob returns a serious answer; they are the children which God hath graciously given thy servant. Jacob speaks of his children,

1. As God's gifts; they are a heritage of the Lord.

2. As choice gifts; he hath graciously given them. Though they were many, and but slenderly provided for, yet he accounts them great blessings.

10. I have seen thy face as though I had seen the face of God - That is, I have seen thee reconciled

John Wesley

to me, and at peace with me, as I desire to see God reconciled.

12. Esau offers himself to be his guide and companion, in token of sincere reconciliation. We never find that Jacob and Esau were so loving with one another as they were now. God made Esau not only not an enemy, but a friend. Esau is become fond of Jacob's company, courts him to mount Seir: let us never despair of any, nor distrust God, in whose hands all hearts are. Yet Jacob saw cause modestly to refute this offer, wherein he shews a tender concern for his own family and flocks, like a good shepherd and a good father. He must consider the children, and the flocks with young, and not lead the one or drive the other too fast. Jacob intimates to him, that it was his design to come to him to mount Seir; and we may presume he did so, after he had settled his concerns elsewhere, though that visit be not recorded.

15. Esau offers some of his men to be his guard and convoy; but Jacob humbly refuseth his offer, only desiring he would not take it amiss that he did not accept it. What needs it? He is under the Divine protection. Those are sufficiently guarded that have God for their guard, and are under a convoy of his hosts, as Jacob was. Jacob adds, only let me find grace in the sight of my Lord - Having thy favour I have all I need, all I desire from thee.

16. And Jacob journeyed to Succoth - Having in a friendly manner parted with Esau, who was gone to his own country, he comes to a place, where he rested, set up booths for his cattle, and other conveniences for himself and family. The place was afterwards known by the name of Succoth, a city in the tribe of Gad, on the other side Jordan; it signifies booths: that when his posterity afterwards dwelt in houses of stone, they might remember that the Syrian ready to perish was their father, who was glad of booths, Deut. xxvi, 5.

18. And Jacob came to Shalem, a city of Shechem - Or rather he came safe, or in peace, to the city of Shechem. After a perilous journey, in which he had met with many difficulties, he came safe at last, into Canaan.

20. He erected an altar -

1. In thankfulness to God for the good hand of his providence over him.

2. That he might keep up religion, and the worship of God in his family. He dedicated this altar to the honour of El-elohe-israel, God-the God of Israel: to the honour of God in general, the only living and true God, the Best of beings, the First of causes: and to the honour of the God of Israel, as a God in covenant with him. God had lately called him by the name of Israel; and now he calls God the God of Israel; though he be called a prince with God, God shall still be a prince with him, his Lord and his God.

XXXIV

In this chapter we have,
1. Dinah debauched, ver. 1, 2-5.
2. A treaty of marriage between her and Shechem who had defiled her, ver. 6-19.
3. The circumcision of the Shechemites, pursuant to that treaty, ver. 20-24.
4. The perfidious and bloody revenge which Simeon and Levi took upon them, ver. 25-31.

1. Dinah was then about fifteen or sixteen years of age when she went out to see the daughters of the land - Probably on some public day. She went to see; yet that was not all, she went to be seen too: she went to see the daughters of the land, but it may be with some thoughts of the sons of the land too.

7. It is called folly in Israel - According to the language of after-times, for Israel was not yet a people, but a family only.

8. Hamor communed - That is, talked. He came to treat with Jacob himself, but he turns them over to his sons. And here we have a particular account of the treaty, in which it is a shame to say the Canaanites were more honest than the Israelites.

18. Hamor and Shechem gave consent themselves to be circumcised. To this perhaps they were moved not only by the strong desire they had to bring about, this match, but by what they might have heard of the sacred and honourable intentions of this sign, in the family of Abraham, which it is probable they had some confused notions of, and of the promises confirmed by it; which made them the more desirous to incorporate with the family of Jacob.

23. Shall not their cattle and their substance be ours? - They observed that Jacob's sons were industrious, thriving people, and promised themselves and their neighbours advantage by an alliance with them: it would improve ground and trade, and bring money into their country.

25. They slew all the males - Nothing can excuse this execrable villainy. It was true Shechem had wrought folly in Israel, in defiling Dinah: but it ought to have been considered how far Dinah herself had been accessary to it. Had Shechem abused her in her mother's tent, it had been another matter; but she went upon his ground, and struck the spark which began the fire. When we are severe upon the sinner, we ought to consider who was the tempter. It was true that Shechem had done ill; but he was endeavouring to atone for it, and was as honest and honourable afterwards as the case would admit. It

was true that Shechem had done ill, but what was that to all the Shechemites? Doth one man sin, and must the innocent fall with the guilty? This was barbarous indeed. But that which above all aggravated the cruelty, was the most perfidious treachery that was in it. The Shechemites had submitted to their conditions, and had done that upon which they had promised to become one people with them. Yet they act as sworn enemies to those to whom they were lately become sworn friends, making as light of their covenant as they did of the laws of humanity. And these are the sons of Israel? Cursed be their anger, for it was fierce.

27. Tho' Simeon and Levi only were the murderers, yet others of the sons of Jacob came upon the slain, and spoiled the city - And so became accessary to the murder.

30. Ye have troubled me, to make me to stink among the inhabitants of the land - That is, You have rendered my family odious among them. And what could be expected but that the Canaanites, who were numerous and formidable, would confederate against him, and he and his little family would become an easy prey to them? I shall be destroyed, I and my house - Jacob knew indeed that God had promised to preserve his house; but he might justly fear that these vile practices of his children would amount to a forfeiture, and cut off the entail. When sin is in the house, there is reason to fear ruin at the door.

31. Should he deal with our sister as with an harlot? - No, he should not; but, if he do, Must they be their own avengers? And nothing less than so many lives, and the ruin of a whole city, serve to atone for the abuse.

XXXV

In this chapter we have,

I. Three communions between God and Jacob.
  1. God ordered Jacob to Beth-el, and in obedience to that order, he purged his house of idols, and prepared for that journey, ver. 1-5.
  2. Jacob built an altar at Beth-el to the honour of God that had appeared to him, and in performance of his vow, ver. 6, 7.
  3. God appeared to him again, and confirmed the change of his name, and the covenant with him, ver 9-13. of which appearance Jacob made a grateful acknowledgement, ver. 14, 15.

II. Three funerals.
  1. Deborah's, ver. 8.
  2. Rachel's, ver. 16-20.
  3. Isaac's, ver. 27-29.

III. Here is also Reuben's incest, ver. 22. and an account of Jacob's sons, ver. 23-26.

1. Arise go to Bethel - Here God minds Jacob of his vow at Beth-el, and sends him thither to perform it, Jacob had said in the day of his distress, If I come again in peace, this stone shall be God's house, chap. xxviii, 22. God had performed his part, had given Jacob more than bread to eat, and raiment to put on; but it should seem he had forgotten his vow, or, at least, deferred the performance of it. And dwell there - That is, Not only go himself, but take his family with him, that they might join with him in his devotions. Put away the strange Gods - Strange God's in Jacob's family! Could such a family, that was taught the knowledge of the Lord, admit them? Could such a master, to whom God had appeared twice, and oftner, connive at them? And be clean, and change your garments - These were ceremonies signifying the purification and change of the heart.

4. And they gave to Jacob - His servants, and even the retainers to his family, gave him all the strange gods, and the ear-rings they wore either as charms, or to the honour of their gods. Jacob took care to bury their images, we may suppose, in some place unknown to them, that they might not afterwards find and return to them.

5. And the terror of God was upon the cities - Though the Canaanites were much exasperated against the sons of Jacob for their barbarous usage of the Shechemites; yet they were so restrained by a divine power, that they could not take this fair opportunity to avenge their neighbours quarrel. God governs the world more by secret terrors on men's minds than we are aware of.

7. He built an altar - And no doubt offered sacrifice upon it, perhaps the tenth of his cattle, according to his vow, I will give the tenth unto thee. And he called the place, That is, the altar, El-beth-el, the God of Beth-el. As when he made a thankful acknowledgement of the honour God had done him in calling him Israel, he worshipped God by the name of El-elohe-israel, so now he was making a grateful recognition of God's former favour at Beth-el, he worships God by the name of El-beth-el, the God of Beth-el, because there God appeared to him.

8. There he buried Deborah, Rebekah's nurse - We have reason to think that Jacob, after he came to Canaan, while his family dwelt near Shechem, went himself to visit his father Isaac at Hebron. Rebekah probably was dead, but her old nurse (of whom mention is made chap. xxiv, 59,) survived her, and Jacob took her to his family. While they were at Beth-el she died, and died lamented, so much lamented, that the oak under which she was buried, was called Allon-bachuth, the oak of weeping.

10. God now confirmed the change of his name. It was done before by the angel that wrestled with him, chap. xxxii, 28, and here it was ratified by the divine majesty, to encourage him against the fear of the Canaanites. Who can be too hard for Israel, a prince with God?

11. He renewed and ratified the covenant with him, by the name of El-Shaddai, I am God Almighty. God All-sufficient, able to make good the promise in due time, and to support thee and provide for thee. Two things are promised him. 1. That he should be the father of a great nation: great in number, a company of nations shall be of thee - Every tribe of Israel was a nation, and all the twelve, a company of nations: great in honour and power, kings shall come out of thy loins. 2. That he should be master of a good land, ver. 12. The land that was given to Abraham and Isaac is here entailed on Jacob and his seed. These two promises had also a spiritual signification, which we may suppose Jacob himself had some notion of: for without doubt Christ is the promised seed, and heaven is the promised land; the former is the foundation, and the latter the top-stone of all God's favours.

13. And God went up from him - Or, from over him - In some visible display of glory, which had hovered over him, while he talked with him.

14. And Jacob set up a pillar - When he was going to Padan-aram he set up that stone which he had laid his head on for a pillar; but now he took time to erect one more stately, and durable, probably inserting that stone into it. And in token of his intending it for a sacred memorial of his communion with God, he poured oil, and the other ingredients of a drink-offering upon it. This stone shall be God's house, that is, shall be set up for his honour, as houses to the praise of their builders; and here he performs it. And he confirmed the name he had formerly given to the place, Beth-el, the house of God. Yet this very place afterwards lost the honour of its name, and became Beth-aven, a house of iniquity, for here it was that Jeroboam set up one of his calves. It is impossible for the best men to entail so much as the profession and form of religion upon a place.

16. She had hard labour - Harder than usual.

17. Rachel had said when she bore Joseph, God shall give me another son, which now the midwife remembers, and tells her, her words were made good. Yet this did not avail; unless God command away fear, no one else can. We are apt in extreme perils to comfort ourselves and our friends with the hopes of a temporal deliverance, in which we may be disappointed; we had better ground our comforts on that which cannot fail us, the hope of eternal life. Rachel had passionately said, Give me children, or else I die; and now she had children (for this was her second) she died.

18. Her dying lips calls her new-born soon Benoni, the son of my sorrow. But Jacob because he would not renew the sorrowful remembrance of his mother's death every time he called his son by name, changed his name, and called him Benjamin, the son of my right hand - That is, very dear to me; set on my right hand for a right hand blessing; the support of my age, like the staff in my hand. Jacob buried her near the place where she died. If the soul be at rest after death, the matter is not great where the body lies. In the place where the tree falls, there let it lie. The Jewish writers say, The death of Deborah and Rachel was to expiate the murder of the Shechemites, occasioned by Dinah, a daughter of the family.

20. And Jacob set up a pillar upon her grave - So that it was known long after to be Rachel's sepulchre, 1 Sam. x, 2, and Providence so ordered it, that this place afterwards fell in the lot of Benjamin. Jacob set up a pillar in remembrance of his joys ver. 14, and here he set up one in remembrance of his sorrows; for as it may be of use to ourselves to keep both in mind, so it may be of use to others to transmit the memorials of both.

21. Israel, a prince with God, yet dwells in tents; the city is reserved for him in the other world.

22. When Israel dwelt in that land - As if he were then absent from his family, which might be the unhappy occasion of these disorders. Though perhaps Bilhah was the greater criminal, yet Reuben's crime was so provoking that for it he lost his birth-right and blessing, chap. xlix, 4. And Israel heard it - No more is said, that is enough; he heard it with the utmost grief and shame, horror and displeasure.

27. And Jacob came unto Isaac his father - We may suppose he had visited him before since his return, for he sore longed after his father's house, but never 'till now brought his family to settle with him, or near him. Probably he did this now upon the death of Rebekah, by which Isaac was left solitary.

28. The age and death of Isaac are here recorded, though it appears by computation that he died not 'till many years after Joseph was sold into Egypt, and much about the time that he was preferred there. Isaac, a mild quiet man, lived the longest of all the patriarchs, for he was one hundred and eighty years old: Abraham was but one hundred and seventy-five. Isaac lived about forty years after he had made his will, chap. xxvii, 2. We shall not die an hour the sooner, but abundance the better, for our timely setting of our heart and house in order. Particular notice is taken of the amicable agreement of

Esau and Jacob in solemnizing their father's funeral, ver. 29, to shew how God had wonderfully changed Esau's mind, since he vowed his brother's murder, upon his father's death, chap. xxvii, 41. God has many ways of preventing ill men from doing the mischief they in tended; he can either tie their hands, or turn their hearts.

XXXVI

In this chapter we have an account of the posterity of Esau, who were from him, were called Edomites;

1. Because he was the son of Isaac, for whose sake this honour is put upon him.
2. Because the Edomites were neighbours to Israel, and their genealogy would be of use to give light to the following stories of what passed between them.
3. To shew the performance of the promise to Abraham, that he should be the father of many nations, and of that answer which Rebekah had from the oracle she consulted, Two nations are in thy womb; and of the blessing of Isaac, Thy dwelling shall be the fatness of the earth. Here are,

I. Esau's wives, ver. 1-5.

II. His remove to mount Seir, ver. 6-8.

III. The names of his sons, ver. 9-14.

IV. The dukes which descended of his sons, ver. 15-19.

V. The dukes of the Horites, ver. 20-30.

VI. The kings and dukes of Edom, ver. 31-43.

1. Who is Edom-That name perpetuated the remembrance of the foolish bargain he made, when he sold his birth-right for that red pottage.

6. Esau had begun to settle among his wife's relations in Seir, before Jacob came from Padan-aram, chap. xxxii, 3. Isaac it is likely, had sent him thither, that Jacob might have the clearer way to the possession of the promised land: yet probably during the life of Isaac, Esau had still some effects remaining in Canaan; but after his death, he wholly withdrew to mount Seir, took with him what came to his share of his father's personal estate, and left Canaan to Jacob, not only because he had the promise of it, but because he saw, if they should both continue to thrive, as they had begun, there would not be room for both.

8. Thus dwelt Esau in mount Seir - Whatever opposition may be made, God's word will take place, and even those that have opposed it will see themselves, some time or other, under a necessity of yielding to it. Esau had struggled for Canaan, but now he retires to mount Seir; for God's counsels shall certainly stand concerning the times before appointed, and the bounds of our habitation.

10. These are the names - Observe here,

1. That only the names of Esau's sons and grand-sons are recorded: not their history, for it is the church that Moses preserves the records of, not of those that were without. The elders only that lived by faith obtained a good report. Nor doth the genealogy go any farther than the third and fourth generation, the very names of all after are buried in oblivion; it is only the pedigree of the Israelites who were to be the heirs of Canaan, and of whom were to come the promised seed, and the holy seed, that is drawn out to any length, as far as there was occasion for it, even of all the tribes till Canaan was divided among them, and of the royal line 'till Christ came.

2. That the sons and grand-sons of Esau are called dukes. Probably they were military commanders, dukes or captains that had soldiers under them; for Esau and his family lived by the sword, chap. xxvii, 40.

3. We may suppose those dukes had numerous families of children and servants. God promised to multiply Jacob and to enrich him, yet Esau increases and is enriched first. God's promise to Jacob began to work late, but the effect of it remained longer, and it had its compleat accomplishment in the spiritual Israel.

20. These are the sons of Seir - In the midst of the genealogy of the Edomites is inserted the genealogy of the Horites, those Canaanites, or Hittites, (compare chap. xxvi, 34,) that were the natives of mount Seir. Mention is made of them, chap. xiv, 6, and of their interest in mount Seir before the Edomites took possession of it, Deut. ii, 12, 22. This comes in here, not only to give light to the story, but to be a standing reflexion upon the Edomites for intermarrying with them, by which it is likely they learned their way, and corrupted themselves. Esau having sold his birth-right, and lost his blessing and

entered into alliance with the Hittites, his posterity and the sons of Seir are here reckoned together. Those that treacherously desert God's church are justly numbered with those that were never in it: apostate Edomites stand on the same ground with accursed Horites. Notice is taken of one Anah, who fed the asses of Zibeon his father, ver. 20, and yet is called duke Anah, ver. 29. Those that expect to rise high should begin low. An honourable descent should not keep men from an honest employment, nor a mean employment baulk any man's preferment.

24. This Anah was not only industrious in his business, but ingenious too, and successful, for he found mules, or, (as some read it) waters, hot baths in the wilderness. Those that are diligent in their business sometimes find more advantages than they expected.

31. By degrees the Edomites worked out the Horites, and got full possession of the country. 1. They were ruled by kings who governed the whole country, and seem to have come to the throne by election, and not by lineal descent: these kings reigned in Edom before there reigned any king over the children of Israel - That is, before Moses's time, for he was king in Jeshurun. God had lately promised Jacob that kings shall come out of his loins: yet Esau's blood becomes royal long before any of Jacob's did. Probably it was a trial to the faith of Israel, to hear of the power of the kings of Edom, while they were bond-slaves in Egypt: but those that look for great things from God must be content to wait for them. God's time is the best time. 2. They were afterward's governed by dukes again, here named, who, I suppose, ruled all at the same time in several places in the country. They set up this form of government, either in conformity to the Horites, who had used it, ver. 29, or God's providence reduced them to it, as some conjecture, to correct them for their unkindness to Israel, in refusing them passage through their country, Num. xx, 18.

43. Mount Seir is called the land of their possession - While the Israelites dwelt in the house of bondage, and their Canaan was only the land of promise, the Edomites dwelt in their own habitations, and Seir was in their possession. The children of this world have their all in hand, and nothing in hope, while the children of God have often their all in hope, and next to nothing in hand. But, all things considered, it is better to have Canaan in promise than mount Seir in possession.

XXXVII

At this chapter begins the story of Joseph, Jacob's eldest son, by his beloved wife Rachel. It is so remarkably divided between his humiliation and his exaltation, that we cannot avoid seeing something of Christ in it, who was first humbled and then exalted; it also shews the lot of Christians, who must through many tribulations enter into the kingdom. In this chapter we have,

I. The malice his brethren bore against him: they hated him, (1.) Because he informed his father of their wickedness, ver. 1, 2. (2.) Because his father loved him, ver. 3, 4. (3.) Because he dreamed of his dominion over them, ver. 5-11.

II. The mischiefs his brethren designed, and did to him. (1.) His visit he made them gave an opportunity, ver. 12-17. (2.) They designed to slay him, but determined to starve him, ver. 18-24. (3.) They changed their purpose, and sold him for a slave, ver. 25- 28. (4.) They made their father believe that he was torn in pieces, ver. 29-35. (5.) He was sold in Egypt to Potiphar, ver. xxxvi, And all this was working together for good.

2. These are the generations of Jacob - It is not a barren genealogy, as those of Esau, but a memorable useful history. Joseph brought to his father their evil report - Jacob's sons did that when they were from under his eye, which they durst not have done if they had been at home with him; but Joseph gave his father an account of their ill carriage, that he might reprove and restrain them.

3. He made him a coat of divers colours - Which probably was significant of farther honours intended him.

5. Though he was now very young, about seventeen years old, yet he was pious and devout, and this fitted him for God's gracious discoveries to him. Joseph had a great deal of trouble before him, and therefore God gave him betimes this prospect of his advancement, to support and comfort him.

8. Shalt thou indeed reign over us? - See here,

1. How truly they interpreted his dream? The event exactly answered this interpretation, chap. xlii, 6, &c.

2. How scornfully they resented it, Shalt thou that art but one, reign over us that are many? Thou that art the youngest, over us that are elder? The reign of Jesus Christ, our Joseph, is despised and striven against by an unbelieving world, who cannot endure to think that this man should reign over them. The dominion also of the upright in the morning of the resurrection is thought of with the utmost disdain.

10. His father rebuked him - Probably to lessen the offense which his brethren would take at it; yet

he took notice of it more than he seemed to do.

18. *And when they saw him afar off they conspired against him* - It was not in a heat, or upon a sudden provocation, that they thought to slay him, but from malice propense, and in cold blood.

21. *And Reuben heard it* - God can raise up friends for his people, even among their enemies. Reuben of all the brothers had most reason to be jealous of Joseph, for he was the first-born, and so entitled to those distinguishing favours which Jacob was conferring on Joseph, yet he proves his best friend. Reuben's temper seems to have been soft and effeminate, which had betrayed him to the sin of uncleanness, while the temper of the two next brothers, Simeon and Levi, was fierce, which betrayed them to the sin of murder, a sin which Reuben startled at the thought of. He made a proposal which they thought would effectually destroy Joseph, and yet which he designed should answer his intention of rescuing Joseph out of their hands, probably hoping thereby to recover his father's favour which he had lately lost; but God over-ruled all to serve his own purpose of making Joseph an instrument to save much people alive. Joseph was here a type of Christ. Though he was the beloved Son of his Father, and hated by a wicked world; yet the Father sent him out of his bosom to visit us; he came from heaven to earth to seek and save us; yet then malicious plots were laid against him; he came to his own, and his own not only received him not, but consulted, This is the heir, come let us kill him. This he submitted to, in pursuance of his design to save us.

24. *They call him into a pit* - To perish there with hunger and cold; so cruel were their tender mercies.

25. *They sat down to eat bread* - They felt no remorse of conscience, which if they had, would have spoiled their stomach to their meat. A great force put upon conscience commonly stupifies it, and for the time deprives it both of sense and speech.

26. *What profit is it if we slay our brother?* - It will be less guilt and more gain to sell him. They all agreed to this. And as Joseph was sold by the contrivance of Judah for twenty pieces of silver, so was our Lord Jesus for thirty, and by one of the same name too, Judas. Reuben it seems, was gone away from his brethren when they sold Joseph, intending to come round some other way to the pit, and to help Joseph out of it. But had this taken effect, what had become of God's purpose concerning his preferment, in Egypt? There are many devices of the enemies of God's people to destroy them, and of their friends to help them, which perhaps are both disappointed, as these here; but the counsel of the Lord that shall stand. Reuben thought himself undone because the child was sold; I, whither shall I go? He being the eldest, his father would expect from him an account of him; but it proved they had all been undone, if he had not been sold.

35. *He refused to be comforted* - He resolved to go down to the grave mourning; Great affection to any creature doth but prepare for so much the greater affliction, when it is either removed from us, or embittered to us: inordinate love commonly ends in immoderate grief.

XXXVIII

How little reason had the Jews, who were so called from this Judah, to boast, as they did, that they were not born of fornication? John viii, 41. We have in this chapter,

I. Judah's marriage and issue, and the untimely death of his two eldest sons, ver. 1-11.

II. Judah's incest with his daughter-in-law Tamar, ver. 12-23.

III. His confusion when it was discovered, ver. 24-26.

IV. The birth of his twin sons in whom his family was built up, ver. 27-30.

1. *Judah went down from his brethren* -- withdrew for a time from his father's family, and got intimately acquainted with one Hirah an Adullamite. When young people that have been well educated begin to change their company, they will soon change their manners, and lose their good education. They that go down from their brethren, that forsake the society of the seed of Israel, and pick up Canaanites for their companions, are going down the hill apace.

2. *He took her*-To wife. His father, it should seem, was not consulted, but by his new friend Hirah.

7. *And Er was wicked in the sight of the Lord* - That is, in defiance of God and his law. And what came of it? Why God cut him off presently, The Lord slew him. The next brother Onan was, according to the ancient usage, married to the widow, to preserve the name of his deceased brother that died childless. This custom of marrying the brother's widow was afterward made one of the laws of Moses, Deut. xxv, 5. Onan, though he consented to marry the widow, yet to the great abuse of his own body, of the wife he had married, and the memory of his brother that was gone, he refused to raise up seed unto his brother. Those sins that dishonour the body are very displeasing to God, and the evidence of vile

actions. Observe, the thing which he did displeased the Lord - And it is to be feared, thousands, especially of single persons, by this very thing, still displeased the Lord, and destroy their own souls.

11. Shelah the third son was reserved for the widow, yet with design that he should not marry so young as his brothers had done, lest he die also. Some think that Judah never intended to marry Shelah to Tamar, but unjustly suspected her to have been the death of her two former husbands, (whereas it was their own wickedness that slew them) and then sent her to her father's house, with a charge to remain a widow. If so, it was an inexcusable piece of prevarication; however Tamar acquiesced, and waited for the issue.

14. Some excuse this by suggesting that she believed the promise made to Abraham and his seed, particularly that of the Messiah, and that she was therefore desirous to have a child by one of that family, that she might have the honour, or at least stand fair for the honour of being the mother of the Messiah. She covered her with a veil - It was the custom of harlots in those times to cover their faces, that tho' they were not ashamed, yet they might seem to be so: the sin of uncleanness did not then go so bare-faced as it now doth.

17. A kid from the flock - A goodly price at which her chastity and honour were valued! Had the consideration been thousands of rams, and ten thousand rivers of oil, it had not been a valuable consideration. The favour of God, the purity of the soul, the peace of the conscience, and the hope of heaven: are too precious to be exposed to sale at any such rates. He lost his Jewels by the bargain: He sent the kid according to his promise, to redeem his pawn, but the supposed harlot could not be found. He sent it by his friend, (who was indeed his back-friend, because he was aiding and abetting in his evil deeds) the Adullamite; who came back without the pledge. 'Tis a good account, if it be but true, of any place that which they here gave, that there is no harlot in this place, for such sinners are the scandals and plagues of any place. Judah sits down content to lose his signet and his bracelets, and forbids his friend to make any further enquiry.

23. Lest we be shamed - Either,
1. Lest his sin should come to be known publicly, Or
2. Lest he should be laughed at as a fool for trusting a whore with his signet and his bracelets. He expresses no concern about the sin, only about the shame. There are many who are more solicitous to preserve their reputation with men, than to secure the savour of God, lest we be shamed goes farther with them than lest we be damned.

28. It should seem the birth was hard to the mother, by which she was corrected for her sin: the children also, like Jacob and Esau, struggled for the birth-right, and Pharez who got it, is ever named first, and from him Christ descended. He had his name from his breaking forth before his brother; this breach be upon thee - The Jews, as Zarah, bid fair for the birth-right, and were marked with a scarlet thread, as those that come out first; but the Gentiles, like Pharez, or a son of violence got the start of them, by that violence which the kingdom of heaven suffers, and attained to the righteousness which the Jews came short of: yet when the fulness of time is come, all Israel shall be saved. Both these sons are named in the genealogy of our saviour, Matt. i, 3, to perpetuate the story, as an instance of the humiliation of our Lord Jesus.

XXXIX

At this chapter we return to the story of Joseph. We have him here,

I. A servant, a slave in Potiphar's house, ver. 1. and yet there greatly honoured and favoured, (1.) By the providence of God, which made him in effect a master, ver. 2-6. (2.) By the grace of God, which made him more than conqueror over a strong temptation, ver. 7-12.

II. We have him a sufferer, falsely accused, ver. 13-18. Imprisoned, ver. 19, 20. And yet his imprisonment made both honourable and comfortable by the tokens of God's special presence with him, ver. 21-23.

1. The Jews have a proverb, If the world did but know the worth of good men, they would hedge them about with pearls. Joseph was sold to an officer of Pharaoh, with whom he might get acquainted with public persons, and public business, and so be fitted for the preferment he was afterwards designed for. What God intends men for, he will be sure, some way or other, to qualify them for.

2. Those that can separate us from all our friends, cannot deprive us of the gracious presence of our God. When Joseph had none of his relations with him, he had his God with him, even in the house of the Egyptian: Joseph was banished from his father's house, but the Lord was with him. It is God's presence with us that makes all we do prosperous. Those that would prosper, must therefore make God their friend; and those that do prosper, must therefore give God the praise.

6. He knew not ought he had, save the bread which he did eat - The servant had all the care and

trouble of the estate, the master had only the enjoyment of it; an example not to be imitated by any master, unless he could be sure that he had one like Joseph for a servant.

9. How can I sin against God - Not only how shall I do it and sin against my master, my mistress, myself, my own body and soul, but against God? - Gracious souls look upon this as the worst thing in sin, that it is against God, against his nature and his dominion, against his love and his design. They that love God, for this reason hate sin.

10. He hearkened not to her, so much as to be with her. Those that would be kept from harm, must keep themselves out of harm's way.

12. When she laid hold on him, he left his garment in her hand - He would not stay to parley with the temptation, but flew out from it with the utmost abhorrence, he left his garment as one escaping for his life.

20. Where the king's prisoners were bound - Potiphar, it is likely, chose that prison because it was the worst; for there the irons entered into the soul, Psalm cv, 18, but God designed it to pave the way to his enlargement. Our Lord Jesus, like Joseph was bound, and numbered with the transgressors.

21. But the Lord was with Joseph and shewed him mercy. God despiseth not his prisoners, Psalm lxix, 33. No gates nor bars can shut out his gracious presence from his people. God gave him favour in the sight of the keeper of the prison - God can raise up friends for his people even where they little expect them. The keeper saw that God was with him, and that every thing prospered under his hand, and therefore intrusted him with the management of the affairs of the prison.

XL

In this chapter things are working towards Joseph's advancement.

I. Two of Pharaoh's servants are committed to prison, and there, to Joseph's care, and so became witnesses of his extraordinary conduct, ver. 1-4.

II. They dreamed each of them a dream, which Joseph interpreted, ver. 5-19. and they verified the interpretation, ver. 20-22.

III. Joseph recommends his case to one of them whose preferment he foresaw, ver. 14, 15. but in vain, ver. 23.

1. We should not have had this story of Pharaoh's butler and baker recorded in scripture, if it had not been serviceable to Joseph's preferment. The world stands for the sake of the church, and is governed for its good. Observe,

1. Two of the great officers of Pharaoh's court having offended the king are committed to prison. Note, High places are slippery places; nothing more uncertain than the favour of princes. Those that make God's favour their happiness, and his service their business, will find him a better master than Pharaoh was, and not so extreme to mark what they do amiss. Many conjectures there are concerning the offense of these servants of Pharaoh; some make it no less than an attempt to take away his life; others no more but the casual lighting of a fly into his cup, and a little sand in his bread: whatever it was, Providence, by this means, brought them into the prison where Joseph was.

4. The captain of the guard, which was Potiphar, charged Joseph with them - Which intimates that he began now to be reconciled to him.

6. They were sad - It was not the prison that made them sad; they were pretty well used to that, but the dream. God has more ways than one to sadden the spirits of those that are to be made sad. Those sinners that are hardy enough under outward trouble, yet God can find a way to trouble them, and take off their wheels, by wounding their spirits, and laying a load upon them.

8. Do not interpretations belong to God? - He means the God whom he worshipped, to the knowledge of whom he endeavours hereby to lead them. And if interpretations belong to God, he is a free agent, and may communicate the power to whom he pleases, therefore tell me your dreams.

14. Think on me, when it shall be well with thee - Though the respect paid to Joseph, made the prison as easy to him as a prison could be, yet none can blame him to be desirous of liberty. See what a modest representation he makes of his own case. He doth not reflect upon his brethren that sold him, only saith, I was stolen out of the land of the Hebrews. Nor doth he reflect on the wrong done him in this imprisonment by his mistress that was his persecutor, and his master that was his judge, but mildly avers his own innocency. Here have I done nothing that they should put me into the dungeon - When we are called to vindicate ourselves, we should carefully avoid as much as may be speaking ill of others. Let us be content to prove ourselves innocent, and not fond of upbraiding others with their guilt.

20. He lifted up the head of these two prisoners-That is, arraigned and tried them; and he restored the chief butler, and hanged the chief baker.

XLI

Two things providence is here bringing about.
1. The advancement of Joseph.
2. The maintenance of Jacob and his family in a time of famine; for the eyes of the Lord run to and fro through the earth, and direct the affairs of the children of men. In order to these, here is,

I. Pharaoh's dream, ver. 1-8.

II. The recommendation of Joseph to him for an interpreter, ver. 9-13.

III. The interpretation of the dreams, and the prediction of seven years plenty, and seven years famine in Egypt, with the prudent advice given to Pharaoh thereupon, ver. 14-36.

IV. The preferment of Joseph to a place of the highest power and trust, ver. 37-45.

V. The accomplishment of Joseph's prediction, and his fidelity to his trust, ver. 46-57.

8. His spirit was troubled - It cannot but put us into a concern to receive any extraordinary message from heaven. And his magicians were puzzled; the rules of their art failed them; these dreams of Pharaoh did not fall within the compass of them. This was to make Joseph's performance by the Spirit of God the more admirable.

9. I remember my faults this day - in forgetting Joseph. Some think he means his faults against Pharaoh, for which he was imprisoned, and then he would insinuate, that through Pharaoh had forgiven him, he had not forgiven himself. God's time for the enlargement of his people will appear, at last, to be the fittest time. If the chief butler had at first used his interest for Joseph's enlargement, and had obtained, it is probable, he would have gone back to the land of the Hebrews, and then he had neither been so blessed himself, nor such a blessing to his family. But staying two years longer, and coming out upon this occasion to interpret the king's dreams, way was made for his preferment. The king can scarce allow him time, but that decency required it, to shave himself, and to change his raiment, chap. xli, 14. It is done with all possible expedition, and Joseph is brought in perhaps almost as much surprised as Peter was, Acts xii, 9, so suddenly is his captivity brought back, that he is as one that dreams, Psalm lxxvi, 1. Pharaoh immediately, without enquiring who or whence he was tells him his business, that he expected he should interpret his dream.

16.(1.) He gives honour to God; It is not in me; God must give it. Great gifts then appear most graceful and illustrious, when those that have them use them humbly, and take not the praise of them to themselves, but give it to God, (2.) He shews respect to Pharaoh, and hearty goodwill to him, supposing that the interpretation would be an answer of peace. Those that consult God's oracles may expect an answer of peace.

29. See the goodness of God, in sending the seven years of plenty before those of famine, that provision might be made accordingly. How wonderful wisely has Providence, that great house-keeper, ordered the affairs of this numerous family from the beginning! Great variety of seasons there have been and the produce of the earth sometimes more, and sometimes less; yet take one time with another, what was miraculous concerning the manna, is ordinarily verified in the common course of Providence; He that gathers much has nothing over, and he that gathers little has no lack, Exod. xvi, 18.

30. See the perishing nature of our worldly enjoyments. The great increase of the years of plenty was quite lost and swallowed up in the years of famine; and the overplus of it, which seemed very much, yet did but just serve to keep men alive.

44. Without thee shall no man lift up his hand or foot - All the affairs of the kingdom must pass through his hand. Only in the throne will I be greater than thou - It is probable there were those about court that opposed Joseph's preferment, which occasioned Pharaoh so oft to repeat the grant, and with that solemn sanction, I am Pharaoh. He gave him his own ring as a ratification of his commission, and in token of peculiar favour; or it was like delivering him the great seal. He put fine clothes upon him instead of his prison garments, and adorned him with a chain of gold. He made him ride in the second chariot next his own, and ordered all to do obeisance to him, as to Pharaoh himself; he gave him a new name and such a name as spoke the value he had for him, Zaphnath-paaneah, a Revealer of secrets. He married him honourably to a prince's daughter. Where God had been liberal in giving wisdom and other merits, Pharaoh was not sparing in conferring honours. Now this preferment of Joseph, was, 1st, an abundant recompense for his innocent and patient suffering, a lasting instance of the equity and goodness of providence, and an encouragement to all to trust in a good God. 2ndly, It was typical of the exaltation of Christ, that great revealer of secrets, (John i, 18,) or as some translate Joseph's new name, the saviour of the world. The brightest glories of the upper world are upon him, the highest trusts lodged

in his hand, and all power given him both in heaven and earth. He is gatherer, keeper, and disposer of all the stores of divine grace, and chief ruler of the kingdom of God among men. The work of ministers is to cry before him; Bow the knee; kiss the Son.

50. *Two sons* - In the names he gave them, he owned the divine Providence giving this happy turn to his affairs. He was made to forget his misery, but could he be so unnatural as to forget all his father's house? And he was made fruitful in the land of his affliction. It had been the land of his affliction, and, in some sense, it was still so, for his distance from his father was still his affliction. Ephraim signifies fruitfulness, and Manasseh forgetfulness.

54. *The seven years of dearth began to come* - Not only in Egypt, but in other lands, in all lands, that is, all the neighbouring countries.

XLII

We have in this chapter,

I. The humble application of Jacob's sons to Joseph, to buy corn, ver. 1-6.

II. The fright Joseph put them into, for their trial, ver. 7-20.

III. The conviction they were now under of their sin concerning Joseph long before, ver. 21-24.

IV. Their return to Canaan with corn, and the great distress their good father was in upon the account they gave him of their expedition, ver. 25-38.

1. *Jacob saw that there was corn* - That is, he saw the corn that his neighbours had bought there and brought home.
2. *Get you down thither* - Masters of families must not only pray for daily bread for their families, but must with care and industry provide it.
7. We may well wonder that Joseph, during the twenty years he had been in Egypt, especially during the last seven years that he had been in power there, never sent to his father to acquaint him with his circumstances; nay, 'tis strange that he who so oft went throughout all the land of Egypt, never made a step to Canaan, to visit his aged father. When he was in the borders of Egypt that lay next to Canaan, perhaps it would not have been above three or four days journey for him in his chariot. 'Tis a probable conjecture, that his whole management of himself in this affair was by special direction from heaven, that the purpose of God, concerning Jacob and his family, might be accomplished. When Joseph's brethren came, he knew them by many a good token, but they knew not him, little thinking to find him there.
9. He remembered the dreams, but they had forgot them. The laying up of God's oracles in our hearts will be of excellent use to us in all our conduct. Joseph had an eye to his dreams, which he knew to be divine, in his carriage towards his brethren, and aimed at the accomplishment of them, and the bringing his brethren to repentance; and both those points were gained.
1. He shewed himself harsh with them: the very manner of his speaking, considering the post he was in, was enough to frighten them, for he spake roughly to them - He charged them with ill designs against the government, treated them as dangerous persons, ye are spies, protesting by the life of Pharaoh that they were so. Some make that an oath, others make it no more but a vehement asseveration; however, it was more than yea, yea, and nay, nay, and therefore came of evil.
2. They hereupon were very submissive; they spoke to him with all respect; nay, my Lord. They modestly deny the charge, we are no spies; they tell him their business, they came to buy food, they give a particular account of themselves and their family, ver. 13, and that was it he wanted.
3. He clapt them all up in prison three days.
4. He concluded with them at last, that one of them should be left as a hostage, and the rest should go home and fetch Benjamin. It was a very encouraging word he said, I fear God; q.d. You may assure yourselves, I will do you no wrong, I dare not, for I know that as high as I am, there is one higher than I. With those that fear God we have reason to expect fair dealing: the fear of God will be a check upon those that are in power, to restrain them from abusing their power to oppression and tyranny:
21. *We are very guilty concerning our brother* - We do not read that they said this during their three days imprisonment; but now when the matter was come to some issue, and they saw themselves still embarrassed, they began to relent. Perhaps Joseph's mention of the fear of God, put them upon consideration, and extorted this reflexion.
24. *He took Simeon* - He chose him for the hostage, probably because he remembered him to have been his most bitter enemy, or because he observed him now to be least humbled and concerned. He bound him before their eyes, to affect them all.

28. Their heart failed them, and they were afraid, saying one to another, What is this that God hath done to us? - They knew that the Egyptians abhorred a Hebrew, chap. xliii, 32, and therefore, since they could not expect to receive any kindness from them, they concluded that this was done with a design to pick a quarrel with them, the rather because the man, the Lord of the land, had charged them as spies. Their own conscience were awake, and their sins set in order before them, and this puts them into confusion. When the events of providence concerning us are surprising, it is good to inquire what it is that God has done and is doing with us?

38. My son shall not go down with you - He plainly intimates a distrust of them, remembering that he never saw Joseph since he had been with them; therefore Benjamin shall not go with you.

XLIII

Here the story of Joseph's brethren is carried on.

I. Their melancholy parting with their father Jacob, in Canaan, ver. 1-14.

II. Their meeting with Joseph in Egypt, ver. 15-34.

9. Judah's conscience had lately smitten him for what he had done a great while ago against Joseph; and as an evidence of the truth of his repentance, he is ready to undertake, as far as a man could do it, for Benjamin's security. He will not only not wrong him but will do all he can to protect him. This is such restitution as the case will admit: when he knew not how he could retrieve Joseph, he would make some amends for the irreparable injury he had done him, by doubling his care concerning Benjamin.

11. If it must be so now, take your brother - If no corn can be had but upon those terms, as good expose him to the perils of the journey, as suffer ourselves and families, and Benjamin among the rest, to perish for want of bread: it is no fault, but our wisdom and duty, to alter our resolutions when there is a good reason for so doing: constancy is a virtue, but obstinacy is not: it is God's prerogative to make unchangeable resolves.

12. Take double money - As much again as they took the time before, upon supposition that the price of corn might be risen, or that, if it should be insisted upon, they might pay a ransom for Simeon. And he sent a present of such things as the land afforded, and were scarce in Egypt, the commodities that Canaan exported.

14. God almighty give you mercy before the man! - Jacob had formerly turned an angry brother into a kind one with a present and a prayer, and here he betakes himself to the same tried method. Those that would find mercy with men must seek it of God. He concludes all with this, if I be bereaved of my children, I am bereaved - If I must part with them thus one after another, I acquiesce and say, The will of the Lord be done.

23. Your God, and the God of your father, has given you treasure in your sacks - Hereby he shews that he had no suspicion of dishonesty in them: for what we get by deceit we cannot say God gives it us. He silences their farther enquiry about it: ask not how it came thither, providence brought it you, and let that satisfy you. It appears by what he said, that by his master's instructions he was brought to the knowledge of the true God, the God of the Hebrews. He directs them to look up to God, and acknowledge his providence in the good bargain they had. We must own ourselves indebted to God as our God, and the God of our fathers, (a God in covenant with us and them) for all our successes and advantages, and the kindnesses of our friends; for every creature is that to us, and no more, than God makes it to be.

26. When they brought him the present, they bowed themselves before him, and again, when they gave him an account of their father's health, they made obeisance, and called him, Thy servant, our father - Thus were Joseph's dreams fulfilled more and more; and even the father, by the sons, bowed before him. Probably Jacob had directed them, if they had occasion to speak of him to the man, the Lord of the land, to call him his servant.

29. God be gracious unto thee, my son - Joseph's favour, though he was the Lord of the land, would do him little good, unless God were gracious to him.

33. He placed his brethren according to their seniority, as if he could certainly divine. Some think they placed themselves so according to their custom; but if so, I see not why such particular notice is taken of it, especially as a thing they marvelled at.

34. They drank and were merry - Their cares and fears were now over, and they eat their bread with joy, concluding they were now upon good terms with the man, the Lord of the land. If God accept our works, our present, we have reason to be chearful.

Joseph having entertained his brethren, dismissed them: but here we have them brought back in a greater fright than any they had been in yet. Observe.

I. What method he took, both to humble them farther, and to try their affections to his brother Benjamin, by which he would be able to judge the sincerity of their repentance for what they had done against him. This he contrived to do by bringing Benjamin into distress, ver. 1-17.

II. The good success of the experiment: he found them all heartily concerned, and Judah particularly, both for the safety of Benjamin, and for the comfort of their aged father, ver. 18-34.

5. *Is not this it in which my Lord drinketh? And for which he would search thoroughly* - So it may be rendered.

16. *God hath found out the iniquity of thy servants* - Referring to the injury they had formerly done to Joseph, for which they thought God was now reckoning with them. Even in those afflictions wherein we apprehend ourselves wronged by men, yet we must own that God is righteous, and finds out our iniquity. We cannot judge what men are, by what they have been formerly, not what they will do, by what they have done. Age and experience may make men wiser and better, They that had sold Joseph, yet would not abandon Benjamin.

18. *And Judah said* - We have here a most pathetic speech which Judah made to Joseph on Benjamin's behalf. Either Judah was a better friend to Benjamin than the rest, and more solicitous to bring him off; or he thought himself under greater obligations to endeavour it than the rest, because he had passed his word to his father for his safe return. His address, as it is here recorded, is so very natural, and so expressive of his present passion, that we cannot but suppose Moses, who wrote it so long after, to have written it under the special direction of him that made man's mouth. A great deal of unaffected art, and unstudied rhetoric there is in this speech.

1. He addressed himself to Joseph with a great deal of respect calls him his Lord, himself and his brethren his servants, begs his patient hearing, and passeth a mighty compliment upon him, Thou art even as Pharaoh, whose favour we desire, and whose wrath we dread as we do Pharaoh's.

2. He represented Benjamin as one well worthy of his compassionate consideration, he was a little one, compared with the rest; the youngest, not acquainted with the world, nor inured to hardship, having been always brought up tenderly with his father. It made the case the more piteous that he alone was left of his mother, and his brother was dead, viz. Joseph; little did Judah think what a tender point he touched upon now. Judah knew that Joseph was sold, and therefore had reason enough to think that he was not alive.

3. He urged it closely that Joseph had himself constrained them to bring Benjamin with them, had expressed a desire to see him, had forbidden them his presence, unless they brought Benjamin with them, all which intimated, that he designed him some kindness. And must he be brought with so much difficulty to the preferment of a perpetual slavery? Was he not brought to Egypt in obedience, purely in obedience to the command of Joseph, and would not he shew him some mercy?

4. The great argument he insists upon was the insupportable grief it would be to his aged father, if Benjamin should be left behind in servitude. His father loves him, ver. 20. Thus they had pleaded against Joseph's insisting on his coming down ver. 22. If he should leave his father, his father would die, much more if he now be left behind, never to return. This the old man of whom they spake, had pleaded against his going down. If mischief befall him, ye shall bring down my gray hairs, that crown of glory, with sorrow to the grave. This therefore Judah presseth with a great deal of earnestness, his life is bound up in the lad's life, when he sees that the lad is not with us, he will faint away and die immediately, or will abandon himself to such a degree of sorrow, as will, in a few days, make an end of him, And (lastly) Judah pleads, that, for his part, he could not bear to see this. Let me not see the evil that shall come on my father.

5. Judah, in honour to the justice of Joseph's sentence, and to shew his sincerity in this plea, offers himself to become a bond-man instead of Benjamin. Thus the law would be satisfied; Joseph would be no loser, for we may suppose Judah a more able bodied man than Benjamin; Jacob would better bear that than the loss of Benjamin. Now, so far was he from grieving at his father's particular fondness for Benjamin, than he is himself willing to be a bond-man to indulge it. Now, had Joseph been, as Judah supposed, an utter stranger to the family, yet even common humanity could not but be wrought upon by such powerful reasonings as these; for nothing could be said more moving, more tender; it was enough to melt a heart of stone: but to Joseph, who was nearer a-kin to Benjamin than Judah himself, and who, at this time, felt a greater passion for him and his aged father, than Judah did, nothing could be more pleasingly nor more happily said. Neither Jacob nor Benjamin needed an intercessor with Joseph, for he himself loved them. Upon the whole, let us take notice, (1.) How prudently Judah suppressed all

mention of the crime that was charged upon Benjamin. Had he said any thing by way of acknowledgment of it, he had reflected on Benjamin's honesty. Had he said any thing by way of denial of it, he had reflected on Joseph's justice; therefore he wholly waves that head, and appeals to Joseph's pity. (2.) What good reason dying Jacob had to say, Judah, thou art he whom thy brethren shall praise, chap. xlix, 8, for he excelled them all in boldness, wisdom, eloquence, and especially tenderness for their father and family. (3.) Judah's faithful adherence to Benjamin now in his distress was recompensed long after, by the constant adherence of the tribe of Benjamin to the tribe of Judah, when all the other ten tribes deserted it.

XLV

Joseph let Judah go on without interruption, heard all he had to say, and then answered it all in one word, I am Joseph. Now he found his brethren humbled for their sins, mindful of himself (for Judah had mentioned him twice in his speech) respectful to their father, and very tender of their brother Benjamin: now they were ripe for the comfort he designed them, by making himself known to them. This was to Joseph's brethren as clear shining after rain; nay, it was to them as life from the dead. Here is,

I. Joseph's discovery of himself to his brethren, and his discourse with them upon that occasion, ver. 1-15.

II. The orders Pharaoh gave to fetch Jacob and his family down to Egypt, and Joseph's dispatch of his brethren back to his father with these orders, ver. 16-24.

III. The joyful tidings of this brought to Jacob, ver. 25-28.

1. Judah and his brethren were waiting for an answer, and could not but be amazed to discover, instead of the gravity of a judge, the natural affection of a father or brother. Cause every man to go out - The private conversations of friends are the most free. When Joseph would put on love, he puts off state, which it was not fit his servants should be witnesses of. Thus Christ graciously manifests himself and his loving kindness to his people, out of the sight and hearing of the world. See note at "ver. 2" for continuation to item

2. Tears were the introduction to his discourse. He had dammed up this stream a great while, and with much ado, but now it swelled so high that he could no longer contain, but he wept aloud, so that those whom he had forbid to see him could not but hear him. These were tears of tenderness and strong affection, and with these he threw off that austerity, with which he had hitherto carried himself towards his brethren; for he could bear it no longer. This represents the Divine compassion towards returning penitents, as much as that of the father of the prodigal, Luke xv, 20 Hosea xi, 8, 9. See note at "ver. 3" for continuation to item No. 3

3. He abruptly tells them; I am Joseph - They knew him only by his Egyptian name, Zaphnath-paaneah, his Hebrew name being lost and forgot in Egypt; but now he teaches them to call him by that, I am Joseph: nay, that they might not suspect it was another of the same name, he explains himself. I am Joseph your brother. This would both humble them yet more for their sin in selling him, and encourage them to hope for kind treatment. This word, at first, startled Joseph's brethren, they started back through fear, or at least stood still astonished: but Joseph called kindly and familiarly to them. Come near, I pray you. Thus, when Christ manifests himself to his people he encourages them to draw near to him with a true heart. Perhaps being about to speak of their selling of him, he would not speak aloud, lest the Egyptians should overhear, and it should make the Hebrews to be yet more an abomination to them; therefore he would have them come near, that he might whisper with them, which, now the tide of his passion was a little over, he was able to do, whereas, at first, he could not but cry out.

4. He endeavours to sweep their grief for the injuries they had done him, by shewing them, that, whatever they designed, God meant it for good, and had brought much good out of it. See note at "ver. 1" for start of item, ie. No. 1

5. Be not grieved or angry with yourselves - Sinners must grieve, and be angry with themselves for their sins; yea, though God, by his power, bring good out of them, for that is no thanks to the sinner: but true penitents should be greatly affected with it, when they see God bringing good out of evil. Though we must not with this consideration extenuate our own sins, and so take off the edge of our repentance; yet it may do well thus to extenuate the sins of others, and so take off the edge of our angry resentments. Thus Joseph doth here. His brethren needed not to fear that he would revenge upon them an injury which God's providence had made to turn so much to his advantage, and that of his family. Now he tells them how long the famine was likely to last, five years yet, ver. 6, and what a capacity he was in of being kind to his relations, which is the greatest satisfaction that wealth and power can give to a good man.

8. *See what a favourable colour he puts upon the injury they had done him, God sent me before you* - God's Israel is the particular care of God's providence. Joseph reckoned that his advancement was not so much designed to save a whole kingdom of Egyptians, as to preserve a small family of Israelites; for the Lord's portion is his people: whatever goes with others, they shall be secured. How admirable are the projects of Providence! How remote its tendencies! What wheels are there within wheels; and yet all directed by the eyes in the wheels, and the Spirit of the living Creature! See note at "ver. 1" for start of item, ie. No. [1.] [5.] He promises to take care of his father and all his family, during the rest of the years of famine. (1.) He desires that his father might speedily be made glad with the tidings of his life and honour. His brethren must hasten to Canaan, and acquaint Jacob that his son Joseph was Lord of all Egypt - He knew it would be a refreshing oil to his hoary head, and a sovereign cordial to his spirits. He desires them to give themselves, and take with them to their father, all possible satisfaction of the truth of these surprising tidings.

12. *Your eyes see that it is my mouth* - If they could recollect themselves, they might remember something of his features and speech, and be satisfied. See note at "ver. 1" for (2.) He is very earnest that his father and all his family should come to him to Egypt. *Come down unto me, tarry not* - He allots his dwelling in Goshen, that part of Egypt which lay towards Canaan, that they might be mindful of the country from which they were to come out. He promiseth to provide for him, *I will nourish* - Our Lord Jesus being, like Joseph, exalted to the highest honours and powers of the upper world, it is his will that all that are his should be with him where he is. This is his commandment, that we be with him now in faith and hope, and a heavenly conversation; and this is his promise, that we shall be forever with him.

24. *See that ye fall not out by the way* - He knew they were but too apt to be quarrelsome; and what had lately passed, which revived the remembrance of what they had done formerly against their brother, might give them occasion to quarrel. Now Joseph having forgiven them all, lays this obligation upon them, not to upbraid one another. This charge our Lord Jesus has given to us, that we love one another, that we live in peace, that whatever occurs, or whatever former occurrences are remembered, we fall not out. For,

1. We are brethren, we have all one father.
2. We are his brethren; and we shame, our relation to him, who is our peace, if we fall out.
3. We are all guilty, verily guilty, and instead of quarrelling with one another, have a great deal of reason to fall out with ourselves.
4. We are forgiven of God, whom we have all offended, and therefore should be ready to forgive one another.
5. We are by the way, a way that lies through the land of Egypt, where we have many eyes upon us, that seek occasion and advantage against us; a way that leads to Canaan, where we hope to be forever in perfect peace.

26. *We have here the good news brought to Jacob.* When, without any preamble, his sons came in crying Joseph is yet alive. The very mention of Joseph's name revived his sorrow, so that his heart fainted. It was a good while before he came to himself. He was in such care and fear about the rest of them, that at this time it would have been joy enough to him to hear that Simeon was released, and Benjamin is come safe home; for he had been ready to despair concerning both these; but to bear that Joseph is alive, is too good news to be true; he faints, for he believes it not.

27. *When he saw the waggons his spirit revived* - Now Jacob is called Israel, for he begins to recover his wonted vigour. It pleases him to think that Joseph is alive. He saith nothing of Joseph's glory, which they had told him of; it was enough to him that Joseph was alive: it pleases him to think of going to see him. Though he was old, and the journey long, yet he would go to see Joseph, because Joseph's business would not permit him to come to him. Observe, He will go see him, not I will go live with him; Jacob was old, and did not expect to live long: but I will go see him before I die, and then let me depart in peace; let my eyes be refreshed with this sight before they are closed, and then it is enough, I need no more to make me happy in this world.

XLVI

Jacob is here removing to Egypt in his old age.

I. God sends him thither, ver. 1-4.

II. All his family goes with him, ver. 5-27.

III. Joseph bids him welcome, ver. 28-34.

1. *And Israel came to Beer-sheba, and offered sacrifices to the God of his father Isaac* - He chose that place in remembrance of the communion which his father and grandfather had with God in that

place. In his devotion he had an eye to God as the God of his father Isaac, that is, a God in covenant with him, for by Isaac the covenant was entailed upon him. He offered sacrifices, extraordinary sacrifices, besides those at his stated times. These sacrifices were offered,

    1. By way of thanksgiving for the late blessed change of the face of his family, for the good news he had received concerning Joseph, and the hopes he had of seeing him.

    2. By way of petition for the presence of God with him in his intended journey.

    3. By way of consultation. Jacob would not go on 'till he had asked God's leave.

    2. And God spake unto Israel in the visions of the night - (Probably the next night after he had offered his sacrifices.) Those who desire to keep up communion with God, shall find that it never fails on his side. If we speak to him as we ought, he will not fail to speak to us. God called him by his name, by his old name, Jacob, Jacob, to mind him of his low estate. Jacob, like one well acquainted with the visions of the Almighty, answers, Here am I - Ready to receive orders. And what has God to say to him?

    3. I am God, the God of thy father - That is, I am what thou ownest me to be: thou shalt find me a God of divine wisdom and power engaged for thee: and thou shalt find me the God of thy father, true to the covenant made with him. Fear not to go down into Egypt - It seems though Jacob, upon the first intelligence of Joseph's life and glory in Egypt, resolved without any hesitation I will go and see him, yet upon second thoughts he saw difficulties in it.

    1. He was old, 130 years old; it was a long journey, and he was unfit to travel.

    2. He feared lest his sons should be tainted with the idolatry of Egypt, and forget the God of their fathers.

    3. Probably he thought of what God had said to Abraham concerning the bondage and affliction of his seed.

    4. He could not think of laying his bones in Egypt. But whatever his discouragements were, this was enough to answer them all, Fear not to go down into Egypt.

    4. I will go down with thee into Egypt - Those that go where God sends them shall certainly have God with them. And I will surely bring thee up again - Tho' Jacob died in Egypt, yet this promise was fulfilled,

    1. In the bringing up of his body to be buried in Canaan.

    2. In the bringing up of his seed to be settled in Canaan. Whatever low and darksome valley we are called into, we may be confident if God go down with us, he will surely bring us up again. If he go with us down to death, he will surely bring us up again to glory. And Joseph shall put his hand upon thine eyes - That is a promise that Joseph should live as long as he lived, that he should be with him at his death, and close his eyes with all possible tenderness. Probably Jacob, in the multitude of his thoughts within him, had been wishing that Joseph might do this last office of love for him; and God thus answered him in the letter of his desire. Thus God sometimes gratifies the innocent wishes of his people, and makes not only their death happy, but the very circumstances of it agreeable.

    7. All his seed - 'Tis probable they continued to live together in common with their father, and therefore when he went they all went; which perhaps they were the more willing to do, because, tho' they had heard that the land of Canaan was promised them, yet to this day they had none of it in possession. We have here a particular account of the names of Jacob's family; his sons sons, most of which are afterwards mentioned, as heads of houses in the several tribes. See Num. xxvi, 5, &c. Issachar called his eldest son Tola, which signifies a worm, probably because when he was born he was a little weak child, not likely to live, and yet there sprang from him a very numerous off-spring, 1Ch vii, 2. The whole number that went down into Egypt were sixty-six, to which add Joseph and his two sons, who were there before, and Jacob himself, the head of the family, and you have the number of seventy. 'Twas now 215 years since God had promised Abraham to make of him a great nation, chap. xii, 2, and yet that branch of his seed, on which the promise was entailed, was as yet increased but to seventy, of which this particular account is kept, that the power of God in multiplying these seventy to so vast a multitude, even in Egypt, may be the more illustrious. When he pleases, A little one shall become a thousand.

    30. Now let me die - Not but that it was farther desirable to live with Joseph, and to see his honour and usefulness; but he had so much satisfaction in this first meeting, that he thought it too much to desire or expect any more in this world.

XLVII

In this chapter we have instances,

I. Of Joseph's kindness to his relations, presenting his brethren first, and then his father to Pharaoh, ver. 1-10. setting them in Goshen, and providing for them there, ver. 11, 12. paying his respects to his father when he sent for him, ver. 27-31.

II. Of Joseph's justice between prince and people in a very critical affair; selling Pharaoh's corn to his subjects with reasonable profit to Pharaoh, and yet without any wrong to them, ver. 13-26.

3. *What is your occupation?* - Pharaoh takes it for granted they had something to do. All that have a place in the world should have an employment in it according to their capacity, some occupation or other. Those that need not work for their bread, yet must have something to do to keep them from idleness.

4. *To sojourn in the land are we cane* - Not to settle there forever; only to sojourn, while the famine prevailed so in Canaan, which lay high, that it was not habitable for shepherds, the grass being burnt up much more than in Egypt, which lay low, and where the corn chiefly failed, but there was tolerable good pasture.

8. *How old art thou?* - A question usually put to old men, for it is natural to us to admire old age, and to reverence it. Jacob's countenance no doubt shewed him to be old, for be had been a man of labour and sorrow. In Egypt people were not so long-lived as in Canaan, and therefore Pharaoh looks upon Jacob with wonder.

9. Observe

1. Jacob calls his life a pilgrimage, looking upon himself as a stranger in this world, and a traveler towards another. He reckoned himself not only a pilgrim now he was in Egypt, a strange country in which he never was before, but his life even in the land of his nativity was a pilgrimage.

2. He reckoned his life by days; for even so it is soon reckoned, and we are not sure of the continuance of it for a day to an end, but may be turned out of this tabernacle at less than an hours warning.

3. The character he gives of them was, (1.) That they were few. Though he had now lived 130 years, they seemed to him but as a few days, in comparison of the days of eternity, in which a thousand years are but as one day; (2.) That they were evil. This is true concerning man in general, Job xiv, 1, he is of few days and full of trouble: Jacob's life particularly had been made up of evil days. the pleasantest days of his life were yet before him. (3.) That they were short of the days of his fathers; not so many, not so pleasant as their days. Old age came sooner upon him than it had done upon some of his ancestors.

10. *And Jacob blessed Pharaoh* - Which was not only an act of civility but an act of piety; he prayed for him, as one having the authority of a prophet and a patriarch: and a patriarch's blessing was not a thing to be despised, no not by a potent prince.

21. *He removed them to cities* - He transplanted them, to shew Pharaoh's sovereign power over them, and that they might, in time, forget their titles to their lands, and be the easier reconciled to their new condition of servitude. How hard soever this seems to have been upon them, they themselves were sensible of it as a great kindness, and were thankful they were not worse used.

28. Jacob lived seventeen years after he came into Egypt, far beyond his own expectation: seventeen years he had nourished Joseph, for so old he was when he was sold from him, and now, seventeen years Joseph nourished him. Observe how kindly Providence ordered Jacob's affairs; that when he was old, and least able to bear care and fatigue, he had least occasion for it, being well provided for by his son without his own forecast.

29. *And the time drew nigh that Israel must die* - Israel, that had power over the angel, and prevailed, yet must yield to death. He died by degrees; his candle was not blown out, but gradually burnt down, so that he saw, at some distance, the time drawing nigh. He would be buried in Canaan, not because Canaan was the land of his nativity, but in faith, because it was the land of promise, which he desired thus, as it were to keep possession of 'till the time should come when his posterity should be masters of it: and because it was a type of heaven, that better country, which he was in expectation of. When this was done, Israel bowed himself upon the bed's head - Worshipping God, as it is explained, Heb. xi, 21, giving God thanks for all his favours, and particularly for this, that Joseph was ready, to put his hand upon his eyes. Thus they that go down to the dust should, with humble thankfulness, bow before God, the God of their mercies.

John Wesley

XLVIII

In this chapter Jacob's dying words are recorded, because he speaks by a spirit of prophecy; Abraham's and Isaac's are not. God's gifts and graces shine forth much more in some than in others upon their death-beds. Here is,

I. Joseph hearing of his father's sickness goes to visit him, and takes his two sons with him, ver. 1-2.

II. Jacob solemnly adopts his two sons, and takes them for his own, ver. 3-7.

III. He blesseth them, ver. 8-16.

IV. He explains and justifies the crossing of his hands in blessing them, ver. 17-20.

V. He leaves a particular legacy to Joseph, ver. 21-22.

3. *God blessed me* - And let that blessing be entailed upon them. God had promised him two things, a numerous issue, and Canaan for an inheritance. And Joseph's sons, pursuant hereunto, should each of them multiply into a tribe, and each of them have a distinct lot in Canaan, equal with Jacob's own sons. See how he blessed them by faith in that which God had said to him Heb. xi, 21.

7. Mention is made of the death and burial of Rachel, Joseph's mother, and Jacob's best beloved wife. The removal of dear relations from us is an affliction, the remembrance of which cannot but abide with us a great while. Strong affections in the enjoyment cause long afflictions in the loss.

11. *I had not thought to see thy face*, (having many years given him up for lost) *and lo God hath shewed me also thy seed?* - See here, How these two good men own God in their comforts. Joseph saith, *They are my sons whom God has given me* - And to magnify the favour he adds, *in this place of my banishment, slavery and imprisonment.* Jacob saith here, *God hath shewed me thy seed* - Our comforts are then doubly sweet to us, when we see them coming from God's hand.

15. *The God who fed me all my life long unto this day* - As long as we have lived in this world we have had continual experience of God's goodness to us in providing for the support of our natural life. Our bodies have called for daily food, and we have never wanted food convenient. He that has fed us all our life long will not fail us at last.

16. *The angel who redeemed me from all evil* - A great deal of hardship he had known in his time, but God had graciously kept him from the evil of his troubles. Christ, the angel of the covenant is he that redeems us from all evil. It becomes the servants of God, when they are old and dying, to witness for our God that they have found him gracious. Joseph had placed his children so, as that Jacob's right-hand should be put on the head of Manasseh the eldest, ver. 12, 13, but Jacob would put it on the head of Ephraim the youngest, ver. 14. This displeased Joseph, who was willing to support the reputation of his first-born and would therefore have removed his father's hands, ver. 17, 18, but Jacob gave him to understand that he knew what he did, and that he did it neither by mistake nor in a humour, nor from a partial affection to one more than the other, but from a spirit of prophecy.

19. *Ephraim shall he greater* - When the tribes were mustered in the wilderness Ephraim was more numerous than Manasseh, and had the standard of that squadron, Num. i, 32, 33, 35-ii, 18, 20, and is named first, Psalm lxxx, 2. Joshua was of that tribe. The tribe of Manasseh was divided, one half on one side Jordan, the other half on the other side, which made it the less powerful and considerable. God, in bestowing his blessings upon his people, gives more to some than to others, more gifts, graces and comforts, and more of the good things of this life. And he often gives most to those that are least likely: he chuseth the weak things of the world, raiseth the poor out of the dust. Grace observes not the order of nature, nor doth God prefer those whom we think fittest to be preferred but as it pleaseth him.

21. *I die, but God shall be with you, and bring you again* - This assurance was given them, and carefully preserved among them, that they might neither love Egypt too much when it favoured them, nor fear it too much when it frowned upon them. These words of Jacob furnish us with comfort in reference to the death of our friends: But God shall be with us, and his gracious presence is sufficient to make up the loss. They leave us, but he will never fail us. He will bring us to the land of our fathers, the heavenly Canaan, whither our godly fathers are gone before us. If God be with us while we stay behind in this world, and will receive us shortly to be with them that are gone before to a better world, we ought not to sorrow as those that have no hope.

22. *He bestowed one portion upon him above his brethren.* The lands bequeathed are described to be those which he took out of the hand of the Amorite with his sword and with his bow. He purchased them first, Josh. xxiv, 32, and it seems was afterwards disseized of them by the Amorites, but retook them by the sword, repelling force by force, and recovering his right by violence when he could not otherwise recover it. These lands he settled upon Joseph. Mention is made of this grant, John iv, 5.

Pursuant to it, this parcel of ground was given to the tribe of Ephraim as their right, and the lot was never cast upon it: and in it Joseph's bones were buried, which perhaps Jacob had an eye to as much as to any thing in this settlement. It may sometimes be both just and prudent to give some children portions above the rest: but a grave is that which we can most count upon as our own in this earth.

XLIX

Jacob is here upon his death-bed making his will: what he said here he could not say when he would, but as the Spirit gave him utterance, who chose this time that divine strength might be perfected in this weakness. The twelve sons of Jacob were in their day men of renown; but the twelve tribes of Israel, which descended and were denominated from them, were much more renowned, we find their names upon the gates of the new Jerusalem, Rev. xxi, 12. In the prospect of which their dying father saith something remarkable of each son, or of the tribe that bore his name. Here is,

I. The preface, ver. 1, 2.

II. The prediction concerning each tribe, ver. 3-28.

III. The charge repeated concerning his burial, ver. 29-32.

IV. His death, ver. 33.

1. Gather yourselves together - Let them all be sent for to see their father die, and to hear his dying words. 'Twas a comfort to Jacob, now he was dying, to see all his children about him tho' he had sometimes thought himself bereaved: 'twas of use to them to attend him in his last moments, that they might learn of him how to die, as well as how to live; what he said to each, he said in the hearing of all the rest, for we may profit by the reproofs, counsels and comforts that are principally intended for others. That I may tell you that which shall befall you, not your persons but your posterity, in the latter days - The prediction of which would be of use to those that come after them, for confirming their faith, and guiding their way, at their return to Canaan. We cannot tell our children what shall befall them, or their families, in this world; but we can tell them from the word of God, what will befall them in the last day of all, according as they carry themselves in this world.
2. Hearken to Israel your father - Let Israel that has prevailed with God, prevail with you.
3. Reuben thou art my first-born - Jacob here puts upon him the ornaments of the birth-right, that he and all his brethren might see what he had forfeited and in that might see the evil of his sin. As the first-born he was his father's joy, being the beginning of his strength. To him belonged the excellency of dignity above his brethren, and some power over them.
4. Thou shalt not excel - A being thou shalt have as a tribe, but not an excellency. No judge, prophet, or prince, are found of that tribe, nor any person of renown only Dathan and Abiram, who were noted for their impious rebellion. That tribe, as not aiming to excel, chose a settlement on the other side Jordan. The character fastened upon Reuben, for which he is laid under this mark of infamy, is, that he was unstable as water. His virtue was unstable, he had not the government of himself, and his own appetites. His honour consequently was unstable, it vanished into smoke, and became as water spilt upon the ground. Jacob charges him particularly with the sin for which he was disgraced, thou wentest up to thy father's bed - It was forty years ago that he had been guilty of this sin, yet now it is remembered against him. Reuben's sin left an indelible mark of infamy upon his family; a wound not to be healed without a scar.
5. Simeon and Levi are brethren -- brethren in disposition, but unlike their father: they were passionate and revengeful, fierce and wilful; their swords, that should have been only weapons of defense, were (as the margin reads it) weapons of violence, to do wrong to others, not to save themselves from wrong.
6. They slew a man - Shechem himself, and many others; and to effect that, they digged down a wall, broke the houses to plunder them, and murder the inhabitants. O my soul, come not thou into their secret - Hereby he professeth not only his abhorrence of such practices in general, but his innocency particularly in that matter. Perhaps he had been suspected as under-hand aiding and abetting; he therefore solemnly expresseth his detestation of the fact.
7. Cursed be their anger - Not their persons. We ought always in the expressions of our zeal carefully to distinguish between the sinner and the sin, so as not to love or bless the sin for the sake of the person, nor to hate or curse the person for the sake of the sin. I will divide them - The Levites were scattered throughout all the tribes, and Simeon's lot lay not together, and was so strait that many of that tribe were forced to disperse themselves in quest of settlements and subsistence. This curse was afterwards turned into a blessing to the Levites; but the Simeonites, for Zimri's sin, Num. xxv, 6-14, had

it bound on.

8. Judah's name signifies praise, in allusion to which he saith, Thou art he whom thy brethren shall praise, God was praised for him, chap. xxix, 35, praised by him, and praised in him; and therefore his brethren shall praise him. Thy hand shall be in the neck of thine enemies - This was fulfilled in David, Psalm xviii, 40. Thy father's children shall bow down before thee - Judah was the law-giver, Psalm lx, 7. That tribe led the van through the wilderness, and in the conquest of Canaan, Jude i, 2. The prerogatives of the birth-right which Reuben had forfeited, the excellency of dignity and power, were thus conferred upon Judah. Thy brethren shall bow down before thee, and yet shall praise thee, reckoning themselves happy in having so wise and bold a commander.

9. Judah is a lion's whelp - The lion is the king of beasts, the terror of the forest when he roars; when he seizeth his prey, none can resist him; when he goes up from the prey, none dares pursue him to revenge it. By this it is foretold that the tribe of Judah should become very formidable, and should not only obtain great victories but should peaceably enjoy what was got by those victories. Judah is compared not to a lion rampant, always raging but to a lion couching, enjoying the satisfaction of his success, without creating vexation to others.

10. The scepter shall not depart from Judah till Shiloh come - Jacob here foretels, (1.) That the scepter should come into the tribe of Judah, which was fulfilled in David, on whose family the crown was entailed. (2.) That Shiloh should be of this tribe; that seed in whom the earth should be blessed. That peaceable prosperous one, or, the saviour, so others translate it, shall come of Judah. (3.) That the scepter should continue in that tribe, till the coming of the Messiah, in whom as the king of the church, and the great High-priest, it was fit that both the priesthood and the royalty should determine. Till the captivity, all along from David's time, the scepter was in Judah, and from thence governors of that tribe, or of the Levites that adhered to it, which was equivalent; till Judea became a province of the Roman empire just at the time of our saviour's birth, and was at that time taxed as one of the provinces, Luke ii, 1, and at the time of his death the Jews expressly owned, We have no king but Caesar. Hence it is undeniably inferred against the Jews, that our Lord Jesus is be that should come, and we are to look for no other, for he came exactly at the time appointed. (4.) That it should be a fruitful tribe, especially that it should abound with milk and wine, ver. 11, 12, vines so common, and so strong, that they should tye their asses to them, and so fruitful, that they should load their asses from them; wine as plentiful as water, so that the men of that tribe should be very healthful and lively, their eyes brisk and sparkling, their teeth white. Much of that which is here said concerning Judah is to be applied to our Lord Jesus.

1. He is the ruler of all his Father's children, and the conqueror of all his Father's enemies, and he it is that is the praise of all the saints.

2. He is the lion of the tribe of Judah, as he is called with reference to this, Rev. v, 5, who having spoiled principalities and powers, went up a conqueror, and couched so as none can stir him up when he sat down on the right hand of the Father.

3. To him belongs the scepter, he is the lawgiver, and to him shall the gathering of the people be, as the desire of all nations, Haggai ii, 7, who being lifted up from the earth should draw all men unto him, John xii, 32, and in whom the children of God that are scattered abroad should meet as the center of their unity, John xi, 52.

4. In him there is plenty of all that which is nourishing and refreshing to the soul, and which maintains and chears the divine life in it; in him we may have wine and milk, the riches of Judah's tribe, without money, and without price, Isaiah lv, 1.

13. Zebulon shall dwell at the haven of the sea - This was fulfilled, when 2 or 300 years after, the land of Canaan was divided by lot, and the border of Zebulon went up towards the sea, Josh. xix, 11.

14. Issachar is a strong ass, couching down between two burdens - The men of that tribe shall be strong and industrious, fit for and inclined to labour, particularly the toil of husbandry, like the ass that patiently carries his burden. Issachar submitted to two burdens, tillage and tribute.

16. Daniel shall judge his people - Though Daniel was one of the sons of the concubines, yet he shall be a tribe governed by Judges of his own as well as other tribes; and shall by art and policy, and surprise, gain advantages against his enemies, like a serpent suddenly biting the heel of the traveler.

18. I have waited for thy salvation, Lord - If he must break off here, and his breath will not serve him to finish what he intended, with these words he pours out his soul into the bosom of his God, and even breaths it out. The pious ejaculations of a warm and lively devotion, though sometimes they maybe incoherent, yet they are not impertinent; that may be uttered affectionately, which doth not come in methodically. It is no absurdity, when we are speaking to men, to lift up our hearts to God. The salvation he waited for was, 1st, Christ, the promised seed, whom he had spoken of, ver. 10, now he was going to be gathered to his people, he breathes after him to whom the gathering of the people shall be. 2ndly, Heaven, the better country, which he declared plainly that he sought, Heb. xi, 13, 14, and continued seeking now he was in Egypt.

19. Concerning Gad, he alludes to his name, which signifies a troop, foresees the character of that tribe, that it should be a warlike tribe; and so we find, 1Ch xii, 8, the Gadites were men of war fit for the

battle. He foresees, that the situation of that tribe on the other side Jordan would expose it to the incursions of its neighbours, the Moabites and Ammonites; and that they might not be proud of their strength and valour, he foretells that the troops of their enemies should, in many skirmishes, overcome them; yet, that they might not be discouraged by their defeats, he assures them, that they should overcome at the last, which was fulfilled, when in Saul's time and David's the Moabites and Ammonites were wholly subdued.

20. Concerning Asher, he foretells, That it should be a rich tribe, replenished not only with bread for necessity, but with fatness, with dainties, royal dainties, and these exported out of Asher, to other tribes, perhaps to other lands. The God of nature has provided for us not only necessaries but dainties, that we might call him a bountiful benefactor; yet, whereas all places are competently furnished with necessaries, only some places afford dainties. Corn is more common than spices. Were the supports of luxury as universal as the supports of life, the world would be worse than it is, and that needs not.

21. Naphtali is a hind let loose - Those of this tribe were, as the loosen'd hind, zealous for their liberty, and yet affable and courteous, their language refined, and they complaisant, giving goodly words. Among God's Israel there is to be found a great variety of dispositions, yet all contributing to the beauty and strength of the body. He closes with the blessings of his best beloved sons, Joseph and Benjamin, with these he will breathe his last.

22. Joseph is a fruitful bough, or young tree, for God had made him fruitful in the land of his affliction, as branches of a vine, or other spreading plant, running over the wall.

23. The archer have sorely grieved him - Tho' he now lived at ease and in honour, Jacob minds him of the difficulties he had formerly waded through. He had many enemies here called archers, being skilful to do mischief; they hated him, they shot their poisonous darts at him. His brethren were spiteful towards him, mocked him, stripped him, sold him, thought they had been the death of him. His mistress sorely grieved him, and shot at him, when she solicited his chastity; and then shot at him by her false accusations.

24. But his bow abode in strength - His faith did not fail; he kept his ground, and came off conqueror. The arms of his hands were made strong - That is, his other graces did their part, his wisdom, courage, patience, which are better than weapons of war: By the hands of the mighty God - Who was therefore able to strengthen him; and the God of Jacob, a God in covenant with him. From thence, from this strange method of Providence, he became the shepherd and stone, the feeder and supporter of Israel, Jacob and his family. Herein Joseph was a type of Christ: He was shot at and hated, but born up under his sufferings, and was afterwards advanced to be the shepherd and stone: and of the church in general, hell shoots its arrows against her, but heaven protects and strengthens her.

25. Even by the God of thy father Jacob, who shall help thee - Our experiences of God's power and goodness in strengthning us hitherto, are encouragements still to hope for help from him. He that has helped us, will. And by the Almighty, who shall bless thee; and he only blesseth indeed. Observe the blessings conferred on Joseph; First, Various and abundant blessings. Blessings of heaven above, rain in its season, and fair weather in its season; blessings of the deep that lies under this earth, or with subterraneous mines and springs. Blessings of the womb and the breasts are given when children are safely born and comfortably nursed. Secondly, Eminent and transcendent blessings, which prevail above the blessings of my progenitors - His father Isaac had but one blessing, and when he had given that to Jacob, he was at a loss for a blessing to bestow upon Esau; but Jacob had a blessing for each of his twelve sons, and now at the latter end, a copious one for Joseph. Thirdly, Durable and extensive blessings: unto the utmost bound of the everlasting hills - Including all the products of the most fruitful hills, and lasting as long as they last. Of these blessings it is here said they shall be, so it is a promise; or, let them be, so it is a prayer, on the head of Joseph, to which let them be as a crown to adorn it, and a helmet to protect it.

27. Benjamin shall ravin as a wolf - It is plain, Jacob was guided in what he said by a spirit of prophecy, and not by natural affection, else he would have spoken with more tenderness of his beloved son Benjamin, concerning whom he only foretells, that his posterity should be a warlike tribe, strong and daring, and that they should enrich themselves with the spoil of their enemies, that they should be active in the world, and a tribe as much feared by their neighbours as any other; in the morning he shall devour the prey which he seized and divided over night.

29. I am to be gathered unto my people - Though death separate us from our children, and our people in this world, it gathers us to our fathers, and to our people in the other world. Perhaps Jacob useth this expression concerning death, as a reason why his sons should bury him in Canaan, for (saith he) I am to be gathered unto my people, my soul must be gone to the spirits of just men made perfect, and therefore bury me with my fathers Abraham and Isaac, and their wives.

33. And when Jacob had made an end of commanding of his sons - He addressed himself to his dying work. He put himself into a posture for dying; having sat upon the bed-side to bless his sons, the spirit of prophecy bringing fresh oil to his expiring lamp, when that work was done, he gathered up his feet into the bed, that he might lie along, not only as one patiently submitting to the stroke, but as one

cheerfully composing himself to rest. He then freely resigned his spirits into the hand of God, the father of spirit; he yielded up the ghost; and his separated soul went to the assembly of the souls of the faithful, who after they are delivered from the burden of the flesh are in joy and felicity; he was gathered to his people.

L

Here, is,

I. The preparation for Jacob's funeral, ver. 1-6.

II. The funeral itself, ver. 7-14.

III. The settling of a good understanding between Joseph and his brethren, after the death of Jacob, ver. 15-21.

IV. The age and death of Joseph, ver. 22-26.

    1. And Joseph fell upon his father's face and wept upon him, and kissed him - Joseph shewed his faith in God, and love to his father, by kissing his pale and cold lips, and so giving an affectionate farewell. Probably the rest of Jacob's sons did the same, much moved, no doubt, with his dying words.

    2. He ordered the body to be embalmed, not only because he died in Egypt, and that was the manner of the Egyptians, but because he was to be carried to Canaan, which would be a work of time.

    3. He observed the ceremony of solemn mourning for him. Forty days were taken up in embalming the body, which the Egyptians had an art of doing so curiously, as to preserve the very features of the face unchanged. All this time, and thirty days more, seventy in all, they either confined themselves and sat solitary, or when they went out, appeared in the habit of close mourners, according to the decent custom of the country. Even the Egyptians, many of them, out of the respect they had for Joseph, put themselves into mourning for his father.

    5. He asked and obtained leave of Pharaoh to go to Canaan, to attend the funeral of his father. It was a piece of necessary respect to Pharaoh, that he would not go without leave; for we may suppose, though his charge about the corn was long since over, yet he continued a prime minister of state, and therefore would not be so long absent from his business without license.

    11. The solemn mourning for Jacob gave a name to the place; Abel-mizraim - The mourning of the Egyptians: which served for a testimony against the next generation of the Egyptians, who oppressed the posterity of this Jacob, to whom their ancestors shewed such respect.

    15. Joseph will peradventure hate us - While their father lived, they thought themselves safe under his shadow; but now he was dead, they feared the worst. A guilty conscience exposeth men to continual frights; those that would be fearless must keep themselves guiltless.

    16. Thy father did command - Thus in humbling ourselves to Christ by faith and repentance, we may plead that it is the command of his father and our father we should do so.

    17. We are the servants of the God of thy father - Not only children of the same Jacob, but worshippers of the same Jehovah. Though we must be ready to forgive all that injure us, yet we must especially take heed of bearing malice towards any that are the servants of the God of our father; those we should always treat with a peculiar tenderness, for we and they have the same master. He wept when they spake to him - These were tears of sorrow for their suspicion of him, and tears of tenderness upon their submission.

    19. Am I in the place of God? - He in his great humility thought they shewed him too much respect, and faith to them in effect, as Peter to Cornelius, Stand up, I myself also am a man. Make your peace with God, and then you will find it an easy matter to make your peace with me.

    20. Ye thought evil, but God meant it unto good - In order to the making Joseph a greater blessing to his family than otherwise he could have been.

    21. Fear not, I will nourish you - See what an excellent spirit Joseph was of, and learn of him to render good for evil. He did not tell them they were upon their good behaviour, and he would be kind to them if he saw they carried themselves well: no, he would not thus hold them in suspence, nor seem jealous of them, though they had been suspicious of him. He comforted them, and, to banish all their fears, he spake kindly to them. Those we love and forgive we must not only do well for, but speak kindly to.

    24. I die, but God will surely visit you - To this purpose Jacob had spoken to him, chap. xlviii, 21. Thus must we comfort others with the same comforts wherewith we ourselves have been comforted of God, and encourage them to rest on those promises which have been our support. Joseph was, under God, both the protector and benefactor of his brethren, and what would become of them now he was

dying? Why let this be their comfort, God will surely visit you. God's gracious visits will serve to make up the loss of our best friends, and bring you out of this land - And therefore, they must not hope to settle there, nor look upon it as their rest forever; they must set their hearts upon the land of promise, and call that their home.

25. And ye shall carry up my bones from hence - Herein he had an eye to the promise, chap. xv, 13, 14, and in God's name assures them of the performance of it. In Egypt they buried their great men very honourably, and with abundance of pomp; but Joseph prefers a plain burial in Canaan, and that deferred almost two hundred years, before a magnificent one in Egypt. Thus Joseph by faith in the doctrine of the resurrection, and the promise of Canaan, gave commandment concerning his bones, Heb. xi, 22. He dies in Egypt; but lays his bones at stake, that God will surely visit Israel, and bring them to Canaan.

26. He was put in a coffin in Egypt - But not buried till his children had received their inheritance in Canaan, Josh. xxiv, 32. If the soul do but return to its rest with God, the matter is not great, though the deserted body find not at all, or not quickly, its rest in the grave. Yet care ought to be taken of the dead bodies of the saints, in the belief of their resurrection; for there is a covenant with the dust which shall be remembered, and a commandment given concerning the bones.

John Wesley

NOTES ON THE SECOND BOOK OF MOSES CALLED EXODUS

MOSES having in the first book of his history preserved the records of the church, while it existed in private families, comes, in the second book, to give us an account of its growth into a great nation. The beginning of the former book shews us how God formed the world for himself, the beginning of this shews us how he formed Israel for himself. There we have the creation of the world in history, here the redemption of the world in type. The Greek translators called this book Exodus, which signifies a going out, because it begins with the story of the going out of the children of Israel from Egypt. This book gives us,

I. The accomplishment of the promise made before to Abraham, to chap. xix. and then,

II. The establishment of the ordinances which were afterwards observed by Israel: thence to the end. Moses in this book begins, like Caesar, to write his own commentaries; and gives us the history of those things which he was himself an eye and ear witness of. There are more types of Christ in this book than perhaps in any other book of the Old Testament. The way of man's reconciliation to God, and coming into covenant and communion with him by a Mediator, is here variously represented; and it is of great use to us for the illustration of the New Testament. We have here,

I. God's kindness to Israel, in multiplying them exceedingly, ver. 1-7.

II. The Egyptians wickedness to them;
    1. Oppressing and enslaving them, ver. 8-14.
    2. Murdering their children, ver. 15-22.

I

1. Every man of his household - That is, children and grand-children.

3. And Benjamin - Who tho' youngest of all is placed before Daniel, Naphtali, &c. because they were the children of the hand-maidens.

5. Seventy souls - According to the computation we had, Gen. xlvi, 27, including Joseph and his two sons. This was just the number of the nations by which the earth was peopled, Gen. x, 1-32, for when God separated the sons of Adam, he set the bounds of the people according to the number of the children of Israel, Deut. xxxii, 8.

6. All that generation by degrees wore off: perhaps all Jacob's sons died much about the same time, for there was not past seven years difference in age between the eldest and the youngest of them, except Benjamin.

7. And the children of Israel were fruitful, and increased abundantly - Like fishes or insects, so that they multiplied; and being generally healthful and strong, they waxed exceeding mighty, so that the land was filled with them, at least Goshen, their own allotment. This wonderful increase was the product of the promise long before made to the fathers. From the call of Abraham, when God first told him he would make him a great nation, to the deliverance of his seed out of Egypt, was 430 years; during the first 215 of which, they were increased to 70, but in the latter half, those 70 multiplied to 600,000 fighting men.

8. There arose a new king (after several successions in Joseph's time) which knew not Joseph - All that knew him loved him, and were kind to his relations for his sake; but when he was dead he was soon forgotten, and the remembrance of the good offices he had done was either not retained or not regarded. If we work for men only, our works at farthest will die with us; if for God, they will follow us, Rev. xiv, 13.

10. Come on, let us deal wisely with them, lest they multiply - When men deal wickedly it is common for them to imagine that they deal wisely, but the folly of sin will at last be manifested before all men.

11. *They set over them task-masters, to afflict them* - With this very design. They not only made them serve, which was sufficient for Pharaoh's profit, but they made them serve with rigor, so that their lives became bitter to them; intending hereby to break their spirits, and to rob them of every thing in them that was generous: to ruin their health, and shorten their days, and so diminish their numbers: to discourage them from marrying, since their children would be born to slavery; and to oblige them to desert the Hebrews, and incorporate with the Egyptians. And 'tis to be feared the oppression they were under did bring over many of them to join with the Egyptians in their idolatrous worship; for we read, Josh. xxiv, 14, that they served other gods in Egypt; and we find, Ezek. xx, 8, that God had threatned to destroy them for it, even while they were in the land of Egypt. *Treasure-cities* - To keep the king's money or corn, wherein a great part of the riches of Egypt consisted.

12. *But the more they afflicted them, the more they multiplied* - To the grief and vexation of the Egyptians. Times of affliction, have oft been the church's growing times: Christianity spread most when it was persecuted.

15. *And the king spake to the Hebrew midwives* - The two chief of them. They are called Hebrew midwives, probably not because they were themselves Hebrews; for sure Pharaoh could never expect they should be so barbarous to those of their own nation, but because they were generally made use of by the Hebrews, and being Egyptians he hoped to prevail with them.

16. *The stools* - Seats used on that occasion.

17. *But the midwives feared God* - Dreaded his wrath more than Pharaoh's, and therefore saved the men-children alive.

19. I see no reason we have to doubt the truth of this; it is plain they were now under an extraordinary blessing of increase, which may well be supposed to have this effect, that the women had quick and easy labour, and the mothers and children being both lively, they seldon needed the help of midwives; this these midwives took notice of, and concluding it to be the finger of God, were thereby emboldened to disobey the king, and with this justify themselves before Pharaoh, when he called them to an account for it.

20. *Therefore God dealt well with them* - That is, built them up in families, and blessed their children.

II

This chapter begins the story of Moses, the most remarkable type of Christ as prophet, saviour, law-giver, and mediator, in all the Old Testament. In this chapter we have,

I. The perils of his birth and infancy, ver. 1-4.

II. His preservation through those perils, and the preferment of his childhood and youth, ver. 5-10.

III. The pious choice of his riper years, which was to own the people of God, (1.) He offered them his service, so they would have accepted it, ver. 11-14. (2.) He retired, that he might reserve himself for farther service, ver. 15-22.

IV. The dawning of the day of Israel's deliverance, ver. 23-25.

1. *And there went a man* - Amram, from the place of his abode to another place. *A daughter* - That is, grand-daughter of Levi.

2. *Bare a son* - It seems just at the time of his birth that cruel law was made for the murder of all the male-children of the Hebrews, and many no doubt perished by the execution of it. Moses's parents had Miriam and Aaron, both elder than he, born to them before that edict came out. Probably his mother had little joy of her being with child of him, now this edict was in force. Yet this child proves the glory of his father's house. Observe the beauty of providence: just when Pharaoh's cruelty rose to this height, the deliverer was born. *She hid him three months* - In some private apartment of their own house, though probably with the hazard of their lives had he been discovered. It is said, Heb. xi, 23. That Moses's parents hid him by faith: some think they had a special Revelation that the deliverer should spring from their loins; however, they believed the general promise of Israel's preservation, and in that faith hid their child.

3. *And when she could no longer hide him, she put him in an ark of bulrushes* - By the river side. God put it into their hearts to do this, to bring about his own purposes: that Moses might by this means be brought into the hands of Pharaoh's daughter, and that by his deliverance, a specimen might be given of the deliverance of God's church.

5. *And the daughter of Pharaoh came* - Providence brings no less a person than Pharaoh's daughter just at that juncture, guides her to the place where this poor infant lay, inclines her heart to pity it, which

she dares do, when none else durst. Never did poor child cry so seasonably, as this did; the babe wept, which moved her compassion, as no doubt his beauty did.

10. *And he became her son* - The tradition of the Jews is, that Pharaoh's daughter had no child of her own, and that she was the only child of her father, so that when he was adopted for her son, he stood fair for the crown: however, it is certain he stood fair for the best preferments of the court in due time, and in the mean time had the advantage of the best education, with the help of which, he became master of all the lawful learning of the Egyptians Acts vii, 22. Those whom God designs for great services he finds out ways for to qualify them. Moses, by having his education in a court, is the fitter to be a prince, and king in Jeshurun; by having his education in a learned court, (for such the Egyptian then was) is the fitter to be an historian; and by having his education in the court of Egypt, is the fitter to be employed as an ambassador to that court in God's name. The Jews tell us, that his father at his circumcision called him Joachim, but Pharaoh's daughter called him Moses, Drawn out of the water, so it signifies in the Egyptian language, The calling of the Jewish lawgiver by an Egyptian name is a happy omen to the Gentile world, and gives hopes of that day when it should be said, Blessed be Egypt my people, Isaiah xix, 25. And his tuition at court was an earnest of the performance of that promise, Isaiah xlix, 23. Kings shall be thy nursing fathers, and queens thy nursing mothers.

11. *When Moses was grown he went out unto his brethren, and looked on their burdens* - He looked on their burdens as one that not only pitied them, but was resolved to venture with them, and for them.

12. *He slew the Egyptian* - Probably it was one of the Egyptian task-masters, whom he found abusing his Hebrew slave. By special warrant from heaven (which makes not a precedent in ordinary cases) Moses slew the Egyptian, and rescued his oppressed brother. The Jew's tradition is, that he did not slay him with any weapon, but as Peter slew Ananias and Sapphira, with the word of his mouth.

14. *He said, Who made thee a prince?* - He challengeth his authority; Who made thee a prince? - A man needs no great authority for giving a friendly reproof; it is an act of kindness; yet this man needs will interpret it an act of dominion, and represents his reprover as imperious and assuming. Thus, when people are sick of good discourse, or a seasonable admonition, they will call it preaching, as if a man could not speak a word for God, and against sin, but he took too much upon him. Yet Moses was indeed a prince, and a judge, and knew it, and thought the Hebrews would have understood it; but they stood in their own light, and thrust him away. Acts vii, 25, 27. *Intendest thou to kill me?* - See what base constructions malice puts upon the best words and actions. Moses, for reproving him, is presently charged with a design to kill him.

15. *Moses fled from Pharaoh* - God ordered this for wise ends. Things were not yet ripe for Israel's deliverance. The measure of Egypt's iniquity was not yet full; the Hebrews were not sufficiently humbled, nor were they yet increased to such a multitude as God designed: Moses is to be farther fitted for the service, and therefore is directed to withdraw for the present, till the time to favour Israel, even the set time, come. God guided Moses to Midian, because the Midianites were of the seed of Abraham, and retained the worship of the true God; so that he might have not only a safe, but a comfortable settlement among them; and through this country he was afterwards to lead Israel, which, that he might do the better, he now had opportunity of acquainting himself with it. Hither he came, and sat down by a well; tired and thoughtful, waiting to see which way Providence would direct him. It was a great change with him, since he was but the other day at ease in Pharaoh's court.

17. *Stood up and helped them* - This be did, because wherever he was, as occasion offered itself, he loved to be doing justice, and appearing in the defense of such as he saw injured. He loved to be doing good: wherever the Providence of God call us, we should desire and endeavour to be useful; and when we cannot do the good we would, we must be ready to do the good we can.

18. *Reul or Raguel* (see Num. x, 29,) seems to have been their grandfather and father of Hobab or Jethro, their immediate father.

22. *Gershom* - That is, A stranger there. Now this settlement of Moses in Midian was designed by Providence. To shelter him for the present; God will find hiding places for his people in the day of their distress. It was also designed to prepare him for the services he was farther designed to. His manner of life in Midian, where he kept the flock of his father-in-law would be of use to him, to inure him to hardship and poverty; and to inure him to contemplation and devotion. Egypt accomplished him for a scholar, a gentleman, a statesman, a soldier, all which accomplishments would be afterwards of use to him; but yet lacketh he one thing, in which the court of Egypt could not befriend him. He that was to do all by divine Revelation must know, what it was to live a life of communion with God, and in this he would be greatly furthered by the retirement of a shepherd's life in Midian. By the former he was prepared to rule in Jeshurun, but by the latter he was prepared to converse with God in Mount Horeb. Those that know what it is to be alone with God, are acquainted with better delights than ever Moses tasted in the court of Pharaoh.

23. *The king of Egypt died* - And after him, one or two more of his sons or successors. *And the children of Israel sighed by reason of bondage* - Probably the murdering of their infants did not

continue, that part of their affliction only attended the birth of Moses, to signalize that. And now they were content with their increase, finding that Egypt was enriched by their labour; so they might have them for their slaves, they cared not how many they were. On this therefore they were intent, to keep them all at work, and make the best hand they could of their labour. When one Pharaoh died, another rose up in his place, that was as cruel to Israel as his predecessors. And they cried - Now at last they began to think of God under their troubles, and to return to him from the idols they had served, Ezek. xx, 8. Hitherto they had fretted at the instruments of their trouble, but God was not in all their thoughts. But before God unbound them, he put it into their hearts to cry unto him. It is a sign God is coming towards us with deliverance, when he inclines us to cry to him for it.

24. And God heard their groaning - That is, he made it to appear that he took notice of their complaints. The groans of the oppressed cry loud in the ears of the righteous God, to whom vengeance belongs; especially the groans of God's children, the burdens they groan under, and the blessings they groan after. And God remembered his covenant - Which he seemed to have forgotten, but really is ever mindful of. This God had an eye to, and not to any merit of theirs in what he did for them. And God looked upon the children of Israel - Moses looked upon them and pitied them, but now God looked upon them and helped them. And God had respect unto them - A favourable respect to them as his own. The frequent repetition of the name of God intimates, that now we are to expect something great. His eyes which run to and fro through the earth, are now fixed on Israel, to shew himself strong, to shew himself a God in their behalf.

III

In this chapter we have,

I. The discovery God was pleased to make of his glory to Moses at the bush, ver. 1-5.

II. A general declaration of God's goodwill to his people, who were beloved for the Father's sake, ver. 6.

III. A particular notification of God's purpose concerning the deliverance of Israel out of Egypt.

    1. He assures Moses it should now be done, ver. 7-9.

    2. He gives him a commission to act in it as his ambassador both to Pharaoh, ver. 10, and to Israel, ver. 16.

    3. He answers the objection Moses made of his own unworthiness, ver. 11, 12.

    4. He gives him full instructions what to say, both to Pharaoh and to Israel, ver. 13-18.

    5. He tells him before-hand what the issue would be, ver. 14-22.

    1. Now Moses - The years of Moses's life are remarkably divided into three forties; the first forty he spent as a prince in Pharaoh's court, the second a shepherd in Midian, the third a king in Jeshurun. He had now finished his second forty when he received his commission to bring Israel out of Egypt. Sometimes it is long before God calls his servants out to that work which of old he designed them for. Moses was born to be Israel's deliverer, and yet not a word is said of it to him till he is eighty years of age. Even to Horeb - Horeb and Sinai were two tops of the same mountain.

    2. And the angel of the Lord appeared to him - It was an extraordinary manifestation of the divine glory; what was visible was produced by the ministry of an angel, but he heard God in it speaking to him. In a flame of fire - To shew that God was about to bring terror and destruction to his enemies, light and heat to his people, and to display his glory before all. And the bush burned, and yet was not consumed - An emblem of the church now in bondage in Egypt, burning in the brick-kilns, yet not consumed; cast down, but not destroyed.

    3. I will turn aside and see - He speaks as one inquisitive, and bold in his inquiry; whatever it was, he would if possible know the meaning of it.

    4. When the Lord saw that he turned aside to see it, God called to him - If he had carelessly neglected it, it is likely God had departed and said nothing to him. God called and said, Moses, Moses - This which he heard could not but surprise him much more than what he saw. Divine calls are then effectual, when the spirit of God makes them particular, and calls us as by name. The Word calls, Ho, every one; the Spirit, by the application of that, calls, Ho, such a one; I know thee by name. Here am I - Not only to hear what is said, but to do what I am bidden.

    5. Put off thy shoes from off thy feet - The putting off the shoe was then what the putting off the hat is now, a token of respect and submission. The ground is holy ground, made so by this special manifestation of the divine presence. We ought to approach to God with a solemn pause and preparation; and to express our inward reverence, by a grave and reverent behaviour in the worship of God, carefully avoiding every thing that looks light, or rude.

    6. I am the God of thy father - He lets him know it is God that speaks to him, to engage his

reverence, faith and obedience. Thy father, thy pious father Amram, and the God of Abraham, Isaac, and Jacob, thy ancestors. Engaged to them by solemn covenant, which I am now come to perform. And Moses hid his face, for he was afraid to look upon God - The more we see of God, the more cause we shall see to worship him with reverence and godly fear. And even the manifestations of God's grace should increase our humble reverence of him.

8. I am come down to deliver them - When God doth something very extraordinary, he is said to come down to do it, as Isaiah lxiv, 1. This deliverance was typical of our redemption by Christ, and in that the eternal Word did indeed come down from heaven to deliver us. A large land - So it was, according to its true and ancient bounds, as they are described, Gen. xv, 18, and not according to those narrow limits, to which they were afterwards confined for their unbelief and impiety. A land flowing with milk and honey - A proverbial expression, abounding with the choicest fruits, both for necessity and delight.

10. I will send thee - And the same hand that now fetched a shepherd out of a desert to be the planter of the Jewish church, afterwards fetched fishermen from their ships to be the planters of the Christian church, that the excellency of the power might be of God.

11. Who am I? - He thinks himself unworthy of the honour and unable for the work. He thinks he wants courage, and therefore cannot go to Pharaoh: he thinks he wants conduct, and therefore cannot bring forth the children of Israel out of Egypt; they are unarmed, undisciplined, quite dispirited, utterly unable to help themselves, Moses was incomparably the fittest of any man living for this work, eminent for learning, wisdom, experience, valour, faith, holiness, and yet Who am I? The more fit any person is for service, commonly the less opinion he has of himself.

12. Certainly I will be with thee - Those that are weak in themselves, yet may do wonders being strong in the Lord, and in the power of his might. God's presence puts wisdom and strength into the weak and foolish, and is enough to answer all objections.

13. When they shall say to me, What is his name? What shall I say unto them? - What name shall I use, whereby thou mayest be distinguished from false gods, and thy people may be encouraged to expect deliverance from thee?

14. And God said - Two names God would now be known by.

1. A name that speaks what he is in himself, I am that I am - This explains his name Jehovah, and signifies, 1st, That he is self- existent; he has his being of himself, and has no dependence upon any other. And being self-existent he cannot but be self-sufficient, and therefore all-sufficient, and the inexhaustible fountain of being and bliss. 2ndly, That he is eternal and unchangeable, always the same, yesterday today, and forever: he will be what he will be, and what he is. 3rdly. That he is faithful and true to all his promises, unchangeable in his word as well as in his nature, and not a man that he should lie. Let Israel know this, I am hath sent me unto you.

2. A name that speaks what he is to his people. Lest that name I am should puzzle them, he is farther directed to make use of another name of God, more familiar.

15. The Lord God of our fathers hath sent me unto you - Thus God made himself known, that he might revive among them the religion of their fathers, which was much decayed, and almost lost. And that he might raise their expectations of the speedy performance of the promises made unto their fathers: Abraham, Isaac, and Jacob are particularly named, because with Abraham the covenant was first made, and with Isaac and Jacob oft expressly renewed, and these three were distinguished from their brethren, and chosen to be the trustees of the covenant. This God will have to be his name forever, and it has been, is, and will be his name, by which his worshippers know him, and distinguish him from all false gods.

18. Hath met with us - Hath appeared to us, declaring his will, that we should do what follows.

19. I am sure he will not let you go - God sends his messengers to those whose obstinacy he foresees, that it may appear he would have them turn and live.

22. Everywoman shall ask (not borrow!) jewels. And I will give this people favour in the sight of the Egyptians - God sometimes makes the enemies of his people not only to be at peace with them, but to be kind to them. And he has many ways of balancing accounts between the injured and the injurious, of righting the oppressed, and compelling those that have done wrong to make restitution.

IV

This chapter,

I. Continues and concludes God's discourse with Moses, concerning bringing Israel out of Egypt. [1.] Moses objects the peoples unbelief, ver. 1. and God answers that objection by giving him a power to work miracles: (1.) To turn his rod into a serpent, and then into a rod again, ver. 2-5. (2.) To make his hand leprous, and then whole again, ver. 6-8. (3.) To turn the water into blood, ver. 9. [2.]Moses objects his own slowness of speech, ver. 10. and begs to be excused, ver. 13. But God answers this objection, (1.) By promising him his presence, ver. 11, 12. (2.) By joining Aaron in commission with him, ver. 14-16. (3.) By putting an honour upon the very staff in his hand, ver. 17.

II. Moses's execution of his commission. (1.) He obtains leave of his father-in-law to return into Egypt, ver. 18. (2.) He receives further instructions from God, ver. 19, 21-23. (3.) He hastens his departure, and takes his family with him, ver. 20. (4.) He meets with some difficulty about the circumcising of his son, ver. 24. 26. (5.) He has the satisfaction of meeting his brother Aaron, ver. 27, 28. (6.) He produceth his commission before the elders of Israel, to their great joy, ver. 29-31.

1. They will not hearken to my voice-That is, they would not take his bare word, unless he shewed them some sign. He remembered how they had once rejected him, and feared it would be so again.

2. A rod - Or staff.

5. That they may believe - An imperfect sentence to be thus compleated, This thou shalt do, before them, that they may believe.

6. His hand was leprous, as snow - For whiteness. This signified, That Moses, by the power of God, should bring sore diseases upon Egypt, that at his prayer they should be removed. And that whereas the Israelites in Egypt were become leprous, polluted by sin, and almost consumed by oppression, by being taken into the bosom of Moses they should be cleansed and cured.

8. The voice of the first sign - God's works have a voice to speak to us, which we must diligently observe.

10. O my Lord, I am not eloquent - He was a great philosopher, statesman, and divine, and yet no orator; a man of a clear head, great thought and solid judgment, but had not a voluble tongue, nor ready utterance; and therefore he thought himself unfit to speak before great men, and about great affairs. Moses was mighty in word, Acts vii, 22, and yet not eloquent: what he said was strong and nervous, and to the purpose, and distilled as the dew, Deut. xxxii, 2, though he did not deliver himself with that readiness, ease and fineness that some do.

13. Send by whom thou wilt send - By any but me.

14. And the anger of the Lord was kindled against him - Even self-diffidence when it grows into an extreme, when it either hinders us from duty, or clogs us in duty, is very displeasing to him.

15. I will be with thy mouth and with his mouth - Even Aaron that could speak well, yet could not speak to purpose, unless God were with his mouth; without the constant aids of divine grace, the best gifts will fail.

16. Instead of God - To teach and to command him.

17. Take this rod - The staff or crook he carried as a shepherd, that he might not be ashamed of that mean condition out of which God called him. This rod must be his staff of authority, and must be to him instead, both of sword and scepter.

19. The Lord said unto Moses - This seems to have been a second vision, whereby God calls him to the present execution of the command given before.

20. The rod of God - His shepherd's crook so called, as it was God's instrument in so many glorious works.

21. In thy hand - in thy power: I will harden his heart - After he has frequently harden'd it himself, wilfully shutting his eyes against the light, I will at last permit Satan to harden it effectually.

22. Thus saith the Lord - This is the first time that preface is used by any man, which afterwards is used so frequently by all the prophets: Israel is my son, my first-born - Precious in my sight, honourable, and dear to me.

23. Let my son go - Not only my servant whom thou hast no right to detain, but my son whose liberty and honour I am jealous for. If thou refuse, I will slay thy son, even thy first-born - As men deal with God's people, let them expect to be themselves dealt with.

24. It seems the sin of Moses, was neglecting to circumcise his son, which perhaps was the effect of his being unequally yoked with a Midianite, who was too indulgent of her child, and Moses so of her. The Lord met him, and, probably, by a sword in an angel's hand, sought to kill him - This was a great change. Very lately God was conversing with him as a friend, and now coming forth against him as an enemy. In this case of necessity Zipporah herself circumcised the child without delay; whether with

passionate words, expressing the dislike of the ordinance itself, or at least the administration of it to so young a child.

26. So he let him go - The destroying angel withdrew. But still Zipporah cannot forget, but will unreasonably call Moses a bloody husband, because he obliged her to circumcise the child; and upon this occasion, (it is probable) he sent them back to his father-in-law, that they might not create him any further uneasiness. When we have any special service to do for God, we should remove that as far from us as we can, which is likely to be our hindrance: let the dead bury their dead, but follow thou me.

27. In the mount of God - That is, the place where God had met with him.

28. Moses told Aaron all - Those that are fellow-servants to God in the same work, should use a mutual freedom, and endeavour, rightly and fully to understand one another.

30. Aaron did the signs - By the direction of Moses.

V

Moses and Aaron here deal with Pharaoh to get leave of him to go to worship in the wilderness.

I. They demand leave in the name of God, ver. 1. and he answers their demand with a defiance of God, ver. 2.

II. They beg leave in the name of Israel, ver. 3. and he answers their request with further orders to oppress Israel, ver. 4-9. These cruel orders were,
    1. Executed by the task-masters, ver. 10-14.
    2. Complained of to Pharaoh, but in vain, ver. 15-19.
    3. Complained of by the people to Moses, ver. 20, 21. and by him to God, ver. 22, 23.

1. Thus saith the Lord God of Israel, Let my people go - Moses, in treating with the elders of Israel, is directed to call God the God of their fathers; but, in treating with Pharaoh, they call him the God of Israel, and it is the first time we find him called so in scripture. He is called the God of Israel, the person, Gen. xxxiii, 20, but here it is Israel the people. They are just beginning to be formed into a people when God is called their God. Let my people go - They were God's people, and therefore Pharaoh ought not to detain them in bondage. And he expected services and sacrifices from them, and therefore they must have leave to go where they could freely exercise their religion, without giving offense to, or receiving offense from, the Egyptians.

2. Who is the Lord that I should obey his voice? - Being summoned to surrender, he thus hangs out the flag of defiance. Who is Jehovah? I neither know him nor care for him; neither value nor fear him. It is a hard name that he never heard of before, but he resolves it shall be no bugbear to him. Israel was now a despised, oppressed people, and by the character they bore he makes his estimate of their God, and concludes that he made no better figure among the gods, than his people did among the nations.

3. We pray thee, let us go three days journey into the desert - And that on a good errand, and unexceptionable: we will sacrifice to the Lord our God - As other people do to theirs; lest if we quite cast off his worship, he fall upon us - With one judgment or other, and then Pharaoh will lose his vassals.

5. The people are many - Therefore your injury to me is the greater, in attempting to make them rest from their labours.

6. The task-masters, were Egyptians, the officers were Israelites employed under them.

7. Straw - To mix with the clay, or to burn the brick with.

8. They are idle - The cities they built for Pharaoh, were witnesses for them that they were not idle; yet he thus basely misrepresents them, that he might have a pretense to increase their burdens.

9. Vain words - Those of Moses and Aaron.

14. In thy own people - For if they had given us straw, we should have fulfilled our task.

21. The Lord look upon you, and judge - They should have humbled themselves before God, but instead of that they fly in the face of their best friends. Those that are called to public service for God and their generation, must expect to be tried not only by the threats of proud enemies, but by the unjust and unkind censures of unthinking friends. To put a sword in their hand to slay us - To give them the occasion they have long sought for.

22. He expostulated with him. He knew not how to reconcile the providence with the promise, and the commission he had received. Is this God's coming down to deliver Israel? Must I who hoped to be a blessing to them become a scourge to them? By this attempt to get them out of the pit, they are but sunk the farther into it. Wherefore hast thou so evil entreated this people - Even when God is coming towards his people in ways of mercy, yet sometimes he takes such methods that they may think themselves but ill-treated: when they think so, they should go to God by prayer, and that is the way to have better

treatment in God's good time. *Why is it that thou hast sent me* - Pharaoh has done evil to this people, and not one step seems to be taken towards their deliverance. It cannot but sit very heavy upon the spirits of those whom God employs for him, to see that their labour doth no good, and much more to see that it doth hurt, eventually, though not designedly.

VI

In this chapter,

I. God satisfies Moses as to his complaints, ver. 1.

II. He gives him fuller instructions what to say to the children of Israel, ver. 2-8. but to little purpose, ver. 9.

III. He sends him again to Pharaoh, ver. 10, 11. But Moses objects against that, ver. 12. upon which a strict charge is given to him and his brother, to execute their commission with vigour, ver. 13.

IV. An abstract of the genealogy of the tribes of Reuben and Simeon, to introduce that of Levi, that the pedigree of Moses and Aaron might be cleared, ver. 14-27

V. A repetition of the preceding story, ver. 28-30.

1. *With a strong hand* - That is, being forced to it by a strong hand, he shall let them go.
2. *I am Jehovah* - The same with I am that I am, the fountain of being and blessedness, and infinite perfection. The patriarchs knew this name, but they did not know him in this matter by that which this name signifies. God would now be known by his name Jehovah, that is,
  1. A God performing what he had promised, and so giving being to his promises.
  2. A God perfecting what he had begun, and finishing his own work. In the history of the creation God is never called Jehovah, till the heavens and the earth were finished, Gen. ii, 4. When the salvation of the saints is compleated in eternal life, then he will be known by his name Jehovah, Rev. xxii, 13, in the mean time they shall find him for their strength and support, El-shaddai, a God All-sufficient, a God that is enough.
5. *I have heard the groaning of the children of Israel* - He means their groaning on occasion of the late hardships put upon them. God takes notice of the increase of his people's calamities, and observes how their enemies grow upon them.
6. *I will bring you out: I will rid you: I will redeem you: I will bring you into the land of Canaan; and, I will give it you* - Let man take the shame of his unbelief which needs such repetitions, and let God have the glory of his condescending grace which gives us such repeated assurances. *With a stretched out arm* - With almighty power: A metaphor taken from a man that stretches out his arm, to put forth all his strength.
7. *I will take you to me for a people* - A peculiar people, and I will be to you a God - And more than this we need not ask, we cannot have, to make us happy.
8. *I am the Lord* - And therefore have power to dispose of lands and kingdoms as I please.
9. *But they hearkened not to Moses for anguish of spirit* - That is, They were so taken up with their troubles that they did not heed him.
11. *That he let the children of Israel go* - God repeats his precepts, before he begins his punishments. Those that have oft been called in vain to leave their sins, yet must be called again, and again.
12. *Behold, the children of Israel have not hearkened to me; they gave no heed to what I have said, how then shall Pharaoh hear me?* - If the anguish of their spirit makes them deaf to that which would compose and comfort them, much more will his pride and insolence, make him deaf to that which will but exasperate him. *Who am of uncircumcised lips* - He was conscious to himself that he had not the gift of utterance.
13. *The Lord gave them a charge, both to the children of Israel, and to Pharaoh* - God's authority is sufficient to answer all objections, and binds us to obedience without murmuring or disputing.
14. This genealogy ends in those two great patriots, Moses and Aaron; and comes in here to shew that they were Israelites, bone of their bone, and flesh of their flesh, whom they were sent to deliver, raised up unto them of their brethren, as Christ also should be, who was to be the prophet and priest, the Redeemer and law-giver of the house of Israel, and whose genealogy also like this was to be carefully preserved. The heads of the houses of three of the tribes are here named, agreeing with the accounts we had, Gen. xlvi, 8-27. Reuben and Simeon seem to be mentioned only for the sake of Levi, from whom Moses and Aaron descended, and all the priests of the Jewish church.

16. The age of Levi, Kohath, and Amram, the father, grandfather, and great grandfather of Moses is here recorded; and they all lived to a great age, Levi to one hundred thirty seven, Kohath to one hundred thirty three, and Amram to one hundred thirty seven: Moses himself came much short of them, and fixed seventy or eighty for the ordinary stretch of human life. Psalm xc, 10. For now Israel was multiplied, and become a great nation, and divine Revelation was by the hand of Moses committed to writing, and no longer trusted to tradition; the two great reasons for the long lives of the patriarchs were ceased, and therefore from henceforward fewer years must serve men.

20. His father's sister - That is, kins-woman. So the Hebrew word is frequently used.

23. Aminadab - A prince of the tribe of Judah. The Levites might marry into any tribe, there being no danger of confusion or loss of inheritance thereby.

26. According to their armies - Like numerous armies, in military order, and with great power. In the close of the chapter, he returns to his narrative, from which he had broken off somewhat abruptly ver. 13, and repeats, the charge God had given him to deliver his message to Pharaoh, ver. 29.

29. Speak all that I say unto thee - As a faithful ambassador. Those that go on God's errand must not shun to declare the whole counsel of God.

VII

In this chapter,

I. Moses applies himself to the execution of his commission, ver. 1-7.

II. The dispute between Moses and Pharaoh begins. Moses in God's name demands Israel's release, Pharaoh denies it; the contest is between the power of the great God and the power of a proud prince.

1. Moses confirms the demand he made to Pharaoh by a miracle, turning his rod into a serpent, but Pharaoh hardens his heart, ver. 8-13.

2. He chastiseth his disobedience by a plague, the first of ten, turning the waters into blood; but Pharaoh hardens his heart again, ver. 14-25.

1. I have made thee a God to Pharaoh - That is, my representative in this affair, as magistrates are called gods, because they are God's vicegerents. He was authorized to speak and act in God's name, and endued with a divine power, to do that which is above the ordinary course of nature. And Aaron shall be thy prophet - That is, he shall speak from thee to Pharaoh, as prophets do from God to the children of men. Thou shalt as a God inflict and remove the plagues, and Aaron as a prophet shall denounce them.

7. Moses was fourscore years old - Joseph, who was to be only a servant to Pharaoh, was preferred at thirty years old; but Moses, who was to be a God to Pharaoh, was not so dignified till he was eighty years old. It is fit he should long wait for such an honour, and be long in preparing for such a service.

9. Say unto Aaron, Take thy rod - This Moses ordinarily held in his hand, and delivered it to Aaron upon occasion, for the execution of his commands.

10. And Aaron cast his rod down, and it became a serpent - This was proper not only to affect Pharaoh with wonder, but to strike a terror upon him. This first miracle, though it was not a plague, yet amounted to the threatening of a plague; if it made not Pharaoh feel, it made him fear; this is God's method of dealing with sinners he comes upon them gradually.

11. Moses had been originally instructed in the learning of the Egyptians, and was suspected to have improved in magical arts in his long retirement. The magicians are therefore sent for to vie with him. The two chief of them were Jannes and Jambres. Their rods became serpents; probably by the power of evil angels artfully substituting serpents in the room of the rods, God permitting the delusion to be wrought for wise and holy ends. But the serpent which Aaron's rod was turned into, swallowed up the others, which was sufficient to have convinced Pharaoh on which side the right lay.

13. And he harden'd Pharaoh's heart - That is, permitted it to be hardened.

20. The waters that were in the river were turned into blood - This was a plague justly inflicted upon the Egyptians; for Nilus the river of Egypt was their idol; they and their land had so much benefit by that creature, that they served and worshipped it more than the creator. Also they had stained the river with the blood of the Hebrew children, and now God made that river all bloody; thus he gave them blood to drink, for they were worthy, Rev. xvi, 6. See the power of God. Every creature is that to us which he makes it to be, water or blood. See the mutability of all things under the sun, and what changes we may meet with in them. That which is water to day may be blood to morrow; what is always vain may soon become vexatious. And see what mischievous work sin makes! It is sin that turns our waters into blood.

22. And the magicians did so - By God's permission with their enchantments; and this served Pharaoh for an excuse not to set his heart to this also, (ver. 23,) and a poor excuse it was. Could they have turned the river of blood into water again, it had been something; then they had proved their

power, and Pharaoh had been obliged to them as his benefactors.

25. Seven days were fulfilled - Before this plague was removed.

VIII

Three more of the plagues of Egypt are related in this chapter.

I. That of the frogs, which is,
   1. Threatened, ver. 1-4.
   2. Inflicted, ver. 5, 6.
   3. Mimicked by the magicians, ver. 7.
   4. Removed at the request of Pharaoh, ver. 8-14. who yet hardens his heart, and notwithstanding his promise, ver. 8. refused to let Israel go, ver. 15.

II. The plague of lice, ver. 16, 17. By which,
   1. The magicians were baffled, ver. 18, 19. and yet,
   2. Pharaoh was hardened, ver. 19.

III. That of flies:
   1. Pharaoh is warned of it before, ver. 20, 21. and told that the land of Goshen should be exempt from this plague, ver. 22, 23.
   2. The plague is brought, ver. 24.
   3. Pharaoh treats with Moses, and humbles himself, ver. 25-29.
   4. The plague is thereupon removed, ver. 31. and Pharaoh's heart hardened, ver. 32.

2. All thy borders - All the land that is within thy borders.

3. The River - Nile. Under which are comprehended all other rivers and waters.

9. Glory over me - That is, I yield to thee.

10. And he said, Tomorrow - Why not immediately? Probably he hoped that this night they would go away of themselves, and then he should get clear of the plague, without being obliged either to God or Moses. However, Moses joins issue with him upon it. Be it according to thy word - It shall be done just when thou wouldst have it done, that thou mayst know, that whatever the magicians pretend to, there is none like unto the Lord our God - None has such a command as he has over all creatures, nor is any so ready to forgive those that humble themselves before him. The great design both of judgments and mercies, is to convince us that there is none like the Lord our God; none so wise, so mighty, so good; no enemy so formidable, no friend so desirable, so valuable.

15. But when Pharaoh saw that there was respite, he hardened his heart - Observe he did it himself, not God, any otherwise than by not hindering.

17. The frogs were produced out of the waters, but the lice out of the dust of the earth; for out of any part of the creation God can fetch a scourge wherewith to correct those that rebel against him.

18. And the magicians did so - That is, endeavoured to do so.

19. This is the finger of God - The power of God. The devil's agents, when God permitted them, could do great things; but when he laid an embargo upon them, they could do nothing. The magicians inability in this instance shewed whence they had their ability in the former instances, and that they had no power against Moses but what was given them from above. But Pharaoh's heart was hardened - By himself and the devil.

20. Rise up early - Those that would bring great things to pass for God and their generation must rise early, and redeem time in the morning. Pharaoh was early up at his superstitious devotions to the river; and shall we be for more sleep, and more slumber, when any service is to be done which would pass well in our account in the great day?

21. Flies - Or insects of various kinds; not only flies, but gnats, wasps, hornets; and those probably more pernicious than the common ones were.

22. Know that I am the Lord in the midst of the earth - In every part of it. Swarms of flies, which seem to us to fly at random, shall be manifestly under the conduct of an intelligent mind. Hither they shall go, saith Moses, and thither they shall come, and the performance is punctual according to this appointment; and both compared amount to a demonstration, that he that said it, and he that did it, was the same, even a being of infinite power and wisdom.

23. A division - A wall of partition.

24. There came a grievous swarm of flies - The prince of the power of the air has gloried in being Beel-zebub, the God of flies; but here it is proved that even in that he is a pretender, and an usurper; for even with swarms of flies God fights against his kingdom and prevails.

26. The abomination of the Egyptians - That which they abominate to see killed, because they

worshipped them as gods.

27. As he shall command us - For he has not yet told us what sacrifices to offer.

28. Ye shall not go very far away - Not so far but that he might fetch them back again. It is likely he suspected that if once they left Egypt, they would never come back; and therefore when he is forced to consent that they shall go, yet he is not willing they should go out of his reach. See how ready God is to accept sinners submissions. Pharaoh only says, Intreat for me - Moses promises immediately, I will intreat the Lord for thee; and that he might see what the design of the plague was, not to bring him to ruin, but to repentance.

32. But Pharaoh hardened his heart at this time also - Still it is his own act and deed, not God's.

IX

In this chapter we have an account of three more plagues.

I. Murrain among the cattle, ver. 1-7.

II. Boils upon man and beast, ver. 8-12.

III. Hail, with thunder and lightning. (1.) Warning is given of this plague, ver. 13-21. (2.) It is inflicted to their great terror, ver 22-26. (3.) Pharaoh renews his treaty with Moses, but instantly breaks his word, ver 27-35.

3. The hand of the Lord - Immediately, without the stretching out of Aaron's hand, is upon the cattle, many of which, some of all kinds, shall die by a sort of pestilence. The hand of God is to be acknowledged even in the sickness and death of cattle, or other damage sustained in them; for a sparrow falls not to the ground without our father. And his providence is to be acknowledged with thankfulness in the life of the cattle, for he preserveth man and beast, Psalm xxxvi, 6.

6. All the cattle died - All that were in the field. The creature is made subject to vanity by the sin of man, being liable, according to its capacity, both to serve his wickedness, and to share in his punishment. The Egyptians worshipped their cattle; it was among them that the Israelites learned to make a God of a calf; in that therefore this plague meets with them. But not one of the cattle of the Israelites died - Doth God take care for oxen? Yes, he doth, his providence extends itself to the meanest of his creatures.

9. A boil breaking forth with blains - A burning scab, which quickly raised blisters and blains.

10. Ashes of the furnace - Sometimes God shews men their sin in their punishment: they had oppressed Israel in the furnaces, and now the ashes of the furnace are made as much a terror to them as ever their task-masters had been to the Israelites. This is afterwards called the botch of Egypt, Deut. xxviii, 27, as if it were some new disease, never heard of before, and known ever after by that name.

11. The magicians were forced to retreat, and could not stand before Moses - To which the apostle refers, 2 Tim. iii, 9, when he saith, that their folly was manifested unto all men.

12. Now the Lord hardened Pharaoh's heart - Before he had hardened his own heart, and resisted the grace of God, and now God justly gave him up to his own heart's lusts, to strong delusions, permitting Satan to blind and harden him. Wilful hardness is commonly punished with judicial hardness. Let us dread this as the sorest judgment a man can be under on this side hell.

14. I will find all my plagues upon thy heart - Hitherto thou hast not felt my plagues on thy own person, the heart is put for the whole man.

16. For this cause have I raised thee up - A most dreadful message Moses is here ordered to deliver to him, whether he will hear, or whether he will forbear. He must tell him, that he is marked for ruin: that he now stands as the butt at which God would shoot all the arrows of his wrath. For this cause have I raised thee up to the throne at this time, and made thee to stand the shock of the plagues hitherto, to shew in thee my power - Providence so ordered it, that Moses should have a man of such a fierce and stubborn spirit to deal with, to make it a most signal and memorable instance of the power God has to bring down the proudest of his enemies; that my name, irresistable power, and my inflexible justice, might be declared throughout all the earth - Not only to all places, but through all ages while the earth remains. This will be the event. But it by no means follows, that this was the design of God. We have numberless instances in scripture of this manner of speaking, to denote not the design, but only the event.

17. As yet exaltest thou thyself against my people - Wilt thou not yet submit?

18. Since the foundation thereof - Since it was a kingdom.

29. The earth - The world, the heaven and the earth.

30. Bolled - Grown up into a stalk.

33. Moses went out of the city - Not only for privacy in his communion with God, but to shew that

he durst venture abroad into the field, notwithstanding the hail and lightning, knowing that every hail-stone had its direction from God. Peace with God makes men thunder-proof, for it is the voice of their father. *And spread abroad his hands unto the Lord* - An outward expression of earnest desire, and humble expectation. *He prevailed with God; but he could not prevail with Pharaoh; he sinned yet more, and hardened his heart* - The prayer of Moses opened and shut heaven, like Elijah's. And such is the power of God's two witnesses, Rev. xi, 6. Yet neither Moses nor Elijah, nor those two witnesses, could subdue the hard hearts of men. Pharaoh was frighted into compliance by the judgment, but, when it was over, his convictions vanished.

X

The eighth and ninth plagues are recorded in this chapter.

I. Concerning the plague of locusts, (1.) God instructs Moses in the meaning of these amazing dispensations of his providence, ver. 1, 2. (2.) He threatens the locusts, ver. 3-6. (3.) Pharaoh, at the persuasion of his servants, is willing to treat again with Moses, ver. 7, 8, 9. but they cannot agree, ver. 10, 11, (4.) The locusts come, ver. 12-15. (5.) Pharaoh cries for mercy, ver. 16, 17. whereupon Moses prays for the removal of the plague, and it is done, but Pharaoh's heart is still hardened, ver. 18-20.

II. Concerning the plague of darkness, (1.) 'Tis inflicted, ver. 21-23. (2.) Pharaoh again treats with Moses, but the treaty breaks off, ver. 24-29.

1. These plagues are standing monuments of the greatness of God, the happiness of the church, and the sinfulness of sin; and standing monitors to the children of men in all ages, not to provoke the Lord to jealousy, nor to strive with their Maker. The benefit of these instructions to the world doth sufficiently balance the expence.

3. *Thus saith the Lord God of the Hebrews, How long wilt thou refuse to humble thyself before me?* - It is justly expected from the greatest of men, that they humble themselves before the great God, and it is at their peril if they refuse to do it. Those that will not humble themselves, God will humble.

10. *Let the Lord be so with you, as I will let you go, and your little ones* - He now curses and threatens them, in case they offered to remove their little ones, telling them it was at their peril. Satan doth all he can to hinder those that serve God themselves, from bringing their children in to serve him. He is a sworn enemy to early piety, knowing how destructive it is to the interests of his kingdom.

13. *The east-wind brought the locusts* - From Arabia, where they are in great numbers: And God miraculously increased them.

15. *They covered the face of the earth, and eat up the fruit of it* - The earth God has given to the children of men; yet when God pleaseth he can disturb his possession even by locusts or caterpillars. Herb grows for the service of man; yet, when God pleaseth, those contemptible insect's shall not only be fellow-commoners with him, but shall eat the bread out of his mouth.

17. Pharaoh desires their prayers that this death only might be taken away, not this sin: he deprecates the plague of locusts, not the plague of a hard heart.

19. An east-wind brought the locusts and now a west-wind carried them off. Whatever point of the compass the wind is in, it is fulfilling God's word, and turns about by his counsel; the wind blows where it listeth for us, but not where it listeth for him; he directeth it under the whole heaven.

21. We may observe concerning this plague.

1. That it was a total darkness. We have reason to think, not only that the lights of heaven were clouded, but that all their fires and candles were put out by the damps or clammy vapors which were the cause of this darkness, for it is said, they saw not one another.

2. That it was darkness which might be felt, felt in its causes by their finger-ends, so thick were the fogs, felt in its effects, (some think) by their eyes which were pricked with pain, and made the more sore by their rubbing them. Great pain is spoken of as the effect of that darkness, Rev. xvi, 10, which alludes to this.

3. No doubt it was very frightful and amazing. The tradition of the Jews is, that in this darkness they were terrified by the apparition of evil spirits, or rather by dreadful sounds and murmurs which they made; and this is the plague which some think is intended (for otherwise it is not mentioned at all there) Psalm lxxviii, 49. He poured upon them the fierceness of his anger, by sending evil angels among them; for those to whom the devil has been a deceiver, he will at length be a terror to.

4. It continued three days; six nights in one; so long they were imprisoned by those chains of darkness. *No man rose from his place* - They were all confined to their houses; and such a terror seized them, that few of them had the courage to go from the chair to the bed, or from the bed to the chair. Thus were they silent in darkness, 1 Sam. ii, 9. Now Pharaoh had time to consider, if he would have improved it.

23. *But the children of Israel had light in their dwellings* - Not only in the land of Goshen, where most of them inhabited, but in the particular dwellings which in other places the Israelites had dispersed among the Egyptians, as it appears they had by the distinction afterwards appointed to be put on their door-posts. And during these three days of darkness to the Egyptians, if God had so pleased, the Israelites by the light which they had, might have made their escape, and have asked Pharaoh no leave; but God would bring them out with a high hand, and not by stealth or in haste.

29. *I will see thy face no more* - Namely, after this time, for this conference did not break off till chap. xi, 8, when Moses went out in great anger and told Pharaoh how soon his proud stomach would come down; which was fulfilled chap. xii, 31, when Pharaoh became an humble supplicant to Moses to depart. So that after this interview Moses came no more till he was sent for.

XI

Pharaoh had bid Moses get out of his presence, chap. x, 28. and Moses had promised this should be the last time he would trouble him, yet he refuses to say out what he had to say, before he left him. Accordingly we have in this chapter,

I. The instructions God had given to Moses, which he was now to pursue, ver. 1, 2. together with the interest Israel and Moses had in the esteem of the Egyptians, ver. 3.

II. The last message Moses delivered to Pharaoh, concerning the death of the first-born, ver. 4-8.

III. A repetition of the prediction of Pharaoh's hardening his heart, ver. 9. and the event answering it, ver. 10.

2. *Let every man ask (not borrow!) of his neighbour jewels* - This was the last day of their servitude, when they were to go away, and their masters, who had abused them in their work, would now have defrauded them of their wages, and have sent them away empty, and the poor Israelites were so fond of liberty that they themselves would be satisfied with that, without pay: but he that executeth righteousness and judgment for the oppressed, provided that the labourers should not lose their hire. God ordered them to demand it now at their departure, in jewels of silver, and jewels of gold; to prepare for which, God had now made the Egyptians as willing to part with them upon any terms, as before the Egyptians had made them willing to go upon any terms.

5. The death of the first-born had been threatened, chap. iv, 23, but is last executed, and less judgments tried, which, if they had done the work, would have prevented this. See how slow God is to wrath, and how willing to be met in the way of his judgments, and to have his anger turned away! *That sitteth upon his throne* - That is to set. *The maid-servant behind the mill* - The poor captive slave, employed in the hardest labour.

8. *All these thy servants* - Thy courtiers and great officers: *The people that follow thee* - That are under thy conduct: and command. When Moses had thus delivered his message, he went out from Pharaoh in great anger, though he was the meekest of all the men of the earth. Probably he expected that the very threatening of the death of the first-born should have wrought upon Pharaoh to comply; especially he having complied so far already, and having seen how exactly all Moses's predictions were fulfilled. But it had not that effect; his proud heart would not yield, no not to save all the first-born of his kingdom. Moses hereupon was provoked to a holy indignation, being grieved, as our saviour afterwards, for the hardness of his heart, Mark iii, 5.

This chapter gives an account of one of the most memorable ordinances, and one of the most memorable providences of all that art recorded in the old testament.

I. None of all the ordinances of the Jewish church were more eminent than that of the passover. It consisted of three parts.
  1. The killing and eating of the paschal lamb, ver. 1-6, 8-11.
  2. The sprinkling of the blood upon the doorposts, peculiar to the first passover, ver. 7. with the reason for it, ver. 11-13.
  3. The feast of unleavened bread for seven days after; this points rather at what was to be done after in the observance of this ordinance, ver. 14-20. This institution is communicated to the people, and they instructed in the observance. (1.) Of this first passover, ver. 21-23. (2.) Of the after passovers, ver. 24-27. And the Israelites obedience to these orders, ver. 28.

II. None of all the providences of God concerning the Jewish church was more illustrious, than the deliverance of the children of Israel out of Egypt.
  1. The first-born of the Egyptians are slain, ver. 29, 30.
  2. Orders are given immediately for their discharge, ver. 31-33.
  3. They begin their march,
    1. Loaded with their own effects, ver. 34.
    2. Enriched with the spoils of Egypt, ver. 35, 36.
    3. Attended with a mixed multitude, ver. 37, 38,
    4. Put to their shifts for present supply, ver. 39. This event is dated, ver. 40-42.

III. A recapitulation in the close, 1st. Of this memorable ordinance, with some additions, ver. 43-49; 2ndly. Of this memorable providence, ver. 50, 51.

1. *The Lord spake* - Had spoken, before the three days darkness. But the mention of it was put off to this place, that the history of the plagues might not be interrupted.

2. *This shall be to you the beginning of months* - They had hitherto begun their year from the middle of September, but hence-forward they were to begin it from the middle of March, at least in all their ecclesiastical computations. We may suppose that while Moses was bringing the ten plagues upon the Egyptians, he was directing the Israelites to prepare for their departure at an hour's warning. Probably he had, by degrees, brought them near together from their dispersions, for they are here called the congregation of Israel; and to them, as a congregation, orders are here sent.

3. *Take every man a lamb* - In each of their families, or two or three families, if they were small, join for a lamb. The lamb was to be got ready four days before. and that afternoon they went, they were to kill it, (ver. 6,) as a sacrifice, not strictly, for it was not offered upon the altar, but as a religious ceremony, acknowledging God's goodness to them, not only in preserving them from, but in delivering them by the plagues inflicted on the Egyptians. The lamb so slain they were to eat roasted (we may suppose in its several quarters) with unleavened bread and bitter herbs; they were to eat it in haste, ver. 11, and to leave none of it until the morning; for God would have them to depend upon him for their daily bread. Before they eat the flesh of the lamb, they were to sprinkle the blood upon the door-posts; by which their houses were to be distinguished from the houses of the Egyptians, and so their first-born secured from the sword of the destroying angel. Dreadful work was to be made this night in Egypt; all the first-born both of man and beast were to be slain; and judgment executed upon the gods of Egypt, Num. xxxiii, 4. It is probable the idols which the Egyptians worshipped were defaced, those of metal melted, those of wood consumed, and those of stone broke to pieces. This was to be annually observed as a feast of the Lord in their generations, to which the feast of unleavened bread was annexed, during which, for seven days, they were to eat no bread but what was unleavened, in remembrance of their being confined to such bread for many days after they came out of Egypt, ver. 14- 20. There was much of the gospel in this ordinance: (1.) The paschal lamb was typical. Christ is our passover, 1 Cor. v, 7, and is the Lamb of God, John i, 29. 2. It was to be a male of the first year; in its prime. Christ offered up himself in the midst of his days. It notes the strength and sufficiency of the Lord Jesus, on whom our help was laid. 3. It was to be without blemish, noting the purity of the Lord Jesus, a lamb without spot, 1 Pet. i, 19. 4. It was to be set apart four days before, noting the designation of the Lord Jesus to be a saviour, both in the purpose and in the promise. It is observable, that as Christ was crucified at the passover, so he solemnly entered into Jerusalem four days before, the very day that the paschal lamb was set apart. 5. It was to be slain and roasted with fire, noting the exquisite sufferings of the Lord Jesus, even unto death, the death of the cross. 6. It was to be killed by the whole congregation between the two evenings, that is, between three o'clock and six. Christ suffered in the latter end of the world,

Heb. ix, 26, by the hand of the Jews, the whole multitude of them, Luke xxiii, 18. 7. Not a bone of it must be broken, ver. 46, which is expressly said to be fulfilled in Christ, John xix, 33, 36. (2.) The sprinkling of the blood was typical. 1st, It was not enough that the blood of the lamb was shed, but it must be sprinkled, noting the application of the merits of Christ's death to our souls; 2ndly, It was to be sprinkled upon the door-posts, noting the open profession we are to make of faith in Christ, and obedience to him. The mark of the beast may be received in the forehead, or in the right hand, but the seal of the lamb is always in the forehead, Rev. vii, 3. 3rdly, The blood thus sprinkled was a means of the preservation of the Israelites from the destroying angel. If the blood of Christ be sprinkled upon our consciences, it will be our protection from the wrath of God, the curse of the law, and the damnation of hell. (3.) The solemn eating of the lamb was typical of our gospel duty to Christ. 1st, The paschal lamb was killed not to be looked upon only, but to be fed upon; so we must by faith make Christ ours, as we do that which we eat, and we must receive spiritual strength and nourishment from him, as from our food, and have delight in him, as we have in eating and drinking when we are hungry or thirsty. 2ndly, It was to be all eaten: those that, by faith, feed upon Christ, must feed upon a whole Christ. They must take Christ and his yoke, Christ and his cross, as well as Christ and his crown. 3rdly, It was to be eaten with bitter herbs, in remembrance of the bitterness of their bondage in Egypt; we must feed upon Christ with brokenness of heart, in remembrance of sin. 4thly, It was to be eaten in a departing posture ver. 11, when we feed upon Christ by faith, we must sit loose to the world, and every thing in it. (4.) The feast of unleavened bread was typical of the Christian life, 1 Cor. v, 7, 8. Having received Christ Jesus the Lord, 1st. We must keep a feast, in holy joy, continually delighting ourselves in Christ Jesus; If true believers have not a continual feast, it is their own fault. 2ndly, It must be a feast of unleavened bread, kept in charity, without the leaven of malice, and in sincerity, without the leaven of hypocrisy. All the old leaven of sin must be put far from us, with the utmost caution, if we would keep the feast of a holy life to the honour of Christ. 3rdly, It was to be an ordinance forever. As long as we live we must continue feeding upon Christ, and rejoicing in him always, with thankful mention of the great things he has done for us.

9. Raw - Half roasted, but throughly drest.

10. Ye shall burn with fire - To prevent the profane abuse of it.

11. The Lord's passover - A sign of his passing over you, when he destroyed the Egyptians.

16. An holy convocation - A solemn day for the people to assemble together.

19. A stranger - A proselyte. Heathens were not concerned in the passover.

22. Out of the door of his house - Of that house, wherein he ate the passover: Until the morning - That is, till towards morning, when they would be called for to march out of Egypt. They went out very early in the morning.

23. The destroyer - The destroying angel, whether this was a good or an evil angel, we have not light to determine.

27. The people bowed the head and worshipped - They hereby signified their submission to this institution as a law, and their thankfulness for it as a favour and privilege.

31. Rise up, and get you forth - Pharaoh had told Moses he should see his face no more, but now he sent for him; those will seek God in their distress, who before had set him at defiance. Such a fright he was now in that he gave orders by night for their discharge, fearing lest if he delay'd, he himself should fall next. And that he sent them out, not as men hated (as the Pagan historians have represented this matter) but as men feared, is plain by his request to them.

32. Bless me also - Let me have your prayers, that I may not be plagued for what is past when you are gone.

33. We be all dead men - When death comes unto our houses, it is seasonable for us to think of our own mortality.

34. Their kneading-troughs - Or rather, their lumps of paste unleavened.

37. About six hundred thousand men - The word means strong and able men fit for wars, beside women and children, which we cannot suppose to make less than twelve hundred thousand more. What a vast increase was this to arise from seventy souls, in little more than two hundred years.

38. And a mixed multitude went up with them - Some perhaps willing to leave their country, because it was laid waste by the plagues. But probably the greatest part was but a rude unthinking mob, that followed they knew not why: It is likely, when they understood that the children of Israel were to continue forty years in the wilderness, they quitted them, and returned to Egypt again. And flocks and herds, even very much cattle - This is taken notice of, because it was long ere Pharaoh would give them leave to remove their effects, which were chiefly cattle.

39. Thrust out - By importunate entreaties.

40. It was just four hundred and thirty years from the promise made to Abraham (as the Apostle explains it, Gal. iii, 17,) at his first coming into Canaan, during all which time the Hebrews, were sojourners in a land that was not theirs, either Canaan or Egypt. So long the promise God made to Abraham lay dormant and unfulfilled, but now, it revived, and things began to work towards the

accomplishment of it. The first day of the march of Abraham's seed towards Canaan was four hundred and thirty years (it should seem, to a day) from the promise made to Abraham, Gen. xii, 2. I will make of thee a great nation.

42. This first passover night was a night of the Lord, much to be observed; but the last passover night, in which Christ was betrayed, was a night of the Lord, much more to be observed, when a yoke heavier than that of Egypt was broke from off our necks, and a land better than that of Canaan set before us. That was a temporal deliverance, to be celebrated in their generations; this an eternal redemption to be celebrated world without end.

45. An hired servant - Unless he submit to be circumcised.

47. All the congregation of Israel must keep it - Though it was observed in families apart, yet it is looked upon as the act of the whole congregation. And so the new testament passover, the Lord's supper, ought not to be neglected by any that are capable of celebrating it.

48. No stranger that was uncircumcised might eat of it. Neither may any now approach the Lord's supper who have not first submitted to baptism; nor shall any partake of the benefit of Christ's sacrifice, who are not first circumcised in heart. Any stranger that was circumcised might eat of the passover, even servants. Here is an indication of favour to the poor Gentiles, that the stranger, if circumcised, stands upon the same level with the home-born Israelite; one law for both. This was a mortification to the Jews, and taught them that it was their dedication to God, not their descent from Abraham, that entitled them to their privileges.

XIII

In this chapter we have,

I. The commands God gave to Israel,
   1. To sanctify all their first-born to him, ver. 1, 2.
   2. To remember their deliverance out of Egypt, ver. 3, 4. and in remembrance of it to keep the feast of unleavened bread, ver. 5-8.
   3. To transmit the knowledge of it to their children, ver. 8-10.
   4. To set apart to God the firstlings of their cattle, ver. 11-13. and to explain that also to their children, ver. 14-16.

II. The care God took of Israel when he had brought them out of Egypt.
   1. Chusing their way for them, ver. 17, 18
   2. Guiding them in the way, ver. 20-22. And their care of Joseph's bones, ver. 19.

2. Sanctify to me all the first-born - The parents were not to look upon themselves as interested in their first-born, till they had first solemnly presented them to God, and received them back from him again. It is mine - By a special right, being by my singular favour preserved from the common destruction.

5. When the Lord shall bring you into the land, thou shalt keep this service - 'Till then they were not obliged to keep the passover, without a particular command from God.

7. There shall no leavened bread be seen in all thy quarters - Accordingly the Jews usage was, before the feast of the passover, to cast all the leavened bread out of their houses; either they burnt it, or buried it, or broke it small, and threw it into the wind; they searched diligently with lighted candles in all the corners of their houses, lest any leaven should remain. The strictness enjoined in this matter was designed,
   1. To make the feast the more solemn, and consequently the more taken notice of by the children, who would ask, why is so much ado made?
   2. To teach us how solicitous we should be to put away from us all sin.

9. Upon thy hand, between thine eyes - Proverbial expressions; denoting things which are never out of our thoughts.

13. Thou shalt redeem - The price of the redemption was fixed by the law.

16. For frontlets between thine eyes - As conspicuous as any thing fixt to thy forehead, or between thine eyes.

18. There were many reasons why God led them through the way of the wilderness of the red sea. The Egyptians were to be drowned in the Red-sea, the Israelites were to be humbled, and proved in the wilderness. Deut. viii, 2. God had given it to Moses for a sign, chap. iii, 12, ye shall serve God in this mountain. They had again and again told Pharaoh that they must go three days journey into the wilderness to do sacrifice, and therefore it was requisite they should march that way, else they had justly been exclaimed against as dissemblers. Before they entered the lifts with their enemies, matters must be settled between them and their God; laws must be given, ordinances instituted, covenants sealed; and for

the doing of this it was necessary they should retire into the solitudes of a wilderness, the only closet for such a crowd; the high road would be no proper place for these transactions. The reason why God did not lead them the nearest way, which would have brought them in a few days to the land of the Philistines, was because they were not yet fit for war, much less for war with the Philistines. Their spirits were broke with slavery; the Philistines were formidable enemies; it was convenient they should begin with the Amalekites, and be prepared for the wars of Canaan, by experiencing the difficulties of the wilderness. God is said to bring Israel out of Egypt as the eagle brings up her young ones, Deut. xxxii, 11, teaching them by degrees to fly. They went up harnessed - They went up by five in a rank, so some; in five squadrons, so others. They marched like an army with banners, which added much to strength and honour.

21. And the Lord went before them in a pillar - In the two first stages, it was enough that God directed Moses whither to march; he knew the country, and the road; but now they are come to the edge of the wilderness, they would have occasion for a guide, and a very good guide they had, infinitely wise, kind, and faithful, the Lord went up before them; The Shechinah or appearance of the divine Majesty, which was a precious manifestation of the eternal Word, who in the fulness of time was to be made flesh, and dwell among us. Christ was with the church in the wilderness, 1 Cor. x, 9. What a satisfaction to Moses and the pious Israelites, to be sure that they were under a divine conduct? They need not fear missing their way who were thus led, nor being lost who were thus directed; they need not fear being benighted, who were thus illuminated, nor being robbed, who were thus protected. And they who make the glory of God their end, and the word of God their rule, the spirit of God the guide of their affections, and the providence of God the guide of their affairs, may be confident that the Lord goes before them, as truly is he went before Israel in the wilderness, though not so sensibly. They had sensible effects of God's going before them in this pillar. For, It led them the way in that vast howling wilderness, in which there was no road, no track, no way-marks through which they had no guides. When they marched, this pillar went before them, at the rate that they could follow, and appointed the place of their encampment, as infinite Wisdom saw fit; which eased them from care, and secured them from danger, both in moving, and in resting. It sheltered them from the heat by day, which at sometimes of the year was extreme: And it gave them light by night when they had occasion for it.

22. He took not away the pillar of the cloud, - No not when they seemed to have less occasion for it: it never left them 'till it brought them to the borders of Canaan. It was a cloud which the wind could not scatter. There was something spiritual in this pillar of cloud and fire.

1. The children of Israel were baptized unto Moses in this cloud, 1 Cor. x, 2. By coming under this cloud they signified their putting themselves under the conduct and command of Moses. Protection draws allegiance; this cloud was the badge of God's protection, and so became the bond of their allegiance. Thus they were initiated, and admitted under that government, now when they were entering upon the wilderness.

2. And it signifies the special conduct and protection which the church of Christ is under in this world.

XIV

Here is,

I. The extreme distress that Israel was in at the Red-sea.
    1. Notice given of it to Moses before, ver. 1-4.
    2. The cause of it was Pharaoh's pursuit of them, ver. 5-9.
    3. Israel was in a consternation upon it, ver. 10-12.
    4. Moses endeavours to encourage them, ver. 13, 14.

II. The wonderful deliverance that God wrought for them.
    1. Moses is instructed concerning it, ver. 15-18.
    2. Lines that could not be forced are set between the camp of Israel and Pharaoh's camp, ver. 19, 20.
    3. By the divine power the Red-sea is divided, ver. 21. and is made,
    1. A lane to the Israelites, who marched safely through it, ver. 22- 29. But.
    2. To the Egyptians it was made,
    1. An ambush into which they were drawn, ver. 23-25. And,
    2. A grave in which they were all buried, ver. 26-28.

III. The impressions this made upon the Israelites, ver. 30, 31.

    2. They were got to the edge of the wilderness, chap. xiii, 20, and one stage or two would have

brought them to Horeb, the place appointed for their serving God, but instead of going forward, they are ordered to turn short off, on the right-hand from Canaan, and to march towards the Red-sea. When they were at Etham, there was no sea in their way to obstruct their passage; but God himself orders them into straits, which might give them an assurance, that when his purposes were served, he would bring them out of those straits. Before Pi-hahiroth - Or the straits of Hiroth, two great mountains, between which they marched. Migdol and Baal-zephon were cities of Egypt and probably garrison'd.

3. They are entangled - Inclosed with mountains, and garrisons, and deserts.

5. And it was told the king that the people fled - He either forgot, or would not own that they had departed with his consent; and therefore was willing it should be represented to him as a revolt from their allegiance.

7. Captains over every one of them - Or rather over all of them; distributing the command of them to his several Captains.

8. With an high hand - Boldly, resolutely.

9. Chariots and horsemen - It should seem he took no foot with him, because the king's business required haste.

10. They were sore afraid - They knew the strength of the enemy, and their own weakness; numerous indeed they were, but all foot, unarmed, undisciplined, dispirited, by long servitude, and now pent up, so that they could not escape. On one hand was Pi-hahiroth, a range of craggy rocks unpassable; on the other hand were Migdol and Baal-zephon, forts upon the frontiers of Egypt; before them was the sea, behind them were the Egyptians; so that there was no way open for them but upwards, and thence their deliverance came.

13. Moses answered not these fools according to their folly: Instead of chiding he comforts them, and with an admirable pretense of mind, not disheartened either by the threatenings of Egypt, or the tremblings of Israel, stills their murmuring, Fear ye not, It is our duty, when we cannot get out of our troubles, yet to get above our fears, so that they may only serve to quicken our prayers and endeavours, but may not prevail to silence our faith and hope. Stand still, and think not to save yourselves either by fighting or flying; wait God's orders, and observe them; Compose yourselves, by an entire confidence in God, into a peaceful prospect of the great salvation God is now about to work for you. Hold your peace, you need not so much as give a shout against the enemy: the work shall be done without any concurrence of yours. In times of great difficulty, it is our wisdom to keep our spirits calm, quiet, and sedate, for then we are in the best frame both to do our own work, and to consider the work of God.

15. Wherefore criest thou unto me - Moses though he was assured of a good issue, yet did not neglect prayer. We read not of one word he said in prayer, but he lifted up his heart to God, and God well understood, and took notice of. Moses's silent prayer prevailed more with God, than Israel's loud out-cries. But is God displeased with Moses for praying? No, he asks this question, Wherefore criest thou unto me? Wherefore shouldst thou press thy petition any farther, when it is already granted? Moses has something else to do besides praying, he is to command the hosts of Israel. Speak to them that they go forward - Some think Moses had prayed not so much for their deliverance, he was assured of that; as for the pardon of their murmurings, and God's ordering them to go forward, was an intimation of the pardon. Moses bid them stand still and expect orders from God: and now orders are given. They thought they must have been directed either to the right hand, or to the left; no, saith God, speak to them to go forward, directly to the sea-side; as if there had lain a fleet of transport ships ready for them to embark in. Let the children of Israel go as far as they can upon dry ground, and then God will divide the sea. The same power could have congealed the waters for them to pass over, but infinite wisdom chose rather to divide the waters for them to pass through, for that way of salvation is always pitched upon which is most humbling.

19. The angel of God - Whose ministry was made use of in the pillar of cloud and fire, went from before the camp of Israel, where they did not now need a guide; there was no danger of missing their way through the sea, and came behind them, where now they needed a guard, the Egyptians being just ready to seize the hindmost of them. There it was of use to the Israelites, not only to protect them, but to light them through the sea; and at the same time it confounded the Egyptians, so that they lost sight of their prey, just when they were ready to lay hands on it. The word and providence of God have a black and dark side towards sin and sinners, but a bright and pleasant side towards those that are Israelites indeed.

21. We have here the history of that work of wonder which is so often mentioned both in the Old and New Testament. An instance of God's almighty power in dividing the sea, and opening a passage through the waters. It was a bay, or gulf, or arm of the sea, two or three leagues over. The God of nature has not tied himself to its laws, but when he pleases dispenseth with them, and then the fire doth not burn, nor the water flow. They went through the sea to the opposite shore; they walked upon dry land in the midst of the sea; and the pillar of cloud being their rereward, the waters were a wall to them on their right hand, and on their left. Moses and Aaron it is likely ventured first, into this untrodden path, and then all Israel after them; and this march through the paths of the great waters would make their march

afterwards through the wilderness less formidable. This march through the sea was in the night, and not a moon-shine night, for it was seven days after the full moon, so that they had no light but what they had from the pillar of fire. This made it the more awful, but where God leads us, he will light us; while we follow his conduct we shall not want his comforts.

23. And the Egyptians went in after them into the midst of the sea - They thought, why might they not venture where Israel did? They were more advantageously provided with chariots and horses, while the Israelites were on foot.

24. The Lord - Called the angel before, looked - With indignation, upon the Egyptians, and troubled the Egyptians - With terrible winds and lightnings and thunders, chap. xv, 10, Psalm lxxvii, 18, 19. Also with terror of mind.

25. They had driven furiously, but now they drove heavily, and found themselves embarrassed at every step; the way grew deep, their hearts grew sad, their wheels dropt off, and the axle-trees failed. They had been flying upon the back of Israel as the hawk upon the dove; but now they cried, Let us flee from the face of Israel.

26. And the Lord said unto Moses, Stretch out thy hand over the sea - And give a signal to the waters to close again, as before upon the word of command they had opened to the right and the left. He did so, and immediately the waters returned to their place, and overwhelmed all the host of the Egyptians. Pharaoh and his servants, that had hardened one another in sin, now fell together, and not one escaped. An ancient tradition saith, That Pharaoh's magicians Jannes and Jambres perished with the rest. Now God got him honour upon Pharaoh, a rebel to God, and a slave to his own barbarous passions; perfectly lost to humanity, virtue, and all true honour; here be lies buried in the deep, a perpetual monument of divine justice: here he went down to the pit, though he was the terror of the mighty in the land of the living.

28. After them - That is, after the Israelites.

30. And Israel saw the Egyptians dead upon the shore - The Egyptians were very curious in preserving the bodies of their great men, but here the utmost contempt is poured upon all the grandees of Egypt; see how they lie heaps upon heaps, as dung upon the face of the earth.

31. And Israel feared the Lord, and believed the Lord and his servant Moses - Now they were ashamed of their distrusts and murmurings; and in the mind they were in, they would never again despair of help from heaven; no not in the greatest straits! They would never again quarrel with Moses; nor talk of returning to Egypt. How well were it for us, if we were, always in as good a frame, as we are in sometimes!

XV

In this chapter,

I. Israel looks back upon Egypt with a song of praise for their deliverance. Here is,
    1. The song itself, ver. 1-19.
    2. The solemn singing of it, ver. 20, 21.

II. Israel marches forward in the wilderness, ver. 22. Their discontent at the waters of Marah, ver. 23, 24. and the relief granted them, ver. 25, 26. Their satisfaction in the waters of Elim, ver. 27.

1. Then sang Moses - Moses composed this song, and sang it with the children of Israel. Doubtless he wrote it by inspiration, and sang it on the spot. By this instance it appears that the singing of psalms, as an act of religious worship, was used in the church of Christ before the giving of the ceremonial law, therefore it is no part of it, nor abolished with it: singing is as much the language of holy joy, as praying is of holy desire. I will sing unto the Lord - All our joy must terminate in God, and all our praises be offered up to him, for he hath triumphed - All that love God triumph in his triumphs.

2. Israel rejoiceth in God, as their strength, song, and salvation - Happy therefore the people whole God is the Lord: They are weak themselves, but he strengthens them, his grace is their strength: they are oft in sorrow, but in him they have comfort, he is their song: sin and death threaten them, but he is, and will be, their salvation. He is their fathers God - This they take notice of, because being conscious of their own unworthiness, they had reason to think that what God had now done for them was for their fathers sake, Deut. iv, 37.

3. The Lord is a man of war - Able to deal with all those that strive with their maker.

4. He hath cast - With great force, as an arrow out of a bow, so the Hebrew word signifies.

7. In the greatness of thine excellency - By thy great and excellent power.

8. With the blast of thy nostrils - By thine anger: The depths were congealed - Stood still, as if they had been frozen: In the heart of the sea - The midst of it.

9. My lust - My desire both of revenge and gain.

11. The gods - So called: Idols, or Princes: Glorious in holiness - In justice, mercy and truth: Fearful in praises - To be praised with reverence.

12. The earth swallowed them - Their dead bodies sunk into the sands on which they were thrown, which sucked them in.

13. Thou in thy mercy hast led forth the People - Out of the bondage of Egypt, and out of the perils of the Red-sea. Thou hast guided them to thy holy habitation - Thou hast put them into the way to it, and wilt in due time bring them to the end of that way.

17. Thou shalt bring them in - If he thus bring them out of Egypt, he will bring them into Canaan; for has he begun, and will he not make an end? Thou wilt plant them in the place which thou hast made for thee to dwell in - It is good dwelling where God dwells, in his church on earth, and in his church in heaven. In the mountains - In the mountainous country of Canaan: The sanctuary which thy hands have established - Will as surely establish as if it was done already.

18. The Lord shall reign forever and ever - They had now seen an end of Pharaoh's reign, but time itself shall not put a period to Jehovah's reign, which like himself is eternal.

20. Miriam (or Mary, it is the same name) presided in an assembly of the women, who (according to the common usage of those times) with timbrels and dances, sung this song. Moses led the psalm, and gave it out for the men, and then Miriam for the women. Famous victories were wont to be applauded by the daughters of Israel, 1 Sam. xviii, 6, 7, so was this. When God brought Israel out of Egypt, it is said, Micah vi, 4, he sent before them Moses, Aaron, and Miriam; though we read not of any thing remarkable that Miriam did but this. But those are to be reckoned great blessings to a people, that go before them in praising God.

21. And Miriam answered them - The men: They sung by turns, or in parts.

23. The name of it was called Marah - That is, Bitterness.

25. And he cried unto the Lord - It is the greatest relief of the cares of magistrates and ministers, when those under their charge make them uneasy, that they may have recourse to God by prayer; he is the guide of the church's guides, and to the chief shepherd, the under shepherds must on all occasions apply themselves: And the Lord directed Moses to a tree, which he cast into the waters, and they were made sweet - Some think this wood had a peculiar virtue in it for this purpose, because it is said, God shewed him the tree. God is to be acknowledged, not only in the creating things useful for man, but in discovering their usefulness. But perhaps this was only a sign, and not a means of the cure, no more than the brazen serpent. There he made a statute and an ordinance, and there he proved them - That is, there he put them upon trial, admitted them as probationers for his favour. In short he tells them, ver. 26, what he expected from them, and that was, in one word, obedience. They must diligently hearken to his voice, and give ear to his commandments, and must take care, in every thing, to do that which was right in God's sight, and to keep all his statutes. Then I will put none of these diseases upon thee - That is, I will not bring upon thee any of the plagues of Egypt. This intimates, that if they were disobedient, the plagues which they had seen inflicted on their enemies should be brought on them. But if thou wilt be obedient, thou shalt be safe, the threatening is implied, but the promise is expressed, I am the Lord that healeth thee - And will take care of thee wherever thou goest.

XVI

This chapter gives us an account of the victualling of the camp of Israel.

I. Their complaint for want of bread, ver. 1-3.

II. The notice God gave them of the provision he intended to make for them, ver. 4-12.

III. The sending of the manna, ver. 13-15.

IV. The laws and orders concerning it.
1. That they should gather it daily, ver. 16-21.
2. That they should gather a double portion on the sixth day, ver. 22-26.
3. That they should expect none on the seventh day, ver. 27-31,
4. That they should preserve a pot of it for a memorial, ver 32.

1. A month's provision, it seems, the host of Israel took with them out of Egypt, when they came thence on the 15th day of the first month, which, by the 15th day of the second month, was all spent.

2. Then the whole congregation murmured against Moses and Aaron - God's viceregents among them.

3. They so undervalue their deliverance, that they wish, they had died in Egypt, nay, and died by the hand of the Lord too. That is, by some of the plagues which cut off the Egyptians; as if it were not

the hand of the Lord, but of Moses only, that brought them into this wilderness. 'Tis common for people to say of that pain, or sickness, which they see not second causes of, It is what pleaseth God, as if that were not so likewise which comes by the hand of man, or some visible accident. We cannot suppose they had any great plenty in Egypt, how largely soever they now talk of the flesh-pots, nor could they fear dying for want in the wilderness while they had their flocks and herds with them; but discontent magnifies what is past, and vilifies what is present, without regard to truth or reason. None talk more absurdly than murmurers.

4. Man being made out of the earth, his Maker has wisely ordered him food out of the earth, Psalm civ, 14. But the people of Israel typifying the church of the first-born that are written in heaven, receiving their charters, laws and commissions from heaven, from heaven also they received their food. See what God designed in making this provision for them, that I may prove them whether they will walk in my law or no - Whether they will trust me, and whether they would serve him, and be ever faithful to so good a master.

5. They shall prepare - Lay up, grind, bake or boil.

6. The Lord - And not we, (as you suggest) by our own counsel.

10. The glory of the Lord - An extra-ordinary and sudden brightness.

12. And ye shall know that I am the Lord your God - This gave proof of his power as the Lord, and his particular favour to them as their God; when God plagued the Egyptians, it was to make them know that he is the Lord; when he provided for the Israelites, it was to make them know that he was their God.

13. The quails came up, and covered the camp - So tame that they might take up as many of them as they pleased. Next morning he rained manna upon them, which was to be continued to them for their daily bread.

15. What is this? Manna descended from the clouds. It came down in dew melted, and yet was itself of such a consistency as to serve for nourishing strengthening food, without any thing else: It was pleasant food; the Jews say it was palatable to all, according as their tastes were. It was wholesome food, light of digestion. By this spare and plain diet we are all taught a lesson of temperance, and forbidden to desire dainties and varieties.

16. An omer - The tenth part of an ephah: Near six pints, wine- measure.

19. Let no man leave 'till morning - But let them learn to go to bed and sleep quietly, though they had not a bit of bread in their tent, nor in all their camp, trusting God with the following day to bring them their daily bread. Never was there such a market of provisions as this, where so many hundred thousand men were daily furnished without money, and without price: never was there such an open house kept as God kept in the wilderness for 40 years together, nor such free and plentiful entertainment given. And the same wisdom, power and goodness that now brought food daily out of the clouds, doth in the constant course of nature bring food yearly out of the earth, and gives us all things richly to enjoy.

23. Here is a plain intimation of the observing a seventh day sabbath, not only before the giving of the law upon Mount Sinai, but before the bringing of Israel out of Egypt and therefore from the beginning. If the sabbath had now been first instituted, how could Moses have understood what God said to him, ver. 4, concerning a double portion to be gathered on the sixth day, without making any express mention of the sabbath? And how could the people so readily take the hint, ver. 22, even to the surprize of the rulers, before Moses had declared that it was done with regard to the sabbath, if they had not had some knowledge of the sabbath before? The setting apart of one day in seven for holy work, and in order to that for holy rest, was a divine appointment ever since God created man upon the earth.

34. An omer of this manna was laid up in a golden pot as we are told, Heb. ix, 4, and kept before the testimony, or the ark, when it was afterwards made, The preservation of this manna from waste and corruption, was a standing miracle; and therefore the more proper memorial of this miraculous food. The manna is called spiritual meat, 1 Cor. x, 3, because it was typical of spiritual blessings. Christ himself is the true manna, the bread of life, of which that was a figure, John vi, 49-51. The word of God is the manna by which our souls are nourished, Matt. iv, 4. The comforts of the Spirit are hidden manna, Rev. ii, 17. These comforts from heaven as the manna did, are the support of the divine life in the soul while we are in the wilderness of this world: it is food for Israelites, for those only that follow the pillar of cloud and fire: it is to be gathered; Christ in the word is to be applied to the soul, and the means of grace used: we must every one of us gather for ourselves. There was manna enough for all, enough for each, and none had too much; so in Christ there is a compleat sufficiency, and no superfluity. But they that did eat manna hungered again, died at last, and with many of them God was not well pleased: whereas they that feed on Christ by faith shall never hunger, and shall die no more, and with them God will be forever well pleased. The Lord evermore give us this bread!

Wesley's Notes on the Bible - The Old Testament: Genesis - Ruth
XVII

In this chapter are recorded,

I. The watering of the host of Israel. (1.) In the wilderness they wanted water, ver. 1. (2.) In their want they chide with Moses, ver. 2, 3. (3.) Moses cried to God, ver. 4. (4.) God ordered him to smite the rock, and fetch water out of it; and he did so, ver. 5, 6. (5.) The place named from it, ver. 7.

II. The defeating of the host of Amalek. (1.) The victory obtained by the prayer of Moses, ver. 8-12. (2.) By the sword of Joshua, ver. 13 (3.) A record kept of it, ver.14-16.

1. They journeyed according to the commandment of the Lord, led by the pillar of cloud and fire, and yet they came to a place where there was no water for them to drink - We may be in the way of our duty, and yet meet with troubles, which Providence brings us into for the trial of our faith.

5. Go on before the people - Though they spake of stoning him. He must take his rod with him, not to summon some plague to chastise them, but to fetch water for their supply. O the wonderful patience and forbearance of God towards provoking sinners! He maintains those that are at war with him, and reaches out the hand of his bounty to those that lift up the heel against him. If God had only shewed Moses a fountain of water in the wilderness, as he did to Hagar, not far from hence, Gen. xxi, 19, that had been a great favour; but that he might shew his power as well as his pity, and make it a miracle of mercy, he gave them water out of a rock. He directed Moses whither to go, appointed him to take of the elders of Israel with him, to be witnesses of what was done, ordered him to smite the rock, which he did, and immediately water came out of it in great abundance, which ran throughout the camp in streams and rivers, Psalm lxxviii, 15, 16, and followed them wherever they went in that wilderness: God shewed his care of his people in giving them water when they wanted it; his own power in fetching it out of a rock, and put an honour upon Moses in appointing the water to flow out upon his smiting of the rock. This fair water that came out of the rock is called honey and oil, Deut. xxxii, 13, because the people's thirst made it doubly pleasant; coming when they were in extreme want. It is probable that the people digged canals for the conveyance of it, and pools for the reception of it. Let this direct us to live in a dependance,

1. Upon God's providence even in the greatest straits and difficulties;
2. And upon Christ's grace; that rock was Christ, 1 Cor. x, 4. The graces and comforts of the Spirit are compared to rivers of living waters, John vii, 38, 39; iv, 14. These flow from Christ. And nothing will supply the needs and satisfy the desires of a soul but water out of this rock. A new name was upon this occasion given to the place, preserving the remembrance of their murmuring, Massah - Temptation, because they tempted God, Meribah - Strife, because they chide with Moses.

8. Then Amalek came and fought with Israel - The Amalekites were the posterity of Esau, who hated Jacob because of the birth- right and blessing. They did not boldly front them as a generous enemy, but without any provocation given, basely fell upon their rear, and smote them that were faint and feeble.

9. I will stand on the top of the hill with the rod of God in my land - See how God qualifies his people for, and calls them to various services for the good of his church; Joshua fights, Moses prays, and both minister to Israel. This rod Moses held up, not so much to Israel as to animate them; as to God by way of appeal to him; Is not the battle the Lord's? Is not he able to help, and engaged to help? Witness this rod! Moses was not only a standard-bearer, but an intercessor, pleading with God for success and victory.

10. Hur is supposed to have been the husband of Miriam.

11. And when Moses held vp his hand in prayer (so the Chaldee explains it) Israel prevailed, but when he let down his hand from prayer, Amalek prevailed - To convince Israel that the hand of Moses (with whom they had just now been chiding) contributed more to their safety than their own hands; the success rises and falls, as Moses lifts up or lets down his hand. The church's cause is ordinarily more or less successful, according as the church's friends are more or less fervent in prayer.

13. Though God gave the victory, yet it is said Joshua discomfited Amalek, because Joshua was a type of Christ, and of the same name, and in him it is that we are more than conquerors.

15. And Moses built an altar, and called it Jehovah-niffi - The Lord is my banner. The presence and power of Jehovah was the banner under which they were lifted, by which they were animated, and kept together, and therefore which they erected in the day of their triumph. In the name of our God we must always lift up our banners: He that doth all the work should have all the praise. Write this for a memorial - This is the first mention of writing we find in scripture; and perhaps the command was not given till after the writing of the law on tables of stone.

XVIII

This chapter is concerning Moses himself, and the affairs of his own family.

I. Jethro his father-in-law brings him his wife and children, ver. 1- 6.

II. Moses entertains his father-in-law with great respect, ver. 7. with good discourse, ver. 8-11. with a sacrifice and a feast, ver. 12.

III. Jethro adviseth him about the management of his business as a judge in Israel, to take other Judg. in to his assistance, ver. 13-23. and Moses after some time takes his counsel, ver. 24-26. They part, ver. 27.

1. Jethro to congratulate the happiness of Israel, and particularly the honour of Moses his son-in-law; comes to rejoice with them, as one that had a true respect both for them and for their God. And also to bring Moses's wife and children to him. It seems he had sent them back, probably from the inn where his wife's lothness to have her son circumcised had like to have cost him his life, chap. iv, 25.

3. The name of one was Gershom - A stranger, designing thereby not only a memorial of his own condition, but a memorandum to this son of his, for we are all strangers upon earth.

4. The name of the other was Eliezer - My God a help: it looks back to his deliverance from Pharaoh, when he made his escape after the slaying of the Egyptian; but if this were the son that was circumcised in the inn, I would rather translate it, The Lord is mine help, and will deliver me from the sword of Pharaoh, which he had reason to expect would be drawn against him, when he was going to fetch Israel out of bondage.

11. Now know I that JEHOVAH is greater than all gods - That the God of Israel is greater than all pretenders; all deities, that usurp divine honours: he silenceth them, subdues them all, and is himself the only living and true God. He is also higher than all princes and potentates, who also are called gods, and has both an incontestable authority over them, and an irresistible power to control them; he manages them all as he pleaseth, and gets honour upon them how great soever they are. Now know I: he knew it before, but now he knew it better; his faith grew up to a full assurance, upon this fresh evidence; for wherein they dealt proudly - The magicians or idols of Egypt, or Pharaoh and his grandees, opposing God, and setting up in competition with him, he was above them. The magicians were baffled, Pharaoh humbled, his powers broken, and Israel rescued out of their hands.

12. And Jethro took a burnt offering for God - And probably offered it himself, for he was a priest in Midian, and a worshipper of the true God, and the priesthood was not yet settled in Israel. And they did eat bread before God - Soberly, thankfully, in the fear of God; and their talk such as became saints. Thus we must eat and drink to the glory of God; as those that believe God's eye is upon us.

13. Moses sat to judge the people - To answer enquiries; to acquaint them with the will of God in doubtful cases, and to explain the laws of God that were already given.

15. The people came to inquire of God - And happy was it for them that they had such an oracle to consult. Moses was faithful both to him that appointed him, and to them that consulted him, and made them know the statutes of God, and his laws - His business was not to make laws, but to make known God's laws: his place was but that of a servant.

16. I judge between one and another - And if the people were as quarrelsome one with another as they were with God, he had many causes brought before him, and the more because their trials put them to no expence.

17. Not good - Not convenient either for thee or them.

19. Be thou for them to God-ward - That was an honour which it was not fit any other should share with him in. Also whatever concerned the whole congregation must pass through his hand, ver. 20. But, he appointed Judg. in the several tribes and families, which should try causes between man and man, and determine them, which would be done with less noise, and more dispatch than in the general assembly. Those whose gifts and stations are most eminent may yet be greatly furthered in their work by the assistance of those that are every way their inferiors. This is Jethro's advice; but he adds two qualifications to his counsel. (1.)That great care should be taken in the choice of the persons who should be admitted into this trust; it was requisite that they should be men of the best character.

1. For judgment and resolution, able men: men of good sense, that understood business; and bold men, that would not be daunted by frowns or clamours. Clear heads and stout hearts make good Judges.

2. For piety, such as fear God, who believe there is a God above them, whose eye is upon them, to whom they are accountable, and whose judgment they stand in awe of. Conscientious men, that dare not do an ill thing, though they could do it never so secretly and securely.

3. For honesty, men of truth, whose word one may take, and whose fidelity one may rely upon.

4. For a generous contempt of worldly wealth, hating covetousness, not only not seeking bribes, or

aiming to enrich themselves, but abhorring the thought of it. (2.) That he should attend God's direction in the case, ver. 23. If thou shalt do this thing, and God command thee so - Jethro knew that Moses had a better counsellor than he was, and to his counsel he refers him.

24. So Moses hearkened unto the voice of his father-in-law. When he came to consider the thing, he saw the reasonableness of it, and resolved to put it in practice, which he did soon after, when he had received directions from God. Those are not so wise as they would be thought to be, who think themselves too wise to be counselled; for a wise man will hear, and will increase learning, and not slight good counsel, though given by an inferior.

27. He went into his own land - It is supposed the Kenites mentioned 1 Sam. xv, 6, were the posterity of Jethro, (compare Jude i, 16,) and they are taken under special protection, for the kindness their ancestor shewed to Israel.

XIX

This chapter introduces the giving of the law upon Mount Sinai, which was one of the most sensible appearances of the divine glory that ever was in this lower world. Here are,

I. The circumstances of time and place, ver. 1, 2.

II. The covenant between God and Israel settled in general. The gracious proposal God made to them, ver. 3-6. And their consent to the proposal, ver. 7, 8.

III. Notice given three days before of God's design to give the law out of a thick cloud, ver. 9. Orders given to prepare the people to receive the law, ver. 10-13. and care taken to execute those orders, ver. 14, 15.

IV. A terrible appearance of God's glory, ver. 16-20.

V. Silence proclaimed, and strict charge given to the people to observe a decorum while God spake to them, ver. 20-25.

1. In the third month after they came out of Egypt. It is computed that the law was given just fifty days after their coming out of Egypt, in remembrance of which the feast of Pentecost was observed the fiftieth day after the passover, and in compliance with which the spirit was poured out upon the apostles, at the feast of Pentecost, fifty days after the death of Christ. Mount Sinai was a place which nature, not art, had made conspicuous, for it was the highest in all that range of mountains. Thus God put contempt upon cities and palaces, setting up his pavilion on the top of a mountain, in a barren desert. It is called Sinai, from the multitude of thorny bushes that over-spread it.

3. Thus shalt thou say to the house of Jacob, and the children of Israel - The people are called by the names both of Jacob and Israel, to mind them that they who had lately been as low as Jacob when he went to Padan-aram, were now grown as great as God made him when he came from thence, and was called Israel.

4. Ye have seen what I did unto the Egyptians, and how I bare you on Eagle's wings - An high expression of the wonderful tenderness God shewed for them. It notes great speed; God not only came upon the wing for their deliverance, but he hastened them out, as it were upon the wing. Also that he did it with great ease, with the strength as well as with the swiftness of an eagle. They that faint not, nor are weary, are said to mount up with wings as eagles, Isaiah xl, 31. Especially it notes God's particular care of them, and affection to them. Even Egypt was the nest in which these young ones were first formed as the embryo of a nation: when by the increase of their numbers they grew to some maturity, they were carried out of that nest. I brought you unto myself - They were brought not only into a state of liberty, but into covenant and communion with God. This, God aims at in all the gracious methods of his providence and grace, to bring us back to himself, from whom we have revolted, and to bring us home to himself, in whom alone we can be happy.

5. Then ye shall be a peculiar treasure to me - He doth not instance in any one particular favour, but expresseth it in that which was inclusive of all happiness, that he would be to them a God in covenant, and they should be to him a people. Nay you shall be a peculiar treasure: not that God was enriched by them, as a man is by his treasure, but he was pleased to value and esteem them as a man doth his treasure; they were precious in his sight. He took them under his special care and protection, as a treasure that is kept under lock and key. He distinguished them from, and dignified them above all people, as a people devoted to him, and to his service.

6. A kingdom of priests, a holy nation - All the Israelites, if compared with other people, were priests unto God, so near were they to him, so much employed in his immediate service, and such

intimate communion they had with him. The tendency of the laws given them was to distinguish them from others, and engage them for God as a holy nation. Thus all believers are, through Christ, made to our God kings and priests, Rev. ii, 6, a chosen generation, a royal priesthood, 1 Pet. ii, 9.

7. And Moses laid before their faces all these words - He not only explained to them what God had given him in charge, but put it to their choice, whether they would accept these promises upon these terms or no. His laying it to their faces speaks his laying it to their consciences.

8. And they answered together; all that the Lord hath spoken we will do - Thus accepting the Lord to be to them a God, and giving up themselves to be to him a people.

10. Sanctify the people - As Job before sent and sanctified his sons, Job i, 5. Sanctify them, that is, call them off from their worldly business, and call them to religious exercises, meditation and prayer, that they may receive the law from God's mouth with reverence and devotion. Two things particularly were prescribed as instances of their preparation. 1st, In token of cleansing of themselves from all sinful pollutions, they must wash their clothes. Not that God regards our clothes, but while they were washing their clothes, he would have them think of washing their souls by repentance. It becomes us to appear in clean clothes when we wait upon great men; so clean hearts are required in our attendance on the great God. 2ndly, In token of their devoting themselves entirely to religious exercises upon this occasion they must abstain even from lawful enjoyments during these three days, and not come at their wives.

11. In the sight of all the people - Though they should see no manner of similitude, yet they should see so much as would convince them, that God was among them of a truth. And so high was the top of Mount Sinai, that it is supposed not only the camp of Israel, but even the countries about might discern some extraordinary appearance of glory upon it.

12. Set bounds - Probably he drew a ditch round at the foot of the hill, which none were to pass upon pain of death. This was to intimate, 1st, That awful reverence which ought to possess the minds of all that worship God. 2ndly, The distance which worshippers were kept at under that dispensation, which we ought to take notice of, that we may the more value our privilege under the gospel, having boldness to enter into the holiest by the blood of Jesus, Heb. x, 19.

13. When the trumpet soundeth long - Then let them take their places at the foot of the mount. Never was so great a congregation called together and preached to at once as this was here. No one man's voice could have reached so many, but the voice of God did.

16. Now at length is come that memorable day, in which Israel heard the voice of the Lord God speaking to them out of the midst of the fire and lived, Deut. iv, 33. Never was there such a sermon preached before or since, as this, which was here preached to the church in the wilderness. For, the preacher was God himself, ver. 17, The Lord descended in fire; and ver. 18. The Lord came down upon Mount Sinai. The Shechinah, or glory of the Lord, appeared in the sight of all the people; he shined forth from mount Paran with ten thousand of his saints, attended with a multitude of the holy angels. Hence the law is said to be given by the disposition of angels, Acts vii, 53. He spake from Mount Sinai, hung with a thick cloud, ver. 16, covered with smoke, ver. 18, and made to quake greatly. Now it was that the earth trembled at the presence of the Lord, and the mountains skipped like rams, Psalm cxiv, 4, 7, that Sinai itself, though rough and rocky, melted from before the Lord God of Israel, Jude v, 5. The congregation was called together by the sound of a trumpet exceeding loud, ver. 16, and waxing louder and louder, ver. 19. This was done by the ministry of the angels, and made all the people tremble. The introductions to the service were thunders and lightnings, ver. 16. These have natural causes; but the scripture directs us in a particular manner to take notice of the power of God, and his terror in them. Thunder is the voice of God, and lightning the fire of God, proper to engage both the learning senses of seeing and hearing.

XX

All things being prepared for the solemn promulgation of the divine law, we have in this chapter,

I. The ten commandments as God himself spake them upon Mount Sinai, ver. 1-17.

II. The impressions made upon the people, thereby, ver. 18-21.

III. Some particular instructions which God gave to Moses, relating to his worship, ver. 22-26.

1. God spake all these words - The law of the ten commandments is a law of God's making; a law of his own speaking. God has many ways of speaking to the children of men by his spirit, conscience, providences; his voice in all which we ought carefully to attend to: but he never spake at any time upon any occasion so as he spake the ten commandments, which therefore we ought to hear with the more earnest heed. This law God had given to man before, it was written in his heart by nature; but sin had so defaced that writing, that it was necessary to revive the knowledge of it.

2. I am the Lord thy God - Herein, God asserts his own authority to enact this law; and proposeth himself as the sole object of that religious worship which is enjoined in the four first commandments. They are here bound to obedience.

1. Because God is the Lord, Jehovah, self-existent, independent, eternal, and the fountain of all being and power; therefore he has an incontestable right to command us.

2. He was their God; a God in covenant with them; their God by their own consent.

3. He had brought them out of the land of Egypt - Therefore they were bound in gratitude to obey him, because he had brought them out of a grievous slavery into a glorious liberty. By redeeming them, he acquired a farther right to rule them; they owed their service to him, to whom they owed their freedom. And thus, Christ, having rescued us out of the bondage of sin, is entitled to the best service we can do him. The four first commandments, concern our duty to God (commonly called the first-table.) It was fit those should be put first, because man had a Maker to love before he had a neighbour to love, and justice and charity are then only acceptable to God when they flow from the principles of piety.

3. The first commandment is concerning the object of our worship, Jehovah, and him only, Thou shalt have no other gods before me - The Egyptians, and other neighbouring nations, had many gods, creatures of their own fancy. This law was pre-fixed because of that transgression; and Jehovah being the God of Israel, they must entirely cleave to him, and no other, either of their own invention, or borrowed from their neighbours. The sin against this commandment, which we are most in danger of, is giving that glory to any creature which is due to God only. Pride makes a God of ourselves, covetousness makes a God of money, sensuality makes a God of the belly. Whatever is loved, feared, delighted in, or depended on, more than God, that we make a God of. This prohibition includes a precept which is the foundation of the whole law, that we take the Lord for our God, accept him for ours, adore him with humble reverence, and set our affections entirely upon him. There is a reason intimated in the last words before me. It intimates,

1. That we cannot have any other God but he will know it.

2. That it is a sin that dares him to his face, which he cannot, will not, overlook. The second commandment is concerning the ordinances of worship, or the way in which God will be worshipped, which it is fit himself should appoint. Here is,

1. The prohibition; we are forbidden to worship even the true God by images, ver. 4, 5. First, The Jews (at least after the captivity) thought themselves forbidden by this to make any image or picture whatsoever. It is certain it forbids making any image of God, for to whom can we liken him? Isaiah xl, 18, 25. It also forbids us to make images of God in our fancies, as if he were a man as we are. Our religious worship must be governed by the power of faith, not by the power of imagination. Secondly, They must not bow down to them - Shew any sign of honour to them, much less serve them by sacrifice, or any other act of religious worship. When they paid their devotion to the true God, they must not have any image before them for the directing, exciting, or assisting their devotion. Though the worship was designed to terminate in God, it would not please him if it came to him through an image. The best and most ancient lawgivers among the Heathen forbad the setting up of images in their temples. It was forbidden in Rome by Numa a Pagan prince, yet commanded in Rome by the Pope, a Christian bishop. The use of images in the church of Rome, at this day, is so plainly contrary to the letter of this command, that in all their catechisms, which they put into the hand of the people, they leave out this commandment, joining the reason of it to the first, and so the third commandment they call the second, the fourth the third, &c. only to make up the number ten, they divide the tenth into two. For I the Lord Jehovah, thy God, am a jealous God, especially in things of this nature. It intimates the care he has of his own institutions, his displeasure against idolaters, and that he resents every thing in his worship that looks like, or leads to, idolatry: visiting the iniquity of the fathers upon the children unto the third and fourth generation - Severely punishing. Nor is it an unrighteous thing with God if the parents died in their iniquity, and the children tread in their steps, when God comes, by his judgments, to reckon with them, to bring into the account the idolatries their fathers were guilty of. Keeping mercy for thousands of persons, thousands of generations, of them that love me and keep my commandments - This intimates, that the second commandment, though in the letter of it is only a prohibition of false worship, yet includes a precept of worshipping God in all those ordinances which he hath instituted. As the first commandment requires the inward worship of love, desire, joy, hope, so this the outward worship of prayer and praise, and solemn attendance on his word. This mercy shall extend to thousands, much further than the wrath threatened to those that hate him, for that reaches but to the third or fourth generation.

7. The third commandment is concerning the manner of our worship; Where we have,

1. A strict prohibition. Thou shalt not take the name of the Lord thy God in vain - Supposing that, having taken Jehovah for their God, they would make mention of his name, this command gives a caution not to mention it in vain, and it is still as needful as ever. We take God's name in vain, First, By hypocrisy, making profession of God's name, but not living up to that profession. Secondly, By covenant breaking. If we make promises to God, and perform not to the Lord our vows, we take his

name in vain. Thirdly, By rash swearing, mentioning the name of God, or any of his attributes, in the form of an oath, without any just occasion for it, but to no purpose, or to no good purpose. Fourthly, By false- swearing, which some think is chiefly intended in the letter of the commandment. Fifthly, By using the name of God lightly and carelessly. The profanation of the form of devotion is forbidden, as well as the profanation of the forms of swearing; as also, the profanation of any of those things whereby God makes himself known. For the Lord will not hold him guiltless - Magistrates that punish other offenses, may not think themselves concerned to take notice of this; but God, who is jealous for his honour, will not connive at it. The sinner may perhaps hold himself guiltless, and think there is no harm in it; to obviate which suggestion, the threatening is thus expressed, God will not hold him guiltless - But more is implied, That God will himself be the avenger of those that take his name in vain; and they will find it a fearful thing to fall into the hands of the living God.

8. The fourth commandment concerns the time of worship; God is to be served and honoured daily; but one day in seven is to be particularly dedicated to his honour, and spent in his service. Remember the sabbath day, to keep it holy; in it thou shalt do no manner of work - It is taken for granted that the sabbath was instituted before. We read of God's blessing and sanctifying a seventh day from the beginning, Gen. ii, 3, so that this was not the enacting of a new law, but the reviving of an old law. 1st. They are told what is the day, they must observe, a seventh after six days labour, whether this was the seventh by computation from the first seventh, or from the day of their coming out of Egypt, or both, is not certain. A late pious Writer seems to prove, That the sabbath was changed, when Israel came out of Egypt; which change continued till our Lord rose again: But that then the Original Sabbath was restored. And he makes it highly probable, at least, That the sabbath we observe, is the seventh day from the creation. 2ndly, How it must be observed;

1. As a day of rest; they were to do no manner of work on this day, in their worldly business.

2. As a holy day, set apart to the honour of the holy God, and to be spent in holy exercises. God, by his blessing it, had made it holy; they, by solemn blessing him, must keep it holy, and not alienate it to any other purpose than that for which the difference between it and other days was instituted. 3rdly, Who must observe it? Thou and thy son and thy daughter - The wife is not mentioned, because she is supposed to be one with the husband, and present with him, and if he sanctify the sabbath, it is taken for granted she will join with him; but the rest of the family is instanced in it, children and servants must keep it according to their age and capacity. In this, as in other instances of religion, it is expected that masters of families should take care, not only to serve the Lord themselves, but that their houses also should serve him. Even the proselyted strangers must observe a difference between this day and other days, which, if it laid some restraint upon them then, yet proved a happy indication of God's gracious design, to bring the Gentiles into the church. By the sanctification of the sabbath, the Jews declared that they worshipped the God that made the world, and so distinguished themselves from all other nations, who worshipped gods which they themselves made. God has given us an example of rest after six days work; he rested the seventh day - Took a complacency in himself, and rejoiced in the work of his hand, to teach us on that day, to take a complacency in him, and to give him the glory of his works. The sabbath begun in the finishing of the work of creation; so will the everlasting sabbath in the finishing of the work of providence and redemption; and we observe the weekly sabbath in expectation of that, as well as in remembrance of the former, in both conforming ourselves to him we worship. He hath himself blessed the sabbath day and sanctified it. He hath put an honour upon it; it is holy to the Lord, and honourable; and he hath put blessings into it which he hath encouraged us to expect from him in the religious observation of that day. Let us not profane, dishonour, and level that with common time, which God's blessing hath thus dignified and distinguished.

12. We have here the laws of the second table, as they are commonly called; the six last commandments which concern our duty to ourselves, and one another, and are a comment upon the second great commandment, Thou shalt love thy neighbour as thyself. As religion towards God is, an essential branch of universal righteousness, so righteousness towards men is an essential branch of true religion: godliness and honesty must go together. The fifth commandment is concerning the duties we owe to our relations; that of children to their parents is only instanced in, honour thy father and thy mother, which includes,

1. an inward esteem of them, outwardly expressed upon all occasions in our carriage towards them; fear them, Lev. xix, 3, give them reverence, Heb. xii, 9. The contrary to this is mocking at them or despising them,

2. Obedience to their lawful commands; so it is expounded, Eph. vi, 1-3. Children obey your parents; come when they call you, go where they send you, do what they bid you, do not what they forbid you; and this cheerfully, and from a principle of love. Though you have said you will not, yet afterwards repent and obey.

3. Submission to their rebukes, instructions and corrections, not only to the good and gentle, but also to the froward.

4. Disposing of themselves with the advice, direction and consent of parents, not alienating their

property, but with their approbation.

5. endeavouring in every thing to be the comfort of their parents, and to make their old age easy to them; maintaining them if they stand in need of support. That thy days may be long in the land which the Lord thy God giveth thee - This promise, (which is often literally fulfilled) is expounded in a more general sense Eph. vi, 3. That it may be well with thee, and thou mayst live long on the earth - Those that in conscience towards God keep this and other of God's commandments, may be sure it shall be well with them, and they shall live as long on the earth as infinite wisdom sees good for, them, and what they may seem to be cut short of on earth, shall be abundantly made up in eternal life, the heavenly Canaan which God will give them.

13. Thou shalt not kill - Thou shalt not do any thing hurtful to the health, or life of thy own body, or any other's. This doth not forbid our own necessary defense, or the magistrates putting offenders to death; but it forbids all malice and hatred to any, for he that hateth his brother is a murderer, and all revenge arising therefrom; likewise anger and hurt said or done, or aimed to be done in a passion; of this our saviour expounds this commandment, Matt. v, 22.

14. Thou shalt not commit adultery - This commandment forbids all acts of uncleanness, with all those desires, which produce those acts and war against the soul.

15. Thou shalt not steal - This command forbids us to rob ourselves of what we have, by sinful spending, or of the use and comfort of it by sinful sparing; and to rob others by invading our neighbour's rights, taking his goods, or house, or field, forcibly or clandestinely, over-reaching in bargains, not restoring what is borrowed or found, with-holding just debts, rents or wages; and, which is worst of all, to rob the public in the coin or revenue, or that which is dedicated to the service of religion.

16. Thou shalt not bear false witness - This forbids,

1. Speaking falsely in any matter, lying, equivocating, and any way devising and designing to deceive our neighbour.

2. Speaking unjustly against our neighbour, to the prejudice of his reputation; And

3. (which is the highest offense of both these kinds put together) Bearing false witness against him, laying to his charge things that he knows not, either upon oath, by which the third commandment, the sixth or eighth, as well as this, are broken, or in common converse, slandering, backbiting, tale-bearing, aggravating what is done amiss, and any way endeavouring to raise our own reputation upon the ruin of our neighbour's.

17. Thou shalt not covet - The foregoing commands implicitly forbid all desire of doing that which will be an injury to our neighbour, this forbids all inordinate desire of having that which will be a gratification to ourselves. O that such a man's house were mine! such a man's wife mine! such a man's estate mine! This is certainly the language of discontent at our own lot, and envy at our neighbour's, and these are the sins principally forbidden here. God give us all to see our face in the glass of this law, and to lay our hearts under the government of it!

18. They removed and stood afar off - Before God began to speak, they were thrusting forward to gaze, but now they were effectually cured of their presumption, and taught to keep their distance.

19. Speak thou with us - Hereby they obliged themselves to acquiesce in the mediation of Moses, they themselves nominating him as a fit person to deal between them and God, and promising to hearken to him as to God's messenger.

20. Fear not - That is, Think not that this thunder and fire is, designed to consume you. No; it was intended, (1.) To prove them, to try how they could like dealing with God immediately, without a mediator, and so to convince them how admirably well God had chosen for them in putting Moses into that office. Ever since Adam fled upon hearing God's voice in the garden, sinful man could not bear either to speak to God, or hear from him immediately. (2.) To keep them to their duty, and prevent their sinning against God. We must not fear with amazement; but we must always have in our minds a reverence of God's majesty, a dread of his displeasure, and an obedient regard to his sovereign authority.

21. While the people continued to stand afar off - Afraid of God's wrath, Moses drew near unto the thick darkness; he was made to draw near, so the word is: Moses of himself durst not have ventured into the thick darkness if God had not called him, and encouraged him, and, as some of the Rabbins suppose, sent an angel to take him by the hand, and lead him up.

22. Moses being gone into the thick darkness where God was, God there spoke in his hearing only, all that follows from hence to the end of chap.

23, which is mostly an exposition of the ten commandments; and he was to transmit it to the people. The laws in these verses relate to God's worship. Ye have seen that I have talked with you from heaven - Such was his wonderful condescension; ye shall not make gods of silver - This repetition of the second commandment comes in here, because they were more addicted to idolatry than to any other sin.

24. An altar of earth - It is meant of occasional altars, such as they reared in the wilderness before the tabernacle was erected, and afterwards upon special emergencies, for present use. They are appointed to make these very plain, either of earth or of unhewn stones. That they might not be tempted

to think of a graven image, they must not so much as hew the stones into shape, that they made their altars of, but pile them up as they were in the rough. In all places where I record my name - Or where my name is recorded, that is, where I am worshipped in sincerity, I will come unto thee, and will bless thee.

26. Neither shall thou go at by steps unto mine altar - Indeed afterwards God appointed an altar ten cubits high. But it is probable, they went not up to that by steps, but by a sloping ascent.

XXI

The laws recorded in this chapter relate to the fifth and sixth commandments; and though not accommodated to our constitution, especially in point of servitude yet are of great use for the explanation of the moral law, and the rules of natural justice.

I. Here are several enlargements upon the fifth commandment, which concerns particular relations. (1.) The duty of masters towards their servants, their men servants ver. 2-6. and maid-servants, ver. 7-11. (2.) The punishment of disobedient children that strike their parents, ver. 15. or curse them, ver. 17.

II. Upon the sixth commandment, which forbids all violence offered to the person of man. Here is, (1.) Concerning murder, ver. 12-14. (2.) Man-stealing, ver, 16. (3.) Assault and battery, ver. 18, 19. (4.) Correcting a servant, ver. 20, 21 (5.) Hurting a woman with child, ver. 22, 23. (6.) The law of retaliation, ver. 24, 25. (7.) Maiming a servant, ver. 26, 27. (8.) An ox goring, ver. 26-32. (9.) Damage by opening a pit, ver. 33, 34. (10.) Cattle fighting, ver 35, 36.

1. The first verse is the general title of the laws contained in this and the two following chapters. Their government being purely a theocracy; that which in other states is to be settled by human prudence, was directed among them by a divine appointment. These laws are called judgments; because their magistrates were to give judgment according to them. In the doubtful cases that had hitherto occurred, Moses had particularly inquired of God, but now God gave him statutes in general, by which to determine particular cases. He begins with the laws concerning servants, commanding mercy and moderation towards them. The Israelites had lately been servants themselves, and now they were become not only their own matters, but masters of servants too; lest they should abuse their servants as they themselves had been abused, provision was made for the mild and gentle usage of servants.

2. If thou buy an Hebrew servant - Either sold by him or his parents through poverty, or by the Judges for his crimes, yet even such a one was to continue in slavery but seven years at the most.

6. For ever - As long as he lives, or till the year of Jubilee.

8. Who hath betrothed her to himself - For a concubine, or secondary Wife. Not that Masters always took Maid-servants on these terms.

9. After the manner of daughters - He shall give her a portion, as to a daughter.

20. Direction is given what should be done, if a servant died by his master's correction. This servant must not be an Israelite, but a Gentile slave, as the Negroes to our planters; and it is supposed that he smite him with a rod, and not with any thing that was likely to give a mortal wound, yet if he died under his hand, he should be punished for his cruelty, at the discretion of the Judges, upon consideration of circumstances.

24. Eye for eye - The execution of this law is not put into the hands of private persons, as if every man might avenge himself, which would introduce universal confusion. The tradition of the elders seems to have put this corrupt gloss upon it. But magistrates had an eye to this rule in punishing offenders, and doing right to those that are injured.

XXII

The laws of this chapter relate,

I. To the eighth commandment, concerning theft, ver. 1-4 Trespass by cattle, ver. 5. Damage by fire, ver. 6. Trusts, ver. 7- 13. Borrowing cattle, ver. 14, 15. Or money, ver. 25-27.

II. To the seventh commandment. Against fornication, ver. 16, 17. Bestiality, ver. 19.

III. To the first table. Forbidding witchcraft, ver. 18. Idolatry, ver. 20. Commanding to offer the first-fruits, ver. 29. 30.

IV. To the poor, ver. 21-24.

V. To the civil government, ver. 28.

VI. To the Jewish nation, ver. 13.

1. Five oxen for an ox, and four sheep for a sheep - More for an ox than for a sheep, because the owner, besides all the other profit, lost the daily labour of his ox. If we were not able to make restitution, he must be sold for a slave: the court of judgment was to do it, and it is likely the person robbed received the money. Thus with us in some cases, felons are transported to the Plantations, where only, Englishmen know what slavery is. But let it be observed, the sentence is not slavery, but banishment: nor can any Englishman be sold, unless he first indent himself to the captain that carries him over. 2. If a thief broke a house in the night, and was killed in the doing it, his blood was upon his own head. But if it were in the day-time that the thief was killed, he that killed him was accountable for it, unless it were in the necessary defense of his own life.

3. For he should make full restitution - This law determined: not that he should die.

4. In his hand alive - Not killed, nor sold, as ver. 1, so that the owner recover it with less charge and trouble.

5. He that wilfully put his cattle into his neighbour's field, must make restitution of the best of his own. The Jews hence observed it as a general rule, that restitution must always be made of the best; and that no man should keep any cattle that were likely to trespass upon his neighbour, or do him any damage.

6. He that designed only the burning of thorns might become accessary to the burning of corn, and should not be held guiltless. If the fire did mischief, he that kindled it must answer for it, though it could not be proved that he designed the mischief. Men must suffer for their carelessness, as well as for their malice. It will make us very careful of ourselves, if we consider that we are accountable not only for the hurt we do, but for the hurt we occasion through inadvertency.

7. If a man deliver goods, suppose to a carrier to be conveyed, or to a warehouse-keeper to be preserved, or cattle to a farmer to be fed upon a valuable consideration, and a special confidence reposed in the person they are lodged with; in case these goods be stolen or lost, perish or be damaged, if it appear that it was not by any fault of the trustee, the owner must stand to the loss, otherwise he that has been false to his trust must be compelled to make satisfaction.

14. If a man (suppose) lent his team to his neighbour, if the owner were with it, or were to receive profit for the loan of it, whatever harm befel the cattle the owner must stand to the loss of it: but if the owner were so kind to lend it him gratis, and put such a confidence in him as to trust it from under his own eye, then, if any harm happened, the borrower must make it good. Learn hence to be very careful not to abuse any thing that is lent to us; it is not only unjust but base and disingenuous, we should much rather chuse to lose ourselves, than that any should sustain loss by their kindness to us.

17. If the father refused, he shall pay money - This shews how ill a thing it is, and by no means to be allowed, that children should marry without their parents consent: even here where the divine law appointed the marriage, both as a punishment to him that had done wrong, and a recompence to her that had suffered wrong, yet there was an express reservation for the father's power; if he denied his consent, it must be no marriage.

18. Witchcraft not only gives that honour to the devil which is due to God alone, but bids defiance to the divine providence, wages war with God's government, puts his work into the devil's hand expecting him to do good and evil. By our law, consulting, covenanting with, invocating or employing any evil spirit to any intent whatever, and exercising any enchantment, charm, or sorcery, whereby hurt shall be done to any person, is made felony, without benefit of clergy; also pretending to tell where goods lost or stolen may be found, is an iniquity punishable by the judge, and the second offense with death. This was the case in former times. But we are wiser than our fore-fathers. We believe, no witch

ever did live! At least, not for these thousand years.

21. A stranger must not be abused, not wronged in judgment by the magistrates, not imposed upon in contracts, nor any advantage taken of his ignorance or necessity, no, nor must he be taunted, or upbraided with his being a stranger; for all these were vexations. For ye were strangers in Egypt - And knew what it was to be vexed and oppressed there. Those that have themselves been in poverty and distress, if Providence enrich and enlarge them, ought to shew a particular tenderness towards those that are now in such circumstances as they were in formerly, now doing to them as they then wished to be done by.

22. Ye shall not afflict the widow or fatherless child - That is, ye shall comfort and assist them, and be ready upon all occasions to shew them kindness. In making just demands from them, their condition must be considered who have lost those that should protect them: they are supposed to be unversed in business, destitute of advice, timorous, and of a tender spirit; and therefore must be treated with kindness and compassion, and no advantage taken against them, nor any hardship put upon them, which a husband or a father would have sheltered them from.

25. If thou lend - (1.) They must not receive use for money from any that borrowed for necessity. And such provision the law made for the preserving estates to their families by the year of Jubilee, that a people who had little concern in trade could not be supposed to borrow money but for necessity; therefore it was generally forbidden among themselves; but to a stranger they were allowed to lend upon usury. This law therefore in the strictness of it seems to have been peculiar to the Jewish state; but in the equity of it, it obligeth us to shew mercy to those we have advantage against, and to be content to share with those we lend to in loss as well as profit, if Providence cross them: and upon this condition it seems as lawful to receive interest for my money, which another takes pains with, and improves, as it is to receive rent for my land, which another takes pains with, and improves, for his own use. (2.) They must not take a poor man's bed-clothes in pawn; but if they did, must restore them by bed-time.

28. Thou shalt not revile the gods - That is, the Judges and magistrates. Princes and magistrates are our fathers, whom the fifth commandment obligeth us to honour, and forbids us to revile. St. Paul applies this law to himself, and owns that he ought not to speak evil of the ruler of his people, no, not though he was then his most unrighteous persecutor, Acts xxiii, 5.

29. The first-born of thy sons shalt thou give unto me - And much more reason have we to give ourselves and all we have to God, who spared not his own Son, but delivered him up for us all. The first ripe of their corn they must not delay to offer; there is danger if we delay our duty, lest we wholly omit it; and by slipping the first opportunity in expectation of another, we suffer Satan to cheat us of all our time.

31. Ye shall be holy unto me - And one mark of that honourable distinction is appointed in their diet, which was, that they should not eat any flesh that was torn of beasts - Both because the blood was not duly taken out of it, and because the clean beast was ceremonially defiled, by the touch of the unclean.

XXIII

This chapter concludes the acts that passed in the first session (if I may so call it) upon Mount Sinai. Here are,

I. Some laws of universal obligation, relating especially to the ninth commandment, against bearing false witness, ver. 1. and giving false judgement, ver. 2, 3, 6, 7, 8. Also a law of doing good to our enemies, ver. 4, 5. and not oppressing strangers, ver. 9.

II. Some laws peculiar to the Jews: the sabbatical years, ver. 10, 11. the three annual feasts, ver. 14-17. with laws pertaining thereto.

III. Gracious promises of completing the mercy God had begun for them, upon condition of their obedience, that God would conduct them through the wilderness, ver 20-24. that he would prosper all they had, ver. 25, 26, that he would put them in possession of Canaan, ver. 27-31. But they must not mingle themselves with the nations, ver. 32, 33.

1. Thou shalt not raise, the margin reads, Thou shalt not receive a false report, for sometimes the receiver in this case is as bad as the thief; and a backbiting tongue would not do so much mischief, if it were not countenanced. Sometimes we cannot avoid hearing a false report, but we must not receive it, we must not hear it with pleasure, nor easily give credit to it.

2. Thou shalt not follow a multitude to do evil - General usage will never excuse us in any ill practice; nor is the broad way ever the safer for its being crowded. We must inquire what we ought to do, not what the most do; because we must be judged by our master, not our fellow servants; and it is

too great a compliment, to be willing to go to hell for company.

7. Keep thee far from a false matter - From assisting or abetting an ill thing. Yea, keep thee far from it, dread it as a dangerous snare. I will not justify the wicked - That is, I will condemn him that unjustly condemns others.

9. Thou shalt not oppress the stranger - Though aliens might not inherit lands among them; yet they must have justice done them. It was an instance of the equity of our law, that if an alien be tried for any crime except treason, the one half of his jury, if he desire it, shall be foreigners; a kind provision that strangers may not be oppressed. For ye know the heart of a stranger - You know something of the griefs and fears of a stranger by sad experience.

10. The institution of the sabbatical year was designed,

1. To shew what a plentiful land that was, into which God was bringing them, that so numerous a people could have rich maintenance out of the products of so small a country, without foreign trade, and yet could spare the increase of every seventh year.

2. To teach them a confidence in the Divine Providence, while they did their duty, That as the sixth day's manna served for two days meat, so the sixth year's increase should serve for two years subsistence.

13. In all things that I have said unto you be circumspect - We are in danger of missing our way on the right hand and on the left, and it is at our peril if we do, therefore we have need to look about us. A man may ruin himself through mere carelessness, but he cannot save himself without great care and circumspection; particularly since idolatry was a sin they were much addicted to, and would be greatly tempted to, they must endeavour to blot out the remembrance of the gods of the heathen, and must disuse all their superstitious forms of speech, and never mention them but with detestation. In Christian schools and academies (for it is in vain to think of re-forming the play-houses) it were to be wished that the names and stories of the heathen deities or demons rather were not so commonly and familiarly used.

14. The Passover, Pentecost, and feast of Tabernacles, in spring, summer, and autumn, were the three times appointed for their attendance; not in winter, because travelling was then uncomfortable; nor in the midst of their harvest.

17. All thy males - All that were of competent years, and health and strength, and at their own disposal. 'Tis probable, servants were exempt: for none was to appear without an offering: but most of these had nothing to offer.

19. Some of the Gentiles, at the end of their harvest, seethed a kid in it's dam's milk, and sprinkled that milk-pottage in a magical way upon their gardens and fields, to make them fruitful. But Israel must abhor such foolish customs. Is not this rather forbidden, as having some appearance of cruelty?

20. Behold, I send an angel before thee - The angel of the covenant: Accordingly the Israelites in the wilderness are said to tempt Christ. It is promised that this blessed anger should keep them in the way, though it lay through a wilderness first, and afterwards through their enemies country; and thus Christ has prepared a place for his followers.

21. Beware of him, and obey his voice; provoke him not - It is at your peril if you do; for my name - My nature, my authority is in him.

25. He shall bless thy bread and thy water - And God's blessing will make bread and water more refreshing and nourishing, than a feast of fat things, and wines on the lees, without that blessing. And I will take sickness away - Either prevent it or remove it. Thy land shall not be visited with epidemical diseases, which are very dreadful, and sometimes have laid countries waste.

26. The number of thy days I will fulfill - And they shall not be cut off in the midst by untimely deaths. Thus hath godliness the promise of the life that now is.

27. I will send my fear before thee - And they that fear will soon flee. Hoseats of hornets also made way for the hosts of Israel; such mean creatures can God make use of for the chastising of his people's enemies.

XXIV

Moses as mediator between God and Israel, having received divers laws and ordinances from God in the foregoing chapters, in this chapter,

I. Comes down to the people, acquaints them with the laws he had received, and takes their consent to those laws, ver. 3. writes the laws, and reads them to the people, who repeat their consent, ver. 4, 7. and then by sacrifice, and the sprinkling of blood ratifies the covenant between them and God, ver. 5, 6, 8.

II. He returns to God again, to receive farther directions. When he was dismissed from his former attendance, he was ordered to attend again, ver. 1, 2. He did so with seventy of the elders, to whom God made a discovery of his glory, ver. 9-11. Moses is ordered up into the mount, ver. 12, 13. the rest are ordered down to the people, ver. 14. The cloud of glory is seen by all the people on the top of Mount Sinai, ver. 15-17. and Moses is there with God forty days and forty nights, ver. 18.

1. Worship ye afar off - Before they came near, they must worship. Thus we must enter into God's gates with humble and solemn adorations.

2. And Moses alone shall come near - Being therein a type of Christ, who as the high priest entered alone into the most holy place. In the following verses we have the solemn covenant made between God and Israel and the exchanging of the ratifications: typifying the covenant of grace between God and believers through Christ.

3. Moses told the people all the words of the Lord - He laid before them all the precepts, in the foregoing chapters, and put it to them, whether they were willing to submit to these laws or no? And all the people answered, All the words which the Lord hath said we will do - They had before consented in general to be under God's government; here they consent in particular to these laws now given.

4. And Moses wrote the words of the Lord - That there might be no mistake; as God dictated them on the mount, where, it is highly probable, God taught him the use of letters. These Moses taught the Israelites, from whom they afterwards travelled to Greece and other nations. As soon as God had separated to himself a peculiar people, he governed them by a written word, as he has done ever since, and will do while the world stands. Pillars according to the number of the tribes - These were to represent the people, the other party to the covenant; and we may suppose they were set up over against the altar, and that Moses as mediator passed to and fro between them. Probably each tribe set up and knew its own pillar, and their elders stood by it. He then appointed sacrifices to be offered upon the altar.

6.

1. The blood of the sacrifice which the people offered was (part of it) sprinkled upon the altar, which signified the people's dedicating themselves to God, and his honour. In the blood of the sacrifices, all the Israelites were presented unto God as living sacrifices, Rom. xii, 1.

2. The blood of the sacrifice which God had owned and accepted was (the remainder of it) sprinkled, either upon the people themselves, or upon the pillars that represented them, which signified God's conferring his favour upon them, and all the fruits of that favour, and his giving them all the gifts they could desire from a God reconciled to them, and in covenant with them. This part of the ceremony was thus explained, Behold the blood of the covenant; see here how God sealed to you to be a God, and you seal to be to him a people; his promises to you, and yours to him, are yea and amen. Thus our Lord Jesus, the Mediator of the new covenant (of whom Moses was a type) having offered up himself a sacrifice upon the cross, that his blood might be indeed the blood of the covenant, sprinkled it upon the altar in his intercession (Heb. ix, 12,) and sprinkles it upon his church by his word and ordinances, and the influences and operations of the Spirit of promise by whom we are sealed.

10. They saw the God of Israel - That is, they had some glimpse of his glory, in light and fire, though they saw no manner of similitude. They saw the place where the God of Israel stood, so the seventy, something that came near a similitude, but was not; whatever they saw it was certainly something of which no image or picture could be made, and yet enough to satisfy them that God was with them of a truth. Nothing is described but that which was under his feet, for our conceptions of God are all below him. They saw not so much as God's feet, but at the bottom of the brightness they saw (such as they never saw before or after, and as the foot- stool or pedestal of it) a most rich and splendid pavement, as it had been of sapphires, azure, or sky-coloured. The heavens themselves are the pavement of God's palace, and his throne is above the firmament.

11. Upon the nobles or elders of Israel he laid not his hand - Though they were men, the splendour of his glory did not overwhelm them, but it was so moderated (Job xxxvi, 9,) and they were so strengthened (Dan. x, 19,) that they were able to bear it: nay, though they were sinful men, and obnoxious to God's justice, yet he did not lay his avenging hand upon them, as they feared he would. When we consider what a consuming fire God is, and what stubble we are before him, we shall have

reason to say, in all our approaches to him, It is of the Lord's mercies we are not consumed. They saw God, and did eat and drink; They had not only their lives preserved, but their vigour, courage, and comfort; it cast no damp upon their joy, but rather increased it. They feasted upon the sacrifice before God, in token of their chearful consent to the covenant, their grateful acceptance of the benefits of it, and their communion with God in pursuance of that covenant.

12. Come up to the mount and be there - Expect to continue there for some time.

13. Joshua was his minister or servant, and it would be a satisfaction to him to have him with him as a companion during the six days that he tarried in the mount before God called to him. Joshua was to be his successor, and therefore thus he was honoured before the people, and thus he was prepared by being trained up in communion with God. Joshua was a type of Christ, and (as the learned Bishop Peirson well observes Moses takes him with him into the mount, because without Jesus, in whom are hid all the treasures of wisdom and knowledge, there is no looking into the secrets of heaven, nor approaching the presence of God.

16. A cloud covered the mount six days - A visible token of God's special presence there, for he so shews himself to us, as at the same time to conceal himself from us, he lets us know so much as to assure us of his power and grace, but intimates to us that we cannot find him out to perfection. During these six days Moses staid waiting upon the mountain, for a call into the presence- chamber. And on the seventh day - Probably the sabbath-day, he called unto Moses. Now the thick cloud opened in the sight of all Israel, and the glory of the Lord broke forth like devouring fire.

18. Moses went into the midst of the cloud - It was an extraordinary presence of mind, which the grace of God furnished him with, else he durst not have ventured into the cloud, especially when it broke out in devouring fire. And Moses was in the mount forty days and forty nights - It should seem the six days, were not part of the forty; for during those six days, Joshua was with Moses, who did eat of the manna, and drink of the brook mentioned, Deut. ix, 21, and while they were together, it is probable Moses did eat and drink with him; but when Moses was called into the midst of the cloud, he left Joshua without, who continued to eat and drink daily while he waited for Moses's return, but from thenceforward Moses fasted.

XXV

At this chapter begins an account of the instructions God gave Moses for erecting and furnishing the tabernacle. Here are,

I. Orders given for a collection to be made among the people, ver. 1-9.

II. Particular instructions,
    1. Concerning the ark of the covenant, ver. 10-22.
    2. The table of shew-bread, ver. 23-30.
    3. The golden candlestick, ver. 31-40.

1. Doubtless when Moses went into the midst of the cloud, and abode there so long, he saw and heard glorious things, but they were things which were not lawful or possible to utter; and therefore, in the records he kept of the transactions there, he saith nothing to satisfy curiosity, but writes that only which he was to speak to the children of Israel. Probably there never was any house or temple built for sacred uses, before this tabernacle was erected by Moses. In this God kept his court, as Israel's king, and it was intended for a sign or token of his presence, that while they had that in the midst of them they might never again ask, Is the Lord among us or not? And because in the wilderness they dwelt in tents, even this royal palace was ordered to be a tabernacle too, that it might move with them. And these holy places made with hands were the figures of the true, Heb. ix, 24. The gospel-church is the true tabernacle which the Lord pitched, and not man, Heb. viii, 2. The body of Christ, in and by which he made atonement, was the greater and more perfect tabernacle, Heb. ix, 11. The Word was made flesh, and dwelt among us, as in a tabernacle.

2. Speak unto the children of Israel that they bring me an offering - This offering was to be given willingly, and with the heart. It was not prescribed to them what or how much they must give, but it was left to their generosity, that they might shew their goodwill to the house of God, and the offices thereof.

4. Blue, and purple, and scarlet - Materials of those colours.

5. Shittim-wood - A kind of wood growing in Egypt and the deserts of Arabia, very durable and precious.

8. A sanctuary - A place of public and solemn worship; that I may dwell among them. Not by my essence, which is everywhere; but by my grace and glorious operations.

9. According to all that I shew thee - God shewed him an exact plan of it in little, which he must conform to in all points. And God did not only shew him the model, but gave him also particular

directions how to frame the tabernacle, according to that model, in all the parts of it. When Moses was to describe the creation of the world, tho' it be such a stately and curious fabrick, yet he gave a very short and general account of it; but when he comes to describe the tabernacle, he doth it with the greatest niceness and accuracy imaginable: for God's church and instituted religion is more precious to him than all the rest of the world. And the scriptures were written not to describe to us the works of nature, (a general view of which is sufficient to lead us to the knowledge of the Creator,) but to acquaint us with the methods of grace, and those things which are purely matters of Revelation.

10. The ark was a chest or coffer, in which the two tables of the law, written with the finger of God, were to be deposited. If the Jewish cubit was, as some learned men compute three inches longer than our half-yard, (twenty one inches in all) this chest or cabinet was about fifty-two inches long, thirty-one broad and thirty one deep; it was overlaid within and without with thin plates of gold; it had a crown, or cornish of gold round it; rings and staves to carry it with; and in it he must put the testimony. The tables of the law are called the testimony, because God did in them testify his will; his giving them that law was in token of his favour to them, and their acceptance of it was in token of their subjection to him. This law was a testimony to them to direct them in their duty, and would be a testimony against them if they transgressed. The ark is called the ark of the testimony, chap. xxx, 6, and the tabernacle, the tabernacle of the testimony, Num. x, 11. The tables of the law were carefully preserved in the ark, to teach us to make much of the word of God, and to hide it in our inmost thoughts, as the ark was placed in the holy of holies. It intimates likewise the care which divine providence ever did, and ever will take to preserve the records of divine Rev. in the church, so that even in the latter days there shall be seen in his temple the ark of his testament. See Rev. xi, 19.

17. The mercy-seat was the covering of the ark, made exactly to fit the dimensions of it. This propitiatory covering, as it might well be translated, was a type of Christ the great propitiation, whose satisfaction covers our transgressions, and comes between us and the curse we deserve.

18. The cherubim (Cherubim is the plural of Cherub, not Cherubims) were fixed to the mercy-seat, and of a piece with it, and spread their wings over it. It is supposed these were designed to represent the holy angels, (who always attend the Shechinah, or divine majesty,) not by any effigies of an angel, but some emblem of the angelical nature, probably one or more of those four faces spoken of Ezek. i, 10. Whatever the faces were, they looked one towards another, and both downwards towards the ark, while their wings were stretched out so as to touch one another. It notes their attendance upon the Redeemer, their readiness to do his will, their presence in the assemblies of saints, Psalm lxviii, 17; 1 Cor. xi, 10, and their desire to look into the mysteries of the gospel, which they diligently contemplate, 1 Pet. i, 12. God is said to dwell or sit between the cherubim, on the mercy-seat, Psalm lxxx, 1, and from thence he here promiseth for the future to meet with Moses, and to commune with him. Thus he manifests himself, willing to keep up communion with us, by the mediation of Christ.

23. This table was to stand not in the holy of holies, (nothing was in that but the ark with its appurtenances) but in the outer part of the tabernacle, called the sanctuary or holy place. This table was to be always furnished with the shew-bread, or bread of faces, twelve loaves, one for each tribe, set in two rows, six in a row. As the ark signified God's being present with them, so the twelve loaves signified their being presented to God. This bread was designed to be, a thankful acknowledgment of God's goodness to them in giving them their daily bread, a token of their communion with God; this bread on God's table being made of the same corn as the bread on their own tables. And a type of the spiritual provision which is made in the church, by the gospel of Christ, for all that are made priests to our God.

31. This candlestick had many branches drawn from the main shaft, which had not only bowls to put the oil and the kindled wick in for necessity, but knops made in the form of a pomegranate and flowers for ornament. The tabernacle had no windows, all its light was candle-light, which notes the comparative darkness of that dispensation, while the sun of righteousness was not as yet risen, nor had the day-star from on high visited his church. Yet God left not himself without witness, nor them without instruction; the commandment was a lamp, and the law a light, and the prophets were branches from that lamp, which gave light in their several ages. The church is still dark, as the tabernacle was, in comparison with what it will be in heaven: but the word of God is the candlestick, a light burning in a dark place.

XXVI

Moses here receives instructions,

I. Concerning the inner curtains of the tabernacle, ver. 1-6.

II. Concerning the outer curtains, ver. 7-13.

III. Concerning the cover which was to secure it from the weather, ver. 14.

IV. Concerning the boards which were to support the curtains, ver. 15-30.

V. The partition between the holy place and the most holy, ver. 31-35.

VI. The veil for the door, ver. 36-37. These particulars seem of little use to us now, yet having been of great use to Moses and Israel, and God having thought fit to preserve to us the remembrance of them, we ought not to overlook them.

1. The curtains were to be embroidered with cherubim, to intimate that the angels of God pitched their tents round about the church, Psalm xxxiv, 7. As there were cherubim over the mercy-seat, so there were round the tabernacle. There were to be two hangings, five breadths to each, sewed together, and the two hangings coupled together with golden clasps or tacks, so that it might be all one tabernacle, ver. 6. Thus the churches of Christ, though they are many, yet are one, being fitly joined together in holy love and by the unity of the Spirit, so growing into one holy temple in the Lord. This tabernacle was very strait and narrow, but at the preaching of the gospel, the church is bid to enlarge the place of her tent, and to stretch forth her curtains, Isaiah liv, 2.

14. Badger skins - So we translate it, but it should rather seem to have been some strong sort of leather, (but very fine) for we read of the best sort of shoes made of it. Ezek. xvi, 10.

15. Very particular directions are here given about the boards of the tabernacle, which were to bear up the curtains. These had tenons which fell into the mortaises that were made for them in silver bases. The boards were coupled together with gold rings at top and bottom, and kept firm with bars that run through golden staples in every board. Thus every thing in the tabernacle was very splendid, agreeable to that infant state of the church, when such things were proper to possess the minds of the worshippers with a reverence of the divine glory. In allusion to this, the new Jerusalem is said to be of pure gold, Rev. xxi, 18. But the builders of the gospel church said, Silver and gold have we none; and yet the glory of their building far exceeded that of the tabernacle.

31. The veils are here ordered to be made, one for a partition between the holy place and the most holy, which not only forbad any to enter, but so much as to look into the holiest of all. Under that dispensation divine grace was veiled, but now we behold it with open face. The apostle tells us, this veil, intimated that the ceremonial law could not make the comers thereunto perfect. The way into the holiest was not made manifest while the first tabernacle was standing; life and immortality lay concealed till they were brought to light by the gospel, which was therefore signified by the rending of this veil at the death of Christ. We have now boldness to enter into the holiest in all acts of devotion by the blood of Jesus; yet such as obliges us to a holy reverence, and a humble sense of our distance. Another veil was for the outward door of the tabernacle. Through this the priests went in every day to minister in the holy-place, but not the people, Heb. ix, 6. This veil was all the defense the tabernacle had against thieves and robbers, which might easily be broken through, for it could be neither locked nor bared, and the abundance of wealth in it, one would think, might be a temptation. But by leaving it thus exposed,

1. The priests and Levites would be so much the more obliged to keep a strict watch upon it: and,

2. God would shew his care of his church on earth, though it be weak and defenseless, and continually exposed. A curtain shall be (if God please to make it so) as strong a defense, as gates of brass and bars of iron.

XXVII

In this chapter directions are given,

I. Concerning the brazen altar, ver. 1-8.

II. Concerning the court of the tabernacle, ver. 9-19.

III. Concerning the oil for the lamp, ver. 20-21.

1. As God intended in the tabernacle to manifest his presence among his people, so there they were to pay their devotions to him; not in the tabernacle itself, into that only the priests entered as God's domestic servants, but in the court before the tabernacle, where, as common subjects they attended. There an altar was ordered so be set up, to which they must bring their sacrifices; and this altar was to sanctify their gifts; from hence they were to present their services to God, as from the mercy-seat he gave his oracles to them; and thus a communion was settled between God and Israel.

2. The horns of it, were for ornament and for use; the sacrifices were bound with cords to the horns of the altar, and to them malefactors fled for refuge.

4. The grate was set into the hollow of the altar, about the middle of it, in which the fire was kept, and the sacrifice burnt; it was made of net-work like a sieve, and hung hollow, that the fire might burn the better, and that the ashes might fall through. Now, this brazen altar was a type of Christ dying to make atonement for our sins. Christ sanctified himself for his church as their altar, John xvii, 19, and by his mediation sanctifies the daily services of his people. To the horns of this altar poor sinners fly for refuge, and are safe in virtue of the sacrifice there offered.

9. Before the tabernacle there was to be a court, enclosed with hangings of fine linen. This court, according to the common computation, was 50 yards long, and 25 broad. Pillars were set up at convenient distances, in sockets of brass, the pillars filleted with silver, and silver tenterhooks in them, on which the linen hangings were fastened: the hanging which served for the gate was finer than the rest. This court was a type of the church, enclosed, and distinguished from the rest of the world; the inclosure supported by pillars, noting the stability of the church hung with the clean linen, which is said to be the righteousness of saints, Rev. xix, 8. Yet this court would contain but a few worshippers; thanks be to God, now the inclosure is taken down; and there is room for all that in every place call on the name of Christ.

20. We read of the candlestick in the 25th chapter; here is order given for the keeping of the lamps constantly burning in it. The pure oil signified the gifts and graces of the Spirit, which are communicated to all believers from Christ the good olive, of whose fulness we receive, Zech. iv, 11, 12. The priests were to light the lamps, and to tend them; to cause the lamp to burn always, night and day. Thus it is the work of ministers to preach and expound the scriptures, which are as a lamp to enlighten the church. This is to be a statute forever, that the lamps of the word be lighted as duly as the incense of prayer and praise is offered.

XXVIII

In this and the following chapter care is taken about the priests that were to minister in this holy place. In this chapter,

I. He pitcheth upon the persons who should be his servants, ver. 1.

II. He appoints their livery; their work was holy, and so must their garments be, and answerable to the glory of the house which was now to be erected, ver. 2-5. (1.) He appoints the garments of his head-servant, the high-priest,

    1. An ephod and girdle, ver. 6-14.
    2. A breast-plate of judgement, ver. 16-29. in which must be put the Urim and Thummim, ver. 30.
    3. The robe of the ephod, ver. 31-35.
    4. The mitre, ver. 36-39. (2.) The garments of the inferior priests, ver. 40-43.

1. Aaron and his sons - Hitherto every master of a family was priest to his own family. But now the families of Israel began to be incorporated into a nation, and a tabernacle of the congregation was to be erected, as a visible center of their unity, it was requisite there should be a publick priesthood instituted. Moses, who had hitherto officiated, and is therefore reckoned among the priests of the Lord, Psalm xcix, 6, had enough to do as their prophet, to consult the oracle for them, and as their prince, to judge among them. Nor was he desirous to ingross all the honours to himself, or to entail that of the

priesthood, which alone was hereditary, upon his own family; but was very well pleased to see his brother Aaron invested with this office, and his sons after him; while (how great soever he was) his sons after him would be but common Levites. It is an instance of the humility of that great man, and an evidence of his sincere regard to the glory of God, that he had so little regard to the preferment of his own family. Aaron, that had humbly served as a prophet to his younger brother Moses, and did not decline the office, is now advanced to be a priest to God. God had said to Israel in general, that they should be to him a kingdom of priests; but because it was requisite that those who ministered at the altar should give themselves wholly to the service, God here chose from among them one to be a family of priests, the father and his four sons; and from Aaron's loins descended all the priests of the Jewish church, whom we read of both in the Old Testament and in the New.

2. The priests garments were made for glory and beauty - Some of the richest materials were to be provided, and the belt artists employed in making them, whose skill God, by a special gift, would improve to a very high degree. Eminency, even in common arts, is a gift of God; it comes from him, and, ought to be used for him. The garments appointed were, (1.) Four, which both the high-priest and the inferior priests wore, viz. The linen breeches, the linen coat, the linen girdle which fastened it to them, and the bonnet; that which the high-priest wore is called a mitre. (2.) Four more which were peculiar to the high-priest, the ephod, with the curious girdle of it, the breast-plate of judgment, the long robe, and the golden plate on his forehead. These glorious garments, were appointed,

1. That the priests themselves might be minded of the dignity of their office.

2. That the people might thereby be possessed with a holy reverence of that God whose ministers appeared in such grandeur.

3. That the priests might be types of Christ, and of all Christians who have the beauty of holiness put upon them.

6. The ephod, was the outmost garment of the high-priest; linen ephods were worn by the inferior priests, but this, which the high- priest wore, was called a golden ephod, because there was a great deal of gold woven into it. It was a short coat without sleeves, buttoned close to him with a curious girdle of the same stuff. The shoulder pieces were buttoned together with two precious stones set in gold, one on each shoulder. In allusion to this, Christ our high priest appeared to John, girt about the paps with a golden girdle, such as was the curious girdle of the ephod, Rev. i, 13. Righteousness is the girdle of his loins. He is girt with strength for the work of our salvation. And as Aaron had the names of all Israel upon his shoulders in precious stones, so He presents to himself and to his Father a glorious church, Eph. v, 27. He bears them before the Lord for a memorial, in token of his appearing before God as the representative of all Israel, and an advocate for them.

11. Ouches - Hollow places, such as are made in gold rings, to receive and hold the precious stones.

15. The most considerable of the ornaments of the high priest was this breast-plate, a rich piece of cloth curiously wrought with gold and purple, two spans long, and a span broad; so that, being doubled, it was a span square. In this breast-plate, the tribes of Israel were recommended to God's favour in twelve precious stones. Some question whether Levi had a precious stone with his name on or no; if not Ephraim and Manasseh were reckoned distinct, as Jacob had said they should be, and the high priest himself being head of the tribe of Levi, sufficiently represented that tribe. Aaron was to bear their names for a memorial before the Lord continually, being ordained for men, to represent them in things pertaining to God; herein typifying our great High Priest, who always appears in the presence of God for us. The name of each tribe was engraven in a precious stone, to signify how precious, in God's sight, believers are, and how honourable, Isaiah xliii, 4. The high priest had the names of the tribes both on his shoulders and on his breast, noting both the power and the love with which our Lord Jesus interceeds for us. How near should Christ's name lie to our hearts, since he is pleased to lay our names so near his? And what a comfort is it to us, in all our addresses to God, that the great High Priest of our profession has the names of all his Israel upon his breast, before the Lord, for a memorial, presenting them to God?

30. The Urim and Thummim - By which the will of God was made known in doubtful cases, was put in this breast-plate, which is therefore called the breast-plate of judgment. Urim and Thummim signify light and integrity: many conjectures there are among the learned what they were: we have no reason to think they were any thing that Moses was to make, more than what was before ordered; so that either God made them himself, and gave them to Moses, for him to put into the breast-plate when other things were prepared; or, no more is meant but a declaration of the further use of what was already ordered to be made. The words may be read thus, And thou shalt give, or add, to the breast-plate of judgment, the illuminations and perfections, and they shall be upon the heart of Aaron - That is, he shall be endued with a power of knowing and making known the mind of God in all difficult cases relating either to the civil or ecclesiastical state. Their government was a theocracy; God was their king, the high priest was, under God, their ruler, this Urim and Thummim were his cabinet council: probably Moses wrote upon the breast-plate, or wove into it, these words, Urim and Thummim, to signify, that the high-priest, having on him this breast-plate, and asking council of God in any emergency, should be directed

to those measures, which God would own. If he were standing before the ark, probably he received instructions from off the mercy-seat, as Moses did, chap. xxv, 22. If he were at a distance from the ark, as Abiathar was when he inquired of the Lord for David, 1 Sam. xxiii, 6, then the answer was given either by a voice from heaven, or by an impulse upon the mind of the high priest, which last is perhaps intimated in that expression, he shall bear the judgment of the children of Israel upon his heart. This oracle was of great use to Israel, Joshua consulted it. Num. xxvii, 21, and it is likely, the Judges after him. It was lost in the captivity, and never retrieved after. It was a shadow of good things to come, and the substance is Christ. He is our oracle; by him God in these last days, makes known himself and his mind to us. Divine Revelation centers in him, and comes to us through him; he is the light, the true light, the faithful witness; and from him we receive the Spirit of truth, who leads into all truth. The joining of the breast-plate to the ephod notes, that his prophetical office was founded on his priesthood; and it was by the merit of his death that he purchased this honour for himself, and this favour for us. It was the Lamb that had been slain that was worthy to take the book and to open the seals. Rev. v, 9. The judgment - The breast-plate of judgment: That breast-plate which declared the judgment or mind of God to the Israelites.

31. The robe of the ephod - This was next under the ephod, and reached down to the knees, without sleeves, and was put on over their head, having holes on the sides to put the arms through, or, as Maimonides describes it, was not sewn together on the sides at all. The hole on the top through which the head was put was carefully bound about, that it might not tear in the putting on. The bells gave notice to the people in the outer court, when he went into the holy place to burn incense, that they might then apply themselves to their devotions at the same time, Luke i, 10, in token of their concurrence with him, and their hopes of the ascent of their prayers to God in the virtue of the incense he offered. Aaron must come near to minister in the garments that were appointed him, that he die not. 'Tis at his peril if he attend otherwise than according to the institution.

32. An habergeon - A coat of armour.

33. Pomegranates - The figures of Pomegranates, but flat and embroidered.

36. On the golden plate fixed upon Aaron's forehead, like an half coronet, reaching, as the Jews say, from ear to ear, must be engraven, Holiness to the Lord - Aaron must hereby be minded, that God is holy, and that his priests must be holy. The high priest must be consecrated to God, and so must all his ministrations. All that attend in God's house must have holiness to the Lord engraven upon their foreheads, that is, they must be holy, devoted to the Lord, and designing his glory in all they do. This must appear in their forehead, in an open profession of their relation to God, as those that are not ashamed to own it, and in a conversation answerable to it. It must likewise be engraven like the engravings of a signet, so deep, so durable; not painted, so as it may he washed off, but sincere and lasting.

38. Aaron must have this upon his forehead, that he may bear the iniquity of the holy things, and that they may be accepted before the Lord - Herein he was a type of Christ, the great Mediator between God and man. Thro' him what is amiss in our services is pardoned: even this would be our ruin, if God should enter into judgment with us: but Christ our high priest bears this iniquity; bears it for us, so as to bear it from us. Thro' him likewise what is good is accepted; our persons, our performances are pleasing to God upon the account of Christ's intercession, and not otherwise. His being holiness to the Lord, recommends all those to the divine favour that believe in him. Having such a high priest, we come boldly to the throne of grace.

39. The embroidered coat of fine linen - Was the innermost of the priestly garments, it reached to the feet, and the sleeves to the wrists, and was bound to the body with a girdle or sash of needlework. The mitre or diadem was of linen, such as kings anciently wore in the east, typifying the kingly office of Christ.

43. It shall be a statute forever - That is, It is to continue as long as the priesthood continues. And it is to have its perpetuity in the substance, of which these things were the shadows.

XXIX

Orders are given in this chapter,

I. Concerning the consecration of the priests, and the sanctification of the altar, ver. 1-37.

II. Concerning the daily sacrifice, ver. 38-41. To which gracious promises are annexed, ver. 42-46.

4. They were to be consecrated at the door of the tabernacle - God was pleased to dwell in the tabernacle, the people attending in the courts, so that the door between the court and the tabernacle was the fittest place for them to be consecrated in, who were to mediate between God and man, and to stand between both, and lay their hands (as it were) upon both. Here they were to be washed, signifying that

they must be clean who bear the vessels of the Lord, Isaiah lii, 11. And they were to be clothed with the holy garments, to signify that it was not sufficient for them to put away the pollutions of sin, but they must put on the graces of the Spirit, be clothed with righteousness, Psalm lxxxii, 9. They must be girded, as men prepared and strengthened for their work; and they must be robed and crowned, as men that counted their work and office their true honour.

7. The high priest was to be anointed with the holy anointing oil - That the church might be filled with the sweet favour of his administrations, and in token of the pouring out of the Spirit upon him, to qualify him for his work.

10. There must be a sin-offering, to make atonement for them. The law made them priests that had infirmity; and therefore they must first offer for their own sin, before they could make atonement for the people, Heb. vii, 27, 28. They were to put their hand on the head of their sacrifice; confessing that they deserved to die for their own sin, and desiring that the killing of the beast might be accepted as a vicarious satisfaction. It was used as other sin-offerings were; only, whereas the flesh of other sin-offerings was eaten by the priests, in token of the priests taking away the sin of the people, this was appointed to be all burnt without the camp, to signify the imperfection of the legal dispensation, for the sins of the priests themselves could not be taken away by those sacrifices, but they must expect a better high priest, and a better sacrifice.

15. There must be a burnt-offering, a ram wholly burnt, in token of the dedication of themselves wholly to God, as living sacrifices, kindled with the fire, and ascending in the flame of holy love. This sin-offering must be offered, and then the burnt- offering, for till guilt be removed no acceptable service can be performed.

19. There must be a peace-offering; it is called the ram of consecration, because there was more in this, peculiar to the occasion, than in the other two. In the burnt-offering God had the glory of their priesthood, in this they had the comfort of it. And in token of a mutual covenant between God and them, the blood of this sacrifice was divided between God and them, part of the blood was sprinkled upon the altar round about, and part upon them, upon their bodies, and upon their garments. Thus the benefit of the expiation made by the sacrifice was applied and assured to them, and their whole selves from head to foot sanctified to the service of God. The blood was put upon the extreme parts of the body, to signify, that it was all as it were enclosed and taken in for God, the tip of the ear, and the great toe not excepted. And the blood and oil signified the blood of Christ, and the graces of the Spirit, which constitute and compleat the beauty of holiness, and recommend us to God. The flesh of the sacrifice, with the meat- offering annexed to it, was likewise divided between God and them, that (to speak with reverence) God and they might feast together, in token of friendship and fellowship.

22. Part of it was to be first waved before the Lord, and then burnt upon the altar, these were first put into the hands of Aaron to be waved to and fro in token of their being offered to God, and then they were to be burnt upon the altar, for the altar was to devour God's part of the sacrifice. Thus God admitted Aaron and his sons to wait at his table, taking the meat of his altar from their hands. Here, in a parenthesis as it were, comes in the law concerning the priests part of the peace-offerings afterwards, the breast and shoulder, which were now divided; Moses had the breast, and the shoulder was burnt on the altar with God's part.

31. The other part of the flesh of the ram, and of the bread, Aaron and his sons were to eat at the door of the tabernacle, to signify that he not only called them servants but friends. He supped with them, and they with him. Their eating of the things wherewith the atonement was made, signified their receiving the atonement, their thankful acceptance of the benefit of it, and their joyful communion with God thereupon.

35. Seven days shalt thou consecrate them - Though all the ceremonies were performed on the first day, yet, they were not to look upon their consecration as compleated till the seven days end, which put a solemnity upon their admission, and a distance between this and their former state, and obliged them to enter upon their work with a pause, giving them time to consider the weight of it. This was to be observed in after ages: he that was to succeed Aaron in the high priesthood, must put on the holy garments seven days together, in token of a deliberate advance into his office, and that one sabbath might pass over him, in his consecration. Every day of the seven, in this first consecration, a bullock was to be offered for a sin-offering, which was to intimate, (1.) That though atonement was made, yet they must still keep up a penitent sense of sin, and often repeat the confession of it. (2.) That those sacrifices which were thus offered day by day, could not make the comers there unto perfect, for then they would have ceased to be offered; Heb. x, 1, 2. They must therefore expect the bringing in of a better hope. Now this consecration of the priests was a shadow of good things to come.

1. Our Lord Jesus is the great high priest of our profession, called of God to be so consecrated forevermore, anointed with the Spirit above his fellows, whence he is called Messiah, the Christ; clothed with the holy garments, even with glory and beauty; sanctified by his own blood, not that of bullocks and rams.

2. All believers are spiritual priests, to offer spiritual sacrifices, 1 Pet. ii, 5, washed in the blood of

Christ, and so made to our God priests, Rev. i, 5, 6. They also are clothed with the beauty of holiness, and have received the anointing, 1 John ii, 27. His blood sprinkled upon the conscience, purgeth it from dead works, that they may, as priests, serve the living God. The Spirit of God is called the finger of God (Luke xi, 20, compared with Matt. xii, 28,) and by him the merit of Christ is effectually applied to our souls, as here Moses with his finger was to put the blood upon Aaron. It is likewise intimated that gospel ministers are to be solemnly set apart to the work of the ministry with great deliberation and seriousness, both in the ordainers, and in the ordained, as those that are employed in a great work, and intrusted with a great charge.

36. The consecration of the altar, seems to have been coincident with that of the priests; and the sin-offerings, which were offered every day for seven days together, had reference to the altar, as well as the priests. And atonement was made for the altar. The altar was also sanctified, not only set apart itself to a sacred use, but made so holy as to sanctify the gifts that were offered upon it, Matt. xxiii, 19. Christ is our altar, for our sakes he sanctified himself, that we and our performances might be sanctified and recommended to God, John xvii, 19.

38. This daily service, a lamb offered upon the altar every morning, and every evening, typified the continual intercession which Christ ever lives to make in the virtue of his satisfaction for the continual sanctification of his church: though he offered himself once for all, yet that one offering thus becomes a continual offering. And this teaches us to offer up to God the spiritual sacrifices of prayer and praise every day, morning and evening, in humble acknowledgment of our dependence upon him, and our obligations to him.

40. A tenth deal, or tenth part of an ephah, is about three quarts. A hin is five quarts.

XXX

Moses in this chapter farther instructed, (1.) Concerning the altar of incense, ver. 1-10. (2.) Concerning the ransom money, which the Israelites were to pay when they were numbered, ver. 11-16. (3.) Concerning the laver of brass, ver. 17-21. (4.) Concerning the anointing oil, ver. 22-33. (5.) Concerning the incense and perfume, which was to be burned on the golden altar, ver. 34-38.

1. The altar of incense was to be about a yard high, and half a yard square, with horns at the corners, a golden cornish round it, with rings and staves of gold for the convenience of carrying it, ver. 1- 5. It doth not appear that there was any grate to this altar for the ashes to fall into, that they might be taken away; but when they burn incense, a golden censer was brought, with coals in it, and placed upon the altar, and in that censer the incense was burnt, and with it all the coals were taken away, so that no coals or ashes fell upon the altar. The altar of incense in Ezekiel's temple is double to what it is here, Ezek. xli, 22, and it is there called an altar of wood, and there is no mention of gold, to signify that the incense in gospel times should be spiritual, the worship plain, and the service of God enlarged. It was placed before the veil, on the outside of that partition, but before the mercy-seat, which was within the veil. For though he that ministered at that altar could not see the mercy-seat, the veil interposing, yet he must look towards it, and direct his incense that way, to teach us, that though we cannot with our bodily eyes see the throne of grace, that blessed mercy-seat, yet we must in prayer by faith set ourselves before it, direct our prayer and look up.

7. Aaron was to burn sweet incense upon this altar every morning and every evening, which was intended not only to take away the ill smell of the flesh that was burnt daily on the brazen altar, but for the honour of God, and to shew the, acceptableness of his people's services to him. As by the offerings on the brazen altar satisfaction was made for what had been done displeasing to God, so by the offering on this what they did well was, as it were, recommended to the divine acceptance.

10. This altar was purified with the blood of the sin-offering put upon the horns of it every year, upon the day of atonement. See Lev. xvi, 18,

19. The high priest was to take this in his way as he came out from the holy of holies. This was to intimate, that the sins of the priests who ministered at this altar, and of the people for whom they ministered, put a ceremonial impurity upon it, from which it must be cleansed by the blood of atonement. This altar typified the mediation of Christ: the brazen altar in the court was a type of Christ dying on earth; the golden altar in the sanctuary was a type of Christ interceding in heaven. This altar was before the mercy- seat, for Christ always appears in the presence of God for us; and his intercession is unto God of a sweet smelling savour. And it typified the devotions of the saints, whose prayers are said to be set forth before God as incense, Psalm lxli, 2. As the smoke of the incense ascended, so must our desires, being kindled with the fire of holy love. When the priest was burning incense the people were praying, Luke i, 10, to signify that prayer is the true incense. This incense was a perpetual incense, for we must pray always. The lamps were dressed or lighted at the same time that the incense was burnt, to teach us that the reading of the scriptures (which are our light and lamp) is a part of our daily work, and should ordinarily accompany our prayers and praises. The devotions of sanctified souls are well-

pleasing to God, of a sweet-smelling savour; the prayers of saints are compared to sweet odours, Rev. v, 8, but it is the incense which Christ adds to them that makes them acceptable; and his blood that atones for the guilt which cleaves to our best services. Yet if the heart and life be not holy, even incense is an abomination, Isaiah i, 13.

11. Perhaps the repetition of those words, the Lord spake unto Moses, here and afterwards, ver. 17, 22, 34, intimates, that God did not deliver these precepts to Moses, in a continued discourse, but with many intermissions, giving him time either to write what was said to him, or at least to charge his memory with it.

12. Some think this refers only to the first numbering of them, when the tabernacle was set up, and that this tax was to make up what was wanting in the voluntary contributions. Others think it was to be always when the people were numbered; and that David offended in not demanding it when he numbered the people. But many of the Jewish writers are of opinion, it was to be an annual tribute; only it was begun when Moses first numbered the people. This was that tribute-money which Christ paid lest he should offend his adversaries. The tribute to be paid was half a shekel, about fifteen-pence of our money. In other offerings men were to give according to their ability, but this, which was the ransom of the soul, must be alike for all; for the rich have as much need of Christ as the poor, and the poor are as welcome to him as the rich. And this was to be paid as a ransom of the soul, that there might be no plague among them - Hereby they acknowledged that they received their lives from God, that they had forfeited their lives to him, and that they depended upon his power and patience for the continuance of them; and thus they did homage to the God of their lives, and deprecated those plagues which their sins had deserved. This money was employed in the service of the tabernacle; with it they bought sacrifices, flour, incense wine, oil, fuel, salt, priests garments, and all other things which the whole congregation was interested in.

18. The laver, or font was a large vessel, that would contain a good quantity of water. The foot of brass, it is supposed, was so contrived as to receive the water, which was let out of the laver, by spouts or cocks. They then had a laver for the priests only to wash in, but to us now there is a fountain opened for Judah and Jerusalem, Zech. xiii, 1, an inexhaustible fountain of living water, so that it is our own fault if we remain in our pollution. Aaron and his sons were to wash their hands and feet at this laver every time they went in to minister. For this purpose clean water was put into the laver, fresh every day. Though they washed themselves ever so clean at their own houses, that would not serve, they must wash at the laver. This was designed, to teach them purity in all their ministrations, and to possess them with a reverence of God's holiness, and a dread of the pollutions of sin. They must not only wash and be made clean when they were first consecrated, but they must wash and be kept clean, whenever they went in to minister. He only shall stand in God's holy place that hath clean hands and a pure heart, Psalm xxiv, 3, 4. And it was to teach us, who are daily to attend upon God, daily to renew our repentance for sin, and our believing application of the blood of Christ to our souls for remission.

23. Interpreters are not agreed concerning these ingredients: the spices, which were in all near half a hundred weight, were to be infused in the oil, which was to be about five or six quarts, and then strained out, leaving an admirable smell in the oil. With this oil God's tent and all the furniture of it were to be anointed; it was to be used also in the consecration of the priests. It was to be continued throughout their generations, ver. 31. Solomon was anointed with it, 1 Kings i, 39, and some other of the kings, and all the high priests, with such a quantity of it, as that it ran down to the skirts of the garments; and we read of the making it up, 1 Chron. ix, 30. Yet all agree that in the second temple there was none of this holy oil, which was probably owing to a notion they had, that it was not lawful to make it up; Providence over-ruling that want as a presage of the better unction of the Holy Ghost in gospel-times, the variety of whose gifts was typified by these sweet ingredients.

34. The incense which was burned upon the golden altar was prepared of sweet spices likewise, though not so rare and rich as those which the anointing oil was compounded of. This was prepared once a year, (the Jews say) a pound for each day of the year, and three pound over for the day of atonement. When it was used it was to be beaten very small; thus it pleased the Lord to bruise the Redeemer, when he offered himself for a sacrifice of a sweet smelling savour. Concerning both these preparations the same law is here given, that the like should not be made for any common use. Thus God would preserve in the peoples minds a reverence for his own institutions, and teach us not to profane or abuse any thing whereby God makes himself known.

XXXI

In this chapter,

I. God appoints what workmen should be employed in the building and furnishing the tabernacle, ver. 1-11.

II. He repeats the law of the sabbath, ver. 12-17.

III. He delivers to Moses the two tables of the testimony, ver. 18.

2. See I have called Bezaleel, the grandson of Hur, probably that Hur who had helped to hold up Moses's hand, chap. xvii, 10-12, and was at this time in commission with Aaron for the government of the people in the absence of Moses. Aholiab of the tribe of Dan. is appointed next to Bezaleel, and partner with him. Hiram, who was the head-workman in the building of Solomon's temple, was also of the tribe of Daniel, 2 Chron. ii, 14.

3. And I have filled him with the spirit of God; and ver. 6. In the hearts of all that are wise-hearted I have put wisdom. Skill in common employments is the gift of God; It is he that puts even this wisdom into the inward parts, Job xxxviii, 36. He teacheth the husbandman discretion, Isaiah xxviii, 26, and the tradesman too, and he must have the praise of it.

13. It is a sign between me and you - The institution of the sabbath was a great instance of God's favour, and a sign that he had distinguished them from all other people: and their religious observance of it, was a great instance of their duty to him. God, by sanctifying this day among them, let them know that he sanctified them, and set them apart for his service, otherwise he would not have revealed to them his holy sabbaths to be the support of religion among them. The Jews by observing one day in seven, after six days labour, testified that they worshipped the God that made the world in six days, and rested the seventh; and so distinguished themselves from other nations, who having first lost the sabbath, the memorial of the creation, by degrees lost the knowledge of the creator, and gave the creature the honour due to him alone.

14. It is holy unto you - That is, it is designed for your benefit as well as for God's honour; it shall be accounted holy by you.

15. It is the sabbath of rest, holy to the Lord - It is separated from common use, for the service of God; and by the observance of it we are taught to rest from worldly pursuits, and devote ourselves, and all we are, have, and can do, to God's glory.

16. It was to be observed throughout their generations, in every age, for a perpetual covenant - This was to be one of the most lasting tokens of the covenant between God and Israel.

17. On the seventh day he rested - And as the work of creation is worthy to be thus commemorated, so the great Creator is worthy to be thus imitated, by a holy rest the seventh day.

18. These tables of stone, were not prepared by Moses, but probably by the ministry of angels. They were written with the finger of God - That is, by his will and power immediately, without the use of any instrument. They were written in two tables, being designed to direct us in our duty, towards God, and towards man. And they were called tables of testimony, because this written law testified the will of God concerning them, and would be a testimony against them if they were disobedient.

XXXII

Here is,

I. The sin of Israel, and Aaron particularly in making the golden calf, ver. 1-4. and worshipping it, ver. 5, 6.

II. The notice which God gave of this to Moses, who was now in the mount with him, ver. 7, 8. and the sentence of his wrath against them, ver. 9, 10.

III. The intercession which Moses made for them, ver. 11, 12, 13. and the prevalency of that intercession, ver 14.

IV. His coming down from the mount, and being an eye witness of their idolatry, ver. 15-19. in detestation of which he broke the tables, ver. 19. and burnt the golden calf, ver. 20.

V. The examination of Aaron about it, ver. 21-24.

VI. Execution done upon the ringleaders in the idolatry, ver. 25- 29.

VII. The further intercession Moses made, to turn away the wrath of God from them, ver. 30-32. and a reprieve granted thereupon, reserving them for a further reckoning, ver. 33-35.

1. Up, make us gods which shall go before us. They were weary of waiting for the promised land. They thought themselves detained too long at Mount Sinai. They had a God that stayed with them, but they must have a God to go before them to the land flowing with milk and honey. They were weary of waiting for the return of Moses: As for this Moses, the man that brought us up out of Egypt, we know not what is become of him - Observe how slightly they speak of his person, this Moses: And how suspiciously of his delay, we know not what is become of him. And they were weary of waiting for a divine institution of religious worship among them, so they would have a worship of their own invention, probably such as they had seen among the Egyptians. They say, make us gods which shall go before us. Gods! How many would they have? Is not one sufficient? And what good would gods of their own making do them? They must have such Gods to go before them as could not go themselves farther than they were carried!

2. And Aaron said break off the golden ear-rings - We do not find that he said one word to discountenance their proposal. Some suppose, that when Aaron bid them break off their ear-rings, he did it with design to crush the proposal, believing that, though their covetousness would have let them do it, yet their pride would not have suffered them to part with them.

3. And all the people brake off their ear-rings - Which Aaron melted down, and, having a mold prepared, poured the melted gold into it, and then produced it in the shape of an ox or calf, giving it some finishing strokes with a graving tool.

5. And Aaron built an altar before it, and proclaimed a feast - A feast of dedication; yet he calls it a feast to Jehovah; for, as brutish as they were, they did not design to terminate their adoration in the image; but they made it for a representation of the true God, whom they intended to worship in and through this image. And yet this did not excuse them from gross idolatry, no more than it will excuse the Papists, whose plea it is, that they do not worship the image, but God by the image; so making themselves just such idolaters as the worshippers of the golden calf, whose feast was a feast to Jehovah, and proclaimed to be so, that the most ignorant and unthinking might not mistake it.

6. And they rose up early on the morrow, and offered sacrifice to this new made deity. And the people sat down to eat and drink of the remainder of what was sacrificed, and then rose up to play - To play the fool, to play the wanton. It was strange that any of the people, especially so great a number of them, should do such a thing. Had they not, but the other day, in this very place, heard the voice of the Lord God speaking to them out of the midst of the fire, Thou shalt not make to thyself any graven image? - Yet They made a calf in Horeb, the very place where the law was given It was especially strange that Aaron should be so deeply concerned, should make the calf and proclaim the feast! Is this Aaron the saint of the Lord! Is this he that had not only seen, but had been employed in summoning the plagues of Egypt, and the judgments executed upon the gods of the Egyptians? What! And yet himself copying out the abandoned idolatries of Egypt? How true is it, that the law made them priests which had infirmity, and needed first to offer for their own sins?

8. They have turned aside quickly - Quickly after the law was given them, and they had promised to obey it; quickly after God had done such great things for them, and declared his kind intentions to do greater.

9. It is a stiff-necked people - Unapt to come under the yoke of the divine law, averse to all good, and prone to evil, obstinate to the methods of cure.

10. Let me alone - What did Moses, or what could he do, to hinder God from consuming them? When God resolves to abandon a people, and the decree is gone forth, no intercession can prevent it. But God would thus express the greatness of his displeasure, after the manner of men, who would have none to interceed for those they resolve to be severe with. Thus also he would put an honour upon prayer, intimating, that nothing but the intercession of Moses could save them from ruin, that he might be a type of Christ, by whose mediation alone God would reconcile the world unto himself.

11. And Moses besought the Lord his God - If God would not be called the God of Israel, yet he hoped he might address him as his own God. Now Moses is standing in the gap to turn away the wrath of God. Psalm cvi, 23. He took the hint which God gave him when he said, Let me alone, which, though it seemed to forbid his interceding, did really encourage it, by shewing what power the prayer of faith hath with God.

12. Turn from thy fierce wrath - Not as if he thought God were not justly angry, but he begs that he would not be so greatly angry as to consume them. Let mercy rejoice against judgment; repent of this evil - Change the sentence of destruction into that of correction, against thy people which thou broughtest up out of Egypt - For whom thou hast done so great things? Wherefore should the Egyptians say, For mischief did he bring them out - Israel is dear to Moses, as his kindred, as his charge; but it is the glory of God that he is most concerned for. If Israel could perish without any reproach to God's name, Moses could persuade himself to sit down contented; but he cannot bear to hear God reflected on; and therefore this he insists upon, Lord, What will the Egyptians say? They will say, God was either weak, and could not, or fickle, and would not compleat the salvation he begun.

13. Remember Abraham - Lord, if Israel be cut off, what will become of the promise?

14. And the Lord repented of the evil he thought to do - Though he designed to punish them, yet he would not ruin them. See here, the power of prayer, God suffers himself to be prevailed with by humble believing importunity. And see the compassion of God towards poor sinners, and how ready he is to forgive.

15. On both their sides - Some on one table and some on the other, so that they were folded together like a book, to be deposited in the ark.

16. The writing of God - Very probably the first writing in the world.

19. He saw the calf, and the dancing, and his anger waxed hot - It is no breach of the law of meekness to shew our displeasure at wickedness. Those are angry and sin not, that are angry at sin only. Moses shewed himself angry, both by breaking the tables, and burning the calf, that he might by these expressions of a strong passion awaken the people to a sense of the greatness of their sin. He broke the tables before their eyes, as it is Deut. ix, 17, that the sight of it might fill them with confusion when they saw what blessings they had lost. The greatest sign of God's displeasure against any people is his taking his law from them.

20. He burnt the calf - Melted it down, and then filed it to dust; and that the powder to which it was reduced might he taken notice of throughout the camp, he strawed it upon the water which they all drank of. That it might appear that an idol is nothing in the world, he reduced this to atoms, that it might be as near nothing as could be.

21. What did this people unto thee - He takes it for granted that it must needs be something more than ordinary that prevailed with Aaron to do such a thing? Did they overcome thee by importunity, and hadst thou so little resolution as to yield to popular clamour! Did they threaten to stone thee, and couldest not thou have opposed God's threatenings to theirs?

23. They said, make us Gods - It is natural to us to endeavour thus to transfer our guilt. He likewise extenuates his own share in the sin, as if he had only bid them break off their gold, intending but to make a hasty essay for the present, and childishly insinuates that when he cast the gold into the fire, it came out either by accident, or by the magic art of some of the mixt multitude (as the Jewish writers dream) in this shape. This was all Aaron had to say for himself, and he had better have said nothing, for his defense did but aggravate his offense; and yet as sin did abound, grace did much more abound.

25. The people were naked - Stript of their armour, and liable to insults.

26. Then Moses stood in the gate of the camp, the place of judgment; and said, Who is on the Lord's side? - The idolaters had set up the golden calf for their standard, and now Moses sets up his in opposition to them.

27. Slay every man his brother - That is, Slay all those that you know to have been active for the making and worshipping of the golden calf, though they were your nearest relations or dearest friends. Yet it should seem they were to slay those only whom they found abroad in the street of the camp; for it might be hoped that those who were retired into their tents were ashamed of what they had done.

28. And there fell of the people that day about three thousand men - Probably these were but few in comparison with the many that were guilty; but these were the men that headed the rebellion, and

were therefore picked out to be made examples of; for terror to others.

31. Oh, this people have sinned a great sin - God had first told him of it, ver. 7, and now he tells God of it by way of lamentation. He doth not call them God's people, he knew they were unworthy to be called so, but this people. This treacherous ungrateful people, they have made them gods of gold.

32. If not - If the decree be gone forth, and there is no remedy but they must be ruined, blot me, I pray thee out of the book which thou hast written - That is, out of the book of life. If all Israel must perish, I am content to perish with them. This expression may be illustrated from Rom. ix, 3. For I could wish myself to be an anathema from Christ, for my brethren's sake. Does this imply no more than not enjoying Canaan? Not that Moses absolutely desired this, but only comparatively expresses his vehement zeal for God's glory, and love to his people, signifying, that the very thought of their destruction, and the dishonour of God, was so intolerable to him, that he rather wishes, if it were possible, that God would accept of him, as a sacrifice in their stead, and by his utter destruction, prevent so great a mischief.

33. Whosoever hath sinned, him will I blot out of my book - The soul that sins shall die, and not the innocent for the guilty.

34. My angel shall go before them - Some created angel that was employed in the common services of his kingdom, which intimated that they were not to expect any thing for the future to be done for them out of the common road of providence. When I visit - Hereafter he shall see cause to punish them for other sins, I will visit for this among the rest. From hence the Jews have a saying, that from hence-forward no judgment fell upon Israel, but there was in it an ounce of the powder of the golden calf.

35. And the Lord plagued the people - Probably by the pestilence, or some other infectious disease. Thus Moses prevailed for a mitigation of the punishment, but could not wholly turn away the wrath of God.

XXXIII

In this chapter we have a further account of the mediation of Moses between God and Israel.

I. He brings a very humbling message from God to them, ver. 1, 2, 3, 5. which has a good effect upon then, ver. 4, 6.

II. He settles a correspondence between God and them; and both God and the people signify their approbation of that correspondence, God by descending in a cloudy pillar, and the people by worshipping at the tent-doors, ver. 7-12.

III. He is earnest with God in prayer, and prevails. (1.) For a promise of his presence with the people, ver. 12-17. (2.) For a sight of his glory for himself, ver. 18-23.

5. I will come up - As if he had said, ye deserve that I should do so. Put off thine ornaments, that I may know what to do with thee - That is, put thyself into the posture of a penitent, that the dispute may be determined in thy favour, and mercy may rejoice against judgment.

6. And Israel stript themselves of their ornaments, by the mount; or, as some read it, at a distance from the mount - Stand afar off, like the publican, Luke xviii, 13. God bid them lay aside their ornaments, and they did so; both to shew in general their deep mourning, and in particular to take a holy revenge upon themselves for giving their ear-rings to make the golden calf of.

7. And Moses took the tabernacle - The tent wherein he gave audience, heard causes, and inquired of God, and pitched it without, afar off from the camp - To signify to them that they were unworthy of it. Perhaps this tabernacle was a model of the tabernacle that was afterwards to be erected, a hasty draught from the pattern shewed him in the mount, designed for direction to the workman, and used in the mean time as a tabernacle of meeting between God and Moses about public affairs.

8. And when Moses went out to the tabernacle, the people looked after him - In token of their respect to him whom before they had slighted, and their dependence upon his mediation. By this it appeared, that they were full of concern what would be the issue.

10. And when they saw the cloudy pillar, that symbol of God's presence, give Moses the meeting, they all worshipped every man at his tent door - Thereby they signified, Their humble adoration of the divine majesty. Their thankfulness to God, that he was pleased to shew them this token for good, for if he had been pleased to kill them he would not have shewed them such things as these. And their hearty concurrence with Moses as their advocate, in every thing he should promise for them.

11. And the Lord spake to Moses face to face as a man speaketh to his friend - Which intimates not only that God revealed himself to Moses with greater clearness than to any other of the prophets, but also with greater expressions of particular kindness than to any other. He spake not as a prince to a

subject, but as a man to his friend, whom he loves, and with whom he takes sweet counsel. And he turned again into the camp - To tell the people what hopes he had of bringing this business to a good issue. But because he intended speedily to return to the tabernacle, he left Joshua there.

12. Moses now returned to the door of the tabernacle, as an important supplicant for two favours, and prevails for both: herein he was a type of Christ the great intercessor, whom the Father heareth always. He is earnest with God for a grant of his presence with Israel in the rest of their march to Canaan. Thou sayst, bring up this people - Lord, it is thou thyself that employest me, and wilt thou not own me? I am in the way of my duty, and shall I not have thy presence with me in that way? Yet, Thou hast said, I know thee by name, as a particular friend, and thou hast also found grace in my sight, above any other.

13. Now therefore, if I have found grace in thy sight, shew me thy way - What favour God had expressed to the people they had forfeited the benefit of; and therefore Moses lays the stress of his plea upon what God had said to him. By this therefore he takes hold on God, Lord, if thou wilt do any thing for me, do this for the people. Thus our Lord Jesus, in his intercession, presents himself to the Father, as one in whom he is always well-pleased, and so obtains mercy for us with whom he is justly displeased, Shew me thy way, that I may know thee, that I may find grace in thy sight - He insinuates that the people also, though most unworthy, yet were in some relation to God; consider that this nation is thy people; a people that thou hast done great things for, redeemed to thyself, and taken into covenant with thyself; Lord, they are thy own, do not leave them.

15. And he said, If thy presence go not with me, carry us not up hence - He speaks as one that dreaded the thought of going forward without God's presence.

16. Wherein shall it be known to the nations that have their eyes upon us, that I, and thy people, have found grace in thy sight; so as to be separated from all people upon earth? Is it not that thou goest with us? Nothing short of that can answer these characters.

17. I will do this thing also that thou hast spoken - See the power of prayer! See the riches of God's goodness! See in type the prevalency of Christ's intercession, which he ever lives to make for all those that come to God by him! And the ground of that prevalency, is purely in his own merit, it is because thou hast found grace in my sight. And now God is perfectly reconciled to them, and his presence in the pillar of cloud returns to them.

18. I beseech thee shew me thy glory - Moses had lately been in the mount with God, and had had as intimate communion with God, as ever any man had on this side heaven, and yet he is still desiring a farther acquaintance. Shew me thy glory - Make me to see it; so the word is: make it some way or other visible, and enable me to bear the sight of it. Not that he was so ignorant as to think God's essence could be seen with bodily eyes, but having hitherto only heard a voice out of a pillar of cloud or fire, he desired to see some representation of the divine glory, such as God saw fit to gratify him with.

20. Thou canst not see my face - A full discovery of the glory of God would quite overpower the faculties of any mortal man. I will make all my goodness pass before thee - He had given him wonderful instances of his goodness in being reconciled to Israel; but that was only goodness in the stream, he would shew him goodness in the spring. This was a sufficient answer to his request: Shew me thy glory, saith Moses; I will shew thee my goodness, saith God. God's goodness is his glory; and he will have us to know him by the glory of his mercy, more than by the glory of his majesty. And I will be gracious to whom I will be gracious - In bestowing his gifts, and is not debtor to any, nor accountable to any; all his reasons of mercy are fetched from within himself, not from any merit in his creatures, and I will shew mercy on whom I will shew mercy - For his grace is always free. He never damns by prerogative, but by prerogative he saves.

22. I will put thee in a cleft of the rock - In that he was to be sheltered from the dazzling light, and devouring fire of God's glory. This was the rock in Horeb, out of which water was brought, of which it is said, That rock was Christ, 1 Cor. x, 4. 'Tis in the clefts of this rock that we are secured from the wrath of God, which otherwise would consume us: God himself will protect those that are thus hid: and it is only through Christ that we have the knowledge of the glory of God. None can see that to their comfort, but those that stand upon this rock, and take shelter in it.

23. And I will take away my hand - Speaking after the manner of men. And thou shalt see my back-parts - The face in man is the seat of majesty, and men are known by their faces, in them we take a full view of men; that sight of God Moses might not have, but such a sight as we have of a man who is gone past us, so that we only see his back. Now Moses was allowed to see this only, but when he was a witness to Christ's transfiguration, he saw his face shine as the sun.

XXXIV

Four instances of the return of God's favour we have in this chapter.

I. The orders he gives to Moses to come up to the mount the next morning, and bring two tables of stone with him, ver. 1-4.

II. His meeting him there, and the proclamation of his name, ver. 6-9.

III. The instructions he gave him there, and his converse with him forty days, ver. 10-28.

IV. The honour he put upon him when he sent him down with his face shining, ver. 29-35. In all which God dealt with Moses as a mediator between him and Israel, and a type of the great Mediator.

1. Moses must prepare for the renewing of the tables. Before God himself provided the tables, and wrote on them; now Moses must hew him out the tables, and God would only write upon them. When God was reconciled to them, he ordered the tables to be renewed, and wrote his law in them, which plainly intimates to us, that even under the gospel (of which the intercession of Moses was typical) the moral law should continue to oblige believers. Though Christ has redeemed us from the curse of the law, yet not from the command of it, but still we are under the law to Christ. When our saviour in his sermon on the mount expounded the moral law, and vindicated it from the corrupt glosses with which the scribes and Pharisees had broken it, he did in effect renew the tables, and make them like the first; that is, reduce the law to its primitive sense and intention.

5. The Lord descended - By some sensible token of his presence, and manifestation of his glory. He descended in the cloud - Probably that pillar of cloud which had hitherto gone before Israel, and had the day before met Moses at the door of the tabernacle.

6. And the Lord passed by before him - Fixed views of God are reserved for the future state; the best we have in this world are transient. And proclaimed the name of the Lord - By which he would make himself known. He had made himself known to Moses in the glory of his self-existence, and self-sufficiency, when he proclaimed that name, I am that I am; now he makes himself known in the glory of his grace and goodness, and all- sufficiency to us. The proclaiming of it notes the universal extent of God's mercy; he is not only good to Israel, but good to all. The God with whom we have to do is a great God. He is Jehovah, the Lord, that hath his being of himself, and is the fountain of all being; Jehovah-El, the Lord, the strong God, a God of almighty power himself, and the original of all power. This is prefixed before the display of his mercy, to teach us to think and to speak even of God's goodness with a holy awe, and to encourage us to depend upon these mercies. He is a good God. His greatness and goodness illustrate each other. That his greatness may not make us afraid, we are told how good he is; and that we may not presume upon his goodness, we are told how great he is. Many words are here heaped up to acquaint us with, and convince us of God's goodness.

1st, He is merciful, This speaks his pity, and tender companion, like that of a father to his children. This is put first, because it is the first wheel in all the instances of God's goodwill to fallen man. 2ndly, He is gracious. This speaks both freeness, and kindness: it speaks him not only to have a compassion to his creatures, but a complacency in them, and in doing good to them; and this of his own goodwill, not for the sake of any thing in them. 3rdly, He is long-suffering. This is a branch of God's goodness which our wickedness gives occasion for. He is long-suffering, that is, he is slow to anger, and delays the executions of his justice, he waits to be gracious, and lengthens out the offers of his mercy. 4thly, He is abundant in goodness and truth. This speaks plentiful goodness; it abounds above our deserts, above our conception. The springs of mercy are always full, the streams of mercy always flowing; there is mercy enough in God, enough for all, enough for each, enough forever. It speaks promised goodness, goodness and truth put together, goodness engaged by promise.

5thly, He keepeth mercy for thousands. This speaks,

1. Mercy extended to thousands of persons. When he gives to some, still he keeps for others, and is never exhausted:

2. Mercy entailed upon thousands of generations, even to those upon whom the ends of the world are come; nay, the line of it is drawn parallel with that of eternity itself.

6thly, He forgiveth iniquity, transgression and sin - Pardoning mercy is instanced in, because in that divine grace is most magnified, and because that it is that opens the door to all other gifts of grace. He forgives offenses of all sorts, iniquity, transgression and sin, multiplies his pardons, and with him is plenteous redemption. He is a just and holy God. For, 1st, He will by no means clear the guilty. He will not clear the impenitently guilty, those that go on still in their trespasses; he will not clear the guilty without satisfaction to his justice. 2ndly, He visits the iniquity of the fathers upon the children - Especially for the punishment of idolaters. Yet he keepeth not his anger forever, but visits to the third and fourth generation only, while he keeps mercy for thousands - This is God's name forever, and this is his memorial unto all generations.

8. And Moses made haste, and bowed his head - Thus he expressed his humble reverence and adoration of God's glory, together with his joy in this discovery God had made of himself, and his thankfulness for it. Then likewise he expressed his holy submission to the will of God made known in this declaration, subscribing to his justice as well as mercy, and putting himself and his people Israel under the government of such a God as Jehovah had now proclaimed himself to be. Let this God be our God forever and ever!

9. And he said, I pray thee go among us - For thy presence is all to our safety and success. And pardon our iniquity and our sin - Else we cannot expect thee to go among us. And take us for thine inheritance - Which thou wilt have a particular eye to, and concern for. These things God had already promised Moses; and yet he prays for them, not as doubting the sincerity of God's grants, but as one solicitous for the ratification of them. But it is a strange plea he urges, for it is a stiff-necked people - God had given this as a reason why he would not go along with them, chap. xxxiii, 3. Yea, saith Moses, the rather go along with us; for the worse they are, the more need they have of thy presence. Moses sees them so stiff-necked, that he has neither patience nor power enough to deal with them; therefore, Lord, do thou go among us; else they will never be kept in awe; thou wilt spare, and bear with them, for thou art God and not man.

10. Behold I make a covenant - When the covenant was broke, it was Israel that broke it; now it comes to be renewed, it is God that makes it. If there be quarrels, we must bear all the blame; if there be peace, God must have all the glory. Before all thy people I will do marvels - Such as the drying up of Jordan, the standing still of the sun. Marvels indeed, for they were without precedent, such as have not been done in all the earth; the people shall see, and own the work of the Lord; and they were the terror of their enemies: it is a terrible thing that I will do.

11. Observe that which I command thee - We cannot expect the benefit of the promises, unless we make conscience of the precepts. The two great precepts are,

1. Thou shalt worship no other gods - A good reason is annexed; for the Lord, whose name is Jealous, is a jealous God - As tender in the matters of his worship as the husband is of the honour of the marriage-bed.

2. Thou shalt make thee no molten gods - Thou shalt not worship the true God by images. This was the sin they had lately fallen into, which therefore they are particularly cautioned against. That they might not be tempted to worship other gods, they must not join in affinity or friendship with those that did.

12. Take heed to thyself - It is a sin thou art prone to, and that will easily beset thee; carefully abstain from all advances towards it, make no covenant with the inhabitants of the land - If God in kindness to them drove out the Canaanites, they ought in duty to God not to harbour them: If they espoused their children they would be in danger of espousing their gods. That they might not be tempted to make molten gods, they must utterly destroy those they found, and all that belonged to them, the altars and groves, lest, if they were left standing, they should be brought in process of time either to use them, or to take pattern by them.

21. Here is a repetition of several appointments made before, especially relating to their solemn feasts: when they had made the calf they proclaimed a feast in honour of it; now, that they might never do so again, they are here charged with the observance of the feasts which God had instituted. Thou shalt rest, even in earing-time and in harvest - The most busy times of the year. All wordly business must give way to that holy rest: harvest-work will prosper the better for the religious observation of the sabbath- day in harvest-time. Hereby we must shew that we prefer our communion with God, before either the business or the joy of harvest.

23. Thrice in the year shall all the men-children appear - But it might be suggested, when all the males slain every part were gone up to worship in the place that God should chuse, the country would he left exposed to the insults of their neighbours; and what would become of the poor women and children? Trust God with them.

24. Neither shalt any man desire thy land - Not only they shall not invade it, but they shall not so much as think of invading it. What a standing Miracle was this, for so many Generations?

28. He wrote - God.

29. The skin of his face shone - This time of his being in the mount he heard only the same he had heard before. But he saw more of the glory of God, which having with open face beheld, he was in some measure changed into the same image. This was a great honour done to Moses, that the people might never again question his mission, or think or speak slightly of him. He carried his credentials in his very countenance, some think as long as he lived, he retained some remainders of this glory, which perhaps contributed to the vigour of his old age; that eye could not wax dim which had seen God, nor that face wrinkle which had shone with his glory.

30. And Aaron and the children of Israel saw it, and were afraid - It not only dazzled their eyes,

but struck such an awe upon them as obliged them to retire. Probably they doubted whether it was a token of God's favour, or of his displeasure.

33. And Moses put a veil upon his face - This veil signified the darkness of that dispensation; the ceremonial institutions had in them much of Christ and the gospel, but a veil was drawn over it, so that the children of Israel could not distinctly and steadfastly see those good things to come which the law had a shadow of. It was beauty veiled, gold in the mine, a pearl in the shell; but thanks be to God, by the gospel, the veil is taken away from off the old testament; yet still it remains upon the hearts of those who shut their eyes against the light.

34. When he went before the Lord, he put off the veil - Every veil must be thrown aside when we go to present ourselves unto the Lord. This signified also, as it is explained, 2 Cor. iii, 16, that when a soul turns to the Lord, the veil shall be taken away, that with open face it may behold his glory.

XXXV

The great affair of setting up God's worship is now upon its former channel again.

I. Moses gives Israel those instructions he had received, which required a present observance, (1.) Concerning the sabbath, ver. 1-3. (2.) Concerning the contribution that was to be made for erecting the tabernacle, ver. 4-9. (3.) Concerning the framing of the tabernacle, and the utensils of it, ver. 10-19.

II. The people bring in their contributions, ver. 20-29.

III. The head workmen are nominated, ver. 30-35.

2. Six days shall work be done - Work for the tabernacle, but on the seventh day - You must not strike a stroke, no not at the tabernacle-work; the honour of the sabbath was above that of the sanctuary.

3. Ye shall kindle no fire - For any servile work, as that of smiths or plumbers. We do not find that ever this prohibition extended farther.

21. Everyone whom his spirit made willing - What they did they did cheerfully. They were willing; and it was not any external inducement that made them so, but their spirits. It was from a principle of love to God, and his service; a desire of his presence with them by his ordinances; gratitude for the great things he had done for them; and faith in his promises of what he would do further.

22. Tablets or Lockets.

30. The Lord hath called Bezaleel - And those whom God called by name to this service, he filled with the spirit of God, to qualify them for it. The work was extraordinary which Bezaleel was designed for, and therefore he was qualified in an extraordinary manner for it. Thus when the apostles were appointed to be master-builders in setting up the gospel-tabernacle, they were filled with the spirit of God in wisdom and understanding.

XXXVI

In this chapter,

I. The work of the tabernacle is begun, ver. 1-4.

II. A stop put to the people's contributions, ver. 5-7.

III. A particular account of the making the tabernacle; the fine curtains of it, ver. 8-13. The coarse ones, ver. 14-19. The boards, ver. 20-xxx, The bars, ver. 31-34 The partition veil, ver. 35, 36. and the hangings of the door, ver. 37, 38.

2. And Moses called Bezaleel - "Even those whom God has qualified for, and inclined to the service of the tabernacle, yet must wait for a call to it, either extraordinary, as that of preachers and apostles, or ordinary, as that of pastors and teachers. And observe who they were that Moses called; those in whose heart God had put wisdom for this purpose, beyond their natural capacity, and whose heart stirred him up to come to the work in good earnest." Those are to be called to the building of the gospel tabernacle, whom God has by his grace made in some measure fit for the work, and free to it: ability and willingness, with resolution, are the two things to be regarded in the call of ministers.

35. The veil made for a partition between the holy place and the most holy, signified the darkness and distance of that dispensation compared with the New Testament, which shews us the glory of God more clearly, and invites us to draw near to it; and the darkness and distance of our present state in comparison with heaven, where we shall be ever with the Lord, and see him as he is.

37. An hanging - Which divided the holy place from the court.

XXXVII

Bezaleel and his workmen are still busy, making,

I. The ark with the mercy-seat and the cherubim, ver. 1-9.

II. The table with its vessels, ver. 10-16.

III. The candle-stick with its appurtenances, ver. 17-24.

IV. The golden altar for incense, ver. 25-28.

V. The holy oil and incense, ver. 29. 1-9. These several ornaments where with the tabernacle was furnished, the people were not admitted to see, but the priests only; and therefore it was requisite they should be thus largely described, particularly to them. And Moses would thus shew the great care which he and his workmen took to make every thing exactly according to the pattern shewed him in the mount. Thus he appeals to every reader concerning his fidelity to him that appointed him, in all his house. And thus he teacheth us to have respect to all God's commandments, even to every jot and tittle of them. In these verses we have an account of the making of the ark with its glorious and significant appurtenances, the mercy-seat and the cherubim. Consider these three together, and they represent the glory of a holy God, the sincerity of a holy heart, and the communion that is between them by a Mediator. It is the glory of a holy God that he dwelleth between the cherubim, that is, is continually attended by the blessed angels, whose swiftness was signified by the wings of the cherubim, and their unanimity in their services, by their faces being one towards another. It is the character of an upright heart, that, like the ark of the testimony, it hath the law of God hid and kept in it. By Jesus Christ the great propitiation there is reconciliation made, and a communion settled, between us and God: he interposeth between us and God's displeasure; and through him we become entitled to God's favour.

10. Observe how much the dispensation of the gospel exceeds that of the law. Tho' here was a table furnished, it was only with shew- bread, bread to be looked upon, not to be fed upon, while it was on the table, and afterwards only by the priests: but to the table Christ has spread in the new covenant all good Christians are invited guests, and to them it is said, Eat, O friends, come eat of my bread. What the law gave but a sight of at a distance, the gospel gives the enjoyment of.

17. This candlestick, which was not of wood overlaid with gold, but all beaten-work of pure gold only, signified that light of divine Revelation with which God's church upon earth (which is his tabernacle among men) hath always been enlightened, being always supplied with fresh oil from Christ the good olive, Zech. iv, 2, 3. The bible is a golden candlestick, it is of pure gold; from it light is diffused to every part of God's tabernacle, that by it the spiritual priests may see to do the service of his sanctuary. The candlestick has not only its bowls for necessary use, but its knops and flowers for ornament; many things which God saw fit to beautify his word with, which we can no more give a reason for than for these knops and flowers, and yet must be sure they wert added for good purpose. Let us bless God for this candlestick, have an eye to it continually, and dread the removal of it out of its place!

25. The incense burnt on this altar daily, signified both the prayers of saints, and the intercession of Christ, to which is owing the acceptableness of them.

XXXVIII

Here is an account,

I. Of the making of the brazen altar, ver. 1-7. and the laver, ver. 8.

II. The preparing of the hangings for the inclosing of the court in which the tabernacle was to stand, ver. 9-20.

III. A summary account of the gold, silver and brass that was contributed to, and used in the preparing of the tabernacle, ver. 21-31.

1. The altar of burnt-offering - On this all their sacrifices were offered. Christ was himself the altar to his own sacrifice of atonement, and so he is to all our sacrifices of acknowledgment. We must have

an eye to him in offering them, as God hath in accepting them.

8. This laver signified the provision that is made in the gospel for cleansing our souls from the pollution of sin by the merit of Christ, that we may be fit to serve the holy God in holy duties. This is here said to be made of the looking-glasses of the women that assembled at the door of the tabernacle. It should seem these women were eminent for devotion, attending more constantly at the place of public worship than others, and notice is here taken of it to their honour. These looking-glasses were of the finest brass, burnished for that purpose. In the laver, either they were artfully joined together, or else molten down and cast anew; but it is probable the laver was so brightly burnished that the sides of it still served for looking-glasses, that the priests when they came to wash might there see their faces, and so discover the spots to wash them clean.

9. And he made the court - The walls of the court, were like the rest, curtains, or hangings. This represented the state of the Old Testament church, it was a garden enclosed; the worshippers were then confined to a little compass. But the inclosure being of curtains only, intimated that that confinement of the church to one particular nation was not to be perpetual. The dispensation itself was a tabernacle-dispensation, moveable and mutable, and in due time to be taken down and folded up, when the place of the tent should be enlarged, and its cords lengthened, to make room for the Gentile world.

21. By the hand of Ithamar - Here we have a breviate of the account which by Moses's appointment the Levites took and kept of the gold, silver, and brass, that was brought in for the tabernacle's use, and how it was employed. Ithamar the son of Aaron was appointed to draw up this account. All the gold amounted to twenty nine talents, and seven hundred and thirty shekels over; Which some compute to be about one hundred and fifty thousand pounds worth of gold, according to the present value of it. The silver amounted to about thirty-four thousand pounds of our money. The raising of the gold by voluntary contribution, and of the silver by way of tribute, shews that either way may be taken for the defraying of public expences, provided that nothing be done with partiality.

XXXIX

This chapter gives us an account of the finishing of the work of the tabernacle.

I. The last thing prepared was the holy garments. The ephod, and its curious girdle, ver. 1-5. The onyx stones for the shoulders, ver. 6, 7. The breast-plate with the precious stones in it, ver. 8-21. The robe of the ephod, ver. 22-26. The coats, bonnets and breeches for the inferior priests, ver. 27-29. And the plate of the holy crown, ver. 30, 31.

II. A summary account of the whole work, ver. 32-43.

1. The priests garments are called here clothes of service - Those that wear robes of honour must look upon them as clothes of service; for those upon whom honour is put, from them service is expected. Holy garments were not made for men to sleep in, but to do service in, and then they are indeed for glory and beauty. These also were shadows of good things to come, but the substance is Christ. He is our great high priest; he put upon him the clothes of service when he undertook the work of our redemption; arrayed himself with the gifts and graces of the Spirit, which he received not by measure; charged himself with all God's spiritual Israel, bare them on his shoulder, carried them in his bosom, and presented them in the breast-plate of judgment unto his Father. And, lastly, he crowned himself with holiness to the Lord, consecrated his whole undertaking to the honour of his Fathers holiness. And all true believers are spiritual priests. The clean linen with which all their clothes of service must be made, is the righteousness of saints: and holiness to the Lord must be so written upon their foreheads, that all who converse with them may see they bear the image of God's holiness.

32. Thus was all the work finished - In not much more than five months. Though there was a great deal of fine work, such as used to be the work of time, embroidering, and engraving, not only in gold, but in precious stones, yet they went through with it in a little time, and with the greatest exactness imaginable. The workmen were taught of God, and so were kept from making blunders, which would have retarded them. And the people were hearty and zealous in the work, and impatient till it was finished. God had prepared their hearts, and then the thing was done suddenly, 2 Chron. xxix, 36.

43. And Moses did look upon all the work - Piece by Piece, and behold they had done it according to the pattern shewed him - For the same that shewed him the pattern, guided their hand in the work. And Moses blessed them - He not only praised them, but prayed for them: he blessed them as one having authority. We read not of any wages Moses paid them for their work, but his blessing he gave them. For though ordinarily the labourer be worthy of his hire, yet in this case, they wrought for themselves. The honour and comfort of God's tabernacle among them would be recompence enough. And they had their meat from heaven on free-cost, for themselves and their families, and their raiment waxed not old upon them; so that they neither needed wages, nor had reason to expect any. But indeed

this blessing in the name of the Lord was wages enough for all their work. Those whom God employs he will bless, and those whom he blesseth, they are blessed indeed. The blessing he commands is life forevermore.

XL

In this chapter,

I. Orders are given for setting up the tabernacle, and fixing all the appurtenances of it, ver. 1-8. and the consecrating of it, ver. 8-11. and of the priests, ver. 12-15.

II. Care taken to do all this, and as it was appointed to be done, ver. 16-33.

III. God's taking possession of it by the cloud, ver. 34-38.

2. The time for doing this is, On the first day of the first month - This wanted but fourteen days of a year since they came out of Egypt. Probably the work was made ready just at the end of the year, so that the appointing this day gave no delay. In Hezekiah's time they began to sanctify the temple on the first day of the first month, 2 Chron. xxix, 17. The new moon (which by their computation was the first day of every month) was observed by them with some solemnity; and therefore this first new moon of the year was thus made remarkable.

15. Their anointing shall be an everlasting priesthood - A seal that their priesthood shall continue as long as the Jewish polity lasts. He signifies that this unction should be sufficient for all succeeding priests. None were afterwards anointed but the high- priests.

34. As when God had finished this earth, which he designed for man's habitation, he made man, and put him in possession of it; so when Moses had finished the tabernacle, which was designed for God's dwelling-place among men, God came and took possession of it. By these visible tokens of his coming among them, he testified both the return of his favour, which they had forfeited by the golden calf, and his gracious acceptance of their care and pains about the tabernacle. Thus God shewed himself well- pleased with what they had done, and abundantly rewarded them. A cloud covered the tent - The same cloud which, as the chariot or pavilion of the Shechinah, had come up before them out of Egypt, now settled upon the tabernacle, and hovered over it, even in the hottest and clearest day; for it was none of those clouds which the sun scatters. This cloud was intended to be a token of God's presence, constantly visible day and night to all Israel. A protection of the tabernacle: they had sheltered it with one covering upon another, but after all, the cloud that covered it was its best guard: And a guide to the camp of Israel in their march through the wilderness. While the cloud continued on the tabernacle, they rested; when it removed, they removed and followed it, as being purely under a divine conduct. And the glory of the Lord filled the tabernacle - The Shechinah now made an awful entry into the tabernacle, passing through the outer part of it into the most holy place, and there seating itself between the cherubim. It was in light and fire, and, for ought we know, no other-wise, that the Shechinah made itself visible. With these the tabernacle was now filled; yet as before the bush, so now the curtains were not consumed, for, to those that have received the anointing, the majesty of God is not destroying. Yet now so dazzling was the light, and so dreadful was the fire, that Moses was not able to enter into the tent of the congregation, at the door of which he attended, till the splendour was a little abated, and the glory of the Lord retired within the veil. But what Moses could not do, our Lord Jesus has done, whom God caused to draw near and approach, and as the fore-runner he is for us entered, and has invited us to come boldly even to the mercy-seat. He was able to enter into the holy place not made with hands; he is himself the true tabernacle, filled with the glory of God, even with that divine grace and truth which were figured by this fire and light. In him the Shechinah took up its rest forever, for in him dwells all the fulness of the Godhead bodily.

NOTES ON THE THIRD BOOK OF MOSES CALLED LEVITICUS

THIS book, containing the actions of about one month's space, acquaint us with the Levitical ceremonies used after the tabernacle was erected in the wilderness, and is therefore called Leviticus: It treats of laws concerning persons, and things, clean and unclean; as also purifyings in general once a year, and divers particular cleansings, with a brief repetition of divers laws, together with certain feasts, of seven years rest, of the jubilee, and the redemption of things consecrated to God; but especially of such ceremonies as were used about offerings and sacrifices, which were both expiatory for trespasses committed, whether by the People or the priests; and also eucharistical in the owning of God's blessings. Here are declared also laws for the regulating of these, and prescribing the lawful time for marriages; here is set down how several abominable sins are punishable by the magistrate; and how these things are to be managed by certain persons appropriated to the tribe of Levi, whose office is confirmed from heaven, and the male-administration of it threatened, and the judgment particularly inflicted on Nadab and Abihu for an example. Here are promises, and threatenings, to the observers, or breakers of this law. The records of even these abrogated laws are of use to us, for the strengthening of our faith in it, as the lamb slain from the foundation of the world; and for the increase of our thankfulness to God, for freeing us from that heavy yoke. Directions concerning burnt-offerings: A bullock, ver. 1-9. A sheep, goat, lamb, or kid, ver. 10-13. A turtle dove, or young pigeon, ver. 14-17.

1. Moses - Stood without, Exod. xl, 35, waiting for God's call. The tabernacle - From the mercy-seat in the tabernacle.

2. There are divers kinds of sacrifices here prescribed, some by way of acknowledgment to God for mercies either desired or received; others by way of satisfaction to God for men's sins; others were mere exercises of devotion. And the reason why there were so many kinds of them was, partly a respect to the childish state of the Jews, who by the custom of nations, and their own natural inclinations were much addicted to outward rites and ceremonies, that they might have full employment of that kind in Gods's service, and thereby be kept from temptations to idolatry; and partly to represent as well the several perfections of Christ, the true sacrifice, and the various benefits of his death, as the several duties which men owe to their Creator and Redeemer, all which could not be so well expressed by one sort of sacrifice. Of the flock - Or, Of the sheep; though the Hebrew word contains both the sheep and goats. Now God chose these creatures for his sacrifices, either,

1. In opposition to the Egyptian idolatry, to which divers of the Israelites had been used, and were still in danger of revolting to again, that the frequent destruction of these creatures might bring such silly deities into contempt. Or,

2. Because these are the fittest representations both of Christ and of true Christians, as being gentle, and harmless, and patient, and useful to men. Or,

3. As the best and most profitable creatures, with which it is fit God should be served, and which we should be ready to part with, when God requires us to do so. Or.

4. As things most common, that men might never want a sacrifice when they needed, or God required it.

3. A burnt sacrifice - Strictly so called, such as was to be all burnt, the skin excepted. For every sacrifice was burnt, more or less. The sacrifices signified that the whole man, in whose stead the sacrifice was offered, was to be entirely offered or devoted to God's service; and that the whole man did deserve to be utterly consumed, if God should deal severely with him; and directed us to serve the Lord with all singleness of heart, and to be ready to offer to God even such sacrifices or services wherein we ourselves should have no part or benefit. A male - As being more perfect than the female, Mal. i, 14, and more truly representing Christ. Without blemish - To signify,

1. That God should be served with the best of every kind.

2. That man, represented by these sacrifices, should aim at all perfection of heart and life, and that Christians should one day attain to it, Eph. v, 27.

3. The spotless and compleat holiness of Christ. Of his own will - According to this translation, the place speaks only of free-will offerings, or such as were not prescribed by God to be offered in

course, but were offered by the voluntary devotion of any person, either by way of supplication for any mercy, or by way of thanksgiving for any blessing received. But it may seem improper to restrain the rules here given to free-will offerings, which were to be observed in other offerings also. At the door - In the court near the door, where the altar stood, ver. 5. For here it was to be sacrificed, and here the people might behold the oblation of it. And this farther signified, that men could have no entrance, neither into the earthly tabernacle, the church, nor into the heavenly tabernacle of glory, but by Christ, who is the door, John x, 7, 9, by whom alone we have access to God.

4. He shall put his hand - Both his hands, chap. viii, 14, 18, and chap. xvi, 21. Whereby he signified,

1. that he willingly gave it to the Lord.

2. That he judged himself worthy of that death which it suffered in his stead; and that he laid his sins upon it with an eye to him upon whom God would lay the iniquity of us all, Isaiah liii, 6, and that together with it he did freely offer up himself to God. To make atonement - Sacramentally; as directing his faith and thoughts to that true propitiatory sacrifice which in time was to be offered up for him. And although burnt-offerings were commonly offered by way of thanksgiving; yet they were sometimes offered by way of atonement for sin, that is, for sins in general, as appears from Job i, 5, but for particular sins there were special sacrifices.

5. And he - Either,

1. the offerer, who is said to do it, namely, by the priest; for men are commonly said to do what they cause others to do, as John iv, 1, 2. Or,

2. the priest, as it follows, or the Levite, whose office this was. Shall sprinkle the blood - Which was done in a considerable quantity, and whereby was signified,

1. That the offerer deserved to have his blood spilt in that manner.

2. That the blood of Christ should be poured forth for sinners, and that this was the only mean of their reconciliation to God, and acceptance with him.

6. Pieces - Namely, the head, and fat, and inwards, and legs, ver. 8, 9.

7. Put fire - Or, dispose the fire, that is, blow it up, and put it together, so as it might be fit for the present work. For the fire there used and allowed came down from heaven, chap. ix, 24, and was to be carefully preserved there, and all other fire was forbidden, chap. x, 1, &c.

8. The fat - All the fat was to be separated from the flesh, and to be put together, to increase the flame, and to consume the other parts of the sacrifice more speedily.

9. But the inwards shall he wash - To signify the universal and perfect purity both of the inwards, or the heart, and of the legs, or ways or actions, which was in Christ, and which should be in all Christians. And he washed not only the parts now mentioned, but all the rest, the trunk of the body, and the shoulders. A sweet savour - Not in itself, for so it rather caused a stink, but as it represented Christ's offering up himself to God as a sweet smelling savour.

11. North-ward - Here this and other kinds of sacrifices were killed, chap. vi, 25, and chap. vii, 2, because here seems to have been the largest and most convenient place for that work, the altar being probably near the middle of the east-end of the building, and the entrance being on the south-side. Besides this might design the place of Christ's death both more generally, in Jerusalem, which was in the sides of the north, Psalm xlviii, 2, and more specially, on mount Calvary, which was on the northwest side of Jerusalem.

14. Turtle-doves - These birds were appointed for the poor who could not bring better. And these birds are preferred before others, partly because they were easily gotten, and partly because they are fit representations of Christ's chastity, and meekness, and gentleness, for which these birds are remarkable. The pigeons must be young, because then they are best; but the turtle-doves are better when they are grown up, and therefore they are not confined to that age.

15. His head - From the rest of the body; as sufficiently appears, because this was to be burnt by itself, and the body afterwards, ver. 17. And whereas it is said chap. v, 8. He shall - wring his head from his neck, but shall not divide it asunder, that is spoken not of the burnt-offering as here, but of the sin-offering.

16. With its feathers - Or, with its dung or filth, contained in the crop and in the guts. On the east - Of the Tabernacle. Here the filth was cast, because this was the remotest place from the holy of holies, which was in the west-end; to teach us, that impure things and persons should not presume to approach to God, and that they should be banished from his presence. The place of the ashes - Where the ashes fell down and lay, whence they were afterwards removed without the camp.

17. He shall cleave the bird through the whole length, yet so as not to separate the one side from the other. A sweet savour unto the Lord - Yet after all, to love God with all our hearts, and to love our neighbour as ourselves, is better than all burnt-offerings and sacrifices.

II

Directions concerning the meal-offerings.

I. Of fine flour with oil and frankincense, ver. 1-11.

II. Of the first fruits, ver. 12-16.

1. A meal-offering - (Not meat-offering, an ancient false print, which has run thro' many editions of our bible.) This was of two kinds, the one joined with other offerings, Num. xv, 4, 7, 10, which was prescribed, together with the measure or proportion of it: the other, of which this place speaks, was left to the offerer's good will both for the thing, and for the quantity. And the matter for this offering was things without life, as meal, corn, or cakes. Now this sort of sacrifices were appointed,

    1. because these are things of greatest necessity and benefit to man, and therefore it is meet that God should be served with them, and owned and praised as the giver of them.

    2. In condescension to the poor, that they might not want an offering for God, and to shew that God would accept even the meanest services, when offered with a sincere mind.

    3. These were necessary provisions for the feast which was to be presented to God, and for the use of the priests, who were to attend upon these holy ministrations. He shall pour oil - This may note the graces of the Holy Ghost, which are compared to oil, and anointing with it, Psalm xlv, 7, 1 John ii, 20, and which are necessary to make any offering acceptable to God. Frankincense - Manifestly designed Christ's satisfaction and intercession, which is compared to a sweet odour, Eph. v, 2.

2. He shall take - That priest to whom he brought it, and who is appointed to offer it. The memorial - That part thus selected and offered; which is called a memorial, either

    1. to the offerer, who by offering this part is minded, that the whole of that he brought, and of all which he hath of that kind, is God's to whom this part was paid as an acknowledgment. Or

    2. to God, whom (to speak after the manner of men) this did put in mind of his gracious covenant and promises of favour, and acceptance of the offerer and his offering. A sweet savour unto the Lord - And so are our spiritual offerings, which are made by the fire of holy love, particularly that of almsgiving. With such sacrifices God is well-pleased.

3. Sons - To be eaten by them, chap. vi, 16. Most holy - Or such as were to be eaten only by the priests, and that only in the holy place near the altar.

4. In the oven - Made in the sanctuary for that use.

6. In pieces - Because part of it was offered to God, and part given to the priests.

11. No leaven - Namely, in that which is offered of free-will; for in other offerings it might be used, chap. vii, xxiii. This was forbidden, partly to mind them of their deliverance out of Egypt, when they were forced thro' haste to bring away their meal or dough (which was the matter of this oblation) unleavened; partly to signify what Christ would be, and what they should be, pure and free from all error in the faith and worship of God, and from all hypocrisy, and malice or wickedness, all which are signified by leaven. Nor any honey - Either,

    1. because it hath the same effect with leaven in paste or dough, making it sour, and swelling. Or,

    2. in opposition to the sacrifices of the Gentiles, in which the use of honey was most frequent. Or,

    3. to teach us, that God's worship is not to be governed by men's fancies and appetites but by God's will.

12. Ye may offer them - Or either of them, leaven or honey. They shall not be burnt - But reserved for the priests.

13. Salt - To signify that incorruption of mind, and sincerity of grace, which in scripture is signified by salt, Mark ix, 49, Colossians iv, 6, and which is necessary in all them that would offer an acceptable offering to God. Or in testimony of that communion which they had with God in these exercises of worship; salt being the great symbol of friendship in all nations is called, either,

    1. because it represented the perpetuity of God's covenant with them, which is designed by salt, Num. xviii, 19, 2 Chron. xiii, 5. Or,

    2. because it was so particularly required as a condition of their covenant with God; this being made absolutely necessary in all their offerings; and as the neglect of sacrifices was a breach of covenant on their part, so also was the neglect of salt in their sacrifices.

14. First-fruits - Of thine own free-will; for there were other first-fruits, and that of several sorts, which were prescribed, and the time, quality, and proportion of them appointed by God.

16. Made by fire - The fire denotes that fervency of spirit, which ought to be in all our religious services. Holy love is the fire, by which all our offerings must be made: else they are not of a sweet savour to God.

III

Directions concerning peace-offerings. A bullock or an heifer, ver. 1-5. A lamb, ver. 6-11. A goat, ver. 12-16. No fat or blood to be eaten, ver. 17.

1. A peace-offering - This was an offering for peace and prosperity, and the blessing of God, either,
 1. obtained, and so it was a thank-offering, or,
 2. desired; and so it was a kind of supplication to God. A female - Which were allowed here, tho' not in burnt-offerings, because those principally respected the honour of God, who is to be served with the best; but the peace-offerings did primarily respect the benefit of the offerer, and therefore the choice was left to himself. Burnt-offerings had regard to God, as in himself the best of beings, and therefore were wholly burned. But peace-offerings had regard to God as a benefactor to his creatures, and therefore were divided between the altar, the priest, and the offerer.

2. At the door - Not on the north-side of the altar, where the burnt- offering was killed, as also the sin-offering, and the trespass- offering, but in the very entrance of the court where the brazen altar stood, which place was not so holy as the other; as appears both because it was more remote from the holy of holies, and because the ashes of the sacrifices were to be laid here. And the reason of this difference is not obscure, both because part of this sacrifice was to be waved by the hands of the offerer, chap. vii, 30, who might not come into the court; and because this offering was not so holy as the others, which were to be eaten only by the priest, whereas part of these were eaten by the offerer.

5. Upon the burnt sacrifice - Either,
 1. Upon the remainders of it, which were yet burning; or rather,
 2. After it; for the daily burnt-offering was first to be offered, both as more eminently respecting God's honour; and as the most solemn and stated sacrifice, which should take place of all occasional oblations, and as a sacrifice of an higher nature, being for atonement, without which no peace could be obtained, nor peace offering offered with acceptance.

9. The rump - Which in sheep is fat, and sweet, and in these parts was very much larger and better than ours.

11. Burnt it - The parts now mentioned; the rest fell to the priest, chap. vii, 31. The food - That is, the fuel of the fire, or the matter of the offering. It is called food, Hebrew. bread, to note God's acceptance of it, and delight in it; as men delight in their food.

16. Shall burn them - The parts mentioned, among which the tail is not one, as it was in the sheep, because that in goats is a refuse part. All the fat - This is to be limited,
 1. To those beasts, which were offered or offerable in sacrifice, as it is explained, chap. vii, 23, 25.
 2. To that kind of fat which is above-mentioned, and required to be offered, which was separated, or easily separable from the flesh for the fat which was here and there mixed with the flesh they might eat.

17. All your dwellings - Not only at or near the tabernacle, not only of those beasts which you actually sacrifice, but also in your several dwellings, and of all that kind of beasts. Fat - Was forbidden,
 1. To preserve the reverence of the holy rites and sacrifices.
 2. That they might be taught hereby to acknowledge God as their Lord, and the Lord of all the creatures, who might reserve what he pleased to himself.
 3. To exercise them in obedience to God, and self-denial and mortification of their appetites, even in those things which probably many of them would much desire. Blood - Was forbidden partly to maintain reverence to God and his worship; partly out of opposition to idolaters, who used to drink the blood of their sacrifices; partly with respect to Christ's Blood, thereby manifestly signified. God would not permit the very shadows of this to be used as a common thing. Nor will he allow us, tho' we have the comfort of the atonement made, to assume to ourselves any share in the honour of making it.

IV

Directions concerning sin-offerings; which were intended for sins committed thro' ignorance, either by the priest himself, ver. 1-12. or by the whole congregation, ver. 13-21. or by a ruler, ver. 22-26. or by a private person, ver. 27-35.

1. The Lord spake unto Moses - The laws contained in the three first chapters, seem to have been delivered to Moses at one time. Here begin the laws of another day, which God delivered from between the Cherubim.

2. If a soul sin - This must necessarily be understood of more than common daily infirmities; for if every such sin had required an offering, it had not been possible either for most sinners to bear such a charge, or for the altar to receive so many sacrifices, or for the priests to manage so infinite a work. And

for ordinary sins, they were ceremonially expiated by the daily offering, and by that on the great day of atonement, chap. xvi, 30. Through ignorance - Or, error, either not knowing his act to be sinful, as appears by comparing ver. 13, 14, or not considering it, but falling into sin thro' the power of some sudden passion or temptation, as the Hebrew word signifies, Psalm 1xix, 67. Things which ought not to be done - The words may be rendered, in or about every, or any of the commandments of the Lord which should not be done; or, which concern things that should not be done, namely, in any negative commands. (And there is great reason why a sacrifice should be more necessary for these, than for other sins, because affirmative precepts do not so strictly and constantly bind men as the negative do.) Then he shall offer according to his quality, which is here to be understood out of the following verses.

3. If the priest - That is, the high-priest, who only was anointed after the first time. His anointing is mentioned, because he was not compleat high-priest 'till he was anointed. Do sin - Either in doctrine or practice, which it is here supposed he may do. And this is noted as a character of imperfection in the priesthood of the law, whereby the Israelites were directed to expect another and better high-priest, even one who is holy, harmless, and separate from sinners, Heb. vii, 26. According to the sin of the people - In the same manner as any of the people do; which implies that God expected more circumspection from him, than from the people. But the words may be rendered, to the sin or guilt of the people, which may be mentioned as an aggrevation of his sin, that by it he commonly brings sin, and guilt, and punishment upon the people, who are infected or scandalized by his example. A young bullock - The same sacrifice which was offered for all the people, to shew how much his sin was aggravated by his quality. Sin-offering - Hebrew. sin, which word is oft taken in that sense.

4. On the head - To testify both his acknowledgment of his sin, and faith in God's promise for the expiation of his sins through Christ, whom that sacrifice typified. Kill the bullock - By one of the priests, whom he should cause to do it.

5. To the tabernacle - Into the tabernacle; which was not required nor allowed in any other sacrifice, possibly to shew the greatness of the high-priest's sin, which needed more than ordinary diligence in him, and favour from God to expiate it.

6. Seven times - A number much used in scripture, as a number of perfection; and here prescribed, either to shew that his sins needed more then ordinary purgation, and more exercise of his faith and repentance, both which graces he was obliged to join with that ceremonial rite. Before the veil - The second veil dividing between the holy of holies, which is generally called the veil of the sanctuary.

7. All the blood - All the rest; for part was disposed elsewhere.

12. The whole bullock - So no part of this was to be eaten by the priests, as it was in other sin-offerings. The reason is plain, because the offerer might not eat of his own sin-offering, and the priest was the offerer in this case, as also in the sin-offering for the whole congregation below, of which the priest himself was a member. Shall be carried forth - Not himself, which would have defiled him, but by another whom he shall appoint for that work. Without the camp - To signify either,

1. The abominable nature of sin, especially in high and holy persons, or when it overspreads a whole people. Or,

2. The removing of the guilt or punishment of that sin from the people. Or,

3. That Christ should suffer without the camp or gate. Where the ashes are - For the ashes, though at first they were thrown down near the altar, chap. i, 16, yet afterwards they, together with the filth of the sacrifices, were carried into a certain place without the camp.

13. The whole congregation - The body of the people, or the greater part of them, their rulers concurring with them.

14. A bullock - But if the sin of the congregation was only the omission of some ceremonial duty, a kid of the goats was to be offered, Num. xv, 24.

15. The elders - Who here acted in the name of all the people, who could not possibly perform this act in their own persons.

17. And sprinkle it - It was not to be poured out there, but sprinkled only; for the cleansing virtue of the blood of Christ was sufficiently represented by sprinkling. It was sprinkled seven times: seven is a number of perfection; because God made the world in six days, and rested the seventh. This signified the perfect satisfaction Christ made, and the compleat cleansing of our souls thereby.

18. The altar - Of incense: Which is before the Lord - That is, before the holy of holies, where the Lord was in a more special manner present.

20. For a sin-offering - That is, for the priest's sin-offering, called the first bullock, ver. 21.

24. The burnt-offering - So called by way of eminency, to wit, the daily burnt-offering. It is a sin-offering - And therefore to be killed where the burnt-offering is killed; whereby it is distinguished from the peace-offering, which were killed elsewhere.

26. It shall be forgiven - Both judicially, as to all ecclesiastical censures or civil punishment; and really, upon condition of repentance and faith in the Messiah to come.

28. A female - Which here was sufficient, because the sin of one of those was less than the sin of the ruler, for whom a male was required.

33. He shall slay it - Not by himself, but by the hands of the priest.

35. Burn them - The fat; but he useth the plural number, because the fat was of several kinds, as we saw ver. 8, 9. upon the offerings, together with them, or after them; because the burnt-offerings were to have the first place.

V

Directions concerning trespass-offerings. Both this and the sin-offering were intended to make atonement for sin, but the former was more general: The latter was to be offered only in some particular cases. If a man sinned, By hearing and concealing blasphemy, ver. 1. By touching an unclean thing, ver. 2, 3. By swearing, ver. 4. He was to offer a lamb or kid, ver. 5, 6. Or two young pigeons, ver. 7-10. Or fine flour, ver. 11-13. Or a ram, if he had embezzled holy things, ver. 14-19.

1. And hear - And for that is, as that particle is often used. For this declares in particular what the sin was. Or, namely, that of cursing, or blasphemy, or execration, as the word commonly signifies, and that either against one's neighbour, or against God. This may seem to be principally intended here, because the crime spoken of is of so high a nature, that he who heard it, was obliged to reveal it, and prosecute the guilty. He hath seen - Been present when it was said. Or known - By sufficient information from others. His iniquity - That is, the punishment of it; so that word is oft used, as Gen. xix, 15, Num. xviii, 1.

2. If it be hidden from him - If he do it unawares, yet that would not excuse him, because he should have been more circumspect to avoid all unclean things. Hereby God designed to awaken men to watchfulness against, and repentance for, their unknown, or unobserved sins. He shall be clean - Not morally, for the conscience was not directly polluted by these things, but ceremonially.

3. When he knoweth - As soon as he knoweth it, he must not delay to make his peace with God. Otherwise he shall be guilty - For his violation and contempt of God's authority and command.

4. If a soul swear - Rashly, without consideration either of God's law, or his own power or right, as David did, 1 Sam. xxv, 22. To do evil - To himself, to punish himself either in his body, or estate, or something else which is dear to him. Or rather to his neighbour. And it be hid from him - That is, he did not know, or not consider, that what he swore to do, was or would be impossible, or unlawful: When he discovers it to be so, either by his own consideration, or by information from others, whether it was good or evil which he swore to do.

5. In one of these things - In one of the three forementioned cases, either by sinful silence, or by an unclean touch, or by rash swearing. He shall confess - Before the Lord in the place of public worship. And this confession is not to be restrained to the present case, but by a parity of reason, and comparing of other scriptures, to be extended to other sacrifices for sin, to which this was a constant companion.

6. His trespass-offering - But how comes confession and a sacrifice to be necessary for him that touched an unclean thing, when such persons were cleansed with simple washing, as appears from chap. xi, 25, 28, 32, 40, 43, and Num. xix, 7, 8, 10, 19? This place speaks of him that being so unclean did come into the tabernacle, as may be gathered by comparing this place with Num. xix, 13, which if any man did, knowing himself to be unclean, which was the case there, he was to be cut off for it; and if he did it ignorantly, which is the case here, he was upon discovery of it to offer this sacrifice.

7. Not able - Through poverty. And this exception was allowed also in other sin-offerings. For a sin-offering - Which was for that particular sin, and therefore offered first: before the burnt-offering, which was for sins in general; to teach us not to rest in general confessions and repentance, but distinctly and particularly, as far as we can, to search out, and confess, and loath, and leave our particular sins, without which God will not accept our other religious services.

9. It is a sin-offering - This is added as the reason why its blood was so sprinkled and spilt.

10. According to the manner - Or order appointed by God. The priest shall make an atonement - Either declaratively, he shall pronounce him to be pardoned; or typically, with respect to Christ.

11. The tenth part of an ephah - About six pints. He shall put no oil, neither frankincense - Either to distinguish these from the meal-offerings, chap. ii, 1, or as a fit expression of their sorrow for their sins, in the sense whereof they were to abstain from things pleasant; or to signify that by his sins he deserved to be utterly deprived both of the oil of gladness, the gifts, graces and comforts of the Holy Ghost; and of God's gracious acceptance of his prayers and sacrifices, which is signified by incense, Psalm lxli, 2.

13. As a meal offering - As it was in the meal-offering, where all, except one handful, fell to the share of the priests. And this is the rather mentioned here, because in the foregoing sacrifices, chap. iv, 3, &c. chap. iv, 13, &c. the priest had no part reserved for him.

15. A trespass - Against the Lord and his priests. Through ignorance - For if a man did it knowingly, he was to be cut off, Num. xv, 30. In the holy things - In things consecrated to God, and to holy uses; such as tithes and first-fruits, or any things due, or devoted to God, which possibly a man

might either with-hold, or employ to some common use. A ram - A more chargeable sacrifice than the former, as the sin of sacrilege was greater. With thy estimation - As thou shalt esteem or rate it, thou, O priest; and at present, thou, O Moses, for he as yet performed the priest's part. And this was an additional charge and punishment to him; besides the ram, he was to pay for the holy thing which he had with-held or abused, so many shekels of silver as the priest should esteem proportionable to it.

17. The former law concerns the alienation of holy things from sacred to common use; this may concern other miscarriages about holy things, and holy duties, as may be gathered from ver. 19, where this is said to be a trespass against the Lord, not in a general sense, for so every sin was; but in a proper and peculiar sense.

VI

Further directions concerning trespass-offerings, ver. 1-7. Concerning the burnt-offerings, ver. 8-13. Concerning the meal- offerings, ver. 14-18. Particularly that at the consecration of the priests, ver. 19-23. Concerning the sin-offering, ver. 24-30.

2. If a soul sin - This sin, though directly committed against man, is emphatically said to be done against the Lord, not only in general, for so every sin against man is also against the Lord, but in a special sense, because this was a violation of human society, whereof God is the author, and president, and defender: and because it was a secret sin, of which God alone was the witness and judge: and because God's name was abused in it by perjury. To keep - In trust. Or in fellowship - Hebrew. Or in putting of the hand: that is, commerce or fellowship in trading, which is very usual when one man puts any thing into another's hand, not to keep it, but to improve it for the common benefit of them both, in which cases of partnership it is easy for one to deceive the other, and therefore provision is made against it. And this is called a putting of the hand, because such agreements used to be confirmed by giving or joining their hands together. By violence - Secretly; for he seems to speak here of such sins as could not be proved by witness. Or hath deceived - Got any thing from him by calumny, or fraud, or circumvention; so the word signifies.

3. Swear falsely - His oath being required, seeing there was no other way of discovery left.

4. Is guilty - This guilt being manifested by his voluntary confession upon remorse, whereby he reapeth this benefit, that he only restores the principal with the addition of a fifth part; whereas if he were convicted of his fault, he was to pay double, Exod. xxii, 9.

5. In the day - It must not be delayed, but restitution to man must accompany repentance towards God. Wherever wrong has been done, restitution must be made, and till it is made to the utmost of our power we cannot look for forgiveness; for the keeping of what is unjustly got, avows the taking: And both together make but one continued act of unrighteousness.

9. And the Lord spake - Hitherto he hath prescribed the sacrifices themselves; now he comes to the manner of them. The burnt- offering - The daily one, which Exod. xxix, 38, Num. xxviii, 3, as the following words shew. This was to be so managed and laid on piece after piece, that the fire might be constantly maintained by it. The morning burnt-offerings were to be kept burning all the day from morning to night also; but he mentions not that, because there was such a constant succession of sacrifices in the day-time that there needed no law for feeding and keeping in the fire then; the only danger was for the night, when other sacrifices were not offered, but only the evening burnt-offering, which if it had been consumed quickly, as the morning burnt-offering was, there had been danger of the going out of that fire, which they were commanded diligently and constantly to keep in.

10. The ashes which the fire hath consumed - That is, the wood consumed into ashes.

11. Other garments - Because this was no sacred, but a common work. A clean place - Where no dung or filth was laid. The priest himself was to do all this. God's servants must think nothing below them but sin.

12. It shall not be put out - The fire coming down from heaven, was to be perpetually preserved, and not suffered to go out, partly that there might be no occasion or temptation to offer strange fire; and partly to teach them whence they were to expect the acceptance of all their sacrifices, even from the divine mercy, signified by the fire that came down from heaven which was an usual token of God's favourable acceptance. Every morning - Though the evening also be doubtless intended, yet the morning is only mentioned, because then the altar was cleansed, and the ashes taken away, and a new fire made. Thereon - Upon the burnt- offering, which thereby would be sooner consumed, that the way might be made for other sacrifices.

13. Thus should we keep the fire of holy love ever burning in our hearts.

14. Of the meal-offering - Of that which was offered alone, and that by any of the people, not by the priest, for then it must have been all burnt. This law before delivered, is here repeated for the sake of some additions made to it.

16. His sons - The males only might eat these, because they were most holy things; whereas the

daughters of Aaron might eat other holy things. In the court - In some special room appointed for that purpose. The reason why this was to be eaten only by holy persons, and that in an holy place, is given ver. 17, because it is most holy.

17. It - That part which remains to the priest; for the part offered to God seems not to have been baked at all.

18. Everyone - That is, none should touch, or eat them, but consecrated persons, priests, or their sons.

20. When he is anointed - For high-priest for he only of all the priests was to be anointed in future ages. This law of his consecration was delivered before, and is here repeated because of some additions made to it. Perpetual - Whensoever any of them shall be so anointed. At night - Or, in the evening; the one to be annexed to the morning-sacrifice, the other to the evening- sacrifice, over and besides that meal-offering which every day was to be added to the daily morning and evening sacrifices.

21. Thou - Who art so anointed and consecrated.

23. It shall not be eaten - No part of it shall be eaten by the priest, as it was when the offering was for the people. The reason of the difference is, partly because when he offered it for the people, he was to have some recompence for his pains; partly to signify the imperfection of the Levitical priest, who could not bear their own iniquity; for the priest's eating part of the people's sacrifices did signify his typical bearing of the people's iniquity; and partly to teach the priests and ministers of God, that it is their duty to serve God with singleness of heart, and to be content with God's honour though they have no present advantage by it.

26. For sin - For the sins of the rulers, or of the people, or any of them, but not for the sins of the priests; for then its blood was brought into the tabernacle, and therefore it might not be eaten.

27. Upon any garment - Upon the priest's garment; for it was he only that sprinkled it, and in so doing he might easily sprinkle his garments. In the holy place - Partly out of reverence to the blood of sacrifices, which hereby was kept from a profane or common touch; and partly that such garments might be decent, and fit for sacred administrations.

28. Broken - Because being full of pores, the liquor in which it was sodden might easily sink into it, whereby it was ceremonially holy, and therefore was broken, lest afterwards it should be abused to common uses. Rinsed - And not broken, as being of considerable value, which therefore God would not have unnecessarily wasted. And this being of a more solid substance than an earthen vessel, was not so apt to drink in the moisture.

VII

Further directions, concerning the trespass-offering, ver. 1-7. The burnt-offering and meal-offering, ver. 8-10. The peace- offering, ver. 11-21. Fat and blood again forbidden, ver. 22-27. The priest's share of it, ver. 28-34. The conclusion of these instructions, ver. 35-38.

7. So is - In the matter following, for in other things they differed. The priests shall have it - That part of it, which was by God allowed to the priest.

9. All the meal-offering - Except the part reserved by God, chap. ii, 2, 9. Because these were ready drest and hot, and to be presently eaten; shall be the priests - The priest, who offered it, was in reason to expect, something more than his brethren who laboured not about it; and that he had only in this offering; for the others were equally distributed.

10. Dry - Without oil, or drink-offering, as those chap. v, 11, Num. v, 15. All the sons of Aaron - These were to be equally divided among all the priests. And there was manifest reason for this difference, because these were in greater quantity than the former; and being raw, might more easily be reserved for the several priests to dress it in that way which each of them liked.

13. Leavened bread - Because this was a sacrifice of another kind than those in which leaven was forbidden, this being a sacrifice of thanksgiving for God's blessings, among which leavened bread was one. Leaven indeed was universally forbidden, chap. ii, 11. But that prohibition concerned only things offered and burnt upon the altar, which this bread was not.

14. Of it - That is, of the offering, one of each part of the whole: it being most agreeable to the rules laid down before and afterward, that the priest should have a share in the unleavened cakes and wafers, as well as in the leavened bread.

16. A vow - Offered in performance of a vow, the man having desired some special favour from God, and vowed the sacrifice to God if he would grant it. On the morrow also - Which was not allowed for the thank-offering.

18. Neither shall it be imputed - For an acceptable service to God.

19. And the flesh - Namely of the holy offering, of which he is here treating; and therefore the general word is to be so limited; for other flesh one might eat in this case. That toucheth - After its oblation; which might easily happen, as it was conveyed from the altar to the place where it was eaten:

for it was not eaten in the holy place, as appears, because it was eaten by the priests, together with the offerers, who might not come thither. The flesh - That is, the other flesh; that which shall not be polluted by any unclean touch. All that are clean - Whether priests or offerers, or guests invited to the feast.

20. That eateth - Knowingly; for if it were done ignorantly, a sacrifice was accepted for it. Not being cleansed from his uncleanness according to the appointment, chap. xi, 24, &c. This verse speaks of uncleanness from an internal cause, as by an issue, &c. for what was from an external cause is spoken of in the next verse.

21. Of man - Or, of women, for the word signifies both.

23. The general prohibition of eating fat, chap. iii, 17, is here explained of those kind of creatures which were sacrificed. The fat of others they might eat.

24. He speaks still of the same kinds of beasts, and shews that this prohibition reaches not only to the fat of those beasts which were offered to God, but also of those that died, or were killed at home. And if this seems a superfluous prohibition, since the lean as well as the fat of such beasts were forbidden, chap. xxii, 8, it must be noted, that prohibition reached only to the priests, ver. 4.

29. Shall bring - Not by another, but by himself, that is, those parts of the peace-offering, which are in a special manner offered to God. His oblation unto the Lord - That is, to the tabernacle, where the Lord was present in a special manner. Though part of such offerings might be eaten in any clean place, chap. x, 14, yet not till they had been killed, and part of them offered to the Lord in the place appointed by him for that purpose.

30. His own hands - After the beast was killed, and the parts of it divided, the priest was to put the parts mentioned into the hands of the offerer. Offerings made by fire - So called, not strictly, as burnt-offerings are, because some parts of these were left for the priest, but more largely, because even these peace-offerings were in part, tho' not wholly, burnt. Waved - To and fro, by his hands, which were supported and directed by the hands of the priest.

31. His sons - The portion of every succeeding high-priest and his family.

34. The wave-breast and heave-shoulder - The breast or heart is the seat of wisdom, and the shoulder of strength for action; and these two may denote that wisdom, and power, which were in Christ our high-priest, and which ought to be in every priest.

35. Of the anointing of Aaron - That is, of the priesthood; the sign put for the thing signified; and the anointing by a like figure is put for the part of the sacrifices belonging to the priest by virtue of his anointing. This was their portion appointed them by God in that day, and therefore to be given to them in after ages.

37. Of the consecrations - That is, of the sacrifice offered at the consecration of the priests.

VIII

This chapter gives an account of the consecration of Aaron and his sins before the congregation, Moses washes and dresses them, ver. 1-9. Anoints the tabernacle with its utensils, and Aaron, ver. 10-12. Clothes his sons, ver. 13. Offers for them a sin- offering, ver. 14-17. A burnt-offering, ver. 18-21. The ram of consecration, ver. 22-30. Declares to them God's charge, which they perform, ver. 31-36.

3. All the congregation - The elders who represented all, and as many of the people as would, and could get thither, that all might be witnesses both of Aaron's commission from God, and of his work and business.

12. He poured - In a plentiful manner, as appears from Psalm lxxxiii, 2, whereas other persons and things were only sprinkled with it: because his unction was to typify the anointing of Christ with the Spirit, which was not given by measure to him. A measure of the same anointing is given to all believers.

14. The bullock - There were indeed seven bullocks to be offered at his consecration, one every day; but here he mentions only one, because he here describes only the work of the first day.

17. His hide - Which in the offerings for the people was not burnt, but given to the priest.

18. He brought the ram - Hereby they gave to God the glory of this great honour which was put upon them: and also signified the devoting themselves and all their service to God.

19. He - Either Moses, as in the following clause, or some other person by his appointment; which may be the reason why he is not named here, as he is to the sprinkling of the blood, which was an action more proper to the priest, and more essential to the sacrifice.

29. Moses's part - Who at this time administering the priest's office was to receive the priest's wages.

31. The flesh - That which was left of the ram, and particularly the breast, which was said to be Moses's part, ver. 29, and by him was given to Aaron, that he and his sons might eat of it, in token that they and only they should have the right to do so for the future.

33. *Seven days* - In each of which the same ceremonies were to be repeated, and other rites to be performed. *He* - Either God or Moses; for the words may be spoken by Moses, either in God's name or in his own; Moses speaking of himself in the third person, which is very common in scripture.

36. *So Aaron and his sons did all things* - And thus the covenant of life and peace, Mal. ii, 5, was made with them. But after all the ceremonies used in their consecration, one point was reserved for the honour of Christ's priesthood. They were made priests without an oath; but Christ with an oath, Heb. vii, 21. For neither these priests, nor their priesthood was to continue. But His is a perpetual and unchangeable priesthood.

IX

Moses appoints Aaron to offer various sacrifices, ver. 1-7. Aaron offers for himself, ver. 8-14. Offers for, and blesses the people, ver. 15-22. God signifies his acceptance of their persons and of their sacrifices, ver. 23-24.

1. *On the eighth day* - Namely, from the day of his consecration, or when the seven days of his consecration were ended. The eighth day is famous in scripture for the perfecting and purifying both of men and beasts. See chap. xii, 2, 3; xiv, 8, 9, 10; xv, 13, 14; xxii, 27. *And the elders of Israel* - All the congregation were called to be witnesses of Aaron's installment into his office, to prevent their murmurings and contempt; which being done, the elders were now sufficient to be witnesses of his first execution of his office.

2. *For a sin-offering* - For himself and his own sins, which was an evidence of the imperfection of that priesthood, and of the necessity of a better. The Jewish writers suggest, that a calf was appointed, to remind him of his sin in making the golden calf. Thereby he had rendered himself forever unworthy of the honour of the priesthood: on which he had reason to reflect with sorrow and shame, in all the atonements he made.

3. *A sin-offering* - For the people, for whose sin a young bullock was required, chap. iv, 15, but that was for some particular sin; this was more general for all their sins. Besides, there being an eye here to the priest's consecration and entrance into his office, it is no wonder if there be some difference in these Sacrifices from those before prescribed.

4. *The Lord will appear* - Hebrew. Hath appeared. He speaks of the thing to come as if it were past, which is frequent in scripture, to give them the more assurance of the thing.

5. *Before the tabernacle where God dwelt.*

6. *The glory of the Lord* - The glorious manifestation of God's powerful and gracious presence.

7. *Go and offer* - Moses had hitherto sacrificed, but now he resigns his work to Aaron, and actually gives him that commission which from God he had received for him. *For thyself and for the people* - The order is very observable, first for thyself, otherwise thou art unfit to do it for the people. Hereby God would teach us, both the deficiency of this priesthood, and how important it is that God's ministers should be in the favour of God themselves, that their ministrations may be acceptable to God, and profitable to the people.

9. *The altar* - Of burnt-offering, of which alone he speaks both in the foregoing and following words; and the blood was poured out at the bottom of this altar only, not of the altar of incense, as appears from chap. iv, 7, where indeed there is mention of putting some of the blood upon the horns of the altar of incense, in this case of the priest's sacrificing for his own sins. But there seems to be a double difference,

1. That sacrifice was offered for some particular sin, this for his sins indefinitely.

2. There he is supposed to be compleat in his office, and here he is but entering into his office, and therefore must prepare and sanctify himself by this offering upon the brazen altar in the court, before he can be admitted into the holy place where the altar of incense was. And the like is to be said for the difference between the sin-offering for the people here, and chap. iv, 17, 18.

10. *He burnt it* - By ordinary fire, which was used until the fire came down from heaven, ver. 24, though afterwards it was forbidden. And if it had not been allowed otherwise, yet this being done by Aaron at the command of Moses, and consequently with God's approbation, it was unquestionably lawful. Add to this, that there is nothing said to be consumed by that heavenly fire, but the burnt-offering with the fat belonging to it, namely, that burnt- offering mentioned ver. 16, which therefore is not there said to be burnt, as it is said of the other burnt-offering, ver. 13, and of the rest of the sacrifices in their places.

16. *The burnt-offering* - Which also was offered for the people, as the last mentioned sin-offering was.

17. *Besides the burnt-sacrifice* - Which was to be first offered every morning; for God will not have his ordinary and stated service swallowed up by extraordinary.

19. *That* - Fat. *Which covereth the inwards* - Or the Guts.

22. Aaron lifted up his hands - Which was the usual rite of blessing. By this posture he signified both whence he expected the blessing, and his hearty desire of it for them. And blessed them - In some such manner, as is related, Num. vi, 24, &c. though not in the same form, for it is not probable that he used it before God delivered it And this blessing was an act of his priestly office, no less than sacrificing. And herein be was a type of Christ, who came into the world to bless us, and when he was parting from his disciples, lifted up his hands and blessed them: yea, and in them his whole church, of which they were the elders and representatives. And came down - From the altar; whence he is said to come down, either

1. Because the altar stood upon raised ground, or
2. Because it was nearer the holy place, which was the upper end.

23. And Moses - Went in with Aaron to direct him, and to see him perform those parts of his office which were to be done in the holy place, about the lights, and the table of shew-bread, and the altar of incense, upon which part of the blood of the sacrifices now offered was to be sprinkled, chap. iv, 7, 16. And blessed the people - Prayed to God for his blessing upon them, as this phrase is explained, Num. vi, 23, &c. and particularly for his gracious acceptation of these and all succeeding sacrifices, and for his signification thereof by some extraordinary token. And the glory of the Lord - Either a miraculous brightness shining from the cloudy pillar, as Exod. xvi, 10, or a glorious and visible discovery of God's gracious presence and acceptance of the present service.

24. And there came a fire - In token of God's approbation of the priesthood now instituted, and the sacrifices offered, and consequently of others of the like nature. And this fire now given was to be carefully kept, and not suffered to go out, chap. vi, 13, and therefore was carried in a peculiar vessel in their journeys in the wilderness. From before the Lord - Or, from the presence of the Lord, that is, from the place where God was in a special manner present, either from heaven or from the holy of holies. They shouted - As wondering at, rejoicing in, and blessing God for this gracious discovery of himself, and his favour. This also was a figure of good things to come. Thus the Spirit descended in fire upon the apostles, so ratifying their commission, as this does that of the priests. And the descent of this holy fire into our souls, to kindle in them devout affections, and such an holy zeal as burns up all unholiness, is a certain token of God's gracious acceptance.

X

The death of Nadab and Abihu, and quieting of Aaron, ver. 1-3. Orders given to bury them, and not to mourn, ver. 4-7. A command not to drink wine or strong drink, and to distinguish between holy and unholy, ver. 8-11. Directions concerning the parts of the burnt-offerings which were to be eaten, ver. 12-15. Moses reproves the priests, but is pacified by Aaron, ver. 16-20.

1. Strange fire - Fire so called, because not taken from the altar, as it ought, but from some common fire. Before the Lord - Upon the altar of incense. Which he commanded not - Not commanding may be here put for forbidding, as it is, Jer. xxxii, 35. Now as this was forbidden implicitly; chap. vi, 12, especially when God himself made a comment upon that text, and by sending fire from heaven declared of what fire he there spake; so it is more than probable it was forbidden expressly, though that be not here mentioned, nor was it necessary it should be.

2. From the Lord - From heaven, or rather from the sanctuary. Devoured them - Destroyed their lives; for their bodies and garments were not consumed. Thus the sword is said to devour, 2 Sam. ii, 26. Thus lightning many times kill persons, without any hurt to their garments.

3. The Lord spake - Though the words be not recorded in scripture, where only the heads of discourses are contained, yet it is probable they were uttered by Moses in God's name. Howsoever the sense of them is in many places. I will be sanctified - This may note, either,

1. their duty to sanctify God, to demean themselves with such care, and reverence, and watchfulness, as becomes the holiness of the God whom they serve; whence he leaves them to gather the justice of the present judgment. Or,
2. God's purpose to sanctify himself, to manifest himself to be an holy and righteous God by his severe and impartial punishment of all transgressors, how near soever they are to him. That come nigh me - Who draw near to me, or to the place where I dwell, and are admitted into the holy place, whence others are shut out. It is a description of the priests. I will be glorified - As they have sinned publickly and scandalously, so I will vindicate my honour in a public and exemplary manner, that all men may learn to give me the glory of my holiness by an exact conformity to my laws. And Aaron held his peace - In acknowledgment of God's justice and submission to it. He murmured not, nor replied against God.

4. Moses called Mishael - For Aaron and his sons were employed in their holy ministrations, from which they were not called for funeral solemnities. Brethren - That is, kinsmen, as that word is oft used. Out of the camp - Where the burying-places of the Jews were, that the living might neither be annoyed by the unwholesome scent of the dead, nor defiled by the touch of their graves.

5. **In their coats** - In the holy garments wherein they ministered; which might be done, either,

1. as a testimony of respect due to them, notwithstanding their present failure; and that God in judgment remembered mercy, and when he took away their lives, spared their souls. Or,

2. because being polluted both by their sin, and by the touch of their dead bodies, God would not have them any more used in his service.

6. **Uncover not your head** - That is, give no signification of your sorrow; mourn not for them; partly lest you should seem to justify your brethren, and tacitly reflect upon God as too severe; and partly lest thereby you should be diverted from, or disturbed in your present service, which God expects to be done cheerfully. But **bewail the burning** - Not so much in compassion to them, as in sorrow for the tokens of divine displeasure.

7. **Ye shall not go from the tabernacle** - Where at this time they were, because this happened within seven days of their consecration. **The oil of the Lord is upon you** - You are persons consecrated peculiarly to God's service, which therefore it is just you should prefer before all funeral solemnities.

9. **Drink not wine** - it is not improbable, that the sin of Nadab and Abihu was owing to this very thing. But if not, yet drunkenness is so odious a sin in itself, especially in a minister, and most of all in the time of his administration of sacred things, that God saw fit to prevent all occasions of it. And hence the devil, who is God's ape, required this abstinence from his priests in their idolatrous service.

10. **Between holy and unholy** - Persons and things, which Nadab and Abihu did not.

11. **Ye may teach** - Which drunken persons are very unfit to do.

12. **Eat it** - Moses repeats the command, partly lest their grief should cause them to neglect their meat prescribed by God, (which abstinence would have been both a signification of their sorrow which God had forbidden them, and a new transgression of a divine precept;) and partly to encourage them to go on in their holy services, and not to be dejected, as if God would no more accept them or their sacrifices.

13. **In the holy place** - in the court, near the altar of burnt-offerings.

14. **In a clean place** - In any of your dwellings, or any place in the camp, which was kept clean from all ceremonial defilement. In any place where the women as well as the men might come, for the daughters of the priest might eat these as well as their sons, if they were maids, or widows, or divorced, chap. xxii, 11-13.

16. **He was angry with Eleazar** - He spares Aaron at this time, as overwhelmed with sorrow, and because the rebuking him before his sons might have exposed him to some contempt; but he knew that the reproof though directed to them, would concern him too. **Who were left alive** - And therefore ought to have taken warning.

17. **God hath given it to you** - As a reward of your service, whereby you expiate, bear, and take away their sins, by offering those sacrifices, by which God through Christ is reconciled to the penitent and believing offerers.

18. **The blood was not brought in** - Because Aaron was not yet admitted into the holy place, whither that blood should have been brought, 'till he had prepared the way by the sacrifices which were to be offered in the court.

19. **They have offered** - They have done the substance of the thing, though they have mistaken this one circumstance. **Such things** - Whereby, having been oppressed with grief, it is not strange nor unpardonable if I have mistaken. **Should it have been accepted** - Because it was not to be eaten with sorrow, but with rejoicing and thanksgiving.

20. **He rested satisfied with his answer.** it appeared, that Aaron sincerely aimed at pleasing God: and those who do so, will find he is not extreme to mark what is done amiss.

XI

Of clean and unclean beasts, ver. 1-8. Fishes, ver. 9-12. Fowls, ver. 13-19. Creeping things whether flying, ver. 20-28. or creeping upon the earth, ver. 29-43. An exhortation to holiness, ver. 44, 45. The conclusion, ver. 46, 47.

1. From the laws concerning the priests, he now comes to those which belong to all the people. God spake to both of them, because the cognizance of the following matters belonged to both: the priest was to direct the people about the things forbidden or allowed, where any doubt or difficulty arose; and the magistrate was to see the direction followed.

2. **These are the beasts** - Though every creature of God be good and pure in itself, yet it pleased God to make a difference between clean and unclean, which he did in part before the flood, Gen. vii, 2, but more fully here for many reasons; as,

1. To assert his own sovereignty over man, and all the creatures which men may not use but with God's leave.

2. To keep up the wall of partition between the Jews and other nations, which was very necessary

for many great and wise purposes.

3. That by bridling their appetite in things in themselves lawful, and some of them very desirable, they might be better prepared and enabled to deny themselves in things simply and grossly sinful.

4. For the preservation of their health, some of the creatures forbidden being, though used by the neighbouring nations, of unwholesome nourishment, especially to the Jews, who were very obnoxious to leprosies. To teach them to abhor that filthiness, and all those ill qualities for which some of these creatures are noted.

3. Cloven-footed - That is, divided into two parts only: This clause is added to explain and limit the former, as appears from ver. 26, for the feet of dogs, cats &c. are parted or cloven into many parts. And cheweth the cud - Hebrew. and bringeth up the cud, that is, the meat once chewed, out of the stomach in the mouth again, that it may be chewed a second time for better concoction. And this branch is to be joined with the former, both properties being necessary for the allowed beasts. But the reason hereof must be resolved into the will of the law-giver; though interpreters guess that God would hereby signify their duties, by the first, that of discerning between good and evil; and by the latter, that duty of recalling God's word to our minds and meditating upon it.

4. The camel - An usual food in Arabia, but yielding bad nourishment. Divideth not the hoof - So as to have his foot cloven in two, which being expressed, ver. 3, is here to be understood. Otherwise the camel's hoof is divided, but it is but a small and imperfect division.

5. As for the names of the following creatures, seeing the Jews themselves are uncertain and divided about them, it seems improper to trouble the unlearned readers with disputes about them.

8. Ye shall not touch - Not in order to eating, as may be gathered by comparing this with Gen. iii, 3. But since the fat and skins of some of the forbidden creatures were useful, for medicinal and other good purposes, and were used by good men, it is not probable that God would have them cast away. Thus God forbad the making of images, Exod. xx, 4, not universally, but in order to the worshipping them, as Christian interpreters agree.

9. Fins and scales - Both of them; such fishes being more cleanly, and more wholesome food than others. The names of them are not particularly mentioned, partly because most of them wanted names, the fish not being brought to Adam and named by him as other creatures were; and partly because the land of Canaan had not many rivers, nor great store of fish.

11. Unto you - This clause is added to shew that they were neither abominable in their own nature, nor for the food of other nations; and consequently when the partition-wall between Jews and Gentiles was taken away, these distinctions of meat were to cease.

13. Among the fowls - The true signification of the following Hebrew words is now lost, as the Jews at this day confess; which not falling out without God's singular providence may intimate the cessation of this law, the exact observation whereof since Christ came is become impossible. In general, this may be observed, that the fowls forbidden in diet, are all either ravenous and cruel, or such as delight in the night and darkness, or such as feed upon impure things; and so the signification of these prohibitions is manifest, to teach men to abominate all cruelty or oppression, and all works of darkness and filthiness. The ossifrage and the osprey - Two peculiar kinds of eagles, distinct from that which being the chief of its kind, is called by the name of the whole kind.

15. After his kind - According to the several kinds, known by this general name, which includes, besides ravens properly so called, crows, rooks, pyes, and others.

20. All fowls - Flying things that crawl or creep upon the earth, and so degenerate from their proper nature, and are of a mongrel kind, which may intimate that apostates and mongrels in religion are abominable in the sight of God. Upon all four - Upon four legs, or upon more than four, which is all one to the present purpose.

22. The locust - Locusts, though unusual in our food, were commonly eaten by the Ethiopians, Lybians, Parthians, and other eastern people bordering upon the Jews. And as it is certain the eastern locusts were much larger than ours, so it is probable they were of different qualities, and yielding better nourishment.

23. All other - That is, which have not those legs above and besides their feet mentioned, ver. 21.

24. Unclean - And such were excluded both from the court of God's house, and from free conversation with other men.

25. Beareth - Or, taketh away, out of the place where it may lie, by which others may be either offended, or polluted.

27. Upon his paws - Hebrew. upon his hands, that is, which hath feet divided into several parts like fingers, as dogs, cats, apes, and bears.

34. That on which such water cometh - That flesh or herbs or other food which is dressed in water, in a vessel so polluted, shall be unclean; not so, if it be food which is eaten dry, as bread, or fruits; the reason of which difference seems to be this, that the water did sooner receive the pollution in itself, and convey it to the food so dressed.

36. Of this no reason can be given, but the will of the law-giver and his merciful condescension to

men's necessities, water being scarce in those countries; and for the same reason God would have the ceremonial law of sacrifices, give place to the law of mercy.

37. Seed - Partly because this was necessary provision for man; and partly because such seed would not be used for man's food till it had received many alterations in the earth whereby such pollution was taken away.

38. If any water - The reason of the difference is, because wet seed doth sooner receive, and longer retain any pollution and partly because such seed was not fit to be sown presently, and therefore that necessity which justified the use of the dry seed, could not be pretended in this case.

39. If any beast die - Either of itself, or being killed by some wild beast, in which cases the blood was not poured forth, as it was when they were killed by men either for food or sacrifice.

40. He that eateth - Unwittingly, for if he did it knowingly, it was a presumptuous sin against an express law, Deut. xiv, 21, and therefore punished with cutting off.

41. Every creeping thing - Except those expressly excepted, ver. 29, 30.

42. Upon the belly - As worms and snakes, Upon all four - As toads and divers serpents.

44. Ye shall be holy - By this he gives them to understand, that all these cautions about eating or touching these creatures was not for any real uncleanness in them, but only that by diligent observation of these rules they might learn with greater care to avoid all moral pollutions, and to keep themselves from all filthiness of flesh and spirit, and from all familiar and intimate converse with notorious sinners.

45. That bringeth you up out of Egypt - This was a reason why they should cheerfully submit to distinguishing laws, who had been so honoured with distinguishing favours.

46. This is the law - It was so, as long the Mosaic dispensation lasted. But under the gospel we find it expressly repealed by a voice from heaven, Acts x, 15. Let us therefore bless God, that to us every creature of God is good, and nothing to be refused.

XII

Laws concerning the uncleanness of women in child-birth, ver. 1-5. Concerning their purification, ver. 6-8.

1. From uncleanness contracted by the touching or eating of external things, he now comes to that uncleanness which ariseth from ourselves.

2. Seven days - Not for any filthiness which was either in the conception, or in bringing forth, but to signify the universal and deep pollution of man's nature, even from the birth, and from the conception. Seven days or thereabouts, nature is employed in the purgation of most women. Her infirmity - Her monthly infirmity. And it may note an agreement therewith not only in the time, chap. xv, 19, but in the degree of uncleanness.

4. In the blood of her purifying - In her polluted and separated estate; for the word blood or bloods signifies both guilt, and uncleanness, as here and elsewhere. And it is called the blood of her purifying, because by the expulsion or purgation of that blood, which is done by degrees, she is purified. No hallowed thing - She shall not eat any part of the peace-offerings which she or her husband offered, which otherwise she might have done; and, if she be a priest's wife, she shall not eat any of the tythes or first fruits, or part of the hallowed meats, which at other times she together with her husband might eat.

5. Threescore and six days - The time in both particulars is double to the former, not so much from natural causes, as to put an honour upon the sacrament of circumcision, which being administered to the males, did put an end to that pollution sooner than otherwise had been.

6. For a son or a daughter - For the birth of a son, or of a daughter: but the purification was for herself, as appears from the following verses. A sin-offering - Because of her ceremonial uncleanness, which required a ceremonial expiation.

8. The morality of this law obliges women who have received mercies from God in child-bearing, with all thankfulness to acknowledge his goodness to them, owning themselves unworthy of it, and (which is the best purification) to continue in faith, and love, and holiness, with sobriety.

XIII

Rules whereby the priest was to judge of the leprosy, ver. 1- 44. Directions concerning the leper, ver. 45, 46. Concerning the leprosy in garments, ver. 47-59.

2. In the skin - For there is the first seat of the leprosy, the bright spot shining like the scale of a fish, as it is in the beginning of a leprosy. The priest - The priest was to admit to, or exclude from, the sanctuary, and therefore to examine who were to be excluded.

3. When the hair is turned white - This change of colour was an evidence both of the abundance of excrementious humours, and of the weakness of nature, as we see in old and sick persons. His flesh -

For the leprosy consumed both the skin and the flesh.

4. Seven days - For greater assurance; to teach ministers not to be hasty in their judgments, but diligently to search and examine all things before-hand. The plague is here put for the man that hath the plague.

6. Dark - Contrary to the white colour of the leprosy. But the word may be rendered, have contracted itself, and thus the opposition seems to be most clear as the spreading of itself. He shall wash his clothes - Though it was no leprosy, to teach us, that no sin is so small as not to need to be washed by the blood of Christ, which was the thing designed by all these washings.

10. White in the skin - With a preternatural and extraordinary whiteness. Raw flesh - This shewed it was not a superficial leprosy but one of a deeper and more malignant nature, that had eaten into the very flesh, for which cause it is in the next verse called an old or inveterate leprosy.

13. All his flesh - When it appeared in some one part it discovered the ill humour which lurked within, and withal the inability of nature to expel it; but when it overspread all, it manifested the strength of nature conquering the distemper, and purging out the ill humours into the outward parts.

14. In it - That is in the place where the appearance of leprosy was, when the flesh was partly changed into a whiter colour, and partly kept its natural colour, this variety of colours was an evidence of the leprosy, as one and the same colour continuing, was a sign of soundness.

15. The raw flesh - This is repeated again and again, because raw or living flesh might rather seem a sign of soundness, and the priest might easily be deceived by it, and therefore he was more narrowly to look into it.

16. Unto white - As it is usual with sores, when they begin to be healed, the skin which is white, coming upon the flesh.

21. Dark - Or, and be contracted.

22. A plague - Or the plague of leprosy, of which he is speaking.

24. A hot burning - A burning of fire, by the touch of any hot- iron, or burning coals, which naturally makes an ulcer or sore in which the following spot is.

28. Of the burning - Arising from the burning mentioned, ver. 24.

30. A yellow, thin hair - The leprosy in the body turned the hair white, in the head or beard it turned it yellow. And if a man's hair was yellow before, this might easily be distinguished from the rest, either by the thinness or smallness of it, or by its peculiar kind of yellow, for there are divers kinds of the same colour manifestly differing from one another.

31. No black hair - For had that appeared, it had ended the doubt, the black hair being a sign of soundness and strength of nature, as the yellow hair was a sign of unsoundness.

33. He shall be shaven - For the more certain discovery of the growth or stay of the plague.

36. He shall not seek - He need not search for the hair, or any other sign, the spreading of it being a sure sign of leprosy.

39. If the spots be darkish white - Or, contracted, or confined to the place where they are, and white.

42. It is a leprosy - It is a sign that such baldness came not from age, or any accident, but from the leprosy.

45. His clothes shall be rent - In the upper and fore parts, which were most visible. This was done partly as a token of sorrow, because though this was not a sin, yet it was an effect of sin, and a sore punishment, whereby he was cut off both from converse with men, and from the enjoyment of God in his ordinances; partly as a warning to others to keep at a due distance from him wheresoever he came. And his head bare - Another sign of mourning. God would have men though not overwhelmed with, yet deeply sensible of his judgments. A covering on his upper lip - Partly as another badge of his sorrow and shame, and partly for the preservation of others from his breath or touch. Unclean, unclean - As begging the pity and prayers of others, and confessing his own infirmity, and cautioning those who came near him, to keep at a distance from him.

46. He shall dwell alone - Partly for his humiliation; partly to prevent the infection of others; and partly to shew the danger of converse with spiritual lepers, or notorious sinners.

47. Leprosy in garments and houses is unknown in these times and places, which is not strange, there being some diseases peculiar to some ages and countries. And that such a thing was among the Jews, cannot reasonably be doubted; for, if Moses had been a deceiver, a man of his wisdom, would not have exposed himself to the contempt of his people by giving laws about that which their experience shewed to be but a fiction.

48. In the warp or woof - A learned man renders it in the outside, or in the inside of it. If the signification of these words be doubtful now, as some of those of the living creatures and precious stones are confessed to be, it is not material to us, this law being abolished; it sufficeth that the Jews understood these things by frequent experience.

55. If it have not changed its colour - If washing doth not take away that vicious colour, and restore it to its own native colour.

XIV

The manner of cleansing a leper, ver. 1-9. The sacrifices to be offered for him, ver. 10-32. The management of an house suspected of leprosy, ver. 33-53. The summary of the whole, ver. 54-57.

2. He shall be brought to the priest - Not into the priest's house, but to some place without the camp or city, which the priest shall appoint.

3. Healed by God-For God alone did heal or cleanse him really, the priest only declaratively.

4. Two birds - The one to represent Christ as dying for his sins, the other to represent him as rising again for his purification or justification. Clean - Allowed for food and for sacrifice. Cedar- wood - A stick of cedar, to which the hyssop and one of the birds was tied by the scarlet thread. Cedar seems to be chosen, to note that the leper was now freed from that corruption which his leprosy had brought upon him, that kind of wood being in a manner incorruptible. Scarlet - A thread of wool of a scarlet colour, to represent both the leper's sinfulness, and the blood of Christ, and the happy change of the leper's colour and complexion, which before was wan and loathsome, now sprightly and beautiful. Hyssop - The fragrant smell of which, signified the cure of the leper's ill scent.

5. Killed - By some other man. The priest did not kill it himself, because it was not properly a sacrifice, as being killed without the camp, and not in that place to which all sacrifices were confined. In an earthen-vessel - That is, over running water put in an earthen-vessel - Thus the blood of the bird and the water were mixed together, partly for the conveniency of sprinkling, and partly to signify Christ, who came by water and blood, 1 John v, 6. The running water, that is, spring or river water by its liveliness and motion did fitly signify the restoring of liveliness to the leper, who was in a manner dead before.

7. Into the open field - The place of its former abode, signifying the taking off that restraint which was laid upon the leper.

8. All his hair - Partly to discover his perfect soundness; partly to preserve him from a relapse through any relicks of it which might remain in his hair or in his clothes. Out of his tent - Out of his former habitation, in some separate place, lest some of his leprosy yet lurking in him should break forth to the infection of his family.

9. All his hair - Which began to grow again, and now for more caution is shaved again.

10. Oil is added as a fit sign of God's grace and mercy, and of the leper's healing. A log is a measure containing six egg-shells full.

11. Maketh him clean - The healing is ascribed to God, ver. 13, but the ceremonial cleansing was an act of the priest using the rites which God had prescribed.

12. A trespass-offering - To teach them, that sin was the cause of leprosy, and of all diseases, and that these ceremonial observations had a farther meaning, to make them sensible of their spiritual diseases, that they might fly to God in Christ for the cure of them.

14. The priest shall put it - To signify, that he was now free to hear God's word in the appointed places, and to touch any person or thing without defiling it, and to go whither he pleased.

15. The oil - As the blood signified Christ's blood by which men obtained remission of sins, so the oil noted the graces of the spirit by which they are renewed.

16. Before the Lord - Before the second veil which covered the holy of holies.

17. Upon the blood - Upon the place where that blood was put.

25. The priest shall put the blood - Upon the extremities of the body, to include the whole. And some of the oil was afterwards put in the same places upon the blood. That blood seems to have been a token of forgiveness, the oil of healing: For God first forgiveth our iniquities, and then healeth our diseases. When the leper was anointed, the oil must have blood under it, to signify that all the graces and comforts of the spirit, all his sanctifying influences are owing to the death of Christ. It is by his blood alone that we are sanctified.

36. That all be not made unclean - It is observable here, that neither the people nor the household stuff were polluted till the leprosy was discovered and declared by the priest, to shew what great difference God makes between sins of ignorance, and sins against knowledge.

37. In the walls of the house - This was an extraordinary judgment of God peculiar to this people, either as a punishment of their sins, which were much more sinful and inexcusable than the sins of other nations; or as a special help to repentance, which God afforded them above other people; or as a token of the mischievous nature of sin, typified by leprosy, which did not only destroy persons, but their habitations also: Hollow streaks - Such as were in the bodies of leprous persons.

40. An unclean place - Where they used to cast dirt and filthy things.

57. To teach - To direct the priest when to pronounce a person or house clean or unclean. So it was not left to the priests power or will, but they were tied to plain rules, such as the people might discern no less than the priest.

XV

This chapter contains laws concerning other ceremonial uncleannesses, contracted either by bodily disease, or some natural incidents, whether in men, ver. 1-18, or in women, ver. 19- 33.

2. *A running issue* - Commonly called the running of the reins, a grievous and loathsome disease, which is generally the consequence of sin.

3. *His flesh be stopped* - That is, if it have run, and be stopped in great measure, either by the grossness of the humour, or by some obstructions that it cannot run freely.

7. *The flesh* - That is, any part of his body.

11. *And hath not rinsed* - That is, the person touched, to whom the washing of his hands is prescribed, if speedily done; but if that was neglected, a more labourious course was enjoined.

13. *When he is cleansed* - When his issue hath wholly ceased.

15. *An atonement* - Not as if this was in itself a sin, but only a punishment of sin; though oft-times it was sinful, as being a fruit of intemperance.

18. *A man* - Or, The man, that had such an issue, which is plainly to be understood out of the whole context. For though in some special cases relating to the worship of God, men were to forbear the use of the marriage-bed, yet to affirm that the use of it in other cases did generally defile the persons, and make them unclean till even, is contrary to the whole current of scripture, which affirms the marriage-bed to be undefiled, Heb. xiii, 4, to the practice of the Jews, which is a good comment upon their own laws, and to the light of nature and reason.

19. *And if a woman* - Hebrew. And a woman when she shall have an issue of blood, and her issue shalt be in her flesh, that is, in her secret parts, as flesh is taken, ver. 2. So it notes her monthly disease. *Put apart* - Not out of the camp, but from converse with her husband and others, and from access to the house of God. *Seven days* - For sometimes it continues so long; and it was decent to allow some time for purification after the ceasing of her issue. *Whosoever toucheth her* - Of grown persons. For the infant, to whom in that case she might give suck, was exempted from this pollution by the greater law of necessity, and by that antecedent law which required women to give suck to their own children.

24. *Seven days* - If he did this ignorantly; but if the man and woman did this knowingly, being accused and convicted, they were punished with death, chap. xx, 18, for as there was a turpitude in the action, so it was very prejudicial to the children then begotten, who were commonly weak, or leprous; which was also an injury to the commonwealth of Israel, and redounded to the dishonour of God and of the true religion, that the professors thereof gave such public evidence of their intemperance.

28. *Seven days* - From the stopping of her issue. And this was for trial, whether it was only a temporary obstruction, or a real cessation.

31. *When they defile my tabernacle* - Both ceremonially, by coming into it in their uncleanness, and morally by the contempt of God's express command to cleanse themselves. The grand reason of all these laws was, to separate the children of Israel from their uncleanness. Hereby they were taught their privilege and honour, that they were purified unto God, a peculiar people; for that was a defilement to them, which was not so to others. They were also taught their duty, which was to keep themselves clean from all pollutions.

XVI

The institution of the yearly day of atonement for the whole nation. The whole service is committed to the high-priest, who is,

1. Then only to come into the holy of holies, in his linen garments with a young bullock, ver. 1-4.
2. To offer a goat, and a bullock for a sin-offering, ver. 5-13.
3. To sprinkle the blood before the mercy seat, and upon the altar, ver. 13-19.
4. To confess over the scape-goat, the sins of the people, and then send him into the wilderness, ver. 20-23.
5. To offer the burnt-offerings, ver. 24-28. And,
6. To appoint this day to be a solemn fast, by a statute forever, ver. 29-34.

2. *At all times* - Not whensoever he pleaseth, but only when I shall appoint him, namely, to take down the parts and furniture of it upon every removal, and to minister unto me once in the year. *Lest he die* - For his irreverence and presumption. *In the cloud* - In a bright and glorious cloud, over the mercy-seat, as a token when I would have him come.

3. *With a young bullock* - That is, with the blood of it; the body of it was to be offered upon the altar of burnt-offerings. *A sin- offering* - For his own and family's sins; for a goat was offered for the sins of the people.

4. *The linen coat* - It is observable, the high-priest did not now use his peculiar and glorious robes,

but only his linen garments, which were common to him with the ordinary priests. The reason whereof was, because this was not a day of feasting and rejoicing, but of mourning and humiliation, at which times people were to lay aside their ornaments. These are holy - Because appropriated to an holy and religious use.

8. For the Lord - For the Lord's use by way of sacrifice. Both this and the other goat typified Christ; this in his death and passion for us; that in his resurrection for our deliverance.

11. The bullock - Mentioned in general, ver. 6. The ceremonies whereof are here particularly described. This was a different bullock or heifer from that Num. xix, 2, 5, 9, 10, 17, as appears by comparing the places.

12. Within the veil - That is, into the holy of holies, ver. 2.

13. Upon the fire - Which was in the censer, ver. 12.

14. Upon the mercy-seat - To teach us, that God is merciful to sinners only through and for the blood of Christ. With his face east-ward, or upon the eastern part, towards the people, who were in the court which lay east-ward from the holy of holies, which was the most western part of the tabernacle. This signified that the high-priest in this act represented the people, and that God accepted it on their behalf. Before the mercy-seat - On the ground.

15. Then shall he kill the goat - He went out of the holy of holies, and killed it, and then returned thither again with its blood. And whereas the high-priest is said to be allowed to enter into that place but once in a year, that is to be understood, but one day in a year, though there was occasion of going in and coming out more than once upon that day.

16. Because of the uncleannesses of Israel - For though the people did not enter into that place, yet their sins entered thither, and would hinder the effects of the high-priest's mediation on their behalf if God was not reconciled to them. In the midst of their uncleanness - In the midst of a sinful people, who defile not themselves only, but also God's sanctuary. And God hereby shewed them, how much their hearts needed to be purified, when even the tabernacle, only by standing in the midst of them, needed this expiation.

17. In the tabernacle - In the holy place, where the priests and Levites were at other times. This was commanded for the greater reverence to the Divine Majesty then in a more special manner appearing, and that none of them might cast an eye into the holy of holies, as the high-priest went in or came out.

18. The altar before the Lord - That is, the altar of incense, where the blood of sacrifices was to be put, particularly the blood of the sin-offerings offered upon this day of atonement, and which is most properly said to be before the Lord, that is, before the place where God in a special manner dwelt. His going out relates to the holy of holies, into which he was said to go in, ver. 17.

19. Seven times - To signify its perfect cleansing, (seven being a number of perfection) and our perfect reconciliation by the blood of Christ.

21. All the iniquities - He mentions iniquities, transgressions, and sins, to note sins of all sorts, and that a free and full confession was to be made, and that the smallest sins needed, and the greatest sins were not excluded from, the benefit of Christ's death here represented. On the head - Charging all their sins and the punishment due to them upon the goat, which tho' only a ceremony, yet being done according to God's appointment and manifestly pointing at Christ upon whom their iniquities and punishments were laid, Isaiah liii, 5, 6, it was available for this end. And hence the Heathens took their custom of selecting one beast or man, upon whom they laid all their imprecations and curses, and whom they killed as an expiatory sacrifice for their sins, and to prevent their ruin. A fit man - Hebrew. a man of time, that is, of years and discretion, who may be trusted with this work. Into the wilderness - Which signified the removal of their sins far away both from the people, and out of God's sight. And here the goat being neglected by all men, and exposed to many hazards from wild beasts, which were numerous there, might further signify Christ's being forsaken both by God and by men, even by his own disciples, and the many dangers and sufferings he underwent. The Jews write, that this goat was carried to the mountain called Azazel, whence the goat is so called, ver. 10, and that there he was cast down headlong.

24. He shall put on his linen garments - Not his ordinary priestly linen garments, for he was to leave them in the tabernacle, ver. 23, but the high-priestly garments, called his garments properly, and by way of distinction. And this change of his garments was not without cause. For the common priestly garments were more proper for him in the former part of his ministration, both because he was to appear before the Lord in the most holy place to humble himself and make atonement for his own and for the people's sins, and therefore his meanest attire was most fit, and because he was to lay his hands upon that goat on which all their sins were put, by which touch both he and his garments would be in some sort defiled, and therefore as he washed himself, so we may presume his linen garments were laid by for the washing, as the clothes of him who carried away the scape-goat were washed, ver. 26. And the high-priestly garments were most proper for the latter part of his work, which was of another nature.

29. The seventh month - Answering part to our September and part to our October; when they had gathered in all their fruits, and were most at leisure for God's service: This time God chose for this and

other feasts, herein graciously condescending to men's necessities and conveniences. This feast began in the evening of the ninth day, and continued till the evening of the tenth. Your souls - Yourselves, both your bodies, by abstinence from food and other delights, and your minds by grief for former sins, which though bitter, yet is voluntary in all true penitents, who are therefore here said to afflict themselves, or to be active in the work.

31. A sabbath - Observed as a sabbath-day from all servile works, and diligent attendance upon God's worship.

32. He - The high-priest, who was to anoint his successor.

34. This shall be an everlasting statute - By which were typified the two great gospel privileges; remission of sins, and access to God, both which we owe to the mediation of the Lord Jesus.

XVII

Two prohibitions,

1. That no sacrifice be offered by any but the priests, nor any where but at the door of the tabernacle, ver. 1-9.

2. That no blood be eaten, ver. 10-16.

3. That killeth-Not for common use, for such beasts might be killed by any person or in any place but for sacrifice. In the camp, or out of the camp - That is, anywhere.

4. The tabernacle - This was appointed in opposition to the Heathens, who sacrificed in all places; to cut off occasions of idolatry; to prevent the people's usurpation of the priest's office, and to signify that God would accept of no sacrifices but through Christ and in the Church; (of both which the tabernacle was a type.) But though men were tied to this law, God was free to dispense with his own law, which he did sometimes to the prophets, as 1 Sam. vii, 9, xi, 15. He hath shed blood - He shall be punished as a murderer. The reason is, because he shed that blood, which, though not man's blood, yet was precious, being sacred and appropriated to God, and typically the price by which men's lives were ransomed.

5. They offer - The Israelites, before the building of the tabernacle, did so, from which they are now restrained. Peace- offerings - He nameth not these exclusively from others, as appears from the reason of the law, and from ver. 8, 9, but because in these the temptation was more common in regard of their frequency, and more powerful, because part of these belonged to the offerer, and the pretense was more plausible, because their sanctity was of a lower degree than others, these being only called holy, and allowed in part to the people, whereas the others are called most holy, and were wholly appropriated either to God, or to the priests.

6. Upon the altar - This verse contains a reason of the foregoing law, because of God's propriety in the blood and fat, wherewith also God was well pleased, and the people reconciled. And these two parts only are mentioned, as the most eminent, and peculiar, though other parts also were reserved for God.

7. Unto devils - So they did, not directly or intentionally, but by construction and consequence, because the devil is the author of idolatry, and is eminently served, and honoured by it. And as the Egyptians were notorious for their idolatry, so the Israelites were infected with their leaven, Josh. xxiv, 14, Ezek. xx, 7, xxiii, 2, 3. A whoring - Idolatry, especially in God's people, is commonly called whoredom, because it is a violation of that covenant by which they were peculiarly betrothed or married to God.

10. I will set my face - I will be an enemy to him, and execute vengeance upon him immediately; because such persons probably would do this in private, so that the magistrate could not know nor punish it. Write that man undone, forever undone, against whom God sets his face.

11. Is in the blood - Depends upon the blood, is preserved and nourished by it. The blood maketh atonement - Typically, and in respect of the blood of Christ which it represented, by which the atonement is really made. So the reason is double;

1. because this was eating up the ransom of their own lives, which in construction was the destroying of themselves.

2. because it was ingratitude and irreverence towards that sacred blood of Christ which they ought to have in continual veneration.

15. That eateth - Through ignorance or inadvertency; for if it was done knowingly, it was more severely punished. A stranger - Who is a proselyte to the Jewish religion: other strangers were allowed to eat such things, Deut. xiv, 21, out of which the blood was either not drawn at all, or not regularly.

16. His iniquity - The punishment of it, and therefore must offer a sacrifice for it.

XVIII

A prohibition of conformity to the heathens, ver. 1-5. Particular laws against incest, ver. 6-18. Against unnatural lusts and barbarous idolatries, ver. 19-23. Enforced from the destruction of the Canaanites, ver. 24-30.

2. *Your God* - Your sovereign, and lawgiver. This is often repeated because the things here forbidden were practiced and allowed by the gentiles, to whose custom he opposes divine authority and their obligation to obey his commands.

3. *Egypt and Canaan* - These two nations he mentions, because their habitation and conversation among them made their evil example in the following matters more dangerous. But under them he includes all other nations.

4. *My judgments* - Though you do not see the particular reason of some of them, and though they be contrary to the laws and usages of the other nations.

5. *He shall live in them* - Not only happily here, but eternally hereafter. This is added as a powerful argument why they should follow God's commands, rather than mens examples, because their life and happiness depend upon it. And though in strictness, and according to the covenant of works they could not challenge life for so doing, except their obedience was universal, perfect, constant and perpetual, and therefore no man since the fall could be justified by the law, yet by the covenant of grace this life is promised to all that obey God's commands sincerely.

6. *To uncover their nakedness* - I think Mark. Free has made it highly probable, that this phrase does not mean marriage, but fornication, throughout this chapter. So it unquestionably means in the twentieth chapter.

16. *Thy brother's wife* - God afterwards commanded, that in one case, a man should marry his brother's widow.

18. *Thou shalt not take a wife to her sister* - Perhaps this text doth not simply forbid the taking one wife to another, but the doing it in such a manner or for such an end, that he may vex or punish, or revenge himself of the former; which probably was a common motive amongst that hardhearted people to do so.

19. *As long as she is set apart* - No not to thy own wife. This was not only a ceremonial pollution, but an immorality also, whence it is put amongst gross sins, Ezek. xviii, 6. And therefore it is now unlawful under the gospel.

21. *Pass through fire* - This was done, either by burning them in the fire, or by making them pass between two great fires, which was a kind of consecration of them to that God. *Moloch* - Called also Milcom, was an idol chiefly of the Ammonites. He seems to be the Saturn of the heathens, to whom especially children and men were sacrificed. This is mentioned, because the neighbours of Israel were most infected with this idolatry, and therefore they are particularly cautioned against it, though under this one instance all other idols and acts, or kinds of idolatry, are manifestly comprehended and forbidden.

25. *I visit* - I am about to visit, that is, to punish.

26. *Nor any stranger* - In nation or religion, of what kind soever. For though they might not force them to submit to their religion, yet they might restrain them from the publick contempt of the Jewish laws, and from the violation of natural laws, which, besides the offense against God and nature, were matters of evil example to the Israelites themselves.

29. *Cut off* - This phrase therefore of cutting off, is to be understood variously, either of ecclesiastical, or civil punishment, according to the differing natures of the offenses for which it is inflicted.

XIX

Various Precepts to be holy, ver. 1, 2. To honour parents and sabbaths, ver. 3. To shun idolatry, ver. 4. Duty to eat their peace-offering, ver. 5- 8. To leave gleanings for the poor, ver. 9, 10. Not to steal, lie, swear falsely, or defraud, ver. 11-13. Not to curse the deaf, or put a stumbling-block before the blind, ver. 14. Not to judge unjustly, carry tales, or bear false witness, ver. 15, 16. To reprove sinners, not to revenge themselves; to love their neighbours, ver. 17, 18. Not to mix different things, ver. 19. Not to lie with their bond- maids, ver. 20-22. Not to eat of the fruit of the land for four years, ver. 23-25. Not to eat blood, use enchantments, or heathen customs, ver. 26-28. Or prostitute their daughters, ver. 29. To reverence God and his sanctuary, ver. 30. Not to regard wizards, ver. 31. To honour the aged, ver. 32. Love and right the stranger, ver. 33, 34. Do no injustice, ver. 34, 35, 36.

2. *Be ye holy* - Separated from all the forementioned defilements, and entirely consecrated to God and obedient to all his laws. *I am holy* - Both in my essence, and in all my laws, which are holy and just

and good.

3. *His mother* - The mother is put first, partly because the practice of this duty begins there, mothers, by perpetual converse, being sooner known to their children than their fathers; and partly because this duty is commonly neglected to the mother, upon whom children have not so much dependence as they have upon their father. And this fear includes the two great duties of reverence and obedience. *And keep my sabbaths* - This is added, to shew, that, whereas it is enjoined to parents that they should take care the sabbath be observed both by themselves and their children, it is the duty of children to fear and obey their parents in this matter. But that, if parents should neglect their duty herein, or by their command, counsel, or example, draw them to pollute the sabbath, the children in that case must keep the sabbath, and prefer the command of God before the commands of their parents.

4. *Idols* - The word signifies such as are no Gods, or nothings, as they are called, 1 Cor. viii, 4, many idols having no being, but in the fancy of their worshippers, and all of them having no virtue or power to do good or evil, Isaiah xli, 23.

5. *At your own will* - Or, according to your own pleasure, what you think fit: For though this in general was required, yet it was left to their choice to determine the particulars.

6. *On the morrow* - He speaks here of that sort of peace-offerings, which were offered either by vow or freely for the obtaining of some mercy, for the other sort, which was by way of gratitude for mercies received, were to be eaten the same day.

10. *I am the Lord your God* - Who gave you all these things with a reservation of my right in them, and with a charge of giving part of them to the poor.

12. *Ye shall not swear falsely* - This is added, to shew how one sin draws on another, and that when men will lye for their own advantage, they will easily be induced to perjury. *Profane the name* - By any unholy use of it. So it is an additional precept, thou shalt not abuse my holy name by swearing either falsely or rashly.

14. *Before the blind* - To make them fall. Under these two particulars are manifestly forbidden all injuries done to such as are unable to right or defend themselves; of whom God here takes the more care, because they are not able to secure themselves. *Fear thy God* - Who both can and will avenge them.

15. *The poor* - So as through pity to him to give an unrighteous sentence.

16. *Stand against the blood* - In judgment as a false accuser or false witness, for accusers and witnesses use to stand, whilst the Judges sit in courts of judicature.

17. *Thou shalt not hate* - As thou dost, in effect, if thou dost not rebuke him. *Thy brother* - The same as thy neighbour, that is, every man. If thy brother hath done wrong, thou shalt neither divulge it to others, nor hate him, and smother that hatred by sullen silence; nor flatter him therein, but shalt freely and in love, tell him of his fault. *And not suffer sin upon him* - Not suffer him to lie under the guilt of any sin, which thou by rebuking him, and thereby bringing him to repentance, couldst free him from.

18. *Thy neighbour* - Every man, as plainly appears,

1. By comparing this place with ver. 34, where this law is applied to strangers.

2. Because the word neighbour is explained by another man, chap. xx, 10 Rom. xiii, 8. *As thyself* - With the same sincerity, though not equality of affection.

19. *Thou shalt not let thy cattle gender* - This was prohibited, partly to restrain the curiosity and boldness of men, who might attempt to amend or change the works of God, partly that by the restraint here laid even upon brute-creatures men might be taught to abhor all unnatural lusts, partly to teach the Israelites to avoid mixtures with other nations, either in marriage or in religion, which also may be signified by the following prohibitions.

20. *She shall be scourged* - Hebrew. There shall be a scourging, which probably may belong to both of them, for

1. Both were guilty.

2. It follows, they shall not be punished with death, which may seem to imply that they were to be punished by some other common and considerable punishment, which scourging indeed was, but the paying of a ram was a small penalty and very unsuitable to the greatness of the offense. And the offering of the ram as a trespass offering for the sin against God, is not inconsistent with making satisfaction other ways for the injury done to men, but only added here as farther punishment to the man, either because he only could do this, and not the woman, who being a bondwoman had nothing of her own to offer. Or because his sex and his freedom aggravated his sin. *Not put to death* - Which they should have been, had she been free, Deut. xxii, 23, 24. The reason of this difference is not from any respect which God gives to persons, for bond and free are alike to him, but because bond-women were scarce wives, and their marriages were scarce true-marriages, being neither made by their choice, but their masters authority, nor continued beyond the year of release, but at her master's or husband's pleasure.

23. *As uncircumcised* - That is, As unclean, not to be eaten but cast away. This precept was serviceable,

1. To the trees themselves, which grew the better and faster, being early stript of those fruits, which otherwise would have drawn away much more of the strength from the tree.

2. To men, both because the fruit then was less wholesome, and because hereby men were taught to bridle their appetites; a lesson of great use and absolute necessity in a holy life.

24. Holy - Consecrated to the Lord, as the first-fruits and tithes were, and therefore given to the priests and Levites, Num. xviii, 12, 13 Deut. xviii, 4 yet so that part of them were communicated to the poor widows and fatherless and strangers. See Deut. xiv, 28. To bless the Lord, by whose power and goodness the trees bring forth fruit to perfection.

25. That it may yield the increase - That God may be pleased to give his blessing, which alone can make them fruitful.

26. Any thing with the blood - Any flesh out of which the blood is poured. Neither shall ye use enchantments - It was unpardonable in them, to whom were committed the oracles of God, to ask counsel of the devil. And yet worse in Christians, to whom the son of God is manifested, to destroy the works of the devil. For Christians to have their nativities cast, or their fortunes told, or to use charms for the cure of diseases, is an intolerable affront to the Lord Jesus, a support of idolatry, and a reproach both to themselves, and to that worthy name by which they are called. Nor observe times - Superstitiously, esteeming some days lucky, others unlucky.

27. The corners of your heads - That is your temples, ye shall not cut off the hair of your heads round about your temples. This the Gentiles did, either for the worship of their idols, to whom young men used to consecrate their hair, being cut off from their heads, as Homer, Plutarch and many others write; or in funerals or immoderate mournings, as appears from Isaiah xv, 2 Jer. xlviii, 37. And the like is to be thought concerning the beard or the hair in the corner, that is, corners of the beard. The reason then of this prohibition is because God would not have his people agree with idolaters, neither in their idolatries, nor in their excessive sorrowing, no nor so much as in the appearances of it.

28. Cuttings in your flesh - Which the Gentiles commonly did both in the worship of their idols, and in their solemn mournings, Jer. xvi, 6.

29. Do not prostitute - As the Gentiles frequently did for the honour of some of their idols, to whom women were consecrated, and publickly prostituted.

31. Wizards - Them that have entered into covenant with the devil, by whose help they foretel many things to come, and acquaint men with secret things. See ver. 27 Deut. xviii, 11; 1 Sam. xxviii, 3, 7, 9; 2 Kings xxi, 6.

32. Rise up - To do them reverence when they pass by, for which end they were obliged, as the Jews say, presently to sit down again when they were past, that it might be manifest they arose out of respect to them. Fear thy God - This respect is due to such, if not for themselves, yet for God's sake, who requires this reverence, and whose singular blessing old age is.

33. Vex him - Either with opprobrious expressions, or grievous exactions.

34. As one born among you - Either 1, as to the matters of common right, so it reacheth to all strangers. Or 2, as to church-privileges, so it concerns only those who were proselytes. Ye were strangers - And therefore are sensible of the fears, distresses, and miseries of such, which call for your pity, and you ought to do to them, as you desired others should do to you, when you were such.

35. In mete-yard - In the measuring of lands, or dry things, as cloth, ribband. In measure - In the measuring liquid or such dry things as are only contiguous, as corn or wine.

36. A just ephah and a just hin - These two two measures are named as most common, the former for dry, the latter for moist things, but under them he manifestly comprehends all other measures.

37. Therefore - Because my blessings and deliverances are not indulgences to sin, but greater obligations to all duties to God and men.

XX

Prohibitions against offering children to Moloch, ver. 1-5. Against consulting wizards, ver. 6. Holiness enjoined, ver. 7, 8. Against cursing parents, ver. 9. Against adultery, ver. 10 Against incestuous mixtures, ver. 11-21. Holiness again enjoined, ver. 22-26. Soothsayers to be stoned, ver. 27.

2. The people - Here follow the punishments of the crimes forbidden in the former chapters.

3. I will set my face against that man - Deal with him as an enemy, and make him a monument of my justice. To defile my sanctuary - Because the sanctuary was defiled by gross abominations committed in that city or land where God's sanctuary was: or because by these actions they declared to all men that they esteemed the sanctuary and service of God abominable and vile, by preferring such odious idolatry before it. And to profane my name - Partly by despising it themselves, partly by disgracing it to others, and giving them occasion to blaspheme it, and to abhor the true religion.

4. Hide their eyes - Wink at his fault, and forbear to accuse and punish him.

6. To go a whoring - To seek counsel or help from them.

8. Who sanctify you - Who separate you from all nations, and from their impurities and idolatries, to be a peculiar people to myself; and who give you my grace to keep my statutes.

9. Curseth - This is not here meant of every perverse expression, but of bitter reproaches or imprecations. His blood shall be upon him - He is guilty of his own death: he deserves to die for so unnatural a crime.

12. Confusion - By perverting the order which God hath appointed, and making the same offspring both his own child and his grandchild.

13. Put to death - Except the one party was forced by the other. See Deut. xxii, 25.

14. They - All who consented to it.

15. Slay the beast - Partly for the prevention of monstrous births, partly to blot out the memory of so loathsome a crime.

17. See her nakedness - In this and several of the following verses, uncovering nakedness plainly appears to mean not marriage, but fornication or adultery.

20. They shall die childless - Either shall be speedily cut off ere they can have a child by that incestuous conjunction; if this seem a less crime than most of the former incestuous mixtures, and therefore the magistrate forbear to punish it with death; yet they shall either have no children from such an unlawful bed, or their children shall die before them.

21. His brother's wife - Except in the case allowed by God, Deut. xxv, 5.

27. A man or a woman that hath a familiar spirit, shall surely be put to death - They that are in league with the devil, have in effect made a covenant with death: and so shall their doom be.

XXI

Directions to the priests, ver. 1-9. To the high-priest, ver. 10- 15. None of these must have any blemish, ver. 16-24.

1. Among his people - None of the priests shall touch the dead body, or assist at his funeral, or eat of the funeral feast. The reason of this law is evident, because by such pollution they were excluded from converse with men, to whom by their function they were to be serviceable upon all occasions, and from the handling of holy things. And God would hereby teach them, and in them all successive ministers, that they ought entirely to give themselves to the service of God. Yea, to renounce all expressions of natural affection, and all worldly employments, so far as they are impediments to the discharge of their holy services.

2. Near to him - Under which general expression his wife seems to be comprehended, though she be not expressed. And hence it is noted as a peculiar case, that Ezekiel, who was a priest, was forbidden to mourn for his wife, Ezek. xxiv, 16, &c. These exceptions God makes in condescension to human infirmity, because in such cases it was very hard to restrain the affections. But this allowance concerns only the inferior priest, not the high- priest.

3. That is nigh him - That is, by nearness not of relation, (for that might seem a needless addition) but of habitation, one not yet cut off from the family. For if she was married, she was now of another family, and under her husband's care in those matters.

4. Being - Or, seeing he is a chief man, for such not only the high- priest, but others also of the inferior priests were. He shall not defile himself for any other person whatsoever. To profane himself - Because such defilement for the dead did profane him, or make him as a common person, and consequently unfit to manage his sacred employment.

5. They shall not make baldness - In funerals, as the Heathens did. Though I allow them to defile themselves for some of the dead, yet in no case shall they use these superstitious rites, which also the people were forbidden to do; but the priests in a more peculiar manner, because they are by word and example to teach the people their duty.

6. Holy unto their God - Devoted to God's service, and always prepared for it, and therefore shall keep themselves from all defilements. The name of their God - Which they especially bear. The bread of their God - That is, the shew-bread: or rather, all the other offerings, besides burnt-offerings: which are called bread, because bread is commonly put for all food.

7. Profane - Or defiled, or deflowered, though it were done secretly, or by force: because the priest must take care that all the members of his family be free not only from gross wickedness, but from all suspicions of evil.

8. Thou - O Moses, and whosoever shall succeed in thy place, to whom it belongs to see my laws observed, shall take care that the priest be holy, and do not defile himself by any of these forbidden marriages.

9. And the daughter - And by analogy his son also, and his wife, because the reason of the law here added, concerns all. And nothing is more common than to name one kind for the rest of the same nature, as also is done chap. xviii, 6. She profaneth her father - Exposeth his person and office, and

consequently religion, to contempt.

10. The garments - Those holy garments, which were peculiar to him. Shall not uncover his head - This being then the posture of mourners, chap. x, 6, though afterwards the custom was changed and mourners covered their heads, 2 Sam. xv, 30, Esth vi, 12. Nor rent his clothes - Another expression of mourning.

11. Go in - Into the chamber or house where they lie. This and divers other rites here prescribed were from hence translated by the Heathens into their use, whose priests were put under the same obligations.

12. Out of the sanctuary - To attend the funerals of any person: for upon other occasions he might and did commonly go out. Nor profane the sanctuary - Either by the performance of a civility, or by entering into the sanctuary before the seven days allotted for his cleansing, Num. xix, 11, were expired. The crown of the anointing oil - Or, the crown, the golden plate, which is called the holy crown, Exod. xxix, 6, and the anointing oil of his God are upon him. So there is only an ellipsis of the conjunction and, which is frequent. And these two things, being most eminent, are put for the rest, as the sign is put for the thing signified, that is, for he is God's high-priest.

13. In her virginity - Or, a virgin, partly because as he was a type of Christ, so his wife was a type of the church, which is compared to a virgin, and partly for greater caution and assurance that his wife was not a defiled or deflowered person. Most of these things are forbidden to all the priests; and here to the high-priest, to shew that he also, and he especially is obliged to the same cautions.

15. I the Lord sanctify him - I have separated him from all other men for my immediate service, and therefore will not have that race corrupted.

17. Of thy seed - Whether the high priest, or the inferior ones. That hath - In all successive ages, any defect or excess of parts, any notorious deformity or imperfection in his body. The reason hereof is partly typical, that he, might more fully represent Christ, the great high-priest, who was typified both by the priest and sacrifice, and therefore both were to be without blemish; partly moral, to teach all Christians and especially ministers of holy things, what purity and perfection of heart and life they should labour after, and that notorious blemishes in the mind or conversation, render a man unfit for the ministry of the gospel; and partly prudential, because such blemishes were apt to breed contempt of the person; and consequently, of his function, and of the holy things wherein he ministered. For which reason, such persons as have notorious defects or deformities, are still unfit for the ministry except where there are eminent gifts and graces, which vindicate a man from the contemptibleness of his bodily presence. The particular defect's here mentioned, I shall not enlarge upon because some of the Hebrew words are diversely interpreted, and because the use of these things being abolished, the knowledge of them is not necessary.

18. A flat nose - Most restrain this word to the nose, and to some great deformity relating to it. But according to others, it signifies more generally, a person that wants some member or members, because the next word, to which it is opposed, signifies one that hath more members than he should.

21. A blemish - Any notorious blemish whereby he is disfigured, though not here mentioned.

22. He shall eat - Which a priest having any uncleanness might not do whereby God would shew the great difference between natural infirmities sent upon a man by God, and moral defilements which a man brought upon himself.

23. To the veil - To the second veil which was between the holy and the most holy place, to burn incense, to order the shew-bread, and to dress the lamps, which were nigh unto that veil though without. My altar - The altar of burnt-offering, which was without the sanctuary. The sense is, he shall not execute the priest's office, which was to be done in those two places.

XXII

A priest, having any uncleanness, must not eat of the holy things, ver. 1-7. No priest must eat that which dies of itself, or is torn, ver. 8, 9. No stranger must eat of holy things, ver. 10-13. Of them that do it ignorantly, ver. 14-16. Sacrifices must be without blemish, and of a due age, ver. 17-27. Thank offerings must be eaten the same day, ver. 29, 30. An exhortation to obedience, ver. 31-33.

2. Separate themselves - When any uncleanness is upon them, as appears from ver. 3, 4. From the holy things - From eating of those parts of the offerings, which belong to them. Only of the tithes they might eat. They - The children of Israel. And it ill became the priests to profane or pollute what the people did hallow.

3. Goeth unto the holy things - To eat them, or to touch them; for if the touch of one of the people having his uncleanness upon him defiled the thing he touched, much more was it so in the priest. Cut off - From my ordinances by excommunication: He shall be excluded both from the administration, and from the participation of them.

7. His food - His portion, the means of his subsistence. This may be added, to signify why there

was no greater nor longer a penalty put upon the priests than upon the people in the same case, because his necessity craved some mitigation: tho' otherwise the priests being more sacred persons, deserved a greater punishment.

9. Lest they bear sin - Incur guilt and punishment. For it - For the neglect or violation of it.

10. No stranger - Of a strange family, who is not a priest; but there is an exception to this rule, ver. 11. A sojourner - One that comes to his house and abides there for a season, and eats at his table.

12. A stranger - To one of another family, who is no priest. Yet the priest's wife, though of another family, might eat. The reason of which difference is, because the wife passeth into the name, state and privileges of her husband, from whom the family is denominated.

14. Unto it - Over and above the principle, and besides the ram to be offered to God, chap. v, 15. And shall give unto the priest the holy thing - That is, the worth of it, which the priest was either to take to himself or to offer to God, as the nature of the thing was.

15. They - The people shall not profane them, by eating them: or the priests shall not profane them, that is, suffer the people to profane them, without censure and punishment.

16. They - That is, the priests, shall not (the negative particle being understood out of the foregoing clause) suffer them - That is, the people, to bear the iniquity of trespass - That is, the punishment of their sin, which they might expect from God, and for the prevention whereof the priest was to see restitution made.

18. Strangers - Such as were proselytes.

19. A male - For a burnt-offering, which was always of that kind: but the females were accepted in peace-offerings, and sin- offerings.

25. A stranger's hand - From proselytes: even from those, such should not be accepted, much less from the Israelites. The bread of your God - That is, the sacrifices.

28. In one day - Because it favoured of cruelty.

32. Hallowed, or sanctified, either by you in keeping my holy commands, or upon you in executing my holy and righteous judgments. I will manifest myself to be an holy God that will not bear the transgression of my laws.

XXIII

Directions concerning the sabbath, ver. 1-3. The passover, ver. 4-8. The first fruits, ver. 9-14. The feast of pentecost, ver. 15- 22. of trumpets, ver. 23-25. Of atonement, ver. 26-32. Of tabernacles, ver. 33-44.

2. Ye shall proclaim - Cause to be proclaimed, by the priests. Holy convocations - Days for your assembling together to my worship in a special manner.

3. Ye shall do no work therein - So it runs in the general for the sabbath day, and for the day of expiation, ver. 28, excluding all works about earthly employments whether of profit or of pleasure; but upon other feast days he forbids only servile works, as ver. 7, 21, 36, for surely this manifest difference in the expressions used by the wife God must needs imply a difference in the things. In all your dwellings - Other feasts, were to be kept before the Lord in Jerusalem only, whither all the males were to come for that end; but the sabbath was to be kept in all places, both in synagogues, and in their private houses.

4. These are the feasts of the Lord - Or rather, the solemnities: (for the day of atonement was a fast:) and so the word is used, Isaiah xxxiii, 20, where Zion is called the city of our solemnities.

10. An omer - They did not offer this corn in the ear, or by a sheaf or handful, but, as Josephus, 3. 10 affirms, and may be gathered from chap. ii, 14, 15, 16, purged from the chaff, and dryed, and beaten out.

11. He shall wave the sheaf before the Lord - In the name of the whole congregation, which as it were sanctified to them the whole harvest, and gave them a comfortable use of all the rest. For then we may eat our bread with joy, when God hath accepted our works. And thus should we always begin with God; begin our lives with him, begin every day with him, begin every work and business with him: seek ye first the kingdom of God. The morrow after the sabbath - After the first day of the feast of unleavened bread, which was a sabbath or day of rest, as appears from ver. 7, or upon the sixteenth day of the month. And this was the first of those fifty days, in the close whereof was the feast of pentecost.

13. Two tenth deals - Or, parts, of an ephah, that is, two omers, whereas in other sacrifices of lambs there was but one tenth deal prescribed. The reason of which disproportion may be this, that one of the tenth deals was a necessary attendant upon the lamb, and the other was peculiar to this feast, and was an attendant upon that of the corn, and was offered with it in thanksgiving to God for the fruits of the earth.

14. Bread - Made of new wheat. Nor green ears - Which were usual, not only for offerings to God, but also for man's food.

15. *From the morrow* - From the sixteenth day of the month, and the second day of the feast of unleavened bread inclusively.

16. *A new meal-offering* - Of new corn made into loaves.

18. *One bullock and two rams* - In Num. xxviii, 11, 19, it is two young bullocks and one ram. Either therefore it was left to their liberty to chuse which they would offer, or one of the bullocks there, and one of the rams here, were the peculiar sacrifices of the feast day, and the other were attendants upon the two loaves, which were the proper offering at this time. And the one may be mentioned there, and the other here, to teach us, that the addition of a new sacrifice did not destroy the former, but both were to be offered, as the extraordinary sacrifices of every feast did not hinder the oblation of the daily sacrifice.

19. *One kid* - In chap. iv, 14, the sin-offering for the sin of the people is a bullock, but here a kid; &c. the reason of the difference may be this, because that was for some particular sin of the people, but this only in general for all their sins.

20. *Wave them* - Some part of them in the name of the whole; and so for the two lambs, otherwise they had been too big and too heavy, to be waved. *For the priests* - Who had to themselves not only the breast and shoulder as in others, which belonged to the priest, but also the rest which belonged to the offerer; because the whole congregation being the offerer here, it could neither be distributed to them all, nor given to some without offense to the rest.

21. *An holy convocation* - A sabbath or day of rest, called pentecost; which was instituted, partly in remembrance of the consummation of their deliverance out of Egypt by bringing them thence to the mount of God, or Sinai, as God had promised, and of that admirable blessing of giving the law to them on the 50th day, and forming them into a commonwealth under his own immediate government; and partly in gratitude for the farther progress of their harvest, as in the passover they offered a thank-offering to God for the beginning of their harvest. The perfection of this feast, was the pouring out of the Holy Spirit upon the apostles on this very day, in which the law of faith was given, fifty days after Christ our passover was sacrificed for us. And on that day the apostles, having themselves received the first-fruits of the spirit, begat three thousand souls thro' the word of truth, as the first-fruits of the Christian church.

22. *When ye reap, thou* - From the plural, ye, he comes to the singular, thou, because he would press this duty upon every person who hath an harvest to reap, that none might plead exemption from it. And it is observable, that though the present business is only concerning the worship of God, yet he makes a kind of excursion to repeat a former law of providing for the poor, to shew that our devotion to God is little esteemed by him if it be not accompanied with acts of charity to men.

24. *A sabbath* - Solemnized with the blowing of trumpets by the priests, not in a common way, as they did every first day of every month, but in an extraordinary manner, not only in Jerusalem, but in all the cities of Israel. They began to blow at sun-rise, and continued blowing till sun-set. This seems to have been instituted,

1. To solemnize the beginning of the new year, whereof as to civil matters and particularly as to the Jubilee, this was the first day; concerning which it was fit the people should be admonished, both to excite their thankfulness for God's blessings in the last year, and to direct them in the management of their civil affairs.

2. To put a special honour upon this month. For as the seventh day was the sabbath, and the seventh year was a sabbatical year, so God would have the seventh month to be a kind of sabbatical month, for the many sabbaths and solemn feasts which were observed in this more than in any other month. And by this sounding of the trumpets in its beginning, God would quicken and prepare them for the following sabbaths, as well as that of atonement and humiliation for their sins, as those of thanksgiving for God's mercies.

27. *Afflict your souls* - With fasting, and bitter repentance for all, especially their national sins, among which no doubt God would have them remember their sin of the golden calf. For as God had threatened to remember it in after times to punish them for it, so there was great reason why they should remember it to humble themselves for it.

28. *Whatsoever soul* - Either of the Jewish nation, or religion. Hereby God would signify the absolute necessity which every man had of repentance and forgiveness of sin, and the desperate condition of all impenitent persons.

32. *From even to even* - The day of atonement began at the evening of the ninth day, and continued till the evening of the tenth day. *Ye shall celebrate your sabbath* - This particular sabbath is called your sabbath, possibly to note the difference between this and other sabbaths: for the weekly sabbath is oft called the sabbath of the Lord. The Jews are supposed to begin every day, and consequently their sabbaths, at the evening, in remembrance of the creation, as Christians generally begin their days and sabbaths with the morning in memory of Christ's resurrection.

34. *Of tabernacles* - Of tents or booths or arbours. This feast was appointed to remind them of that time when they had no other dwellings in the wilderness, and to stir them up to bless God, as well for

the gracious protection then afforded them, as for the more commodious habitations now given them; and to excite them to gratitude for all the fruits of the year newly ended, which were now compleatly brought in.

36. Ye shall offer - A several-offering each day. The eighth day - Which though it was not one of the days of this feast strictly taken. Yet in a larger sense it belonged to this feast, and is called the great day of the feast, John vii, 37. And so indeed it was, as for other reasons, so because, by their removal from the tabernacles into fixed habitations, it represented that happy time wherein their 40 years tedious march in the wilderness was ended with their settlement in the land of Canaan, which it was most fit they should acknowledge with such a solemn day of thanksgiving as this was.

37. A sacrifice - A sin-offering, called by the general name, a sacrifice, because it was designed for that which was the principal end of all sacrifices, the expiation of sin.

38. Beside the sabbaths - The offerings of the weekly sabbaths. God will not have any sabbath-sacrifice diminished because of the addition of others, proper to any other feast. And it is here to be noted, that though other festival days are sometimes called sabbaths, yet these are here called the sabbaths of the Lord, in way of contradistinction, to shew that this was more eminently such than other feast days. Your gifts - Which being here distinguished from the free-will-offerings made to the Lord, may note what they freely gave to the priests over and above their first-fruits and tithes or other things which they were enjoined to give.

39. This is no addition of a new, but only a repetition of the former injunction, with a more particular explication both of the manner and reason of the feast. The fruit - Not the corn, which was gathered long before, but that of the trees, as vines, olives, and other fruit-trees: which compleated the harvest, whence this is called the feast of in-gathering.

40. Of goodly trees - Namely, olive, myrtle and pine, mentioned, Neh. viii, 15, 16, which were most plentiful there, and which would best preserve their greenness. Thick trees - Fit for shade and shelter. And willows - To mix with the other, and in some sort bind them together. And as they made their booths of these materials, so they carried some of these boughs in their hands, as is affirmed by Jewish and other ancient writers.

42. In booths - Which were erected in their cities or towns, either in their streets, or gardens, or the tops of their houses. These were made flat, and therefore were fit for the use.

44. The feasts of the Lord - We have reason to be thankful, that the feasts of the Lord, now are not so numerous, nor the observance of them so burdensome and costly; but more spiritual and significant, and surer and sweeter earnests of the everlasting feast, at the last in-gathering, which we hope to be celebrating to eternity.

XXIV

Laws concerning the lamps, ver. 1-4. The shew-bread, ver. 5-9. Blasphemy occasioned by that of Shelomith's son, ver. 10-16. The law of retaliation, ver. 17-22. The blasphemer stoned, ver. 23.

2. To cause the lamps to burn - Hebrew. the lamp: yet ver. 4, it is the lamps: The seven lamps made all one lamp. In allusion to which, the Blessed Spirit is represented, Rev. iv, 5, by seven lamps of fire before the throne. For there are diversities of gifts, but one spirit.

3. Aaron - Either by himself, or by his sons, Exod. xxv, 37.

4. The pure candlestick - So called, partly because it was made of pure gold, partly because it was to be always kept clean.

5. Thou - By the priests or Levites, whose work it was to prepare them, 1Chr ix, 32. Twelve cakes - Representing the twelve tribes.

6. Two rows - Not one above another, but one beside another, as the frankincense put upon each, ver. 7, shews.

7. Pure frankincense - Unmixed and uncorrupted, or of the best sort, to be burnt before the Lord. On the bread - And this was done every time that the bread was changed. For a memorial - For that part which properly belonged to God, whereas the rest belonged to the priests.

8. From the children of Israel - And these cakes are said to be received from or offered by the children of Israel, bought with the money which they contributed. By an everlasting covenant - By virtue of that compact made between me and them, by which they were obliged to keep this amongst other commands, and, they so doing, I am obliged to be their God and to bless them. And this may be here called an everlasting covenant, not only because it was to endure as long as the Jewish polity stood, but also because this was to stand everlastingly, or continually, and therefore the new cakes were first brought before the old were taken away.

9. It - The old bread now to be taken away. Made by fire - The incense was offered by fire, and that for or instead of the bread, and therefore the bread was reputed as if it had been so offered.

10. Whose father was an Egyptian - This circumstance seems noted, partly to shew the danger of

marriages with persons of wicked principles, and partly by this severity against him who was a stranger by the father, and an Israelite by the mother, to shew that God would not have this sin go unpunished amongst his people, what-soever he was that committed it. Went out - Out of Egypt, being one of that mixed multitude, which came out with the Israelites, Exod. xii, 32. It is probable, this was done when the Israelites were near Sinai.

11. The name of the Lord - The words of the Lord, or of Jehovah, are supplied out of ver. 16, where they are expressed; here they are omitted perhaps for the aggravation of his crime. He blasphemed the name so called by way of eminency; that name which is above every name; that name which a man should in some sort tremble to mention; which is not to be named without cause or without reverence. And cursed - Not the Israelite only, but his God also, as appears from ver. 15, 16. And they brought him - Either the people who heard him, or the inferior magistrate, to whom he was first brought.

12. That the mind of the Lord might be shewed - For God had only said in general, that he would not hold such guiltless, that is, he would punish them, but had not declared how he would have them punished by men.

14. Lay their hands upon his head - Whereby they gave public testimony that they heard this person speak such words, and did in their own and all the peoples names, demand justice to be executed upon him, that by this sacrifice God might be appeased, and his judgments turned away from the people, upon whom they would certainly fall if he were unpunished. Stone him - The same punishment which was before appointed for those who cursed their parents.

15. Whosoever curseth his God - Speaketh of him reproachfully. Shall bear his sin - That is, the punishment of it; shall not go unpunished.

16. He that blasphemeth the name of the Lord - This is a repetition of the same sin in other words, which is common. As this law is laid down in general terms, ver. 15, so both the sin and the punishment are particularly expressed, ver. 16. All the congregation - To shew their zeal for God, and to beget in them the greater dread and abhorrence of blasphemy.

17. He that killeth - This law is repeated here, to prevent the mischievous effects of men's striving together, which as here it caused blasphemy, so it might in others lead to murder.

22. One law - That is, in matters of common right, but not as to church privileges.

23. Stone him with stones - This blasphemer was the first that died by the law of Moses. Stephen the first that died for the gospel, died by the abuse of the law. The martyr and the malefactor suffered the same death; but how vast the difference between them.

XXV

In token of his peculiar right to the land of Canaan, God in this chapter appoints,

1. That every seventh year should be a year of rest, ver. 1-7.
2. That every fiftieth year should be a year of jubilee, ver. 8-17. A peculiar blessing annext, ver. 18-22. The land sold may be redeemed: if not, it shall revert at the year of jubilee, only with some exceptions, ver. 23-34. Usury forbidden, ver. 35-38. Jewish servants to be released at the jubilee, ver. 39. but heathens might be retained, ver. 40-46. Of an Israelite that sold himself to a stranger, ver. 47-55.

1. In Mount Sinai - That is, near Mount Sinai. So the Hebrew particle beth is sometimes used. So there is no need to disturb the history in this place.

2. When ye come into the land - So as to be settled in it; for the time of the wars was not to be accounted, nor the time before Joshua's distribution of the land among them. Keep a sabbath - That is, enjoy rest and freedom from plowing, and tilling. Unto the Lord - In obedience and unto the honour of God. This was instituted,

1. For the assertion of God's sovereign right to the land, in which the Israelites were but tenants at God's will.
2. For the trial of their obedience.
3. For the demonstration of his providence as well in general towards men, as especially towards his own people.
4. To wean them from inordinate love, and pursuit of worldly advantages, and to inure them to depend upon God alone, and upon God's blessing for their subsistence.
5. To put them in mind of that blessed and eternal rest provided for all good men.
4. A sabbath of rest to the land - They were neither to do any work about it, nor expect any harvest from it. All yearly labours were to be intermitted in the seventh year, as much as daily labours on the seventh day.
5. Of its own accord - From the grains that fell out of the ears the last reaping time. Thou shalt not reap - That is, as thy own peculiarly, but only so as others may reap it with thee, for present food. Undressed - Not cut off by thee, but suffered to grow for the use of the poor.
6. The sabbath of the land - That is, the growth of the sabbath, or that fruit which groweth in the

sabbatical year. *For thy servant* - For all promiscuously, to take food from thence as they need it.

9. *The jubilee* - Signified the true liberty from our spiritual debts and slaveries to be purchased by Christ, and to be published to the world by the sound of the gospel. *The seventh month* - Which was the first month of the year for civil affairs; the jubilee therefore began in that month; and, as it seems, upon this very tenth day, when the trumpet sounded, as other feasts generally began when the trumpet sounded. *In the day of atonement* - A very fit time, that when they fasted and prayed for God's mercy to them in the pardon of their sins, then they might exercise their charity to men in forgiving their debts; and to teach us, that the foundation of all solid comfort must be laid in repentance and atonement for our sins through Christ.

10. *The fiftieth year* - The year of jubilee was not the forty and ninth year, as some learned men think, but precisely the fiftieth. The old weekly sabbath is called the seventh day, because it truly was so, being next after the six days of the week and distinct from them all: and the year of release is called the seventh year, ver. 4, as immediately following the six years, ver. 3, and distinct from them all. And in like manner the jubilee is called the fiftieth year, because it comes next after seven tines seven or forty-nine years, ver. 8, and is distinct from them all. *Unto all the inhabitants* - Understand such as were Israelites; principally to all servants, even to such as would not and did not go out at the seventh year, and to the poor, who now were acquitted from all their debts, and restored to their possessions. *Jubilee* - So called either from the Hebrew word Jobel which signifies first a ram, and then a ram's horn, by the sound whereof it was proclaimed; or from Jubal the inventor of musical instruments, Gen. iv, 21, because it was celebrated with music and all expressions of joy. *Unto his possession* - Which had been sold or otherwise alienated from him. This law was not at all unjust, because all buyers and sellers had an eye to this condition in their bargains; but it was expedient in many regards, as

1. To mind them that God alone was the Lord and proprietor both of them and of their lands, and they only his tenants; a point which they were very apt to forget.

2. That hereby inheritances, families, and tribes, might be kept entire and clear until the coming of the Messiah, who was to be known as by other things, so by the tribe and family out of which he was to come. And this accordingly was done by the singular providence of God until the Lord Jesus did come. Since which time those characters are miserably confounded: which is no small argument that the Messiah is come.

3. To set bounds both to the insatiable avarice of some, and the foolish prodigality of others, that the former might not wholly and finally swallow up the inheritances of their brethren, and the latter might not be able to undo themselves and their posterity forever, which was a singular privilege of this law and people. *His family* - From whom he was gone, being sold to some other family either by himself or by his father.

12. *It shall be holy* - So it was, because it was sequestered in great part from worldly employments and dedicated to God, and to the exercise of holy joy and thankfulness; and because it was a type of that holy and happy jubilee which they were to expect and enjoy under the Messiah. *The increase thereof* - Such things as it produced of itself. *Out of the field* - Whence they in common with others might take it as they needed it; but must not put it into barns, See ver. 5, and Exod. xxiii, 11.

14. *Ye shall not oppress* - Neither the seller by requiring more, nor the buyer by taking the advantage from his brother's necessities to give him less than the worth of it.

15. *Years of fruits* - Or, fruitful years; for there were some unfruitful years; those wherein they were not allowed to sow or reap.

16. *Years of fruits* - Or, For the number of the fruits. The meaning is, he selleth not the land, but only the fruits thereof, and that for a certain time.

21. *For three years* - Not compleatly, but in great part, namely, for that part of the 6th year which was between the beginning of harvest and the beginning of the 7th year, for the whole 7th year, and for that part of the 8th year which was before the harvest, which reached almost until the beginning of the ninth year. This is added to shew the equity of this command. As God would hereby try their faith and obedience, so he gave them an eminent proof of his own exact providence and tender care over them in making provisions suitable to their necessities.

22. *Old fruit* - Of the sixth year principally, if not solely.

23. *For ever* - So as to be forever alienated from the family of him that sells it. Or, absolutely and properly, so as to become the property of the buyer: Or, to the extermination or utter cutting off, namely, of the seller, from all hopes and possibility of redemption. *The land is mine* - Procured for you by my power, given to you by my grace and bounty, and the right of propriety reserved by me. *With me* - That is, in my land or houses: thus he is said to sojourn with another that dwells in his house. Howsoever in your own or other mens opinions you pass for lords and proprietors, yet in truth, ye are but strangers and sojourners, not to possess the land forever, but only for a season, and to leave it to such as I have appointed for it.

24. *A redemption* - A right of redemption in the time and manner following.

25. *If any of his kin come* - Or, If the redeemer come, being near akin to him, who in this was an

eminent type of Christ, who was made near akin to us by taking our flesh, that he might perform the work of redemption for us.

27. The years of the sale - That is, from the time of the sale to the jubilee. See above, ver. 15, 16. The overplus - That is, a convenient price for the years from this redemption to the jubilee.

28. Go out - That is, out of the buyer's hand, without any redemption money.

30. It shall not go out - The reasons before alledged for lands do not hold in such houses; there was no danger of confusion in tribes or families by the alienation of houses. The seller also had a greater propriety in houses than in lands, as being commonly built by the owner's cost and diligence, and therefore had a fuller power to dispose of them. Besides, God would hereby encourage persons to buy and possess houses in such places, as frequency and fulness of inhabitants in cities, was a great strength, honour and advantage to the whole land.

31. In the villages - Because they belonged to and were necessary for the management of the lands.

34. May not be sold - Not sold at all, partly, because it was of absolute necessity for them for the keeping of their cattle, and partly because these were no enclosures, but common fields, in which all the Levites that lived in such a city had an interest, and therefore no particular Levite could dispose of his part in it.

35. A sojourner - Understand it of proselytes only, for of other strangers they were permitted to take usury, Deut. xxiii, 20.

36. Of him - That is, of thy brother, whether he be Israelite, or proselyte. Or increase - All kinds of usury are in this case forbidden, whether of money, or of victuals, or of any thing that is commonly lent by one man to another upon usury, or upon condition of receiving the thing lent with advantage and overplus. If one borrow in his necessity, there can be no doubt but this law is binding still. But it cannot be thought to bind, where money is borrowed for purchase of lands, trade, or other improvements. For there it is reasonable, that the lender share with the borrower in the profit.

39. As a bond-man - Neither for the time, forever, nor for the manner, with the hardest and vilest kinds of service, rigorously and severely exacted.

41. Then shall he depart - Thou shalt not suffer him or his to abide longer in thy service, as thou mightest do in the year of release, Exod. xxi, 2, 6.

42. They are my servants - They, no less than you, are members of my church and people; such as I have chosen out of all the world to serve me here, and to enjoy me hereafter, and therefore are not to be oppressed, neither are you absolute lords over them to deal with them as you please.

43. Fear thy God - Though thou dost not fear them who are in thy power, and unable to right themselves, yet fear that God who hath commanded thee to use them kindly, and who can and will avenge their cause, if thou oppress them.

47. The flock - Hebrew. root, that is, one of the root or flock. So the word root is elsewhere used for the branch or progeny growing from it. He seems to note one of a foreign race and country, transplanted into the land of Israel, and there having taken root amongst the people of God, yet even such an one, though he hath some privilege by it, shall not have power to keep an Hebrew servant from the benefit of redemption.

50. According to the time of an hired servant - Allowance shall be made for the time wherein he hath served, proportionable to that which is given to an hired servant for so long service, because his condition is in this like theirs; it is not properly his person, but his work and labour that was sold.

53. In thy sight - Thou shalt not suffer this to be done, but whethe thou art a magistrate, or a private person, thou shalt take care according to thy capacity to get it remedied.

XXVI

A general enforcement of the preceding laws, by promises of reward, and threats of punishment: Wherein is,

I. A repetition of some principal commandments, ver. 1, 2.

II. A promise of all good to the obedient, ver. 3-13.

III. A threatening of terrible judgments to the disobedient, ver. 14- 39.

IV. A promise of mercy to the penitent, ver. 40-46.

1. An image - Or pillar, that is, to worship it, or bow down to it, as it follows. Otherwise this was not simply prohibited, being practiced by holy men, both before and after this law.

2. My sanctuary - By purging and preserving it from all uncleanness, by approaching to it and

managing all the services of it with reverence, and in such manner only as God hath appointed.

4. Rain - Therefore God placed them not in a land where there were such rivers as the Nile, to water it and make it fruitful, but in a land which depended wholly upon the rain of heaven, the key whereof God kept in his own hand, that so he might the more effectually oblige them to obedience, in which their happiness consisted.

5. The vintage - That is, you shall have so plentiful an harvest, that you shall not be able to thresh out your corn in a little time, but that work will last till the vintage.

6. The sword - That is, war, as the sword is oft taken. It shall not enter into it, nor have passage through it, much less shall your land be made the seat of war.

8. Five - A small number; a certain number for an uncertain.

9. Establish my covenant - That is, actually perform all that I have promised in my covenant made with you.

10. Bring forth - Or, cast out, throw them away as having no occasion to spend them, or give them to the poor, or even to your cattle, that you may make way for the new corn, which also is so plentiful, that of itself it will fill up your barns.

11. I will set - As I have placed it, so I will continue it among you, and not remove it from you, as once I did upon your miscarriage, Exod. xxxiii, 7.

12. I will walk among you - As I have hitherto done, both by my pillar of cloud and fire, and by my tabernacle, which have walked or gone along with you in all your journeys, and staid among you in all your stations, to protect, conduct, instruct, and comfort you. And I will own you for that peculiar people which I have singled out of mankind, to bless you here and to save you hereafter.

13. Upright - With heads lifted up, not pressed down with a yoke. It notes their liberty, security, confidence and glory.

15. Break my covenant - Break your part of that covenant made between me and you, and thereby discharge me from the blessings promised on my part.

16. That shall consume the eyes, and cause sorrow of heart - Two remarkable effects of this distemper, when it continues long. It eminently weakens the sight, and sinks the spirit. All chronical diseases are here included in the consumption, all acute in the burning ague or fever. 19. The pride of your power - That is, your strength of which you are proud, your numerous and united forces, your kingdom, yea, your ark and sanctuary. I will make your heaven as iron - The heavens shall yield you no rain, nor the earth fruits.

20. In vain - in plowing, and sowing, and tilling the ground.

25. The quarrel of my covenant - That is, my quarrel with you for your breach of your covenant made with me.

26. When I have broken the staff of your bread - By sending a famine or scarcity of bread, which is the staff and support of man's present life. Ten women - That is, ten or many families, for the women took care for the bread and food of all the family. By weight - This is a sign and consequence both of a famine, and of the baking of the bread of several families together in one oven, wherein each family took care to weigh their bread, and to receive the same proportion which they put in.

29. The flesh of your sons - Through extreme hunger. See Lam. iv, 10.

30. High places - In which you will sacrifice after the manner of the Heathens. The carcases of your idols - So he calls them, either to signify that their idols how specious soever or glorious in their eyes, were in truth but lifeless and contemptible carcases; or to shew that their idols should be so far from helping them, that they should be thrown down and broken with them, and both should lie together in a forlorn and loathsome state.

31. Sanctuaries - God's sanctuary, called sanctuaries here, as also Psalm 7iii, 17; 7iv, 7 Jer. li, 51 Ezek. xxviii, 18, because there were divers apartments in it, each of which was a sanctuary, or, which is all one, an holy place, as they are severally called. And yours emphatically, not mine, for I disown and abhor it, and all the services you do in it, because you have defiled it. I will not smell - Not own or accept them. Your sweet odours - Either of the incense, or of your sacrifices, which when offered with faith and obedience, are sweet and acceptable to me.

32. Who dwell therein - Having driven you out and possessed your places.

33. After you - The sword shall follow you into strange lands, and you shall have no rest there.

34. The land shall enjoy her sabbaths - It shall enjoy those sabbatical years of rest from tillage, which you through covetousness would not give it.

37. When none pursueth - Your guilt and fear causing you to imagine that they do pursue when indeed they do not.

39. Pine away - Be consumed and melt away by degrees through diseases, oppressions, griefs, and manifold miseries.

40. If they shall confess their iniquity, and the iniquity of their fathers, with their trespass which they have trespassed against me - That is, with their prevarication with me and defection from me to idolatry, which by way of eminency he calls their trespass: and that also they have walked contrary to

me, ver. 41, and that I also have walked contrary unto them, and have brought them into the land of their enemies - That is, that they are not come into these calamities by chance, nor by the misfortune of war, but by my just judgment upon them. And, if then their uncircumcised, that is, impure, carnal, profane, and impenitent hearts be humbled, that is, subdued, purged, reformed: if to this confession they add sincere humiliation and reformation, I will do what follows.

41. If they accept of - The meaning is, if they sincerely acknowledge the righteousness of God and their own wickedness, and patiently submit to his correcting hand; if with David they are ready to say, it is good for them that they are afflicted, that they may learn God's statutes, and yield obedience to them for the future, which is a good evidence of true repentance.

42. I will remember my covenant - So as to make good all that I have promised in it. For words of knowledge or remembrance in scripture, commonly denote affection and kindness. I will remember the land - Which now seems to be forgotten and despised, as if I had never chosen it to be the peculiar place of my presence and blessing.

44. For I am the Lord their God - Therefore neither the desperateness of their condition, nor the greatness of their sins, shall make me wholly make void my covenant with them and their ancestors, but I will in due time remember them for good, and for my covenant's sake return to them in mercy. From this place the Jews take great comfort, and assure themselves of deliverance out of their present servitude and misery. And from this, and such other places, St. Paul concludes, that the Israelitish nation, tho' then rejected and ruined, should be gathered again and restored.

46. These are the laws which the Lord made between him and the children of Israel - Hereby his communion with his church is kept up. He manifests not only his dominion over them, but his favour to them, by giving them his law. And they manifest not only their holy fear, but their holy love by the observance of it. And thus it is made between them rather as a covenant than as a law: for he draws them with the cords of a man.

XXVII

Laws concerning persons sanctified to God, ver. 1-8. Concerning cattle, ver. 9-13. Concerning houses and lands, ver. 14-25. An exception concerning firstlings, ver. 26-27. Concerning what was devoted, ver. 28, 29. Concerning tithes, ver. 30-34.

2. A singular vow-Or, an eminent, or hard vow, not concerning things, which was customary, but concerning persons, which he devoted to the Lord, which was unusual and difficult: yet there want not instances of persons who devoted either themselves or their children, and that either more strictly, as the Nazarites, and the Levites, 1 Sam. i, 11, and for these there was no redemption admitted, but they were in person to perform the service to which they were devoted: or more largely, as some who were not Levites, might yet through zeal to God, or to obtain God's help, which they wanted or desired, devote themselves or their children to the service of God and of the sanctuary, tho' not in such a way as the Levites, which was forbidden, yet in some kind of subserviency to them. And because there might be too great a number of persons thus dedicated, which might be burdensome to the sanctuary, an exchange is allowed, and the priests are directed to receive a tax for their redemption. By thy estimation - Thine, O man that vowest, as appears from ver. 8, where his estimation is opposed to the priest's valuation. Nor was there any fear of his partiality in his own cause, for the price is particularly limited. But where the price is undetermined, there, to avoid that inconveniency, the priest is to value it, as ver. 8, 12.

3. Unto sixty years - Which is the best time for strength and service, and therefore prized at the highest rate.

4. Thirty shekels - Less than the man's price, because she is inferior to him both in strength and serviceableness.

5. Five years old - At which age they might be vowed by their parents, as appears from 1 Sam. i, 11-28, tho' not by themselves; and the children were obliged by their parents vow, which is not strange considering the parents right to dispose of their children so far as is not contrary to the mind of God.

8. Than thy estimation - If he be not able to pay the price which thou, according to the rules here given, requirest of him.

9. Whereof men bring an offering - That is, a clean beast. Giveth - Voweth to give: Shall be holy - Consecrated to God, either to be sacrificed, or to be given to the priest, according to the manner of the vow, and the intention of him that voweth.

10. He shall not alter it, nor change it - Two words expressing the same thing more emphatically, that is, he shall in no wise change it, neither for one of the same, nor of another kind: partly because God would preserve the reverence of consecrated things, and therefore would not have them alienated, and partly to prevent abuses of them who on this pretense might exchange it for the worse. It and the exchange - That is, both the thing first vowed, and the thing offered or given in exchange. This was inflicted upon him as a just penalty for his levity in such weighty matters.

11. *Unclean* - Either for the kind, or for the quality of it; if it were such an one as might not be offered.

14. *Sanctify his house* - By a vow, for of that way and manner of sanctification he speaks in this whole chapter.

15. *The fifth part* - Which he might the better do, because the priests did usually put a moderate rate upon it.

16. *Of his possession* - That is, which is his by inheritance, because particular direction is given about purchased lands, ver. 22. And he saith, part of it, for it was unlawful to vow away all his possessions, because thereby he disabled himself from the performance of divers duties, and made himself burdensome to his brethren. According to the seed - That is, according to the quantity and quality of the land, which is known by the quantity of seed which it can receive and return. Fifty-shekels - Not to be paid yearly, 'till the year of jubilee, but once for all, as is most probable,

1. Because here is no mention of any yearly payment, but only of one payment.

2. Because it is probable that lands were moderately valued, that men might be rather encouraged to make such vows, than deterred by excessive impositions. But if this were yearly rent, it was an excessive rate, and much more than the land ordinarily yielded. For an omer is but the tenth part of an ephah, about a pottle of our measure, which quantity of seed would not extend very far, and in some lands would yield but an inconsiderable crop, especially in barley, which was cheaper than wheat and which for that reason, among others, may be mentioned rather than wheat.

17. *From the year of jubilee* - That is, immediately after the year of jubilee is past. According to thy estimation - Now mentioned, of fifty shekels for an omer of barley seed. It shall stand - That is, that price shall be paid without diminution.

18. *After the jubilee* - That is, some considerable time after. The defalcation from the full price of fifty shekels shall be more or less as the years are more or fewer.

20. *If he will not redeem it* - When the priest shall set a price upon it, and offer it to him in the first place to redeem it: or, rather and, for this seems to be added by way of accumulation, if he, that is, the priest, of whom he might have redeemed it, upon his refusal, offers it to sale, and have sold the field to another man - He shall forever lose the benefit of redemption.

21. *When it goeth out* - That is, out of the possession of the other man to whom the priest sold it. The possession shall be the priests - For their maintenance. Nor is this repugnant to that law, that the priests should have no inheritance in the land, Num. xviii, 20, for that is only spoken of, the tribe of Levi in general, in reference to the first division of the land, wherein the Levites were not to have a distinct part of land, as other tribes had; but this doth not hinder, but some particular lands might be vowed and given to the priests, either for their own benefit, or for the service of the sanctuary.

22. *His possession* - His patrimony or inheritance.

23. *Thy estimation* - That is, the price which thou, O Moses, by my direction hast set in such cases. To the jubilee - As much as it is worth, for that space of time between the making of the vow and the year of jubilee: for he had no right to it for any longer time, as the next verse tells us. As an holy thing - As that which is to be consecrated to God instead of the land redeemed by it.

25. *The shekel* - About 2s. 6d.

26. *No man shall sanctify it* - By vow; because it is not his own, but the Lord's already, and therefore to vow such a thing to God is a tacit derogation from, and an usurpation of the Lord's right, and a mocking of God by pretending to give what we cannot withhold from him. Or ox or sheep - Under these two eminent kinds he comprehends all other beasts which might be sacrificed to God, the firstlings whereof could not be redeemed but were to be sacrificed; whereas the firstlings of men were to be redeemed, and therefore were capable of being vowed, as we see, 1 Sam. i, 11.

27. *An unclean beast* - That is, if it be the first-born of an unclean beast, as appears from ver. 26, which could not be vowed, because it was a first-born, nor offered, because it was unclean, and therefore is here commanded to be redeemed or sold. It shall be sold - And the price thereof was given to the priests, or brought into the Lord's treasury.

28. *No devoted thing* - That is, nothing which is absolutely devoted to God with a curse upon themselves or others, if they disposed not of it according to their vow; as the Hebrew word implies. Most holy - That is, only to be touched or employed by the priests, and by no other persons; no not by their own families, for that was the state of the most holy things.

29. *Devoted of men* - Not by men, as some would elude It; but of men, for it is manifest both from this and the foregoing verses, that men are here not the persons devoting, but devoted to destruction, either by God's sentence, as idolaters, Exod. xxii, 20 Deut. xxiii, 15, the Canaanites, Deut. xx, 17, the Amalekites, Deut. xxv, 19, and 1 Sam. xv, 3, 26, Benhaded, 1 Kings xx, 42, or by men, in pursuance of such a sentence of God, as Num. xxi, 2, 3; xxxi, 17, or for any crime of an high nature, as Jude xxi, 5 Josh. xvii, 15. But this is not to be generally understood, as some have taken it, as if a Jew might by virtue of this Text, devote his child or his servant to the Lord, and thereby oblige himself to put them to death. For this is expressly limited to all that a man hath, or which is his, that is, which he hath a power

over. But the Jews had no power over the lives of their children or servants, but were directly forbidden to take them away, by that great command, thou shalt do no murder. And seeing he that killed his servant casually by a blow with a rod was surely to be punished, as is said, Exod. xxi, 20, it could not be lawful wilfully to take away his life upon pretense of any such vow as this. But for the Canaanites, Amalekites, &c. God the undoubted Lord of all men's lives, gave to the Israelites a power over their persons and lives, and a command to put them to death. And this verse may have a special respect to them or such as them.

30. The tithe - There are divers sorts of tithes, but this seems to be understood only of the ordinary and yearly tithes belonging to the Levites, as the very expression intimates, and the addition of the fifth part in case of redemption thereof implies.

32. Under the rod - Either,

1. The tither's rod, it being the manner of the Jews in tithing to cause all their cattle to pass through some gate or narrow passage, where the tenth was marked by a person appointed for that purpose and reserved for the priest. Or

2. the shepherd's rod, under which the herds and flocks passed, and by which they were governed and numbered. See Jer. xxxiii, 13 Ezek. xx, 37.

34. These are the commandments which the Lord commanded Moses for the children of Israel in M/ount Sinai - This has reference to the whole book. Many of these commandments are moral: others ceremonial and peculiar to the Jewish economy: Which yet are instructive to us, who have a key to the mysteries that are contained in them. Upon the whole, we have cause to bless God, that we are not come to Mount Sinai, that we are not under the dark shadows of the law, but enjoy the clear light of the gospel. The doctrine of our reconciliation to God by a Mediator, is not clouded with the smoke of burning sacrifices, but cleared by the knowledge of Christ, and him crucified. And we may praise him, that we are not under the yoke of the law, but under the sweet and easy instructions of the gospel, which pronounces those the true worshippers, that worship the Father in spirit and in truth, by Christ only, who is our priest, temple, altar, sacrifice, purification and all.

NOTES ON THE FOURTH BOOK OF MOSES CALLED NUMBERS

THIS book is thus entitled, because of the numbers of the children of Israel, so often mentioned therein, an eminent accomplishment of God's promise to Abraham, that his seed should be as the stars of heaven for multitude. It also relates two numberings of them, one at Mount Sinai, chap. 1. the other, thirty-nine years after. And there are not three men of the same in the last account that were in the first. The book is almost equally divided, between histories and laws intermixed. An abstract of much of this book we have in a few words, Psalm xcv, 10. Forty years long was I grieved with this generation: and an application of it to ourselves, Heb. iv, 1. Let us fear lest we come short!

I

Orders given to Moses to number the people, ver. 1-4. Persons named to assist him therein, ver. 5-16. The particular number of each tribe, ver. 17-43. The sum of all together, ver. 44-46. The Levites excepted, ver. 47-54.

1. In the wilderness - Where now they had been a full year or near it, as may be gathered by comparing this place with Exod. xix, 1; xl, 17.

2. Take the sum - This is not the same muster with that Exod. xxxviii, 26, as plainly appears, because that was before the building of the tabernacle, which was built and set up on the first day of the first month, Exod. xl, 2, but this was after it, on the first day of the second month. And they were for different ends; that was to tax them for the charges of the tabernacle; but this was for other ends, partly that the great number of the people might be known to the praise of God's faithfulness, in making good his promises of multiplying them, and to their own encouragement: partly for the better ordering their camp and march, for they were now beginning their journey; and partly that this account might be compared with the other in the close of the book, where we read that not one of all this vast number, except Caleb and Joshua were left alive; a fair warning to all future generations to take heed of rebelling against the Lord. It is true, the sums and numbers agree in this and that computation, which is not strange, because there was not much time between the two numberings, and no eminent sin among the people in that interval, whereby God was provoked to diminish their numbers. Some conceive that in that number, Exod. xxx, 11-16 and xxxviii, 25, 26, the Levites were included, which are here excepted, ver. 47, and that in that interval of time, there were grown up as many more men of those years as there were Levites of the same age. Israel - So the strangers mixed with them, were not numbered. Their fathers - The people were divided into twelve tribes, the tribes into great families, ver. xxvi, 5, these great families into lesser families called the houses of their fathers, because they were distinguished one from another by their fathers.

5. Reuben - The tribes are here numbered according to the order or quality of their birth, first the children of Leah, then of Rachel, and then of the handmaids.

12. Deuel - Called Reuel, chap. iii, 14, the Hebrew letters Daleth and Resh being often changed.

19. He numbered them - For ought that appears in one day.

20. By their generations - That is, the persons begotten of Reuben's immediate children, who are here subdivided into families, and they into houses, and they into particular persons.

27. Threescore and fourteen thousand - Far more than any other tribe, in accomplishing Jacob's prophecy, Gen. xlix, 8-12.

33. Ephraim - Above 8000 more than Manasseh, towards the accomplishment of that promise, Gen. xlviii, 20, which the devil in vain attempted to defeat by stirring up the men of Gath against them, 1Chr vii, 21, 22.

37. Thirty five thousand - The smallest number, except one, though Benjamin had more immediate children than any of his brethren, Gen. xlvi, 21, whereas Daniel had but one immediate son, Gen. xlvi, 23, yet now his number is the biggest but one of all the tribes, and is almost double to that of Benjamin. Such great and strange changes God easily can, and frequently doth make in families, 1 Sam. ii, 5. And therefore let none boast or please themselves too much in their numerous offspring.

49. Levi - Because they were not generally to go out to war, which was the thing principally eyed in this muster, ver. 3, 20, 45, but were to attend upon the service of the tabernacle. They that minister upon holy things, should not entangle themselves in secular affairs. The ministry itself is work enough for a whole man, and all little enough to be employed in it.

50. The tabernacle of testimony - So called here, and Exod. xxxviii, 21, because it was made chiefly for the sake of the ark of the testimony, which is often called the testimony.

51. That cometh nigh - The stranger elsewhere is one of another nation, here one of another tribe. So as to do the offices mentioned, ver. 50.

53. No wrath - From God, who is very tender of his worship, and will not suffer the profaners of it go unpunished! whose wrath is called simply wrath by way of eminency, as the most terrible kind of wrath.

II

Orders concerning the camp,
1. A general order, ver. 1, 2.
2. Particular directions for posting each of the tribes, in four squadrons. In the vanguard, on the east, Judah, Issachar, and Zebulun, ver. 3-9. In the right wing, southward, Reuben, Simeon, and Gad, ver. 10-16. The tabernacle in the midst, ver. 17. In the rear, westward, Ephraim, Manasseh, and Benjamin, ver. 18-24. In the left wing, northward, Daniel, Asher, and Naphtali, ver. 25-31. The conclusion of the appointment, ver. 32-34.

2. His own standard - It is manifest there were four great standards or ensigns, which here follow, distinguished by their colours or figures; also there were other particular ensigns belonging to each of their fathers houses or families. Far off - Partly out of reverence to God and his worship, and the portion, allotted to it, and partly for caution, lest their vicinity to it might tempt them to make too near approaches to it. It is supposed they Were at 2000 cubits distance from it, which was the space between the people and the ark; and it is not improbable, because the Levites encamped round about it, between them and the tabernacle. It is observable, those tribes were placed together, that were nearest of kin to each other. Judah, Issachar, and Zebulun were the three youngest sons of Leah, and Issachar and Zebulun would not grudge to be under Judah, their elder brother. Reuben and Simeon would not be content with their place. Therefore Reuben, Jacob's eldest son, is chief of the next squadron. Simeon doubtless is willing to be under him. And Gad, the son of Leah's handmaid, is fitly added to him, in Levi's room. Ephraim Manasseh, and Benjamin are all the posterity of Rachel. Daniel the eldest son of Bilhah leads the rest; to them are added the two younger sons of the handmaids. So much of the wisdom of God appears even in these smaller circumstances!

3. Judah - This tribe was in the first post, and in their marches led the van, not only because it was the most numerous, but chiefly because Christ, the Lion of the tribe of Judah, was to descend from it: Yea, from the loins of Nahshon, who is here appointed the chief captain of it.

17. In the midst - This is not to be understood strictly, but largely; for in their march they were divided, and part of that tribe marched next after Judah, chap. x, 17, and the other part exactly in the midst of the camp.

18. Ephraim - Who is here preferred before his brother, according to the prophecy, Gen. xlviii, 19, 20.

31. The Camp of Daniel - The strongest camp next after Judah, and therefore he comes in the rear, as Judah marched in the front, that the tabernacle might be best guarded where there was most danger.

III

In this chapter we have an account,
1. Of the priests, ver. 1-4.
2. The work of the Levites, taken instead of the first-born, ver. 5- 13.
3. Of the number, place and charge of each family; the Gershonites, ver. 14-26. The Kohathites, ver. 27-32. The Merarites, ver. 33-39.
4. Of the first-born, ver. 40-51.

1. These - Which follow in this chapter. The generations - The kindred or family. Moses his family and children are here included under the general name of the Amramites, ver. 27, which includes all the children and grand-children of Amram, the persons only of Aaron and Moses being excepted. And the generations of Moses are thus obscurely mentioned, because they were but common Levites, the priesthood being given solely to Aaron's posterity, whence Aaron is here put before Moses, who elsewhere is commonly named after him. In Sinai - Nadab and Abihu, were then alive, though dead at

the time of taking this account.

4. *In the sight of Aaron* - Under his inspection and direction, and as their father's servants or ministers in the priest's office.

6. *Present them* - Offer them to the Lord for his special service. This was promised to them before, and now actually conferred.

7. *His charge* - That is, Aaron's, or those things which are committed principally to Aaron's care and oversight. *Of the congregation* - That is, of all the sacrifices and services which are due to the Lord from all the people, because the people might not perform them, in their own persons, therefore they were to be performed by some particular persons in their stead; formerly by the first-born, chap. viii, 16, and now by the Levites. *Before the tabernacle* - Not within the tabernacle, for the care of the things within the holy place was appropriated to the priests, as the care of the most holy place was to the high-priest.

8. *Of the children of Israel* - Those things which all the children of Israel are in their several places and stations obliged to take care of, though not in their persons, yet by others in their stead.

9. *Given to him* - To attend upon him and observe his orders, and ease him of his burden.

10. *The stranger* - That is, every one who is of another family than Aaron's; yea, though he be a Levite. *That cometh nigh* - To execute any part of the priest's office.

12. *The first-born* - Who were God's property, Exod. xiii, 12, and to whom the administration of holy things was formerly committed, which now was taken away from them, either because they had forfeited this privilege by joining with the rest of their brethren in the idolatrous worship of the calf, or because they were to be mainly concerned in the distribution and management of the inheritances which now they were going to possess, and therefore could not be at leisure to attend upon the service of the sanctuary: and God would not commit it to some other persons in each tribe, which might be an occasion of idolatry, confusion, division, and contempt of sacred things, but to one distinct tribe, which might be entirely devoted to that service, and particularly to the tribe of Levi; partly out of his respect to Moses and Aaron, branches of this tribe; partly as a recompence of their zeal for God against idolaters, and partly because it was the smallest of the tribes, and therefore most likely to find both employment in, and maintenance for the work.

15. *From a month old* - Because at that time the first-born, in whose stead the Levites came, were offered to God. And from that time the Levites were consecrated to God, and were, as soon as capable, instructed in their work. Elsewhere they are numbered from twenty-five years old, when they were entered as novices into part of their work, chap. viii, 24, and from thirty years old, when they were admitted to their whole office.

25. *The tabernacle* - Not the boards, which belonged to Merari, ver. 36, but the ten curtains. *The tent* - The curtains of goats hair. *The coverings* - That is, the coverings of rams-skins and badgers-skins.

26. *The cords* - By which the tabernacle was fastened to the pins, and stretched out, Exod. xxxv, 18.

27. *Of Kohath* - This family had many privileges above the others: of that were Moses and Aaron, and all the priests: they had the chief place about the tabernacle, and the care of the most holy things here, and in the land of Canaan they had twenty three cities, which were almost as many as both their brethren received. Yet the posterity of Moses were not at all dignified or distinguished from other Levites. So far was he from seeking any advantage or honour for his own family.

28. *Keeping* - That is, appointed for that work, as soon as they were capable of it. *Of the sanctuary* - That is, of the holy things contained in or belonging to the sanctuary.

31. *The hanging* - Which covered the most holy place, for all other hangings belonged to the Gershonites. *The service* - That is, all the other furniture belonging to it.

32. *Chief* - Next under the high-priest; whence he is called the second priest, 2 Kings xxv, 18, and in case of the high-priest's absence by sickness or other necessary occasions, he was to perform his work, and he had a superiority over all the rest of the priests and Levites. *The chief of the Levites* - That is, over those three persons, who were each the chief of their several families, ver. 24, 31, 34.

38. *For the charge* - Either in their stead, that charge which they were obliged to keep, if God had not committed it to those: or for their benefit; for their preservation, as the word may be rendered.

39. *Two and twenty thousand* - If the particular numbers mentioned ver. 22, 28, 34, be put together, they make 22,300. But the odd 300 are omitted here, either according to the use of the holy scripture, where in so great numbers small sums are commonly neglected, or, because they were the first-born of the Levites, and therefore belonged to God already, and so could not be given to him again instead of the other first-born. If this number of first-born seem small to come from 22,000 Levites, it must be considered, that only such first-born are here named as were males, and such as continued in their parents families, not such as had erected new families of their own. Add to this, that God so ordered things by his wise providence for divers weighty reasons, that this tribe should be much the least of all the tribes, as is evident by comparing the numbers of the other tribes, from twenty years old, chap. i, 3-49, with the number of this from a month old; and therefore it is not strange if the number of

their first-born be less than in other tribes.

41. Instead of the first-born - Such as are now alive of them, but those which should be born of them hereafter are otherwise disposed. Of the Levites - Not that they were to be taken from the Levites, or to be sacrificed to God, any more than the Levites themselves were; but they together with the Levites were to be presented before the Lord by way of acknowledgment, that the Levites might be set apart for God's service, and their cattle for themselves as God's ministers, and for their support in God's work.

46. For those that are to be redeemed - 'Tis probable, in the exchange they began with the eldest of the first-born, and so downwards, so that those were to be redeemed, who were the two hundred, seventy three youngest of them.

47. Five shekels - Which was the price paid for the redemption of a first-born a month old.

IV

A command to number the Levites from thirty to fifty years old, ver. 1-3. The charge of the Kohathites, ver. 4-20. Of the Gershonites, ver. 21-28. Of the Merarites, ver. 29-33. The number of each, ver. 34-45. Of all in general, ver. 46-49.

3. From thirty - This age was prescribed, as the age of full strength of body, and therefore most proper for their labourious work of carrying the parts and vessels of the tabernacle, and of maturity of judgment, which is necessary for the right management of holy services. Whence even John and Christ entered not upon their ministry till that age. Indeed their first entrance upon their work was at their 25th year, when they began as learners, and acted under the inspection and direction of their brethren; but in their 30th year they were compleatly admitted to a full discharge of their whole office. But David, being a prophet, and particularly directed by God in the affairs of the temple, made a change in this matter, because the magnificence of the temple, and the great multitude of sacred utensils and sacrifices, required a greater number of attendants than formerly was necessary. Until fifty - When they were exempted from the toilsome work of carrying burdens, but not discharged from the honourable and easy work done within the tabernacle, chap. viii, 26. All that enter - That is, that do and may enter, having no defect, nor other impediment.

5. They shall take down - For upon this necessary occasion the inferior priests are allowed to come into the holy of holies, which otherwise was peculiar to the high-priest. The covering veil - The second veil, wherewith the ark was covered while the tabernacle stood, Exod. xl, 3. Cover the ark - Because the Levites, who were to carry the ark, might neither see, nor immediately touch it.

6. Badgers-skins - Whereby the ark was secured from the injuries of the weather.

7. The dishes - Upon which the shew-bread was put. Continual bread - So called because it was continually to be there, even in the wilderness; where though they had only manna for themselves, yet they reserved corn for the weekly making of these loaves, which they might with no great difficulty procure from some of the people bordering upon the wilderness.

11. The golden altar - All covered with plates of gold.

12. The instruments of ministry - The sacred garments used by the priests in their holy ministrations. Cover them - All these coverings were designed,

1. For safety, that these holy things might not be filled by rain, or tarnished by the sun.

2. For decency, most of them had a cloth of blue, or purple, or scarlet over them; the ark, a cloth wholly of blue, perhaps an emblem of the azure skies, which are spread between us and the Majesty on high;

3. For concealment. It was a fit sign of the darkness of that dispensation. The holy things were then covered. But Christ hath now destroyed the face of the covering.

13. The altar - Hence we may conclude, that they did offer sacrifices at other times, though not so constantly and diligently, as they did in Canaan. Moreover the taking away of the ashes only doth sufficiently imply that the fire was preserved, which as it came down from heaven, Lev. ix, 24. So it was by God's command to be continually fed, and kept burning, and therefore doubtless was put into some vessel, which might be either fastened to the altar and put within this covering, or carried by some person appointed thereunto.

15. Bear it - Upon their shoulders. Afterward the priests themselves, being multiplied, carried these things, though the Levites also were not excluded. They shall not touch - Before they are covered.

16. Eleazar - He himself is to carry these things, and not to commit them to the sons of Kohath. The oversight - The care that all the things above mentioned be carried by the persons and in the manner expressed.

18. Cut not off - Do not by your neglect provoke God to cut them off for touching the holy things.

19. To his service - To that which is peculiarly allotted to him, the services, and burdens being equally distributed among them.

25. *The curtains* - The curtains or covering of goats-hair. *The tabernacle* - The ten curtains which covered the boards of the tabernacle; for the boards themselves were carried by the Merarites. *His covering* - The covering of rams-skins which was put next over those ten curtains.

26. *Which is round about* - Which court compassed both the tabernacle and the altar.

28. *Under the hand* - Under his conduct and direction.

31. *The sockets* - Which were as the feet upon which the pillars stood.

32. *Ye shall reckon* - Every part and parcel shall be put in an inventory; which is required here rather than in the fore-going particulars; because these were much more numerous than the former; because being meaner things, they might otherwise have been neglected; and also to teach us, that God esteems nothing small in his service, and that he expects his will should be observed in the minutest circumstances. The death of the saints is represented us the taking down of the tabernacle. The immortal soul, like the most holy things, is first covered and taken away, carried by angels unseen, and care is taken also of the body, the skin and flesh, which are as the curtains, the bones and sinews, which are as the bars and pillars. None of these shall be lost. Commandment is given concerning the bones, a covenant made with the dust. They are in safe custody, and shall be produced in the great day, when this tabernacle shall be set up again, and these vile bodies made like the glorious body of Jesus Christ.

44. *Three thousand* - Here appears the wisdom of Divine Providence, that whereas in the Kohathites and Gershonites, whose burdens were fewer and easier, there were but about a third part of them fit for service; the Merarites, whose burdens were more and heavier, had above half of them fit for this work.

V

A command to remove the unclean out of the camp, ver. 1-4. Laws concerning restitution, ver. 5-10. The law concerning a woman suspected of adultery, ver. 11-31.

3. *That they defile not the camp* - By which God would intimate the danger of being made guilty by other mens sins, and the duty of avoiding intimate converse with wicked men. *I dwell* - By my special and gracious presence.

6. *Any sin that men commit* - Hebrew. any sins of men, that is, sins against men, as deceits or wrongs, whereby other men are injured, of which he manifestly speaks. *Against the Lord* - Which words may be added, to shew that such injuries done to men are also sins against God, who hath commanded justice to men, as well as religion to himself. *Guilty* - That is, shall be sensible of his guilt, convicted in his conscience.

7. *They shall confess their sin* - They shall not continue in the denial of the fact, but give glory to God, and take shame to themselves by acknowledging it. *The principal* - That is, the thing he took away, or what is equivalent to it. *And add* - Both as a compensation to the injured person for the want of his goods so long, and as a penalty upon the injurious dealer, to discourage others from such attempts.

8. *No kinsman* - This supposes the person injured to be dead or gone, into some unknown place, and the person injured to be known to the injurer. *To the priest* - Whom God appointed as his deputy to receive his dues, and take them to his own use, that so he might more cheerfully and entirely devote himself to the ministration of holy things. This is an additional explication to that law, Lev. vi, 2, and for the sake thereof it seems here to be repeated.

9. *Unto the priest* - To offer by his hands.

10. *Every man's hallowed things* - Understand this not of the sacrifices, because these were not the priest's peculiar, but part of them was offered to God, and the remainder was eaten by the offerer as well as by the priest; but of such other things as were devoted to God, and could not be offered in sacrifice; as suppose a man consecrated an house to the Lord, this was to be the priest's.

12. *If a man's wife* - This law was given partly to deter wives from adulterous practices, and partly to secure wives against the rage of their hard-hearted husbands, who otherwise might upon mere suspicions destroy them, or at least put them away. There was not like fear of inconveniences to the husband from the jealousy, of the wife, who had not that authority and power, and opportunity for the putting away or killing the husband, as the husband had over the wife. *Go aside* - From the way of religion and justice, and that either in truth, or in her husband's opinion.

15. *The man shall bring her to the priest* - Who first strove to persuade her to own the truth. If she did, she was not put to death, (which must have been, if it had been proved against her) but only was divorced and lost her dowry. *Her offering* - By way of solemn appeal to God, whom hereby she desired to judge between her and her husband, and by way of atonement to appease God, who had for her sins stirred up her husband against her. *He shall pour no oil* - Both because it was a kind of sin-offering, from which these were excluded, and because she came thither as a delinquent, or suspected of delinquency, unpleasing both to God and men; as one that wanted that grace and amiableness and joy which oil signified, and that acceptance with God which frankincense denoted, Psalm lxli, 2. Bringing

iniquity to remembrance - Both to God before whom she appeared as a sinner, and to her own conscience, if she was guilty; and, if she were not guilty of this, yet it reminded her of her other sins, for which this might be a punishment.

16. Before the Lord - That is, before the sanctuary where the ark was.

17. Holy water - Water of purification appointed for such uses. This water was used, that if she were guilty, she might be afraid to add profaneness to her other crime. An earthen vessel - Because, after this use, it was to be broken in pieces, that the remembrance of it might be blotted out as far as was possible. Dust - An emblem of vileness and misery. From the floor of the tabernacle - Which made it holy dust, and struck the greater terror into the woman, if she were guilty.

18. Before the Lord - Before the tabernacle with her face towards the ark. Uncover her head - Partly that she might be made sensible how manifest she and all her ways were to God; partly in token of her sorrow for her sin, or at least for any cause of suspicion which she had given. In her hands - That she herself might offer it, and thereby call God to be witness of her innocency. Bitter - So called either from the bitter taste which the dust gave it, or from the bitter effects of it upon her, if she were guilty. That causeth the curse - Not by any natural power, but by a supernatural efficacy.

19. By an oath - To answer truly to his question, or to declare whether she be guilty or no, and after such oath shall say as follows.

21. An oath - That is, a form of cursing, that when they would curse a person, they may wish that they may be as miserable as thou wast. Thy thigh - A modest expression, used both in scripture, as Gen. xlvi, 26, Exod. i, 5, and other authors. To rot - Hebrew. to fall, that is, to die or waste away. To swell - Suddenly and violently till it burst, which the Jews note was frequent in this case. And it was a clear evidence of the truth of their religion.

22. Amen, amen - That is, so let it be if I be guilty. The word is doubled by her as an evidence of her innocency, and ardent desire that God would deal with her according to her desert.

23. In a book - That is, in a scroll of parchment, which the Hebrews commonly call a book. Blot them out - Or scrape them out and cast them into the bitter water. Whereby it was signified, that if she was innocent, the curses should be blotted out and come to nothing; and, if she were guilty, she should find in her the effects of this water which she drank, after the words of this curse had been scraped and put in.

24. To drink - That is, after the jealousy-offering was offered.

28. Conceive seed - That is, shall bring forth children, as the Jews say, in case of her innocency, she infallibly did, yea though she was barren before.

31. Guiltless - Which he should not have been, if he had either indulged her in so great a wickedness, and not endeavoured to bring her to repentance or punishment, or cherished suspicions in his breast, and thereupon proceeded to hate her or cast her off. Whereas now, whatsoever the consequence is, the husband shall not be censured for bringing such curses upon her, or for defaming her, if she appear to be innocent. Her iniquity - That is, the punishment of her iniquity, whether she was false to her husband, or by any light carriage gave him occasion to suspect her.

VI

The law of the Nazarites. What they were to abstain from, ver. 1-8. How to be cleansed from casual uncleanness, ver. 9-12. How to be discharged from their vow, ver. 13-21. The form of blessing the people, ver. 22-27.

2. Man or woman - For both sexes might make this vow, if they were free and at their own disposal: otherwise their parents or husbands could disannul the vow. A vow of a Nazarite - Whereby they sequestered themselves from worldly employments and enjoyments, that they might entirely consecrate themselves to God's service, and this either for their whole lifetime, or for a less and limited space of time.

3. Nor eat grapes - Which was forbidden him for greater caution to keep him at the farther distance from wine.

4. All the days of his separation - Which were sometimes more, sometimes fewer, as he thought fit to appoint.

5. No razor - Nor scissors, or other instrument to cut off any part of his hair. This was appointed, partly as a sign of his mortification to worldly delights and outward beauty; partly as a testimony of that purity which hereby he professed, because the cutting off the hair was a sign of uncleanness, as appears from ver. 9, partly that by the length of his hair he might be constantly minded of his vow; and partly that he might reserve his hair entirely for God, to whom it was to be offered. Holy - That is, wholly consecrated to God and his service, whereby he shews that inward holiness was the great thing which God required and valued in these, and consequently in other rites and ceremonies.

7. His father - Wherein he was equal to the high-priest, being, in some sort, as eminent a type of

Christ, and therefore justly required to prefer the service of God, to which he had so fully given himself, before the expressions of his affections to his dearest and nearest relations. The consecration - That is, the token of his consecration, namely, his long hair.

9. He shall shave his head - Because his whole body, and especially his hair was defiled by such an accident, which he ought to impute either to his own heedlessness, or to God's providence so ordering the matter, possibly for the punishment of his other sins, or for the quickening him to more purity and detestation of all dead works, whereby he would be defiled.

11. A sin-offering - Because such a pollution was, though not his sin, yet the chastisement of his sin. He sinned - That is, contracted a ceremonial uncleanness, which is called sinning, because it was a type of sin, and a violation of a law, tho' through ignorance and inadvertency. Hallow - Begin again to hallow or consecrate it.

12. The days of his separation - As many days as he had before vowed to God. Lost - Hebrew. fall, to the ground, that is, be void or of none effect.

14. A sin-offering - Whereby he confessed his miscarriages, notwithstanding the strictness of his vow and all the diligence which he could use, and consequently acknowledged his need of the grace of God in Christ Jesus the true Nazarite. For peace- offerings - For thankfulness to God, who had given him grace to make and in some measure to keep such a vow. So he offered all the three sorts of offerings, that he might so far fulfil all righteousness and profess his obligation to observe the will of God in all things.

15. Their meal-offering - Such as generally accompanied the sacrifices.

18. At the door - Publickly, that it might be known that his vow was ended, and therefore he was at liberty as to those things from which he had restrained himself for a season, otherwise some might have been scandalized at his use of his liberty. The fire - Upon which the flesh of the peace-offerings was boiled.

19. The shoulder - The left-shoulder, as it appears from ver. 20, where this is joined with the heave-shoulder, which was the right- shoulder, and which was the priests due in all sacrifices, Lev. vii, 32, and in this also. But here the other shoulder was added to it, as a special token of thankfulness from the Nazarites for God's singular favours vouchsafed unto them. The hands - That he may give them to the priest, as his peculiar gift.

20. May drink wine - And return to his former manner of living.

21. That his hand shall get - Besides what he shall voluntarily give according to his ability.

23. On this wise - Hebrew. Thus, or in these words: yet they were not tied to these very words; because after this we have examples of Moses and David and Solomon, blessing the people in other words.

24. Bless thee - Bestow upon you all manner of blessings, temporal and spiritual. Keep thee - That is, continue his blessings to thee, and preserve thee in and to the use of them; keep thee from sin and its bitter effects.

25. Shine upon thee - Alluding to the shining of the sun upon the earth, to enlighten, and warm, and renew the face of it. The Lord love thee, and make thee know that he loves thee. We cannot but be happy, if we have God's love; and we cannot but be easy, if we know that we have it.

26. Lift up his countenance - That is, look upon thee with a chearful and pleasant countenance, as one that is well pleased with thee and thy services. Peace - Peace with God, with thy own conscience, and with all men; all prosperity is comprehended under this word.

27. Put my name - Shall call them by my name, shall recommend them to me as my own people, and bless them and pray unto me for them as such; which is a powerful argument to prevail with God for them.

VII

The offerings of the princes upon the dedication of the tabernacle, ver. 1-9. Upon the dedication of the altar, ver. 10-88, Which God graciously accepts, ver. 89.

1. On the day - It seems day is for time, and on the day, for about the time. For all the princes did not offer these things upon one and the same day, but on several days, as here it follows. And so this chapter comes in its proper place, and those things were done in the second month of the second year after the tabernacle and altar, and all other instruments thereof were anointed, as is here expressed; and after the Levites were separated to the service of the tabernacle, and appointed to their several works, which was done about a month after the tabernacle was erected, and after the numbering of the people, chap. i, 2-49, when the princes here employed in the offerings were first constituted; and after the disposal of the tribes about the tabernacle, the order of which is here observed in the time of their offerings.

2. Offered - In the manner and days hereafter mentioned.

3. Waggons - For the more convenient and safe carriage of such things as were most cumbersome.

5. According to his service - More or fewer, as the nature of their service and of the things to be carried required.

9. Upon their shoulders - Because of the greater worth and holiness of the things which they carried.

10. The altar - Of burnt-offerings, and incense too, as appears from the matter of their offerings. Not for the first dedication of them, for it is apparent they were dedicated or consecrated before this time by Moses and Aaron: but for a farther dedication of them, these being the first offerings that were made for any particular persons or tribes. In the day - That is, about the time, as soon as it was anointed.

11. On his day - And in this offering they followed the order of their camp, and not of their birth.

13. Charger - A large dish or platter; to be employed about the altar of burnt-offering, or in the court; not in the sanctuary, for all its vessels were of gold.

17. Peace-offerings - Which are more numerous because the princes and priests, and some of the people made a feast before the Lord out of them.

87. Their meal-offering - Which was not mentioned before, because it was sufficiently understood from the law which required it.

88. After it was anointed - Which words are very conveniently added to explain in what sense he had so oft said, that this was done in the day when it was anointed, namely, not exactly, but in a latitude, a little after that it was anointed.

89. To speak with him - To consult God upon occasion. The mercy-seat - Which Moses standing without the veil could easily hear. And this seems to be added in this place, to shew that when men had done their part, God was not wanting in the performance of his part, and promise. God's speaking thus to Moses by an audible voice, as if he had been cloathed with a body, was an earnest of the incarnation of the Son of God, when in the fulness of time the Word should be made flesh, and speak in the language of the sons of men. That he who spake to Moses was the Eternal Word, was the belief of many of the ancients. For all God's communion with man is by his Son, who is the same yesterday, today and forever.

VIII

Directions concerning the lamps, ver. 1-4. Concerning cleansing the Levites, ver. 5-8. Concerning the presenting them to God, ver. 9-22. Concerning their age and service, ver. 23-26.

2. When thou lightest the lamps - The priests lighted the middle lamp from the fire of the altar; and the rest one from another; signifying that all light and knowledge comes from Christ, who has the seven spirits of God, figured by the seven lamps of fire. Over against the candlestick - On that part which is before the candlestick, Hebrew. over against the face of the candlestick - That is, in that place towards which the candlestick looked, or where the candlestick stood in full view, that is, upon the north- side, where the table of shew-bread stood, as appears from hence, because the candlestick stood close to the boards of the sanctuary on the south-side, Exod. xxvi, 35. And thus the lights were on both sides of the sanctuary, which was necessary, because it was dark in itself, and had no window.

4. Of beaten gold - Not hollow, but solid gold, beaten out of one piece, not of several pieces joined or soldered together.

7. Of purifying - Hebrew. of sin, that is, for the expiation of sin. This water was mixed with the ashes of a red heifer, chap. xix, 9, which therefore may seem to have been prescribed before, though it be mentioned after; such kind of transplacings of passages being frequent in scripture. Shave all their flesh - This external rite signified the cutting off their inordinate desire of earthly things and that singular purity of heart and life which is required in the ministers of God.

8. A young bullock - The same sacrifice which was offered for a sin-offering for the whole congregation, because the Levites came in the stead of all the first-born, who did in a manner represent the whole congregation.

10. The children of Israel - Not all of them, which was impossible, but some in the name of all the princes or chiefs of each tribe, who used to transact things in the name of their tribes. Put their hands - Whereby they signified their transferring that right of ministering to God from the first-born in whose hands it formerly was, to the Levites, and their entire resignation and dedication of them to God's service.

11. For an offering - Hebrew. for a wave-offering. Not that Aaron did so wave them, which he could not do, but that he caused them to imitate that motion, and to wave themselves toward the several parts of the world: whereby they might signify their readiness to serve God, according to their capacity wheresoever they should be.

12. Lay their hands - To signify that they were offered by them and for them.

13. Set the Levites before Aaron - Give the Levites to them, or to their service. Unto the Lord -

For to him they were first properly offered, and by him given to the priests in order to his service.

15. Go in - Into the court, where they were to wait upon the priests at the altar of burnt-offering; and, at present, into the tabernacle, to take it down and set it up.

19. To do the service of Israel - To serve God in their stead, to do what otherwise they had been obliged to do in their own persons. To make an atonement - Not by offering sacrifices, which the priests alone might do, but by assisting the priests in that expiatory work, and by a diligent performance of all the parts of their office, whereby God was pleased both with them and with the people. That there be no plague - This is added as a reason why God appointed them to serve in the tabernacle, that they might guard it, and not suffer any of the people to come near it, or meddle with holy things, which if they did, it would certainly bring a plague upon them.

26. In the tabernacle - By way of advice, and assistance in lesser and easier works.

IX

Orders concerning eating the passover on the 14th day of the first month, ver. 1-5. On the 14th day of the second month, by those who had been hindered, ver. 8-12. Concerning the negligent and the stranger, ver. 13, 14. Concerning the pillar of cloud and fire, ver. 15-23

1. In the first month - And therefore before the numbering of the people, which was not till the second month, chap. i, 1, 2. But it is placed after it, because of a special case relating to the passover, which happened after it, upon occasion whereof he mentions the command of God for keeping the passover in the wilderness, which was done but once, and without this command they had not been obliged to keep it at all, till they came to the land of Canaan.

6. They came - For resolution of their difficulty.

7. An offering - Which if we neglect, we must be cut off, and if we keep it in these circumstances, we must also be cut off. What shall we do?

10. Unclean or in a journey - Under these two instances the Hebrews think that other hindrances of like nature are comprehended; as if one be hindered by a disease, or by any other such kind of uncleanness; which may seem probable both from the nature of the thing, and the reason of the law which is the same in other cases.

14. A stranger - Who is a proselyte.

15. Namely, the tent of the testimony - Or, the tabernacle above the tent of the testimony, that is, that part of the tabernacle in which was the testimony, or the ark of the testimony; for there the cloudy pillar stood. This was an evident token of God's special presence with, and providence over them. And this cloud was easily distinguished from other clouds, both by its peculiar figure and by its constant residence in that place. Fire - That they might better discern it and direct themselves and their journeys or stations by it. Had it been a cloud only, it had scarce been visible by night: And had it been a fire only, it would have been scarce discernable by day. But God was pleased to give them sensible demonstrations, that he kept them night and day.

17. Was taken up - Or, ascended on high, above its ordinary place, by which it became more visible to all the camp.

18. The motion or stay of the cloud is fitly called the command of God, because it was a signification of God's will and their duty.

19. The charge - That is, the command of God, that they should stay as long as the cloud stayed.

21. When the cloud abode - This is repeated again and again, because it was a constant miracle, and because it is a matter we should take particular notice of, as highly significant and instructive. It is mentioned long after by David, Psalm cv, 39, and by the people of God after their captivity, Neh. ix, 19. And the guidance of this cloud is spoken of, as signifying the guidance of the Blessed Spirit, Isaiah lxiii, 14. The Spirit of the Lord caused him to rest, and so didst thou lead the people. And thus, in effect, does he guide, all those, who commit their ways unto the Lord. So that they may well say, Father, thy will be done! Dispose of me and mine as thou pleasest. Here I am, waiting on my God, to journey and rest at the commandment of the Lord. What thou wilt, and where thou wilt: only let me be thine, and always in the way of my duty.

X

Orders concerning the silver trumpets, ver. 1-10. The removal of the Israelites to Paran, ver. 11-28. The treaty of Moses with Hobab, ver. 29-32. His prayer at the removal and resting of the ark, ver. 33-36.

2. Two trumpets - For Aaron's two sons: though afterwards the number of the trumpets was much increased, as the number of the priests also was. These trumpets were ordained, both for signification of

the great duty of ministers, to preach the word; and for use, as here follows.

6. For their journeys - As a sign for them to march forward, and consequently for the rest to follow them.

9. Ye shall be saved - If you use this ordinance of God with trust and dependance upon God for help.

10. In the days of your gladness - Days appointed for rejoicing and thanksgiving to God for former mercies, or deliverances. Your solemn days - Your stated festivals. For a memorial - That God may remember you for good to accept and bless you. God then takes pleasure in our religious exercises, when we take pleasure in them. Holy work should be done with holy joy.

12. Paran - From which they travelled to other places, and then returned into it again, chap. xii, 16.

21. The others - The Gershonites, and Merarites, who therefore marched after the first camp, a good distance from, and before the Kohathites, that they might prepare the tabernacle for the reception of its utensils, which the Kohathites brought some time after them.

29. Raguel - Called also Reuel, Exod. ii, 18, who seems to be the same with Jethro; it being usual in scripture for one person to have two or three names. And therefore this Hobab is not Jethro, but his son, which may seem more probable, because Jethro was old and unfit to travel, and desirous, as may well be thought, to die in his own country, whither he returned, Exod. xviii, 27, but Hobab was young and fitter for these journeys, and therefore entreated by Moses to stay and bear them company.

30. I will not go - So he might sincerely say, though afterward he was overcome by the persuasions of Moses.

31. Thou mayest be to us instead of eyes - To direct and guide us: for though the cloud determined them to a general place, yet many particulars might be unknown to Moses, wherein Hobab, having long lived in those parts, might be able to advise him, as concerning the conveniences of water for their cattle, concerning the safety or danger of the several parts, by reason of serpents or wild-beasts, or enemies, in the parts adjoining to them, that so they might guard themselves better against them. Or, this is to be understood of his directing them not so much in their way. as about great and difficult matters, wherein the counsel he had from God did not exclude the advice of men, as we see in Hobab's father Jethro, Exod. xviii, 19-27. And it is probable, this was the wise son of a wise father.

33. Three days - With continued journeys; only it seems probable, that the cloud made little pauses that they might have time for sleep and necessary refreshments. The ark went before them - Altho' in their stations it was in the middle, yet in their marches it went before them; and the cloud was constantly over the ark whether it stood or went; therefore the ark is said to go before and direct them, not as if the ark could be seen of all the camps, which being carried only upon mens shoulders was impossible; but because the cloud, which always attended upon the ark, and did, together with the ark, constitute, in a manner, one sign of God's presence, did lead and direct them. To search out - A metaphorical expression, for discovering to them; for the ark could not search, and God, who knew all places and things, needed not to search.

34. By day - And by night too, as was expressed before. So we must learn to compare places of scripture, and to supply the defects of one out of another, as we do in all authors.

36. Return - Or, give rest, that is, a safe and quiet place, free from enemies and dangers.

XI

The punishment of the murmurers stopt by the prayer of Moses, ver. 1-3. The fresh murmuring of the people, ver. 4-6. The description of manna, ver. 7-9. The murmuring of Moses, ver. 10- 16. God's answer, ver. 16-23. The appointment of the seventy elders, ver. 24-30. Quails sent with a plague, ver. 31-35.

1. Complained - Or, murmured, the occasion whereof seems to be their last three days journey in a vast howling wilderness, and thereupon the remembrance of their long abode in the wilderness, and the fear of many other tedious journeys, whereby they were like to be long delayed from coming to the land of milk and honey, which they thirsted after. The fire of the Lord - A fire sent from God in an extraordinary manner, possibly from the pillar of cloud and fire, or from heaven. The uttermost parts - Either because the sin began there among the mixed multitude, or in mercy to the people, whom he would rather awaken to repentance than destroy; and therefore he sent it into the skirts and not the midst of the camp.

2. The people - The murmurers, being penitent; or others for fear.

3. Taberah - This fire; as it was called Kibroth-hattaavah from another occasion, ver. 34, 35, and chap. xxxiii, 16. It is no new thing in scripture for persons and places to have two names. Both these names were imposed as monuments of the peoples sin and of God's just judgment.

4. Israel also - Whose special relation and obligation to God should have restrained them from such carriage. Flesh - This word is here taken generally so as to include fish, as the next words shew.

They had indeed cattle which they brought out of Egypt, but these were reserved for breed to be carried into Canaan, and were so few that they would scarce have served them for a month.

5. Freely - Either without price, for fish was very plentiful, and fishing was there free, or with a very small price. And this is the more probable because the Egyptians might not taste of fish, nor of the leeks and onions, which they worshipped for Gods, and therefore the Israelites, might have them upon cheap terms.

6. Our soul - Either our life, as the soul signifies, Gen. ix, 5, or our body, which is often signified by the soul. Dried away - Is withered and pines away; which possibly might be true, through envy and discontent, and inordinate appetite.

7. As coriander-seed - Not for colour, for that is black, but for shape and figure. Bdellium - Is either the gum of a tree, of a white and bright colour, or rather a gem or precious stone, as the Hebrew doctors take it; and particularly a pearl wherewith the Manna manifestly agrees both in its colour, which is white, Exod. xvi, 14, and in its figure which is round.

8. Fresh oil - Or, of the most excellent oil; or of cakes made with the best oil, the word cakes being easily supplied out of the foregoing member of the verse; or, which is not much differing, like wafers made with honey, as it is said Exod. xvi, 31. The nature and use of Manna is here thus particularly described, to shew the greatness of their sin in despising such excellent food.

10. In the door of his tent - To note they were not ashamed of their sin.

11. Not found favour - Why didst thou not hear my prayer, when I desired thou wouldest excuse me, and commit the care of this unruly people to some other person.

12. Have I begotten them? - Are they my children, that I should be obliged to provide food and all things for their necessity and desire?

14. To bear - The burden of providing for and satisfying them. Alone - Others were only assistant to him in smaller matters; but the harder and greater affairs, such as this unquestionably was, were brought to Moses and determined by him alone.

15. My wretchedness - Hebrew. my evil, my torment, arising from the insuperable difficulty of my office and work of ruling this people, and from the dread of their utter extirpation, and the dishonour which thence will accrue to God and to religion, as if, not I only, but God also were an impostor.

16. To be elders - Whom thou by experience discernest to be elders not only in years, and name, but also in wisdom and authority with the people. And according to this constitution, the Sanhedrim, or great council of the Jews, which in after-ages sat at Jerusalem, and was the highest court of the judgment among them, consisted of seventy men.

17. I will come down - By my powerful presence and operation. I will put it on them - That is, I will give the same spirit to them which I have given to thee. But as the spirit was not conveyed to them from or through Moses, but immediately from God, so the spirit or its gifts were not by this means impaired in Moses. The spirit is here put for the gifts of the spirit, and particularly for the spirit of prophecy, whereby they were enabled, as Moses had been and still was, to discern hidden and future things, and resolve doubtful and difficult cases, which made them fit for government. It is observable, that God would not, and therefore men should not, call any persons to any office for which they were not sufficiently qualified.

18. Sanctify themselves - Prepare to meet thy God, O Israel, in the way of his judgments. Prepare yourselves by true repentance, that you may either obtain some mitigation of the plague, or, whilst your bodies are destroyed by the flesh you desire and eat, your souls may be saved from the wrath of God. Sanctifying is often used for preparing, as Jer. vi, 4; xii, 3. In the ears of the Lord - Not secretly in your closets, but openly and impudently in the doors of your tents, calling heaven and earth to witness.

20. At your nostrils - Which meat violently vomited up frequently doth. Thus God destroys them by granting their desires, and turns even their blessings into curses. Ye have despised the Lord - You have lightly esteemed his bounty and manifold blessings, you have slighted and distrusted his promises and providence after so long and large experience of it. Who is among you - Who is present and resident with you to observe all your carriage, and to punish your offenses. This is added as a great aggravation of the crime, to sin in the presence of the judge. Why came we forth out of Egypt? - Why did God do us such an injury? Why did we so foolishly obey him in coming forth?

21. Six hundred thousand footmen - Fit for war, besides women and children. That Moses speaks this as distrusting God's word is evident; and that Moses was not remarkably punished for this as he was afterward for the same sin, chap. xx, 12, may be imputed to the different circumstances of this and that sin: this was the first offense of the kind, and therefore more easily passed by; that was after warning and against more light and experience. This seems to have been spoken secretly: that openly before the people; and therefore it was fit to be openly and severely punished to prevent the contagion of that example.

24. Moses went out - Out of the tabernacle, into which he entered to receive God's answers from the mercy-seat. The seventy men - They are called seventy from the stated number, though two of them were lacking, as the Apostles are called the twelve, Matt. xxvi, 20, when one of that number was absent.

Round the tabernacle - Partly that the awe of God might be imprinted upon their hearts, that they might more seriously undertake and more faithfully manage their high employment, but principally, because that was the place where God manifested himself, and therefore there he would bestow his spirit upon them.

25. Rested on them - Not only moved them for a time, but took up his settled abode with them, because the use and end of this gift was perpetual. They prophesied - Discoursed of the word and works of God in a marvelous manner, as the prophets did. So this word is used, 1 Sam. x, 5, 6 Joel ii, 28; 1 Cor. xiv, 3. Yet were they not hereby constituted teachers, but civil magistrates, who together with the spirit of government, received also the spirit of prophesy, as a sign and seal both to themselves and to the people, that God had called them to that employment. They did not cease - Either for that day, they continued in that exercise all that day, and, it may be, all the night too, as it is said of Saul, 1 Sam. xix, 24, or, afterwards also, to note that this was a continued gift conferred upon them to enable them the better to discharge their magistracy; which was more expedient for them than for the rulers of other people, because the Jews were under a theocracy or the government of God, and even their civil controversies were decided out of that word of God which the prophets expounded.

26. In the camp - Not going to the tabernacle, as the rest did, either not having seasonable notice to repair thither: or, being detained in the camp by sickness, or some urgent occasion, not without God's special providence, that so the miracle might be more evident. Were written - In a book or paper by Moses, who by God's direction nominated the fittest persons.

27. Told Moses - Fearing lest his authority should be diminished by their prophesying; and thereby taking authority to themselves without his consent.

28. One of his young men - Or, one of his choice ministers, which may be emphatically added, to note that even great and good men may mistake about the works of God. Forbid them - He feared either schism, or sedition, or that by their usurpation of authority, independently upon Moses, his power and esteem might be lessened.

29. Enviest thou for my sake - Art thou grieved because the gifts and graces of God are imparted to others besides me? Prophets - He saith prophets, not rulers, for that he knew was absurd and impossible. So we ought to be pleased, that God is glorified and good done, tho' to the lessening of our own honour.

30. Into the camp - Among the people, to exercise the gifts and authority now received.

31. A wind from the Lord - An extraordinary and miraculous wind both for its vehemency and for its effects. Quails - God gave them quails once before, Exod. xvi, 13, but neither in the same quantity, nor with the same design and effect as now. From the sea - Principally from the Red-sea, and both sides of it where, by the reports of ancient Heathen writers, they were then in great numbers, and, no doubt, were wonderfully increased by God's special providence for this very occasion. Two cubits high - Not as if the quails did cover all the ground two cubits high for a day's journey on each side of the camp, for then there had been no place left where they could spread them all abroad round about the camp; but the meaning is, that the quails came and fell down round about the camp for a whole day's journey on each side of it, and that in all that space they lay here and there in great heaps, which were often two cubits high.

32. Stood up - Or rather rose up, which word is often used for beginning to do any business. All that night - Some at one time, and some at the other, and some, through greediness or diffidence, at both times. Ten homers - That is, ten ass loads: which if it seem incredible, you must consider,

1. That the gatherers here were not all the people, which could not be without great inconveniences, but some on the behalf of all, while the rest were exercised about other necessary things. So the meaning is not, that every Israelite had so much for his share, but that every collector gathered so much for the family, or others by whom he was intrusted.

2. That the people did not gather for their present use only, but for a good while to come, and being greedy and distrustful of God's goodness, it is not strange if they gathered much more than they needed.

3. That the word, rendered homers, may signify heaps, as it doth, Exod. viii, 14 Judg. xv, 16 Hab. iii, 15, and ten, is often put for many, and so the sense is, that every one gathered several heaps. If yet the number seems incredible, it must be farther known,

4. That Heathen and other authors affirm, in those eastern and southern countries quails are innumerable, so that in one part of Italy, within the compass of five miles, there were taken about an hundred thousand of them every day for a month together. And Atheneus relates, that in Egypt, a country prodigiously populous, they were in such plenty, that all those vast numbers of people could not consume them, but were forced to salt and keep them for future use. They spread them - That so they might dry, salt and preserve them for future use, according to what they had seen in Egypt.

33. Chewed - Hebrew. cut off, namely from their mouths. A very great plague - Probably the pestilence. But the sense is, before they had done eating their quails, which lasted for a month. Why did God so sorely punish the peoples murmuring for flesh here, when he spared them after the same sin,

Exod. xvi, 12. Because this was a far greater sin, and aggravated with worse circumstances; proceeding not from necessity, as that did, when as yet they had no food, but from mere wantonness, when they had Manna constantly given them; committed after large experience of God's care and kindness, after God had pardoned their former sins, and after God had in a solemn and terrible manner made known his laws to them.

34. Kibroth-hattaavah - Hebrew. the graves of lust, that is, of the men that lusted, as it here follows. And it notes that the plague did not seize upon all that eat of the quails, for then all had been destroyed, but only upon those who were inordinate both in the desire and use of them.

XII

Miriam and Aaron murmur against Moses, ver. 1-3. God calls them to an account for it, ver. 4-9. Miriam becoming leprous, Aaron humbles himself, and Moses prays for her, ver. 10-13. She is healed, but shut out of the camp for seven days, ver. 14-16.

1. Miriam - Miriam seems to be first named, because she was the first mover of the sedition; wherefore she is more eminently punished. The Ethiopian - Either,

1. Zipporah, who is here called an Ethiopian, in the Hebrew a Cushite, because she was a Midianite: the word Cush being generally used in scripture, not for Ethiopia properly so called below Egypt, but for Arabia. If she be meant, probably they did not quarrel with him for marrying her, because that was done long since, but for being swayed by her and her relations, by whom they might think he was persuaded to chose seventy rulers, by which co-partnership in government they thought their authority and reputation diminished. And because they durst not accuse God, they charge Moses, his instrument, as the manner of men is. Or,

2. some other woman, whom he married either whilst Zipporah lived, or rather because she was now dead, though that, as many other things, be not recorded. For, as the quarrel seems to be about his marrying a stranger, it is probable it was a fresh occasion about which they contended. And it was lawful for him as well as any other to marry an Ethiopian or Arabian woman, provided she were, a sincere proselyte.

2. By us - Are not we prophets as well as he? so Aaron was made, Exod. iv, 15, 16, and so Miriam is called, Exod. xv, 20. And Moses hath debased and mixed the holy seed, which we have not done. Why then should he take all power to himself, and make rulers as he pleaseth, without consulting us. The Lord heard - Observed their words and carriage to Moses.

3. Meek - This is added as the reason why Moses took no notice of their reproach, and why God did so severely plead his cause. Thus was he fitted for the work he was called to, which required all the meekness he had. And this is often more tried by the unkindness of our friends, than by the malice of our enemies. Probably this commendation was added, as some other clauses were, by some succeeding prophet. How was Moses so meek, when we often read of his anger? But this only proves, that the law made nothing perfect.

4. Suddenly - To stifle the beginnings of the sedition, that this example might not spread amongst the people. Come out - Out of your private dwellings, that you may know my pleasure and your own doom.

5. In the door - While they stood without, not being admitted into the tabernacle, as Aaron used to be; a sign of God's displeasure.

6. Among you - if you be prophets, yet know there is a difference among prophets, nor do I put equal honour upon all of them.

7. In all my house - That is, whom I have set over all my house, my church and people, and therefore over you; and who hath discharged his office faithfully, and not partially as you falsely accuse him.

8. Mouth to mouth - That is, distinctly, by an articulate voice; immediately, not by an interpreter, nor by shadows and representations in his fancy, as it is in visions and dreams; and familiarly. Apparently - Plainly and certainly. Dark speeches - Not in parables, similitudes, dark resemblances; as by shewing a boiling pot, an almond tree, &c. to Jeremiah, a chariot with wheels, &c. to Ezekiel. The similitude - Not the face or essence of God, which no man can see and live, Exod. xxxiii, 20, but some singular manifestation of his glorious presence, as Exod. xxxiii, 11, 20. Yea the Son of God appeared to him in an human shape, which he took up for a time, that he might give him a foretaste of his future incarnation. My servant - Who is so in such an eminent and extraordinary manner.

9. He departed - From the door of the tabernacle, in token of his great displeasure, not waiting for their answer. The removal of God~s presence from us, is the saddest token of his displeasure. And he never departs, till we by our sin and folly drive him from us.

10. From the tabernacle - Not from the whole tabernacle, but from that part, whither it was come, to that part which was directly over the mercy-seat, where it constantly abode. Leprous - She, and not

Aaron, either because she was chief in the transgression or because God would not have his worship interrupted or dishonoured, which it must have been if Aaron had been leprous. White - This kind of leprosy was the most virulent and incurable of all. It is true, when the leprosy began in a particular part, and thence spread itself over all the flesh by degrees, and at last made it all white, that was an evidence of the cure of the leprosy, Lev. xiii, 12, 13. But it was otherwise when one was suddenly smitten with this universal whiteness.

11. Lay not the sin - Let not the guilt and punishment of this sin rest upon us, upon her in this kind, upon me in any other kind, but pray to God for the pardon and removal of it.

12. As one dead - Because part of her flesh was putrefied and dead, and not to be restored but by the mighty power of God. Like a still-born child, that hath been for some time dead in the womb, which when it comes forth, is putrefied, and part of it consumed.

14. Spit in her face - That is, expressed some eminent token of indignation and contempt, which was this, Job xxx, 10 Isaiah l, 6. Ashamed - And withdraw herself, from her father's presence, as Jonathan did upon a like occasion, 1 Sam. xx, 34. So though God healed her according to Moses's request, yet he would have her publickly bear the shame of her sin, and be a warning to others to keep them from the same transgression.

15. Journeyed not - Which was a testimony of respect to her both from God and from the people, God so ordering it, partly lest she should be overwhelmed by such a publick rebuke from God, and partly lest, she being a prophetess, the gift of prophesy should come into contempt.

16. Paran - That is, in another part of the same wilderness.

XIII

The sending of the spies into Canaan, ver. 1-17. The instructions given them, ver. 18-20. Their journey and return, ver. 21-25. Their report, ver. 26-33.

1. Speak unto Moses - In answer to the peoples petition about it, as is evident from Deut. i, 22. And it is probable, the people desired it out of diffidence of God's promise.

2. A ruler - A person of wisdom and authority.

8. Oshea - Called also Joshua, ver. 16.

11. Of Joseph - The name of Joseph is elsewhere appropriated to Ephraim, here to Manasseh; possibly to aggravate the sin of the ruler of this tribe, who did so basely degenerate from his noble ancestor.

16. Jehoshua - Oshea notes a desire of salvation, signifying, Save we pray thee; but Jehoshua, or Joshua, includes a promise of salvation, He will save. So this was a prophecy of his succession to Moses in the government, and of the success of his arms. Josh. is the same name with Jesus, of whom Joshua was a type. He was the saviour of God's people from the powers of Canaan, Christ from the powers of hell.

17. Southward - Into the southern part of Canaan, which was the nearest part, and the worst too, being dry and desert, and therefore fit for them to enter and pass through with less observation. Into the mountain - Into the mountainous country, and thence into the valleys, and so take a survey of the whole land.

18. What it is - Both for largeness, and for nature and quality.

19. In tents - As the Arabians did; or in unwalled villages, which, like tents, are exposed to an enemy.

20. Fat - Rich and fertile.

21. Zin - In the south of Canaan, differing from the wilderness of Sin, which was nigh unto Egypt. To Hamath - From the south they passed through the whole land to the northern parts of it; Rehob was a city in the northwest part, Hamath, a city in the northeast.

22. By the south - Moses having described their progress from south to north, more particularly relates some memorable places and passages. They came - Hebrew. He came, namely, Caleb, as appears from Josh. xiv, 9, 12, 14. For the spies distributed their work among them, and went either severally, or by pairs; and it seems the survey of this part was left to Caleb. Anak - A famous giant, whole children these are called, either more generally, as all giants sometimes were, or rather more specially because Arbah, from whom Hebron was called Kiriath-arbah, was the father of Anak, Josh. xv, 13. And this circumstance is mentioned as an evidence of the goodness of that land, because the giants chose it for their habitation. Before Zoan - This seems to be noted to confront the Egyptians, who vainly boasted of the antiquity of their city Zoan above all places.

23. Upon a staff - Either for the weight of it, considering the, length of the way they were to carry it, or for the preservation of it whole and entire. In those eastern and southern countries there are vines and grapes of an extraordinary bigness as Strabo and Pliny affirm.

24. Eschol - That is, a cluster of grapes.

25. *They returned after forty days* - 'Tis a wonder the people had patience to stay forty days, when they were just ready to enter Canaan, under all the assurances of success they could have from the Divine power, proved by a constant series of miracles, that had hitherto attended them. But they distrusted God, and chose to be held in suspence by their own counsels, rather than to rest upon God's promise! How much do we stand in our own light by unbelief?

26. *Kadesh* - Kadesh-barnea, which some confound with Kadesh in the wilderness of Sin, into which they came not 'till the fortieth year after their coming out of Egypt, as appears from chap. xxxiii, 37, 38, whereas they were in this Kadesh in the second year, and before they received the sentence of their forty years abode in the wilderness.

27. *They told him* - In the audience of the people.

29. *The Amalekites in the south* - Where we are to enter the land, and they who were so fierce against us that they came into the wilderness to fight with us, will, without doubt, oppose us when we come close by their land, the rather, to revenge themselves for their former loss. Therefore they mention them, though they were not Canaanites. *In the mountains* -In the mountainous country, in the southeast part of the land, so that you cannot enter there without great difficulty, both because of the noted strength and valour of those people, and because of the advantage they have from the mountains. *By the sea* - Not the mid-land sea, which is commonly understood by that expression, but the salt or dead sea, as appears,

1. Because it is that sea which is next to Jordan,

2. Because the Canaanites dwelt principally in those parts, and not near the mid-land sea. So these guard the entrance on the east- side, as the others do on the south.

30. *Caleb* - Together with Joshua, as is manifest from chap. xiv, 6, 7, 30, but Caleb alone is here mentioned, possibly because he spake first and most, which he might better do, because he might be presumed to be more impartial than Joshua, who being Moses's minister might be thought to speak only what he knew his master would like. *Stilled the people* -Which implies either that they had began to murmur, or that by their looks and carriage, they discovered the anger which boiled in their breasts. *Before Moses* - Or, towards Moses, against whom they were incensed, as the man who had brought them into such sad circumstances. *Let us go up and possess it* - He does not say, Let us go up and conquer it. He looks on that to be as good as done already: but, Let us go up and possess it! There is nothing to be done, but to enter without delay, and take the possession which our great Lord is now ready to give us! Thus difficulties that lie in the way of salvation, vanish away before a lively faith.

31. *The men* - All of them, Joshua excepted. *Stronger* - Both in stature of body and numbers of people. Thus they question the power, and truth, and goodness of God, of all which they had such ample testimonies.

32. *Eateth up its inhabitants* - Not so much by civil wars, for that was likely to make their conquest more easy; but rather by the unwholesomeness of the air and place, which they guessed from the many funerals, which, as some Hebrew writers, not without probability affirm, they observed in their travels through it: though that came to pass from another cause, even from the singular providence of God, which, to facilitate the Israelites conquest, cut off vast numbers of the Canaanites either by a plague, or by the hornet sent before them, as is expressed, Josh. xxiv, 12.

XIV

The murmuring of the people against Moses and Aaron, ver. 1-4. Their fruitless endeavour to still them, ver. 5-10. God's threatening utterly to destroy them, ver. 11-12. The intercession of Moses, ver. 13-19. The decree that all that generation should die in the wilderness, ver. 20-35. The immediate death of the spies, ver. 36-39. The ill success of those who would go up notwithstanding, ver. 40-45.

2. *Against Moses and Aaron* - As the instruments and occasions of their present calamity. *That we had died in this wilderness* - It was not long before they had their desire, and did die in the wilderness.

3. *The Lord* - From instruments they rise higher, and strike at God the cause and author of their journey: by which we see the prodigious growth and progress of sin when it is not resisted. *A prey* - To the Canaanites whose land we were made to believe we should possess.

4. *A captain* - Instead of Moses, one who will be more faithful to our interest than he. *Into Egypt* - Stupendous madness! Whence should they have protection against the hazards, and provision against all the wants of the wilderness? Could they expect either God's cloud to cover and guide them, or Manna from heaven to feed them? Who could conduct them over the Red-sea? Or, if they went another way, who should defend them against those nations whose borders they were to pass? What entertainment could they expect from the Egyptians, whom they had deserted and brought to so much ruin?

5. *Fell on their faces* - As humble and earnest suppliants to God, the only refuge to which Moses resorted in all such straits, and who alone was able to govern this stiff-necked people. *Before all the assembly* -That they might awake to apprehend their sin and danger, when they saw Moses at his

prayers, whom God never failed to defend, even with the destruction of his enemies.

6. Rent their clothes - To testify their hearty grief for the peoples blasphemy against God and sedition against Moses, and that dreadful judgment which they easily foresaw this must bring upon the congregation.

8. Delight in us - If by our rebellion and ingratitude we do not provoke God to leave and forsake us.

9. Bread - We shall destroy them as easily as we eat our bread. Their defense - Their conduct and courage, and especially God, who was pleased to afford them his protection 'till their iniquities were full, is utterly departed from them, and hath given them up as a prey to us. With us - By his special grace and almighty power, to save us from them and all our enemies. Only rebel not against the Lord - Nothing can ruin sinners but their own rebellion. If God leaves them, 'tis because they drive him from them, and they die, because they will die.

10. Appeared - Now in the extremity of danger to rescue his faithful servants, and to stop the rage of the people. In the tabernacle - Upon or above the tabernacle, where the cloud usually resided, in which the glory of God appeared now in a more illustrious manner. When they reflected upon God, his glory appeared not, to silence their blasphemies: but when they threatened Caleb and Joshua, they touched the apple of his eye, and his glory appeared immediately. They who faithfully expose themselves for God, are sure of his special provision.

12. I will smite them - This was not an absolute determination, but a commination, like that of Nineveh's destruction, with a condition implied, except there be speedy repentance, or powerful intercession.

16. Not able - His power was quite spent in bringing them out of Egypt, and could not finish the work he had begun and had sworn to do.

17. Be great - That is appear to be great, discover its greatness: namely, the power of his grace and mercy, or the greatness of his mercy, in pardoning this and their other sins: for to this the following words manifestly restrain it, where the pardon of their sins is the only instance of this power both described in God's titles, ver. 18, and prayed for by Moses ver. 19, and granted by God in answer to him, xiv, 20. Nor is it strange that the pardon of sin, especially such great sins, is spoken of as an act of power in God, because undoubtedly it is an act of omnipotent and infinite goodness.

18. Visiting the iniquity - These words may seem to be improperly mentioned, as being a powerful argument to move God to destroy this wicked people, and not to pardon them. It may be answered, that Moses useth these words together with the rest, because he would not sever what God had put together. But the truer answer seems to be, that these words are to be translated otherwise, And in destroying he will not utterly destroy, though he visit the iniquity of the fathers upon the children, unto the third and fourth generation.

20. I have pardoned - So far as not utterly to destroy them.

21. With the glory of the Lord - With the report of the glorious and righteous acts of God in punishing this rebellious people.

22. My glory - That is, my glorious appearances in the cloud, and in the tabernacle. Ten times - That is, many times. A certain number for an uncertain.

24. Caleb - Josh. is not named, because he was not now among the people, but a constant attendant upon Moses, nor was he to be reckoned as one of them, any more than Moses and Aaron were, because he was to be their chief commander. He had another spirit - Was a man of another temper, faithful and courageous, not acted by that evil spirit of cowardice, unbelief, disobedience, which ruled in his brethren but by the spirit of God. Fully - Universally and constantly, through difficulties and dangers, which made his partners halt. Whereinto he went - In general, Canaan, and particularly Hebron, and the adjacent parts, Josh. xiv, 9.

25. In the valley - Beyond the mountain, at the foot whereof they now were, ver. 40. And this clause is added, either

1. As an aggravation of Israel's misery and punishment, that being now ready to enter and take possession of the land, they are forced to go back into the wilderness or

2. As an argument to oblige them more willingly to obey the following command of returning into the wilderness, because their enemies were very near them, and severed from them only by that Idumean mountain, and, if they did not speedily depart, their enemies would fall upon them, and so the evil which before they causelessly feared would come upon them; they, their wives and their children, would become a prey to the Amalekites and Canaanites, because God would not assist nor defend them. By the way of the Red-sea - That leadeth to the Red-sea, and to Egypt, the place whither you desire to return.

28. As ye have spoken - When you wickedly wished you might die in the wilderness.

30. You - Your nation; for God did not swear to do so to these particular persons.

32. Your carcases - See with what contempt they are spoken of, now they had by their sin made themselves vile! The mighty men of valour were but carcases, now the Spirit of the Lord was departed

from them! It was very probably upon this occasion, that Moses wrote the ninetieth psalm.

33. Forty years - So long as to make up the time of your dwelling in the wilderness forty years; one whole year and part of another were past before this sin or judgment. Your whoredoms - The punishment of your whoredoms, of your apostacy from, and perfidiousness against your Lord, who was your husband, and had married you to himself.

34. Each day for a year - So there should have been forty years to come, but God was pleased mercifully to accept of the time past as a part of that time. Ye shall know my breach of promise - That as you have first broken the covenant between you and me, by breaking the conditions of it, so I will make it void on my part, by denying you the blessings promised in that covenant. So you shall see, that the breach of promise wherewith you charged me, lies at your door, and was forced from me by your perfidiousness.

37. By the plague - Either by the pestilence, or by some other sudden and extraordinary judgment, sent from the cloud in which God dwelt, and from whence he spake to Moses, and wherein his glory at this time appeared before all the people, ver. 10, who therefore were all, and these spies among the rest, before the Lord.

38. But Joshua and Caleb lived still - Death never misses his mark, nor takes any by oversight who are designed for life, tho' in the midst of those that are to die.

39. And the people mourned greatly - But it was now too late. There was now no place for repentance. Such mourning as this there is in hell; but the tears will not quench the flames.

40. Gat them up - Designed or prepared themselves to go up.

45. The Canaanites - Largely so called, but strictly the Amorites. Hormah - A place so called afterwards, ver. 3, from the slaughter or destruction of the Israelites at this time.

XV

Laws, concerning meal-offerings and drink offerings, ver. 1- 16. Concerning dough for heave-offerings, ver. 17-21. Sacrifices for sins of ignorance, ver. 22-29. Concerning presumptuous sinners, ver. 30, 31. An instance in the sabbath-breaker, ver. 32- 36. Concerning fringes on the borders of their garments, ver. 37- 41.

2. I give you - Will certainly give you, not withstanding this great provocation. And for their better assurance hereof he repeats and amplifies the laws of sacrifices, whereby through Christ he would be reconciled to them and theirs upon their repentance.

3. A sacrifice - A peace-offering.

4. A tenth deal - The tenth part of an Ephah, that is, about five pints. An hin contained about five quarts.

6. Two tenth-deals - Because this belonged to a better sacrifice than the former; and therefore in the next sacrifice of a bullock, there are three tenth deals. So the accessory sacrifice grows proportionably with the principal.

8. Peace-offerings - Such as were offered either freely or by command, which may be called peace-offerings or thank- offerings, by way of eminency, because such are offered purely by way of gratitude to God, and with single respect to his honour, whereas the peace-offerings made in performance of a vow were made and offered, with design of getting some advantage by them.

12. Their number - As many cattle as ye sacrifice, so many meal and drink-offerings ye shall offer.

15. Before the Lord - As to the worship of God: his sacrifices shall be offered in the same manner and accepted by God upon the same terms, as yours: which was a presage of the future calling of the Gentiles. And this is added by way of caution, to shew that strangers were not upon this pretense to partake of their civil privileges.

19. When ye eat - When you are about to eat it: for before they eat it, they were to offer this offering to God. The bread - That is, the bread-corn.

20. The threshing floor - That is, of the corn in the threshing floor, when you have gathered in your corn.

22. All these commandments - Those now spoken of, which concern the outward service of God, or the rites or ceremonies belonging to it. And herein principally this law may seem to differ from that Lev. iv, 13, which speaks of some positive miscarriage, or doing that which ought not to have been done, about the holy things of God; whereas this speaks only of an omission of something which ought to have been done about holy ceremonies.

30. Reprocheth the Lord - He sets God at defiance, and exposeth him to contempt, as if he were unable to punish transgressors.

32. On the sabbath-day - This seems to be added as an example of a presumptuous sin: for as the law of the sabbath was plain and positive, so this transgression of it must needs be a known and wilful sin.

33. To all the congregation - That is, to the rulers of the congregation.

34. They - That is, Moses and Aaron, and the seventy rulers. What should be done - That is, in what manner he was to be cut off, or by what kind of death he was to die, which therefore God here particularly determines: otherwise it was known in general that sabbath-breakers were to be put to death.

38. Fringes - These were certain threads or ends, standing out a little further than the rest of their garments, lest there for this use. In the borders - That is, in the four borders or quarters, as it is, Deut. xxii, 12. Of their garments - Of their upper garments. This was practiced by the Pharisees in Christ's time, who are noted for making their borders larger than ordinary. A ribband - To make it more obvious to the sight, and consequently more serviceable to the use here mentioned. Of blue - Or, purple.

39. For a fringe - That is, the ribband, shall be unto you, shall serve you for a fringe, to render it more visible by its distinct colour, whereas the fringe without this was of the same piece and colour with the garment, and therefore less observeable. That ye seek not - Or, inquire not for other rules and ways of serving me than I have prescribed you. Your own heart, and eyes - Neither after the devices of your own hearts, as Nadab and Abihu did when they offered strange fire; nor after the examples of others which your eyes see, as you did when you were set upon worshipping a calf after the manner of Egypt. The phylacteries worn by the Pharisees in our Lord's time, were a different thing from these. Those were of their own invention: these were a divine institution.

40. Be ye holy - Purged from sin and sincerely devoted to God.

41. I am the Lord your God - Though I am justly displeased with you for your frequent rebellions, for which also I will keep you forty years in the wilderness, yet I will not utterly cast you off, but will continue to be your God.

XVI

Korah, Dathan and Abiram, rise up against Moses, ver. 1-4. Moses reasons with them, ver. 5-11. Sends for Dathan and Abiram, who refuse to come, ver. 12-14. His proposal to Korah, ver. 15-19. The punishment of the rebels, ver. 20-35. Their censers preserved for a memorial, ver. 36-40. A new insurrection stopped by a plague, ver. 41-45. Aaron stays the plague, ver. 46- 50.

1. The son of Izhar - Amram's brother, Exod. vi, 18, therefore Moses and he were cousin germans. Moreover, Izhar was the second son of Kohath, whereas Elizaphan, whom Moses had preferred before him, and made prince or ruler of the Kohathites, chap. iii, 30, was the son of Uzziel, the fourth son of Kohath. This, the Jewish writers say, made him malcontent, which at last broke forth into sedition. Sons of Reuben - These are drawn into confederacy with Korah, partly because they were his next neighbours, both being encamped on the south-side, partly in hopes to recover their rights of primogeniture, in which the priesthood was comprehended, which was given away from their father.

2. Rose up - That is, conspired together, and put their design in execution. Before Moses - Not obscurely, but openly and boldly, not fearing nor regarding the presence of Moses.

3. They - Korah, Dathan and Abiram, and the rest, who were all together when Moses spake those words, ver. 5-7, but after that, Dathan and Abiram retired to their tents, and then Moses sent for Korah and the Levites, who had more colourable pretenses to the priesthood, and treats with them apart, and speaks what is mentioned, ver. 8-11. Having dispatched them, he sends for Dathan and Abiram, ver. 12, that he might reason the case with them also apart. Against Aaron - To whom the priesthood was confined, and against Moses, both because this was done by his order, and because before Aaron's consecration Moses appropriated it to himself. For whatever they intended, they seem not now directly to strike at Moses for his supreme civil government, but only for his influence in the disposal of the priesthood. Ye take too much - By perpetuating the priesthood in yourselves and family, with the exclusion of all others from it. All are holy - A kingdom of priests, an holy nation, as they are called, Exod. xix, 6, a people separated to the service of God, and therefore no less fit to offer sacrifice and incense, than you are. Among them - By his tabernacle and cloud, the tokens of his gracious presence, and therefore ready to receive sacrifices from their own hands. Ye - Thou Moses, by prescribing what laws thou pleasest about the priesthood, and confining it to thy brother; and thou Aaron by usurping it as thy peculiar privilege.

4. On his face - Humbly begging that God would direct and vindicate him. Accordingly God answers his prayers, and strengthens him with new courage, and confidence of success.

5. Tomorrow - Hebrew. In the morning, the time appointed by men for administering justice, and chosen by God for that work. Some time is allowed, partly that Korah and his company might prepare themselves and their censers, and partly to give them space for consideration and repentance. He will cause him - He will by some evident token declare his approbation of him and his ministry.

8. Ye sons of Levi - They were of his own tribe, nay, they were God's tribe. It was therefore the worse in them thus to mutiny against God and against him.

9. To minister to them - So they were the servants both of God and of the church, which was an high dignity, though not sufficient for their ambitious minds.

11. Against the Lord - Whose chosen servant Aaron is. You strike at God through Aaron's sides.

12. Dathan and Abiram - To treat with them and give them, as he had done Korah and his company, a timely admonition. Come up - To Moses's tabernacle, whither the people used to go up for judgment. Men are said in scripture phrase to go up to places of judgment.

14. These men - Of all the people who are of our mind: wilt thou make them blind, or persuade them that they do not see what is visible to all that have eyes, to wit, that thou hast deceived them, and broken thy faith and promise given to them?

15. Respect not their offering - Accept not their incense which they are now going to offer, but shew some eminent dislike of it. He calls it their offering, though it was offered by Korah and his companions, because it was offered in the name and by the consent of all the conspirators, for the decision of the present controversy between them and Moses. I have not hurt one of them - I have never injured them, nor used my power to defraud or oppress them, as I might have done; I have done them many good offices, but no hurt: therefore their crime is without any cause or provocation.

16. Before the Lord - Not in the tabernacle, which was not capable of so many persons severally offering incense, but at the door of the tabernacle, where they might offer it by Moses's direction upon this extraordinary occasion. This work could not be done in that place, which alone was allowed for the offering up of incense; not only for its smallness, but also because none but priests might enter to do this work. Here also the people, who were to be instructed by this experiment, might see the proof and success of it.

18. Fire - Taken from the altar which stood in that place, for Aaron might not use other fire. And it is likely the rememberance of the death of Nadab and Abihu deterred them from offering any strange fire.

19. Against them - That they might be witnesses of the event, and, upon their success, which they doubted not of, might fall upon Moses and Aaron. And it seems by this that the people were generally incensed against Moses, and inclined to Korah's side. The glory appeared -In the cloud, which then shone with greater brightness and majesty, as a token of God's approach and presence.

22. The spirits - And this is no empty title here, but very emphatical. Thou art the maker of spirits, destroy not thy own workmanship! O thou who art the preserver of men, and of their spirits, the Lord of spirits, Job xii, 10, who as thou mayst justly destroy this people, so thou canst preserve whom thou pleasest: the father of spirits, the souls. Deal mercifully with thy own children: the searcher of spirits, thou canst distinguish between those who have maliciously railed this tumult, and those whose ignorance and simple credulity hath made them a prey to crafty seducers. Of all flesh - Of all mankind: the word flesh is often put for men. One man - Korah, the ringleader of this sedition.

24. The congregation - Whom for your sakes I will spare upon the condition following.

25. Unto Dathan - Because they refused to come to him. The elders - The seventy rulers, whom he carried with him for the greater solemnity of the action, and to encourage them in their work, notwithstanding the obstinate and untractable nature of the people they were to govern.

27. Stood in the door - An argument of their foolish confidence, obstinacy and impenitency, whereby they declared that they neither feared God, nor reverenced man.

28. All these works - As the bringing of the people out of Egypt; the conducting of them through the wilderness; the exercising authority among them; and giving laws to them concerning the priesthood.

29. The death of all men - By a natural death. The visitation of all men - By plague, or sword, or some usual judgment. The Lord hath not sent me - I am content that you take me for an imposter, falsely pretending to be sent of God.

32. All that appertained unto Korah - That is, all his family which were there, women, children, and servants; but his sons, who were spared, chap. xxvi, 11, 58; 1 Chron. vi, 22, 37, were absent either upon some service of the tabernacle, or upon some other occasion, God so ordering it by his providence either because they disliked their fathers act, or upon Moses's intercession for them. This expression may intimate, that Korah himself was not here, but that he continued with his two hundred and fifty men before the Lord, where they were waiting for God's decision of the controversy. Nor is it probable that their chief captain would desert them, and leave them standing there without an head, especially, when Aaron his great adversary, abode there still, and did not go with Moses to Dathan. And Korah may seem to have been consumed with those two hundred and fifty. And so much is intimated, ver. 40, that no stranger come near to offer incense before the Lord, that he be not as Korah, and as his company, that is, destroyed, as they were, by fire from the Lord. And when the Psalmist relates this history, Psalm cvi, 17-18, the earth's swallowing them up is confined to Dathan and Abiram, Psalm cvi, 17, and for all the rest of that conspiracy it is added, Psalm cvi, 18. And a fire was kindled in their company, the flame burnt up the wicked.

33. Into the pit - Into the earth, which first opened itself to receive them, and then shut itself to

destroy them.

35. From the Lord - From the cloud, wherein the glory of the Lord appeared.

37. To Eleazer - Rather than to Aaron, partly because the troublesome part of the work was more proper for him, and partly lest Aaron should be polluted by going amongst those dead carcasses; for it is probable this fire consumed them, as lightning sometimes doth, others, by taking away their lives, and leaving their bodies dead upon the place. Out of the burning - From among the dead bodies of those men who were burnt. Yonder - Far from the altar and sanctuary, into an unclean place, where the ashes were wont to be cast: by which God shews his rejection on of their services. They are hallowed - By God's appointment, because they were presented before the Lord by his express order, ver. 16, 17.

38. Their own souls - That is, their own lives: who were the authors of their own destruction. The altar - Of burnt-offerings, which was made of wood, but covered with brass before this time, Exod. xxvii, 1, 2, to which this other covering was added for farther ornament, and security against the fire, continually burning upon it. A sign - A warning to all strangers to take heed of invading the priesthood.

40. To him - To Eleazer. These words belong to ver. 38, the meaning is, that Eleazer did as God bade him.

41. On the morrow - Prodigious wickedness and madness so soon to forget such a terrible instance of Divine vengeance! The people of the Lord - So they call those wicked wretches, and rebels against God! Tho' they were but newly saved from sharing in the same punishment, and the survivors were as brands plucked out of the burning, yet they fly in the face of Moses and Aaron, to whose intercession they owe their preservation.

42. They - Moses and Aaron, who in all their distresses made God their refuge.

43. Moses and Aaron came - To hear what God, who now appeared, would say to them.

45. They fell upon their faces - To beg mercy for the people; thus rendering Good for Evil.

46. Incense - Which was a sign of intercession, and was to be accompanied with it. Go unto the congregation - He went with the incense, to stir up the people to repentance and prayer, to prevent their utter ruin. This he might do upon this extraordinary occasion, having God's command for his warrant, though ordinarily incense was to be offered only in the tabernacle.

48. The living - Whereby it may seem that this plague, like that fire, chap. xi, 1, began in the uttermost parts of the congregation, and so proceeded destroying one after another in an orderly manner, which gave Aaron occasion and direction so to place himself, as a mediator to God on their behalf.

XVII

The blossoming of Aaron's rod, ver. 1-9. It is laid up for a memorial, ver. 10, 11. The people are terrified, ver. 12, 13.

2. Of every one - Not of every person, but of every tribe. A rod - That staff, or rod, which the princes carried in their hands as tokens of their dignity and authority. Every man's name - Every prince's: for they being the first-born, and the chief of their tribes might above all others pretend to the priesthood, if it was communicable to any of their tribes, and besides each prince represented all his tribe: so that this was a full decision of the question. And this place seems to confirm, that not only Korah and the Levites, but also those of other tribes contested with Moses and Aaron about the priesthood, as that which belonged to all the congregation they being all holy.

3. Aaron's name - Rather than Levi's, for that would have left the controversy undecided between Aaron and the other Levites, whereas this would justify the appropriation of the priesthood to Aaron's family. One rod - There shall be in this, as there is in all the other tribes, only one rod, and that for the head of their tribe, who is Aaron in this tribe: whereas it might have been expected that there should have been two rods, one for Aaron, and another for his competitors of the same tribe. But Aaron's name was sufficient to determine both the tribe, and that branch or family of the tribe, to whom this dignity should be affixed.

4. Before the testimony - That is, before the ark of the testimony, close by the ark. I will meet with you - And manifest my mind to you, for the ending of this dispute.

6. Among their rods - Was laid up with the rest, being either one of the twelve, as the Hebrew affirm, or the thirteenth, as others think.

8. Into the tabernacle - Into the most holy place, which he might safely do under the protection of God's command, though otherwise none but the high-priest might enter there, and that once in a year.

10. To be kept for a token - it is probable, the buds and blossoms and fruit, all which could never have grown together, but by miracle, continued fresh, the same which produced them in a night preserving them for ages.

12. We perish - Words of consternation, arising from the remembrance of these severe and repeated judgments, from the threatening of death upon any succeeding murmurings, and from the sense of their own guilt and weakness, which made them fear lest they should relapse into the same

miscarriages, and thereby bring the vengeance of God upon themselves.

13. Near - Nearer than he should do; an error which we may easily commit. Will God proceed with us according to his strict justice, till all the people be cut off?

XVIII

The Work of the priests and Levites, ver. 1-7. The maintenance of the priests, ver. 8-20. Of the Levites, ver. 21-24. The portion they are to pay to the priests, ver. 25-32.

1. Shall bear the iniquity of the sanctuary - Shall suffer the punishment of all the usurpations, or pollutions of the sanctuary, or the holy things, by the Levites, or any of the people, because you have power from me to keep them all within their bounds. Thus the people are in good measure secured against their fears. Also they are informed that Aaron's high dignity was attended with great burdens, having not only his own, but the people's sins to answer for; and therefore they had no such reason to envy him, if the benefits and dangers were equally considered. The iniquity of your priesthood - That is, Of all the errors committed by yourselves, or by you permitted in others in things, belonging to your priesthood.

2. Unto thee - About sacrifices and offerings and other things, according to the rules I have prescribed them. The Levites are said to minister to Aaron here, to the church, chap. xvi, 9, and to God, Deut. x, 8. They shall not contend with thee for superiority, as they have done, but shall be subordinate to thee. Thy sons with thee - Or, both to thee, and to thy sons with thee: Which translation may seem to be favoured by the following words, before the tabernacle, which was the proper place where the Levites ministered. Besides, both the foregoing words, and the two following verses, entirely speak of the ministry of the Levites, and the ministry of the priests is distinctly spoken of, ver. 5.

3. They charge - That is, that which thou shalt command them and commit unto them.

5. The sanctuary - Of the holy, and of the most holy place.

6. To you they are given as a gift - We are to value it as a great gift of the divine bounty, to have those joined to us, that will be helpful and serviceable to us, in the service of God.

7. The altar - Of burnt-offering. Within the veil - This phrase here comprehends both the holy and the most holy place. As a gift which I have freely conferred upon you, and upon you alone; and therefore let no man henceforth dare either to charge you with arrogance in appropriating this to yourselves, or to invade your office.

8. I have given them - Not only the charge, but the use of them for thyself and family. By reason of the anointing - That is, because thou art priest, and art to devote thyself wholly to my service.

9. Most holy - Such as were to be eaten only by the priests, and that in the sanctuary. Reserved - That is, such sacrifices or parts of sacrifices as were not burnt in the fire. Render unto me - By way of compensation for a trespass committed against me, in which case a ram was to be offered, which was a most holy thing, and may be particularly designed here.

10. In the most holy place - In the court of the priests, where there were places for this use, which is called the most holy place, not simply and absolutely, but in respect of the thing he speaks of because this was the most holy of all the places appointed for eating holy things, whereof some might be eaten in any clean place in the camp, or in their own house.

13. Whatsoever is first ripe - Not only the first-fruits of the oil and wine, and wheat now mentioned, but all other first-fruits of all other grains, and all fruit trees. Clean - And none else, because these were first offered to God, and by consequence given to priests; but for those which were immediately given to the priests, the clean and unclean might eat of them.

14. Devoted - Dedicated to God by vow or otherwise, provided it be such a thing as might be eaten: for the vessels or treasures of gold and silver which were dedicated by Joshua, David, or others, were not the priests, but appropriated to the uses of the temple.

15. Of men - Which were offered to God in his temple, and to his service and disposal.

16. Those that are to be redeemed - Namely, of men only, not of unclean beasts, as is manifest from the time and price of redemption here mentioned, both which agree to men; the time, ver. 16, the price, chap. iii, 46, 47, but neither agree to unclean beasts, which were to be redeemed with a sheep, Exod. xiii, 13, and that after it was eight days old.

17. Holy - Namely, in a peculiar manner, consecrated to an holy use, even to be sacrificed to God. Deut. xv, 19.

18. The flesh - All the flesh of them, and not only some parts, as in other sacrifices.

19. A covenant of salt - A durable and perpetual covenant; so called here and 2 Chron. xiii, 5, either, because salt is a sign of incorruption, as being of singular use to preserve things from corruption: or, because it is ratified on their part by salt, which is therefore called the salt of the covenant, for which the priests were obliged to take care, that it should never be lacking from any meat-offering, Lev. ii, 13. And this privilege conferred upon the priests is called a covenant because it is given them conditionally,

upon condition of their service, and care about the worship of God.

20. In their land - In the land of the children of Israel. You shall not have a distinct portion of land, as the other tribes shall. The reason of this law, was, partly because God would have them wholly devoted to his service, and therefore free from worldly incumbrances; partly, because God had abundantly provided for them otherwise, by tithes and first-fruits and oblations; and partly that by this means being dispersed among the several tribes, they might have the better opportunity for teaching and watching over the people. I am thy part - I have appointed thee a liberal maintenance out of my oblations.

21. The tenth - For the tithes were all given to the Levites, and out of their tithes the tenth was given to the priests.

22. Nigh - So nigh as to do any proper act to the priests or Levites.

23. Their iniquity - The punishment due not only for their own, but also for the people's miscarriage, if it be committed through their connivance or negligence. And this was the reason why the priests withstood King Uzziah, when he would have burnt incense to the Lord.

24. An heave-offering - An acknowledgment that they have all their land and the fruits of it from God's bounty. Note the word heave-offering, which is for the most part understood of a particular kind of offerings heaved or lifted up to the Lord, is here used for any offering.

26. Ye shall offer up an heave-offering - They who are employed in assisting the devotions of others, must be sure to pay their own as an heave-offering. Prayers and praises, or rather the heart lifted up in them, are now our heave-offerings.

27. As though it were the corn - It shall be accepted of you as much as if you offered it out of your own lands and labours.

28. To Aaron - And to his children, who were all to have their share herein.

29. Your gifts - Not only out of your tithes, but out of the other gifts which you receive from the people, and out of those fields which shall belong to your cities. Offer - To the priest. As many gifts, so many heave-offerings; you shall reserve a part out of each of them for the priest. The hallowed part - the tenth part, which was the part or proportion that God hallowed or sanctified to himself as his proper portion.

31. Every place - In every clean place, and not in the holy place only.

32. Neither shall ye pollute the holy things - As you will do, if you abuse their holy offerings, by reserving that entirely to yourselves, which they offer to God to be disposed as he hath appointed, namely, part to you, and part to the priests.

XIX

The manner of preparing the water of purification, ver. 1-10. Of using it, ver. 11-22.

2. Red - A fit colour to shadow forth the bloody nature of sin, and the blood of Christ, from which this water and all other rites had their purifying virtue. No blemish - A fit type of Christ. Upon which never came yoke - Whereby may be signified, either that Christ in himself was free from all the yoke or obligation of God's command, till for our sakes he put himself under the law; or that Christ was not forced to undertake our burden and cross, but did voluntarily chuse it. He was bound and held with no other cords but those of his own love.

3. Eleazar - Who was the second priest, and in some cases, the deputy of the high-priest. To him, not to Aaron, because this service made him unclean for a season, and consequently unfit for holy ministrations, whereas the high-priest was, as far as possibly he could, to be preserved from all sorts of defilement, fit for his high and holy work. Without the camp -Partly because it was reputed an unclean and accursed thing, being laden with the sins of all the people; and partly to signify that Christ should suffer without the camp, in the place where malefactors suffered.

4. Before the tabernacle - Or, towards the tabernacle, standing at a good distance from it, even without the camp, yet turning and looking towards it. For here is no intimation that he went into the camp before this work was done, but rather the contrary is implied, ver. 7. And because being defiled by this work he could not come near the tabernacle, it was sufficient for him to turn and look towards it. This signified his presenting this blood before the Lord by way of atonement for his and the people's sins, and his expectation of acceptance and pardon only from God, and from his mercy-seat in the tabernacle. And this typified the satisfaction that was made to God, by the death of Christ, who by the eternal Spirit offered himself without spot to God, and did as it were sprinkle his own blood before the sanctuary, when he said, Into thy hands I commend my spirit!

5. Burn the heifer - To signify the sharp and grievous sufferings of Christ for our sins. Her blood - All of it, but what was spent in sprinkling.

6. Cedar-wood, hyssop, scarlet - All which are here burnt, and as it were offered to God, that they might be sanctified to this holy use for the future; for of these kinds of things was the sprinkle made

wherewith the unclean were sprinkled, Lev. xiv, 4.

7. Shall be unclean - Partly to teach us the imperfection of the Levitical priesthood, in which the priest himself was defiled by some parts of his work, and partly to shew that Christ himself, though he had no sin of his own, yet was reputed by men, and judged by God, as a sinful person, by reason of our sins which were laid upon him.

9. For a water - Or, to the water, that is, to be put to the water, or mixed with it. Of separation - Appointed for the cleansing of them that are in a state of separation, who for their uncleanness are separated from the congregation. It is a purification for sin - Hebrew. a sin, that is, an offering for sin, or rather a mean for expiation or cleansing of sin. And this was a type of that purification for sin, which our Lord Jesus made by his death.

10. The stranger - A proselyte.

12. With it - With the water of separation. On the third day - To typify Christ's resurrection on that day by which we are cleansed or sanctified.

13. Whosoever toucheth - If this transgression be done presumptuously; for if it was done ignorantly, he was only to offer sacrifice. Defiled -By approaching to it in his uncleanness: for holy things or places were ceremonially defiled with the touch of any unclean person or thing. Is upon him - He continues in his guilt, not now to be washed away by this water, but to be punished by cutting off.

16. With a sword - Or by any other violent way.

17. Running water - Waters flowing from a spring or river, which are the purest. These manifestly signify God's spirit, which is oft compared to water, and by which alone true purification is obtained. Those who promise themselves benefit by the righteousness of Christ, while they submit not to the influence of his spirit, do but deceive themselves; for they cannot be purified by the ashes, otherwise than in the running water.

20. That shall not purify himself - Shall contemptuously refuse to submit to this way of purification.

21. Shall wash his clothes - Because he is unclean. It is strange, that the same water should cleanse one person, and defile another. But God would have it so, to teach us that it did not cleanse by any virtue in itself, or in the work done, but only by virtue of God's appointment: to mind the laws of the imperfection of their priesthood, and their ritual purifications and expiations, and consequently of the necessity of a better priest and sacrifice and way of purifying; and to shew that the efficacy of God's ordinances doth not depend upon the person or quality of his ministers, because the same person who, was polluted himself could and did cleanse others. He that toucheth the water - Either by sprinkling of it, or by being sprinkled with it; for even he that was cleansed by it, was not fully cleansed as soon as he was sprinkled, but only at the even of that day.

22. The unclean person - Not he who is so only by touching the water of separation, ver. 21, but he who is so by the greater sort of uncleanness, which lasted seven days, and which was not removed without the use of this water of purification.

XX

This chapter begins the history of the fortieth year of the Israelites wandering in the wilderness. Little is recorded of them from the beginning of their second year till this, which brought them to the borders of Canaan. Here is,
1. The death of Miriam, ver. 1.
2. The fetching water out of the rock, ver. 2-13.
3. The treaty with the Edomites, ver. 14-21.
4. The death of Aaron and installment of Eleazar, ver. 22-29.

1. Then - To wit, after many stations and long journeys here omitted, but particularly described, chap. xxxiii, 1-49. Zin - A place near the land of Edom, distinct and distant from that Sin, Exod. xvi, 1. The first month - Of the fortieth year, as is evident, because the next station to this was in mount Hor, where Aaron died, who died in the fifth month of the fortieth year, chap. xxxiii, 38. Moses doth not give us an exact journal of all occurrences in the wilderness, but only of those which were most remarkable, and especially of those which happened in the first and second, and in the fortieth year. Miriam died - Four months before Aaron, and but a few more before Moses.

2. No water - Which having followed them through all their former journeys, began to fail them here, because they were now come near countries, where waters might be had by ordinary means, and therefore God would not use extraordinary, lest he should seem to prostitute the honour of miracles. This story, though like that, Exod. xvii, 1-7, is different from it, as appears by divers circumstances. It is a great mercy, to have plenty of water; a mercy which if we found the want of, we should own the worth of.

3. Before the Lord - Suddenly, rather than to die such a lingering death. Their sin was much

greater than that of their parents, because they should have taken warning by their miscarriages, and by the terrible effects of them, which their eyes had seen.

8. *The rod* - That which was laid up before the Lord in the tabernacle; whether it was Aaron's rod, which was laid up there, chap. xvii, 10, or Moses's rod by which he wrought so many miracles. For it is likely, that wonder-working rod, was laid up in some part of the tabernacle, though not in or near the ark, where Aaron's blossoming rod was put.

9. *From before the Lord* - Out of the tabernacle.

12. *Ye believed me not* - But shewed your infidelity: which they did, either by smiting the rock, and that twice, which is emphatically noted, as if he doubted whether once smiting would have done it, whereas he was not commanded to smite so much as once, but only to speak to it: or by the doubtfulness of these words, chap. xx, 10. Must we fetch water out of the rock? which implies a suspicion of it, whereas they should have spoken positively and confidently to the rock to give forth water. And yet they did not doubt of the power of God, but of his will, whether he would gratify these rebels with this farther miracle, after so many of the like kind. *To sanctify me* - To give me the glory of my power in doing this miracle, and of my truth in punctually fulfilling my promise, and of my goodness in doing it notwithstanding the peoples perverseness. *In the eyes of Israel* - This made their sin scandalous to the Israelites, who of themselves were too prone to infidelity; to prevent the contagion, God leaves a monument of his displeasure upon them, and inflicts a punishment as publick as their sin.

13. *Meribah* - That is, strife. *In them* - Or, among them, the children of Israel, by the demonstration of his omnipotency, veracity, and clemency towards the Israelites, and of his impartial holiness and severity against sin even in his greatest friends and favourites.

14. *All the travel* - All the wanderings and afflictions of our parents and of us their children, which doubtless have come to thine ears.

16. *An Angel* - The Angel of the Covenant, who first appeared to Moses in the bush, and afterward in the cloudy pillar, who conducted Moses and the people out of Egypt, and through the wilderness. For though Moses may be called an angel or messenger yet it is not probable that he is meant, partly because Moses was the person that sent this message; and partly because another angel above Moses conducted them, and the mention hereof to the Edomites, was likely to give more authority to their present message. *In Kadesh* - Near, the particle in being so often used.

17. *The wells* - Or, pits, which any of you have digged for your private use, not without paying for it, ver. 19, but only of the waters of common rivers, which are free to all passengers. No man's property ought to be invaded, under colour of religion. Dominion is founded in providence, not in Grace.

18. *By me* - Through my country: I will not suffer thee to do so: which was an act of policy, to secure themselves from so numerous an host.

19. *Said* - That is, their messengers replied what here follows.

23. *And the Lord spake unto Moses and Aaron* - So these two dear brothers must part! Aaron must die first: but Moses is not likely to be long after him. So that it is only for a while, a little while, that they are separated.

24. *Because they rebelled* - This was one but not the only reason. God would not have Moses and Aaron to carry the people into Canaan, for this reason also, to signify the insufficiency of the Mosaical law and Aaronical priesthood to make them perfectly happy, and the necessity of a better, and to keep the Israelites from resting in them, so as to be taken off from their expectation of Christ.

26. *His garments* - His priestly garments, in token of his resignation of his office. *Put them on Eleazar* - By way of admission and inauguration to his office.

27. *In the sight of all the congregation* - That their hearts might be more affected with their loss of so great a pillar, and that they all might be witnesses of the translation of the priesthood from Aaron to Eleazar.

28. *And Moses stript Aaron* - And Death will strip us. Naked we came into the world: naked we must go out. We shall see little reason to be proud of our cloaths, our ornaments, or marks of honour, if we consider how soon death will strip us of all our glory, and take the crown off from our head! *Aaron died there* - He died in Mosera, Deut. x, 6. Mosera was the general name of the place where that station was, and mount Hor a particular place in it. Presently after he was stript of his priestly garments, he laid him down and died. A good man would desire, if it were the will of God, not to outlive his usefulness. Why should we covet to continue any longer in this world, than while we may do God and our generation some service?

29. *Saw* - Understood by the relation of Moses and Eleazar, and by other signs. *Thirty days* - The time of publick and solemn mourning for great persons.

Wesley's Notes on the Bible - The Old Testament: Genesis - Ruth

XXI

The defect of Arad, ver. 1-3. The people murmur and are plagued with fiery serpents, ver. 4-6. They are healed by looking on the brazen serpent, ver. 7-9. They journey forward, ver. 10-20. Conquer Sihon, ver. 21-31. And Og, ver. 33-35.

1. King Arad - Or rather, the Canaanite King of Arad: for Arad is not the name of a man, but of a city or territory. And he seems to be called a Canaanite in a general sense, as the Amorites and others. The south - Of Canaan, towards the east, and near the dead sea. Of the spies - Not of those spies which Moses sent to spy the land, for that was done thirty eight years before this, and they went so privately, that the Canaanites took no notice of them, nor knew which way they came or went; but of the spies which he himself sent out to observe the marches and motions of the Israelites. Took some of them prisoners - Which God permitted for Israel's humiliation, and to teach them not to expect the conquest of that land from their own wisdom or valour.

2. I will utterly destroy them - I will reserve no person or thing for my own use, but devote them all to total destruction.

3. They utterly destroyed them - Neither Moses nor the whole body of the people did this but a select number sent out to punish that king and people, who were so fierce and malicious that they came out of their own country to fight with the Israelites in the wilderness; and these, when they had done this work, returned to their brethren into the wilderness. But why did they not all now go into Canaan, and pursue this victory? Because God would not permit it, there being several works yet to be done, other people must be conquered, the Israelites must be farther humbled and tried and purged, Moses must die, and then they shall enter, and that in a more glorious manner, even over Jordan, which shall be miraculously dried up, to give them passage. Hormah - That is, utter destruction.

4. By way of the Red-sea - Which leadeth to the Red-sea, as they must needs do to compass the land of Edom. Because of the way - By reason of this journey, which was long and troublesome, and unexpected, because the successful entrance and victorious progress which some of them had made in the borders of Canaan, made them think they might have speedily gone in and taken possession of it, and so have saved the tedious travels and farther difficulties, into which Moses had again brought them.

5. Against God - Against Christ, their chief conductor, whom they tempted, 1 Cor. x, 19. Thus contemptuously did they speak of Manna, whereas it appears it yielded excellent nourishment, because in the strength of it they were able to go so many and such tedious journeys.

6. Fiery serpents - There were many such in this wilderness, which having been hitherto restrained by God, are now let loose and sent among them. They are called fiery from their effects, because their poison caused an intolerable heat and burning and thirst, which was aggravated with this circumstance of the place, that here was no water, ver. 5.

8. A fiery serpent - That is, the figure of a serpent in brass, which is of a fiery colour. This would require some time: God would not speedily take off the judgment, because he saw they were not throughly humbled. Upon a pole - That the people might see it from all parts of the camp, and therefore the pole must be high, and the serpent large. When he looketh - This method of cure was prescribed, that it might appear to be God's own work, and not the effect of nature or art: and that it might be an eminent type of our salvation by Christ. The serpent signified Christ, who was in the likeness of sinful flesh, though without sin, as this brazen serpent had the outward shape, but not the inward poison, of the other serpents: the pole resembled the cross upon which Christ was lifted up for our salvation: and looking up to it designed our believing in Christ.

9. He lived - He was delivered from death, and cured of his disease.

10. In Oboth - Not immediately, but after two other stations mentioned, chap. xxxiii, 43, 44.

12. The valley of Zared - Or rather, by the brook of Zared, which ran into the dead sea.

13. On the other side - Or rather, on this side of Arnon, for so it now was to the Israelites, who had not yet passed over it. Between Moab and the Amorites - Though formerly it and the land beyond it belonged to Moab, yet afterwards it had been taken from them by Sihon. This is added to reconcile two seemingly contrary commands of God, the one that of not meddling with the land of the Moabites, Deut. ii, 9, the other that of going over Arnon and taking possession of the land beyond it, Deut. ii, 24, because, saith he, it is not now the land of the Moabites, but of the Amorites.

14. The book of the wars of the Lord - This seems to have been some poem or narration of the wars and victories of the Lord, either by: or relating to the Israelites: which may be asserted without any prejudice to the integrity of the holy scripture, because this book doth not appear to have been written by a prophet, er to be designed for a part of the canon, which yet Moses might quote, as St. Paul doth some of the heathen poets. And as St. Luke assures us, that many did write an history of the things done, and said by Christ, Luke i, 1, whose writings were never received as canonical, the like may be conceived concerning this and some few other books mentioned in the old testament. The brooks - The brook, the plural number for the singular, as the plural number rivers is used concerning Jordan, Psalm

John Wesley

7iv, 15, and concerning Tigris, Nahum ii, 6, and concerning Euphrates, Psalm lxxxvii, 1, all which may be to called because of the several little streams into which they were divided.

15. Ar - A chief city in Moab.

16. Beer - This place and Mattanah, Nahaliel, and Bamoth named here, ver. 19, are not mentioned among those places where they pitched or encamped, chap. xxxiii, 1-49. Probably they did not pitch or encamp in these places, but only pass by or through them. I will give them water - In a miraculous manner. Before they prayed, God granted, and prevented them with the blessings of goodness. And as the brasen serpent was the figure of Christ, so is this well a figure of the spirit, who is poured forth for our comfort, and from him flow rivers of living waters.

17. Spring up - Hebrew. ascend, that is, let thy waters, which now lie hid below in the earth, ascend for our use. It is either a prediction that it should spring up, or a prayer that it might.

18. With their staves - Probably as Moses smote the rock with his rod, so they struck the earth with their staves, as a sign that God would cause the water to flow out of the earth where they smote it, as he did before out of the rock. Perhaps they made holes with their staves in the sandy ground, and God caused the water immediately to spring up.

20. Pisgah - This was the top of those high hills of Abarim.

21. Sent messengers - By God's allowance, that so Sihon's malice might be the more evident and inexcusable, and their title to his country more clear in the judgment of all men, as being gotten by a just war, into which they were forced for their own defense.

22. Let me pass - They spoke what they seriously intended and would have done, if he had given them quiet passage.

24. From Arnon - Or, which reached from Arnon; and so here is a description or limitation of Sihon's conquest and kingdom, that is, extended only from Arnon, unto the children of Ammon; and then the following words, for the border of the children of Ammon was strong, come in very fitly, not as a reason why the Israelites did not conquer the Ammonites, for they were absolutely forbidden to meddle with them, Deut. iii, 8, but as a reason why Sihon could not enlarge his conquests to the Ammonites, as he had done to the Moabites. Jabbok - A river by which the countries of Ammon and Moab were in part bounded and divided. Strong - Either by the advantage of the river, or by their strong holds in their frontiers.

26. Was the city of Sihon - This is added as a reason why Israel took possession of this land, because it was not now the land of the Moabites, but in the possession of the Amorites. The former king -The predecessor of Balak, who was the present king. See the wisdom of providence, which prepares long before, for the accomplishing God's purposes in their season! This country being designed for Israel, is before-hand put into the hand of the Amorites, who little think they have it but as trustees, till Israel comes of age. We understand not the vast reaches of providence: but known unto God are all his works!

27. In Proverbs - The poets or other ingenious persons, of the Amorites or Canaanites, who made this following song of triumph over the vanquished Moabites: which is here brought in, as a proof that this was now Sihon's land, and as an evidence of the just judgment of God in spoiling the spoilers, and subduing those who insulted over their conquered enemies. Come into Heshbon - These are the words either of Sihon speaking to his people, or of the people exhorting one another to come and possess the city which they had taken. Of Sihon - That which once was the royal city of the king of Moab, but now is the city of Sihon.

28. A fire - The fury of war, which is fitly compared to fire. Out of Heshbon - That city which before was a refuge and defense to all the country, now is turned into a great annoyance. It hath consumed Ar -This may be understood not of the city Ar, but of the people or the country subject or belonging to that great and royal city. The lords of the high places - The princes or governors of the strong holds, which were frequently in high places, especially in that mountainous country, and which were in divers parts all along the river Arnon. So the Amorites triumphed over the vanquished Moabites. But the triumphing of the wicked is short!

29. People of Chemosh - The worshippers of Chemosh: so the God of the Moabites was called. He, that is, their God, hath delivered up his own people to his and their enemies; nor could he secure even those that had escaped the sword, but suffered them to be carried into captivity. The words of this and the following verse seem to be not a part of that triumphant song made, by some Amoritish poet, which seems to be concluded, ver. 28, but of the Israelites making their observation upon it. And here they scoff at the impotency not only of the Moabites, but of their God also, who could not save his people from the sword of Sihon and the Amorites.

30. Though you feeble Moabites, and your God too, could not resist Sihon, we Israelites, by the help of our God, have shot, with success and victory, at them, at Sihon and his Amorites. Heshbon - The royal city of Sihon, and by him lately repaired, Is perished - Is taken away from Sihon, and so is all his country, even as far as Dibon.

32. Jaazer - One of the cities of Moab formerly taken from them by Sihon, and now taken from

him by the Israelites.

33. Og - Who also was a king of the Amorites. And it may seem that Sihon and Og were the leaders or captains of two great colonies which came out of Canaan, and drove out the former inhabitants of these places. Bashan - A rich country, famous for its pastures and breed of cattle, and for its oaks.

XXII

Balak's fear of Israel, ver. 1-4. His message to Balaam, who refuses to come, ver. 5-14. On the second message he goes, ver. 15-21. He is rebuked by an angel, ver. 22-35. His interview with Balak, ver. 36-41.

1. The plains of Moab - Which still retained their ancient title, though they had been taken away from the Moabites by Sihon, and from him by the Israelites. By Jericho - That is, over against Jericho.

3. Sore afraid - As it was foretold both in general of all nations, Deut. ii, 25, and particularly concerning Moab, Exod. xv, 15.

4. The elders - Called the kings of Midian, chap. xxxi, 8, and princes of Midian, Josh. xiii, 21, who though divided into their kingdoms yet were now united upon the approach of the Israelites their common enemy, and being, as it seems, a potent and crafty people, and neighbours to the Moabites, these seek confederacy with them. We read of Midianites near Mount Sinai, Exod. ii, and iii, which seem to have been a colony of this people, that went out to seek new quarters, as the manner of those times was, but the body of that people were seated in those parts. Lick up - That is, consume and utterly destroy, in which sense the fire is said to lick up the water and sacrifices, 1 Kings xviii, 38. All that are round about us - All our people, who live in the country adjoining to each city, where the princes reside.

5. Balaam - Who is called a prophet, 2Pet ii, 16, because God was pleased to inspire and direct him to speak the following prophecies. Indeed many of the Jewish writers say, that Balaam had been a great prophet, who for the accomplishment of his predictions, and the answers of his prayers, had been looked upon justly as a man of great interest with God. However it is certain, that afterwards for his covetousness, God departed from him. Beor - Or, Bosor, 2Pet ii, 15, for he had two names, as many others had. Pethor - A city in Mesopotamia. By the river - By Euphrates, which is called the river, by way of eminency, and here the river of Balaam's land or country, to wit, of Mesopotamia.

6. Curse them for my sake and benefit; use thy utmost power, which thou hast with thy Gods, to blast and ruin them. We may smite them - Thou by thy imprecations, and I by my sword.

8. This night - The night was the time when God used to reveal his mind by dreams. The Lord - Hebrew. Jehovah, the true God, whom he here mentions, either for his own greater reputation, as if he consulted not with inferior spirits, but with the supreme God; or rather because this was Israel's God, and the only possible way of ruining them was by engaging their God against them: as the Roman and other Heathens, when they went to besiege any city, used enchantments to call forth that God under whose peculiar protection they were. Of Moab - And of Midian too.

9. What men are these - He asks this that Balaam by repeating the thing in God's presence might be convinced and ashamed of his sin and folly, in offering his service in such a business: and for a foundation to the following answer.

20. If the men come - On this condition he was to go.

22. Because he went - Because he went of his own accord, with the princes of Moab, and did not wait till they came to call him, which was the sign and condition of God's permission, but rather himself rose and called them. The apostle describes Balaam's sin here to be, that he ran greedily into an error for reward, Jude i, 11. For an adversary - To oppose, if not to kill him. His servants with him - The rest of the company being probably gone before them. For in those ancient times there was more of simplicity, and less of ceremony, and therefore it is not strange that Balaam came at some distance, after the rest, and attended only by his own servants.

28. Opened the mouth - Conferred upon her the power of speech and reasoning for that time.

29. Balaam said - Balaam was not much terrified with the ass's speaking, because perhaps he was accustomed to converse with evil spirits, who appeared to him and discoursed with him in the shape of such creatures. Perhaps he was so blinded by passion, that he did not consider the strangeness of the thing.

31. On his face - In token of reverence and submission.

32. Thy way is perverse - Springing from covetousness.

33. I had slain thee - I had slain thee alone, and not her, therefore her turning aside and falling down was wholly for thy benefit, not for her own, and thy anger against her was unjust and unreasonable.

35. Go with the men - I allow thee to go, upon the following terms.

36. In the utmost coast - Not far from the camp of the Israelites, whom he desired him to curse.

40. The princes - Whom the king had left to attend him.

41. The high places of Baal - Consecrated to the worship of Baal, that is, of Baal Peor, who was their Baal or God. The utmost part - That is, all that people, even to the utmost and remotest of them, as appears by comparing this with, chap. xxiii, 13. He hoped that the sight of such a numerous host ready to break in upon his country would stir up his passion.

XXIII

Balaam's first attempt to curse Israel, turned into a blessing, ver. 1-10. His second attempt with like success, ver. 11-24. The preparation for a third attempt, ver. 25-30.

1. Build seven altars - To the true God, otherwise he would not have mentioned it to God, as an argument why he should grant his requests, as he doth, ver. 4. And though Balak was averse from God and his worship, yet he would be easily overruled by Balaam, who doubtless told him that it was in vain to make an address to any other than the God of Israel, who alone was able either to bless or curse them as he pleased. Seven - This being the solemn and usual number in sacrifices.

3. Stand by thy burnt-offering - As in God's presence, as one that offers thyself as well as thy sacrifices to obtain his favour. I will go - To some solitary and convenient place, where I may prevail with God to appear to me. Sheweth me - Reveals to me, either by word or sign. An high place - Or, into the plain, as that word properly signifies.

7. His parable - That is, his oracular and prophetical speech; which he calls a parable, because of the weightiness of the matter, and the liveliness of the expressions which is usual in parables. Jacob - The posterity of Jacob.

9. The rocks - Upon which I now stand. I see him - I see the people, according to thy desire, ver. 41, but cannot improve that sight to the end for which thou didst design it, to curse them. The people shall dwell alone - This people are of a distinct kind from others, God's peculiar people, separated from all other nations, as in religion and laws, so also in divine protection; and therefore enchantments cannot have that power against them which they have against other persons and people.

10. The dust - The numberless people of Jacob or Israel, who according to God's promise, are now become as the dust of the earth. Of the righteous - Of this righteous and holy people. The sense is, they are not only happy above other nations in this life, and therefore in vain should I curse them, but they have this peculiar privilege, that they are happy after death: their happiness begins where the happiness of other people ends; and therefore I heartily wish that my soul may have its portion with theirs when I die. Was not God now again striving with him, not only for the sake of Israel, but of his own soul?

12. Must I not - Ought I not? Is it not my duty? Canst thou blame me for it?

13. Thou shalt not see them all - Perhaps he thought the sight of all them might discourage him, or as it did before, raise his fancy to an admiration of the multitude and felicity of the people.

15. While I meet the Lord - To consult him, and to receive an answer from him.

18. Rise up - This word implies the diligent attention required; rouse up thyself and carefully mind what I say.

19. That he should lie - Break his promises made to his people for their preservation and benediction. Repent - Change his counsels or purposes; unless he see iniquity in Jacob.

21. Iniquity - Not such as in the Canaanites: Such as he will punish with a curse, with utter destruction. The Lord is with him - He hath a favour for this people, and will defend and save them. The shout of a king - That is, such joyful and triumphant shouts as those wherewith a people congratulate the approach and presence of their King: when he appears among them upon some solemn occasion, or when he returns from battle with victory. This expression implies God's being their King and ruler, and their abundant security and confidence in him.

22. Out of Egypt - Namely, by a strong hand, and in spite of all their enemies, and therefore it is in vain to seek or hope to overcome them. He - Israel, whom God brought out of Egypt, such change of numbers being very common in the Hebrew language. The sense is, Israel is not now what he was in Egypt, a poor, weak, dispirited, unarmed people, but high and strong and invincible. An unicorn - The word may mean either a rhinoceros, or a strong and fierce kind of wild goat. But such a creature as an unicorn, as commonly painted, has no existence in nature.

23. Against Jacob - Nor against any that truly believe in Christ. What hath God wrought - How wonderful and glorious are those works which God is now about to do for Israel! These things will be a matter of discourse and admiration to all ages.

24. As a great Lion - As a lion rouseth up himself to fight, or to go out to the prey, so shall Israel stir up themselves to warlike attempts against their enemies. He shall not lie down - Not rest or cease from fighting and pursuing.

28. Peor - An high place called Beth-peor, Deut. iii, 29. That is, the house or temple of Peor, because there they worshipped Baal- peor.

XXIV

Balaam inspired by God, blesses Israel again, ver. 1-9. Answers Balak's reproof, ver. 10-13. Utters several prophecies, ver. 14-24 Goes home, ver. 25.

1. At other times - In former times. Toward the wilderness - Where Israel lay encamped, expecting what God of his own accord would suggest to him concerning this matter.

2. Came upon him - Inspired him to speak the following words.

3. Whose eyes are open - Hebrew. Who had his eyes shut, but now open. The eyes of his mind, which God had opened in a peculiar and prophetical manner, whence prophets are called Seers, 1 Sam. ix, 9. It implies that before he was blind and stupid, having eyes, but not seeing nor understanding.

4. The vision - So called properly, because he was awake when this was revealed to him: A trance - Or, extasy, fainting and falling upon the ground, as the prophets used to do.

6. As the valleys - Which often from a small beginning are spread forth far and wide. As gardens - Pleasant and fruitful and secured by a fence. As lign-aloes - An Arabian and Indian tree of a sweet smell, yielding shade and shelter both to man and beast; such is Israel, not only safe themselves, but yielding shelter to all that join themselves to them. Which the Lord hath planted - Nature, not art.

7. He shall pour the water - That is. God will abundantly water the valleys, gardens, and trees, which represent the Israelites; he will wonderfully bless his people, not only with outward blessings, of which a chief one in those parts was plenty of water, but also with higher gifts and graces, with his word and spirit, which are often signified by water, and at last with eternal life, the contemplation whereof made Balaam desire to die the death of the righteous. His seed shall be in many waters - This also may be literally understood of their seed, which shall be sown in waterish ground, and therefore bring forth a better increase. His King - That is, the King of Israel, or their chief governor. Than Agag - Than the King of the Amalekites, which King and people were famous and potent in that age, as may be guessed by their bold attempt upon so numerous a people as Israel. And it is probable, that Agag was the common name of the Amalekitish Kings, as Abimelech was of the Philistines, and Pharaoh of the Egyptians, and Caesar of the Romans.

9. He lay down - Having conquered his enemies the Canaanites, and their land, he shall quietly rest and settle himself there.

11. The Lord - Whose commands thou hast preferred before my desires and interest; and therefore seek thy recompence from him, and not from me.

17. I shall see him - Or, I have seen, or do see the star, and scepter as it here follows, that is, a great and eminent prince, which was to come out of Israel's loins, the Messiah, as both Jewish and Christian interpreters expound it, who most eminently and fully performed what is here said, in destroying the enemies of Israel or of God's church, here described under the names of the nearest and fiercest enemies of Israel: And to him alone agrees the foregoing verb properly, I shall see him, in my own person, as every eye shall see him, when he comes to judgment. Not now - Not yet, but after many ages. A star - A title often given to, princes and eminent persons, and particularly to the Messiah, Rev. ii, 28; xxii, 16. A scepter - That is, a scepter-bearer, a king or ruler, even that scepter mentioned Gen. xlix, 10. The corners - The borders, which are often used in scripture for the whole country to which they belong. Of Sheth - This seems to be the name of some then eminent, though now unknown place or prince in Moab; there being innumerable instances of such places or persons sometime famous, but now utterly lost as to all monuments and remembrances of them.

18. A possession - Which was also foretold, Gen. xxv, 23, and in part fulfilled, 2 Sam. viii, 14; 1 Chron. xviii, 13, but more fully by Christ, Amos ix, 12 Obad. i, 18, who shall subdue and possess all his enemies; here signified by the name of Edom, as Jacob or Israel, his brother, signifies all his church and people. Seir - A part and, mountain of Edom.

19. Out of Jacob - Out of Jacob's loins. He that shall have dominion - David, and especially Christ. Of the city - Or from or out of this city, that is, the cities, the singular number for the plural. He shall not subdue those Moabites and Edomites which meet him in the field, but he shall pursue them even to their strongest holds and cities.

20. He looked on Amalek - From the top of Pisgah, which was exceeding high, and gave him the prospect of part of all these kingdoms. The first - Hebrew. the firstfruits; so called either, because they were the first of all the neighbouring nations which were embodied together in one government: or, because he was the first who fought against Israel and was vanquished by them. That victory was an earnest and first-fruit of the large harvest of victories which the Israelites should in due time get over all their enemies. He shall perish forever - He began with God and with Israel, but God will end with him, and the firm purpose of God is, that he shall be utterly destroyed; so that Saul lost his kingdom for not executing this decree, and God's command pursuant thereunto.

21. The Kenites - The posterity or kindred of Jethro; not that part of them which dwelt among the Israelites, to whom the following words do not agree, but those of them who were mingled with the

Amalekites and Midianites. Thy nest - Thy dwelling-place, so called, either because it was in an high place, as nests commonly are: or in allusion to their name, for ken in Hebrew signifies a nest.

22. The Kenite - Hebrew. Kain, that is, the Kenite, so called, either by a transposition of letters, which is very usual in the Hebrew tongue; or from the name of some eminent place where they lived, or person from whom they were descended, though now the memory of them be utterly lost, as it hath fared with innumerable other places and persons, famous in their generations, mentioned in ancient Heathen writers. Shall be wasted - Shall be by degrees diminished by the incursions of divers enemies, till at last the Assyrian comes to compleat the work and carries them into captivity. For the Kenites who lived partly among the ten tribes, and partly with the two tribes, were carried captive with them, part by Salmaneser, the King of Assyria, and part by Nebuchadnezzar, who also is called an Assyrian, Ezra vi, 22 Isaiah lii, 4.

23. Who shall live - How calamitous and miserable will the state of the world be, when the Assyrian, and after him the Chaldean, shall over-turn all these parts of the world? Who will be able to keep his heart from fainting under such grievous pressures? Nay, how few will escape the destroying sword?

24. Chittim - A place or people so called from Chittim the son of Javan, Gen. x, 4, whose posterity were very numerous, and were first seated in the lesser Asia, and from thence sent forth colonies into the islands of the Aegean sea, and into Cyprus, afterwards into Macedonia and other parts of Greece, and then into Italy. Whence it comes to pass that by this name is understood sometimes Macedonia, as 1 Maccabees. i. 1, and 1 Maccabees. viii. 5, sometimes Italy, as Dan. xi, 29, 30, and sometimes both, as in this place: for he speaks here of the scourge that God hath appointed for the Assyrian after he had done God's work in punishing of his people and the bordering nations. Now although the Assyrian and Chaldean empire was subdued by the Medes and Persians, yet the chief afflictions of that people came from two hands, both beyond the sea and brought to them by ships; first from the Grecians under Alexander and his successors, by whom that people were grievously oppressed and wasted; then from the Romans, who subdued all the Grecian empire, one great part whereof were the Assyrians largely so called. Eber - The posterity of Eber, the Hebrew, who were the chief and flower of Eber's children. He also - Not the Hebrew: they shall have a better end; all Israel shall be saved; but the afflicter or scourge of Ashur and Eber, namely, the Grecian and Roman empire. Thus Balaam, instead of cursing the church, curses Amalek, the first, and Rome, the last enemy of it!

25. To his place - To Mesopotamia; tho' afterwards he returned to the Midianites, and gave them that devilish counsel which was put in practice, chap. xxv, 16-18.

XXV

The sin of Israel, ver. 1-3. Their punishment, ver. 4, 5. The zeal of Phinehas, with the promise annext to it, ver. 6-15. The command to slay the Midianites, ver. 16-18.

1. Shittim - And this was their last station, from whence they passed immediately into Canaan. This is noted as a great aggravation of their sin, that they committed it, when God was going to put them into the possession of their long-expected land. The people - Many of them. Whoredom - Either because they prostituted themselves to them upon condition of worshipping their God: or because their filthy God was worshipped by such filthy acts, as Priapus and Venus were. The daughters of Moab - And of Midian too; for both these people being confederated in this wicked design, the one is put for the other, and the daughters of Moab may be named, either because they began the transgression, or because they were the chief persons, possibly, the relations or courtiers of Balak.

2. They - The Moabites being now neighbours to the Israelites, and finding themselves unable to effect their design by war and witchcraft, fell another way to work, by contracting familiarity with them, and, perceiving their evil inclinations, they, that is, their daughters, invited them. Unto the sacrifices - Unto the feasts which were made of their parts of the sacrifices, after the manner of the Jews and Gentiles too, the participation whereof, was reckoned a participation in the worship of that God to whom the sacrifices were offered. Of their gods - Of their God, Baal-peor, the plural Elohim being here used, as commonly it is, for one God.

3. Joined himself - The word implies a forsaking God to whom they were joined and a turning to, and strict conjunction with, this false God. Baal-peor - Called Baal, by the name common to many false Gods, and especially to those that represented any of the heavenly bodies, and Peor, either from the hill Peor, where he was worshipped, chap. xxiii, 28, rather from a verb signifying to open and uncover, because of the obscene posture in which the idol was set, as Priapus was: or because of the filthiness which was exercised in his worship.

4. Take all the heads - Take, that is, apprehend, all the heads, that is, the chief, of the people, such as were chief in this transgression, and in place and power, who are singled out to this exemplary punishment for their concurrence with others in this wickedness, which was more odious and

mischievous in them. Hang them up before the Lord - To the vindication of God's honour and justice. Against the sun - Publickly, as their sin was publick and scandalous, and speedily, before the sun go down.

5. Everyone his men - Those under his charge, for as these seventy were chosen to assist Moses in the government, so doubtless the care and management of the people was distributed among them by just and equal proportions.

6. One came - This was done, when Moses had given the charge to the Judges, and, as it may seem, before the execution of it; otherwise it is probable he would not have been so foolish to have run upon certain ruin, when the examples were frequent before his eyes. To his brethren -- into the camp of the Israelites. In the sight of Moses - An argument of intolerable impudence and contempt of God and of Moses. Weeping - Bewailing the wickedness of the people, and the dreadful judgments of God, and imploring God's mercy and favour.

8. Thrust them thro' - Phineas was himself a man in great authority, and did this after the command given by Moses to the rulers to slay these transgressors, and in the very sight, and no doubt by the consent of Moses himself, and also by the special direction of God's spirit.

9. Twenty four thousand - St. Paul says twenty three thousand, 1 Cor. x, 8. The odd thousand here added were slain by the Judges according to the order of Moses, the rest by the immediate hand of God, but both sorts died of the plague, the word being used, as often it is, for the sword, or hand, or stroke of God.

12. My covenant of peace - That is, the covenant of an everlasting priesthood, as it is expounded, ver. 13, which is called a covenant of peace, partly with respect to the happy effect of this heroical action of his, whereby he made peace between God and his people; and partly with regard to the principal end of the priestly office, which was constantly to do that which Phinehas now did, even to meditate between God and men, to obtain and preserve his own and Israel's peace and reconciliation with God, by offering up sacrifices and incense, and prayers, to God on their behalf, as also by turning them away from iniquity, which is the only peace- breaker, and by teaching and pressing the observation of that law, which is the only bond of their peace.

13. At everlasting priesthood - To continue as long as the law and common-wealth of the Jews did. But this promise was conditional, and therefore might be made void, by the miscarriages of Phinehas's sons, as it seems it was, and thereupon a like promise was made to Eli of the line of Ithamar, that he and his should walk before the Lord, namely, in the office of high- priest, forever, which also for his and their sins was made void, 1 Sam. ii, 30. And the the priesthood returned to Phinehas's line in the time of Solomon, 1 Kings ii, 26, 27, 34.

17. The Midianites - And why not the Moabites. It is probable the Midianites were most guilty, as in persuading Balak to send for Balaam, chap. xxii, 4, 7. So in the reception of Balaam after Balak had dismissed him, chap. xxxi, 8, and in farther consultation with him, and in contriving the means for the executing of this wicked plot.

18. With their wiles - For under pretense of kindred and friendship and leagues, which they offered to them, instead of that war which the Israelites expected, they sought only an opportunity to insinuate themselves into their familiarity, and execute their hellish plot of bringing that curse upon the Israelites, which they had in vain attempted to bring another way.

XXVI

Orders for numbering the people, ver. 1-4. Their families and number, ver. 5-51. Directions for dividing the land between them, ver. 52-55. The families and number of the Levites, ver. 56- 62. Notice taken of the death of them that were first numbered, ver. 62-65.

2. Take the sum - They were numbered twice before, Exod. xxx, 11, 12 chap. i, 1, 2. Now they are numbered a third time, to demonstrate the faithfulness of God, both in cutting all those off whom he had threatened to cut off, chap. xiv, 29, and in a stupendous increase of the people according to his promise, notwithstanding all their sins, and the sweeping judgments inflicted upon them; and to prepare the way for the equal division of the land, which they were now going to possess.

7. Families - The chief houses, which were subdivided into divers lesser families. Forty three thousand seven hundred and thirty - Whereas in their last numbering they were forty six thousand five hundred; for Korah's conspiracy, as well as other provocations of theirs, had cut off many of them.

10. With Korah - According to this translation Korah was not consumed by fire with his two hundred and fifty men, but swallowed up by the earth. But others rather think he was devoured by the fire, and render these words, and the things of Korah, or belonging to Korah, namely, his tent and goods, and family, children excepted, as here follows. A sign - God made them a monument or example, to warn others not to rebel against God, or magistracy, nor to usurp the priestly office.

11. Died not - God being pleased to spare them, because they disowned their father's fact, and

separated themselves both from his tent and company. Hence the sons of Korah are mentioned, 1 Chron. vi, 22, 38, and often in the book of Psalms.

12. Jachin - Called also Jarib, 1 Chron. iv, 24. And such names might be either added or changed upon some special occasion not recorded in scripture.

14. Twenty two thousand and two hundred - No tribe decreased so much as Simeon's. From fifty nine thousand and three hundred it sunk to twenty two thousand and two hundred, little more than a third part of what it was. One whole family of that tribe, (Ohad mentioned Exod. vi, 15) was extinct in the wilderness. Some think most of the twenty four thousand, cut off by the plague for the iniquity of Peor, were of that tribe. For Zimri, a ring-leader in that iniquity, was a prince of that tribe. Simeon is not mentioned in Moses's blessing, Deut. xxxiii, 1-29. And the lot of that tribe in Canaan was inconsiderable, only a canton out of Judah's lot, Josh. xix, 9.

18. Children of Gad - Fewer by above five thousand than there were in their last numbering.

22. The families of Judah - About two thousand more than they were, chap. i, 27, whereas the foregoing tribes were all diminished.

34. Fifty two thousand and seven hundred - Whereas they were but thirty two thousand and two hundred, in chap. i, 35. So they are now increased above twenty thousand, according to that prophecy, Gen. xlix, 22.

38. The sons of Benjamin - Who were ten, Gen. xlvi, 21, whereof only five are here mentioned, the rest probably, together with their families, being extinct.

43. Threescore and four thousand and four hundred - All from one son and family, whereas of Benjamin who had ten sons, and five families, there were only forty five thousand and six hundred, to shew that the increase of families depends singly upon God's blessing and good pleasure.

51. These were the numbered - Very nigh as many as there were before, chap. i, 46. So wisely and marvelously did God at the same time manifest his justice in cutting off so vast a number; his mercy in giving such a speedy and numerous supply; and his truth in both.

53. The land shall be divided - The land was divided into nine parts and an half, respect being had in such division to the goodness as well as to the largeness of the several portions, and the lot gave each tribe their part. Of names - Of persons, the share of each tribe was divided amongst the several families, to some more, to some less, according to the number of the persons of each family. And withal, if one of the portions proved too large or too little for the families and persons of that tribe, they might give part of their portion to another tribe, (as Simeon and Daniel had part of Judah's share) or take away a part from the portion belonging to another tribe.

55. By lot - For the tribes, not for the several families; for the distribution of it to them was left to the rulers wisdom according to the rule now given.

56. Many and few - That share, which shall by lot fall to each tribe, shall be distributed to the several families and persons in such proportions as their numbers shall require.

65. Not left a man - Only of the Levites, who being not guilty of that sin did not partake of their judgment.

XXVII

The case of Zelophehad's daughters determined, ver. 1-11. Notice given to Moses of his death, ver. 12-14. His successor provided. ver. 15-23.

2. By the door of the tabernacle - Nigh unto which it seems was the place where Moses and the chief rulers assembled for the administration of publick affairs, which also was very convenient, because they had frequent occasion of recourse to God for his direction.

3. In his own sin - For his own personal sins. It was a truth, and that believed by the Jews that death was a punishment for mens own sins.

4. Be done away - As it will be, if it be not preserved by an inheritance given to us in his name and for his sake. Hence some gather, that the first son of each of these heiresses was called by their father's name, by virtue of that law, Deut. xxv, 6, whereby the brother's first son was to bear the name of his elder brother, whose widow he married. Give us a possession - In the land of Canaan upon the division of it, which though not yet conquered, they concluded would certainly be so, and thereby gave glory to God.

10. No brethren -- nor sisters, as appears from ver. 8.

11. A statute of judgment - A statute or rule, by which the magistrates shall give judgment in such cases.

12. Abarim - The whole tract of mountains was called Abarim, whereof one of the highest was called Nebo, and the top of that Pisgah.

13. Thou shalt be gathered unto thy people - Moses must die: but death does not cut him off; it only gathers him to his people, brings him to rest with the holy patriarchs that were gone before him.

Abraham, Isaac and Jacob were his people, the people of his choice, and to them death gathered him.

15. And Moses spake unto the Lord - Concerning his successor. We should concern ourselves both in our prayers and in our endeavours for the rising generation, that God's kingdom may be advanced among men, when we are in our graves.

16. The Lord of the spirits of all flesh - God of all men: the searcher of spirits, that knowest who is fit for this great employment; the father and giver and governor of spirits, who canst raise and suit the spirits of men to the highest and hardest works.

17. Go out before them - That is, who may wisely conduct them in all their affairs, both when they go forth to war, or upon other occasions, and when they return home and live in peace. A metaphor from shepherds, who in those places used not to go behind their sheep, as ours now do, but before them, and to lead them forth to their pasture, and in due time to lead them home again.

18. The spirit - The spirit of government, of wisdom, and of the fear of the Lord. Lay thy hand - By which ceremony Moses did both design the person and confer the power, and by his prayers, which accompanied that rite, obtain from God all the spiritual gifts and graces necessary for his future employment.

19. Before all the congregation - That they may be witnesses of the whole action, and may acknowledge him for their supreme ruler. Give him charge - Thou shalt give him counsels and instructions for the right management of that great trust.

20. Put some of thine honour - Thou shalt not now use him as a servant, but as a brother and thy partner in the government, that the people being used to obey him while Moses lived, might do it afterward the more cheerfully.

21. Who shall ask counsel for him - When he requires him to do so, and in important and difficult matters. Of Urim - Urim is put for both Urim and Thummim. Before the Lord - Ordinarily in the tabernacle near the second veil setting his face to the ark. At his word - The word of the Lord, delivered to him by the high priest.

22. And Moses did as the Lord commanded him - It had been little to resign his honour to a son of his own. But with his own hands, first to ordain Eleazar high-priest, and now Joshua chief ruler, while his own children had no preferment at all, but were left in the rank of common Levites: this was more to his glory than the highest advancement of his family could have been. This shews him to have had a principle which raised him above all other lawgivers, who always took care to establish their families in some share of the greatness themselves possessed.

XXVIII

Laws concerning the daily, ver. 1-8. Weekly, ver. 9-10. Monthly, ver. 11-15. Yearly sacrifices, ver. 16-31.

2. Command the children of Israel - God here repeats some of the former laws about sacrifices, not without great reason, partly because they had been generally discontinued for thirty eight years together; partly because the generation to which the former laws had been given about these things was wholly dead, and it was fit the new generation should be instructed about them, as their parents were; partly to renew their testimonies of God's grace and mercy, notwithstanding their frequent forfeitures thereof by their rebellion: and principally because they were now ready to enter into that land, in which they were obliged to put these things in practice.

7. In the holy place - Upon the altar of burnt offerings, which was in the court of the priests, nigh to the entrance into the sanctuary.

17. The feast - Namely, of unleavened bread.

23. In the morning - And that in the evening too, as is evident from other scriptures; but the morning-sacrifice alone is mentioned, because the celebration of the feast began with it, and principally because this alone was doubtful, whether this might not be omitted when so many other sacrifices were offered in that morning, whereas there was no question but the evening sacrifice should be offered, when there were none other to be offered.

26. The day of the first fruits - In the feast of pentecost, Acts ii, 1. Your weeks - The seven weeks which you are to number from the passover.

XXIX

Offerings to be made in the seventh month,
1. At the feast of trumpets, ver. 1-6.
2. In the day of atonement, ver. 7-11.
3. At the feast of tabernacles, ver. 12-40.

6. Of the month - Belonging to every new moon.
7. Afflict your souls - Yourselves, by fasting and abstinence from all delightful things, and by compunction for your sins, and the judgments of God, either deserved by you or inflicted upon you.
12. Seven days - Not by abstaining so long from all servile work, but by offering extraordinary sacrifices each day. This was the Feast of Tabernacles. And all the days of their dwelling in booths, they must offer sacrifices. While we are in these tabernacles, 'tis our interest as well as duty, to keep up our communion with God. Nor will the unsettledness of our outward condition, excuse our neglect of God's worship.

XXX

A general rule, vows must be performed, ver. 1-3. Particular exceptions, of the vow of a daughter, not allowed by the father, ver. 3-5. And the vow of a wife, not allowed by her husband, 6-16.

5. In the days - Speedily, or without delay, allowing only convenient time for deliberation. And it is hereby intimated, that the day or time he had for disallowing her vow, was not to be reckoned from her vowing, but from his knowledge of her vow. The Lord shall forgive - Or, will forgive her not performing it. But this should be understood only of vows which could not be performed without invading the father's right; for if one should vow to forbear such, or such a sin, and all occasions or means leading to it, and to perform such, or such duties, when he had opportunity, no father can discharge him from such vows. If this law does not extend to children's marrying without the parent's consent, so far as to put it in the power of the parent, to disannul the marriage, (which some think it does) yet certainly it proves the sinfulness of such marriages, and obliges those children to repent and humble themselves before God and their parents.
9. Widow or divorced - Though she be in her father's house, whither such persons often returned.
10. If she vowed - If she that now a widow, or divorced, made that vow while her husband lived with her; as suppose she then vowed, that if she was a widow, she would give such a proportion of her estate to pious or charitable uses, of which vow she might repent when she came to be a widow, and might believe or repented she was free from it, because that vow was made in her husband's lifetime; this is granted, in case her husband then disallowed it; but denied, in case by silence, or otherwise he consented to it.
13. To afflict her soul - Herself by fasting, by watching, or the like. And these words are added to shew that the husband had this power not only in those vows which concerned himself or his estate, but also in those which might seem only to concern her own person, or body, and the reason is, because the wife's person or body being the husband's right; she might not do any thing to the injury of her body without his consent.
15. After he hath heard - And approved them by his silence from day to day, if after that time he shall hinder it, which he ought not to do: her non-performance of her vow shall be imputed to him, not to her.

XXXI

God commands Moses to avenge Israel of the Midianites, ver. 1, 2. Moses sends them to the war, ver. 3-6. They slay the Midianites, ver. 7-12. He reproves them for sparing the women, ver. 13-18. Directions for purifying themselves, ver. 19-24. The distribution of the spirit, ver. 25-47. The free-will-offering of the officers, ver. 48-54.

3. Avenge ye the Lord - For the affront which they offered to God, by their own idolatry and lewdness, and by seducing God's people into rebellion against him. God's great care was to avenge the Israelites, ver. 2, and Moses's chief desire was to avenge God rather than himself or the people.
5. Twelve thousand - God would send no more, though it is apparent the Midianites were numerous and strong, because he would exercise their trust in him, and give them an earnest of their Canaanitish conquests.
6. Them and Phinehas - Who had the charge not of the army, as general, (an office never committed to a priest in all the Old Testament) but of the holy instruments, and was sent to encourage,

and quicken, them in their enterprize. The holy instruments - The holy breast-plate, wherein was the Urim and Thummim, which was easily carried, and very useful in war upon many emergent occasions.

7. All the males - Namely all who lived in those parts, for colonies of them, were sent forth to remoter places, which therefore had no hand either in their former sin, or in this present ruling. And herein they did according to God's own order concerning such people, Deut. xx, 13, only their fault was, that they did not consider the special reason which they had to involve the women in the destruction.

13. Without the camp - Partly to put respect upon them, and congratulate with them for their happy success; and partly to prevent the pollution of the camp by the untimely entrance of the warriors into it.

17. The little ones - Which they were forbidden to do to other people, Deut. xx, 14, except the Canaanites, to whom this people had equaled themselves by their horrid crimes, and therefore it is not strange, nor unjust, that God, the supreme Lord of all mens lives, who as he gives them, so may take them away when he pleaseth, did equal them in the punishment. Every woman -Partly for punishment, because the guilt was general, and though some of them only did prostitute themselves to the Israelites, yet the rest made themselves accessary by their consent or approbation; and partly, for prevention of the like mischief from such an adulterous generation.

20. Your raiment - Namely, your spoil and prey. All work - All which had contracted some ceremonial uncleanness either from the dead bodies which wore them, or the tents or houses where they were, in which such dead bodies lay, or from the touch of the Israelitish soldiers, who were legally defiled by the slaughters they made.

27. Two parts - The congregation hath some share, because the warriors went in the name of all, and because all having been injured by the Midianites, all were to have some share in the reparations: but the warriors who were but 12000, have a far greater share than their brethren, because they underwent greater pains and dangers.

29. An heave-offering - In thankfulness to God for their preservation and good success.

30. One of fifty - Whereas the former part was one of five hundred; the reason of the difference is, partly, because this was taken out of the peoples portion, whose hazards being less than the others, their gains also in all reason were to be less: partly because this was to be distributed into more hands, the Levites being now numerous, whereas the priests were but few.

50. An atonement - For their error noted, ver. 14, 15, 16, and withal for a memorial, or by way of gratitude for such a stupendous assistance and deliverance. We should never take any thing to ourselves in war or trade, of which we cannot in faith consecrate a part to God, who hates robbery for burnt-offerings. But when God has remarkably preserved and succeeded us, he expects we should make some particular return of gratitude to him.

XXXII

The request of Reuben and Gad for an inheritance on this side Jordan, ver. 1-5. Moses's misconstruction of it, ver. 6-15. Their explication of it, ver. 16-19. The grant of their petition, ver. 20-42.

1. Jazer - A city and country of the Amorites; Gilead - A mountainous country, famous for pasturage

6. Ye sit here - In ease and peace, while your brethren are engaged in a bloody war.

12. The Kenezite - So called from Kenaz, his grand-father.

15. All this people - Who being moved by your counsel and example, will refuse to go over Jordan.

17. We ourselves - Either all, or as many as shall be thought necessary, leaving only so many as may be necessary to provide for the sustenance and defense of our wives and children here.

20. Before the Lord - Before the ark, which was the token of God's presence. He alludes either to the order of the tribes in their march, whereby Reuben and Gad marched immediately before the ark, or to the manner of their passage over Jordan, wherein the ark went first into Jordan, and stood there while all the tribes marched over Jordan by and before it, and these amongst the rest, as is expressly noted in these very words, that they passed over before the Lord, Josh. iv, 13.

22. Before the Lord - By his presence and gracious and powerful assistance.

23. Your sin - The punishment of your sin. Sin will certainly find out the sinner sooner or later. It concerns us therefore to find our sins out, that we may repent of them and forsake them, lest our sins find us out, to our confusion and destruction.

30. They shall have possession - They shall forfeit their possessions in Gilead, and be constrained to go over Jordan, and to seek possessions there among their brethren.

31. As the Lord hath said - Either at this time by thy mouth: or formerly, where he commanded us, as well as our brethren to go into Canaan and possess it.

34. Built - Repaired and fortified. For they neither had need nor leisure as yet to do more, the old cities not being burnt and ruined, as divers in Canaan were.

38. Their names changed - Either because conquerers of places used to do so: or because the names of other Gods (which Nebo and Baal-meon unquestionably were) were not to be mentioned, Exod. xxiii, 13.

40. Machir - Not to Machir himself, who doubtless was long since dead, but the family or posterity of Machir.

42. Nobah - Who, though not else where named, was doubtless an eminent person of the tribe of Manasseh. 'Tis observable, that these tribes, as they were placed before the other tribes, so they were displaced before them. They were carried captive by the king of Assyria, some years before the other tribes. Such a proportion does providence frequently observe, in balancing prosperity and adversity.

XXXIII

An account of the marches and encampments of the Israelites, from Egypt to Canaan, ver. 1-49. A strict command to drive out all the Canaanites.

2. And Moses wrote their goings out - When they set out, God ordered him to keep a journal of all the remarkable occurrences in the way, that it might be a satisfaction to himself and an instruction to others. It may be of use to Christians, to preserve an account of the providences of God concerning them, the constant series of mercies they have experienced, and especially those turns which have made some days of their lives more remarkable.

4. On their gods - Their false gods, namely those beasts which the brutish Egyptians worshipped as gods, which were killed with the rest, for the first-born both of men and beasts were then killed. Probably their images likewise were thrown down, as Dagon afterward before the ark.

10. By the Red-sea - By another part of that sea which they passed over.

48. Shittim - The place where the people sinned in the matter of Peor, is here called Abel-Shittim - Abel signifies mourning; and probably this place was so called, from the mourning of Israel for that sin, and the heavy punishment inflicted on the sinners.

52. Drive out - Not by banishing, but by destroying them. Pictures - Which seem to have been stones curiously engraven, and set up for worship. High Places - Chapels, altars, groves, or other means of worship there set up.

XXXIV

Directions concerning the bounds of Canaan, ver. 1-15. Concerning the division of it, ver. 16-29.

2. Coasts - Or limits or bounds, to wit, of the land beyond Jordan. Which are here particularly described,

1. to direct and bound them in their wars and conquests, that they might not seek the enlargement of their empire, after the manner of other nations, but be contented with their own portion.

2. To encourage them in their attempt upon Canaan, and assure them of their success. There was a much larger possession promised them, if they were obedient, even to the river Euphrates. But this, which is properly Canaan, lay in a very little compass. 'Tis but about an hundred and fifty miles in length, and about fifty in breadth. This was that little spot of ground, in which alone for many ages God was known! But its littleness was abundantly compensated by its fruitfulness: otherwise it could not have sustained so numerous a nation. See, how little a share of the world God often gives to his own people! But they that have their portion in heaven, can be content with a small pittance of this earth.

3. Your fourth quarter - Which is here described from east to west by divers windings and turnings, by reason of the mountains and rivers. The salt sea - So called from the salt and sulphurous taste of its waters. Eastward - That is, at the eastern part of that sea, where the eastern and southern borders meet.

4. From the south - Or, on the south, that is, proceeding onward towards the south. Azmon - Which is at the west-end of the mount of Edom.

5. The river of Egypt - Called Sihor, Josh. xiii, 3, which divided Egypt from Canaan. The sea - The midland sea, called the sea emphatically, whereas the other seas, as they are called, are indeed but lakes.

6. The great sea - This midland sea from the south to the north, so far as it runs parallel with mount Libanus.

7. Hor - Not that Hor where Aaron died, which was southward, and bordering upon Edom, but another mountain, and, as it is conceived, the mountain of Libanus, which is elsewhere mentioned as the northern border of the land, and which, in regard of divers parts, or by divers people, is called by divers

names, and here Hor, which signifies a mountain, by way of eminency.

17. Eleazar - Who was to act in God's name, to cast lots, to prevent contentions, to consult with God in cases of difficulty, to transact the whole business in a solemn and religious manner.

19. Judah - The order of the tribes is here different from that, chap. i, 7, 26, and in other places, being conformed to the order of their several inheritances, which afterwards fell to them by lots. Which is an evident demonstration of the infinite wisdom of God's providence, and of his peculiar care over his people.

XXXV

Forty eight cities assigned to the Levites, of which six were cities of refuge, ver. 1-15. In what cases it was not allowed to flee to these, ver. 16-21. In what cases it was allowed, ver. 22- 24. Laws concerning them, ver. 25-34.

3. For the cattle - For pasturage for their cattle: where they might not build houses, nor plant gardens, orchards or vineyards, no nor sow corn, for which they were abundantly provided out of the first-fruits. And these suburbs did not belong to the Levites in common, but were distributed to them in convenient proportions.

4. A thousand cubits - In the next verse it is two thousand. But this verse and the next do not speak to the same thing; this speaks of the space from whence the suburbs shall be measured, the next speaks of the space unto which that measure shall be extended; and the words may very well be read thus. And the suburbs - Shall be from the wall of the city and from without it, or, from the outward parts of it, even from a thousand cubits round about. Which are mentioned not as the thing measured, but as the space from which the measuring line should begin. And then it follows, ver. 5. And ye shall measure from without the city, (not from the wall of the city, as said before ver. 4, but from without it, that is, from the said outward space of a thousand cubits without the wall of the city round about) on the east side two thousand cubits. So in truth there were three thousand cubits from the wall of the city, whereof one thousand probably were for out-houses, stalls for cattle, gardens, vineyards and olive-yards, and the other two thousand for pasture, which are therefore called the field of the suburbs, Lev. xxv, 34, by way of distinction from the suburbs themselves, which consist of the first thousand cubits from the wall of the city.

6. Cities for refuge - Or, of escape for manslayers: And these cities are assigned among the Levites, partly because they might be presumed to be the most proper and impartial Judges between man-slayers, and wilful murderers; partly because their presence and authority would more effectually bridle the passions of the avenger of blood who might pursue him thither; and perhaps to signify, that it is only in Christ (whom the Levitical priests represented) that sinners find refuge and safety from the destroyer.

11. Unawares - Not wilfully, designedly or maliciously, but through mistake or indiscretion.

12. From the avenger - Hebrew. from the redeemer, or, from the next kinsman, to whom by the law belonged the right of redemption of the lands of; and vindication of the injury done to, the person deceased. Die not - Be not killed by the avenger meeting him in some other place. Before the congregation - Before the Judges or elders who were appointed in every city for the decision of criminal causes, who were to examine, and that publickly before the people, whether the murder was wilful or casual.

14. On this side Jordan - Because that land was as long as Canaan, though not so broad, and besides these might be convenient for many of them that lived in Canaan.

16. If he smite him - Wittingly and wilfully, though not with premeditated malice. He shall be put to death - Yea though he were fled into the city of refuge.

19. He shall slay him - Either by himself, as the following words shew; so it is a permission, that he may do it without offense to God or danger to himself: or by the magistrate, from whom he shall demand justice: so it is a command.

24. Then - If the man-slayer flee to to the city of refuge.

26. He shall abide in it - Be confined to it, partly to shew the hatefulness of murder in God's account by so severe a punishment, inflicted upon the very appearance of it, and partly for the security of the man-slayer, lest the presence of such a person, and his conversation among the kindred of the deceased, might occasion reproach and blood-shed. The death of the high- priest - Perhaps to shew that the death of Christ (the true High- priest, whom the others represented) is the only means whereby sins are pardoned and sinners set at liberty.

27. Not guilty - Not liable to punishment from men, though not free of guilt before God. This God ordained to oblige the man- slayer to abide in his city of refuge.

XXXVI

An inconvenience if heiresses should marry into another tribe, ver. 1-4. An appointment that they should marry in their own tribe, ver. 5-9. Zelophehad's daughters marry their cousins, ver. 10-12. The conclusion, ver.13.

2. *Our brother* - Our kinsman.

6. *To the family* - They seem hereby to be confined not only to the same tribe, but also to the family of their tribe, as appears from the reason of the law, for God would have the inheritance of families as well as tribes kept entire and unmixed.

8. *The inheritance of his fathers* - This law was not general to forbid every woman to marry into another tribe, as may be reasonably concluded from the practice of so many patriarchs, kings, priests, and other holy men, who have married women of other tribes, yea sometimes of other nations, but restrained to heiresses, or such as were likely to be so. But if they had brethren, they were free to marry into any tribe, yet so that, if their brethren died, the inheritance went from them to the next a-kin of their father's tribe and family. And the principal reason why God was solicitous to preserve tribes and families unmixed was, that the tribe and family too, out of which the Messiah was to come, and by which he should be known, might be evident and unquestionable.

NOTES ON THE FIFTH BOOK OF MOSES CALLED DEUTERONOMY

THE Greek interpreters call this book Deuteronomy, that is, The second law, or a second edition of the law, because it is a repetition of many of the laws, (as well as much of the history contained in the three foregoing books. They to whom the first law was given were all dead, and a new generation sprung up, to whom God would have it repeated by Moses himself, that it might make the deeper impression upon them. It begins with a brief rehearsal of the most remarkable events, that had befallen them since they came from mount Sinai. In the fourth chapter begins a pathetic exhortation to obedience: From the 12th to the 27th are repeated many particular laws, inforced in the 27th and 28th with promises and threatnings, which are formed into a covenant, chap. 29, 30. Care is taken in chap. 31. to perpetuate the remembrance of these things among them, particularly by a song, chap. 32 concluded with a blessing, chap. 33. All this was delivered by Moses to Israel, in the last month of his life. See how busy this great and good Man was to do good, when he knew his time was short.

I

The preface, fixing the time and place, ver. 1-5. Israel commanded to march, ver. 6-8. Judges provided, ver. 9-1; 3. They come to Kadesh-barnea, ver. 19-21. Spies sent, their report, the people's murmuring, ver. 22-33. The sentence passed upon them, ver. 34-40. They are smitten by the Amorites, and remain at Kadesh, ver. 41-46.

1. All Israel - Namely, by the heads or elders of the several tribes, who were to communicate these discourses to all the people. In the wilderness - In the plain of Moab, as may appear by comparing this with ver. 5, and Num. xxii, 1, and chap. xxxiv, 8. The word Suph here used does not signify the Red-Sea, which is commonly called jam-suph, and which was at too great a distance, but some oiher place now unknown to us, (as also most of the following places are) so called from the reeds or flags, or rushes (which that word signifies) that grew in or near it. Paran - Not that Num. x, 12, which there and elsewhere is called the Wilderness of Paran, and which was too remote, but some other place called by the same name. Laban, Hazeroth, and Dizahab - These places seem to be the several bounds, not of the whole country of Moab, but of the plain of Moab, where Moses now was.
2. There are eleven days journey - This is added to shew that the reason why the Israelites, in so many years were advanced no farther from Horeb, than to these plains, was not the distance of the places but because of their rebellions. Kadesh-barnea - Which was not far from the borders of Canaan.
3. The eleventh month - Which was but a little before his death. All that the Lord had given him in commandment - Which shews not only that what he now delivered was in substance the same with what had formerly been commanded, but that God now commanded him to repeat it. He gave this rehearsal and exhortation by divine direction: God appointed him to leave this legacy to the church.
4. Og - His palace or mansion-house was at Astaroth, and he was slain at Edrei.
7. To the mount of the Amorites - That is, to the mountainous country where the Amorites dwelt, which is opposed to the plain, where others of them dwelt. And this is the first mentioned, because it was in the borders of the land.
8. Before you - Hebrew. Before your faces; it is open to your view, and to your possession; there is no impediment in the way.
9. At that time - That is, about that time, namely, a little before their coming to Horeb.
12. Your burden - The trouble of ruling and managing so perverse a people. Your strife - Your contentions among yourselves, for the determnination whereof the elders were appointed.
15. Officers - Inferior officers, that were to attend upon the superior magistrates, and to execute their decrees.
16. The stranger - That converseth or dealeth with himn. To Such God would have justice equally adtninistred as to his own people, partly for the honour of religion, and partly for the interest which every man hath in matters of common right.
17. Respect persons - Hebrew. Not know, or acknowledge faces, that is, not give sentence

according to the outward qualities of the person, as he is poor or rich, your friend or enemy, but purely according to the merit of the cause. For which reason some of the Grecian law-givers ordered that the Judges should give sentence in the dark where they could not see mens faces. The judgment is God's - It is passed in the name of God, and by commission from him, by you as representing his person, and doing his work; who therefore will defend you therein against all your enemies, amid to whom you must give an exact account.

18. All the things which ye shall do - I delivered unto you, and especially unto your Judges, all the laws, statutes, and judgments revealed unto me by the Lord in Horeb.

24. Eshcol - That is, of grapes, so called from the goodly cluster of grapes which they brought from thence.

28. Greater - In number and strength and valour.

31. Bare thee - Or, carried thee, as a father carries his weak and tender child in his arms, through difficulties and dangers, gently leading you according as you are able to go, and sustaining you by his power and goodness.

32. Ye did not believe the Lord - So they could not enter in, because of unbelief. It was not any other sin shut them out of Canaan, but their disbelief of that promise, which was typical of gospel grace: to signify that no sin will ruin us but unbelief, which is a sin against the remedy; and therefore without remedy.

33. Your words - That is to say, your murmurings, your unthankful, impatient, distrustful and rebellious speeches.

36. Save Caleb - Under whom Josh. is comprehended, though not here expressed, because he was not now to be one of the people, but to be set over them as a chief governor.

37. For your sakes - Upon occasion of your wickedness and perverseness, by which you provoked me to speak unadvisedly.

38. Who standeth - Who is now thy servant.

44. As bees - As bees which being provoked come out of their hives in great numbers, and with great fury pursue their adversary and disturber.

II

Their march from Kadesh-barnea, ver. 1-3. A charge not to trouble the Edomites, ver. 4-8. Nor the Moabites, ver. 9-12. (They pass the river Zered, ver. 13-16.) Nor the Ammonites, ver. 17-23. A command to attack Sihon, ver. 24-26. The conquest of his kingdom, ver. 27-37

1. Mount Seir - The mountainous country of Seir or Edom. Many days - Even for thirty eight years.

3. Northward - Towards the land of the Amorites and Canaanites.

6. Buy meat - For thongh the manna did yet rain upon them, they were not forbidden to buy other meats when they had opportunity, but only were forbidden greedily to hunger after them when they could not obtain them. Buy water - For water in those parts was scarce, and therefore private persons did severally dig pits for their particular use.

7. The Lord hath blessed thee - By God's blessing thou art able to buy thy conveniences, and therefore thy theft and rapine will be inexcusable, because without any pretense of necessity. He knoweth - Hebrew. He hath known, that is, observed, or regarded with care and kindness, which that word often notes. Which experience of God's singular goodness to thee, should make thee rely on him still, and not use any unjust practice to procure what thou wantest or desirest.

8. We turned - From our direct road which lay through Edom.

9. Ar - The chief city of the Moabites, here put for the whole country which depended upon it. The children of Lot - So called to signify that this preservation, was not for their sakes, for they were a wicked people, but for Lot's sake whose memory God yet honours.

10. The Emims - Men terrible for stature and strength, as their very name imparts, whose expulsion by the Moabites is here noted as a great encouragement to the Israelites, for whose sake he would much more drive out the wicked and accursed Canaanites.

12. Which the Lord gave - The past tense is here put for the future, will give after the manner of the prophets.

23. The Caphtorim - A people a-kin to the Philistines, Gen. x, 14, and confederate with them in this enterprize, and so dwelling together, and by degrees uniting together by marriages, they became one people. Caphtor - Which is by the learned thought to be Cappadocia: whither these people might make an expedition out of Egypt, either because of the report of the great riches of part of that country which drew others thither from places equally remote, or for some other reason now unknown.

25. Under heaven - The following words rest rain the sentence to those nations that heard of them.

28. On my feet - Or, with my company who are on foot: which is added significantly, because if

their army had consisted as much of horsemen as many other armies did, their passage through his land might have been more mischievous and dangerous.

29. As the children of Esau did - They did permit them to pass quietly by the borders, though not through the heart of their land, and in their passage the people sold them meat and drink, being it seems more kind to them than their king would have had them; and therefore they here ascribe this favour not to the king, though they are now treating with a king, but to the people, the children of Esau.

30. Hardened his spirit - That is, suffered it to be hardened.

34. Utterly destroyed - By God's command, these being a part of those people who were devoted by the Lord of life and death, to utter destruction for their abominable wickedness.

37. Of Jabbok - That is, beyond Jabbok: for that was the border of the Ammomites.

III

The conquest of Og and his country, ver. 1-11. The distribution of it to the two tribes and an half, ver. 12-17. On condition of assisting their brethren, ver. 18-20. Joshua encouraged, ver. 21- 22. Moses prays that he may go into Canaan, v. 23-25. But is refused, yet permitted to see it, ver. 26-29.

8. On this side Jordan - So it was when Moses wrote this book; but afterward when Israel passed over Jordan it was called the land beyond Jordan.

9. Sirion - Elsewhere called Mount Gilead, and Lebanon, and here Shenir, and Sirion, which several names are given to this one mountain partly by several people, and partly in regard of several tops and parts of it.

10. All Gilead - Gilead is sometimes taken for all the Israelites possessions beyond Jordan, and so it comprehends Bashan; but here for that part of it which lies in and near mount Gilead, and so it is distinguished from Bashan and Argob.

11. In Rabbath - Where it might now be, either because the Ammonites in some former battle with Og, had taken it as a spoil: or because after Og's death, the Ammonites desired to have this monument of his greatness, and the Israelites permitted them to carry it away to their chief city. Nine cubits - So his bed was four yards and an half long, and two yards broad.

14. Unto this day - This must be put among those passages which were not written by Moses, but added by those holy men, who digested the books of Moses into this order, and inserted some few passages to accommodate things to their own time and people.

15. Gilead - That is, the half part of Gilead. To Machir - That is, unto the children of Machir, son of Manasseh, for Machir was now dead.

16. Half the valley - Or rather to the middle of the river: for the word rendered half signifies commonly middle, and the same Hebrew word means both a valley and a brook or river. And this sense is agreeable to the truth, that their land extended from Gilead unto Arnon, and, to speak exactly, to the middle of that river; for as that river was the border between them and others, so one half of it belonged to them, as the other half did to others, Josh. xii, 2. The same thing is expressed in the same words in the Hebrew which are here, though our translators render the self- same words there, from the middle of the river, which here they render, half of the valley. There the bounds of Sihon's kingdom, which was the same portion here mentioned as given to Reuben and Gad, are thus described, from Aroer, which is upon the bank of the river of Arnon, and from the middle of the river, and from half Gilead, even unto the river Jabbok, which is the border of the children of Ammon.

17. The plain - The low country towards Jordan. The sea of the plain - That is, that salt sea, which before that dreadful conflagration was a goodly plain.

18. You - Namely, the Reubenites and Gadites. All that are meet - In such number as your our brethren shall judge necessary. They were in all above an hundred thousand. Forty thousand of them went over Jordan before their brethren.

23. I besought the Lord - We should allow no desire in our hearts, which we cannot in faith offer unto God by prayer.

24. Thou hast begun to shew thy servant thy greatness - Lord, perfect what thou hast begun. The more we see of God's glory in his works, the more we desire to see. And the more we are affected with what we have seen of God, the better we are prepared for farther discoveries.

25. Let me go over - For he supposed God's threatening might be conditional and reversible, as many others were. That goodly mountain -Which the Jews not improbably understood of that mountain on which the temple was to be built. This he seems to call that mountain, emphatically and eminently, that which was much in Moses's thoughts, though not in his eye.

28. He shall go over - It was not Moses, but Joshua or Jesus that was to give the people rest, Heb. iv, 8. 'Tis a comfort to those who love mankind, when they are dying and going off, to see God's work likely to be carried on by other hands, when they are silent in the dust.

IV

An exhortation to obedience, ver. 1-13. A warning against idolatry, ver. 14-28. A promise upon repentance, ver. 29-40. Cities of refuge appointed, ver. 41-43. The place where Moses repeated the law, ver. 44-49.

1. The statutes - The laws which concern the worship and service of God. The judgments - The laws concerning your duties to men. So these two comprehend both tables, and the whole law of God.

6. In the sight of the nations - For though the generality of Heathens in the latter ages, did through inveterate prejudices condemn the laws of the Hebrew, yet it is certain, the wisest Heathens did highly approve of them, so that they made use of divers of them, and translated them into their own laws and constitutions; and Moses, the giver of these laws, hath been mentioned with great honour for his wisdom and learning by many of them. And particularly the old Heathen oracle expressly said, that the Chaldeans or Hebrew, who worshipped the uncreated God, were the only wise men.

7. So nigh - By glorious miracles, by the pledges of his special presence, by the operations of his grace, and particularly by his readiness to hear our prayers, and to give us those succors which we call upon him for.

8. So righteous - Whereby he implies that the true greatness of a nation doth not consist in pomp or power, or largeness of empire, as commonly men think, but in the righteousness of its laws.

10. Thou stoodest - Some of them stood there in their own persons, though then they were but young, the rest in the loins of their parents.

11. The midst of heaven - Flaming up into the air, which is often called heaven.

12. No similitude - No resemblance or representation of God, whereby either his essence, or properties, or actions were represented, such as were usual among the Heathens.

14. Statutes and judgments - The ceremonial and judicial laws which are here distinguished from the moral, or the ten commandments.

15. In Horeb - God, who in other places and times did appear in a similitude in the fashion of a man, now in this most solemn appearance, when he comes to give eternal laws for the direction of the Israelites in the worship of God, and in their duty to men, purposely avoids all such representations, to shew that he abhors all worship of images, or of himself by images of what kind soever, because he is the invisible God, and cannot be represented by any visible image.

16. Lest ye corrupt yourselves - Your ways, by worshipping God in a corrupt manner.

19. Driven - Strongly inclined. Which the Lord hath divided unto all nations - Which are not Gods, but creatures, made not for the worship, but for the use of men; yea, of the meanest and most barbarous people under heaven, and therefore cannot without great absurdity be worshipped, especially by you who are so much advanced above other nations in wisdom and knowledge, and in this, that you are my peculiar people.

24. A consuming fire - A just and terrible God, who, notwithstanding his special relation to thee, will severely punish thee, if thou provoke him. A jealous God - Who being espoused to thee, will be highly incensed against thee, (if thou follow after other lovers, or commit whoredom with idols) and will bear no rival or partner.

28. Ye shall serve Gods - You shall be compelled by men, and given up by me to idolatry. So that very thing which was your choice, shall be your punishment: it being just and usual for God to punish one sin by giving men up to another.

29. If from thence thou seek the Lord - Whatever place we are in, we may from thence seek him. There is no part of the earth which has a gulf fixt between it and heaven.

30. In the latter days - In succeeding ages.

32. The one side of heaven - That is, of the earth under heaven. Ask all the inhabitants of the world.

33. And live - And was not overwhelmed and consumed by such a glorious appearance.

34. By temptations - Temptations is the general title, which is explained by the following particulars, signs, and wonders, &c. which are called temptations, because they were trials both to the Egyptians and Israelites, whether they would be induced to believe and obey God or no. By terrors - Raised in the minds of the Egyptians, or, by terrible things done among them.

37. In his sight - Keeping his eye fixed upon him, as the father doth on his beloved child.

44. This is the law - More punctually expressed in the following chapter, to which these words are a preface.

V

The general intent of the Ten Commandments as a covenant between God and Israel, ver. 1-5. The Commandments, ver. 6-21. God writes them, and grants the people's request, that he would speak by Moses, ver. 22-28. Exhortations to obedience, ver. 29- 33.

1. All Israel - Namely by their elders, who were to impart it to the rest.

3. Not with our fathers - Only: but with us, who are all alive - He saith not, that all who made the covenant at Sinai are now alive, but this covenant was made with all that are now alive; which is most true, for it was made with the elders in their persons, and with the rest in their parents, who covenanted for them.

4. Face to face - Personally and immediately, not by the mouth or ministry of Moses; plainly and certainly, as when two men talk face to face; freely and familiarly, so as not to overwhelm and confound you.

5. Between the Lord and you - As a mediator between you, according to your desire. The word of the Lord - Not the ten commandments, which God himself uttered, but the following statutes and judgments.

7. There being little said, concerning the spiritual sense of the Ten Commandments, in the notes on the twentieth of Exodus, I think it needful to add a few questions here, which the reader may answer between God and his own soul. Thou shalt have none other gods before me - Hast thou worshipped God in spirit and in truth? Hast thou proposed to thyself no end besides him? Hath he been the end of all thy actions? Hast thou sought for any other happiness, than the knowledge and love of God? Dost thou experimentally know the only true God, and Jesus Christ whom he hath sent? Dost thou love God? Dost thou love him with all thy heart, with all thy soul, and with all thy strength; so as to love nothing else but in that manner and degree which tends to increase thy love of him? Hast thou found happiness in God? Is he the desire of thine eyes, the joy of thy heart? If not, thou hast other gods before him.

8. Thou shalt not make any graven image - Hast thou not formed any gross image of God in thy mind? Hast thou always thought of him as a pure spirit, whom no man hath seen, nor can see? And hast thou worshipped him with thy body, as well as with thy spirit, seeing both of them are God's?

11. Thou shalt not take the name of the Lord thy God in vain - Hast thou never used the name of God, unless on solemn and weighty occasions? Hast thou then used it with the deepest awe? Hast thou duly honoured his word, his ordinances, his ministers? Hast thou considered all things as they stand in relation to him, and seen God in all? Hast thou looked upon heaven as God's throne? Up on earth as God's footstool? On every thing therein as belonging to the great king? On every creature as full of God?

12. Keep the sabbath-day, to sanctify it - Dost thou do no work on this day, which can be done as well on another? Art thou peculiarly careful on this day, to avoid all conversation, which does not tend to the knowledge and love of God? Dost thou watch narrowly over all that are within thy gates, that they too may keep it holy? And dost thou try every possible means, to bring all men, wherever you are, to do the same?

16. honour thy father and mother - Hast thou not been irreverent or undutiful to either? Hast thou not slighted their advice? Hast thou cheerfully obeyed all their lawful commands? Hast thou loved and honoured their persons? Supplied their wants, and concealed their infirmities? Hast thou wrestled for them with God in prayer? Hast thou loved and honoured thy prince, and avoided as fire all speaking evil of the ruler of thy people? Have ye that are servants done all things as unto Christ? Not with eye-service, but in singleness of heart? Have ye who are masters, behaved as parents to your servants, with all gentleness and affection? Have ye all obeyed them that watch over your souls, and esteemed them highly in love for their work's sake?

17. Thou shalt not kill - Have you not tempted any one, to what might shorten his life? Have you tempted none to intemperance? Have you suffered none to be intemperate under your roof, or in your company? Have you done all you could in every place, to prevent intemperance of all kinds! Are you guilty of no degree of self-murder? Do you never eat or drink any thing because you like it, although you have reason to believe, it is prejudicial to your health? Have you constantly done whatever you had reason to believe was conducive to it? Have you not hated your neighbour in your heart? Have you reproved him that committed sin in your sight? If not, you have in God's account hated him, seeing you suffered sin upon him. Have you loved all men as your own soul? As Christ loved us? Have you done unto all men, as in like circumstances, you would they should do to you? Have you done all in your power to help your neighbours, enemies as well as friends? Have you laboured to deliver every soul you could from sin and misery? Have you shewed that you loved all men as yourself, by a constant, earnest endeavour, to fill all places with holiness and happiness, with the knowledge and love of God?

18. Neither shalt thou commit adultery - If thou hast not been guilty of any act of uncleanness, hath thy heart conceived no unclean thought? Hast thou not looked on a woman so as to lust after her?

John Wesley

Hast thou not betrayed thy own soul to temptation, by eating and drinking to the full, by needless familiarities, by foolish talking, by levity of dress or behaviour? Hast thou used all the means which scripture and reason suggest, to prevent every kind and degree of unchastity? Hast thou laboured, by watching, fasting, and prayer, to possess thy vessel in sanctification and honour?

19. Neither shalt thou steal - Have you seriously considered, that these houses, lands, money, or goods, which you are used to call your own, are not your own, but belong to another, even God? Have you ever considered, that God is the sole proprietor of heaven and earth? The true owner of every thing therein? Have you considered, that he has only lent them to you? That you are but a steward of your Lord's goods? And that he has told you expressly the uses and purposes for which he intrusts you with them? Namely, for the furnishing first yourselves, and then as many others as you can, with the things needful for life and godliness? Have you considered, that you have no right at all, to apply any part of them to any other purpose? And that if you do, you are as much a robber of God, as any can be a robber of you?

20. Neither shalt thou bear false witness against thy neighbour - Have you not been guilty of evil-speaking? Of needlessly repeating the real fault of your neighbour? If I see a man do an evil thing, and tell it to another, unless from a full and clear conviction, that it is necessary to mention it just then, for the glory of God, the safety or good of some other person, or for the benefit of him that hath done amiss; and unless I then do it only so far, as is necessary to these ends, that is evil-speaking. O beware of this! It is scattering abroad arrows, fire-brands, and death.

21. Neither shalt thou covet any thing that is thy neighbour's - The plain meaning of this is, thou shalt not desire any thing that is not thy own, any thing which thou hast not. Indeed why shouldst thou? God hath given thee whatever tends to thy one end, holiness. Thou canst not deny it, without making him a liar: and: when any thing else will tend thereto, he will give thee that also. There is therefore no room to desire any thing which thou hast not. Thou hast already every thing that is really good for thee, wouldst thou have more money, more pleasure, more praise still? Why this is not good for thee. God has told thee so, by withholding it from thee. O give thyself up to his wise and gracious disposal!

22. Out of the midst of the fire, of the cloud, and of the thick darkness - That was a dispensation of terror, designed to make the gospel of grace the more welcome, and to be a specimen of the terrors of the judgment-day. He added no more - He ceased for that time to speak immediately, and with that loud voice unto the people; for the rest were delivered to Moses, and by him communicated unto them. This he did to shew the preeminence of that law above the rest, and its everlasting obligation.

25. Why should we die? - For though God hath for this season kept us alive, yet we shall never be able to endure any further discourse from him in such a terrible manner, but shall certainly sink under the burden of it.

26. Flesh - Is here put for man in his frail, corruptible, and mortal state.

29. O that there were such an heart in them! - A heart to fear God, and keep his commandments forever! The God of heaven is truly and earnestly desirous of the salvation of poor sinners. He has given abundant proof that he is so: he gives us time and space to repent; by his mercies invites us to repentance, and waiteth to be gracious: has sent his son to redeem us, published a general offer of pardon, promised his spirit to those that pray for him; and has said, yea and sworn, that he hath no pleasure in the death of a sinner!

VI

A persuasive to obedience, ver. 1-3. The first truth, God is One, the first duty, to love him, ver. 4, 5. The means hereto, ver. 6-9. A caution not to forget God in prosperity, ver. 10-13. Not to worship idols, or tempt God, ver. 14-16. Exhortation to obedience, ver. 17-19. And to teach their children, ver. 20-25.

5. And thou shalt love the Lord thy God with all thine heart - And is this only an external commandment? Can any then say, that the Sinai - covenant was merely external? With all thy heart - With an entire love. He is One; therefore our hearts must be united in his love. And the whole stream of our affections must run toward Him. O that this love of God may be shed abroad in our hearts.

7. Teach them diligently - Hebrew. whet, or sharpen them, so as they may pierce deep into their hearts. This metaphor signifies the manner of instructing them, that it is to be done diligently, earnestly, frequently, discreetly.

8. Thou shalt bind them - Thou shalt give all diligence, and use all means to keep them in thy remembrance, as men often bind something upon their hands, or put it before their eyes to prevent forgetfulness of a thing which they much desire to remember.

13. Shalt swear by his name - When thou hast a call and just cause to swear, not by idols, or any creatures.

15. Among you - Hebrew. In the midst of you, to see and observe all your ways and your turnings

aside to other Gods.

16. Ye shall not tempt - Not provoke him, as the following instance explains. Sinners, especially presumptuous sinners, are said to tempt God, that is, to make a trial of God, whether he be, so wise as to see their sins, so just and true and powerful as to take vengeance on them, concerning which they are very apt to doubt because of the present impunity and prosperity of many such persons.

17. Ye diligently keep - Negligence will ruin us: but we cannot be saved without diligence.

25. It shall be our righteousness - Hebrew. Righteousness shall be to us. We shall be owned and pronounced by God to be righteous and holy persons, if we sincerely obey him, otherwise we shall be declared to be unrighteous and ungodly. Or, mercy shall be to us, or with us. For as the Hebrew word rendered righteousness is very often put for mercy, (as Psalm xxiv, 5; xxxvi, 10; li, 14 Prov. x, 2; xi, 4 Dan. ix, 16) so this sense seems best to agree both with the scripture use of this phrase, (in which righteousness, seldom or never, but grace or mercy frequently, is said to be to us or with us) and with the foregoing verse and argument God, saith he, chap. v, 24, commanded these things for our good, that he might preserve us alive, as it is this day. And, saith he in this verse, this is not all; for as he hath done us good, so he will go on to do us more and more good, and God's mercy shall be to us, or with us, in the remainder of our lives, and forever, if we observe these commandments.

VII

A command to destroy the Canaanites, with all pertaining to their idols, ver. 1-5. And to obey God, considering their relation to him, ver. 6-11. Promises to the obedient, ver. 12-15. A repetition of the command, utterly to destroy the Canaanites, with all the monuments of their idolatry, ver. 16-26.

1. Seven nations - There were ten in Gen. xv, 19-21. But this being some hundreds of years after, it is not strange if three of them were either destroyed by foreign or domestick wars, or by cohabitation and marriage united with, and swallowed up in the rest.

4. To serve other Gods - That is, there is manifest danger of apostacy and idolatry from such matches. Which reason doth both limit the law to such of these as are unconverted (otherwise Salmon married Rahab, Matt. i, 5) and enlarge it to other idolatrous nations, as appears from 1 Kings xi, 2 Ezra ix, 2 Neh. xiii, 23.

5. Their graves - Which idolaters planted about the temples and altars of their Gods. Hereby God designed to take away whatsoever might bring their idolatry to remembrance, or occasion the reviving of it.

7. The fewest - To wit, at that time when God first declared his choice of you for his peculiar people, which was done to Abraham. For Abraham had but one son concerned in this choice and covenant, namely, Isaac, and that was in his hundredth year; and Isaac was sixty years old ere he had a child, and then had only two children; and though Jacob had twelve sons, it was a long time before they made any considerable increase. Nor do we read of any great multiplication of them 'till after Joseph's death.

8. The Lord loved you - It was his free choice without any cause or motive on your part.

10. Them that hate him - Not only those who hate him directly and properly, (for so did few or none of the Israelites to whom he here speaks,) but those who hate him by construction and consequence; those who hate and oppose his people, and word, those who wilfully persist in the breach of God's commandments. To their face - That is, openly, and so as they shall see it, and not be able to avoid it. Slack - So as to delay it beyond the fit time or season for vengeance, yet withal he is long-suffering, and slow to anger.

12. The covenant and the mercy - That is, the covenant of mercy, which he out of his own mere grace made with them.

13. He will love thee - He will continue to love thee, and to manifest his love to thee.

15. The diseases of Egypt - Such as the Egyptians were infected with, either commonly, or miraculously. It seems to refer not only to the plagues of Egypt, but to some other epidemic disease, which they remembered to have prevailed among the Egyptians, and by which God had chastised them for their national sins. Diseases are God's servants, which go where he sends them, and do what he bids them.

19. The temptations - The trials and exercises of thy faith and obedience to my commands.

24. No man shall stand - This promise is made upon condition of their performance of their duty, which they neglecting, justly lose the benefit of it.

25. The silver or gold - Wherewith the idols are covered or adorned, nor consequently any other of their ornaments. This he commands to shew his utter detestation of idolatry, and to cut off all occasions of it.

VIII

An exhortation to obedience, in consideration of past and promised mercies, ver. 1-9. A caution not to forget God in prosperity, ver. 10-18. A threatening, in case of apostacy, ver. 19, 20.

1. Live - Live comfortably and happily.
2. All the way - All the events which befell three in the way, the miraculous protections, deliverances, provisions, instructions which God gave thee; and withal the frequent and severe punishments of thy disobedience. To know - That thou mightest discover to thyself and others that infidelity, inconstancy, hypocrisy, and perverseness, which lay hid in thy heart; the discovery whereof was of singular use both to them, and to the church of God in all succeeding ages. It is good for us likewise to remember all the ways both of God's providence and grace, by which he has led us hitherto through the wilderness, that we may trust him, and cheerfully serve him.
3. By every word - That is, by every or any thing which God appoints for this end, how unlikely so-ever it may seem to be for nourishment; seeing it is not the creature, but only God's command and blessing upon it, that makes it sufficient for the support of life.
5. As a man chastiseth his son - That is, unwillingly, being constrained by necessity; moderately, in judgment remembering mercy; and for thy reformation not thy destruction.
7. Depths - Deep wells or springs, or lakes, which were numerous and large.
9. Whose stones are iron - Where are mines of iron in a manner as plentiful as stones, and upon which travelers must tread, as in other parts they do upon stones.
10. Bless the Lord - Solemnly praise him for thy food; which is a debt both of gratitude and justice, because it is from his providence and favour that thou receivest both thy food and refreshment and strength by it. The more unworthy and absurd is that too common profaneness of them, who, professing to believe a God, from whom all their comforts come, grudge to own him at their meals, either by desiring his blessing before them, or by offering due praise to God after them.
14. Lifted up - As if thou didst receive and enjoy these things, either, by thy owns wisdom, and valour, and industry, or for thy own merit.
16. That he might humble thee - By keeping thee in a constant dependence upon him for every day's food, and convincing thee what an impotent, helpless creature thou art, having nothing whereon to subsist, and being supported wholly by the alms of divine goodness from day to day. The mercies of God, if duly considered, are as powerful a mean to humble us as the greatest afflictions, because they increase our debts to God, and manifest our dependance upon him, and by making God great, they make us little in our own eyes. To do thee good - That is, that after he hath purged and prepared thee by afflictions, thou mayest receive and enjoy his blessings with less disadvantage, whilst by the remembrance of former afflictions. thou art made thankful for them, and more cautious not to abuse them.

IX

A promise of Canaan, ver. 1-3. A caution, not to ascribe this to their own merit, ver. 4-6. A rehearsal of their various rebellions, ver. 7-24. and of Moses's intercession for them, ver. 25-29.

1. Hear, O Israel - This seems to be a new discourse, delivered at some distance of time from the former, probably on the next sabbath-day. This day - That is, shortly, within a little time, the word day being often put for time. Nations - That is, the land of those nations. Mightier than thyself - This he adds, that they might not trust to their own strength, but rely upon God's help for the destroying them, and, after the work was done, might ascribe the glory of it to God alone, and not to themselves.
2. Who can stand - This seems to be a proverb used in those times.
5. Not for thy righteousness - Neither for thy upright heart, nor holy life, which are the two things which God above all things regards. And consequently he excludes all merit. And surely they who did not deserve this earthly Canaan, could not merit the kingdom of glory. To perform the word - To shew my faithfulness in accomplishing that promise which I graciously made and confirmed with my oath.
6. Stiff-necked - Rebellious and perverse, and so destitute of all pretense of righteousness. And thus our gaining possession of the heavenly Canaan, must be ascribed to God's power, not our own might, and to God's Grace, not our own merit. In him we must glory.
8. In Horeb - When your miraculous deliverance out of Egypt was fresh in memory; when God had but newly manifested himself to you in so stupendous and dreadful a manner, and had taken you into covenant with himself, when God was actually conferring farther mercies upon you.
10. With the finger of God - Immediately and miraculously, which was done not only to procure the greater reverence to the law, but also to signify, that it is the work of God alone to write this law upon the tables of men's hearts. In the day of the assembly - That is, when the people were gathered by

God's command to the bottom of Mount Sinai, to hear and receive God's ten commandments from his own mouth.

14. *Let me alone!* - Stop me not by thy intercession.

17. *I brake them before your eyes* - Not by an unbridled passion, but in zeal for God's honour, and by the direction of God's spirit, to signify to tine people, that the covenant between God and them contained in those tables was broken and they were now cast out of God's favour, and could expect nothing from him but fiery indignation.

18. *I fell down* - In a way of humiliation and supplication, on your behalf.

21. *Into the brook* - That there might be no monument or remembrance of it left.

25. *I fell down forty days* - The same as were mentioned before, ver. 18, as appears by comparing this with Exodus, where this history is more fully related, and where this is said to be done twice only.

26. *Through thy greatness* - Through the greatness of thy power, which appeared most eminently in that work.

27. *Thy servants* - That is, the promise made and sworn to thy servants.

29. *Thy people* - Whom thou hast chosen to thyself out of all mankind, and publickly owned them for thine, and hast purchased and redeemed them from the Egyptians.

X

God's mercy, in renewing the two tables, ver. 1-5. In leading Israel forward, and chusing the tribe of Levi for his own, ver. 6-9. In accepting the intercession as Moses, ver. 10-11. An exhortation to fear, love, and serve God, ver. 12-22.

2. *I will write on the tables* - Tho' the tables were broken, because they broke his commandment, they were now renewed, in proof that his wrath was turned away. And thus God's writing his law in our inward parts, is the surest proof of our reconciliation to him.

6. This following history comes in manifestly by way of parenthesis, as may appear from ver. 10, where he returns to his former discourse; and it seems to be here inserted as an evidence of God's gracious answer to Moses's prayers, and of his reconciliation to the people, notwithstanding their late and great provocation. For, saith he, after this they proceeded by God's guidance in their journeys, and though Aaron died in one of them, yet God made up that breach, and Eleazar came in his place, and ministered as priest, one branch of which office was to intercede for the people.

8. *At that time* - About that time, that is, when I was come down from the mount, as was said, ver. 5. *To stand before the Lord* - A phrase used concerning the prophets, 1 Kings xvii, 1; xviii, 15, this being the posture of ministers. Hence the angels are said to stand, 2Chr xviii, 18 Luke i, 19. *To bless* - The people, by performance of those holy ministrations for the people, and giving those instructions to them, to which God's blessing was promised; and this they did in God's name, that is, by command, and commission from him.

9. *The Lord is his inheritance* - That is, the Lord's portion, namely, tithes and offerings, which belong to God, are given by him to the Levites for their subsistence, from generation to generation.

11. *Take thy journey before the people* - 'Twas fit that he who had saved them from ruin by his intercession, should have the conduct and command of them. And herein he was a type of Christ, who, as he ever lives to make intercession for us, so has all power in heaven and in earth.

12. *What doth he require* - By way of duty and gratitude for such amazing mercies.

14. *The heaven* - The airy and starry heaven. *The heaven of heavens* - The highest or third heaven, called the heaven of heavens for its eminency. *All that therein is* - With all creatures and all men, which being all his, he might have chosen what nation he pleased to be his people.

15. *To love them* - He shews that God had no particular obligation to their fathers, any more than to other persons or people, all being equally his creatures, and that his choice of them out of and above all others, proceeded only from God's good pleasure.

16. *Circumcise* - Rest not in your bodily circumcision, but seriously set upon that substantial work which is signified thereby: cleanse your hearts from all filthiness and superfluity of naughtiness, fitly compared to the foreskin, which if not cut off, made persons profane, unclean and odious in the sight of God.

17. *Regardeth not persons* - Whether Jews or Gentiles, but deals justly and equally with all sorts of men; and as whosoever fears and obeys him shall be accepted, so all incorrigible transgressors shall be severely punished, and you no less than other people: therefore do not flatter yourselves as if God would bear with your sins because of his particular kindness to you or to your fathers.

18. *He doth execute* - That is, plead their cause, and give them right against their potent adversaries, and therefore he expects you should do so too.

20. *To him shalt thou cleave* - With firm confidence, true affection, and constant obedience.

21. *Thy praise* - The object and matter of thy praise, as Exod. xv, 2, whom thou shouldest ever

praise.

XI

Moses exhorts them to obedience by rehearsing God's works, ver. 1-7. By describing the goodness of the land, ver. 8-12. By promises and threats, ver. 13-17. An exhortation to teach their children, closed with a promise, ver. 18-25. A blessing and a curse, ver. 26-32.

2. Know - That is, acknowledge and consider it with diligence and thankfulness.

4. Unto this day - The effect of which destruction continueth to this day, in their weakness and fear, and our safety from their farther attempts against us.

7. Your eyes have seen - All of them had seen some, and some of them had seen all the great things done in Egypt and at the Red- sea, and in the Wilderness. What our eyes have seen, especially in our early days, should be improved by us long after.

10. With thy foot - That is, with great pains and labour of thy feet, partly by going up and down to fetch water and disperse it, and partly by digging furrows with thy foot, and using engines for distributing the water, which engines they thrust with their feet. For tho' the river Nile did once in a year overflow the grounds, and made them fruitful, yet often it failed them, at least in part, and then they were put to great pains about their ground. And when it did overflow sufficiently, and left its mud upon the earth, yet that mud was in a little time hardened, and needed another watering, and much digging and labour both of the hand and feet, especially in places more remote from that river; which inconvenience Canaan was free from.

11. Of hills and valleys - And therefore much more healthful than Egypt was, which as it was enriched, so it was annoyed with the Nile, which overflowed the land in summer time, and thereby made the country both unpleasant and unhealthful. And health being the greatest of all outward blessings, Canaan must therefore needs be a more desirable habitation than Egypt. The rain of heaven - Which is more easy, being given thee without thy charge or pains; more sweet and pleasant, not hindering thy going abroad upon thy occasions, as the overflow of the Nile did, whereby the Egyptians were confined in a great measure to their houses; more safe and healthful, being free from that mud which attends upon the waters of the Nile; and more certain too, the former and the latter rain being promised to be given to them in their several seasons, upon condition of their obedience, which condition, tho' it may seem a clog and inconvenience, yet indeed was a great benefit, that by their own necessities and interest they might be obliged to that obedience, upon which their happiness depended both for this life and the next.

12. Careth for - In a special manner watering it immediately as it were by his own hand, without man's help, and giving peculiar blessings to it, which Egypt enjoys not. To the end of the year - To give it the rain, and other blessings proper to the several seasons. But all these mercies, and the fruitfulness of the land consequent upon them, were suspended upon their disobedience. And therefore it is not at all strange that some later writers, describe the land of Canaan as a barren soil, which is, so far from affording ground to question the authority of the scriptures, that it doth much more confirm it, this, being an effect of that threatning that God would turn a fruitful land into barrenness for the wickedness of these that dwell in it, Psalm cvii, 34.

14. The ruin of your land - Which is, proper to your land, not common to Egypt, where, as all authors agree, there is little rain. The first rain fell in seed time, to make the corn spring, the other a little before harvest, to ripen it.

15. I will send grass in thy fields - So godliness has here the promise of the life which now is. But the favour of God puts gladness into the heart, more than the increase of corn, wine and oil.

17. Shut up the heaven - Which is compared sometimes to a great store-house wherein God lays up his treasures of rain, Job xxxviii, 22, the doors whereof God is said to open when he gives rain, and to shut when he witholds it.

18. Lay up - Let us all observe these three rules,

1. Let our hearts be filled with the word of God. Lay up these words in your hearts, as in a store-house, to be used upon all occasions.

2. Let our eyes be fixed upon the word of God: Bind them for a sign upon your hand, which is always in view, and as frontlets between your eyes, which you cannot avoid the sight of.

3. Let our tongues be employed about the word of God, especially with our children, who must be taught this, as far more needful than the rules of decency, or the calling they are to live by.

21. As the days of heaven - As long as the heaven keeps its place and continues its influences upon earth.

24. Every place - Not absolutely, as the Rabbins fondly conceit, but in the promised land, as it is restrained in the following words; either by possession, or by dominion, namely, upon condition of your obedience. The wilderness - Of Sin, on the south-side. To Lebanon - Which was on the north border.

Euphrates - On the east. So far the right of dominion extended, but that their sins cut them short: and so far Solomon extended his dominion. The uttermost sea - The western or midland sea.

26. I set before you - I propose them to your choice.

28. Which ye have not known - Which you have no acquaintance with, nor experience of their power, or wisdom, or goodness, as you have had of mine.

29. Put - Hebrew. Thou shalt give, that is, speak or pronounce, or cause to be pronounced. So the word to give is used, chap. xiii, 1, 2Job xxxvi, 3 Prov. ix, 9. This is, more particularly expressed, chap. xxvii, 12, 13.

30. Over against - Looking toward Gilgal, tho' at some considerable distance from it. Beside the plains of Moreh - This was one of the first places that Abram came to in Canaan. So that in sending them thither to hear the blessing and the curse, they were minded of the promise made to Abram in that very place, Gen. xii, 6, 7.

XII

A command, to destroy all relicks of idolatry, ver. 1-3. To worship God in his own place, and according to his own appointment, ver. 4-14. A permission to eat flesh, but not blood, ver. 15, 16. Directions to eat the tithe in the holy place, and to take care of the Levite, ver. 17-19. A farther permission to eat flesh, but not blood, ver. 20-25. A direction to eat holy things in the holy place, ver. 26-28. Farther cautions against idolatry, ver. 20-32.

2. All the places - Temples, chapels, altars, groves, as appears from other scriptures. Green-tree - As the Gentiles consecrated divers trees to their false gods, so they worshipped these under them.

3. Pillars - Upon which their images were set. Names - That is, all the memorials of them, and the very names given to the places from the idols.

4. Not do so - That is, not worship him in several places, mountains, and groves.

5. To put his name there - That is, to set up his worship there, and which he shall call by his name, as his house, or his dwelling- place; namely, where the ark should be, the tabernacle, or temple: which was first Shiloh, and then Jerusalem. There is not one precept in all the law of Moses, so largely inculcated as this, to bring all their sacrifices to that one altar. And how significant is, that appointment? They must keep to one place, in token of their belief. That there is one God, and one Mediator between God and man. It not only served to keep up the notion of the unity of the godhead, but the one only way of approach to God and communion with him in and by his son.

6. Thither bring your burnt-offerings - Which were wisely appropriated to that one place, for the security of the true religion, and for the prevention of idolatry and superstition, which might otherwise more easily have crept in: and to signify that their sacrifices were not accepted for their own worth, but by God's gracious, appointment, and for the sake of God's altar, by which they were sanctified, and for the sake of Christ, whom the altar manifestly represented. Your heave-offerings - That is, your first-fruits, of corn, and wine, and oil, and other fruits. And these are called the heave-offerings of their hand, because the offerer was first to take these into his hands, and to heave them before the Lord, and then to give them to the priest. Your free-will-offerings - Even your voluntary oblations, which were not due by my prescription, but only by your own choice: you may chuse what kind of offering you please to offer, but not the place where you shall offer them.

7. There - Not in the most holy place, wherein only the priests might eat, but in places allowed to the people for this, end in the holy city. Ye shall eat - Your part of the things mentioned, ver. 6. Before the Lord - In the place of God's presence, where God's sanctuary shall be.

8. Here - Where the inconveniency of our abode, and the uncertainty of our abode, would not permit exact order in sacrifices and feasts and ceremonies, which therefore God was then pleased to dispense with; but, saith he, he will not do so there. Right in his own eyes - Not that universal liberty was given to all persons to worship how they listed; but in many things their unsettled condition gave opportunity to do so.

11. His name - His majesty and glory, his worship and service, his, special and gracious presence. Your choice vows - Hebrew. the choice of your vows, that is, your select or chosen vows; so called, because things offered for vows, were to be perfect, whereas defective creatures were accepted in free-will-offerings.

12. Your daughters - Hence it appears, that though the males only were obliged to appear before God in their solemn feasts, yet the women also were permitted to come.

13. Thy burnt-offerings - Nor the other things mentioned above, this one and most eminent kind being put for all the rest.

17. Within thy gates - That is, in your private habitations, here opposed to the place of God's worship.

20. Enlarge thy border - Which will make it impossible to bring all the cattle thou usest to the

tabernacle.

21. If the place be too far - Being obliged to carry their sacrifices to the place of worship, they might think themselves obliged to carry their other cattle thither to be killed. They are therefore released from all such obligations, and left at liberty to kill them at home, whether they lived nearer that place, or farther from it; only the latter is here mentioned, as being the matter of the scruple. As I have commanded - In such a manner as the blood may be poured forth.

22. As the roe-buck - As common or unhallowed food, tho' they be of the same kind with the sacrifices which are offered to God. The unclean - Because there was, no holiness in such meat for which the unclean might be excluded from it.

27. The flesh - Excepting what shall be burned to God's, honour, and given to the priest according to his appointment.

30. By following them - By following the example they left, when their persons are destroyed.

XIII

Enticers to idolatry to be stoned, ver. 1-11. Idolatrous cities to be entirely destroyed, ver. 12-18.

1. A dreamer of dreams - One that pretends God hath revealed himself to him by visions or dreams. Giveth a sign or wonder - That is, shall foretell some strange and wonderful thing.

3. Thou shalt not hearken to that prophet - Not receive his doctrine, though the sign come to pass. For although when such a sign or wonder foretold did not follow or come to pass, it was a sign of a false prophet, yet when it did come to pass, it was no sufficient sign of a true one, especially, in such a case. There are many things, which may be wrought by evil spirits, God so permitting it for wise and just reasons, not only for the trial of the good, but also for the punishment of ungodly men. Proveth you - That is, trieth your faith and love and obedience. To know - Namely, judicially, or in a publick manner, so as both you and others may know and see it, that so the justice of his judgments upon you may be more evident and glorious.

5. To thrust - This phrase notes the great force and power of seducers to corrupt men's minds. So shalt thou put the evil away - Thou shalt remove the guilt, by removing the guilty.

6. The son of thy mother - This is added, to restrain the signification of the word brother, which is often used generally for one near a-kin, and to express the nearness of the relation, the mother's, side being usually the ground of the most fervent affection. Thy daughter - Thy piety must overcome both thy affection, and thy compassion to the weaker sex. The father and mother are here omitted, because they are sufficiently contained in the former examples.

8. Conceal him - That is, smother his fault, hide or protect his person, but shalt accuse him to the magistrate, and demand justice upon him.

9. Thou shalt kill him - Not privately, which pretense would have opened the door to innumerable murders, but by procuring his death by the sentence of the magistrate. Thou shalt cast the first stone at him, as the witness was to do.

13. Children of Belial - It signifies properly persons without yoke, vile and wretched miscreants, lawless and rebellious, that will suffer no restraint, that neither fear God, nor reverence man. From among you - That is, from your church and religion. It notes a separation from them, not in place (as appears by their partnership with their fellow citizens both in the sin and punishment) but in heart, doctrine and worship.

14. Inquire - This is, meant of the magistrate, to whose office this properly belongs, and of whom he continues to speak in the same manner, thou, ver. 15, 16. The Jewish writers say, the defection of a city is to be tried by the great sanhedrim. If it appear, that they are thrust away to idolatry, they send two learned men, to admonish them. If they repent, all is well: is not, all Israel must go up and execute this sentence. Tho' we do not find this law put in execution, in all the history of the Jewish church, yet for neglecting the execution of it on inferior cities, God himself by the army of the Chaldeans, executed it on Jerusalem, the head city, which was utterly destroyed, and lay in ruins for seventy years.

15. The inhabitants - Namely, all that are guilty, not the innocent part, such as disowned this apostacy, who doubtless by choice, at least upon warning, would come out of so wicked a place. Utterly - The very same punishment which was, inflicted upon the cities of the cursed Canaanites, to whom having made themselves equal in sin, it is but just God should equal them in punishment.

16. For the Lord - For the satisfaction of God's justice, the maintainance of his honour and authority, and the pacification of his offended majesty. It shall not be built - It shall be an eternal monument of God's justice, and terror to after ages.

17. Multiply thee - So thou shalt have no loss of thy numbers by cutting off so many people.

XIV

Directions, concerning mourning, ver. 1, 2. Concerning clean and unclean meats, ver. 3-21. Concerning tithes, ver. 29.

1. Of the Lord - Whom therefore you must not disparage by unworthy or unbecoming practices. Ye shall not cut yourselves - Which were the practices of idolaters, both in the worship of their idols, in their funerals, and upon occasion of public calamities. Is not this like a parent's charge to his little children, playing with knives, "Do not cut yourselves!" This is, the intention of those commands, which obliges us to deny ourselves. The meaning is, Do yourselves no harm! And as this also is, the design of cross providences, to remove from us those things by which we are in danger of doing ourselves harm.

3. Abominable - Unclean and forbidden by me, which therefore should be abominable to you.

22. All the increase - This is to be understood of the second tithes, which seem to be the same with the tithes of the first year, mentioned ver. 28.

25. In thine hand - That is, in a bag to be taken into thy hand and carried with thee.

27. Thou shalt not forsake him - Thou shalt give him a share in such tithes or in the product of them.

28. At the end of three years - That is, in the third year, as it is, expressed, chap. xxvi, 12. The same year - This is added to shew that he speaks of the third year, and not of the fourth year, as some might conjecture from the phrase, at the end of three years.

XV

Orders concerning the release of debts every seventh year, ver. 1-6. Concerning lending, ver. 7-11. Concerning the release of servants, ver. 12-18. Concerning the firstlings, ver. 19-23.

1. At the end - That is, in the last year of the seven, as is, most evident from ver. 9. And this year of release, as it is, called below, ver. 9, is the same with the sabbatical year, Exod. xxiii, 11.

2. Every creditor - Here is, a law for poor, insolvent debtors. Every seventh year was a year of release, when among other acts of grace, this was one, that every Israelite, who had borrowed money, and had not been able to pay it before, should this year be released from it. And tho' if he was able, he was bound in conscience to pay it afterwards, yet it could not be recovered by law. His brother - This is added to limit the word neighbour, which is more general, unto a brother, in nation and religion, an Israelite. The Lord's release - Or, a release for the Lord, in obedience to his command, for his honour, and as an acknowledgment of his right in your estates, and of his kindness in giving and continuing them to you.

4. Save when there shall be no poor - The words may be rendered thus, as in the margin of our Bibles, To the end that there be no poor among you. And so they contain a reason of this law, namely, that none be impoverished and ruined by a rigid exaction of debts.

8. Open thine hand wide - That is, deal bountifully and liberally with him.

9. Beware - Suppress the first risings of such uncharitableness. It be sin - That is, it be charged upon thee as a sin.

10. Thine heart shall not be grieved - That is, thou shalt give, not only with an open hand, but with a willing and chearful mind, without which thy very charity is uncharitable, and not accepted by God.

11. The poor shall never cease - God by his providence will so order it, partly for the punishment of your disobedience, and partly for the trial and exercise of your obedience to him and charity to your brother.

12. If thy brother be sold - Either by himself, or his parents, or as a criminal. Six years - To be computed from the beginning of his servitude, which is everywhere limited to the space of six years.

15. The Lord redeemed thee - And brought thee out with riches, which because they would not, God gave thee as a just recompense for thy service; and therefore thou shalt follow his example, and send out thy servant furnished with all convenient provisions.

17. For ever - All the time of his life, or, at least, 'till the year of jubilee. Likewise - That is, either dismiss her with plenty, or engage her to perpetual servitude, in the same manner and by the same rites.

19. All the firstling males thou shalt sanctify - Giving them to God on the eighth day. And thou shalt do no work with the female firstlings of the cow, nor shear those of the sheep. Even these must be offered to God as peace-offerings, or used in a religious feast.

20. Year by year - Namely, in the solemn feasts which returned upon them every year.

XVI

A repetition of the laws concerning the passover, ver. 1-8. The feast of pentecost, ver. 9-12 That of tabernacles, ver. 13-15. All the males are to attend them, ver. 16, 17. An appointment of Judges and officers, ver. 18-20. A caution against groves and images, ver. 21, 22.

1. Observe the month of Abib - Or of new fruits, which answers to part of March and part of April, and was by a special order from God made the beginning of their year, in remembrance of their deliverance out of Egypt. By night - In the night Pharaoh was forced to give them leave to depart, and accordingly they made preparation for their departure, and in the morning they perfected the work.

2. The passover - That is, the feast of the passover, and so the place may be rendered, thou shalt therefore observe the feast of the passover unto the Lord thy God, with sheep, and with oxen, as is prescribed, Num. xxviii, 18, &c.

3. With it - Or, in it, that is, during the time of the feast of the passover. Bread of affliction - Bread which is not usual nor pleasant, to put thee in mind both of thy miseries endured in Egypt; and of thy hasty coming out of it, which allowed thee no time to leaven or prepare thy bread.

4. Any of the flesh - That is, of the passover properly so called.

5. Of thy gates - That is, of thy cities.

6. There - Namely, in the court of the tabernacle or temple. This he prescribed, partly that this great work might be done with more solemnity in such manner as God required; partly, because it was not only a sacrament, but also a sacrifice, and because here was the sprinkling of blood, which is the essential part of a sacrifice; and partly to design the place where Christ, the true passover or lamb of God, was to be slain. At the season - About the time you were preparing yourselves for it.

7. In the morning - The morning after the seventh day. Thy tents - That is, thy dwellings, which he calls tents, as respecting their present state, and to put them in mind afterwards when they were settled in better habitations, that there was a time when they dwelt in tents.

8. Six days - Namely, besides the first day, on which the passover was killed.

9. To put the sickle - That is, to reap thy corn, thy barley, when the first-fruits were offered.

10. Of weeks - Of pentecost. Thou shalt give - Over and besides what was appointed.

17. Thou shalt rejoice - In God and the effects of his favour, praising him with a glad heart.

18. Judges - Chief magistrates to examine and determine causes and differences. Officers - Who were subordinate to the other to bring causes and persons before him, to acquaint people with the sentence of the Judges, and to execute their sentence. Thy gates - Thy cities, which he here calls gates, because there were seats of judgment set. Pursuant to this law, in every town which contained above an hundred and twenty families, there was a court of twenty three Judges; in the smaller towns, a court of three Judges.

19. Wrest judgment - Not give an unjust sentence. A gift doth blind the eyes - Biasseth his mind, that he cannot discern between right and wrong. The words - That is the sentence, of those Judges who are used to do righteous things, it makes them give wrong judgment.

20. That which is altogether just - Hebrew. righteousness, righteousness, that is, nothing but righteousness in all causes and times, and to all persons equally.

21. Thou shalt not plant - Because this was the practice of idolaters, and might be an occasion of reviving idolatry.

XVII

A charge, concerning sacrifices, ver. 1. Concerning putting idolaters to death, ver. 2-7. Concerning the decision of cases by the sanhedrim, ver. 8-13. Concerning the choice and duty of a king, ver. 14-20.

1. Bullock or sheep - Either greater or smaller sacrifices, all being comprehended under the two most eminent kinds.

2. In transgressing his covenant - That is, in idolatry, as it is explained ver. 3, which is called a transgression of God's covenant made with Israel, both because it is a breach of their faith given to God and of that law which they covenanted to keep; and because it is a dissolution of that matrimonial covenant with God, a renouncing of God and his worship, and a chusing other Gods.

3. The host of heaven - Those glorious creatures, which are to be admired as the wonderful works of God, but not to be set up in God's stead. By condemning the most specious of all idolaters, he intimates, how absurd a thing it is to worship stocks and stones, the works of men's hands. I have not commanded - That is, I have forbidden. Such negative expressions are emphatical.

6. Witnesses - Namely, credible and competent witnesses. The Jews rejected the testimonies of children, women, servants, familiar friends or enemies, persons of dissolute lives or evil fame.

7. First upon him - God thus ordered it, for the caution of witnesses, that, if they had thro' malice

or wrath accused him falsely, they might now be afraid to imbrue their hands in innocent blood; and for the security and satisfaction of the people in the execution of this punishment.

8. For thee - He speaks to the inferior magistrates, who were erected in several cities. If thou hast not skill to determine, between blood and blood - That is, in capital causes. Between plea and plea - In civil causes, about words or estates. Between stroke and stroke - In criminal causes, concerning blows, or wounds inflicted by one man upon another. Matters of controversy - That is, such things being doubtful, and the magistrates divided in their opinions about it. Chuse - Namely to set up his tabernacle, or temple there; because there was the abode, both of their sanhedrim, which was constituted of priests and civil magistrates, and of the high-priests, who were to consult God by Urim, in matters which could not be decided otherwise.

9. Unto the priests - That is, unto the great council, which consisted chiefly of the priests and Levites, as being the best expositors of the laws of God, by which all those controversies were to be decided. And the high-priest was commonly one of that number, understood here under the priests, whereof he was the chief. The judge - Probably the high-priest, to whom it belonged to determine, some at least, of those controversies, and to expound the law of God. And he may be distinctly named, tho' he be one of the priests, because of his eminency, and to shew that amongst the priests, he especially was to be consulted in such cases. The sentence of judgment - Hebrew. The word, or matter of judgement, that is, the true state of the cause, and what judgment or sentence ought to be given in it.

10. Thou - Thou shalt pass sentence: he speaks to the inferior magistrates; who were to give sentence, and came hither to be advised about it.

11. Thou shalt do - In particular suits between man and man, altho' the judge be hereby confined to his rule in giving the sentence, yet it seems but fit and reasonable that people should be bound simply to acquiesce in the sentence of their last and highest judge, or else there would have been no end of strife.

12. Do presumptuously - That will proudly and obstinately oppose the sentence given against him. The evil - The evil thing, that scandal, that pernicious example.

13. When thou shalt - He only foresees and foretells what they would do, but doth not approve of it. Yea when they did this thing for this very reason, he declares his utter dislike of it, 1 Sam. viii, 7.

15. Thy God shall chuse - Approve of, or appoint. So it was in Saul and David. God reserved to himself the nomination both of the family, and of the person. Thy brethren -- of the same nation and religion; because such a person was most likely to maintain true religion, and to rule with righteousness, gentleness, and kindness to his subjects; and that he might be a fit type of Christ their supreme king, who was to be one of their brethren.

16. He shall not multiply horses - Tho' he might have horses for his own use, yet he was not to have many horses for his officers and guard, much less for war, lest he should trust in them. The multiplying horses is also forbidden, lest it should raise too great a correspondence with Egypt which furnished Canaan with them. The Lord hath said - The Lord hath now said to me, and I by his command declare it to you. Ye shall no more return that way - Into Egypt, lest ye be again infected with her idolatries.

17. Turn away - From God and his law.

18. He shall write - With his own hand, as the Jews say. Out of that - Out of the original, which was carefully kept by the priests in the sanctuary, that it might be a perfect copy, and that it might have the greater influence upon him, coming to him as from the hand and presence of God.

19. All the days of his life - 'Tis not enough to have Bibles, but we must use them, yea, use them daily. Our souls must have constant meals of that manna, which if well digested, will afford them true nourishment and strength.

20. If his heart be not lifted up - He intimates, that the scriptures diligently read, are a powerful means to keep him humble, because they shew him in that, tho' a king, he is subject to an higher monarch, to whom he must give an account of all his administrations, and receive from him his sentence agreeable to their quality, which is sufficient to abate the pride of the haughtiest person in the world.

XVIII

Rules concerning priests and Levites, ver. 1-8. Cautions against witchcraft, ver. 9-14. A promise of Christ, ver. 15-19. The punishment and mark of a false prophet, ver. 20-22.

1. His inheritance - The Lord's portion or inheritance, which God had reserved to himself, as tithes and first fruits, and other oblations distinct from those which were made by fire.

3. The maw - The Hebrew word here rendered maw or stomach, may have another signification, and some render it the breast, others take it for the part, which lies under the breast.

6. With all the desire of his mind - With full purpose to fix his abode, and to spend his whole time and strength in the service of God. It seems, the several priests were to come from their cities to the

temple by turns, before David's time; and it is certain they did so after it. But if any of them were not contented with this attendance upon God in his tabernacle, or temple, and desired more entirely and constantly to devote himself to God's service there, he was permitted so to do, because this was an eminent act of piety joined with self - denial, to part with those great conveniences which he enjoyed in the city of his possession.

8. Like portions - With their brethren who were in actual ministration: as they share with them in the work, so shall they in the encouragements. Beside that which cometh - The reason of this law was, because he that waited on the altar, ought to live by the altar: and because it was fit he should keep his money, wherewith he might redeem what he sold, if afterwards he saw occasion for it. Mr. Henry adds a remarkable note here: especially considering he wrote threescore years ago. "A hearty, pious zeal to serve God and his church, tho' it may a little encroach upon a settled order, and there may be somewhat in it that looks irregular, yet ought to be gratified, and not discouraged. He that loves dearly to be employed in the service of the sanctuary: in God's name let him minster. He shall be as welcome to God as the Levites, whose course it was to minister, and should be so to them."

10. Useth divination - Foretelleth things secret or to come, by unlawful arts and practices. An observer of times - Superstitiously pronouncing some days lucky, and others unlucky. Or, an observer of the clouds or heavens, one that divineth by the motions of the clouds, by the stars, or by the flying or chattering of birds, all which Heathens used to observe. An inchanter - Or, a conjecturer, that discovers hidden things by a superstitious use of words or ceremonies, by observation of water or smoke or any contingencies. A witch - One that is in covenant with the devil.

11. A charmer - One that charmeth serpents or other cattle. Or, a fortune-teller, that foretelleth the events of men's lives by the conjunctions of the stars. Spirits - Whom they call upon by certain words or rites. A wizard - Hebrew. a knowing man, who by any forbidden way's undertakes the Revelation of secret things. A necromancer - One that calleth up and inquireth of the dead.

13. Perfect - Sincerely and wholly his, seeking him and cleaving to him and to his word alone, and therefore abhorring all commerce and conversations with devils.

14. Hath not suffered thee so to do - Hath not suffered thee to follow these superstitious and diabolical practices, as he hath suffered other nations to do, but hath instructed thee better by his word and spirit, and will more fully instruct thee by a great prophet.

15. Will raise up - Will produce and send into the world in due time. A prophet like unto me - Christ was truly, and in all commendable parts like him, in being both a prophet and a king and a priest and mediator, in the excellency of his ministry and work, in the glory of his miracles, in his familiar and intimate converse with God.

19. I will require it - I will punish him severely for it. The sad effect of this threatning the Jews have felt for above sixteen hundred years together.

22. If the thing - Which he gives as a sign of the truth of his prophecy. The falsehood of his prediction shews him to be a false prophet. Presumptuously - Impudently ascribing his own vain and lying fancies to the God of truth.

XIX

Of the cites of refuge, ver. 1-10. Of wilful murderers, ver. 11-13. Of removing land-marks, ver. 14. Of witnesses, true, ver. 15. Of false, ver. 16-21

2. In the midst of the land - Namely, beyond Jordan, as there were three already appointed on this side Jordan: In the midst of the several parts of their land, to which they might speedily flee from all the parts of the land.

3. Prepare thee a way - Distinguish it by evident marks, and make it plain and convenient, to prevent mistakes and delays.

8. Enlarge thy coast - As far as Euphrates.

9. If thou shalt keep all these commandments - But the Jewish writers themselves own, that the condition not being performed, the promise of enlarging their coast was not fulfilled, so that there was no need for three more cities of refuge. Yet the holy, blessed God, say they, did not command it in vain, for in the day's of Messiah the Prince, they shall be added. They expect it in the letter: but we know, it has in Christ its spiritual accomplishment. For the borders of the Gospel- Israel are inlarged according to the promise: and in the Lord our righteousness, refuge is provided for all that by faith fly to him.

15. Rise - Or be established, accepted, owned as sufficient: it is the same word which in the end of the verse is rendered, be established.

16. A safe witness - A single witness, though he speak truth, is not to be accepted for the condemnation of another man, but if he be convicted of false witness, this is sufficient for his own condemnation.

21. Eye for eye - What punishment the law allotted to the accused, if he had been convicted, the

same shall the false accuser bear.

XX

The exhortation of the priest to them who were going to battle, ver. 1-4. The dismission of them who were engaged in business, or faint-hearted, ver. 5-9. How they were to treat distant cities, ver. 10-15. The cities of the Canaanites, ver. 16-18. Fruit-trees not to be destroyed, ver. 19, 20.

2. *Speak unto the people* - Probably to one regiment of the army after another.

5. *What man* - This and the following exceptions are to be understood only of a war allowed by God, not in a war commanded by God, not in the approaching war with the Canaanites, from which even the bridegroom was not exempted, as the Jewish writers note.

6. *A vineyard* - This and the former dispensation were generally convenient, but more necessary in the beginning of their settlement in Canaan, for the encouragement of those who should build houses or plant vineyards, which was chargeable to them, and beneficial to the common-wealth. *Eaten of it* - Hebrew. made it common, namely, for the use of himself and family and friends, which it was not, 'till the fifth year.

9. *Make captains* - Or rather, as the Hebrew hath it, they shall set or place the captains of the armies in the head or front of the people under their charge, that they may conduct them, and by their example encourage their soldiers. It is not likely they had their captains to make when they were just going to battle.

16. *Nothing* - No man. For the beasts, some few excepted, were given them for a prey.

19. *Thou shalt not destroy* - Which is to be understood of a general destruction of them, not of the cutting down some few of them, as the conveniency of the siege might require. *Man's life* - The sustenance or support of his life.

XXI

The expiation of an uncertain murder, ver. 1-9. The usage of a captive taken to wife, ver. 10-14. The first-born to not to be disinherited, ver. 15-17. A stubborn son to be put to death, ver. 18-21. Bodies of malefactors to be buried, ver. 22. 23.

1. *The field* - Or, in the city, or any place: only the field is named, as the place where such murders are most commonly committed.

2. *Thy elders and Judges* - Those of thy elders who are Judges: the Judges or rulers of all the neighbouring cities. *Measure* - Unless it be evident which city is nearest; for then measuring was superfluous.

3. *Which hath not drawn in the yoke* - A fit representative of the murderer, in whose stead it was killed, who would not bear the yoke of God's laws. A type also of Christ, who was under the yoke, but what he had voluntarily taken upon himself.

4. *A rough valley* - That such a desert and horrid place might beget an horror of murder and of the murderer. *Strike off the neck* - To shew what they would and should have done to the murderer if they had found him.

5. *Every controversy* - Of this kind: every controversy which shall rise about any stroke, whether such a mortal stroke as is here spoken of, or any other stroke or wound given by one man to another.

7. *They shall answer* - To the priests who shall examine them. *This blood* - This about which the present enquiry is made: or this which is here present: for it is thought the corps of the slain man was brought into the same place where the heifer was slain. Nor have we seen or understood how or by whom this was done.

8. *Forgiven* - Though there was no mortal guilt in this people, yet there was a ceremonial uncleanness in the land, which was to be expiated and forgiven.

10. *Enemies* - Of other nations, but not of the Canaanites.

11. *Hast a desire unto her* - Or, hast taken delight in her: which may be a modest expression for lying with her, and seems probable, because it is said, ver. 14, that he had humbled her. And here seem to be two cases supposed, and direction given what to do in both of them,

1. that he did desire to marry her, of which he speaks, ver. 11-13.
2. that he did not desire this, of which he speaks, ver. 14.

12. *She shall shave her head* - In token of her renouncing her heathenish idolatry and superstition, and of her becoming a new woman, and embracing the true religion.

13. *Raiment of captivity* - Those sordid raiments which were put upon her when she was taken captive. *Bewail her father and mother* - Either their death, or which was in effect the same, her final separation from them.

14. If thou have no delight in her - If thou dost not chuse to marry her. Thou shalt not make merchandise of her - Make gain of her, either by using her to thy own servile works, or by prostituting her to the lusts or to the service of others.

15. Two wives - This practice, though tolerated, is not hereby made lawful; but only provision is made for the children in this case. Hated - Comparatively, that is, less loved.

19. His father and mother - The consent of both is required to prevent the abuse of this law to cruelty. And it cannot reasonably be supposed that both would agree without the son's abominable and incorrigible wickedness, in which case it seems a righteous law, because the crime of rebellion against his own parents did so fully signify what a pernicious member he would be in the commonwealth of Israel, who had dissolved all his natural obligations. Unto the elders - Which was a sufficient caution to preserve children from the malice of any hard-hearted parents, because these elders were first to examine the cause with all exactness, and then to pronounce the sentence.

20. A glutton and a drunkard - Under which two offenses others of a like or worse nature are comprehended.

22. On a tree - Which was done after the malefactor was put to death some other way, this publick shame being added to his former punishment.

23. He is accursed of God - He is in a singular manner cursed and punished by God's appointment with a most shameful kind of punishment, as this was held among the Jews and all nations; and therefore this punishment may suffice for him, and there shall not be added to it that of lying unburied. And this curse is here appropriated to those that are hanged, to so signify that Christ should undergo this execrable punishment, and be made a curse for us, Gal. iii, 13, which though it was to come in respect to men, yet was present unto God. Defiled - Either by inhumanity towards the dead: or by suffering the monument of the man's wickedness, and of God's curse, to remain publick a longer time than God would have it, whereas it should be put out of sight, and buried in oblivion.

XXII

Laws for preserving stray or fallen cattle, ver. 1-4. For a distinction of apparel between women and men, ver. 5. For compassion even toward birds, ver. 6, 7. Of battlements on houses, ver. 8. Against improper mixtures, ver. 9-11. Of fringes, ver. 12. Of a wife, falsely accused, ver. 13-19. Justly accused, ver. 20, 21. The punishment of adultery, rape, fornication, ver. 22-29. Of incest, ver. 30.

1. Thy brother's - Any man's. Thou shalt not hide thyself - Dissemble or pretend that thou dost not see them; or pass them by as if thou hadst not seen them.

2. To thine own house - To be used like thine own cattle.

3. Hide thyself - Dissemble that thou hast found it. Or, hide it, that is, conceal the thing lost.

5. Shall not wear - Namely, ordinarily or unnecessarily, for in some cases this may be lawful, as to make an escape for one's life. Now this is forbidden, both for decency sake, that men might not confound those sexes which God hath distinguished, that all appearance of evil might be avoided, such change of garments carrying a manifest sign of effeminacy in the man, of arrogance in the woman, of lightness and petulancy in both; and also to cut off all suspicions and occasions of evil, which this practice opens a wide door to.

7. Let the dam go - Partly for the bird's sake, which suffered enough by the loss of its young; for God would not have cruelty exercised towards the brute creatures: and partly for mens sake, to refrain their greediness, that, they should not monopolize all to themselves, but leave the hopes of a future seed for others.

8. A battlement - A fence or breastwork, because the roofs of their houses were made flat, that men might walk on them. Blood - The guilt of blood, by a man's fall from the top of thy house, thro' thy neglect of this necessary provision. The Jew's say, that by the equity of this law, they are obliged, and so are we, to fence or remove every thing, whereby life may he endangered, as wells, or bridges, lest if any perish thro' our omission, their blood be required at our hand.

9. Divers seeds - Either

1. With two kinds of seed mixed and sowed together between the rows of vines in thy vineyard: which was forbidden to be done in the field, Lev. xix, 19, and here, in the vineyard. Or,

2. With any kind of seed differing from that of the vine, which would produce either herbs, or corn, or fruit-bearing trees, whose fruit might be mingled with the fruit of the vines. Now this and the following precepts, tho' in themselves small and trivial, are given, according to that time and state of the church, for instructions in greater matters, and particularly to commend to them simplicity in all their carriage towards God and man, and to forbid all mixture of their inventions with God's institutions in doctrine or worship. Defiled - Legally and morally, as being prohibited by God's law, and therefore made unclean; as on the contrary, things are sanctified by God's word, allowing and approving them, 1 Tim. iv, 5.

10. *An ox and an ass* - Because the one was a clean beast, the other unclean whereby God would teach men to avoid polluting themselves by the touch of unclean persons or things.

12. *Fringes* - Or laces, or strings, partly to bring the commands of God to their remembrance, as it is expressed, Num. xv, 38, and partly is a public profession of their nation and religion, whereby they might be distinguished from strangers, that so they might be more circumspect to behave as became the people of God, and that they should own their religion before all the world. *Thou coverest thyself* - These words seem restrictive to the upper garment wherewith the rest were covered.

13. *If any man take a wife* - And afterward falsely accuse her- What the meaning of that evidence is, by which the accusation was proved false, the learned are not agreed. Nor is it necessary for us to know: they for whom this law was intended, undoubtedly understood it.

19. *The father* - Because this was a reproach to his family, and to himself, as such a miscarriage of his daughter would have been ascribed to his evil education.

24. *She cried not* - And therefore is justly presumed to have consented to it.

26. *Even so* - Not an act of choice, but of force and constraint.

27. *The damsel cried* - Which is in that case to be presumed; charity obliging us to believe the best, 'till the contrary be manifest.

29. *Fifty shekels* - Besides the dowry, as Philo, the learned Jew notes, which is here omitted, because that was customary, it being sufficient here to mention what was peculiar to this case. *His wife* - If her father consented to it.

30. *Take* - To wife. So this respects the state, and the next branch speaks of the act only.

XXIII

Who are to be excluded the congregation of rulers, ver. 1-6. An Edomite and an Egyptian not to be abhorred, ver. 7, 8. No uncleanness to be in the camp, ver. 9-14. Of servants, escaped from their masters, ver. 15, 16. Laws, against sodomy and whoredom, ver. 17, 18. Against usury, ver. 19, 20. Against the breach of vows, ver. 21-23. The liberty which might be taken in another's field or vineyard, ver. 24, 25.

1. *He that is wounded* - A phrase denoting an eunuch. *Shall not enter into the congregation of the Lord* - Shall not be admitted to honours and offices either in the church or commonwealth of Israel; and so the congregation of the Lord doth not here signify, the body of the people, but the society of the elders or rulers of the people. Add to this, that the Hebrew word, Kahal, generally signifies a congregation or company of men met together; and therefore this cannot so conveniently be meant of all the body of the people, which could never meet in one place, but of the chief rulers, which frequently did so. Nor is it strange that eunuchs are excluded from government, both because such persons are commonly observed to want that courage which is necessary for a governor, because as such persons ordinarily were despicable, so the authority in their hands was likely to be exposed to the same contempt.

2. *The congregation* - Taking the word as in the former verse.

3. *For ever* - This seems to note the perpetuity of this law, that it should be inviolably observed in all succeeding ages.

4. *They met you not with bread and water* - As the manner of those times was to wait and provide for strangers and travelers, which was the more necessary, because in those times and countries, there were no public houses of entertainment. Their fault then was unmercifulness to strangers and afflicted persons, which was aggravated both by their relation to the Israelites, as being the children of Lot, and by the special kindness of God, and of the Israelites to them, in not fighting against them.

6. *Thou shalt not seek their peace* - That is, make no contracts either by marriages or leagues, or commerce with them, but rather constantly keep a jealous eye over them, as enemies who will watch every opportunity to ensnare or disturb thee. This counsel was now the more necessary, because a great part of the Israelites lived beyond Jordan in the borders of those people, and therefore God sets up this wall of partition betwixt them, as well knowing the mischief of bad neighbours, and Israel's proneness to receive infection from them. Each particular Israelite is not hereby forbidden to perform any office of humanity to them, but the body of the nation are forbidden all familiar conversation with them.

7. *Thou wast a stranger* - And didst receive habitation, protection and provision from them a long time, which kindness thou must not forget for their following persecution. It is ordinary with men, that one injury blots out the remembrance of twenty courtesies; but God doth not deal so with us, nor will he have us to deal so with others, but commands us to forget injuries, and to remember kindnesses.

8. *In their third generation* - Supposing their grandfather, or great-grandfather turned proselyte, and the children continue in that faith received by such ancestors.

9. *Keep from every wicked thing* - Then especially take heed, because that is a time of confusion and licentiousness; when the laws of God and man cannot be heard for the noise of arms; because the

success of thy arms depends upon God's blessing, which wicked men have no reason to expect; and because thou dost carry thy life in thy hand, and therefore hast need to be well prepared for death and judgment.

13. Cover - To prevent the annoyance of ourselves or others; to preserve and exercise modesty and natural honesty; and principally that by such outward rites they might be innured to the greater reverence of the Divine Majesty, and the greater caution to avoid all real and moral uncleanness.

15. The servant - Of such as belonged to the Canaanites, or other neighbouring nations, because if he had lived in remote countries, it is not probable that he would flee so far to avoid his master, or that his master would follow him so far to recover him. For the Canaanites this sentence was most just, because both they and theirs were all forfeited to God and Israel, and whatsoever they enjoyed was by special indulgence. And for the other neighbours it may seem just also, because both masters and servants of these and other nations are unquestionably at the disposal of the Lord their maker and sovereign ruler. Understand it likewise of such as upon enquiry appear to have been unjustly oppressed by their masters. Now it is not strange if the great God, who hates all tyranny, and styles himself the refuge of the oppressed doth interpose his authority to rescue such persons from their cruel masters.

17. No whore - No common prostitute, such as were tolerated and encouraged by the Gentiles, and used even in their religious worship. Not that such practices were allowed to the strangers among them, as is evident from many scriptures and reasons, but that it was in a peculiar manner, and upon special reasons, forbidden to them, as being much more odious in them than in strangers.

18. The hire of a whore - This is opposed to the practice of the Gentiles, who allowed both such persons and the oblations they made out of their infamous gains; and some of them kept lewd women, who prostituted themselves in the temples, to the honour of their false Gods, and offered part of their profit to them. Or the price of a dog - It seems to mean, of a whoremonger or sodomite. Such are called dogs, Rev. xxii, 15. And it is not improbable they are called so here. From these God would not accept of any offering.

19. Thou shalt not lend upon usury to thy brother - To an Israelite. They held their estates immediately from God, who while he distinguished them from all other people, might have ordered, had he pleased, that they should have all things in common. But instead of that, and in token of their joint interest in the good land he had given them, he only appointed them, as there was occasion, to lend to one another without interest. This among them would be little or no loss to the lender, because their land was so divided, their estates so settled, and there was so little a merchandise among them, that it was seldom or never they had occasion to borrow any great sums, but only for the subsistence of their family, or some uncommon emergence. But they might lend to a stranger upon usury, who was supposed to live by trade, and therefore got by what he borrowed: in which case 'tis just, the lender should share in the gain. This usury therefore is not oppressive: for they might not oppress a stranger.

21. Not slack - Not delay: because delays may make them both unable to pay it, and unwilling too.

23. A free-will-offering - Which though thou didst really make, yet being made, thou art no longer free, but obliged to perform it.

24. At thy pleasure - Which was allowed in those parts, because of the great plenty and fruitfulness of vines there.

XXIV

Of Divorce, ver. 1-4. New-married men discharged from the war, ver. 5. Of pledges, ver. 6. 10-13. Of man-stealers, ver. 7. Of the leprosy, ver. 8, 9. Of daily wages, ver. 14, 15. None to be punished for another's sin, ver. 16. Of justice and mercy to the widow, fatherless and stranger, ver. 17-22.

1. Some uncleanness - Some hateful thing, some distemper of body or quality of mind not observed before marriage: or some light carriage, as this phrase commonly signifies, but not amounting to adultery. Let him write - This is not a command as some of the Jews understood it, nor an allowance and approbation, but merely a permission of that practice for prevention of greater mischiefs, and this only until the time of reformation, till the coming of the Messiah when things were to return to their first institution and purest condition.

4. May not - This is the punishment of his levity and injustice in putting her away without sufficient cause, which by this offer he now acknowledgeth. Defiled - Not absolutely, as if her second marriage were a sin, but with respect to her first husband, to whom she is as a defiled or unclean woman, that is, forbidden things; forbidden are accounted and called unclean, Judg. xiii, 7, because they may no more be touched or used than an unclean thing. Thou shalt not cause the land to sin - Thou shalt not suffer such lightness to be practiced, lest the people be polluted, and the land defiled and accursed by that means.

5. Business - Any publick office or employment, which may cause an absence from or neglect of his wife. One year - That their affections may be firmly settled, so as there may be no occasions for the

divorces last mentioned.

6. Mill-stone - Used in their hand-mills. Under this, he understands all other things necessary to get a livelihood, the taking away whereof is against the laws both of charity and prudence, seeing by those things alone he can be enabled both to subsist and to pay his debts. Life - His livelihood, the necessary support of his life.

10. Thou shalt not go in - To prevent both the poor man's reproach by having his wants exposed, and the creditor's greediness which might be occasioned by the sight of something which he desired, and the debtor could not spare.

11. The pledge - He shall chuse what pledge he pleases, provided it be sufficient for the purpose.

12. Thou shalt not sleep - But restore it before night, which intimates that he should take no such thing for pledge, without which a man cannot sleep.

13. Bless thee - Bring down the blessing of God upon thee by his prayers: for though his prayers, if he be not a good man, shall not avail for his own behalf, yet they shall avail for thy benefit. It shall be right - Esteemed and accepted by God as a work of righteousness, or mercy.

15. At this day - At the time appointed, weekly or daily.

16. Not put to death - If the one be free from the guilt of the others sin, except in those cases where the sovereign Lord of life and death, before whom none is innocent, hath commanded it, as chap. xiii, 1-18 Josh. vii, 24. For though God do visit the father's sins upon the children, Exod. xx, 5, yet he will not suffer men to do so.

17. Raiment - Not such as she hath daily and necessary use of, as being poor. But this concerns not rich persons, nor superfluous raiment.

XXV

Stripes not to exceed forty, ver. 1-3. The ox not to be muzzled, ver. 4. Of marrying the brother's widow, ver. 5-10. Of an immodest woman, ver. 11, 12. Of just weights and measures, ver. 13-16. Amalek to be destroyed, ver. 17-19.

1. Justify - Acquit him from guilt and false accusations, and free him from punishment.

2. Beaten - Which the Jews say was the case of all those crimes which the law commands to be punished, without expressing the kind or degree of punishment. Before his face - That the punishment may be duly inflicted, without excess or defect. And from this no person's rank or quality exempted him, if he was a delinquent.

3. Forty stripes - It seems not superstition, but prudent caution, when the Jews would not exceed thirty-nine stripes, lest through mistake or forgetfulness they should go beyond their bounds, which they were commanded to keep. Should seem vile - Should be made contemptible to his brethren, either by this cruel usage of him, as if he were a brute beast: or by the deformity or infirmity of body which excessive beating might produce.

4. He treadeth out the corn - Which they did in those parts, either immediately by their hoofs on by drawing carts or other instruments over the corn. Hereby God taught them humanity, even to their beasts that served them, and much more to their servants or other men who laboured for them, especially to their ministers, 1 Cor. ix, 9.

5. Together - In the same town, or at least country. For if the next brother had removed his habitation into remote parts, on were carried thither into captivity, then the wife of the dead had her liberty to marry the next kinsman that lived in the same place with her. One - Any of them, for the words are general, and the reason of the law was to keep up the distinction of tribes and families, that so the Messiah might be discovered by the family from which he was appointed to proceed; and also of inheritances, which were divided among all the brethren, the first-born having only a double portion. A stranger - To one of another family.

6. That his name be not put out - That a family be not lost. So this was a provision that the number of their families might not be diminished.

9. Loose his shoe - As a sign of his resignation of all his right to the woman, and to her husband's inheritance: for as the shoe was a sign of one's power and right, Psalm lx, 8; cviii, 9, so the parting with the shoe was a token of the alienation of such right; and as a note of infamy, to signify that by this disingenuous action he was unworthy to be amongst free-men, and fit to be reduced to the condition of the meanest servants, who used to go barefoot, Isaiah xx, 2, 4.

10. His name - That is, his person, and his posterity also. So it was a lasting blot.

13. A great and a small - The great to buy with, the small for selling.

17. Out of Egypt - Which circumstance greatly aggravates their sin, that they should do thus to a people, who had been long exercised with sore afflictions, to whom pity was due by the laws of nature and humanity, and for whose rescue God had in so glorious a manner appeared, which they could not be ignorant of. So this was barbarousness to Israel, and setting the great Jehovah at defiance.

XXVI

A form of confession made by him that offered the first-fruits, ver. 1-11. A prayer to be made after the disposal of the third year's tithe, ver. 12-15. He binds all these precepts upon them, by the divine authority, and the covenant between God and them, ver. 16-19.

2. Thou shalt take - This seems to be required of each master of a family, either upon his first settlement, or once every year at one of their three feasts, when they were obliged to go up to Jerusalem.

5. A Syrian - So Jacob was, partly by his original, as being born of Syrian parents, as were Abraham and Rebecca, both of Chaldea or Mesopotamia, which was a part of Syria largely so called, partly by his education and conversation; and partly by his relations, his wives being such, and his children too by their mother's. Ready to perish - Either through want and poverty; (See Gen. xxviii, 11, 20; xxxii, 10,) or through the rage of his brother Esau, and the treachery of his father-in-law Laban.

10. It - The basket of first-fruits, ver. 2.

11. Thou shalt rejoice - Thou shalt hereby enabled to take comfort in all thy employments, when thou hast sanctified them by giving God his portion. It is the will of God, that we should be chearful not only in our attendance upon his holy ordinances, but in our enjoyment of the gifts of his providence. Whatever good thing God gives us, we should make the most comfortable use of it we can, still tracing the streams to the fountain of all consolation.

12. The year of tithing - Hebrew. the year of that tithe, so called, either

1. because these tithes were gathered only in that year. Or rather,

2. because then only they were so bestowed; and whereas these second tithes for two years together were eaten only by the owners and Levites, and that in Jerusalem, in the third year they were eaten also by the strangers, fatherless, and widows, and that in their own dwellings.

13. Before the Lord - In thy private addresses to God; for this is to be said presently upon the distribution of these tithes, which was not done at Jerusalem, but in their own private gates or dwellings. And this is to be spoken before the Lord, that is, solemnly, seriously, and in a religious manner, with due respect to God's presence, and will, and glory.

14. In my mourning - In sorrow, or grieving that I was to give away so much of my profits to the poor, but I have cheerfully eaten and feasted with them, as I was obliged to do. Unclean use - For any common use; for any other use than that which thou hast appointed, which would have been a pollution of them. For the dead - For any funeral pomp or service; for the Jews used to send in provisions to feast with the nearest relations of the party deceased; and in that case both the guests and food were legally polluted, Num. xix, 11, 14, and therefore the use of these tithes in such cases had been a double fault, both the defiling of sacred food, and the employing those provisions upon sorrowful occasions, which by God's express command were to be eaten with rejoicing.

15. Look down - After that solemn profession of their obedience to God's commands, they are taught to pray for God's blessing whereby they are instructed how vain and ineffectual the prayers of unrighteous or disobedient persons are.

17. Avouched - Or, declared, or owned.

18. Avouched thee - Hath owned thee for such before all the world by eminent and glorious manifestations of his power and favour, by a solemn entering into covenant with thee, and giving peculiar laws, promises, and privileges to thee above all mankind.

XXVII

A command to write all the law upon stones, ver. 1-8. A charge to Israel, to obey God, ver. 9-10. To pronounce a blessing on mount Gerizzim, and a curse on mount Ebal, ver. 11-13. To the Levites, to pronounce the whole curse, ver. 14-26.

2. On that day - About that time, for it was not done 'till some days after their passing over. 3. This law - The law properly so called, that is, the sum and substance of the precepts or laws of Moses, especially such as were moral, particularly the decalogue. Write it, that thou mayest go in - As the condition of thy entering into the land. For since Canaan is given only by promise, it must be held by obedience.

4. Mount Ebal - The mount of cursing. Here the law is written, to signify that a curse was due to the violators of it, and that no man could expect justification from the works of the law, by the sentence whereof all men are justly accused, as being all guilty of the transgression of it in one kind and degree or other. Here the sacrifices are to be offered, to shew that there is no way to be delivered from this curse, but by the blood of Christ, which all these sacrifices did typify, and by Christ's being made a curse for us.

6. Whole stones - Rough, not hewed or polished. By the law written on the stones, God spake to

them: by the altar and sacrifices upon it, they spake to God: and thus was communion kept up between them and God.

9. *The people of the Lord* - By thy solemn renewing of thy covenant with him.

12. *Upon mount Gerizzim* - These words may be rendered beside or near to mount Gerizzim. There were in Canaan two mountains that lay near together, with a valley between, one called Gerizzim, the other Ebal. On the sides of these which faced each other, all the tribes were to be drawn up, six on a side, so that in the valley they came near each other, so near that the priests standing between them, might be heard by them that were next them on both sides. Then one of the priests, or perhaps more, at some distance from each other, pronounced with a loud voice, one of the curses following. And all the people who stood on the foot and side of mount Ebal, (those farther off taking the signal from those who were nearer) said Amen! Then the contrary blessing was pronounced, "Blessed is he that doth so or so:" To which all who stood on the foot and side of mount Gerizzim, said, Amen! *Simeon* - All these were the children of the free-women, Leah and Rachel, to shew both the dignity of the blessings above the curses, and that the blessings belong only to those who are evangelically such, as this is expounded and applied, Gal. iv, 22, even to those that receive the Spirit of adoption and liberty. Joseph is here put for both his sons and tribes Manasseh and Ephraim, which are reckoned as one tribe, because Levi is here numbered; but when Levi is omitted, as it is where the division of the land is made, there Manasseh and Ephraim pass for two tribes.

13. *To curse* - Of the former tribes, 'tis said, they stood to bless the people: of these, that they stood to curse. Perhaps the different way of speaking intimates, That Israel in general were an happy people, and should ever be so, if they were obedient. And to that blessing, they on mount Gerizzim said, Amen! But the curses come in, only as exceptions to the general rule: "Israel is a blessed people: but if there be any even among them, that do such and such things, they have no part or lot in this matter, but are under a curse." This shews how ready God is to bestow the blessing: if any fall under the curse, they bring it on their own head. Four of these are children of the bond-woman, to shew that the curse belongs to those of servile and disingenuous spirits. With these are joined Reuben, who by his shameful sin fell from his dignity, and Zebulun, the youngest of Leah's children, that the numbers might be equal.

14. *The Levites* - Some of the Levites, namely, the priests, who bare the ark, as it is expressed Josh. viii, 33, for the body of the Levites stood upon mount Gerizzim, ver. 12. But these stood in the valley between Gerizzim and Ebal, looking towards the one or the other mountain as they pronounced either the blessings or the curses.

15. *Cursed* - The curses are expressed, but not the blessings. For as many as were under the law, were under the curse. But it was an honour reserved for Christ to bless us; to do that which the law could not do. So in his sermon on the mount, the true mount Gerizzim, we have blessings only. *The man* - Under this particular he understands all the gross violations of the first table, as under the following branches he comprehends all other sins against the second table. *Amen* - 'Tis easy to understand the meaning of Amen to the blessings. But how could they say it to the curses? It was both a profession of their faith in the truth of it, and an acknowledgment of the equity of these curses. So that when they said Amen, they did in effect Say, not only, it is certain it shall be so, but it is just it should be so.

16. *Light* - Or, despiseth in his heart: or reproacheth or curseth, secretly: for if the fact was notorious, it was punished with death.

17. *Out of the way* - That misleadeth simple souls, giving them pernicious counsel, either for this life, or for the next.

24. *Smiteth* - That is, killeth. This includes murder under colour of law, which is of all others the greatest affront to God. Cursed therefore is he that any ways contributes to accuse, or convict, or condemn an innocent person.

26. *Confirmeth not* - Or, performeth not. To this we must all say, Amen! Owning ourselves to be under the curse, and that we must have perished forever, if Christ had not redeemed us from the curse of the law, by being made a curse for us.

XXVIII

The blessings of obedience, personal, family and national, ver. 1-14. The curses of the disobedient; their extreme vexation, ver. 15-44. Their utter ruin and destruction, ver. 45-68.

2. *Overtake thee* - Those blessings which others greedily follow after, and never overtake, shall follow after thee, and shall be thrown into thy lap by special kindness.

3. *In the city, and in the field* - Whether they were husbandmen or tradesmen, whether in the town or country, they should be preserved from the dangers of both, and have the comforts of both. How constantly must we depend upon God, both for the continuance and comfort of life! We need him at every turn: we cannot be safe, if he withdraw his protection, nor easy, if he suspends his savour: but if he bless us, go where we will, 'tis well with us.

5. Store - Store-house, it shall always be well replenished and the provision thou hast there shall be preserved for thy use and service.

6. Comest in - That is, in all thy affairs and administrations.

9. Establish thee - Shall confirm his covenant with thee, by which he separated thee to himself as an holy and peculiar people.

10. Of the Lord - That you are in truth his people and children: A most excellent and glorious people, under the peculiar care and countenance of the great God.

11. The same things which were said before are repeated, to shew that God would repeat and multiply his blessings upon them.

12. His treasure - The heaven or the air, which is God's storehouse, where he treasures up rain or wind for man's use.

13. The head - The chief of all people in power, or at least in dignity and privileges; so that even they that are not under thine authority shall reverence thy greatness and excellency. So it was in David's and Solomon's time, and so it should have been much oftner and much more, if they had performed the conditions.

15. Overtake thee - So that thou shalt not be able to escape them, as thou shalt vainly hope and endeavour to do. There is no running from God, but by running to him; no flying from his justice, but by flying to his mercy.

20. Vexation - This seems chiefly to concern the mind, arising from the disappointment of hopes and the presages of its approaching miseries. Rebuke - Namely, from God, not so much in words as by his actions, by cross providences, by sharp and sore afflictions.

23. Brass - Like brass, hard and dry, and shut up from giving rain. Iron - Hard and chapt and barren.

24. Dust - Either thy rain shall be as unprofitable to thy ground and seed as if it were only so much dust. Or instead of rain shall come nothing but dust from heaven, which being raised and carried up by the wind in great abundance, returns, and falls upon the earth as it were in clouds or showers.

27. The botch of Egypt - Such boils and blains as the Egyptians were plagued with, spreading from head to foot: The emerodes - Or piles.

28. Blindness - Of mind, so that they shall not know what to do: Astonishment - They shall be filled with wonder and horror because of the strangeness and soreness of their calamities.

29. Grope at noon day - In the most clear and evident matters thou shalt grossly mistake. Thy ways - Thy counsels and enterprizes shall be frustrated and turn to thy destruction.

32. Unto another people - By those who have conquered them, and taken them captives, who shall give or sell them to other persons. Fail - Or, be consumed, partly with grief and plentiful tears; and partly with earnest desire, and vain and long expectation of their return. No might - No power to rescue, nor money to ransom them.

33. Which thou knowest not - Which shall come from a far country, which thou didst not at all expect or fear, and therefore will be the more dreadful when they come; a nation whose language thou understandest not, and therefore canst not plead with them for mercy, nor expect any favour from them.

34. Thou shalt be mad for the sight of thine eyes - Quite put out of the possession of their own souls; quite bereaved of all comfort and hope, and abandoned to utter despair. They that walk by sight, and not by faith, are in danger of losing reason itself, when all about them looks frightful; and their condition is bad indeed, who are mad for the sight of their eyes.

36. Thy king - The calamity shall be both universal, which even thy king shall not be able to avoid, much less the subjects, who have far less advantage and opportunity for escape; and irrecoverable, because he who should protect or rescue them is lost with them, Lam. iv, 10. Wood and stone - So what formerly was their choice and delight now becomes their plague and misery. And this doubtless was the condition of many Israelites under the Assyrian and Balylonish captivities.

43. Within thee - Within thy gates; who formerly honoured and served thee, and were some of them glad of the crumbs which fell from thy table.

45. Moreover all these curses - It seems Moses has been hitherto foretelling their captivity in Babylon, by which even after their return, they were brought to the low condition mentioned, ver. 44. But in the following he foretells their last destruction by the Romans. And the present deplorable state of the Jewish nation, so exactly answers this prediction, that it is an incontestable proof of the truth of the prophecy, and consequently of the divine authority of the scriptures. And this destruction more dreadful than the former shews, that their sin in rejecting Christ, was more provoking to God than idolatry itself, and left them more under the power of Satan. For their captivity in Babylon cured them effectually of idolatry in seventy years. But under this last destruction, they continue above sixteen hundred years incurably averse to the Lord Jesus.

46. They - These curses now mentioned. A wonder - Signal and wonderful to all that hear of them. 'Tis amazing, a people so incorporated, should be so universally disperst! And that a people scattered in all nations, should not mix with any, but like Cain, be fugitives and vagabonds, and yet so marked as to

be known.

54. Evil - Unkind, envious, covetous to monopolize these dainty bits to themselves, and grudging that their dearest relations should have any part of them.

56. Evil - Unmerciful: she will desire or design their destruction for her food.

57. Her young one - Hebrew. after-birth: that which was loathsome to behold, will now be pleasant to eat; and together with it she shall eat the child which was wrapt up in it, and may be included in this expression. Which she shall bear - Or, which she shall have born, that is, her more grown children. She shall eat them - This was fulfilled more than once, to the perpetual reproach of the Jewish nation. Never was the like done either by Greek or Barbarian. See the fruit of being abandoned by God!

63. To destroy you - His just indignation against you will be so great, that it will be a pleasure to him to take vengeance on you. For though he doth not delight in the death of a sinner in itself, yet he doth delight in glorifying his justice upon incorrigible sinners, seeing the exercise of all his attributes must needs please him, else he were not perfectly happy.

65. Neither shall thy foot have rest - Ye shall have no settlement in the land whither you are banished, but there you shall be tossed about from place to place, and sold from person to person, or Cain - like, wander about.

66. Thy life shall hang in doubt - Either because thou art in the hands of thy enemies that have power, and want no will, to destroy thee: or because of the terrors of thy own mind, and the guilt of thy conscience making thee to fear, even where no fear is.

68. Into Egypt - Which was literally fulfilled under Titus, when multitudes of them were carried thither in ships, and sold for slaves. And this expression seems to mind them of that time when they went over the sea without ships, God miraculously drying up the sea before them, which now they would have occasion sadly to remember. By the way - Or, to the way. And the way seems not to be meant here of the usual road-way from Canaan to Egypt, which was wholly by land, but to be put for the end of the way or journey, even the land of Egypt, for to this, and not to the road- way between Canaan and Egypt, agree the words here following, whereof I speak unto thee, thou shalt see it, (that is, Egypt) no more again. No man shall buy you - Either because the number of your captives shall be so great, that the market shall be glutted with you; or because you shall be so loathsome and contemptible that men shall not be willing to have you for slaves. And this was the condition of the Jews after the destruction of Jerusalem, as Josephus the Jew hath left upon record. Let us all learn hence, to stand in awe and not to sin. I have heard of a wicked man (says Mr. Henry) who on reading these threatenings, was so enraged, that he tore the leaf out of his bible. But to what purpose is it, to deface a copy, while the original remains unchangeable? By which it is determined, that the wages of sin is death: yea, a death more dreadful than all that is here spoken!

XXIX

The preface of God's covenant, ver. 1. A recital of his dealings with them, ver. 2-8. A solemn exhortation to keep covenant with God, ver. 9-17. A severe threatning to them that break it, ver. 18-28. The end of the revealed will of God, ver. 29.

1. These are the terms or conditions upon which God hath made, that is renewed his covenant with you. The covenant was but one in substance, but various in the time and manner of its dispensation.

4. Yet the Lord - That is, you have perceived and seen them with the eyes of your body, but not with your minds and hearts; you have not yet learned rightly to understand the word and works of God, so as to know them for your good, and to make a right use of them, and to comply with them: which he expresseth thus, the Lord hath not given you, &c. not to excuse their wickedness, but to direct them to whom they must have recourse for a good understanding of God's works; and to intimate that although the hearing ear, and the seeing eye, be the workmanship of God, yet their want of his grace was their own fault, and the just punishment of their former sins; their present case being like theirs in Isaiah's time, who first shut their own eyes and ears that they might not see and hear, and would not understand, and then by the righteous judgment of God, had their eyes and ears closed that they should not see and hear, and understand. God's readiness to do us good in other things, is a plain evidence, that if we have not grace, that best of gifts, 'tis our own fault and not his: he would have gathered us, and we would not.

6. Ye have not eaten bread - Common bread purchased by your own money, or made by your own hands, but heavenly and angelical bread. Neither drank wine - But only water out of the rock. The Lord - Omnipotent and all-sufficient for your provision without the help of any creatures, and your God in covenant with you who hath a true affection to you, and fatherly care of you.

11. Thy stranger - Such strangers as had embraced their religion: all sorts of persons, yea, even the meanest of them.

12. Into covenant and into his oath - Into covenant, confirmed by a solemn oath.

13. That he may establish thee - Here is the summary of that covenant whereof Moses was the

mediator, and in the covenant relation between God and them, all the precepts and promises of the covenant are included. That they should be established for a people to him, to fear, love, obey, and be devoted to him, and that he should be to them a God, to make them holy and happy; and a due sense of the relation we stand in to God as our God, and the obligation we are under to him as his people, is enough to bring us to all the duties, and all the comforts of the covenant. And does this covenant include nothing spiritual? nothing that refers to eternity?

15. So also - With your posterity. For so the covenant was made at first with Abraham and his seed, by which as God engaged himself to continue the blessing of Abraham upon his posterity, so he also engaged them to the same duties which were required of Abraham. So it is even among men, where a king confers an estate upon a subject and forever enjoy that benefit, are obliged to the same conditions. It may likewise include those who were then constrained to be absent, by sickness, or any necessary occasion. Nay one of the Chaldee pharaphrasts reads it, all the generations that have been from the first days of the world, and all that shall arise to the end of the whole world, stand with us here this day. And so taking this covenant as a typical dispensation of the covenant of grace, 'tis a noble testimony to the Mediator of that covenant, who is the same yesterday, to day, and forx ever. 16. Egypt - Where you have seen their idolatries, and learned too much of them, as the golden calf shewed, and therefore have need to renew your covenant with God; where also we were in dreadful bondage whence God alone hath delivered us, to whom therefore we are deeply obliged, and have all reason to renew our covenant with him. Through the nations - With what hazard, if God had not appeared for us!

18. A root - An evil heart inclining you to such cursed idolatry, and bringing forth bitter fruits.

19. Of this curse - Of that oath where-in he swore he would keep covenant with God, and that with a curse pronounced against himself if he did not perform it. Bless himself - Flatter himself in his own eyes, with vain hopes, as if God did not mind such things, and either could not, or would not punish them. Peace - Safety and prosperity. My own heart - Though I do not follow God's command, but my own devices. To add drunkenness to thirst - The words may be rendered, to add thirst to drunkenness, and so the sense may be, that when he hath multiplied his sins, and made himself as it were drunk with them, yet he is not satisfied therewith, but still whets his appetite, and provokes his thirst after more, as drunkards often use means to make themselves thirst after more drink.

20. Shall smoke - Shall burn and break forth with flame and smoke as it were from a furnace.

21. Unto evil - Unto some peculiar and exemplary plague; he will make him a monument of his displeasure to the whole land.

23. Salt and burning - Is burnt up and made barren, as with brimstone and salt.

26. Whom God had not given to them - For their worship, but hath divided them unto all nations, for their use and service. So he speaks here of the sun and moon and stars, which were the principal gods worshipped by the neighbouring nations.

29. The secret things - Having mentioned the amazing judgments of God upon the whole land and people of Israel, and foreseeing the utter extirpation which would come upon them for their wickedness, he breaks out into this pathetic exclamation, either to bridle their curiosity, who would be apt to inquire into the time and manner of so great an event; or to quiet his own mind, and satisfy the scruples of others, who perceiving God to deal so severely with his own people, when in the meantime he suffered those nations which were guilty of grosser atheism and idolatry, might thence take occasion to deny his providence or question the equity of his proceedings. To this he answers, that the ways and judgments of God, tho' never unjust, are often times hidden from us, unsearchable by our shallow capacities, and matter for our admiration, not our enquiry. But the things which are revealed by God and his word, are the proper object of our enquiries, that thereby we may know our duty, and be kept from such terrible calamities as these now mentioned.

XXX

Promises upon their repentance, ver. 1-10. The righteousness of faith set before them, ver. 11-14. Life and death offered to their choice, ver. 15-20.

1. The blessing - When thou art obedient. The curse - When thou becomest rebellious.

6. And the Lord - Or, For the Lord will circumcise thine heart, will by his word and spirit change and purge thy heart from all thine idolatry and wickedness, and incline thy heart to love him. God will first convert and sanctify them, the fruit whereof shall be, that they shall return and obey God's commandments, ver. 8, and then shall prosper in all things, ver. 9. This promise principally respects the times of the gospel, and the grace which was to be then imparted to all Israel by Christ.

9. For good - Whereas thou did formerly receive these mercies for thy hurt, now thou shalt have them for thy good, thy heart shall be so changed that thou shalt not now abuse them, but employ them to the service of God the giver. Over thee for good - To do thee good; as he did rejoice to destroy thee.

10. If thou wilt hearken - This is added to warn them that they should not receive the grace of God

in vain, and to teach them that the grace of God doth not discharge man's obligation to his duty, nor excuse him for the neglect of it. It is observable, that Moses calls God, the Lord thy God twelve times in these ten verses. In the threatnings of the former chapter, he is all along called the Lord, a God of power, and the judge of all. But in the promises of this chapter, the Lord thy God, a God of grace, and in covenant with thee.

11. This commandment - The great command of loving and obeying God, which is the sum of the law, of which yet he doth not here speak, as it is in itself, but as it is molified and accompanied with the grace of the gospel. The meaning is, that tho' the practice of God's laws be now far from us, and above our strength, yet, considering the advantage of gospel grace, whereby God enables us to do our duty, it is near and easy to us, who believe. And so this well agrees with Rom. x, 6, &c. where St. Paul applies this place to the righteousness of faith. Is not hidden - Hebrew. Is not too wonderful for thee, not too hard for thee to know and do. The will of God, which is but darkly manifested to other nations, Acts xvii, 27, is clearly and fully revealed unto thee: thou canst not pretend ignorance or invincible difficulty.

12. In heaven - Shut up there, but it hath been thence delivered and published in thy hearing.

13. Neither beyond the sea - The knowledge of this commandment is not to be fetched from far distant places, to which divers of the wise Heathens travelled for their wisdom; but it was brought to thy very doors and ears, and declared to thee in this wilderness.

14. In thy mouth - Thou knowest it so well, that it is the matter of thy common discourse. In thy heart - In thy mind, (as the heart is very commonly taken) to understand and believe it. In a word, the Law is plain and easy: but the gospel is much more so.

19. Chuse life - They shall have life that chuse it: they that chuse the favour of God, and communion with him, shall have what they chuse. They that come short of life and happiness, must thank themselves only. They had had them, if they had chosen them, when they were put to their choice: but they die, because they will die.

20. That thou mayest love the Lord thy God - Here he shews them in short, what their duty is; To love God as the Lord, a being most amiable, and as their God, a God in covenant with them: as an evidence of their love, to obey his voice in every thing, and by constancy in this love and obedience, to cleave to him all their days. And what encouragement had they to do this? For he is thy life and the length of thy days - He gives life, preserves life, restores life, and prolongs it, by his power, tho' it be a frail life, and by his presence, tho' it be a forfeited life. He sweetens life by his comforts, and compleats all in life everlasting.

XXXI

Moses encourages the people and Joshua, ver. 1-8. 23. Delivers to the priests the law, to be read every seventh year, ver. 9-13. God informs Moses of his approaching death, and the future apostasy of Israel, ver. 14-18. Orders him to write a song, which should be a testimony against them, ver. 19-22. Moses gives the law to the Levites to lay up beside the ark, and bids them assemble the people to hear his song, ver. 24-30.

1. Went and spake - Continued to speak, an usual Hebrew phrase.

2. Go out and come in - Perform the office of a leader or governor, because the time of my death approaches.

9. This law - Largely so called, the whole law or doctrine delivered unto Moses contained in these five books. To the priests - That they might keep it carefully and religiously, and bring it forth upon occasion, and read it, and instruct the people out of it. The elders - Who were assistants to the priests, to take care that the law should be kept, and read, and observed.

10. The year of release - When they were freed from debts and troubles, and cares of worldly matters, and thereby fitter to attend on God and his service.

11. Thou shalt read - Thou shalt cause it to be read by the priest or Levites; for he could not read it himself in the hearing of all Israel, but this was to be done by several persons, and so the people met in several congregations.

12. Together - Not in one place. But into divers assemblies or synagogues. Women who hereby are required to go to Jerusalem at this solemnity, as they were permitted to do in other solemnities. Children - Such of them as could understand, as appears from Neh. viii, 2, 3, the pious Jews doubtless read it daily in their houses, and Moses of old time was read in the synagogues every sabbath day. But once in seven years, the law was thus to be read in public, to magnify it and make it honourable.

14. Give him a charge - Immediately from myself for his greater encouragement, and to gain him more authority with the people.

16. The strangers of the land - That is, of the Canaanites, who will be turned out of their possessions, and become as strangers in their own land. This aggravates their folly to worship such gods as could neither preserve their friends, nor annoy their enemies.

17. Hide my face - Withdraw my favour and help. Whatever outward troubles we are in if we have but the light of God's countenance, we are safe. But if God hide his face from us then we are undone.

19. Write this song - Which is contained chap. xxxii, 1-43, and is put into a song that it may be better learned, and more fixed in their minds and memories. Put it in their mouths - Cause them to learn it, and sing it one to another, to oblige them to more circumspection. A witness - Of my kindness in giving them so many blessings, of my patience in bearing so long with them, of my clemency in giving them such fair and plain warnings, and my justice in punishing such an incorrigible people.

21. Their imaginations - Inclinations to Idolatry, which they do not check, as they ought; and some of them do not only cherish it in their hearts, but as far as they can and dare, secretly practice it, as may be gathered from Amos v, 25 Acts vii, 43.

25. The Levites - The priests, ver. 9, who also were Levites.

26. Take this book - Probably the very same book, which (after having been some way misplaced) was found in the house of the Lord, in the days of Josiah, and publickly read by the king himself, for a witness against a people, who were then almost ripe for ruin. In the side - In the outside, in a little chest fixed to it, for nothing but the tables of stone were contained in the ark, 1 Kings viii, 9, here it was kept for greater security and reverence. A witness against thee - Against thy people, to whom he turns his speech that they might be the more affected with it.

XXXII

The song of Moses contains the preface, ver. 1, 2. A high character of God, ver. 3-6. A recital of the great things God had done for them, and as their carriage toward him, ver. 7-18. A prediction of judgments for their aggravated impieties, ver. 19-35. A promise of vengeance upon their enemies, and deliverance for a remnant, ver. 36-43. An exhortation annext, ver. 44-47. Orders given to Moses, to go up to the mount and die, ver. 48-52.

1. O heavens, O earth - You lifeless and senseless creatures, which he calls upon partly to accuse the stupidity of Israel, that were more dull of hearing than these: and partly as witnesses of the truth of his sayings and the justice of God's proceedings against them.

2. As the rain - Look what effect rain and dew have upon herbs and grass which they make fresh and fragrant and growing, the same effect may my discourse have upon your hearts, that is, to make them soft and pliable and fruitful.

3. The name of the Lord - His glorious excellencies and righteous actions, by which he hath made himself known as a man is known by his name, and by which it will appear both that there is no blame to be laid upon him whatsoever befalls you, and that it is gross madness to forsake such a God for dumb idols. Ascribe ye - As I am about to publish the majesty and glory of God, so do you also acknowledge it.

4. A rock - As for the stability of his nature, and invincibleness of his power, so also for his fixedness and immutability in his counsels and promises and ways; so that is there shall be a sad change in your affairs, remember that this proceeds from yourselves and from the change of your ways towards God, and not from God, in whom there is no variableness or shadow of change, James i, 17. His work - All his works and actions are unblameable, perfect, wise and righteous. His ways - All his administrations in the world and particularly with you are managed with wisdom and justice. A God of truth - Constant to his promises: you cannot accuse him of any unfaithfulness to this day.

5. They - The Israelites. Their spot - The wickedness with which they are stained, is not of his children - Plainly shews they are not his children, but the devil's. God's children have no such spot. Indeed this text does not affirm, they have any spot at all. Perverse - Froward and untractable: Crooked - Irregular and disorderly.

6. O foolish people and unwise! - Fools and double fools! Fools indeed, to disoblige one, on whom you so entirely depend! Who hath bewitched you! To forsake your own mercies for lying vanities! Bought thee - That hath redeemed thee from Egyptian bondage. Made thee - Not only in a general by creation, but in a peculiar manner by making thee his peculiar people. Established - That is, renewed and confirmed his favour to thee, and not taken it away, which thou hast often provoked him to do.

7. The days of old - The events of ancient days or former ages, and thou wilt find that I had a respect unto thee not only in Abraham's time, but long before it.

8. Their inheritance - When God by his providence allotted the several parts of the world to several people, which was done Gen. x, 1-32 Gen. xi, 1-9. When he separated - Divided them in their languages and habitations according to their families. He set the bounds - That is, he disposed of the several lands and limits of the people so as to reserve a sufficient place for the great numbers of the people of Israel. And therefore he so guided the hearts of several people, that the posterity of Canaan, which was accursed of God, and devoted to ruin, should be seated in that country which God intended

for the children of Israel, that so when their iniquities were ripe, they might be rooted out, and the Israelites come in their stead.

9. His people - It is no wonder God had so great a regard to this people, for he chose them out of all mankind to be his peculiar portion.

10. He found him - Not by chance, but as it were looking out and seeking for him. He did indeed manifest himself to him in Egypt, but it was in the wilderness at Sinai, God found him in an eminent manner, and revealed his will to him, and entered into covenant with him, and imparted himself and his grace and blessing to him. By this word he also signifies both their lost condition in themselves, and that their recovery was not from themselves, but only from God who sought and found them out by his grace. In the waste howling wilderness - In a place destitute of all the necessaries and comforts of life, which also was a type of that desolate and comfortless condition in which all men are before the grace of God finds them out; where instead of the voices of men, is nothing heard but the howlings and yellings of ravenous birds and beasts. He led them - He conducted them frons place to place by his cloudy pillar and providence. Or, he compassed him about, by his provident care, watching over him and preserving him on every side. As the apple of his eye - As men use to keep the apple of their eye, that is, with singular care and diligence, this being as a most tender, so a most useful part.

11. Her nest - Her young ones in the nest; which she by her cry and motion provoketh to fly. Her wings - As preparing herself to fly. On her wings - Or, as on her wings, that is, gently, and tenderly and safely too, as if she carried them not in her claws for fear of hurting them, but upon her wings. Some say, the eagle doth usually carry her young ones upon her wings.

12. Did lead them - When they were shut up in Egypt as in their nest whence they durst not venture to fly nor stir, he taught and encouraged and enabled them to fly out from that bondage, he dealt tenderly with them, bearing with their infirmities, keeping them from all harms. With him - To assist him at that work or to deliver them. The more unworthy they in giving to idols a share in that worship which they owe to God only.

13. The high places - To conquer their strongest holds, which often are in the mountains, and their cities fenced with walls of greatest height and strength. To ride upon, in scripture phrase, is to subdue or conquer. Out of the rock - This being a land flowing with honey, where the bees made honey in the holes of rocks, or in the trees that grew upon or among the rocks. Out of the flinty rocks - The olive-trees grow and bear most fruit in rocky or hilly places.

14. Fat of lambs - For though the fat wherewith the inward parts were covered was not to be eaten by them, but offered to God, yet that fat which was mixed with the flesh they might eat, as the Jewish doctors note. Basham - A place famous for excellent cattle. Fat of kidneys of wheat - With the finest of the grains of wheat; compared to kidneys for their shape and largeness.

15. Jeshurun - Israel whom he calls right or upright, (as the word signifies) partly by way of instruction to mind them what they professed and ought to be; and partly by way of exprobration, to shew them what a shame it was to degenerate so much from their name and profession. Kicked - As well fed cattle use to do: he grew insolent and rebellious against God and against his word and spirit.

16. To jealousy - To anger and fury, for jealousy is the rage of a man. And withall it implies the ground of his anger, their falseness to God whom they had accepted as their husband, and their spiritual whoredom with other gods.

17. Unto devils - Unto idols, which the devils brought into the world in opposition to God, in and by which the devils often manifested themselves to men, and gave them answers, and received their worship. The Gentiles pretended to worship God in those idols, and the devils which inspired them, deluded the nations with pretenses that they were a sort of lower gods. Moses takes off this mark, and shews the Israelites that these pretended gods were really devils, and therefore that it was the height of madness to honour or worship them. Not to God - For God utterly rejected those sacrifices which they offered to him together with idols. They knew not - Or, who never knew them, that is, never shewed any kindness to them, or did them any good: New gods - Not simply or absolutely, for some of these had been worshipped for many generations, but comparatively to the true God, who is the ancient of days, chap. vii, 9, and who was worshipped from the beginning of the world. Feared not - Served not, worshipped not.

18. Of the rock - Of God, one of whose titles this is, or of Christ, who is called the rock, 1 Cor. x, 4, whom the Israelites tempted.

19. His sons and daughters - Such they were by calling and profession.

20. I will see - I will make them and others see, what the fruit of such actions shall be. No faith - No fidelity: perfidious, that have broken their covenant so solemnly made with me.

21. I will move them to jealousy with those that are not a people - With the Heathen nations, who are none of my people, who scarce deserve the name of a people, as being without the knowledge and fear of God, which is the foundation of all true policy and government, and many of them destitute of all government, laws and order. And yet these people I will take in your stead, receive them and reject you; which, when it came to pass how desperately did it provoke the Jews to jealousy? A foolish nation - So

the Gentiles were both in the opinion of the Jews and in truth and reality, notwithstanding all their pretenses to wisdom, there being nothing more foolish or brutish than the worship of idols.

22. A fire is kindled - Great and grievous judgments shall be inflicted, which often come under the name of fire. Are they proud of their plenty? It shall burn up the increase of the earth. Are they confident of their strength? It shall destroy the very foundations of the mountains. It shall burn unto the lowest hell: it shall bring them to the very depth of misery in this world, which yet will be but a faint resemblance of their endless misery in the next.

23. Spend mine arrows - Even empty my quiver, and send upon them all my plagues, which, like arrows shot by a skilful and strong hand, shall speedily reach and certainly hit and mortally wound them.

24. With hunger - With famine, which burns and parches the inward parts, and make the face black as a coal, Lam. iv, 8. Burning heat - From fevers or carbuncles, or other inflaming distempers.

27. The wrath - Their rage against me, as it is expressed, Isaiah xxxvii, 28, 29, their furious reproaches against my name, as if I were cruel to my people or unable to deliver them. The fear hereof is ascribed to God after the manner of men. Strangely - Insolency and arrogantly above what they used to do.

28. Void of counsel - Their enemies are foolish people, and therefore make so false and foolish a judgment upon things.

29. They - Israel. Latter end - What their end will be, and that tho' God spare them long, yet at last judgment will certainly overtake them.

30. One - Israelite. Their rock - Their God, who was their refuge and defense. Sold them - Namely, for bond-slaves, had given themselves up into their enemies hands. Shut them up - As it were in the net which their enemies had laid for them.

31. Being Judges - Who by their dear bought experience have been forced to acknowledge that our God was far stronger than they and their false gods together.

32. For - As if he had said, This is the reason why their rock hath shut them up. Their vine is of the vine of Sodom - The people of Israel, which I planted as a choice vine, are now degenerated and become like the vine of Sodom, their principles and practices are all corrupt and abominable. Bitter - Their fruits are loathsome to me, mischievous to others, and at last will be pernicious to themselves.

34. This - All their wickedness mentioned before. My long suffering towards them may make them think I have forgotten their sins, but I remember them punctually, they are sealed up as in a bag, Job xiv, 17, and as men seal up their treasures.

35. Their feet shall slide - They who now think they stand fast and unmoveable, shall fall into utter destruction. In due time - Though not so soon as some may expect, yet in that time when it shall be most proper, when they have filled up the measure of their sins. At hand - Hebrew. is near. So the scripture often speaks of those things which are at many hundred years distance, to signify, that though they may be afar off as to our measures of time, yet in God's account they are near, they are as near as may be, when the measure of their sins is once full, the judgment shall not be deferred.

36. For - Or, nevertheless, having spoken of the dreadful calamity which would come upon his people, he now turns his discourse into a more comfortable strain, and begins to shew that after God had sorely chastised his people, he would have mercy upon them and turn their captivity. Judge his people - Shall plead their cause, shall protect and deliver them. Repent - Of the evils he hath brought upon them. None shut up - Either in their strong cities or castles or other hiding places, or in the enemies hands or prisons, whence there might be some hope or possibility of redemption; and none left, as the poor and contemptible people are neglected and usually left by the conquerors in the conquered land, but all seem to be cut off and destroyed.

37. He shall say - The Lord, before he deliver his people, will first convince them of their former folly in forsaking him and following idols.

38. Which did eat - That is, to whom you offered sacrifices and oblations after the manner of the Gentiles. Help you - If they can.

39. See now - Learn by your own sad experience what vain and impotent things idols are. I am he - The only true, omnipotent and irresistible God.

40. I lift up my hand - I solemnly swear, that I will do what here follows. I live - As sure as I live.

41. If I whet my sword - If once I begin to prepare for war and for the execution of my sentence. Judgment - Of the instruments of judgment, of the weapons of war. A metaphor from warriors, that take their weapons into their hand, when they intend to fight.

42. Captives - Whom my sword hath sorely wounded, though not utterly killed. From the beginning - When once I begin to revenge myself and my people upon mine and their enemies, I will go on and make a full end.

43. Rejoice - He calls upon the nations to rejoice and bless God for his favours, and especially for the last wonderful deliverance which shall be given to the Jews, when they shall be converted to the gospel in the last days; which they have all reason to do, because of that singular advantage which all

nations will have at that time and upon that occasion.

44. *He and Hoshea* - Or Joshua. Probably Moses spoke it to as many as could hear him, while Josh. in another assembly at the same time delivered it to as many as his voice would reach. Thus Joshua, as well as Moses, would be a witness against them, if ever they forsook God.

47. *Not vain* - It is not an unprofitable or contemptible work I advise you to, but well worthy of your most serious care.

48. *That self-same day* - Now he had finished his work, why should he desire to live a day longer? He had indeed formerly desired and prayed, that he might go over Jordan: but now he is entirely satisfied, and saith no more of that matter.

49. *Nebo* - A ridge or top of the mountains of Abarim.

51. *Because ye trespassed* - God reminds him of the sin he had committed long before. It is good for the holiest of men to die repenting, even of their early sins.

52. *Yet thou shalt see the land* - And see it as the earnest of that better country, which is only seen with the eye of faith. What is death to him who has a believing prospect and a steadfast hope of eternal life?

XXXIII

The blessing of Moses. He pronounces them all blessed, in what God had done for them, already, ver. 1-5. He pronounces a blessing upon each tribe, ver. 6-25. He pronounces them all in general blessed, on account of what God would be to them, and do for them, if they were obedient, ver. 26-29.

1. *Moses blessed Israel* - He is said to bless them, by praying to God with faith for his blessing upon them; and by foretelling the blessings which God would confer upon them. And Moses calls himself here the man of God, that is, the servant or prophet of God, to acquaint them that the following prophecies were not his own inventions, but divine inspirations. *The children of Israel* - The several tribes: only Simeon is omitted, either in detestation of their parent Simeon's bloody carriage, for which Jacob gives that tribe a curse rather than a blessing, in Gen. xlix, 5-7. Or, because that tribe had no distinct inheritance, but was to have its portion in the tribe of Judah, Josh. xix, 1.

2. *The Lord came* - Namely, to the Israelites, manifested himself graciously and gloriously among them. *From Sinai* - Beginning at Sinai, where the first appearance of God was, and so going on with them to Seir and Paran. *And rose up* - He appeared or shewed himself, as the sun doth when it riseth. *From Seir* - From the mountain or land of Edom, to which place the Israelites came, Num. xx, 14, &c. and from thence God led them on towards the land of promise, and then gloriously appeared for them in subduing Sihon and Og before them. But because the land of Edom is sometimes taken more largely, and so reacheth even to the Red-sea, and therefore Mount Sinai was near to it, and because Paran was also near Sinai, being the next station into which they came from the wilderness of Sinai: all this verse may belong to God's appearance in Mount Sinai, where that glorious light which shone upon Mount Sinai directly, did in all probability scatter its beams into adjacent parts, such as Seir and Paran were. And if so, this is only a poetical expression of the same thing in divers words, and God coming or rising or shining from or to or in Sinai and Seir and Paran note one and the same illustrious action of God appearing there with ten thousands of his saints or holy angels, and giving a fiery law to them. *Paran* - A place where God eminently manifested his presence and goodness both in giving the people flesh which they desired, and in appointing the seventy elders and pouring forth his spirit upon them. *With ten thousands of saints* - That is, with a great company of holy angels, Psalm lxviii, 17 Dan. vii, 10, which attended upon him in this great and glorious work of giving the law, as may be gathered from Acts vii, 53 Gal. iii, 19. *From his right hand* - Which both wrote the law and gave it to men. An allusion to men who ordinarily write and give gifts with their right hand. *A fiery law* - The law is called fiery, because it is of a fiery nature purging and searching and inflaming, to signify that fiery wrath which it inflicteth upon sinners for the violation of it, and principally because it was delivered out of the midst of the fire.

3. *The people* - The tribes of Israel. The sense is, this law, though delivered with fire and smoke and thunder, which might seem to portend nothing but hatred and terror, yet in truth was given to Israel, in great love, as being the great mean of their temporal and eternal salvation. Yea, he embraced the people, and laid them in his bosom! so the word signifies, which speaks not only the dearest love, but the most tender and careful protection. *All God's saints or holy ones, that is, his people, were in thy hand*, that is, under God's care to protect, direct and govern them. These words are spoken to God: the change of persons, his and thy, is most frequent in the Hebrew tongue. This clause may farther note God's kindness to Israel, in upholding them when the fiery law was delivered, which was done with so much terror that not only the people were ready to sink under it, but even Moses did exceedingly fear and quake. But God sustained both Moses and the people, in or by his hand, whereby he in a manner covered them that no harm might come to them. *At thy feet* - Like scholars to receive instructions. He alludes to the place where the people waited when the law was delivered, which was at the foot of the

mount. Everyone - Of the people will receive or submit to thy instructions and commands. This may respect either, the peoples promise when they heard the law, that they would hear and do all that was commanded. Or, their duty to do so.

4. Moses - He speaks this of himself in the third person, which is very usual in the Hebrew language. The law is called their inheritance, because the obligation of it was hereditary, passing from parents to their children, and because this was the best part of their inheritance, the greatest of all those gifts which God bestowed upon them.

5. He was king in Jeshurun - Moses was their king not in title, but in reality, being under God, their supreme governor, and law giver. Gathered together - When the princes and people met together for the management of public affairs, Moses was owned by them as their king and lawgiver. 6. Let Reuben live - Though Reuben deserve to be cut off or greatly diminished and obscured, according to Jacob's prediction, Gen. xlix, 4, yet God will spare them and give them a name and portion among the tribes of Israel, and bless them with increase of their numbers. All the ancient paraphrasts refer this to the other world, so far were they from expecting temporal blessings only. Let Reuben live in life eternal, says Onkelos, and not die the second death. Let Reuben live in this world, so Jonathan and the Jerusalem Targum, and not die that death which the wicked die in the world to come.

7. Hear, Lord - God will hear his prayer for the accomplishment of those great things promised to that tribe, Gen. xlix, 8-12. This implies the delays and difficulties Judah would meet with, that would drive him to his prayers, which would be with success. Unto his people - When he shall go forth to battle against his enemies and shall fall fiercely upon them, as was foretold, Gen. xlix, 8, 9. Bring him back with honour and victory, to his people, to the rest of his tribe who were left at home when their brethren went to battle: and to his brethren the other tribes of Israel. Let his hands be sufficient for him - This tribe shall be so numerous and potent that it shall suffice to defend itself without any aid, either from foreign nations or from other tribes; as appeared when this tribe alone was able to grapple with nine or ten of the other tribes. From his enemies - Thou wilt preserve this tribe in a special manner, so that his enemies shall not be able to ruin it, as they will do other tribes, and that for the sake of the Messiah who shall spring out of it.

8. Let thy Urim - The Thummim and the Urim, which are thine, O Lord by special institution and consecration, (by which he understands the ephod in which they were put, and the high priesthood, to which they were appropriated, and withal the gifts and graces signified by the Urim and Thummim, and necessary for the discharge of that high-office) shall be with thy holy one, that is, with that priest, whom thou hast consecrated to thyself, and who is holy in a more peculiar manner than all the people were; that is, the priesthood shall be confined to and continued in Aaron's family. Whom thou didst prove - Altho' thou didst try him, and rebuke him, yet thou didst not take away the priesthood from him. At Massah - Not at that Massah mentioned Exod. xvii, 7, which is also called Meribah, but at that other Meribah, Num. xx, 13. Thou didst strive - Whom thou didst reprove and chastise.

9. I have not seen him - That is, I have no respect unto them. The sense is, who followed God and his command fully, and executed the judgment enjoined by God without any respect of persons, Exod. xxxii, 26, 27. They kept thy covenant - When the rest broke their covenant with God by that foul sin of idolatry with the calf, that tribe kept themselves pure from that infection, and adhered to God and his worship.

11. His substance - Because he hath no inheritance of his own and therefore wholly depends upon thy blessing. The work of his hands - All his holy administrations, which he fitly calls the work of his hands, because a great part of the service of the Levites and priests was done by the labour of their hand and body, whereas the service of evangelical ministers is more spiritual and heavenly. Smite - He pray's thus earnestly for them, because he foresaw they who were to teach and reprove, and chastise others would have many enemies, and because they were under God, the great preservers and upholders of religion, and their enemies were the enemies of religion itself.

12. Of Benjamin - Benjamin is put next to Levi, because the temple, where the work of the Levites lay, was upon the edge of the lot of this tribe. And 'tis put before Joseph, because of the dignity of Jerusalem, (part of which was in this lot) above Samaria, which was in the tribe of Ephraim: likewise because Benjamin adhered to the house of David and to the temple of God, when the rest of the tribes deserted both. The beloved of the Lord - So called in allusion to their father Benjamin who was the beloved of his father Jacob; and because of the kindness of God to this tribe which appeared both in this, that they dwelt in the best part of the land, as Josephus affirms, and in the following privilege. Shall dwell in safety by him - Shall have his lot nigh to God's temple, which was both a singular comfort and safeguard to him. Shall cover - Shall protect that tribe continually while they cleave to him. He - The Lord shall dwell, that is, his temple shall be placed, between his shoulders, that is, in his portion, or between his border's as the word shoulder is often used. And this was truly the situation of the temple, on both sides whereof was Benjamin's portion. And though Mount Zion was in the tribe of Judah, yet mount Moriah, on which the temple was built, was in the tribe of Benjamin.

13. And of Joseph - Including both Ephraim and Manasseh. In Jacob's blessing that of Joseph's is

the largest. And so it is here. His land - His portion shall be endowed with choice blessings from God. Of heaven - That is, the precious fruits of the earth brought forth by the influences of heaven, the warmth of the sun, and the rain which God will send from heaven. The deep - The springs of water bubbling out of the earth: perhaps it may likewise refer to the great deep, the abyss of waters, which is supposed to be contained in the earth.

14. By the sun - Which opens and warms the earth, cherishes and improves and in due time ripens the seeds and fruits of it. The moon - Which by its moisture refreshes and promotes them. Hebrew. Of the moons, or months, that is, which it bringeth forth in the several months or seasons of the year.

15. The chief things - That is, the excellent fruits, as grapes, olives, figs, &c. which delight in mountains, growing upon, or the precious minerals contained in, their mountains and hills called ancient and lasting, that is, such as have been from the beginning of the world, and are likely to continue to the end of it, in opposition to those hills or mounts which have been cast up by man.

16. And for - And in general for all the choice fruits which the land produceth in all the parts of it, whither hills or valleys. Fulness thereof - That is, the plants and cattle and all creatures that grow, increase, and flourish in it. The good will - For all other effects of the good will and kindness of God who not long since did for a time dwell or appear in the bush to me in order to the relief of his people, Exod. iii, 2. Of Joseph - That is, of Joseph's posterity. Him that was separated from his brethren -- his brethren separated him from them by making him a slave, and God distinguished him from them by making him a prince. The preceeding words might be rendered, My dweller in the bush. That was an appearance of the divine majesty to Moses only, in token of his particular favour. Many a time had God appeared to Moses; but now he is just dying, he seems to have the most pleasing remembrance, of the first time that he saw the visions of the Almighty. It was here God declared himself the God of Abraham, Isaac and Jacob, and so confirmed the promise made to the father, that promise which our Lord shews, reaches as far as the resurrection and eternal life.

17. His glory is like the firstling of his bullock - Or young bull, which is a stately creature, and was therefore formerly used as an emblem of royal majesty. This seems to note the kingdom which Ephraim should obtain in Jeroboam and his successors. His horns - His strength and power shall be very great. The people - All that shall oppose him, and particularly the Canaanites. The ten thousands - Of the land of Canaan. Though Manasseh be now more numerous, yet Ephraim shall shortly outstrip him, as was foretold Gen. xlviii, 17-19.

18. Rejoice - Thou shalt prosper and have cause of rejoicing. In thy going out -

1. To war, as this phrase is often used.

2. To sea, in way of traffick, because their portion lay near the sea. And in both respects his course is opposite to that of Issachar, who was a lover of peace and pasturage. He is here joined with Zebulun, both because they were brethren by father and mother too, and because their possessions lay near together. In thy tents - Thou shalt give thyself to the management of laud and cattle, living quietly in thy own possessions.

19. They - Zebulun of whom Moses takes more special notice. And so having dispatched Issachar in two words, he returns to Zebulun. The people - the Gentiles, either those of Galilee, which was called Galilee of the Gentiles, who were their neighbours; or people of other nations, with whom they had commerce, which they endeavoured to improve in persuading them to worship the true God. The mountain - That is, to the temple, which Moses knew was to be seated upon a mountain. Sacrifices of righteousness - Such as God requires. Their trafficking abroad with Heathen nations shall not make them forget their duty at home, nor shall their distance from the place of sacrifice hinder them from coming to it to discharge that duty. Of the abundance of the sea - They shall grow rich by the traffick of the sea, and shall consecrate themselves and their riches to God. Hid in the sand - Such precious things as either

1. Are contained in the sand of the sea and rivers, in which sometimes there is mixed a considerable quantity of gold and silver. Or,

2. Such as grow in the sea, or are fetched from the sandy bottom of it, as pearls, coral, ambergrease. Or,

3. Such as being cast into the sea by shipwreck are cast upon the shore by the workings of the sea. It were well, if the enlargement of our trade with foreign countries, were made to contribute to the spreading of the gospel.

20. Enlargeth - That bringeth him out of his straits amid troubles, which he was often engaged in, because he was encompassed with potent enemies. As a lion - Safe and secure from his enemies, and terrible to them when they rouse and molest him. Teareth the arm - Utterly destroys his enemies, both the head, the seat of the crown, their dignity and principality, and the arm, the subject of strength and instrument of action; both chief princes, and their subjects.

21. The first part - The first fruits of the land of promise, the country of Sihon, which was first conquered, which he is said to provide for himself, because he desired and obtained it of Moses. Of the law-giver - Of Moses, whose portion this is called, either because this part of the land beyond Jordan

was the only part of the land which Moses was permitted to enter upon: or because it was given him by Moses, whereas the portions beyond Jordan were given to the several tribes by Joshua according to the direction of the lot. Seated - Hebrew. hid or protected: for their wives and children were secured in their cities, while many of their men went over to the war in Canaan. He came - He went, or he will go, to the war in Canaan, with the princes, or captains, or rulers of the people of Israel, that is, under their command and conduct, as indeed they did; or with the first of the people; or, in the front of the people, as the Syriack renders it; for this tribe and their brethren whose lot fell beyond Jordan, were to march into Canaan before their brethren. He executed - The just judgment of God against the Canaanites, as the rest of the Israelites did.

22. A lion's whelp - Courageous, and generous, and strong, and successful against his enemies. Which leapeth - From Bashan, because there were many and fierce lions in those parts, whence they used to come forth and leap upon the prey. Or this may refer either to the particular victories obtained by Samson, who was of the tribe of Daniel, or to a more general achievement of that tribe, when a party of them surprised Laish, which lay in the farthest part of the land of Canaan from them. And the mountain of Bashan lying not far from that city, from whence they probably made their descent upon it, thus leaping from Basham.

23. Satisfied with favour - With the favour of God. That only is the favour that satisfies the soul. They are happy indeed that have the favour of God; and they shall have it, that place their satisfaction in it. And full with the blessing of the Lord - Not Only with corn, wine and oil, the fruit of the blessing, but with the blessing itself, the grace of God, according to his promise and covenant. Possess thou the west and the south - Or, the sea and the south. This is not to be understood of the place, that his lot should fall there, for he was rather in the east and north of the land; but of the pleasures and commodities of the west or of the sea, which were conveyed to him from his neighbour Zebulun; and of the south, that is, from the southern tribes and parts of Canaan, which were brought to him down the river Jordan, and both sorts of commodities were given him in exchange for the fruitful rich soil which he had in great abundance.

24. Let Asher - Who carries blessedness in his very name, be blessed with children - He shall have numerous, strong and healthful children. Acceptable to his brethren -- by his sweet disposition and winning carriage. In oil - He shall have such plenty of oil that he may not only wash his face, but his feet also in it.

25. Iron and brass - The mines of iron and copper, which were in their portion, whence Sidon their neighbour was famous among the Heathens for its plenty of brass, and Sarepta is thought to have its name from the brass and iron which were melted there in great quantity. Thy strength shall be - Thy strength shall not be diminished with age, but thou shalt have the vigour of youth even in thine old age: thy tribe shalt grow stronger and stronger.

26. There us none - These are the last words that ever Moses wrote, perhaps the greatest writer that ever lived upon the earth. And this man of God, who had as much reason to know both as ever any mere man had, with his last breath magnifies both the God of Israel, and the Israel of God. Unto the God of Jeshurun, who to help thee, rideth upon the heaven, and with the greatest state and magnificence, on the sky. Riding on the heaven denotes the greatness and glory, in which he manifests himself to the upper world, and the use he makes of the influences of heaven and the products of the clouds, in bringing to pass his own counsels in this lower world. All these he manages and directs, as a man doth the horse he rides on.

27. The eternal God - He who was before all worlds, and will be, when time shall be no more: Is thy refuge - Or, thy habitation or mansion-house (so the word signifies) in whom thou art safe, and easy, and at rest, as a man is in his own house. Every true Israelite is at home in God: the soul returns to him, and reposes in him. And they that make him their habitation shall have all the comforts and benefits of an habitation in him. And underneath are the everlasting arms - The almighty power of God, which protects and comforts all that trust in him, in their greatest straits and distresses. He shall thrust out the enemy from before thee - Shall make room for thee by his resistless power, and shall say, Destroy them - Giving thee not only a commission but strength to put it in execution. And, has he not given the same commission and the same strength to believers, to destroy all sin?

28. Alone - Either

1. Tho' they be alone, and have no confederates to defend them, but have all the world against them, yet my single protection shall be sufficient for them. Or,

2. Distinct and separated from all other nations, with whom I will not have them mingle themselves. The fountain - That is, the posterity of Jacob, which flowed from him as waters from a fountain, in great abundance. The fountain is here put for the river or streams which flow from it, as Jacob or Israel who is the fountain is often put for the children of Israel. His heavens - That is, those heavens or that air which hangs over his land.

29. The shield of they help - By whom thou are sufficiently guarded against all assailants; and the sword of thy excellency - Or, thy most excellent sword, that is, thy strength and the author of all thy

past or approaching victories. Those in whose hearts is the excellency of holiness, have God himself for their shield and sword. They are defended by the whole armour of God: His word is their sword, and faith their shield. And thine enemies shall be found liars unto thee - Who said they would destroy thee: or at least, that they would never submit: and thou shalt tread upon their high places - Their strong holds, palaces and temples. Thus shall the God of peace tread Satan under the feet of all believers, and that shortly.

XXXIV

Moses having finished his testimony, finishes his life. This chapter was probably added by Samuel, who wrote by divine authority what he found in the records of Joshua, and his successors the Judges. Here is, The view Moses had of the land, ver. 1-4. His death, burial, and age, ver. 5-7. Israel's mourning for him, ver. 8. His successor, ver. 9. His character, ver. 10-12.

1. And Moses went up - When he knew the place of his death he cheerfully mounted a steep hill to come to it. Those who are well acquainted with another world, are not afraid to leave this. When God's servants are sent for out of the world, the summons runs go up and die! Unto Daniel - To that city which after Moses's death was called so.

2. All Naphtali - The land of Naphtali, which together with Daniel, was in the north of Canaan, as Ephraim and Manasseh were in the midland parts, and Judah on the south, and the sea, on the west. So these parts lying in the several quarters are put for all the rest. He stood in the east and saw also Gilead, which was in the eastern part of the land, and thence he saw the north and south and west. The utmost sea - The midland sea, which was the utmost bound of the land of promise on the west.

3. The south - The south quarter of the land of Judah, which is towards the salt sea, the city of palm-trees - Jericho, so called from the multitude of palm-trees, which were in those parts, as Josephus and Strabo write. From whence and the balm there growing it was called Jericho, which signifies, odouriferous or sweet smelling.

4. I have caused thee to see it - For tho' his sight was good, yet he could not have seen all Canaan, an hundred and sixty miles in length, and fifty or sixty in breadth, if his sight had not been miraculously assisted and enlarged. He saw it at a distance. Such a sight the Old Testament believers had of the kingdom of the Messiah. And such a sight believers have now of the glory that shall be revealed. Such a sight have we now, of the knowledge of the glory of the Lord, which shall cover the earth. Those that come after us shall undoubtedly enter into that promised land: which is a comfort to us, when we find our own carcases falling in this wilderness.

5. So Moses the servant of the Lord died - He is called the servant of the Lord, not only as a good man, (all such are his servants) but as a man eminently useful, who had served God's counsels in bringing Israel out of Egypt, and leading them thro' the wilderness. And it was more his honour, to be the servant of the Lord, than to be king in Jeshurun. Yet he dies. Neither his piety nor his usefulness would exempt him from the stroke of death. God's servants must die, that they may rest from their labours, receive their recompense, and make room for others. But when they go hence, they go to serve him better, to serve him day and night in his temple. The Jews say, God sucked his soul out of his body with a kiss. No doubt he died in the embraces of his love.

6. He - The Lord, buried him either immediately, or by the ministry of angels, whereof Michael was the chief or prince. Of his sepulchre - Of the particular place where he was buried: which God hid from the Israelites, to prevent their superstition and idolatry, to which he knew their great proneness. And for this very reason the devil endeavoured to have it known and contended with Michael about it, Jude i, 9. God takes care even of the dead bodies of his servants. As their death is precious, so is their dust. Not one grain of it shall be lost, but the covenant with it shall be remembered.

7. His eye was not dim - By a miraculous work of God in mercy to his church and people.

8. Thirty day's - Which was the usual time of mourning for persons of high place and eminency. 'Tis a debt owing to the surviving honour of deceased worthies, to follow them with our tears, as those who loved and valued them, are sensible of the loss, and humbled for the sins which have provoked God to deprive us of them.

9. Wisdom - And other gifts and graces too, but wisdom is mentioned as being most necessary for the government to which he was now called. Upon him - And this was the thing which Moses at that time asked of God for him.

10. Whom the Lord - Whom God did so freely and familiarly converse with.

12. Moses was greater than any other of the prophets of the Old Testament. By Moses God gave the law, and molded and formed the Jewish church. By the other prophets he only sent particular

reproofs, directions and predictions. But as far as the other prophets came short of him, our Lord Jesus went beyond him. Moses was faithful as a servant, but Christ as a son: his miracles more illustrious, his communion with the father more intimate: for he is in his bosom from eternity. Moses lies buried: but Christ is sitting at the right-hand of God, and of the increase of his government there shall be no end.

NOTES ON THE BOOK OF JOSHUA

IN this book and those that follow to the end of Esther, we have the history of the Jewish nation. These books, to the end of the second book of Kings, the Jewish writers call, the first book of the prophets: as being wrote by prophets, men divinely inspired. Indeed it is probable they were collections of the authentic records of the nation, which some of the prophets were divinely directed and assisted to put together. It seems the substance of the several histories was written under divine direction, when the events had just happened, and long after put into the form wherein they stand now, perhaps all by the same hand. In the five books of Moses we had a full account of the rise and constitution of the Old Testament church, the miracles by which it was built up, and the laws and ordinances by which it was to be governed. And any nation that had statutes and judgments so righteous, one would think, should have been very holy. But alas! a great part of the history is a representation of their sins and miseries. For the law made nothing perfect; that was to be done by the bringing in of the better hope. The book of Joshua, if not written by him, was at least collected out of his journals or memoirs. It contains the history of Israel under the command of Joshua: how he presided over them,

1. In their entrance into Canaan, chap. i-v.
2. In their conquest of Canaan, chap. vi-xii.
3. In the distribution of the land among the tribes of Israel, chap. xiii-xxi.
4. In the establishment of religion among them, chap. 21-24. In all which he was a great example of wisdom, courage, fidelity and piety. And in this history we may see,

1. Much of God and his providence; his power in the kingdom of nature; his justice in punishing the Canaanites; his faithfulness to his covenant with the patriarchs; his kindness to his people:
2. Much of Christ and his grace: Joshua being in many respects an eminent type of him.

I

In this chapter,
1. God appoints Joshua to govern in the stead of Moses, and gives him instructions and encouragement, ver. 1-9.
2. He enters on his office immediately, giving orders to the officers, and to the two tribes and an half, ver. 10-15.
3. The people accept him as their governor, ver. 16-18

1. After the death of Moses - Either immediately after it, or when the days of mourning for Moses were expired. Joshua was appointed and declared Moses's successor in the government before this time; and here he receives confirmation from God therein. The servant of the Lord - This title is given to Moses here and ver. 2, as also Deut. xxxiv, 5, and is repeated not without cause, to reflect honour upon him, to give authority to his laws and writings, in publishing whereof he acted as God's servant, in his name: and that the Israelites might not think of Moses above what was meet, remembering that he was not the Lord himself, but only the Lord's servant; and therefore not to be too pertinaciously followed in all his institutions when the Lord himself should come and abolish part of the Mosaical dispensation; it being but reasonable that he who was only a servant in God's house, should give place to him who was the son, and heir, and Lord of it. The Lord spake - Either in a dream or vision, or by Urim, Num. xxvii, 21. Moses's minister - Who had waited upon Moses in his great employments, and thereby been privy to his manner of government, and so prepared for it.

2. Now therefore arise - Let not the withering of the most useful hands be the weakening of ours. When God has work to do, he will either find or make instruments fit to carry it on. Moses the servant is dead; but God the master is not: he lives forever. This Jordan - Which is now near thee, which is the only obstacle in thy way to Canaan. Which I give - That is, am now about to give thee actual possession of it, as I formerly gave a right to it by promise.

3. Every place - That is, within the following bounds.

4. This Lebanon - Emphatically, as being the most eminent mountain in Syria, and the northern border of the land: or this which is within thy view. Hittites - Of the Canaanites, who elsewhere are all called Amorites; (Gen. xv, 16) and here Hittites, the Hittites being the most considerable and formidable

of all. The greater - The midland sea, great in itself, and especially compared with those lesser collections of waters, which the Jews called seas. "But the Israelites never possessed all this land." I answer:

1. That was from their own sloth and cowardice, and disobedience to God, and breach of those conditions upon which this promise was suspended:

2. Though their possessions extended not to Euphrates, yet their dominion did, and all those lands were tributary to them in David's and Solomon's time.

5. With Moses - To assist him against all his enemies, and in all the difficulties of governing this stiff-necked people, which Joshua might justly fear no less than the Canaanites. Forsake thee - I will not leave thee destitute either of inward support, or of outward assistance.

6. Be strong and of a good courage - Joshua, though a person of great courage and resolution, whereof he had given sufficient proof, yet needs these exhortations, partly because his work was great, and difficult, and long, and in a great measure new; partly because he had a very mean opinion of himself, especially if compared with Moses; and remembering how perverse and ungovernable that people were, even under Moses, he might very well suspect the burden of ruling them would be too heavy for his shoulders.

7. Commanded thee - Remember, that though thou art the commander of my people, yet thou art my subject, and obliged to observe all my commands. To the right hand or to the left - That is, in any kind, or upon any pretense; which plainly shews, that God's assistance promised to him and the Israelites, was conditional, and might justly be withdrawn upon their breach of the conditions. Whithersoever thou goest - That is, whatsoever thou doest. Mens actions are often compared to ways, or steps by which they come to the end they aim at.

8. Out of thy mouth - That is, thou shalt constantly read it, and upon occasion discourse of it, and the sentence which shall come out of thy mouth, shall in all things be given according to this rule. Day and night - That is, diligently study, and upon all occasions consider what is God's will and thy duty. The greatness of thy place and employments shall not hinder thee from this work, because this is the only rule of all thy private actions, and publick administrations.

9. I commanded thee - I whom thou art obliged to obey: I who can carry thee through every thing I put thee upon: I of whose faithfulness and almighty power thou hast had large experience?

10. The officers of the people - These who commanded under Joshua, in their respective tribes and families, attended him for orders, which they were to transmit to the people.

11. Prepare you victuals - For although Manna was given them to supply their want of ordinary provisions in the wilderness; yet they were allowed, when they had opportunity, to purchase other provisions, and did so, Deut. ii, 6, 28. And now having been some time in the land of the Amorites, and together with Manna used themselves to other food, which that country plentifully supplied them with; they are warned to furnish themselves therewith for their approaching march. Three days - These words, though placed here, seem not to have been delivered by Joshua 'till after the return of the spies; such transpositions being frequent in scripture. And hence it comes, that these three days mentioned here below, after the history of the spies, are again repeated chap. iii, 2.

13. Commanded you - His charge to you, and your promise to him. Rest - That is, a place of rest, as that word signifies.

14. Before their brethren -- in the front of all of them; which was but reasonable; because they had the advantage of their brethren, having actually received their portion, which their brethren had only in hope, because they were freed from those impediments which the rest were exposed to, their wives, and children, and estates being safely lodged; and to prevent their withdrawing themselves from the present service, which they otherwise would have had temptation to do, because of the nearness of their habitations. Armed - For by this time they were well furnished with arms, which they had either from the Egyptians, Amalekites, or Amorites, from whom they had taken them; or by purchase from those people by whose borders they passed. Men of valour - All such were obliged to go over if occasion required it, but Joshua took only some of them, because they were sufficient for his purpose, and because some were fit to be left, both to secure their own wives, children, and possessions, and to prevent their enemies on that side from giving them disturbance in their enterprise upon Canaan.

16. And they answered - Not the two tribes and an half only, but the officers of all the people, in their name, concurring with the divine appointment, by which Joshua was set over them. Thus must we swear allegiance to our Lord Jesus, as the captain of our salvation.

17. Unto thee - The same obedience which we owed, to Moses, we promise unto thee. With Moses - This is not a limitation of their obedience, as if they would not obey him any longer than he was prosperous, but an additional prayer for him. As we have hereby promised thee our obedience, so our prayer shall be, that God would bless and prosper thee, as he did Moses.

II

Joshua sends spies to Jericho, ver. 1. Rahab receives and conceals them, ver. 2-7. Her agreement with them for the safety of herself and family, ver. 8-21. The return of the spies, and the account given by them, ver. 22-24.

1. Sent - Or, had sent. Two men - Not twelve, as Moses did, because those were to view the whole land, these but a small parcel of it. To spy - That is, to learn the state of the land and people. It is evident Joshua did not this out of distrust; it is probable, he had God's command and direction in it for the encouragement of himself and his army. Secretly - With reference not to his enemies, that being the practice of all spies, but to the Israelites; a good caution to prevent the inconveniency which possibly might have arisen, if their report had been discouraging. Jericho - That is, the land about Jericho, together with the city. Hebrew. The land and Jericho, that is, especially Jericho. Harlot's - So the Hebrew word is used, Judg. xi, 1, and so it is rendered by two apostles, Heb. xi, 31 James ii, 25, such she either now was, or rather, had been formerly. Lodged - Or, lay down; as the same word is rendered, ver. 8, composed themselves to rest; but they were hindered from that intention.

2. To night - This evening.

3. Probably Israel had but one friend in all Jericho: and God directed them to her! Thus what seems to be most accidental, is often over-ruled, to serve the great ends of providence. And those that acknowledge God in their ways, he will guide them with his eye.

4. And the woman - Or, But the woman had taken - and had hid them, before the messengers came from the king; as soon as she understood from her neighbours, that there was a suspicion of the matter, and guessed that search would be made. And this is justly mentioned as a great and generous act of faith, Heb. xi, 31, for she apparently ventured her life upon a steadfast persuasion of the truth of God's word and promise given to the Israelites. Whence they were - Her answer contained in these and the following words, was false, and therefore unquestionably sinful; tho' her intention was good therein. But it is very probable, she being an Heathen, might think, that an officious lie is not unlawful.

6. Roof - Which was flat after their manner. Upon the roof - That they might be dried by the heat of the sun.

7. Fords - Or passages, that is, the places where people used to pass over Jordan, whether by boats or bridges. The gate - Of the city, to prevent the escape of the spies, if peradventure Rahab was mistaken, and they yet lurked therein.

8. Laid down - To sleep as they intended.

9. Your terror - That is, the dread of you.

11. Melted - That is, were dissolved, lost all courage.

12. By the Lord - By your God who is the only true God: so she owns his worship, one eminent act whereof is swearing by his name. My father's house - My near kindred, which she particularly names, ver. 13, husband and children it seems she had none. And for herself, it was needless to speak, it being a plain and undeniable duty to save their preserver. True token - Either an assurance that you will preserve me and mine from the common ruin: or a token which I may produce as a witness of this agreement, and a means of my security. This is all that she asks. But God did for her more than she could ask or think. She was afterwards advanced to be a princess in Israel, the wife of Salmon and one of the ancestors of Christ.

13. All that they have - That is, their children, as appears from chap. vi, 23.

14. For yours - We will venture our lives for the security of yours. Our business - That is, this agreement of ours, and the condition of it, lest others under this pretense, should secure themselves. By which they shew both their piety and prudence in managing their oath with so much circumspection, that neither their own consciences might be ensnared, nor the publick justice obstructed.

15. Town-wall - Which gave her the opportunity of dismissing them when the gates were shut. Upon the wall - Her particular dwelling was there: which may possibly be added, because the other part of her house was reserved for the entertainment of strangers.

16. The mountain - That is, to some of the mountains wherewith Jericho was encompassed, in which also there were many caves where they might lurk. Three days - Not three whole days, but one whole day, and part of two days.

17. Said - Or, had said; namely, before she let them down; it being very improbable, either that she would dismiss them before the condition was agreed on; or that she would discourse with them, or they with her, about such secret and weighty things after they were let down, when others might overhear them. Blameless - That is, free from guilt or reproach if it be violated, namely, if the following condition be not observed.

18. Into the land - That is, over Jordan, and near the city. This line of scarlet - Probably the same with which she was about to let them down. Window - That it may be easily discerned by our soldiers.

19. Upon his head - The blame of his death shall rest wholly upon himself, as being occasioned by

his own neglect of the means of safety. Our head - We are willing to bear the sin, and shame, and punishment of it. Be upon him - So as to kill him.

21. In the window - Forthwith, partly that the spies might see it hung out before their departure, and so the better know it at some distance; partly lest some accident might occasion a neglect about it.

22. Three days - Supporting themselves there with the provisions, which Rahab had furnished them with. The ways - That is, in the road to Jordan, and the places near it, but not in the mountains.

23. Passed over - Jordan unto Joshua.

III

The people decamp from Shittim, and are directed to follow the ark, and sanctify themselves, ver. 1-5. The priests are ordered to go first, ver. 6. Joshua being encouraged and directed as God, tells the people what God is about to do, ver. 7 - 13. Jordan is divided, and Israel marches through, ver. 14-17

1. In the morning - Not after the return of the spies, but after the three days, chap. i, 11, as it follows, ver. iii, 2. Lodge there - That night, that they might go over in the day time, that the miracle might be more evident and unquestionable, and strike the greater terror into their enemies.

2. After three days - Either at the end of them, or upon the last of them. Through the host - The second time to give them more particular directions, as they had given them a general notice, chap. i, 10, 11.

3. Commanded the people - In Joshua's name, and by his authority. Priests and Levites - Who were not only Levites, but priests also. For altho' the Levites were to carry the ark, Num. iv, 1-15, yet the priests might perform that office, and did so upon some solemn occasions. Go after it - Towards Jordan, to go over it in such a manner as I am about to describe. 'Till this time the ark went in the middle of the cloudy pillar, now it goes in the front. Probably the pillar of fire and cloud was still hovering over the ark.

4. Two thousand cubits - A thousand yards, at which distance from it the Israelites seem to have been encamped in the wilderness. And because they generally went from their tents to the ark to worship God, especially on the sabbath-days; hence it hath been conceived, that a sabbath-day's journey reached only to two thousand cubits. But that may be doubted; for those who encamped nearest the ark, were at that distance from it, and came so far; but the rest were farther from it, and their sabbath-day's journey was considerably longer. Near unto it - Partly from the respect they should bear to the ark; but chiefly, that the ark marching so far before you into the river, and standing still there 'till you pass over, may give you the greater assurance of your safe passage. Ye have not passed this way heretofore - While we are here, we must expect unusual events, to pathways that we have not passed before: and much more when we go hence, when we pass thro' the valley of the shadow of death. But if we have the assurance of God's presence, what have we to fear?

5. And Joshua said - Or rather, had said, the day before their passage; for it follows, tomorrow. Sanctify yourselves - Both in soul and body, that you may be meet to receive such a favour, and with more reverence observe this great work, and fix it in your hearts.

6. Take up - Namely, upon your shoulders; for so they were to carry it, Num. vii, 9. Before the people - Not in the middle of them, as you used to do.

7. Magnify thee - That is, to gain thee authority among them, as the person whom I have set in Moses's stead, and by whom I will conduct them to the possession of the promised land.

8. The brink - Hebrew. to the extremity, so far as the river then spread itself, which was now more than ordinary, ver. 15. In Jordan - Within the waters of Jordan, in the first entrance into the river; Where they stood for a season, 'till the river was divided, and then they went into the midst of it, and there abode 'till all the people were passed over. 9. Come hither - To the ark or tabernacle, the place of public assemblies. The Lord your God - Who is now about to give a proof that he is both the Lord, the omnipotent governor of heaven and earth, and all creatures; and your God, in covenant with you, having a tender care and affection for you.

10. Ye shall know - By experience and sensible evidence. The living God - Not a dull, dead, senseless God, such as the gods of the nations are; but a God of life, and power, and activity to watch over you, and work for you. Among you - Is present with you to strengthen and help you.

12. Twelve men - For the work described, chap. iv, 2, 3.

13. The ark of the Lord - That so it may appear this is the Lord's doing, and that in pursuance of his covenant made with Israel. Of all the earth - The Lord of all this globe of earth and water, who therefore can dispose of this river and the adjoining land as he pleaseth. Cut off - The waters which now are united now shall be divided, and part shall flow down the channel towards the dead sea, and the other part that is nearer the spring of the river, and flows down from it, shall stand still. An heap - Being as it were congealed, as the Red-Sea was, Exod. xv, 8, and so kept from overflowing the country.

15. All the time of harvest - This is meant not of wheat-harvest, but of the barley-harvest, as is

manifest from their keeping the passover at their first entrance, chap. v, 10, which was kept on the fourteenth day of the first month, when they were to bring a sheaf of their first-fruits, which were of barley. So that this harvest in those hot countries fell very early in the spring, when rivers used to swell most; partly because of the rains which have fallen all the winter, partly because of the snows which melt and come into the rivers. And this time God chose that the miracle might be more glorious, more amazing and terrible to the Canaanites; and that the Israelites might be entertained at their first entrance with plentiful and comfortable provisions.

16. Adam - The city Adam being more obscure, is described by its nearness to a more known place, then eminent, but now unknown. The meaning is, that the waters were stopped in their course at that place, and so kept at a distance from the Israelites whilst they passed over. Against Jericho - Here God carried them over, because this part was,

1. The strongest, as having in its neighbourhood an eminent city, a potent king, and a stout and war-like people.

2. The most pleasant and fruitful, and therefore more convenient both for the refreshment of the Israelites after their long and tedious marches, and for their encouragement.

17. Stood firm - That is, in one and the same place and posture; their feet neither moved by any waters moving in upon them, nor sinking into any mire, which one might think was at the bottom of the river. And this may be opposed to their standing on the bank of the water when they came to it, commanded, ver. 8, which was but for a while, 'till the waters were divided and gone away; and then they were to go farther, even into the midst of Jordan, where they are to stand constantly and fixedly, as this Hebrew word signifies, until all were passed over. The midst of Jordan - In the middle and deepest part of the river.

IV

Twelve stones taken up out of the midst of Jordan, and twelve set up there for a memorial, ver. 1-9. The march of the people through Jordan, ver. 10-13. God magnifies Joshua, who commands the priests to come out of Jordan, ver. 14-17. The waters close again, ver. 18, 19. Joshua erects twelve stones for a memorial, ver. 20-24.

1. Spake - This was commanded before, chap. iii, 12, and is here repeated with enlargement, as being now to be put in execution.

2. Out of every tribe a man - For the greater evidence, and the more effectual spreading the report of this marvelous work among all the tribes.

3. Lodge this night - That is, in Gilgal, as is expressed below, ver. 19, 20.

4. Prepared - That is, appointed for that work, and commanded to be ready for it.

5. Before the ark - That is, go back again to the place where the ark stands.

6. A sign - A monument or memorial of this day's work.

9. Twelve stones - These stones are not the same with those which a man could carry upon his shoulder, ver. 5. They might be very much larger; and being set up in two rows one above another, might be seen, at least when the water was low, especially where it was shallow, as it was ordinarily, though not at this time, when Jordan overflowed all its banks. Add to this, that the waters of Jordan are very clear; therefore these stones might be seen in it, either by those who stood upon the shore, because the river was not broad; or by those that passed in boats. Unto this day - This might be written, either

1. by Joshua who probably wrote this book near 20 years after this was done: or,

2. by some other holy man divinely inspired, who inserted this and some such passages both in this book and in the writings of Moses.

10. Commanded Joshua - Not particularly, but in general; because he commanded Joshua to observe and do all that God had commanded him by Moses, and all that he should command him any other way. Hasted - That is, passed over with haste, an argument of their fear, or weakness of their faith; as on the contrary, the priests are commended that they stood firm, and settled in their minds, as well as in the posture of their bodies.

13. Before the Lord - Either,

1. before the ark, or,

2. in the presence of God who observed whether they would keep their covenant made with their brethren, or not.

16. Out of Jordan - For being now in the middle, and deepest place of the river, they are most properly said to go up to the land.

17. The priests - Who stayed contentedly in the river, 'till God by Joshua called them out.

18. Their place - Returned into their proper channel, according to their natural and usual course.

19. The first month - Namely, of Nisan, which wanted but five days of forty years from the time of their coming out of Egypt, which was on the fifteenth day of this month. So punctual is God in the

performing of his word, whether promised or threatened. And this day was very seasonable for the taking up of the lambs which were to be used four days after, according to the law, Exod. xii, 3, 6. Gilgal - A place afterwards so called, chap. v, 9.

20. In Gilgal - Probably in order, like so many little pillars, to keep up the remembrance of this miraculous benefit.

23. Before us - That is, myself and Caleb, and all of us here present; for this benefit, though done to their fathers, is justly said to be done to themselves, because they were then in their parent's loins. It greatly magnifies later mercies, to compare them with former mercies; for hereby it appears, that God is the same yesterday, today and forever.

V

The Canaanites terrified, ver. 1. Circumcision renewed, ver. 2- 9. The passover kept, ver. 10. The Israelites eat corn, and the manna ceases, ver. 11-12. Christ appears to Joshua, ver. 13-15.

1. Amorites - These and the Canaanites are mentioned for all the rest, as being the chief of them for number, and power, and courage. Westward - This is added to distinguish them from the other Amorites, eastward from Jordan, whom Moses had subdued. Canaanites - So the proper place of this nation was on both sides of Jordan. The sea - The midland sea, all along the coast of it, which was the chief seat of that people, though divers colonies of them were come into, and settled in other places. Jordan - Which was their bulwark on the east-side, where the Israelites were; for it is very probable they had taken away all bridges near those parts; and the Israelites having been so long in that neighbouring country, and yet not making any attempt upon them, they were grown secure; especially now, when Jordan swelled beyond its ordinary bounds; and therefore they did not endeavour to hinder their passage. Melted - They lost all their courage, and durst attempt nothing upon the Israelites; not without God's special providence, that the Israelites might quietly participate of the two great sacraments of their church, circumcision and the passover, and thereby be prepared for their high and hard work, and for the possession of the holy and promised land; which would have been defiled by an uncircumcised people.

2. At that time - As soon as ever they were come to Gilgal, which was on the tenth day; and so this might be executed the eleventh day, and that in the morning: on the thirteenth day they were sore of their wounds, and on the fourteenth day they recovered, and at the even of that day kept the passover. Make - Or, prepare, or make ready, as this word sometimes used. As it was not necessary for those who had such knives already to make others for that use; so it is not probable that such were commanded to do so, but only to make them sharp and fit for that work. The second time - He calleth this a second circumcision, not as if these same persons had been circumcised before, but with respect to the body of the people, where of one part had been circumcised before, and the other at this time, which is called a second time, in relation to some former time wherein they were circumcised, either, in Egypt, when many of the people, who possibly for fear or favour of the Egyptians, had neglected this duty, were by the command of Moses circumcised. Or at Sinai, when they received the passover, Num. ix, 5, which no uncircumcised person might do.

3. And circumcised - That is, he caused this to be done; and, because it was to be done speedily, the passover approaching, it was necessary to use many hands in it. Children of Israel - That is, such of them as were uncircumcised. And, though it be not mentioned, it is more than probable, that the Israelites beyond Jordan were circumcised at the same time.

4. Out of Egypt - This is to be restrained to such as were then above twenty years old, and such as were guilty of that rebellion, Num. xiv, 1-25, as it is expressed below, ver. 6.

5. Them - Either their parents, or the rulers of Israel, by Divine permission and indulgence; because they were now on a journey, in which case the passover also might be neglected, Num. ix, 10, 13. Rather, it was a continued token of God's displeasure against them, for their unbelief and murmuring: a token that they should never have the benefit of that promise, whereof circumcision was the seal.

6. The people - The Hebrew word commonly signifies the Gentiles; so he calls them, to note that they were unworthy the name of Israelites. Shew them - That is, not give them so much as a sight of it, which he granted to Moses, much less the possession.

7. Circumcised - Which God would have done,

1. As a testimony of God's reconciliation to the people, and that he would not farther impute their parents rebellion to them.

2. Because the great impediment of circumcision was now removed, their continued travels, and frequent and uncertain removal.

3. To prepare them for the approaching passover.

4. To distinguish them from the Canaanites, into whose land they were now come.

5. To ratify the covenant between God and them, whereof circumcision was a sign and seal, to

assure them that God would now make good his covenant, in giving them this land; and to oblige them to perform all the duties to which that covenant bound them, as soon as they came into Canaan, Exod. xii, 25 Lev. xxiii, 10 Num. xv, 2.

8. Whole - Free from that pain and soreness which circumcision caused, it was indeed an act of great faith, to expose themselves to so much pain and danger too, in this place where they were hemmed in by Jordan and their enemies.

9. The reproach of Egypt - That is, uncircumcision, was both in truth, and in the opinion of the Jews, a matter of great reproach, and although this was a reproach common to most nations of the world, yet it is particularly called the reproach of Egypt, either,

1. because the other neighbouring nations, being the children of Abraham by the concubines, are supposed to have been circumcised, which the Egyptians at this time were not, as may be gathered from Exod. ii, 6, where they knew the child to be an Hebrew by this mark. Or

2. because they came out of Egypt, and were esteemed to be a sort of Egyptians, Num. xxii, 5, which they justly thought a great reproach; but by their circumcision they were now distinguished from them, and manifested to be another people. Or

3. because many of them lay under this reproach in Egypt, having wickedly neglected this duty there for worldly reasons; and others of them continued in the same shameful condition for many years in the wilderness. Gilgal - That is, rolling.

10. The passover - Which was their third passover: the first was in Egypt, Exod. xii, 11-24, the second at Mount Sinai, Num. ix, 1-5, the third here; for in their wilderness travels, these and all other sacrifices were neglected, Amos v, 25. While they were in the wilderness, they were denied the comfort of this ordinance, as a farther token of God's displeasure. But now God comforted them again, after the time that he had afflicted them.

11. Old corn - The corn of the last year, which the inhabitants of those parts had left in their barns, being fled into their strong cities, or other remoter parts. The morrow - That is, on the sixteenth day; for the passover was killed between the two evenings of the fourteenth day, and was eaten in that evening or night, which, according to the Jewish computation, whereby they begin their days at the evening, was a part of the fifteenth day, all which was the feast of the passover; and so the morrow of the sixteenth day, was the morrow after the passover, when they were obliged to offer unto God the first sheaf, and then were allowed to eat of the rest. Parched corn - Of that year's corn. which was most proper for that use. Self-same day - Having an eager desire to enjoy the fruits of the land. And this corn came very seasonably; for after the passover, they were to keep the feast of unleavened bread, which they could not do, when they had nothing but manna to live upon.

12. The manna ceased - Which God now withheld, to shew that Manna was not an ordinary production of nature, but an extraordinary and special gift of God to supply their necessity. And because God would not be prodigal of his favours, by working miracles where ordinary means were sufficient. The morrow - That is, on the seventeenth day.

13. By Jericho - Hebrew. In Jericho, that is, in the territory adjoining to it; whither he went to view those parts, and discern the fittest places for his attempt upon Jericho. A man - One in the appearance of a man. Drawn - In readiness to fight, not, as Joshua thought, against him, but for him and his people.

14. As captain - I am the chief captain of this people, and will conduct and assist thee and them in this great undertaking. Now this person is not a created angel, but the son of God, who went along with the Israelites in this expedition, as their chief and captain. And this appears,

1. By his acceptance of adoration here, which a created angel durst not admit of, Rev. xxii, 8, 9.

2. Because the place was made holy by his presence, ver. 15, which was God's prerogative, Exod. iii, 5.

3. Because he is called the Lord, Hebrew. Jehovah, chap. vi, 2. My Lord - I acknowledge thee for my Lord and captain, and therefore wait for thy commands, which I am ready to obey.

15. From thy foot - In token of reverence and subjection. Holy - Consecrated by my presence. The very same orders which God gave to Moses at the bush, when he was sending him to bring Israel out of Egypt, he here gives to Joshua, for the confirming his faith, that as he had been with Moses, so he would be with him.

VI

Directions given to Joshua concerning Jericho, ver. 1-5. The people compass the city seven days, ver. 6-14. The taking it, with the charge to destroy it utterly, ver. 15-21. The preservation of Rahab and her relations, ver. 22-25. A curse pronounced on any that should rebuild it, ver. 26, 27.

3. Round about the city once - At a convenient distance, out of the reach of their arrows. Six days - Every day once. This and the following course might seem ridiculous and absurd, and is therefore prescribed by God, that they might learn to take new measures of things, and to expect success not from

their own valour, or skill, but merely from God's appointment and blessing; and in general, not to judge of any of God's institutions by mere carnal reason, to which divers of their ceremonies would seem no less foolish than this action.

5. The wall - Not all of it; which was unnecessary, and might have given the people better opportunity of escaping, but only a considerable part of it, where the Israelites might fitly enter: for Rahab's house was not overthrown, ver. 22. Flat - Hebrew. under it, it was not battered down with engines which would have made part of it fall out of its place; but it fell of its own accord, and therefore in the place it did formerly stand in. God chose this way, to try the faith and obedience of the people: whether they would observe a precept, which to human policy seemed foolish, and believe a promise, which seemed impossible to be performed: whether they could patiently bear the reproaches of their enemies, and patiently wait for the salvation of God. Thus by faith, not by force, the walls of Jericho fell down.

6. Of rams horns - Of the basest matter, and the dullest sound, that the excellency of the power might be of God.

7. Him that is armed - God would have them armed both for the defense of themselves and the ark, in case the enemies should make a sally upon them, and for the execution of the Lord's vengeance upon that city.

9. The rereward - Which being opposed to the armed men, may seem to note the unarmed people, who were desirous to be spectators of this wonderful work.

10. Ye shall not shout - Because shouting before the time appointed, would be ineffectual, and so might give them some discouragement, and their enemies matter of insulting.

16. Shout - To testify your faith in God's promise, and thankfulness for this glorious mercy; to encourage yourselves and brethren, and to strike a terror into your enemies. Given you the city - It is given to them, to be devoted to God, as the first, and perhaps the worst of all the cities of Canaan.

17. Accursed - That is, devoted to utter destruction. This he speaks by direction from God, as is evident from 1 Kings xvi, 34. To the Lord - Partly because the first-fruits were appropriated to God; partly lest the soldiers being glutted with the spoil of the rich city, should grow sluggish in their work; and partly to strike the greater terror into the rest of their enemies.

18. A curse - By provoking God to punish them for your sin, in which they may be one way or other involved; or the whole camp having sins of their own, God might take what occasion he saw fit to inflict this punishment.

19. Vessels of brass and iron - Except that of which images were made, which were to be utterly destroyed. Unto the Lord - Being first made to pass through the fire, Num. xxxi, 22, 23. Treasury of the Lord - To be employed wholly for the uses of the tabernacle, not to be applied to the use of any private person or priest.

21. Young and old - Being commanded to do so by the sovereign Lord of every man's life; and being informed by God before that the Canaanites were abominably wicked, and deserved the severest punishments. As for the infants, they were guilty of original sin, and otherwise at the disposal of their creator; but if they had been wholly innocent, it was a great favour to them to take them away in infancy, rather than reserve them to those dreadful calamities which those who survived them were liable to.

22. Harlot's house - Which together with the wall upon which it leaned, was left standing, by a special favour of God to her.

23. Without the camp of Israel - 'Till they were cleansed from the impurities of their Gentile state, and instructed in the Jewish religion, and solemnly admitted into that church, for which Rahab's good counsel and example had doubtless prepared them.

25. The harlot olive - For that general command of rooting out the Canaanites seems to have had some exception, in case any of them had sincerely and seasonably cast off their wickedness, and submitted to the Israelites.

26. Adjured them - Or, made them to fear; caused the people, or some in the name of all, to swear for the present and succeeding generations, and to confirm their oath by a curse. Before the Lord - That is, from God's presence, and by his sentence, as they are said to cast lots before the Lord, chap. xviii, 8, 10, that is, expecting the design from God. He intimates, that he doth not utter this upon a particular dislike of that place, but by divine inspiration. God would have the ruins of this city remain as a standing monument of God's justice against this wicked and idolatrous people, and of his almighty power in destroying so great and strong a city by such contemptible means. Buildeth - That is, that shall attempt to build it. So this curse is restrained to the builder, but no way belongs to those who should inhabit it after it was built, as is evident from 2 Kings iv, 18 Luke xix, 1, 5. In his youngest son - That is, he shall lose all his children in the work, the first at the beginning, others in the progress of it by degrees, and the youngest in the close of it, when the gates use to be set up. This was fulfilled, 1 Kings xvi, 34.

27. The word of the Lord was with him - (So the Chaldee:) Even Christ himself, the same that was

with Moses. Nothing makes a man appear more truly great, than to have the evidences of God's presence with him.

VII

We have here the sin of Achan in taking the accursed thing, ver. 1. The defeat of Israel before Ai, ver. 2-5. Joshua's humiliation and prayer, ver. 6-9. God's directions to him, ver. 10- 15. The discovery, conviction, and execution of the criminal, ver. 16-26.

1. The children of Israel - That is, one of them, by a very usual figure, as Matt. xxvi, 8, where that is ascribed to the disciples, which belonged to Judas only, John xii, 4. Accursed thing - That is, in taking some of the forbidden and accursed goods. Zabdi - Called also Zimri, 1 Chron. ii, 6. Zerah - Or, Zarah, who was Judah's immediate son, Gen. xxxviii, 30, who went with Judah into Egypt: and so for the filling up the 256 years that are supposed to come between that and this time, we must allow Achan to be, now an old man, and his three ancestors to have begotten each his son at about sixty years of age; which at that time was not incredible nor unusual. Against the children of Israel - Why did God punish the whole society for this one man's sin? All of them were punished for their own sins, whereof each had a sufficient proportion; but God took this occasion to inflict the punishment upon the society, partly because divers of them might be guilty of this sin, either by coveting what he actually did, or by concealing his fault, which it is probable could not be unknown to others; or by not sorrowing for it, and endeavouring to purge themselves from it: partly to make sin the more hateful; as being the cause of such dreadful judgments: and partly to oblige all the members of every society to be more circumspect in ordering their own actions, and more diligent to prevent the miscarriages of their brethren, which is a great benefit to them, and to the whole society.

2. To Ai - They were not to go into the city of Ai, but into the country belonging to it, to understand the state of the place; and the people.

3. Go up - Which was done by the wise contrivance of Divine providence, that their sin might be punished, and they awaked and reformed with as little mischief and reproach, as might be: for if the defeat of these caused so great a consternation in Joshua, it is easy to guess what dread it would have caused in the people if a host had been defeated.

4. They fled - Not having courage to strike a stroke, which was a plain evidence that God had forsaken then; and an useful instruction, to shew them what they were when God left them: and that it was God, not their own valour, that gave the Canaanites into their hands.

5. About thirty and six men - A dear victory to them, whereby Israel was awakened and reformed, and they hardened to their own ruin. The going down - By which it seems it was a down-hill way to Jericho, which was nearer Jordan. As water - Soft and weak, and full of fluctuation and trembling.

6. Rent his clothes - In testimony of great sorrow, for the loss felt, the consequent mischief feared, and the sin which he suspected. His face - In deep humiliation and fervent supplication. Until the eventide - Continuing the whole day in fasting and prayer. Put dust upon their heads - As was usual in case of grief and astonishment.

7. Over Jordan - This and the following clause, tho' well intended, yet favour of human infirmity, and fall short of that reverence and modesty, and submission, which he owed to God; and are mentioned as instances that the holy men of God were subject to like passions and infirmities with other men.

8. What shall I say - In answer to the reproaches of our insulting enemies. When Israel - God's people, which he hath singled out of all nations for his own.

9. Thy great name - Which will upon this occasion be blasphemed and charged with inconstancy, and with inability to resist them, or to do thy people that good which thou didst intend them. The name of God is a great name, above every name. And whatever happens, we ought to pray, that this may not be polluted. This should be our concern more than any thing else: on this we should fix our eye: and we cannot urge a better plea than this, Lord, what wilt thou do for thy great name? Let God in all be glorified, and then welcome his whole will!

10. Upon thy face - This business is not to be done by inactive supplication, but by vigourous endeavours for reformation.

11. Israel - Some or one of them. Transgressed my covenant - That is, broken the conditions of my covenant which they have promised to perform, whereof this was one, not to meddle with the accursed thing. Stolen - That is, taken my portion which I had reserved, chap. vi, 19. Dissembled - Covered the fact with deep dissimulation. Possibly Achan might be suspected, and being accused, had denied it. Among their own stuff - Converted it to their own use, and added obstinacy to the crime.

12. Were accursed - They have put themselves out of my protection, and therefore are liable to the same destruction which belongs to this accursed people.

13. Sanctify yourselves - Purify yourselves from that defilement which you have all in some sort contracted by this accursed fact, and prepare yourselves to appear before the Lord, expecting the

sentence of God for the discovery and punishment of the sin, and that the guilty person might hereby be awakened, and brought to a free confession of his fault. And it is a marvelous thing that Achan did not on this occasion acknowledge his crime; but this is to be imputed to the heart-hardening power of sin, which makes men, grow worse and worse; to his pride, being loath to take to himself the shame of such a mischievous and infamous action; and to his vain conceit, whereby he might think others were guilty as well as he, and some of them might be taken, and he escape.

14. The Lord taketh - Which shall be declared guilty by the lot, which is disposed by the Lord, Prov. xvi, 33, and which was to be cast in the Lord's presence before the ark. Of such use of lots, see 1 Sam. xiv, 41, 42 Jonah i, 7 Acts i, 26.

15. Shall be burnt with fire - As persons and things accursed were to be. All that he hath - His children and goods, as is noted, ver. 24, according to the law, Deut. xiii, 16. Wrought folly - So sin is often called in scripture, in opposition to the idle opinion of sinners, who commonly esteem it to be their wisdom. In Israel - That is, among the church and people of God who had such excellent laws to direct them, and such an all-sufficient and gracious God to provide for them, without any such unworthy practices. It was sacrilege, it was invading God's rights, and converting to a private use that which was devoted to his glory, which was to be thus severely punished, for a warning to all people in all ages, to take heed how they rob God.

17. The family - Either,

1. the tribe or people, as the word family sometimes signifies, or,

2. the families, as ver. 14, the singular number for the plural, the chief of each of their five families, Num. xxvi, 20, 21. Man by man - Not every individual person, as is evident from ver. 18, but every head of the several houses, or lesser families of that greater family of the Zarhites, of which see 1 Chron. ii, 6.

19. My son - So he calls him, to shew, that this severe inquisition and sentence did not proceed from any hatred to his person, which he loved as a father doth his son, and as a prince ought to do each of his subjects. The Lord God of Israel - As thou hast highly dishonoured him, now take the blame to thyself, and ascribe unto God the glory of his omniscience in knowing thy sin, of his justice in punishing it in thee, and others for thy sake; of his omnipotency, which was obstructed by thee; and of his kindness and faithfulness to his people, which was eclipsed by thy wickedness; all which will now be evident by thy sin confessed and punished.

20. Indeed I have sinned - He seems to make a sincere and ingenuous confession, and loads his sin with all just aggravations. Against the Lord - Against his express command, and glorious attributes. God of Israel - The true God, who hath chosen me and all Israel to be the people of his peculiar love and care.

21. When I saw - He accurately describes the progress of his sin, which began at his eye, which he permitted to gaze upon them, which inflamed his desire, and made him covet them; and that desire made him take them; and having taken, resolve to keep them; and to that end hide them in his tent. Babylonish garment - Which were composed with great art with divers colours, and of great price, as appears both from scripture, and Heathen authors. Two hundred shekels - To wit, in weight, not in coin; for as yet they received and payed money by weight. The silver under it - That is, under the Babylonish garment; covered with it, or wrapt up in it.

22. Sent messengers - That the truth of his confession might be unquestionable, which some, peradventure might think was forced from him. And they ran - Partly longing to free themselves and all the people from the curse under which they lay; and partly that none of Achan's relations might get thither before them, and take away the things. It was hid - That is, the parcel of things mentioned, ver. 21 and 24.

23. Before the Lord - Where Joshua and the elders continued yet in their assembly waiting for the issue.

24. His sons, and his daughters - Their death was a debt they owed to their own sins, which debt God may require when he pleaseth; and he could not take it in more honourable circumstances than these, that the death of a very few in the beginning of a new empire, and of their settlement in the land, might be useful to prevent the deaths of many thousands who took warning by this dreadful example, whom, if the fear of God did not, yet the love of their own, and of their dear children's lives would restrain from such pernicious practices. And it is very probable they were conscious of the fact, as the Jewish doctors affirm. If it be pretended that some of them were infants; the text doth not say so, but only calls them sons and daughters. And considering that Achan was an old man, as is most probable, because he was the fifth person from Judah, it seems most likely, that the children were grown up, and so capable of knowing, and concealing, or discovering this fact. His oxen, and his asses, and his sheep - Which, though not capable of sin, nor of punishment, properly so called, yet as they were made for man's use, so they are rightly destroyed for man's good; and being daily killed for our bodily food, it cannot seem strange to kill them for the instruction of our minds, that hereby we might learn the contagious nature of sin, which involves innocent creatures in its plagues; and how much sorer

punishments are reserved for man, who having a law given to him, and that excellent gift of reason and will to restrain him from the transgressions of it, his guilt must needs be unspeakably greater, and therefore his sufferings more severe and terrible. Farther, by this enumeration it appears, that he had no colour of necessity to induce him to this fact.

25. With stones - And burned him with fire; which is easily understood both out of the following words, and from God's command to do so. They were stoned (which was the punishment of such offenders, Lev. xxiv, 14 Num. xv, 35,) and not burned to death; but God would have their dead carcases burned to shew his utmost detestation of such persons as break forth into sins of such a public scandal and mischief.

26. A great heap of stones - As a monument of the sin and judgment here mentioned, that others might be warned by the example; and as a brand of infamy, as chap. viii, 29; 2 Sam. xviii, 17. The valley of Achor - Or, the valley of trouble, from the double trouble expressed, ver. 25.

VIII

Here is God's encouragement to Joshua, ver. 1, 2. Joshua's orders to the men of war, ver. 3-8. The stratagem succeeds, ver. 9- 22. Joshua takes and destroys the city, ver. 23-29. The solemn writing and reading of the law before all Israel, ver. 30-35.

1. Take all the people - That all of them might be partakers of this first spoil, and thereby encouraged to proceed in their work. The weak multitude indeed were not to go, because they might have hindered them in the following stratagem; and it was but fit that the military men who run the greatest hazards, should have the precedency in the spoils.

2. To Ai - That is, the city and people of Ai. Unto Jericho and her king - That is, overcome and destroy them. This was enjoined to chastise their last insolence, and the triumphs and blasphemies which doubtless their success had produced: and to revive the dread and terror which had been impressed upon the Canaanites by Jericho's ruin, and had been much abated by the late success of Ai.

3. To go up against Ai - That is, to consider about this expedition; not as if all the people of war did actually go up, which was both unnecessary and burdensome: but it seems to be resolved by Joshua and all the council of war, that the thirty thousand here following should be selected for the enterprize. Either, 1, the thirty thousand now mentioned; or, 2. part of them; namely, such as were to lie in wait; and these were only five thousand men, as is expressed, ver. 12.

4. Them - The same party last spoken of, even the five thousand mentioned ver. 12, there are only two parties engaged in the taking of Ai, and but one ambush, as plainly appears by comparing ver. 9, with ver. 12, which speaks only of five thousand, who are justly supposed to be a part of those thirty thousand named, ver. 3.

5. That are - Or, that shall be: for at present he sent them away, ver. 9, but the next morning followed, and joined himself with them, ver. 10, 11. That we - I and the twenty five thousand with me.

9. Sent them - The same party. Among the people - Hebrew. that people, the people of war as they are called, ver. 11, that is, the main body of the host consisting of thirty thousand.

10. The people - Hebrew. that people, not all the people of Israel; which was needless, and required more time than could now be spared; but the rest of that host of thirty thousand, whereof five thousand were sent away; the remainder are numbered, to see whether some of them had not withdrawn themselves, taking the advantage of the night, and of the design of laying an ambush; and that it might be evident, this work was done without any loss of men, whereby they might be encouraged to trust in God, and to proceed resolutely in their work. The elders of Israel - The chief magistrates and rulers of Israel under Joshua; and these, I suppose, went with Joshua, and with the army, to take care that the cattle and the spoil of the city, which was given by God to all Israel for a prey, ver. 2, 27, might be justly and equally divided between those that went to battle, and the rest of the people.

11. That were with him - Namely, the thirty thousand mentioned, ver. 3, or the most of them.

12. And he took - Or rather, but he had taken, namely, out of the said number of thirty thousand, for this is added by way of recapitulation and farther explication of what is said in general, ver. 9.

13. Joshua went - Namely, accompanied with a small part of the host now mentioned, that is, very early in the morning, when it was yet dark, as is said in a like case, John xx, 1, whence it is here called night, though it was early in the morning, as is said, ver. 10, for it seems most probable, that all was done in one night's space, and in this manner; Joshua sends away the ambush by night, ver. 3, and lodgeth that night with twenty-five thousand men, ver. 9, not far from the city. But not able or willing to sleep all night, he rises very early, ver. 10, and numbers his men, which by the help of the several officers was quietly done, and so immediately leads them towards Ai; and while it was yet duskish or night, he goes into the midst of the valley, ver. 13, and when the day dawns he is discovered by the king and people of Ai, who thereupon rose up early to fight with them, ver. 14. The valley - Which was near the city, thereby to allure them forth.

John Wesley

14. His people - Namely, all his men of war, for the rest were left in Ai, ver. 16. At a time appointed - At a certain hour agreed upon between the king and people of Ai, and of Bethel too, who were their confederates in this enterprize, as it may seem from ver. 17. Possibly they might appoint the same hour of the day on which they had fought against Israel with good success, looking upon it as a lucky hour. Before the plain - That is, towards or in sight of that plain or valley in which the Israelites were, that so they might put themselves in battle-array. Against him - The former success having made him secure, as is usual in such cases; God also blinding his mind, and infatuating him, as he useth to do with those whom he intends to destroy.

15. Made as if they were beaten - That is, fled from them, as it were for fear of a second blow. The wilderness - Which lay between Ai and Jericho, whither they now seemed to flee.

16. All the people - Namely, all that were able to bear arms, for old men and children were unfit for the pursuit or fight; and that they were yet left, may seem from ver. 24, 25.

17. Not a man - Namely, fit for war. Bethel - Which, being a neighbouring city, and encouraged by the former success, had sent some forces to assist them; and now, upon notice sent to them of the flight of their common enemies, or upon some other signal given, all their men of war join with those of Ai in the pursuit.

18. Stretch out the spear - This was, either,

1. for a sign to his host present with him, to stop their flight, and make head against the pursuers: or,

2. for a signal to the liers in wait, or,

3. as a token of God's presence and assistance with them, and of their victory.

19. Set the city on fire - Not all of it, as appears from ver. 28, and because then they had lost that prey which God had allowed them; but part of it, enough to raise a smoke, and give notice to their brethren of their success.

21. All Israel - That is, all the Israelites there present.

22. The other - They who lay in ambush.

23. Took alive - Reserving him to a more ignominious punishment.

24. Smote it - That is, the inhabitants of it, the men, who through age or infirmity were unfit for war, and the women, ver. 25.

25. Of Ai - Not strictly, but largely so called, who were now in Ai, either as constant and settled inhabitants, or as sojourners and such as came to them for their help.

26. Drew not his hand back - He kept his hand and spear in the same posture, both stretched out and lifted up, as a sign both to encourage them, and to direct them to go on in the work.

29. Hanged on a tree - He dealt more severely with the kings of Canaan than with the people, because the abominable wickedness of that people was not restrained and punished (as it should have been) but countenanced and encouraged by their evil examples; and because they were the principal authors of the destruction of their own people, by engaging them in an obstinate opposition against the Israelites. Down from the tree - According to God's command in that case, Deut. xxi, 22. The gate of the city - Which place he chose either as most commodious, now especially when all the city within the gate was already turned in to an heap of stones and rubbish; or because this was the usual place of judgment; and therefore proper to bear the monument of God's just sentence against him, not without reflection upon that injustice which he had been guilty of in that place.

30. Then - Namely, after the taking of Ai. For they were obliged to do this, when they were brought over Jordan into the land of Canaan, Deut. xi, 29; xxvii, 2, 3, which is not to be understood strictly, as if it were to be done the same day; for it is manifest they were first to be circumcised, and to eat the passover, which they did, and which was the work of some days; but as soon as they had opportunity to do it, which was now when these two great frontier cities were taken and destroyed, and thereby the coast cleared, and the bordering people under great consternation, so that all the Israelites might securely march thither. And indeed this work was fit to be done as soon as might be, that thereby they might renew their covenant with God, by whose help alone they could expect success in their great and difficult enterprize. Built an altar - Namely, for the offering of sacrifices, as appears from the following verse. Mount Ebal - God's altar was to be but in one place, Deut. xii, 13, 14, and this place was appointed to be mount Ebal, Deut. xxvii, 4, 5, which also seems most proper, that in that place whence the curses of the law were denounced against sinners, there might also be the tokens and means of grace, and peace, and reconciliation with God, for the removing of the curses, and the procuring of God's blessing to sinners.

32. Upon the stones - Not upon the stones of the altar, which were to be rough and unpolished, ver. 31, but upon other stones, smooth and plaistered, as is manifest from Deut. xxvii, 2. The law of Moses - Not certainly the whole five books of Moses, for what stones and time would have sufficed for this, but the most weighty parts of the law, and especially the law of the ten commandments.

33. All Israel - That is, the whole congregation, old and young, male and female. That side - Some on one side of it, and some on the other. Mount Gerizim - These two places were in the tribe of

Ephraim, not far from Shechem, as appears both from scripture, and from other authors. Bless - Or curse, which is easily understood out of the following verse.

34. Afterward - After the altar was built, and the stones plaistered and writ upon. He read - That is, he commanded the priests or Levites to read, Deut. xxvii. 14. Blessings and cursings - Which words came in not by way of explication, as if the words of the law were nothing else besides the blessings and curses; but by way of addition, to note that these were read over and above the words of the law.

35. Read not - Therefore he read not the blessings and curses only, as some think, but the whole law, as the manner was when all Israel, men and women, were assembled together, or the ten commandments. Among them - Who were proselytes, for no others can be supposed to be with them at this time.

IX

The confederacy of the kings of Canaan against Israel, ver. 1, 2. The confederacy of the Gibeonites with Israel, ver. 3-18. Their employment, ver. 19-27.

2. Together - They entered into a league to do this. Tho' they were many kings of different nations, and doubtless of different interests, often at variance with each other, yet they are all determined to unite against Israel. O that Israel would learn this of Canaanites, to sacrifice private interests to the public good, and to lay aside all animosities among themselves, that they may cordially unite against the common enemy.

3. Gibeon - A great and royal city of the Hivites.

4. Been ambassadors - Sent from a far country.

6. The camp at Gilgal - The place of their head-quarters. Men of Israel - To those who used to meet in council with Joshua, to whom it belonged to make leagues, even the princes of the congregation. Now therefore - Because we are not of this people, whom, as we are informed, you are obliged utterly to destroy.

7. The Hivites - That is, the Gibeonites who were Hivites, chap. xi, 19. Among us - That is, in this land, and so are of that people with whom we are forbidden to make any league or covenant.

8. Thy servants - We desire a league with you upon your own terms; we are ready to accept of any conditions. From whence came ye - For this free and general concession gave Joshua cause to suspect that they were Canaanites.

9. Name of the Lord - Being moved thereunto by the report of his great and glorious nature and works; so they gave them hopes that they would embrace their religion. In Egypt - They cunningly mention those things only which were done some time ago, and say nothing of dividing Jordan, or the destruction of Jericho and Ai, as if they lived so far off that the fame of those things had not yet reached them.

13. The bottles - Leathern bottles.

14. The men - That is, the princes. Their victuals - That they might examine the truth of what they said. The mouth of the Lord - As they ought to have done upon all such weighty occasions. So they are accused of rashness and neglect of their duty. For though it is probable, if God had been consulted, he would have consented to the sparing of the Gibeonites; yet it should have been done with more caution, and an obligation upon them to embrace the true religion. In every business of importance, we should stay to take God along with us, and by the word and prayer consult him. Many a time our affairs miscarry, because we asked not counsel at the mouth of the Lord. Did we acknowledge him in all our ways, they would be more safe, easy and successful.

15. To let them live - That is, they should not destroy them. That this league was lawful and obliging, appears,

1. Because Joshua and all the princes, upon the review concluded it so to be, and spared them accordingly.

2. Because God punished the violation of it long after, 2 Sam. xxi, 1.

3. Because God is said to have hardened the hearts of all other cities, not to seek peace with Israel, that so he might utterly destroy them, chap. xi, 19, 20, which seems to imply that their utter destruction did not necessarily come upon them by virtue of any peremptory command of God, but by their own obstinate hardness, whereby they refused to make peace with the Israelites.

16. Three days - That is, at the last of them, or upon the third day, as it is said, ver. 17.

17. And Kirjath-jearim - Which cities were subject to Gibeon, the royal city, chap. x, 2.

18. Against the princes - Both from that proneness which is in people to censure the actions of their rulers; and from their desire of the spoil of these cities.

21. Unto all the congregation - That is, Let them be public servants, and employed in the meanest offices, (one kind being put for all the rest) for the use of the congregation; to do this partly for the sacrifices and services of the house of God, which otherwise the Israelites themselves must have done;

partly for the service of the camp or body of the people; and sometimes, even to particular Israelites.

22. Called for them - Probably not only the messengers, but the elders of Gibeon were now present.

23. Ye are cursed - You shall not escape the curse of God which by divine sentence belongs to all the Canaanites; but only change the quality of it, you shall feel that curse of bondage, which is proper to your race by virtue of that ancient decree, Gen. ix, 25. Bond-men - The slavery, which is upon you shall be entailed on your posterity. The house of my God - This only service they mention here, because it was their durable servitude, being first in the tabernacle, and then in the temple, whence they were called Nethinim, 1 Chron. ix, 2 Ezra ii, 43, whereas their servitude to the whole congregation in a great measure ceased when the Israelites were dispersed to their several habitations.

25. In thine hand - That is, in thy power to use us as thou wilt. Unto thee - We refer ourselves to thee and thy own piety, and probity, and faithfulness to thy word and oath; if thou wilt destroy thy humble suppliants, we submit. Let us in like manner submit to our Lord Jesus, and refer ourselves to him; saying, We are in thy hand; do unto us as seemeth right unto thee. Only save our souls: give us our lives for a prey; and let us serve thee, just as thou wilt!

27. The altar of the Lord - By which appears, that they were not only to do this service in God's house, but upon all other occasions, as the congregation needed their help.

X

In this chapter we have an account of the confederacy against Gibeon, and the request of the Gibeonites to Joshua, ver. 1-6. Of Joshua's marching and defeating the confederate kings, ver. 7-11. Of the sun's standing still, ver. 12-14. Of the execution of the kings, ver. 15-27. Of the taking their cities, and conquering all that country, ver. 28-42. Of the return of the army to Gilgal, ver. 43.

1. Among them - That is, were conversant with them, had submitted to their laws, and mingled interests with them.

2. Thy - That is, he and his people, the king being spoken of ver. 1, as a publick person representing all his people. Royal cities - Either really a royal city, or equal to one of the royal cities, though it had no king, but seems to have been governed by elders, chap. ix, 11.

3. Adoni-zedek sent - Either because he was superior to them, or because he was nearest the danger, and most forward in the work.

5. Of the Amorites - This name being here taken largely for any of the Canaanites, as is frequent; for, to speak strictly, the citizens of Hebron here mentioned, ver. 3, were Hittites. It is reasonably supposed, that the Amorites being numerous and victorious beyond Jordan poured forth colonies into the land of Canaan, subdued divers places, and so communicated their name to all the rest.

6. Slack not thy hand - Do not neglect or delay to help us. Whom thou art obliged to protect both in duty as thou art our master; and by thy owns interest, we being part of thy possessions; and in ingenuity, because we have given ourselves to thee, and put ourselves under thy protection. In the mountains - In the mountainous country.

7. Joshua ascended - Having no doubt asked advice of God first, which is implied by the answer God gives him, ver. 8. All the mighty men - That is, an army of the most valiant men picked out from the rest; for it is not probable, either that he would take so many hundred thousands with him, which would have hindered one another, or that he would leave the camp without an army to defend it.

9. Came suddenly - Though assured by God of the victory, yet he uses all prudent means. All night - It is not said, that he went from Gilgal to Gibeon in a night's space; but only that he travelled all night; unto which you may add part either of the foregoing or of the following day. It is true, God had promised, that he would without fail deliver the enemies into his hand. But God's promises are intended, not to slacken, but to quicken our endeavours. He that believeth doth not make haste, to anticipate providence; but doth make haste to attend it, with a diligent, not a distrustful speed.

10. At Gibeon - Hebrew. in Gibeon, not in the city, but in the territory belonging to it.

11. Great stones - That is, hailstones of extraordinary greatness, cast down with that certainty, as to hit the Canaanites and not their pursuers the Israelites. Josephus affirms, that thunder and lightning were mixed with the hail, which may seem probable from Hab. iii, 11. They had robbed the true God of his honour, by worshipping the host of heaven, and now the hosts of heaven fights against them, and triumphs in their ruin. Beth-horon lay north of Gibeon, Azekah and Makkedah, south, so that they fled each way. But which way soever they fled, the hailstones pursued them. There is no fleeing out of the hands of God!

12. Spoke Joshua - Being moved to beg it out of zeal to destroy God's enemies, and directed to it by the motion of God's spirit, and being filled with holy confidence of the success, he speaks the following words before the people, that that they might be witnesses. In the sight - That is, in the presence and audience of Israel. Over Gibeon - That is, in that place and posture in which now it stands

towards, and looks upon Gibeon. Let it not go down lower, and by degrees, out of the sight of Gibeon. It may seem, that the sun, was declining, and Joshua perceiving that his work was great and long, and his time but short, begs of God the lengthening out of the day, and that the sun and moon might stop their course, He mentions two places, Gibeon and Ajalon, not as if the sun stood over the one and the moon over the other, which is absurd especially these places being so near the one to the other; but partly to vary the phrase, as is common in poetical passages; partly because he was in his march in the pursuit of his enemies, to pass from Gibeon to Ajalon; and he begs that he may have the help of longer light to pursue them, and to that end that the sun might stand still, and the moon also; not that he needed the moon's light, but because it was fit, either that both sun and moon should go, or that both should stand still to prevent disorder in the heavenly bodies. The prayer is thus express with authority, because it was not an ordinary prayer, but the prayer of a prophet, divinely inspired at this very time for this purpose. And yet it intimates to us the prevalency of prayer in general, and may mind us of that honour put upon prayer, concerning the work of my hands command you me.

13. Avenged them on their enemies - That is, till they had utterly destroyed them. Book of Jasher - This book was written and published before Joshua wrote his, and so is fitly alluded here. But this, as well as some other historical books, is lost, not being a canonical book, and therefore not preserved by the Jews with the same care as they were. The sun stood - Here is no mention of the moon, because the sun's standing was the only thing which Joshua desired and needed; and the moon's standing he desired only by accident to prevent irregularity in the motions of those celestial lights. And if it seem strange to any one, that so wonderful a work should not be mentioned in any Heathen writers; he must consider, that it is confessed by the generality of writers, Heathens and others, that there is no certain history or monument in Heathen authors of any thing done before the Trojan war, which was a thousand years after Joshua's time; and that all time before that, is called by the most learned Heathens, the uncertain, unknown, or obscure time. A whole day - That is, for the space of a whole day. Understand an artificial day between sun-rising and sun-setting; for that was the day which Joshua needed and desired, a day to give him light for his work.

14. No day like that - Namely, in those parts of the world in which he here speaks, vain therefore is that objection, that the days are longer near the northern and southern poles, where they are constantly longer at certain seasons, and that by the order of nature; whereas the length of this day was purely contingent, and granted by God in answer to Joshua's prayer. The Lord hearkened to a man - Namely, in such a manner to alter the course of nature, and of the heavenly bodies, that a man might have more time to pursue and destroy his enemies. The Lord fought - This is added as the reason why God was so ready to answer Joshua's petition, because he was resolved to fight for Israel, and that in a more than ordinary manner. But this stupendous miracle was designed for something more, than to give Israel light to destroy the Canaanites. It was designed to convince and confound those idolaters, who worshipped the sun and moon, by demonstrating, that these also were subject to the command of the God of Israel: as also to signify, that in the latter days, when the world was covered with darkness, the sun of righteousness, even our Joshua, should arise, and be the true light of the world. To which we may add, that when Christ conquered our enemies upon the cross, the miracle wrought on the sun was the reverse of this. It was then darkened, as if going down at noon. For Christ needed not the light of the sun, to compleat his victory: so he made darkness his pavilion.

15. Joshua returned - Not upon the same day, but after he had dispatched the matter which here follows; as appears by ver. 43, where the very same words are repeated. And they are put here to close the general discourse of the fight which begun ver. 10, and ends here; which being done he particularly describes some remarkable passages, and closeth them with the same words.

16. A cave - A place of the greatest secrecy; but there is no escaping the eye or hand of God. At Makkedah - Hebrew. in Makkedah, not in the city, for that was not yet taken; but in the territory of it.

19. Enter their cities - Whereby they will recover their strength, and renew the war. God hath delivered them - Your work will be easy, God hath already done the work to your hands.

20. The children of Israel - That is, a party of them by the command of Joshua; for Joshua himself went not with them, but abode in the siege before Makkedah, ver. 21.

21. To the camp - To the body, of the army which were engaged there with Joshua to besiege that place. None moved his tongue - Not only their men of war could not find their hands, but they were so confounded, that they could not move their tongues in way of insult, as doubtless they did when the Israelites were smitten at Ai; but now they were silenced as well as conquered: they durst no more provoke the Israelites.

24. Put your feet on the necks - This he did not from pride and contempt; but as a punishment of their impious rebellion against their Sovereign Lord; in pursuance of that curse of servitude due to all this people, and as a token to assure his captains, that God would subdue the proudest of them under their feet.

27. Took them down - That neither wild beasts could come to devour them, nor any of their people to give them honourable burial. Thus that which they thought would have been their shelter, was made

their prison first, and then their grave. So shall we surely be disappointed, in whatever we flee to from God.

28. And that day - On which the sun stood still. Nor is it strange that so much work was done, and places so far distant taken in one day, when the day was so long, and the Canaanites struck with such a terror.

29. All Israel - Namely, who were with him in this expedition.

35. On that day - On which they first attempted it.

36. Unto Hebron - The conquest of Hebron is here generally related, afterwards repeated, and more particularly described, chap. xv, 13, 14.

37. All the cities - Which were subject to its jurisdiction; this being, it seems, a royal city as Gibeon was, ver. 2, and having cities under it as that had.

38. Joshua returned - He is said to return thither, not as if he had been there before, but because having gone as far westward and southward as he thought fit, even as far as Gaza, ver. 41, he now returned towards Gilgal, which lay north-ward and eastward from him, and in his return fell upon Debir.

40. All that breathed - That is, all mankind, they reserved the cattle for their own uses. As God had commanded - This is added for the vindication of the Israelites, whom God would not have to suffer in their reputation for executing his commands; and therefore he acquits them of that cruelty, which they might be thought guilty of, and ascribes it to his own just indignation. And hereby was typified the final destruction of all the impenitent enemies of the Lord Jesus, who having slighted the riches of his grace, must forever feel the weight of his wrath.

41. Kadesh-barnea - Which lay in the south of Canaan, Num. xxxiv, 4 Deut. i, 19 chap. xv, 3. Gaza - Which was in the southwest of Canaan. So he here signifies, that Joshua did in this expedition subdue all those parts which lay south and west from Gilgal. Goshen - Not that Goshen in Egypt, but another in Judah.

XI

The confederacy of many kings against Israel, ver. 1-5. God's encouragement to Joshua, and his conquest of them and their cities, ver. 6-20. The destruction of the Anakims, ver. 21-23.

1. Hazor - The chief city of those parts, ver. 10. Had heard - This was a remarkable instance of the wisdom and goodness of Divine Providence, which so governed the minds of the Canaanites, that they were not all united under one king, but divided amongst many petty kings; and next, that these did not all unanimously join their counsels and forces together to oppose the Israelites at their first entrance, but quietly suffered the destruction of their brethren, thereby preparing the way for their own.

2. On the north - The general designation of all the particular places following: they were in the northern parts of Canaan, as those mentioned chap. x, 1-43, were in the southern parts; in the mountain, either in or near the mountain of Lebanon, called the mountain by way of eminency; or in the mountainous country. Cinneroth - Hebrew. in the plain lying southward from Cinneroth, or the lake of Genesareth. Dor - A place upon the coast of the midland-sea.

3. The Canaanite - The Canaanites properly so called, lived part of them on the east near Jordan, and part on the west near the sea, and both are here united. The Hivite - That dwelt under mount Hermon in the north of Canaan, whereby they are differenced from those Hivites who lived in Gibeon. Mizpeh - That Mizpeh which was in the northern part of Gilead. But there are other cities called by that name, which signifying a watching-place, might be easily applied to several places of good prospect.

5. Merom - A lake made by the river Jordan in the northern part of it, which was in the territory of the King of Schimron, near Hazor, Jabin's royal city, and almost in the middle of these confederate kings.

6. Hough their horses - Cut their hamstrings that they may my be unfit for war. For God forbad them to keep many horses, now especially, that they might not trust to their horses, nor ascribe the conquest of the land to their own strength, but wholly to God, by whose power alone a company of raw and unexperienced footmen were able to subdue so potent a people, who besides their great numbers, and giants, and walled cities, had the advantage of many thousands of horses and chariots.

7. Suddenly - When they least expected them, intending there to refresh, and prepare, and order themselves for the offensive war which they designed.

8. Great Zidon - A great city in the northwest part of Canaan, upon the sea. Misrephoth-maim - A place not far from Zidon, supposed to be so called from the salt or glass which they made there. Valley of Mizpeh - Under mount Hermon, as appears by comparing this with ver. 3, and 17. where it seems to be called the valley of Lebanon. This lay on the east, as Zidon did on the west; and so it seems they fled several ways, and the Israelites also divided themselves into two bodies, one pursuing east, and the other west.

10. The king - In his royal city, to which he fled out of the battle. Head of these kingdoms - Not of

all Canaan, but of all those who were confederate with him in this expedition.

11. *Not any left* - That is, no human person.

13. *In their strength* - Hebrew. with their fence, walls or bulwarks, that is, which were not ruined with their walls in taking them. *Save Hazor* - Because this city began the war, and being the chief and royal city, might renew the war. If the Canaanites should ever seize upon it: which in fact they did, and settled there, under a king of the same name, Judg. iv, 2.

16. *All that land* - Of Canaan, whose parts here follow. *The hill* - Or, the mountain, that is, the mountainous country, namely, of Judea. A considerable part of Judea was called the hilly or the mountainous country, Luke i, 39, 65. *The south country* - That is, not only the mountainous part, but all the country of Judea, which lay in the southern part of Canaan, and often comes under the name of the south. *The vale* - The low countries. *The plain* - The fields or campaign grounds. *The mountain of Israel* - The mountains or mountainous country of Israel.

17. *To Seir* - That is, To the country of Seir or Edom; namely, that part of it which was south from Judea, not that which was eastward from it, as appears from hence, that here is mention of the two extreme bounds of the land conquered by Joshua; whereof the other which follows being in the north, this must needs be in the south of the land. *Baal-Gad* - A part of mount Lebanon.

18. *A long time* - For divers years together, as is evident by the following history. And this is here expressed, lest it should be thought that as all these wars are here recorded in a short narration, so they were dispatched in a short time. And God would have the land to be conquered gradually, for many weighty reasons;

1. Lest the sudden extirpation of those nations should have made a great part of the land desert, and thereby have increased the number of wild beasts, Deut. vii, 22.

2. Lest being done suddenly and easily, it should soon be forgotten and despised, as the nature of man is apt to do in those cases.

3. That by long exercise the Israelites might grow skilful in the art of war.

4. For the trial and exercise of their patience and courage, and trust in God.

5. To oblige them to the greater care to please God, whom they yet need for their help against their enemies.

19. *All other* - Namely, all that were taken by Joshua, were taken by the sword, and therefore it is no wonder that the war was long, when the enemy was so obstinate.

20. *To harden their hearts* - It was the design of God's providence not to soften their hearts to a compliance with the Israelites, but to give them up to their own animosity, pride, confidence and stubbornness; that so their abominable and incorrigible wickedness might be punished, and that the Israelites might not be mixed with them, but be entire among themselves in the possession of the land.

21. *At that time* - In that war, but in divers years. *The mountain* - Or, mountains, the singular number for the plural; these barbarous and monstrous persons either chose to live in the dens or caves, which were frequent in the mountains of those parts, or else they were driven thither by the arms and success of the Israelites. *From Debir* - From the territories belonging to these cities, as we have often seen in this history, cities mentioned for the country subject to them. *The mountains of Israel* - It doth not follow from hence, that this book was written by some other person long after Joshua's death, even after the division of the Israelites into two kingdoms. of Israel and Judah; but only that this was one of those clauses which were added by Ezra or some other prophet; though that be not necessary: for since it was evident to Joshua, from Gen. xlix, 10, &c. that the tribe of Judah was to be the chief of all these tribes, and some dawnings of its eminency appeared in that time, in their having the first lot in the land of Canaan, chap. xv, 1, and the largest inheritance, chap. xix, 9, it is no wonder that it is mentioned apart, and distinguished from the rest of the tribes of Israel, though that also be one of them. But how could Joshua utterly destroy these, when Caleb and Othniel destroyed some of them after Joshua's death? chap. xiv, 12 Judg. i, 10-12. This might be, either

1. Because these places being in part destroyed and neglected by the Israelites, were repossessed by the giants, and by them kept 'till Caleb destroyed them. Or rather

2. Because this work, though done by the particular valour of Caleb, is ascribed to Joshua as the general of the army, according to the manner of all historians; and therefore it is here attributed to Joshua, though afterwards, that Caleb might not lose his deserved honour, the history is more particularly described, and Caleb owned as the great instrument of it, chap. xiv, 6-15 and Judg. i, 12-20.

23. *The whole land* - That is, the greatest and best part of it, for some parts are expressly excepted in the following history. *All that the Lord said unto Moses* - God had promised to drive out the nations before them. And now the promise was fulfilled. Our successes and enjoyments are then doubly comfortable, when we see them flowing to us from the promise. This is according to what the Lord hath said: our obedience is acceptable, when it has an eye to the precept. And if we make a conscience of our duty, we need not question the performance of the promise.

XII

The conquests of Israel, under Moses, ver. 1-6. Under Joshua, ver. 7-24.

1. Plain on the east - On the east of Jordan, called the plain, Deut. i, 1.
2. Middle of the river - It is not unusual even among us, for a river to be divided between two lords, and for their territories or jurisdictions to meet in the middle of the river: and besides, here is a very particular reason for this expression, because the city Ar, which was no part of Sihon's dominions, but belonged to the Moabites, Deut. ii, 9, 18, was in the middle of the river Arnon, Deut. ii, 36; iii, 16, and therefore the middle of the river is properly here mentioned, as the bound of Sihon's dominion on that side. Half Gilead - Hebrew. and the half Gilead, that is, half of the country of Gilead; this doth not denote the bound from which his dominion began, but the country, over which his dominion was, which began at Arnon, and took in half Gilead, and ended at Jabbok, beyond which was the other half of Gilead which belonged to Og.
3. On the east - Which words describe the situation not of the sea of Cinneroth, which was part of the western border of Sihon's dominion, but of the plain, which is here said to lie eastward from the sea of Cinneroth, and also eastward from the salt sea. And this was indeed the situation of the plains of Moab, which are here spoken of; they lay between the two seas, that of Cinneroth and the salt sea, and eastward to them both. Sea of the plain - The salt sea was a famous plain, pleasant and fruitful, before it was turned into a sea.
4. Ashtaroth and Edrei - Sometimes at the one, sometimes at the other city; both being his royal mansions. But Israel made one grave serve him, who could not be contented with one palace.
6. Smile - Fresh mercies must not drown the remembrance of former mercies: nor must the glory of the present instruments of good to the church, diminish the just honour of those that went before them. Joshua's services were confessedly great. But let not those under Moses be forgotten. Both together proclaim God to be the Alpha and Omega of his peoples salvation.
8. The wilderness - This word here and elsewhere in scripture notes not a land wholly desert and uninhabited, but one thin of inhabitants, as 1 Kings ii, 34; ix, 18 Matt. iii, 1, 3. The Gargashites either were now incorporated with some other of these nations, or as the tradition of the Jews is, upon the approach of Israel under Joshua, they all withdrew and went unto Africk, leaving their land to be possessed by the Israelites, with whom they saw, it was fruitless to contend.
23. King of Gilgal - Not of that Gilgal where Joshua first lodged after his passage over Jordan; where it doth not appear, that there was either king or city; but of a city of the same name, probably in Galilee towards the sea, where divers people might possibly resort for trade and merchandise, over whom this was a king, as formerly Tidal seems to have been, Gen. xiv, 1.
24. Thirty one - Each being king only of one city or small province belonging to it, which was by the wise and singular providence of God, that they might be more easily conquered. But what a fruitful land must Canaan then be, which could subsist so many kingdoms! And yet at this day it is one of the most barren and despicable countries in the world. Such is the effect of the curse it lies under, since its inhabitants rejected the Lord of glory!

XIII

God informs Joshua what parts of the land were yet unconquered, and orders him to divide what was conquered, ver. 1-7. A repetition of the division made by Moses, first, in general, ver. 8-14. then in particular: the lot of Reuben, ver. 15-23. Of Gad, ver. 24-28. Of the half tribe of Manasseh, ver. 29-33.

1. Thou art old - Therefore delay not to do the work which I have commanded thee to do. It is good for those that are stricken in years, to be remembered that they are so: that they may be quickened to do the work of life, and prepare for death which is coming on apace.
2. Remaineth - Unconquered by thee, and to be conquered by the Israelites, if they behave themselves aright. All Geshuri - A people in the northeast of Canaan, as the Philistines are on the southwest.
3. Counted to the Canaanites - That is, which though now possessed by the Philistines, who drove out the Canaanites the old inhabitants of it, Deut. ii, 23 Amos ix, 7, yet is a part of the land of Canaan, and therefore belongs to the Israelites. The Avites - Or, the Avims, as they are called, Deut. ii, 23, who though they were expelled out of their ancient seat, and most of them destroyed by the Caphtorims or Philistines, as is there said, yet many of them escaped, and planted themselves not very far from the former.
4. From the south - That is, from those southern parts of the sea-coast, now possessed by the Philistines, all the more northern parts of the sea-coast being yet inhibited by the Canaanites, almost as far as Sidon. The Amorites - The Amorites were a very strong and numerous people, and we find them

dispersed in several parts, some within Jordan, and some without it, some in the south and others in the north, of whom he speaks here.

6. Will I drive out - Whatever becomes of us, however we may be laid aside as broken vessels, God will do his work in his own time. I will do it by my word; so the Chaldee here, as in many other places: by the eternal word, the captain of my host. But the promise of driving them out from before the children of Israel, supposes that the Israelites must use their own endeavours, must go up against them. If Israel, thro' sloth or cowardice let them alone, they are not likely to be driven out. We must go forth on our Christian warfare, and then God will go before us.

8. Which Moses gave them - By my command, and therefore do not thou disturb them in their possessions, but proceed to divide the other possessions to the rest.

9. Medeba unto Dibon - Two cities anciently belonging to the Moabites, and taken from them by the Amorites, Num. xxi, 30, and from them by the Israelites; and after the Israelites were gone into captivity, recovered by the first possessors, the Moabites.

11. And Maacathites - Whose land God had given to the Israelites without Jordan, though they had not yet used the gift of God, nor taken possession of it, as is noted, ver. 13.

12. These did Moses smite - Not all now mentioned, but Sihon and Og, and their people, and the generality of them.

14. He gave - That is, Moses. None inheritance - Namely, in the land beyond Jordan, where yet a considerable part of the Levites were to have their settled abode. This is mentioned as the reason both why Moses gave all that land to the Reubenites and Gadites and Manassites; and why Joshua should divide the land only into nine parts and an half, as was said, ver. 7, because Levi was otherwise provided for. Made by fire - Which are here put for all the sacrifices and oblations, including first-fruits and tithes, that were assigned to the Levites; and this passage is repeated, to prevent those calumnies and injuries which God foresaw the Levites were likely to meet with, from the malice, envy and covetousness of their brethren.

15. According to their families - Dividing the inheritance into as many parts as they had families; but this is only spoken of the greater families; for the lesser distributions to the several small families was done by inferior officers, according to the rules which Moses gave them.

19. In the mount of the valley - In the mountain bordering upon that valley, which then was famous among the Israelites; whether that where Moses was buried, which was near to Beth-peor, Deut. xxxiv, 1, 6, or some other. And this clause is thought to belong to all the cities now mentioned.

21. Cities of the plain - Opposed to the cities of the mountain of the valley. All the kingdom of Sihon - A great part of it; in which sense we read of all Judea, and all the region round about Jordan, Matt. iii, 5, and all Galilee, Matt. iv, 23. Whom Moses smote - Not in the same time or battle, as appears by comparing Num. xxi, 23, 24, with Num. xxxi, 8, but in the same manner. And they are here mentioned, partly because they were slain not long after, and upon the same occasion, even their enmity against Israel; and partly because of their relation and subjection to Sihon. Dukes of Sihon - But how could they be so, when they were kings of Midian? Num. xxxi, 8. There were divers petty kings in those parts, who were subject to greater kings; and such these were, but are here called dukes or princes of Sihon, because they were subject and tributaries to him, and therefore did one way or other assist Sihon in this war, though they were not killed at this time. It is probable, that when Sihon destroyed those Moabites which dwelt in these parts, he frighted the rest of them, and with them their neighbours and confederates, the Midianites, into some kind of homage, which they were willing to pay him. Dwelling in the country - Hebrew. inhabiting that land, namely Midian, last mentioned; whereby he signifies, that tho' they were subject to Sihon, yet they did not dwell in his land, but in another.

22. Were slain by them - This was recorded before, Num. xxxi, 8, and is here repeated, because the defeating of Balaam's purpose to curse Israel, and the turning that curse into a blessing, was such an instance of the power and goodness of God, as was fit to be had in everlasting remembrance.

23. The border thereof - That is, those cities or places which bordered upon Jordan.

25. The cities of Gilead - That is, all the cities of eminency; all the cities properly so called, which lay in that part of Gilead; and so this may well agree with ver. 31, where half the country of Gilead is said to be given to the Manassites; but there is no mention of any cities there. The land of the children of Ammon - Not of that which was now theirs, for that they were forbidden to meddle with, but of that which was anciently theirs, 'till taken from them by the Amorites, from whom the Israelites took it. Aroer - The border between them and Moab. Rabbah - The chief city of the Ammonites.

26. Ramath-mizpeh - Called Ramoth-Gilead, or Ramoth in Gilead. Mahanaim - Exclusively; for Mahanaim was in the portion of Manasseh, beyond Jabbok, which was the border of Gad and Manasseh.

27. The rest of the kingdom - The northern part of his kingdom.

29. Of Manasseh - Not that thou desired it, as Reuben and Gad did, Num. xxxii, 1, but partly as a recompence to Machir the Manassite, for his valiant acts against Og; and partly for the better defense of the other two tribes, by so considerable an accession to them, which also was without any

inconvenience to them, because the country was too large for the two tribes of Reuben and Gad.

30. Of Jair - Who, though of the tribe of Judah, by the father, 1 Chron. ii, 21, 22, yet is called the son of Manasseh, Num. xxxii, 41, because he married a daughter of Manasseh, and wholly associated himself with those valiant Manassites; and with their help took sixty cities or great towns, Deut. iii, 4, 14, which thence were called the towns of Jair.

31. Children of Machir - Whom before he called the children of Manasseh, he now calls the children of Machir, because Machir was the most eminent, and as it may seem, the only surviving son of Manasseh, Num. xxvi, 29; 1 Chron. vii, 14-16.

XIV

The method of dividing the land, ver. 1-5. Caleb demands Hebron, ver. 6-12. which Joshua grants, ver. 13-15.

1. Eleazar the priest - He best understood the laws of God by which this division was to be regulated. Heads of the fathers - Twelve persons, each the head of his tribe, who were appointed and named by God, Num. xxxiv, 19, and if any of them were now dead, no doubt Joshua and Eleazar, by God's direction, put others in their stead.

2. By lot - This course God ordained, partly to prevent discontents, enmities and quarrels among the tribes, and partly to demonstrate the truth and wisdom of his providence, by which alone those parts fell to each of them, which Jacob long since, and Moses lately, foretold; so that as a learned man saith, he must be more stupid than stupidity, that doth not acknowledge a Divine hand in this matter. The lot did only determine the several parts to the several tribes, but did not precisely fix all the bounds of it; these might be either enlarged or diminished according to the greater or smaller number of the tribes.

4. Were two tribes - That is, had the portion of two tribes, and therefore though Levi was excluded, there remained nine tribes and a half, to be provided for in Canaan.

5. They - That is, the persons named, ver. 5, who acted in the name of the children of Israel, divided it, either now, or presently after.

6. Then - When Joshua and the rest were consulting about the division of the land, though they did not yet actually divide it. The heads of that tribe who were willing thus to shew respect to him; and to testify their consent, that he should be provided for by himself, and that they would not take it as any reflection on the rest of the tribe. In Gilgal - Where the division of the land was designed and begun, though it was executed and finished at Shiloh. The Kenezite - Of the posterity of Kenaz. The Lord said - In general, the promise he made us of possessing this land; and for my part, that which is expressed here, ver. 9.

7. As it was in mine heart - I spake my opinion sincerely, without flattery and fear, when the other spies were biased by their own fears, and the dread of the people, to speak otherwise than in their consciences they believed.

8. I wholly followed the Lord - Which self-commendation is justifiable, because it was necessary, as being the ground of his petition. Therefore it was not vain glory in him to speak it: no more than it is for those, who have God's spirit witnessing with their spirits, that they are the children of God, humbly and thankfully to tell others, for their encouragement, what God hath done for their souls.

10. Forty-five years - Whereof thirty- eight years were spent in the wilderness, and seven since they came into Canaan. The longer we live the more sensible we should be, of God's goodness to us in keeping us alive! Of his care in prolonging our frail lives, his patience in prolonging our forfeited lives! And shall not the life thus kept by his providence, be devoted to his praise?

11. For war - Not only for counsel, but for action; for marching and fighting. And therefore this gift will not be cast away upon an unprofitable and unserviceable person. To go out, and to come in - To perform all the duties belonging to my place. Moses had said, that at eighty years old, even our strength is labour and sorrow. But Caleb was an exception to this rule: At eighty-five years old, his strength was still ease and joy. This he got by following the Lord fully.

12. This mountain - That is, this mountainous country. He names the country rather than the cities, because the cities were given to the Levites, chap. xxi, 11, 13. Thou heardest - Didst understand, both by the reports of others, and by thy own observation. Hearing, the sense by which we get knowledge, is often put for knowing or understanding. If the Lord will be with me - A modest and pious expression, signifying both the absolute necessity of God's help, and his godly fear, lest God for his sins should deny his assistance to him; for although he was well assured in general, that God would crown his people with success in this war, yet he might doubt of his particular success in this or that enterprize. To drive them out - Out of their fastnesses where they yet remain, Caleb desires this difficult work as a testimony of his own faith, and as a motive to quicken his brethren to the like attempts.

13. Blessed him - Prayed to God to bless and help him according to his own desire.

15. A great man - In stature, and strength, and dignity, and authority, as being the progenitor of

Anak, the father of those famous giants called Anakims.

XV

The bounds of the inheritance of Judah, ver. 1-12. The assignment of Hebron to Caleb and his family, ver. 13-19. The cities of Judah, ver. 20-63.

1. The lot - For the general understanding of this, it must be known
1. That casting lots was transacted with great seriousness and solemnity, in God's presence, with prayer and appeal to him for the decision of the matter.
2. That although exact survey of this land was not taken 'till chap. xviii, 4, 5, yet there was, and must needs be a general description of it, and a division thereof into nine parts and an half; which, as far as they could guess, were equal either in quantity or quality.
3. That the lot did not at this time so unchangeably determine each tribe, that their portion could neither be increased or diminished; as is manifest, because after Judah's lot was fixed, Simeon's lot was taken out of it, chap. xix, 9, though after the land was more distinctly known and surveyed, it is likely the bounds were more certain and fixed.
4. That the lot determined only in general what part of the land belonged to each tribe, but left the particulars to be determined by Joshua and Eleazar. For the manner of this, it is probably conceived, that there was two pots, into one of which were put the names of all the tribes, each in a distinct paper, and into the other the names of each portion described; then Eleazar or some other person, drew out first the name of one of the tribes out of one pot, and then the name of one portion out of the other, and that portion was appropriated to that tribe. And with respect to these pots, in the bottom of which the papers lay, these lots are often said to come up, or come forth. Of Judah - Whose lot came out first by God's disposition, as a note of his preeminency above his brethren. Of Edom - Which lay southeast from Judah's portion. Judah and Joseph were the two sons of Jacob, on whom Reuben's forfeited birthright devolved. Judah had the dominion entailed upon him, and Joseph the double portion. Therefore these two tribes are first seated: and on them the other seven attended.
2. The bay - Hebrew. the tongue: either a creek or arm of that sea; or a promontory, which by learned authors is sometimes called a tongue. Every sea is salt, but this had an extraordinary saltness, the effect of that fire and brimstone which destroyed Sodom and Gomorrah: the ruins of which lie buried at the bottom of this dead water, which never was moved itself by any tides, nor had any living thing in it.
5. The end of Jordan - That is, the place where Jordan runs into the salt-sea.
6. The stone of Bohan - A place so called, not from Bohan's dwelling there, (for the Reubenites had no portion on this side Jordan) but from some notable exploit which he did there, though it is not recorded in scripture.
8. Went up - Properly; for the line went from Jordan and the salt sea, to the higher grounds nigh Jerusalem; and therefore the line is said to go down, chap. xviii, 16, because there it takes a contrary course, and goes downward to Jordan and the sea. Valley of Hinnom - A very pleasant place, but afterward made infamous. Of the Jebusites - Of the city of the Jebusites, which was anciently called Jebussi. Jerusalem - It may seem hence, that Jerusalem properly, or at least principally, belonged to Benjamin; and yet it is ascribed to Judah also; either because a part of the city was allotted to Judah; or because the Benjamites desired the help and conjunction of this powerful tribe of Judah, for the getting and keeping of this most important place. And when the Benjamites had in vain attempted to drive out the Jebusites, this work was at last done by the tribe of Judah, who therefore had an interest in it by the right of war; as Ziglag which belonged to the tribe of Simeon, being gotten from the Philistines by David, was joined by him to his tribe of Judah, 1 Sam. xxvii, 6.
10. Mount Seir - Not that of Edom, but another so called from some resemblance it had to it.
13. He - Joshua. City of Arba - Or, Kirjath-arba. Not the city, which was the Levites, but the territory of it, chap. xxi, 13.
14. Drove thence - That is, from the said territory, from their caves and forts in it. These giants having either recovered their cities, or defended themselves in the mountains. Three sons of Anak - Either the same who are mentioned, Num. xiii, 33, and so they were long-lived men, such as mainly were in those times and places: or their sons, called by their father's names, which is very usual.
15. Debir - The same mentioned above, ver. 7. The name was Kirjath-sepher - This clause seems to be added to distinguish this from the other Debir subdued by Joshua, chap. x, 38, 39.
16. To wife - Which is to be understood with some conditions, as, if he were one who could marry her by God's law; and if she were willing; for though parents had a great power over their children, they could not force them to marry any person against their own wills. He might otherwise be an unfit and unworthy person; but this was a divine impulse, that Othniel's valour might be more manifest, and so the way prepared for his future government of the people, Judg. iii, 9.

John Wesley

18. As she came - Or, as she went, namely, from her father's house to her husband's, as the manner was. She moved him - She persuaded her husband, either,

1. That he would ask: or rather,

2. That he would suffer her to ask, as she did. She lighted - That she might address herself to her father in an humble posture, and as a suppliant, which he understood by her gesture.

19. A blessing - That is, a gift, as that word signifies, Gen. xxxiii, 11. A south land - That is, a dry land, much exposed to the south wind, which in those parts was very hot and drying, as coming from the deserts of Arabia. Springs of water - That is, a field, wherein are springs of water, which in that country were of great price; she begs a well moistened field, which also might give some relief to that which was dry and barren. Upper and nether springs - Or two fields, one above and the other below that south and dry ground which she complained of, that by this means it might be watered on both sides.

32. Twenty nine - Here are thirty seven or thirty eight cities named before; how then are they only reckoned twenty nine? There were only twenty nine of them, which either,

1. properly belonged to Judah; the rest fell to Simeon's lot; or

2. Were cities properly so called, that is, walled cities, or such as had villages under them, as it here follows; the rest being great, but unwalled towns, or such as had no villages under them.

48. The mountains - That is, in the higher grounds called mountains or hills, in comparison of the sea-coast.

55. Ziph - Which gave its name to the neighbouring mountains, 1 Sam. xxvi, 1.

62. City of salt - So called either from the salt sea, which was near it; or from the salt which was made in, or about it.

63. Inhabitants of Jerusalem - For though Jerusalem was in part taken by Joshua before this; yet the upper and stronger part of it, called Zion, was still kept by the Jebusites, even until David's time; and it seems from thence they descended to the lower town called Jerusalem, and took it so that the Israelites were forced to win it a second time; yea, and a third time also: for afterwards it was possessed by the Jebusites, Judg. xix, 11; 2 Sam. v, 6, 7. Could not drive them out - Namely, because of their unbelief, as Christ could do no mighty work, because of the peoples unbelief, Mark vi, 5, 6 Matt. xiii, 58, and because of their sloth, and cowardice, and wickedness, whereby they forfeited God's help. The children of Judah - The same things which are here said of the children of Judah, are said of the Benjamites, Judg. i, 21. Hence ariseth a question, To which of the tribes Jerusalem belonged? It seems probable, that part of it, and indeed the greatest part, stood in the tribe of Benjamin; and hence this is mentioned in the list of their cities, and not in Judah's list; and part of it stood in Judah's share, even mount Moriah, on which the temple was built; and Mount Zion, when it was taken from the Jebusites. To this day - When this book was written, whether in Joshua's life, which continued many years after the taking of Jerusalem; or after his death, when this clause was added by some other man of God. But this must be done before David's time, when the Jebusites were quite expelled, and their fort taken.

XVI

The lot of Ephraim and Manasseh, ver. 1-4. Of Ephraim in particular, ver. 5-10

1. Children of Joseph - That is, of Ephraim, and the half tribe of Manasseh, which are here put together in one; because in these first verses he speaks of them in common; and then of their several portions.

4. Manasseh - That is, half Manasseh. Their inheritance - Their several portions which here follow. It is said, they took their inheritance, which also Judah had done before them, because the tribes of Judah and Joseph did take their inheritances before the rest; and it was fit they should do so, for the security of the main camp, and the body of the people which were at Gilgal, chap. xviii, 5.

5. East-side - That is, the northeast side. It is no wonder, if some of these descriptions are dark to us at this distance of time; there having been so many alterations made in places, and so many circumstances, being now altogether undiscoverable. But this is certain, that all the descriptions here mentioned, were then evident to the Israelites, because these were the foundations of all the possessions which then they took, and peaceably possessed in succeeding ages.

6. Toward the sun - The midland sea, towards the west.

7. To Jericho - Not to the city of Jericho, which belonged to Benjamin's lot, chap. xviii, 21, but to its territory.

9. The separate cities - That is, besides those cities which were within Ephraim's bounds, he had some other cities, to which all of all their territories were annexed out Manasseh's portion, because his tribe was all here, and was larger than Manasseh's.

XVII

The families of Manasseh, ver. 1-6. The country that fell to their lot, ver. 7-18. Their request for more land, ver. 14-18.

1. The first born of Joseph - The sense is, though Ephraim was to be more potent and numerous, yet Manasseh was the first-born, and had the privilege of the first-born, which was translated to Joseph, namely, a double portion; and therefore though this was but half the tribe of Manasseh, yet they are not made intimates to Ephraim, but have a distinct lot of their own, as their brethren, or other half tribe had beyond Jordan. For Machir - The only son of Manasseh, who therefore is here, put for the whole tribe. The first-born - So even only sons are sometimes called, as Matt. i, 25. He - That is, Machir, had given great proof of his valour (though the particular history be not mentioned) and his posterity were no degenerate sons, but had his valiant blood still running in their veins. Gilead and Bashan - Part of these countries; for part of them was also given to the Reubenites, and part to the Gadites. This may be added as a reason, either,

1. why he got those places from the Amorites: or
2. why they were allotted to him or his posterity, because this was a frontier country, and the out-works to the land of Canaan, and therefore required valiant persons to defend it.

2. A Lot - A distinct inheritance. The rest - Namely, those of them which had not received their possessions beyond Jordan. Male-children - This expression is used to bring in what follows, concerning his female children.

4. He - That is, Eleazar, or Joshua, with the consent of the princes appointed for that work.

5. Ten portions - Five for the sons, and five for the daughters; for as for Hepher, both he and his son Zelophehad was dead, and that without sons, and therefore had no portion; but his daughters had several portions allotted to them.

6. The daughters - Not less than the son, so the sex was no bar to their inheritance.

9. Three cities - Tappuah, and the cities upon the coast descending to the river, &c. last mentioned. Among the cities of Manasseh - That is, are intermixed with their cities, which was not strange nor unfit, these two being linked together by a nearer alliance than the rest.

10. His border - Manasseh's, whose portion is here described, and whose name was last mentioned. In Asher - That is, upon the tribe of Asher; for though Zebulon came between Asher and them for the greatest part of their land; yet it seems there was some necks of land, both of Ephraim's and of Manasseh's, which jutted out farther than the rest, and touched the borders of Asher. And it is certain there were many such incursions of the land of one tribe upon some parcels of another, although they were otherwise considerably distant one from the other.

11. Manasseh had in Issachar and in Asher - As Ephraim had some cities in the tribe of Manasseh, and as it was not unusual, when the place allotted to any tribe was too narrow for it, and the next too large, to give away part from the larger to the less portion; nay, sometimes one whole tribe was taken into another; as Simeon's was into Judah's portion, when it was found too large for Judah. Inhabitants of Dor - Not the places only, but the people; whom they spared and used for servants. Three countries - The words may be rendered, the third part of that country; and so the meaning may be, that the cities and towns here mentioned are a third part of that country, that is, of that part of Issachar's and Asher's portion, in which those places lay.

14. Children of Joseph - That is, of Ephraim and Manasseh. Spake unto Joshua - That is, expostulated with him, when they went and saw that portion which was allotted them, and found it much short of their expectation. One portion - Either,

1. because they really had but one lot, which was afterwards divided by the arbitrators between them. Or,
2. because the land severally allotted to them, was but little enough for one of them.

15. A great people - He retorts their own argument; seeing thou art a great and numerous people, turn thy complaints into action, and enlarge thy borders by thy own hand, to which thou mayest confidently expect God's assistance. The wood-country - To the mountain, as it is called, ver. 18, where among some towns there is much wood-land, which thou mayest without much difficulty possess, and so get the more room. And cut down - The wood, for thy own advantage; in building more cities and towns; and preparing the land for pasture and tillage. The Perizzites - Supposed to be a savage and brutish kind of people, that lived in woods and mountains. Giants - Who lived in caves and mountains, now especially when they were driven out of their cities. If mount Ephraim - Or, seeing mount Ephraim is too narrow for thee, as thou complainest; take to thyself the rest of that hilly and wood country. Mount Ephraim was a particular portion of the land, belonging to the tribe of Ephraim. And this seems to be here mentioned, for all the portion allotted to Ephraim and Manasseh, as appears from their complaint, which was not, that this part, but that their whole portion was too strait for them.

16. Is not enough - Hebrew. the hill will not be found, that is, obtained by us; those fierce and

strong people the Perizzites and the giants will easily defend themselves, and frustrate our attempts, having the advantage of the woods and mountains. The Canaanites that dwell - That is, and if thou sayest, that if the hill either cannot be conquered, or is not sufficient for us, we may go down and take more land out of the pleasant and fruitful valleys, we shall meet with no less difficulty there than in the mountains. Chariots of iron - Not all made of iron, but armed with iron, not only for defense, but for offense also, having as it were scythes and swords fastened to them, to cut down all that stood in their way.

17. One lot only - Thou needest and deservedst more than that lot, of which thou art actually possessed, and thou hast power to get more; which if thou endeavourest to do, God will bless thee, and give thee more.

18. The out-goings of it - The valleys and fields belonging or adjoining to it, for there the Canaanites were, ver. 16.

XVIII

The setting up of the tabernacle at Shiloh, ver. 1. Joshua's stirring up the seven remaining tribes to look after their lot, ver. 2- 7. The division of the land into several lots assigned to those several tribes, ver. 8-10. The lot of Benjamin, ver. 11-28.

1. Set up the tabernacle - By God's appointment. It was removed from Gilgal, partly for the honour and conveniency of Joshua, that he being of the tribe of Ephraim, and seating himself there, might have the opportunity of consulting with God as often as he needed; and partly for the conveniency of all the tribes, that being in the center of them, they might more easily resort to it from all places. Here the tabernacle continued for above three hundred years, even 'till Samuel's days, 1 Sam. i, 3. Shiloh was the name given to the Messiah in dying Jacob's prophecy. So the pitching the tabernacle in Shiloh intimated to the Jews, that in that Shiloh whom Jacob spoke of, all the ordinances of this worldly sanctuary should have their accomplishment, in a greater and more perfect tabernacle.

3. How long are you slack - This slackness is supposed to arise from an opinion of the impossibility of making any regular distribution of the parts, 'till the whole were more exactly surveyed, which accordingly is here done. Likewise, being weary of war, and having sufficient plenty of all things, they were unwilling to run into new hazards.

4. Three men - Three, not one, for more exact observation both of the measure and quality of the several portions, and for greater assurance of their care and faithfulness in giving in their account. Of each tribe - One of each of these tribes, who were yet unprovided for.

5. Seven parts - Which were of equal extent or worth: for no tribe was so great, but one of these parts in its full extent would abundantly suffice them; and there was no reason why the portions should be greater or less according as the tribes at present were more or fewer in number, because of the various changes which happened therein successively; it being usual for one tribe to be more numerous than another in one age, which was fewer in the next. And if the several tribes had increased more, and not diminished their numbers by their sins, they might have sent forth colonies, and taken any part of the land, even as far as Euphrates, all which the Lord of the whole earth had given them a right to, which when they pleased they might take possession of. Judah shall abide on the south - They shall not be disturbed in their possession, but shall keep it, except some part of it shall be adjudged to another tribe. Joseph on the north - In respect of Judah, not of the whole land; for divers other tribes were more northern than they.

6. Before the Lord - That is, before the ark or tabernacle, that God may be witness and judge, and author of the division, that each may be contented with his lot, and that your several possessions may be secured to you as things sacred.

9. By cities - Or, according to the cities, to which the several parties or territories belonged.

11. And the children of Joseph - Wherein we see the wisdom of Divine Providence, this being the only place in which that prophecy, Deut. xxxiii, 12, could have been accomplished. Providence cast Benjamin next to Joseph on the one hand, because Benjamin was own and only brother to Joseph, and next to Judah on the other hand, that this tribe might hereafter unite with Judah, in an adherence to the throne of David, and the temple at Jerusalem.

14. Kirjath-jearim - The Israelites changed the name, to blot out the remembrance of Baal.

16. The end of the mountain - The place where the mountain ends, and the valley begins. Before the valley - That is, in the prospect of that valley. In the valley on the north - Which extends unto this other valley on the north-side of it. Of Jebusi - To that part where the Jebusites lived, which was in and near Jerusalem.

21. Jericho - For tho' the city was destroyed, the territory remained.

Wesley's Notes on the Bible - The Old Testament: Genesis - Ruth
XIX

The lot of Simeon, ver. 1-9. Of Zebulon, ver. 10-16. Of Issachar, ver. 17-23. Of Asher, ver. 24-31. Of Naphtali, ver. 32- 39. Of Daniel, ver. 40-48. The inheritance assigned to Joshua and his family, ver. 49-51.

1. Within the inheritance of Judah - This was so ordered by God's providence, partly to fulfil that threatning that he would divide and scatter this tribe in Israel, Gen. xlix, 7, which was hereby done in part, because they had no distinct lot, but were as inmates to Judah; partly, because now upon the more exact survey of the land, it appeared, that the part given to Judah did far exceed the proportion which they needed, or which the other tribes could expect. And this was the least of the tribes, Num. xxvi, 14, and therefore fittest to be put within another tribe.

11. Toward the sea - The lot of this tribe was washed by the midland sea on the west, and by the sea of Tiberias on the east, answering Jacob's prophecy, Zebulun shall be an haven of ships; trading ships on the great sea, and fishing ships on the sea of Galilee. Before Jokneam - Supposed to be Kishon.

15. Beth-lehem - Not that where Christ was born, which was in Judah, but another. Twelve cities - There are more numbered here, but the rest either were not cities properly so called, or were not within this tribe, but only bordering upon it, and belonging to other tribes.

18. Jezreel - The royal city, 1 Kings xxi, 1. This tribe, because it lay between Benjamin on the south, and Zebulun on the north, is not here described by its borders, which were the same with theirs; but by some of its cities.

26. Carmel west-ward - Or, Carmel by the sea, to distinguish it from Carmel in the tribe of Judah. This was a place of eminent fruitfulness, agreeable to the prophecy concerning Asher, Gen. xlix, 20.

27. Cubal - A city so called. Left hand - That is, on the north, which, when men look towards the east, as is usual, is on their left hand.

28. Kenah - Namely, Kenah the greater, in the upper Galilee; not Kenah the less, which was in the lower Galilee. Zidon - Called great for its antiquity, and riches, and glory. The city either was not given to the Israelites, or at least was never possessed by them; not without a singular providence of God, that they might not by the opportunity of so good a port, be engaged in much commerce with other nations; from which, together with wealth, that great corrupter of mankind, they might contract their errors and vices.

29. To Ramah - From the north southward. To Tyre - Exclusively, for this city was no part of the land given them. But this was not the same city we read of afterwards. For that was built on an island, this on the continent. Probably into these strong holds Tyre and Sidon, many of the Canaanites fled, when Joshua invaded them.

30. Twenty two cities - Here are more named, but some of them were not within this tribe, but only bordering places.

33. Their coast - Their northern border drawn from west to east, as appears, because when this coast is described and brought to its end, the coast is said to turn from the east westward, ver. 34. The out-goings - The end of that coast.

35. Cinnereth - Whence the lake of Cinnereth or Genesareth received its name.

41. Of their inheritance - Which is here described only by its cities, not its borders, which are in part the same with Judah's, and their inheritance is in good part taken out of Judah's too large portion; as appears from divers of the cities here mentioned, which are also reckoned in Judah's portion.

47. Went up to fight - This was done after Joshua's death, and seems to be here inserted, that all the chief places where the Danites dwelt, tho' far distant, might be mentioned together; and to give an account of this strange accident, why they removed from their appointed portion to so remote a place; which may be this, that being much molested by their bad neighbours, they thought fit to go to some place remote from them, which also they were in a manner constrained to do, because otherwise they must have taken some part of the portions of other tribes, whereas now going to the very utmost northern point of the land, they took that which did not belong to any other tribe.

49. The children of Israel - That is, they are said to give it, because the whole land was given to Joshua, and Eleazar, and the princes, as joint trustees, acting in the name, and for the good of the people: so that even Joshua could take nothing without their gift.

50. The word of The Lord - As God had promised, or commanded; either formerly, or at this time by Eleazar. He built - That is, repaired and enlarged it, in which sense Nebuchadnezzar is said to have built Babylon, Dan. iv, 30.

John Wesley

XX

The laws concerning the cities of refuge, ver. 1-6. The appointment of those cities, ver. 7-9.

2. Appoint - The possessions being now divided among you, reserve some of them for the use which I have commanded. Cities of refuge - Designed to typify the relief which the gospel provides for poor, penitent sinners, and their protection from the curse of the law and the wrath of God, in our Lord Jesus, to whom believers fly for refuge.

3. Unwittingly - Hebrew. Through ignorance, or error, or mistake, and without knowledge. The same thing twice repeated to cut off all the expectations that wilful murderers might have of protection here; God having declared, that such should be taken even from his altar, that they might be killed. It is strange that any Christians should make their sanctuaries give protection to such persons whom God hath so expressly excepted from it! Avenger - The nearest kinsman, who had right or power to demand, or take vengeance of the slaughter.

4. The gate - Where the Judges used to sit. His cause - Shall give them a true relation of the fact, and all its circumstances. They shall take him - If they are satisfied in the relation he makes, concerning the fact, otherwise it had been a vain thing to examine. Give a place - Which they might well allow him, because God gave them the city with a reservation for such persons.

6. Stand - Which was the posture of the accused and accusers. The congregation - The council appointed to judge of these matters, not the council of the city of refuge, for they had examined him before, ver. 4, but of the city to which he belonged, or in or nigh which the fact was committed, as appears from Num. xxxv, 25.

7. And they appointed - Concerning these cities note,

1. That they were all upon mountains, that they might be seen at a great distance, and so direct those who fled thither.

2. That they were seated at convenient distance one from another, for the benefit of the several tribes; for Kedesh was in the north, Hebron in the south, and Shechem between them.

3. That they all belonged to the Levites; partly that these causes might be more impartially examined, and justly determined by them who are presumed best able to understand the law of God, and most obliged to follow it and not to be biass'd by any affection or corrupt interest, and partly, that their reputation with the people, and their good counsels, might lay a restraint upon revengeful persons, who might be inclined to follow the man-slayer thither, and endeavour to kill him there. It was likewise an advantage to the poor refugee, that when he might not go up to the house of the Lord, yet he had the servants of God's house with him, to instruct him, and pray for him, and help to make up the want of public ordinances.

8. They assigned - Or, had assigned or given; for they were given by Moses, Deut. iv, 41, &c. or, they applied them to that use to which Moses designed them.

9. The stranger - Not only proselytes, but others also; because this was a matter of common right, that a distinction might be made between casual man-slayers, and wilful murderers.

XXI

The motion of the Levites, to have their cities appointed, which is done, ver. 1-8. A catalogue of those cities, ver. 9-42. A testimony, that God had fulfilled his word, ver. 43-45.

1. Then - When the whole land was distributed to the several tribes, but not actually possessed by them; which was the proper season for them to put in their claim. Fathers of the Levites-The fathers of the Levites were Kohath, Gershom, and Merari, and the heads of these were the chief persons now alive of these several families.

2. The Lord commanded - Observe: the maintenance of ministers is not an arbitrary thing, left purely to the good will of the people. No: as the God of Israel commanded, that the Levites should be provided for, so hath the Lord Jesus ordained, (and a perpetual ordinance it is) that they who preach the gospel should live of the gospel.

3. The children of Israel gave - Probably they gave the Levites promiscuously such cities as God commanded, and the lot appropriated them to their several houses or families. Out of their inheritance - That is, out of their several possessions; that the burden might be equally divided; and, that the Levites being dispersed among the several tribes, according to Jacob's prediction, Gen. xlix, 7, might more easily, and effectually teach the Israelites God's law and judgments, which they were engaged to do, Deut. xxxiii, 10, and that the people might upon all occasions resort to them, and inquire the meaning of the law at their mouths. And suburbs - Not only the use, but the absolute dominion of them, as is manifest both from ver. 11, 12, where a distinction is made between the city and suburbs of Hebron, and the fields and villages thereof; (the former given to the Levites, the latter to Caleb;) and from the return

of these cities in the Jubilee, unto the Levites as to their proper owners, Lev. xxv, 33, 34.

4. Judah, Simeon, and Benjamin - Which three tribes were nearest the temple, where their business lay. Thirteen cities - For though the priests were now few enough for one city, yet respect was to be had to their succeeding numbers; this division being made for all future generations. And seeing the Levites might sell their houses until the Jubilee, Lev. xxv, 33, much more might they let them; and therefore it is probable their cities were not long uninhabited, many being inclined to dwell with them by virtue of relations contracted with them; or out of respect to the service of God, and the good of their souls.

5. Children of Kohath - Who were of Aaron's family. Ephraim, Daniel, and Manesseh - Which tribes are nearest to the three former, and so the Kohathites are placed next to their brethren the Aaronites. Ten cities - Fewer than they gave out of the three former tribes, because their inheritance was less than the former.

9. Judah and Simeon - These are mentioned together, because the cities of Simeon lay within Judah's portion.

10. Families - That is, of the family, the plural number for the singular, which is not unusual.

12. The fields and villages - That is, all beyond the two thousand cubits expressed, Num. xxxv, 5. This is here mentioned, not as his peculiar case, but as one eminent instance, to shew, that it was so in all the rest of the cities here named; that the fields and villages thereof still belonged to the several tribes from whom the cities and their suburbs were taken; and to make the rest of the Israelites more cheerfully resign part of their possessions to the Levites, because even Caleb did so, though his possession had been long before promised, and now actually given to him by God's special command, as a mark of honour and compensation for his long and faithful service.

16. And Ain - Ain and Gibeon, and some others here named are not named, 1 Chron. vi, 59. Either they were destroyed in some of those invasions wherewith their land was grievously wasted before that time; or they appear there under other names.

20. Which remained - Over and above those who were priests.

25. Half the tribe - Namely, that half which dwelt in Canaan.

41. Forty eight cities - Why hath this tribe, which was the least of all, more cities than any of them? First, it doth not appear that they had more: for though all the cities of the Levites be expressed, it is not so with the other tribes, but divers of their cities are omitted. Secondly, the Levites were confined to their cities and suburbs; the rest had large territories belonging to their cities, which also so they were in a capacity of improving, which the Levites were not; so that one of their cities might be more considerable than divers of the Levites. Thirdly, God, was pleased to deal liberally with his ministers, to put honour on those whom he foresaw many would be prone to despise; and, that being free from outward distractions, they might more entirely and fervently devote themselves to the service of God.

43. All the land - He gave them the right to all, and the actual possession of the greatest part of it, and power to possess the rest, as soon as it was needful for them, which was when their numbers were increased, and the absolute dominion of all the people remaining in it.

44. Gave them rest - Namely, all the days of Joshua; for afterwards it was otherwise with them.

45. All came to pass - Such an acknowledgment as this, here subscribed by Joshua, in the name of all Israel, we afterward find made by Solomon; and all Israel did in effect say amen to it, 1 Kings viii, 56. The inviolable truth of God's promise, and the performance of it to the uttermost, is what all believers in Christ have been always ready to bear their testimony to. And if in any thing it has seemed to come short, they have been as ready to take all the blame to themselves.

XXII

Joshua's dismission of the two tribes and an half, and their return to their own country, ver. 1-9. The altar they built on that side of Jordan, which offended the other tribes, ver. 10-20. Their apology, with which the rest were satisfied, ver. 21-34.

4. Your tents - That is, to your settled habitations. Tho' their affections to their families could not but make them very desirous to return, yet like good soldiers, they would not move 'till they had orders from their general. So, tho' we desire to be at home with Christ ever so much, yet we must stay here till our warfare is accomplished, wait for a due discharge, and not anticipate the time of our removal.

5. Take heed - Watch over yourselves and all your actions. Commandment and law - Two words expressing the same thing, the law of commandments delivered by Moses. All your heart and soul - With the whole strength of your minds, and wills, and affections.

8. With your brethren -- that is, with them who stayed beyond Jordan for the defense of their land, and wives, and children, who therefore were to have a share, though not an equal share with these. But for them, 1 Sam. xxx, 24, their share was equal, because their danger was equal.

10. Built an altar - About that time when they came to them, they designed it, and as soon as they were got over Jordan, which was in a very little time, they effected and perfected it. They built it, no

John Wesley

doubt, on their own side of the water: for how could they build on other men's land, without their consent? And it is said, in the following verse, to be over against the land of Jordan. Nor would there have been cause to suspect that it was designed for sacrifice, if they had not built it among themselves.

11. At the passage - Where they passed over Jordan, either at their first entrance into Canaan, or afterwards, and usually.

12. The children of Israel - Not in their own persons, not by their elders, who used to transact all affairs of this kind in the name of all the people. Against them - As apostates from God, according to God's command in that case, Deut. xiii, 13. &c.

16. The congregation - Who do and are resolved to cleave unto that God from whom you have revolted. What trespass - How heinous a crime is this! This day - That is, so soon after God hath obliged you by such wonderful favours, and when God is now conducting you home to reap the fruits of all your pains and hazards. Rebel - With a design to rebel against God, and against his express command of worshipping him at one only altar.

17. Of Peor - That is, of our worshipping of Baal-peor, Num. xxv, 3. Probably this is mentioned the rather, because Phinehas, the first commissioner in this treaty, had signalized himself in that matter: and because they were now at or near the very place, where that iniquity was committed. Are not cleansed - For though God had pardoned it, as to the national punishment of it, Num. xxv, 11, yet they were not yet throughly purged from it; partly because the shame and blot of that odious practice was not yet wiped off: and partly, because some of that corrupt leaven still remained among them, and though smothered for a time, yet was ready to break forth upon all occasions, See chap. xxiv, 33. And God also took notice of these idolatrous inclinations in particular persons, and found out ways to punish them.

18. Tomorrow - That is, suddenly, as that word is often used. Congregation - With you for doing so, and with us for suffering, or not punishing it.

19. Be unclean - If you apprehend it to be so for want of the tabernacle and altar there; as the following words imply: if you now repent of your former choice in preferring the worldly commodities of that country before the advantage of God's presence, and more frequent opportunities of his service. Among us - We will readily resign part of our possessions to you for the prevention of this sin and mischief. Against us - For all the tribes were united in one body politick, and made one commonwealth, and one church; and each tribe was subject to the laws and commands of the whole society, and of the chief ruler or rulers thereof; so its disobedience to their just commands was properly rebellion against them.

20. Of Zerah - That is, one of his posterity. Not alone - But brought destruction upon his whole family, and part of our forces sent against Ai.

22. The Lord - That Jehovah, whom we no less than you acknowledge and adore as the God of gods, infinitely superior to all that are called gods. The multiplying of his titles, and the repetition of these words, shew their zeal and earnestness in this matter. He knoweth - To him we appeal who knoweth all things, and the truth of what we are now saying. Not only our present words, but our future and constant course shall satisfy all Israel of our perseverance in the true religion. In rebellion - If this have been done by us with such design, or in such a manner. Save us not - Thou, O Lord, to whom we have appealed, and without whom we cannot be saved and preserved, save us not from any of our enemies, nor from the sword of our brethren. It is a sudden apostrophe to God, usual in such vehement speeches.

23. Require it - That is, call us to an account and punish us for it.

24. With the Lord - You have no relation to him, nor interest in him, or his worship.

25. A border - To shut you out of the land of promise, and consequently from the covenant made between God and our fathers. No part - Nothing to do with him; no right to serve him or expect favour from him. Cease from fearing the Lord - For they that are cut off from public ordinances, usually by degrees lose all religion. It is true, the form and profession of godliness, may be kept without the life and power of it. But the life and power will not long be kept, without the form and profession of it.

27. Before him - That we and ours may have and hold our privilege of serving and worshiping God, not upon this altar, but in the place of God's presence, in your tabernacle, and upon your altar.

28. The pattern - An exact representation and resemblance. A witness - That we both serve one God, and approve and make use of one and the same altar.

30. Pleased them - They were fully satisfied with this answer.

31. Is among us - By his gracious presence, and preventing goodness, in keeping you from so great an offense, and all of us from those calamities that would have followed it. Hand of the Lord - That is, from the wroth and dreadful judgments of God, by avoiding that sin which would have involved both you and us in a most bloody war; you have delivered us from the evils we feared. He that prevents an approaching disease or mischief, doth as truly deliver a man from it, as he that cures or removes it after it hath been inflicted.

33. Destroy the land - As they were by the law of God obliged to do, if they had been guilty and persisted therein; as afterwards they did the tribe of Benjamin for the same reason.

34. *The altar Ed* - That is, a witness: a witness of the relation they stood in to God and Israel, and of their concurrence with the other tribes in the common faith, that Jehovah he is God. It was a witness to posterity, of their care to transmit their religion pure and entire; and would be a witness against them, if ever they should turn from following the Lord their God.

XXIII

Joshua reminds the people, assembled for that purpose, of what God had done, and what he would do for them, ver. 1-5. Exhorts them resolutely to persevere in their duty to God, ver. 6- 8. which he enforces by former benefits, and by promises, ver. 9- 11. and by threatnings, ver. 12-16.

1. *A long time* - About fourteen years after it.
2. *Joshua called* - Either to his own city, or rather to Shiloh, the usual place of such assemblies, where his words being uttered before the Lord, were likely to have the more effect upon them. *All Israel* - Not all the people in their own persons, but in their representatives, by their elders, heads, Judges and officers. Probably he took the opportunity, of one of the three great feasts. You will not have me long to preach to you; therefore observe what I say, and lay it up for the time to come.
3. *Because of you* - For your good, that you might gain by their losses.
4. *That remain* - Not yet conquered. *An inheritance* - You shall certainly subdue them, and inherit their hand, as you have done the rest, if you be not wanting to yourselves. *All the nations* - That is, with the land of those nations; the people put for their land, as we have seen before; and as sometimes on the contrary, the land is put for the people. *The great sea* - Where the Philistines, your most formidable adversaries yet survive; but them also and their land I have given to you, and you shall undoubtedly destroy them, if you will proceed vigourously in your work.
6. *Very courageous* - For it will require great courage and resolution to execute all the commands of Moses, and particularly, that of expelling and destroying the residue of the Canaanites. *The right hand or the left* - That is, in one kind or other, by adding to the law, or diminishing from it.
7. *Come not* - That is, avoid all familiar converse and contracts, but especially marriages with them. *Name their gods* - To wit, unnecessarily and familiarly, lest the mention of them breed discourse about them, and so by degrees bring to the approbation and worship of them. *Nor cause* - Nor require nor compel the Gentiles to swear by them, as they used to do; especially in leagues and contracts. It is pity, that among Christians, the name of the Heathen God's are so commonly used, especially in poems. Let those names which have been set up in rivalship with God, be forever loathed and lost. *Nor bow* - Neither give them any inward reverence, or outward adoration. Here is an observable gradation, whereby he shews what notable progress sin usually makes, and what need there is to look to the beginnings of it, forasmuch as a civil and common conversation with their persons was likely to bring them, and indeed did actually bring them, by insensible steps, to the worship of their gods. So it is no wonder, if some things not simply and in themselves evil, be forbidden by God, as here the naming of their gods is, because they are occasions and introductions to evil.
8. *Cleave to the Lord* - By constant obedience, entire affection, faithful service and worship of him alone. *To this day* - To wit, since you came in to Canaan; since which time the body of the people (for of them he speaks, not of every particular person) had behaved themselves much better than they did in the wilderness, and had not been guilty of any gross and general apostacy from God, or rebellion against him.
9. *No man* - To wit, whom you have invaded; otherwise some of those people did yet remain unconquered.
10. *He fighteth* - Impute not this therefore to your own valour, as you will be apt to do, but to God's gracious and powerful assistance.
11. *Take heed* - Now it requires more watchfulness and diligence than it did in the wilderness, because your temptations are now stronger; from the examples and insinuations of your bad neighbours, the remainders of this wicked people; and from your own peace and prosperity: and the pride, security, forgetfulness of God, and luxury, which usually attend that condition.
12. *Go back* - From God, and from his worship and service.
13. *Traps to you* - By your converse with them, you will be drawn by degrees into their errors, and impieties, and brutish lusts. *Thorns in your eyes* - When they have seduced, and thereby weakened you, then they will molest and vex you, no less than a severe scourge doth a man's sides which are lashed by it, or than a small thorn doth the eye when it is got within it. *Till ye perish* - They shall so persecute you, and fight against, you with such success, that you shall be forced to quit your own land, and wander you know not whither; which must needs be very terrible to them to think of, when they compared this present ease, and plenty and safety, with the pains, and weariness, and hazards, and wants of their former wanderings.
14. *Of all the earth* - That is, of all flesh, or of all men; the way which all men go; I am about to

die, as all men must. To die is, to go a journey, a journey to our long home. And Joshua himself, tho' he could so ill be spared, cannot be exempted from this common lot. He takes notice of it, that they might look on these as his dying words, and regard them accordingly. Ye know - That is, you know assuredly; your own experience puts it out of all question.

15. Evil things - The accomplishment of God's promise is a pledge that he will also fulfil his threatnings; both of them depending upon the same ground, the faithfulness of God.

16. It will aggravate their perdition, that the land from which they shall perish is a good land, and a land which God himself had given them: and which therefore he would have secured to them, if they had not thrown themselves out of it. "Thus the goodness of the heavenly Canaan, says Mr. Henry, and the free and sure grant God has made of it, will aggravate the misery of those that shall forever be shut out and perish from it. Nothing will make them see how wretched they are, so much as to see, how happy they might have been." Might have been! What on the supposition of absolute decrees? How happy might a person not elected have been? And if he was elected, how could he be wretched for ever? What art of man can reconcile these things? Again, shall any of the elect perish forever? or has God made to any others, a free and sure grant of the heavenly Canaan? If not, how can the misery of those that perish be aggravated, by a free and sure grant which they never had any share in?

XXIV

Joshua assembling the people, recounts what great things God had done for them, ver. 1-13. Exhorts them to serve God, which they engage to do, ver. 14-28. His age, death, and burial, ver. 29-31. The burying of Joseph's bones, ver. 32. The death and burial of Eleazar, ver. 33.

1. All Israel - Namely, their representatives. Shechem - To the city of Shechem, a place convenient for the purpose, not only because it was a Levitical city, and a city of refuge, and a place near Joshua's city, but especially for the two main ends for which he summoned them thither.

1. For the solemn burial of the bones of Joseph, and the rest of the patriarchs, for which this place was designed.

2. For the solemn renewing of their covenant with God; which in this place was first made between God and Abraham, Gen. xii, 6, 7, and afterwards renewed by the Israelites at their first entrance into the land of Canaan, between the two mountains of Ebal and Gerizzim, chap. viii, 30, &c. which were very near Shechem: and therefore this place was most proper, both to remind them of their former obligations to God, and to engage them to a farther ratification of them. Before God - As in God's presence, to hear what Joshua was to speak to them in God's name, and to receive God's commands from his mouth. He had taken a solemn farewell before: but as God renewed his strength, he desired to improve it for their good. We must never think our work for God done, 'till our life is done.

2. The people - To the elders, by whom it was to be imparted to all the rest, and to as many of the people as came thither. He spake to them in God's name, and as from him, in the language of a prophet, Thus saith the Lord. Jehovah, the great God, and the God of Israel, whom you are peculiarly engaged to hear. The flood - Or, the river, namely, Euphrates, so called by way of eminency. They served - That is, Both Abraham and Nahor were no less idolaters than the rest of mankind. This is said to prevent their vain boasting in their worthy ancestors, and to assure them that whatsoever good was in, or had been done by their progenitors, was wholly from God's free grace, and not for their own merit or righteousness.

3. I took - I snatched him out of that idolatrous place, and took him into acquaintance and covenant with myself, which was the highest honour and happiness he was capable of. And led - That is I brought him after his father's death into Canaan, Gen. xii, 1, and I conducted and preserved him in all his travels through the several parts of Canaan. And multiplied - That is, gave him a numerous posterity, not only by Hagar and Keturah, but even by Sarah and by Isaac. Gave Isaac - By my special power and grace to be heir of my covenant, and all my promises, and the seed in or by which all the nations were to be blessed.

4. Mount Seir - That he might leave Canaan entire to his brother Jacob and his posterity, Gen. xxxvi, 7, 8. Into Egypt - Where they long lived in grievous bondage; which God having delivered us from, I shall now pass it over. 7. Your eyes - He speaketh this to the elders, ver. 1, who were so, not only by power and dignity, but many of them by age; and there being now not sixty years past since those Egyptian plagues, it is very probable that a considerable number of those present, had seen those things in Egypt, and being not twenty years old, were exempted from that dreadful sentence passed upon all who were older, Num. xiv, 29.

9. Balak warred - Balak warred, tho' not by open force, yet by crafty counsel and warlike stratagems, by wicked devices.

10. Unto Balaam - Who hereby appears to have desired of God leave to curse Israel; and therefore it is not strange, that God who permitted him simply to go, was highly angry with him for going with so

wicked an intent, Num. xxii, 20, 22, 32. Delivered you - That is, from Balak's malicious design against you.

11. Deliver them - Namely, successively; for in these few words he seems to comprise all their wars, which being so fresh in their memory, he thought it needless particularly to mention.

12. Sent the hornet - When they were actually engaged in battle with the Canaanites. These dreadful swarms which first appeared in their war with Sihon and Og, tormented them with their stings and terrified them with their noise, so that they became an easy prey to Israel. God had promised to do this for them, Exod. xxiii, 27, 28, and here Joshua observes the fulfilling the promise.

14. The gods - Whereby it appears, that although Joshua had doubtless prevented and purged out all public idolatry, yet there were some of them who practiced it in their private houses and retirements. Your fathers - Terah, and Nahor, and Abraham, as ver. 2, and other of your ancestors. In Egypt - See Ezek xxiii, 3, 8, 19, 21, 27. Under these particulars, no doubt he comprehends all other false gods, which were served by the nations amongst whom they were, but only mentions these, as the idols which they were in more danger of worshipping than those in Canaan; partly because those of Canaan had been now lately and palpably disgraced by their inability to preserve their worshippers from total ruin; and partly, because the other idols came recommended to them by the venerable name of antiquity, and the custom of their forefathers.

15. Seem evil - Unjust, unreasonable or inconvenient. Choose ye - Not that he leaves them to their liberty, whether they would serve God or idols; for Joshua had no such power himself, nor could give it to any other; and both he and they were obliged by the law of Moses, to give their worship to God only, and to forbear all idolatry in themselves, and severely to punish it in others; but it is a powerful insinuation, whereby he both implies, that the worship of God is so highly reasonable, necessary and beneficial; and the service of idols so absurd, and vain, and pernicious, that if it were left free for all men to take their choice, every man in his right wits must needs chuse the service of God, before that of idols; and provokes them to bind themselves faster to God by their own choice. He will - But know this, if you should all be so base and brutish, as to prefer senseless and impotent idols, before the true and living God, it is my firm purpose, that I will, and my children, and servants (as far as I can influence them) shall be constant and faithful to the Lord. And that, whatever others do. They that resolve to serve God, must not start at being singular in it. They that are bound for heaven must be willing to swim against the stream, and must do, not as most do, but as the best do.

19. Ye cannot - He speaks not of an absolute impossibility, (for then both his resolution to serve God himself, and his exhortation to them had been vain) but of a moral impossibility, or a very great difficulty, which he alledgeth not to discourage them from God's service, but to make them more considerate in obliging themselves; and more resolved in answering their obligations. The meaning is, God's service is not, as you seem to fancy, a slight and easy thing, but it is a work of great difficulty, and requires great care, and courage and resolution; and when I consider the infinite purity of God, that he will not be mocked or abused; and withal your proneness to superstition and idolatry, even during the life of Moses, and in some of you, while I live, and while the obligations which God had laid upon you in this land, are fresh in remembrance; I cannot but fear that after my decease you will think the service of God burdensome, and therefore will cast it off and revolt from him, if you do not carefully avoid all occasions of idolatry. A jealous God - In the Hebrew, He is the holy Gods, holy Father, holy Son, holy Spirit. He will not endure a partner in his worship; you can not serve him and idols together. Will not forgive - If you who own yourselves his people and servants, shall wilfully transgress his laws, he will not let this go unpunished in you, as he doth in other nations; therefore consider what you do, when you take the Lord for your God; weigh your advantages and inconveniences together; for as if you be sincere and faithful in God's service, you will have admirable benefits by it; so if you be false to your professions, and forsake him whom you have so solemnly avouched to be your God, he will deal more severely with you than with any people in the world.

20. Will turn - That is, he will alter his course and the manner of his dealing with you, and will be as severe as ever he was kind and gracious. He will repent of his former kindnesses, and his goodness abused will be turned into fury.

21. The Lord - Namely, him only, and not strange gods.

22. Against yourselves - This solemn profession will be a swift witness against you, if hereafter you apostatize from God.

23. Strange gods - Those idols which you either brought out of Egypt, or have taken in Canaan, which some of you keep contrary to God's command, whether for the preciousness of the matter, or rather for some secret inclination to superstition and idolatry.

25. A statute - He set or established that covenant with them, that is, the people, for a statute or an ordinance, to bind themselves and their posterity unto God forever.

26. These words - That is, this covenant or agreement of the people with the Lord. In the book - That is, in the volume which was kept in the ark, Deut. xxxi, 9, 26, whence it was taken and put into this book of Joshua: this he did for the perpetual remembrance of this great and solemn action, to lay the

greater obligation upon the people to be true to their engagement; and as a witness for God, against the people, if afterward he punished them for their defection from God, to whom they had so solemnly and freely obliged themselves. Set it up - As a witness and monument of this great transaction, according to the custom of those ancient times. Possibly this agreement was written upon this stone, as was then usual. By the sanctuary - That is, near the place where the ark and tabernacle then were; for tho' they were forbidden to plant a grove of trees near unto the altar, as the Gentiles did, yet they might for a time set up an altar, or the ark, near a great tree which had been planted there before.

27. It hath heard - It shall be as sure a witness against you, as if it had heard. This is a common figure, whereby the sense of hearing is often ascribed to the heavens and the earth, and other senseless creatures.

32. The bones of Joseph - Joseph died two hundred years before in Egypt, but gave commandment concerning his bones, that they should not rest in a grave, 'till Israel rested in the land of promise. Now therefore they were deposited in that piece of ground, which his father gave him near Shechem. One reason why Joshua called all Israel to Shechem, might be to attend Joseph's bones to the grave. So that he now delivered as it were both Joseph's funeral sermon, and his own farewell sermon. And if it was in the last year of his life, the occasion might well remind him, of his own death now at hand. For he was just of the same age with his illustrious ancestor, who died being one hundred and ten years old, Gen. i, 26.

33. Given him - By special favour, and for his better conveniency in attending upon the ark, which then was, and for a long time was to be in Shiloh, near this place: whereas the cities which were given to the priests, were in Judah. Benjamin, and Simeon, which were remote from Shiloh, tho' near the place where the ark was to have its settled abode, namely, at Jerusalem. It is probable Eleazar died about the same time with Joshua, as Aaron did in the same year with Moses. While Joshua lived, religion was kept up, under his care and influence, but after he and his contemporaries were gone, it swiftly went to decay. How well is it for the gospel church, that Christ, our Joshua, is still with it by his Spirit, and will be always, even to the end of the world?

NOTES ON THE BOOK OF JUDGES

This book contains the history of the Israelites under the Judges, which lasted two hundred and ninety nine years: under Othniel, forty, under Ehud, eighty, under Barak, forty, under Gideon, forty, under Abimelek, three, under Tola, twenty-three, under Jair, twenty-two, under Jephtha, six, under Ibzan, seven, under Elon, ten, under Abdon, eight, under Samson, twenty. As for the years of their servitude, they coincide with the years of some or other of the Judges. In the five last chapters we have an account of some memorable events, which happened in the days when the Judges ruled. As to the state of Israel during this period,

1. They were miserably corrupted, and miserably oppressed. Yet we may hope, the tabernacle service was kept up, and that many attended it.

2. It seems, each tribe had its government within itself, and acted separately, without any common head. This occasioned many differences among themselves.

3. The government of the Judges was not constant but occasional. By their judging Israel is meant chiefly, their avenging Israel of their enemies, and purging them from their idolatries.

4. During the government of the Judges, God was in an especial manner the king of Israel. It is not improbably supposed, that the prophet Samuel was the penman of this book.

I

The conquests made by Judah and Simeon, ver. 1-20. Benjamin failed, ver. 21. The house of Joseph took Bethel, ver. 22-26. But Manasseh did not drive out the Canaanites, ver. 27, 28. Nor Ephraim, ver. 29. Nor Zebulun, ver. 30. Nor Asher, ver. 31, 32. Nor Naphtali, ver. 33. Nor Daniel, ver. 34-36.

1. After the death - Not long after it; for Othniel, the first judge, lived in Joshua's time. Asked the Lord - Being assembled together at Shiloh, they inquired of the high-priest by the Urim and the Thummim. Against the Canaanites first - Finding their people multiply exceedingly, and consequently the necessity of enlarging their quarters, they renew the war. They do not inquire who shall be captain general to all the tribes; but what tribe shall first undertake the expedition, that by their success the other tribes may be encouraged to make the like attempt upon the Canaanites in their several lots.

2. Judah - The tribe of Judah is chosen for the first enterprise, because they were both most populous, and so most needing enlargement; and withal most valiant, and therefore most likely to succeed: for God chooseth fit means for the work which he designs. Moreover the Canaanites were numerous and strong in those parts, and therefore to be suppressed, before they grew too strong for them.

3. To Simeon - As nearest to him both by relation, being his brother by both parents, and by habitation. The Canaanites - Specially so called, because they are distinguished from the Perizzites, ver. 4.

4. In Bezek - Not in the city, for that was not yet taken, ver. 5, but in the territory of it.

5. Adoni-bezek - The Lord or king of Bezek; as his name signifies. In Bezek - Whither he fled when he lost the field. Against him - That is, against the city wherein he had encamped himself, and the rest of his army.

6. Great toes - And this they did, either by the direction of God, or upon notice of his former tyranny and cruelty.

7. Threescore and ten - Which is not strange in those times and places. For it is well known, that anciently each ruler of a city, or great town, was called a king, and had kingly power in that place; and many such kings we meet with in Canaan: and it is probable, that some years before, kings were more numerous there, 'till the greater devoured many of the less. Under my table - An act of barbarous inhumanity thus to insult over the miserable, joined with abominable luxury.

8. And took - Yet some of the inhabitants retired into the castle, and held out there 'till David's time.

10. Judah went - Under the conduct of Caleb, as is recorded, ver. 14, &c., for that relation, and this, are doubtless one and the same expedition, and it is mentioned there by anticipation.

16. Moses's father-in-law - That is, of Jethro, so called from the people whom he descended, Num. xxiv, 21, 22. And, whatsoever he did, it is evident, that his posterity came into Canaan with the Israelites, and were there seated with them, see chap. iv, 11, 17; v, 24; 1 Sam. xv, 6; 1 Chron. ii, 1-54, 55. City of palm-trees - That is, from Jericho, so called, Deut. xxxiv, 3, not the city which was destroyed, but the territory belonging to it, where it seems they were seated, in a most pleasant, and fruitful, and safe place, according to the promise made by Moses to their father, Num. x, 29-32, and whence they might remove, either to avoid the neighbouring Canaanites; or out of love to the children of Judah. South of Arad - In the southern part of the land of Canaan, where Arad was, Num. xxi, 1. They went - That is some of them, for others of them dwelt in a contrary quarter, in the most northern part of the land. Among the people - Hebrew. that people, namely, those children of Judah that lived there.

17. Judah went with Simeon - According to his promise, ver. 3, and the laws of justice and gratitude. Hormah - Either,

1. The same place so called, Num. xxi, 3, and so what was there vowed, is here executed: or,

2. Some other place called by the same name upon the like occasion, which was frequent among the Hebrew. This seems more probable.

18. Judah took - It is only said, they took the cities, and probably contented themselves with making them tributary; but it is not said that they slew the people, as they ought to have done; and as it is said of the other cities here. And the people being thus spared, did by God's just judgment recover their strength, and expel the Jews out of their cities. It is farther observable, that Ekron here taken, was one of Dan's cities, ver. 43, and it was taken here by Judah and Simeon, partly out of love for their brother Daniel, and partly to secure their new conquests, and other adjoining territories, from such potent neighbours.

19. Could not drive - Because of their unbelief, whereby they distrusted God's power to destroy those who had chariots of iron, and so gave way to their own fear and sloth, whereby God was provoked to withdraw his helping hand.

22. House of Joseph - That is, the tribe of Ephraim.

24. The entrance - On which side it is weakest, that we might best invade and take it.

25. His family - Together with his estate, as the following verse manifests.

26. The Hittites - Where the Hittites seated themselves after they were driven out of Canaan, which seems to be northward from Canaan, and near upon it.

27. Manasseh - That is, that half of this tribe which dwelt in Canaan.

29. In Gezer - Which they possessed 'till Solomon's time, 1 Kings ix, 16.

34. The valley - That is, into the plain country; which was the occasion of that expedition for the getting new quarters, of which we read ver. 47, 48 and chap. xviii, 1-31.

35. House of Joseph - That is, of the Ephraimites, who helped their brethren the Danites against the Amorites.

36. Akrabbim - Which was in the southern part of Canaan, Josh. xv, 2, 3 , from whence it went up towards the north. This is added to shew the great power and large extent of this people.

II

An angel reproves Israel, who bewail their sins, ver. 1-5. They served God during the life of Joshua and his contemporaries, ver. 4-9. Their frequent revolts to idolatry, ver. 10-19. God stops their success, ver. 20-23.

1. The angel - Christ the angel of the covenant, often called the angel of the Lord, to whom the conduct of Israel out of Egypt into Canaan, is frequently ascribed. He alone could speak the following words in his own name and person; whereas created angels and prophets universally usher in their message with, Thus saith the Lord, or some equivalent expression. And this angel having assumed the shape of a man, it is not strange that he imitates the motion of a man, and comes as it were from Gilgal to the place where now they were: by which motion he signified, that he was the person that brought them to Gilgal, the first place where they rested in Canaan, and there protected them so long, and from thence went with them to battle, and gave them success. Bochim - A place so called by anticipation; it seems to be no other than Shiloh, where it is probable, the people were met together upon some solemn festival. I said - That is, I promised upon condition of your keeping covenant with me.

2. Done this - That is, disobeyed these express commands.

3. I said - With myself, I have now taken up this peremptory resolution.

4. Wept - Some of them from a true sense of their sins; others from a just apprehension of their approaching misery.

5. Bochim - That is, Weepers. They sacrificed - For the expiation of their sins, by which they had provoked God to this resolution.

6. *Let the people go* - When he had distributed their inheritances, and dismissed them severally to take possession of them. This was done before this time, whilst Joshua lived; but is now repeated to discover the time, and occasion of the peoples defection from God, and of God's desertion of them.

10. *Knew not* - Which had no experimental, nor serious and affectionate knowledge of God, or of his works.

11. *In the sight* - Which notes the heinousness and impudence of their sins, above other peoples; because God's presence was with them, and his eye upon them in a peculiar manner, which also they were not ignorant of, and therefore were guilty of more contempt of God than other people. *Baalim* - False gods. He useth the plural number, because the gods of the Canaanites, and adjoining nations, which Israel worshipped, were most of them called by the name of Baal.

13. *Baal and Ashtaroth* - That is, the sun and moon, whom many Heathens worshipped, tho' under divers names; and so they ran into that error which God had so expressly warned them against, Deut. iv, 19. Baalim signifies lords, and Ashtaroth, blessed ones, he-gods and she-gods. When they forsook Jehovah, they had gods many and lords many, as a luxuriant fancy pleased to multiply them.

14. *Sold them* - That is, delivered them up, as the seller doth his commodities unto the buyer.

15. *Whithersoever they went* - That is, Whatsoever expedition or business they undertook; which is usually signified by going out, and coming in.

16. *Raised up* - By inward inspiration and excitation of their hearts, and by outward designation testified by some extra- ordinary action. *Judges* - Supreme magistrates, whose office it was, under God, and by his particular direction, to govern the commonwealth of Israel by God's laws, and to protect and save them from their enemies, to preserve and purge religion, and to maintain the liberties of the people against all oppressors.

17. *Their Judges* - Who admonished them of their sin and folly, and of the danger and misery which would certainly befall them.

18. *It repented the Lord* - That is, the Lord changed his course and dealings with them, as penitent men use to do; removed his judgments, and returned to them in mercy.

19. *Returned* - To their former, and usual course. *Their fathers* - In Egypt, or in the wilderness. *Their own doings* - That is, from their evil practices, which he calls their own, because they were agreeable to their own natures, which in all mankind are deeply and universally corrupted, and because they were familiar and customary to them.

22. *May prove* - That I may try and see whether Israel will be true and faithful to me, or whether they will suffer themselves to be corrupted by the counsels and examples of their bad neighbours.

III

A general account of Israel's enemies, ver. 1-7. A particular account of Othniel, ver. 8-11, Of Ehud, ver. 12-30. and of Shamgar, ver. 31.

1. *Had not known* - That is, such as had no experience of those wars, nor of God's extraordinary power and providence manifested in them.

2. *Teach them war* - That by the neighbourhood of such warlike enemies, they might be purged from sloth and security, and obliged them to innure themselves to martial exercises, and to stand continually upon their guard, and consequently to keep close to that God whose assistance they had so great and constant need of.

3. *Five lords* - Whereof three had been in some sort subdued, chap. i, 18. but afterwards recovered their strength. *Canaanites* - Properly so called, who were very numerous, and dispersed through several parts of the land, whence they gave denomination to all the rest of the people. *Zidonions* - The people living near Zidon, and subject to its jurisdiction. *Baal-hermon* - Which was the eastern part about Lebanon.

4. *To know* - That is, that they and others might know by experience.

6. *Served their gods* - Were drawn to idolatry by the persuasions and examples of their yoke-fellows.

7. *And the groves* - That is, in the groves, in which the Heathens usually worshipped their Baalim or idols.

8. *Served* - That is, were made subject to him. Mesopotamia was that part of Syria which lay between the two great rivers, Tigris and Euphrates. This lay at such a distance, that one would not have thought Israel's trouble should have come from such a far country: which shews so much the more of the hand of God in it.

9. *Cried* - That is, prayed fervently for deliverance.

10. *Came upon him* - With extraordinary influence, endowing him with singular wisdom and courage, and stirring him up to this great undertaking. *Judged Israel* - That is, pleaded and avenged the cause of Israel against their oppressors.

11. Forty years - It rested about forty years, or the greatest part of forty years: it being most frequent in scripture to use numbers in such a latitude. Nor is it unusual either in scripture, or in other authors, for things to be denominated from the greater part; especially, when they enjoyed some degrees of rest and peace even in their times of slavery.

12. Strengthened Eglon - By giving him courage, and power, and success against them.

13. City of Palm-trees - That is, Jericho. Not the city which was demolished, but the territory belonging to it. Here he fixed his camp, for the fertility of that soil, and because of its nearness to the passage over Jordan, which was most commodious both for the conjunction of his own forces which lay on both sides of Jordan; to prevent the conjunction of the Israelites in Canaan with their brethren beyond Jordan; and to secure his retreat into his own country.

14. Eighteen years - The former servitude lasted but eight years; this eighteen: for if smaller troubles do not the work, God will send greater.

15. A Benjamite - This tribe was next to Eglon, and doubtless most afflicted by him; and hence God raiseth a deliverer. Left handed - Which is here noted, as a considerable circumstance in the following story.

16. A cubit length - Long enough for his design, and not too long for concealment. His right thigh - Which was most convenient both for the use of his left hand, and for avoiding suspicion.

17. The present - Which was to be paid to him as a part of his tribute.

18. Sent the people - He accompanied them part of the way, and then dismissed them, and returned to Eglon alone, that so he might have more easy access to him.

19. Turned again - As if he had forgot some important business. Keep silence - 'Till my servants be gone: whom he would not have acquainted with a business which he supposed to be of great importance.

20. A summer parlor - Into which he used to retire from company: which is mentioned as the reason why his servants waited so long ere they went in to him, ver. 25. A message - To be delivered not in words, but by actions. He designedly uses the name Elohim, which was common to the true God, and false ones; and not Jehovah, which was peculiar to the true God; because Ehud not knowing whether the message came; not from his own false God, he would more certainly rise, and thereby give Ehud more advantage for his blow; whereas he would possibly shew his contempt of the God of Israel by sitting still to hear his message. He arose - In token of reverence to God.

23. Went forth - With a composed countenance and gait, being well assured, that God, who by his extraordinary call had put him upon that enterprise, would by his special providence carry him through it. Upon him - Upon or after himself. Locked them - Either pulling it close after him, as we do when doors have spring locks; or taking the key with him.

24. Covereth his feet - This phrase is used only here, and 1 Sam. xxiv, 3. A late judicious interpreter expounds it, of composing himself to take a little sleep, as was very usual to do in the day-time in those hot countries. And when they did so in cool places, such as this summer parlor unquestionably was, they used to cover their feet. And this may seem to be the more probable, both because the summer parlor was proper for this use, and because this was a more likely reason of their long waiting at his door, lest they should disturb his repose. And this sense best agrees with Saul's case in the cave, when being asleep, David could more securely cut off the lap of his garment.

25. Ashamed - Or, confounded, not knowing what to say or think; lest they should either disturb him, or be guilty of neglect towards him. A key - Another key, it being usual in princes courts to have divers keys for the same door.

27. The children of Israel - Whom doubtless he had prepared by his emissaries gathered together in considerable numbers.

28. Fords of Jordan - Where they passed over Jordan, that neither the Moabites that were got into Canaan, might escape, nor any more Moabites come over Jordan to their succor.

30. Fourscore years - Chiefly that part of it which lay east of Jordan: for the other side of the country, which lay southwest, was even then infested by the Philistines.

31. An ox goad - As Samson did a thousand with the jaw-bone of an ass; both being miraculous actions, and not at all incredible to him that believes a God, who could easily give strength to effect this. It is probable Shamgar was following the plough, when the Philistines made an inroad into the country. And having neither sword nor spear, when God put it into his heart to oppose them, he took the instrument that was next at hand. It is no matter how weak the weapon is, if God direct and strengthen the arm.

Wesley's Notes on the Bible - The Old Testament: Genesis - Ruth
IV

Israel revolting from God is oppressed by Jabin, ver. 1-3. Deborah concerts their deliverance with Barak, ver. 4-9. Barak takes the field and conquers, ver. 10-16. Sisera flies and is killed, ver. 17-21. Barak sees him, and Israel is delivered, ver. 22-24.

2. Of Canaan - That is, of the land where most of the Canaanites, strictly so called, now dwelt, which seems to be in the northern part of Canaan. This seems to be of the posterity of that Jabin, whom Joshua slew, Josh. xi, 11, who watched all opportunities to recover his ancient possessions, and to revenge his own and his father's quarrel. In Hazor - In the territory or the kingdom of Hazor, which might now be restored to its former largeness and power. Of the Gentiles - So called, because it was much frequented and inhabited by the Gentiles; either by the Canaanites, who being beaten out of their former possessions, seated themselves in those northern parts; or by other nations coming there for traffick, whence Galilee, where this was, is called Galilee of the Gentiles.

3. Mightily oppressed - More than former tyrants; from his malice and hatred against the Israelites; and from God's just judgment, the growing punishment being suitable to their aggravated wickedness.

4. A prophetess - As there were men-prophets, so there were also women-prophetesses, as Miriam, Exod. xv, 20. Huldah, 2 Kings xxii, 14, and divers others; but the word prophets or prophetesses is ambiguous, sometimes being used of persons extraordinarily inspired by God, and endowed with the power of working miracles, and foretelling things to come; and sometimes of persons endowed with special gifts or graces, for the better understanding and discoursing about the word and mind of God. Of this sort were the sons of the prophets, or such as were bred in the schools of the prophets. who are often called prophets, as 1 Sam. x, 5, 10. And because we read nothing of Deborah's miraculous actions, perhaps she was only a woman of eminent holiness, and knowledge of the holy scriptures, by which she was singularly qualified for judging the people according to the laws of God. Judged Israel - That is, determined causes and controversies arising among the Israelites, as is implied, ver. 5. And this Jabin might suffer to be done, especially by a woman. Yet the frequent discharge of this part of the judge's office, whereby she gained great power and authority with the people, did notably (though not observed by the tyrant) prepare the way for her sliding into the other part of her office, which was to defend and rescue the people from their enemies.

5. And she dwelt - Or, she sat: she had her judgment-seat in the open air, under the shadow of that tree; which was an emblem of the justice she administered there: thriving and growing against opposition, as the palm-tree does under pressures. Came to her - To have their suits and causes determined by her sentence.

6. Called Barak - By virtue of that power which God had given her, and the people owned in her. Kedesh Naphtali - So called, to distinguish it from other places of that name, one in Judah, and another in Issachar. Hath not the Lord, &c. - That is, assuredly God hath commanded thee; this is not the fancy of a weak woman, which peradventure thou mayst despise; but the command of the great God by my mouth. Mount Tabor - A place most fit for his purpose, as being in the borders of divers tribes, and having a large plain at the top of it, where he might conveniently marshal and discipline his army. Naphtali and Zebulun - These she names because they were nearest and best known to Barak, and therefore soonest brought together, because they were nearest to the enemy, and therefore might speedily be assembled, whilst the other tribes, being at a distance, had better opportunity of gathering forces for their succor; and because these had most smarted under this oppressor, who was in the heart of their country; but these are not named exclusively, as appears by the concurrence of some other tribes.

7. Draw to Thee - By my secret and powerful providence, ordering and over-ruling his inclinations that way. In fixing the very place, she gave him a sign, which might confirm his faith, when he came to engage.

8. I will not go - His offer to go with her, shews the truth of his faith, for which he is praised, Hebrew xi, 32, but his refusal to go without her, shews the weakness of his faith, that he could not trust God's bare word, as he ought to have done, without the pledge of the presence of his prophetess.

10. Ten thousand at his feet - That is, who followed him; possibly he intimates that they were all foot-men; and so this is emphatically added, to signify by what contemptible means God overthrew Sisera's great host.

11. Heber - The husband of Jael. Of Hobab - Called also Jethro. The Kenites - From the rest of his brethren, who lived in the wilderness of Judah. His tent - That is, his dwelling, which probably was in tents, as shepherds used.

12. They - That is, this people dwelling there, or his spies.

14. Up - Hebrew. arise, delay not. If we have ground to believe, that God goes before us, we may well go on with courage and cheerfulness. Gone before thee - Namely, as general of thine army, to fight

for thee. Went down - He doth not make use of the advantage which he had of the hill, where he might have been out of the reach of his iron chariots, but boldly marcheth down into the valley, to give Sisera the opportunity of using all his horses and chariots, that so the victory might he more glorious.

15. Discomfited - With great terror and noise, as the word signifies, probably with thunder and lightning, and hail-stones, poured upon them from heaven, as is implied, chap. v, 20. Edge of the sword - That is, by the sword of Barak and his army, whose ministry God used; but so, that they had little else to do, but to kill those whom God by more powerful arms had put to flight. On his feet - That he might flee away more secretly in the quality of a common soldier, whereas his chariot would have exposed him to more observation.

16. Left - In the field; for there were some who fled away, as Sisera did.

17. The tent of Jael - For women had their tents apart from their husbands. And here he thought to lurk more securely than in her husband's tent. Peace - Not a covenant of friendship, which they were forbidden to make with that cursed people, but only a cessation of hostilities, which he afforded them because they were peaceable people, abhorring war, and wholly minding pasturage, and were not Israelites, with whom his principal quarrel was; and especially by God's over-ruling disposal of his heart to favour them who were careful to keep themselves uncorrupted with Israel's sins, and therefore preserved from their plagues.

18. Fear not - This was a promise of security, and therefore she cannot be excused from dissimulation and treachery.

19. A bottle of milk - As a signification of greater respect. Covered him - Upon pretense of hiding him.

21. A nail of the tent - Wherewith they used to fasten the tent, which consequently was long and sharp. This might seem a very bold attempt, but it must be considered, that she was encouraged to it, by observing that the heavens and all the elements conspired against him, as one devoted to destruction. In the following son, Deborah doth not commend Jael's words, ver. 18. Turn in my Lord, fear not; but only her action: touching which, this one consideration may abundantly suffice to stop the mouths of objectors. It cannot be denied, that every discourse which is recorded in scripture, is not divinely inspired, because some of them were uttered by the devil, and others by holy men, but mistaken. This being so, the worst that any can infer from this place is, that this song, tho' indited by a good woman, was not divinely inspired, but only composed by a person transported with joy for the deliverance of God's people, but subject to mistake; who therefore, out of zeal to commend the instrument of so great a deliverance, might overlook the indirectness of the means, and commend that which should have been disliked, And if they farther object, that it was composed by a prophetess, and therefore must be divinely inspired; it may be replied, that every expression of a true prophet was not divinely inspired; as is evident from Samuel's mistake concerning Eliab, whom he thought to be the Lord's anointed, 1 Sam. xvi, 6. This is said upon supposition that Jael acted deceitfully in this affair; but if we suppose, which is much more likely, that Jael fully intended to afford Sisera the shelter and protection which he sought of her, but was afterwards by the immediate direction of heaven ordered to kill him, the whole difficulty vanishes, and the character both of Jael and of Deborah remains unimpeached.

V

Deborah's song begins with praise, ver. 1-3. Compares God's present appearance for them with his appearance on Mount Sinai, ver. 4-5. Describes the condition they were in before, ver. 6-8. Calls all the delivered to join in praise, ver. 9-13. Commends those tribes that were forward in the war, and censures those that declined the service, ver. 14-19. Takes notice how God fought for them, and how Jael slew Sisera, ver. 20-30. Concludes with prayer, ver.. 31.

1. Deborah - The composer of this song.

2. The Lord-Give him the praise who hath done the work. The people - Chiefly Zebulun and Naphtali. Offered themselves - When neither Deborah nor Barak had any power to compel them.

3. The princes - You especially that live near, and have evil designs against Israel, know this for your caution, and terror too, if you presume to molest them. God of Israel - Who, as you see by this plain instance, is both able and resolved to defend them from all their enemies.

4. Edom - Seir and Edom are the same place; and these two expressions note the same thing, even God's marching in the head of his people, from Seir or Edom, towards the land of Canaan: while the Israelites were encompassing mount Seir, there were none of the following effects; but when once they had done that, and got Edom on their backs, then they marched directly forward towards the land of Canaan. The prophetess being to praise God for the present mercies, takes her rise higher, and begins her song with the commemoration of the ancient deliverances afforded by God to his people, the rather because of the great resemblance this had with them, in the miraculous manner of them. The earth trembled - God prepared the way for his people, and struck a dread into their enemies, by earth-quakes

as well as by other terrible signs. Dropped water - That is, thou didst send storms and tempests, thunder and lightning, and other tokens of thy displeasure upon thine enemies.

5. Melted - Or, flowed, with floods of water powered out of the clouds upon them, and from them flowing down in a mighty stream upon the lower grounds, and carrying down part of the mountains with it. Sinai - She slides into the mention of a more ancient appearance of God for his people in Sinai; it being usual in scripture repetitions of former actions, to put divers together in a narrow compass. The sense is, No wonder that the mountains of the Amorites and Canaanites melted and trembled, when thou didst lead thy people toward them; for even Sinai itself could not bear thy presence, but melted in like manner before thee.

6. Jael - Jael, though an illustrious woman, effected nothing for the deliverance of God's people, 'till God raised me up. By-ways - Because of the Philistines and Canaanites, who, besides the public burdens which they laid upon them, waited for all opportunities to do them mischief secretly; their soldiers watching for travelers in common roads, as is usual with such in times of war; and, because of the robbers even of their own people, who having cast off the fear of God, and there being no king in Israel to punish them, broke forth into acts of injustice and violence, even against their own brethren.

7. Ceased - The people forsook all their unfortified towns, not being able to protect them from military insolence. A mother - That is, to be to them as a mother, to instruct, and rule, and protect them, which duties a mother owes to her children.

8. Chose - They did not only submit to idolatry when they were forced to it by tyrants, but they freely chose it. New gods - New to them, and unknown to their fathers, and new in comparison of the true and everlasting God of Israel, being but of yesterday. The gates - That is, in their walled cities, which have gates and bars; gates are often put for cities; then their strong holds fell into the hands of their enemies. Was there a shield - There was not, the meaning is not, that all the Israelites had no arms, but, either they had but few arms among them, being many thousands of them disarmed by the Canaanites and Philistines, or that they generally neglected the use of arms, as being without all hope of recovering their liberty.

9. My heart is toward - I honour and love those, who being the chief of the people in wealth and dignity, did not withdraw themselves from the work, as such usually do; but exposed themselves to the same hazards, and joined with their brethren in this noble but dangerous attempt. The Lord - Who inclined their hearts to this undertaking, and gave them success in it. As she gives instruments their due, so she is careful the sovereign cause lose not his glory.

10. Speak - Celebrate the praise of our mighty God. That ride on white asses - That is, magistrates and nobles, who used to do so, chap. x, 4; xii, 14. That walk - That is, you that can safely travel in those high ways, which before you durst neither ride nor walk in: so great and mean persons are jointly excited to praise God.

11. From the noise - From the triumphant noise and shout of archers, rejoicing when they meet with their prey. Of drawing water - At those pits or springs of water, which were precious in those hot countries, to which the people's necessities forced them to resort, and nigh unto which the archers usually lurked, that they may shoot at them, and kill and spoil them. There - When they come to those places with freedom and safety, which before they could not, they shall with thankfulness rehearse this righteous and gracious work of God, in rescuing his people. Of the villages - Whom she mentions, because as their danger was greater, ver. 7, so was their deliverance. Gates - Of their cities, which were the chief places to which both city and country resorted for public business and matters of justice, from which they they had been debarred by their oppressors; but now they had free access and passage, either in or out of the gates, as their occasions required; and they who had been driven from their cities, now returned to them in peace and triumph; so the citizens deliverance is celebrated here, as the country-mens is in the foregoing words.

12. Awake - Stir up thyself and all that is within thee, to admire and praise the Lord. This work needs and well deserves the utmost liveliness and vigour of soul. Lead captivity captive - How could this be done, when there was none of them left? chap. iv, 16.

1. None were left to make head against them.
2. None is often put for few, and those few might be taken after the battle, and carried captive, and led in triumph.

13. He made him, &c. - Thus God did not only preserve the poor and despised remnant of his people, from the fury of the oppressor, and from the destruction which Sisera designed, but also gave them the victory, and thereby the dominion over the nobles of Canaan, who were combined against them. Me - Tho' but a weak woman.

14. Ephraim - Now she relates the carriage of the several tribes in the expedition; and she begins with Ephraim. A root - Of the Ephraimites. By root she seems to mean a branch, as that word is sometimes used. By which also she may note the fewness of those that came out of Ephraim, yielding but one branch or an handful of men to this service. Amalek - The constant enemy of the Israelites, who were confederate with their last oppressors the Moabites, chap. iii, 13, and in all probability took their

John Wesley

advantage now against the Israelites in the southern or middle parts of Canaan, while their main force was drawn northward against Jabin and Sisera. Against these therefore Ephraim sent forth a party, and so did Benjamin. Benjamin - Benjamin followed Ephraim's example. The people - Among the people of Benjamin, with whom these few Ephraimites united themselves in this expedition. Machir - That is, out of the tribe of Manasseh, which are elsewhere called by the name of Machir, namely, out of the half tribe which was within Jordan; for of the other she speaks, ver.

17. Governors - Either civil governors, princes and great persons, who were as ready to hazard themselves, as the meanest: or military officers, valiant and expert commanders, such as some of Machir's posterity are noted to have been. Writer - That is, even the Scribes, who gave themselves to study and writing, whereby they were exempted from military service, did voluntarily enter into this service.

15. With Deborah - Ready to assist her. Issachar - Hebrew. and Issachar, that is, the tribe or people of Issachar, following the counsel and example of their princes. Barak - That is, they were as hearty and valiant as Barak their general; and as he marched on foot against their enemies horses and chariots, and that into the valley, where the main use of horses and chariots lies; so did they with no less courage and resolution. Divisions - Or, separations, not so much one from another, (for they seem to be all so well agreed in abiding at home with their sheep) as all from their brethren, from whom they were divided no less in their designs and affections, than in their situation by the river Jordan: and they would not join their interests and forces with them in this common cause. Great thoughts - Or, great searchings, great and sad thoughts, and debates, and perplexities of mind among the Israelites, to see themselves deserted by so great and potent a tribe as Reuben was.

16. Why abodest - Why wast thou so unworthy and cowardly, that thou wouldest not engage thyself in so just, so necessary, and so noble a cause, but didst prefer the care of this sheep, and thy own ease and safety, before this generous undertaking? Reuben thought neutrality their wisest course; being very rich in cattle, Num. xxxii, 1. They were loath to run the hazard of so great a loss, by taking up arms against so potent an enemy as Jabin: and the bleatings of their sheep were so loud in their ears, that they could not hear the call of Deborah and Barak.

17. Gilead - Sometimes taken strictly for that part of the land beyond Jordan which fell to the half-tribe of Manasseh, and sometimes both for that part of Manasseh's, and for Gad's portion, as Josh. xiii, 24-25, 29-31, and so it seems to be understood here; and the land Gilead is here put for the people or inhabitants of it, Gad and Manasseh. Beyond Jordan - In their own portions, and did not come over Jordan to the help of the Lord, and of his people, as they ought to have done. In ships - Daniel, whose coast was near the sea, was wholly intent upon his merchandise, and therefore could not join in this land expedition. Sea-shore - Where their lot lay. His breaches - Either in the creeks of the sea, or, in their broken and craggy rocks and caves.

18. Jeoparded - Hebrew. despised, comparatively; they chose rather to venture upon a generous and honourable death, than to enjoy a shameful and servile life. High-places - That is, upon that large and eminent plain in the top of mount Tabor, where they put themselves in battle array, and expected the enemy; though when they saw they did not come up to them, they marched down to meet them.

19. The kings - There were divers petty kings in those parts who were subject to Jabin. Megiddo - Taanah and Megiddo were two eminent cities, not far from mount Tabor, nor from the river Kishon. No gain - They fought without pay, whether from mere hatred of the Israelites, and a desire to be revenged upon them: or from a full hope and confidence of paying themselves abundantly out of Israel's spoils.

20. From heaven - Or, they from heaven, or the heavenly host fought, by thunder, and lightning, and hail-stones, possibly mingled with fire. The stars - Raising these storms by their influences, which they do naturally. Courses - Or, from their paths, or stations. As soldiers fight in their ranks and places assigned them, so did these.

21. River of Kishon - Which, though not great in itself, was now much swelled by the foregoing storm and rain, and therefore drowned those who being pursued by the hand of God, and by the Israelites, were forced into it, and thought to pass over it, as they did before. Ancient river - So called, either, first, in opposition to those rivers which are of a later date, being made by the hand and art of man. Or, secondly, because it was a river anciently famous for remarkable exploits, for which it was celebrated by the ancient poets or writers, though not here mentioned. Trodden down - Thou, O Deborah, though but a weak woman, hast by God's assistance subdued a potent enemy. Such abrupt speeches are frequent in poetical scriptures.

22. Horses hoofs - Their horses, in which they put most confidence, had their hoofs, which are their support and strength, broken, either by dreadful hail-stones, or rather, by their swift and violent running over the stony grounds, when they fled with all possible speed from God and from Israel. Pransings - Or because of their fierce or swift courses. Mighty ones - Of their strong and valiant riders, who forced their horses to run away as fast as they could.

23. Meroz - A place then, no doubt, eminent and considerable, tho' now there be no remembrance of it left, which possibly might be the effect of this bitter curse; as God curseth Amalek in this manner,

that he would utterly blot out their remembrance. And this place above all others may be thus severely cursed; because it was near the place of the fight, and therefore had the greatest opportunity and obligation to assist their brethren. *The angel, &c.* - She signifies, that this curse proceeded not from her ill-will towards that place, but from divine inspiration; and that if all the rest of the song should be taken but for the breathings of a pious soul, but liable to mistake, yet this branch of it was immediately directed to her by the Lord, the angel of the covenant. *Of the Lord* - Of the Lord's people: for God takes what is done for, or against his people, as if it was done to himself. The cause between God and the mighty, the principalities and powers of the kingdom of darkness, will not admit of a neutrality.

24. *Blessed* - Celebrated, and endowed with all sorts of blessings more than they. *In the tent* - In her tent or habitation, in her house and family, and all her affairs: for she and hers dwelt in tents. The tent is here mentioned as an allusion to the place where the fact was done.

25. *Butter* - Or, cream, that is, the choicest of her milk: so the same thing is repeated in different words. *Lordly dish* - Which you are not to understand of such a costly dish as the luxury of after ages brought in, which is not agreeable to the simplicity either of this family, or of those ancient times; but of a comely and convenient dish, the best which she had, and such as the better sort of persons then used. Probably Jael at that time intended him no other than kindness, 'till God by an immediate impulse on her mind, directed her to do otherwise.

28. *Looked out* - Expecting to see him returning: for she concluded, that he went forth not so much to fight, as to take the spoil.

30. *Have they not, &c.* - That is, it is certain they have got the prey, only they tarry to distribute it, according to every man's quality and merit.

31. *So let* - That is, so suddenly, so surely, so effectual and irrecoverably. Deborah was a prophetess and this prayer was a prediction, that in due time all God's enemies shall perish. *In his might* - When he first riseth, and so goeth on in his course, which he doth with great might, even as a strong man that runneth a race, and so as no creature can stop, or hinder him; even so irresistible let thy people be. Such shall be the honour and such the joy of all that love God in sincerity, and they shall shine forever as the sun in the kingdom of their father.

VI

The calamities of Israel by the Midianites, ver. 1-6. The message God sent them by a prophet, ver. 7-10. God's commission to Gideon, confirmed by a sign, ver. 11-24. He breaks down the altar of Baal, ver. 25-32. The preparation for war, and encouragement by another sign, ver. 33-40.

1. *Of Midian* - For although the generality of the Midianites had been cut off by Moses about two hundred years ago, yet many of them doubtless fled into the neighbouring countries, whence afterwards they returned into their own land, and in that time might easily grow to be a very great number; especially, when God furthered their increase, that they might be a scourge for Israel when they transgressed. Let all that sin, expect to suffer: let all that turn to folly, expect to return to misery.

3. *Children of the east* - That is, the Arabians, who are commonly called the children of the east. Not all the Arabians; but the eastern part of them.

4. *Unto Gaza* - That is, from the east, on which side they entered, to the well, where Gaza was, near the sea: so they destroyed the whole land.

5. *Without number* - That is, so many that it was not easy to number them. And not in a regular army to engage, but in a confused swarm, to plunder the country. Yet Israel, being forsaken of God, had not spirit to make head against them; God fighting against them with those very terrors, with which otherwise he would have fought for them.

8. *A prophet* - We have reason to hope, God is designing mercy for us, if we find he is by his grace preparing us for it.

10. *Not obeyed my voice* - He intends to bring them to repentance. And our repentance is then genuine, when he sinfulness of sin, as disobedience to God, is that in it which we chiefly lament.

11. *In Ophrah* - In Manasseh: there was another Ophrah in Benjamin, Josh. xviii, 23. *The Abiezrite* - Of the posterity of Abiezer. *Threshed* - Not with oxen, as the manner was, Deut. xxv, 4, but with a staff to prevent discovery. *Wine-press* - In the place where the wine-press stood, not in the common floor.

12. *Is with thee* - That is, will assist thee against thine enemies. *Man of valour* - To whom I have given strength and courage for this end.

13. *With us* - The angel had said, Peace be with Thee: but he expostulates for All: herding himself with all Israel, and admitting no comfort, but what they might be sharers in.

14. *Looked* - With a settled and pleasant countenance, as a testimony of his favour, and readiness to help him. *Go* - Or, go now, in thy might: in the strength which thou hast already received, and dost now farther receive from me. *Have not I sent thee* - I do hereby give thee command and commission for

this work. God's fitting men for his work, is a sure evidence of his calling them to it.

15. My family - Hebrew. my thousand: for the tribes were distributed into several thousands, whereof each thousand had his peculiar governor. Is poor - That is, weak and contemptible. The least - Either for age, or fitness for so great a work.

16. As one man - As easily, as if they were all but one man.

17. That thou - That it is thou, an angel or messenger sent from God, that appears to me, and discourseth with me. Or, a sign of that which thou talkest with me; that is, that thou wilt by me smite the Midianites.

18. My present - A repast for the angel, whom he thought to be a man. Set it - That thou mayest eat and refresh thyself.

19. An ephah - The choicest part of a whole ephah; as also he brought to him the best part of a kid dressed; for a whole ephah, and a whole kid had been superfluous, and improper to provide for one man.

21. Consumed the flesh - By which, he shewed himself to be no man that needed such provisions, but the Son of God; and by this instance of his omnipotency, gave him assurance, that he both could, and would consume the Midianites.

22. Alas - I am an undone man: I must die, and that speedily; for that he feared, ver. 23, according to the common opinion in that case.

23. Said unto him - Perhaps by an audible voice. Peace be to thee - Thou shalt receive no hurt by this vision; but only peace, that is, all the blessings needful for thy own happiness, and for the present work.

24. There - On the top of the rock, as is evident from ver. 26, where that which is here expressed only in general, is more particularly described. Jehovah-shalom - That is, the Lord's peace; the sign or witness of God's speaking peace to me, and to his people: or the place where he spake peace to me, when I expected nothing but destruction.

25. The second bullock - He was to offer one for himself, the other for the sins of the people, whom he was to deliver. 'Till sin be pardoned thro' the great sacrifice, no good is to be expected. Thy father hath - Which thy father built in his own ground, tho' for the common use of the city. The grove - Planted by the altar for idolatrous uses, as the manner of idolaters was. This action might seem injurious to his father's authority; but God's command was a sufficient warrant, and Gideon was now called to be the supreme magistrate, whereby he was made his father's superior, and was authorized to root out all idolatry, and the instruments thereof.

26. Of this rock - Hebrew. of this strong hold: for in that calamitous time the Israelites retreated to such rocks, and hid and fortified themselves in them. Ordered place - That is, in a plain and smooth part of the rock, where an altar may be conveniently built. And offer - Gideon was no priest, nor was this the appointed place of sacrifice; but God can dispense with his own institutions, though we may not; and his call gave Gideon sufficient authority.

27. Ten men - Whom doubtless he had acquainted with his design, and the assurance of success in it, whereby they were easily induced to assist him. He feared - Not so much, lest he should suffer for it, as lest he should be prevented from doing it.

28. Was offered - Not upon Baal's altar, for which it was designed; but upon an altar erected in contempt of Baal.

30. They said - Probably some of the persons employed in it.

31. Will ye plead - Why are you so zealous in pleading for that Baal, for the worship whereof you suffer such grievous calamities at this day? It is plain, that Joash had been a worshipper of Baal: but probably he was now convinced by Gideon. He that will plead - He that shall farther plead for such a God as this, deserves to die for his folly and impiety. It is not probable, that this was all which he said for his son: but it is usual in scripture to give only short hints of things which were more largely discoursed. While it is morning - That is, instantly, without delay. Let him plead - As the God of Israel hath often done when any indignity or injury hath been done him. But Baal hath now shewed, that he is neither able to help you, nor himself; and therefore is not worthy to be served any longer. This resolute answer was necessary to stop the torrent of the peoples fury; and it was drawn from him, by the sense of his son's extreme danger; and by the confidence he had, that God would plead his son's cause, and use him for the rescue of his people.

32. He called - Joash called Gideon so, chap. viii, 29, in remembrance of this noble exploit, and to put a brand upon Baal. Jerub-baal - That is, Let Baal plead. It is a probable conjecture, that that Jerombalus, whom Sanchoniathon, (one of the most ancient of all the Heathen writers) speaks of as a priest of Jao, (a corruption of Jehovah) and to whom he was indebted for a great deal of knowledge, was this Jerub-baal.

33. Of Jezreel - Not Jezreel in Judah, but another in the borders of Manasseh and Issachar, which was not far distant from Ophrah, where Gideon dwelt.

34. The spirit came - Inspiring him with extraordinary wisdom, and courage, and zeal to vindicate God's honour, and his country's liberty. The Hebrew is, The Spirit of the Lord clothed Gideon; clothed

him as a robe, to put honour upon him; clothed him as a coat of mail to put a defense upon him. Those are well clad that are thus clothed. Abiezer - That is, the Abiezrites, his kindred, and their servants, and others; who finding no harm coming to him for destroying Baal, but rather a blessing from God, in giving him strength and courage for so great an attempt, changed their minds, and followed him as the person by whose hands God would deliver them.

35. All Manasseh - On Both sides of Jordan. Unto Asher, &c. - Because these tribes were nearest, and so could soonest join with him; and were nearest the enemy also, ver. 33, and therefore were most sensible of the calamity, and would in all reason be most forward to rescue themselves from it.

36. Gideon said - In a way of humble supplication, for the strengthening his own faith, and for the greater encouragement of his soldiers in this great attempt.

37. On all the earth - That is, upon all that spot of ground which encompasses the fleece.

39. On the ground - Which was more preternatural than the former instance, because if there be any moisture, such bodies as fleeces of wool are likely to drink it up.

40. And God did so - See how tender God is, even of the weak; and how ready to condescend to their infirmities! These signs were very expressive. They are going to engage the Midianites. Could God distinguish between a small fleece of Israel, and the vast floor of Midian? Yes, by this token it appears that he can. Is Gideon desirous, that the dew of divine grace might descend on himself in particular? He sees the fleece wet with dew, to assure him of it. Does he desire, that God will be as the dew to all Israel? Behold all the ground is wet!

VII

God's direction to Gideon for modelling his army, ver. 1-8. The dream of the Midianite, ver. 9-15. His manner of attacking the camp of Midian, ver. 16-20. Their total overthrow, ver. 21-25.

2. Too many - For my purpose; which is, so to deliver Israel, that it may appear to be my own act, that so I may have all the glory, and they may be the more strongly obliged to serve me. This may help us to understand those providences, which sometimes seem to weaken the church of Christ. Its friends are too many, too mighty, too wise, for God to work deliverance by. God is taking a course to lessen them, that he may be exalted in his own strength.

3. Mount Gilead - Not mount Gilead beyond Jordan; for both the camps of the Israelites and the Midianites were on this side Jordan: but another mount Gilead in the tribe of Manasseh. There returned - These finding their whole army very small, in comparison of their enemies, who were a hundred and thirty five thousand, chap. viii, 10, and they, no doubt well armed and disciplined, and encouraged by long success; whereas the Israelites were dispirited with long servitude, and many of them unarmed, lost the courage which they had at first.

4. The water - Either that which ran from the well of Harod, mentioned ver. 1, or some other brook.

6. That lapped - Taking up a little water in the palm of their hands.

7. His own place - That is, to his own home. By this farther distinction it was proved, that none should be made use of, but,

1. Men that were hardy, that could endure fatigue, without complaining of thirst or weariness:

2. Men that were hasty, that thought it long, 'till they were engaged with the enemy, and so just wetted their mouth and away, not staying for a full draught. Such as these God chuses to employ, that are not only well affected, but zealously affected to his work.

8. Their trumpets - That is the trumpets belonging to the whole army, which he retained for the use following.

9. The same night - After he had dismissed all but the three hundred. The Lord said - In a dream or vision of the night.

11. Thine hand strengthened - Thou wilt be encourage to proceed, notwithstanding the smallness of thy number.

13. A cake - A weak and contemptible thing; and in itself as unable to overthrow a tent, as to remove a mountain; but being thrown by a divine hand, it bore down all before it.

14. His fellow answered, &c. - As there are many examples of significant dreams, given by God to Heathens, so some of them had the gift of interpreting dreams; which they sometimes did by divine direction as in this case.

15. He worshipped-He praised God for this special encouragement.

16. Three companies - To make a shew of a vast army. Within the pitchers - Partly to preserve the flame from the wind and weather; and partly to conceal it, and surprise their enemy with sudden flashes of light.

17. Look on me - For though two hundred of his men were placed on other sides of the camp; yet they were so disposed, that some persons, set as watchmen, might see what was done, and give notice to

the rest to follow the example.

18. Of Gideon - He mentions his own name, together with God's, not out of arrogance, as if he would equal himself with God; but from prudent policy, because his name was grown formidable to them, and so was likely to further his design. See ver. 14.

19. Middle watch - That is, of the second watch; for though afterward the night was divided into four watches by the Romans, Matt. xiv, 25, yet in more ancient times, and in the eastern parts, it was divided into three: he chose the dark and dead of the night, to increase their terror by the trumpets, whose sound would then be loudest, and the lamps, whose light would then shine most brightly, to surprise them, and conceal the smallness of their numbers.

21. They stood - As if they had been torch-bearers to the several companies.

22. Against his fellow - They slew one another, because they suspected treachery, and so fell upon those they first met with; which they might more easily do, because they consisted of several nations, because the darkness of the night made them unable to distinguish friends from foes, because the suddenness of the thing struck them with horror and amazement; and because God had infatuated them, as he had done many others.

24. The waters - That is, the passes over those waters to which they are like to come. Jordan - The fords of Jordan, which they must pass over into their own country.

25. The other side of Jordan - For Gideon in the pursuit had passed over Jordan. Oreb and Zeeb had probably taken shelter, the one in a rock, the other by a wine-press. But the places of their shelter were made the places of their slaughter, and the memory of it preserved in the names of the places.

VIII

Gideon pacifies the Ephraimites, ver. 1-3. Pursues the Midianites, ver. 4-12. Chastises the men of Succoth and Penuel, ver. 13-17. Slays the two kings of Midian, ver. 18-21. Declines the government of Israel, ver. 22, 23. Makes an ephod, ver. 24-27. Keeps the country quiet forty years, ver. 28. Dies, leaving a numerous family, ver, 29-32. Israel quickly forget God and him, ver. 33-35.

1. Why haft thou, &c. - Why hast thou neglected and despised us, in not calling us in to thy help, as thou didst other tribes? These were a proud people, puffed up with a conceit of their number and strength, and the preference which Jacob gave them above Manasseh, of which tribe Gideon was, who by this act had seemed to advance his own tribe, and to depress theirs.

2. What have I, &c. - What I have done in cutting off some of the common soldiers, is not to be compared with your destroying their princes; I began the war, but you have finished. The gleaning - What you have gleaned or done after me, Of Abiezer - That is, of the Abiezrites, to whom he modestly communicates the honour of the victory, and does not arrogate it to himself.

3. Was abated - His soft and humble answer allayed their rage.

4. Passed over - Or, had passed over. 6. Are the hands, &c. - Art thou so foolish, to think with thy three hundred faint and weary soldiers, to conquer and destroy an host of fifteen thousand Men? Thus the bowels of their compassion were shut up against their brethren. Were these Israelites! Surely they were worshippers of Baal, or in the interest of Midian.

8. Penuel - Another city beyond Jordan; both were in the tribe of Gad.

9. Your tower - Your confidence in which makes you thus proud and presumptuous.

10. That drew sword - That is, persons expert and exercised in war, besides the retainers to them.

11. That dwelt in tents - That is, of the Arabians, so fetching a compass, and falling upon them where they least expected it. Was secure - Being now got safe over Jordan, and a great way from the place of battle; and probably, supposing Gideon's men to be so tired with their hard service, that they would have neither strength nor will to pursue them so far.

13. Before the sun was up - By which it might be gathered, that he came upon them in the night, which was most convenient for him who had so small a number with him; and most likely to terrify them by the remembrance of the last Night's sad work.

14. He described - He told him their names and qualities.

17. Slew the men of the city - Not all of them; probably those only who had affronted him.

18. What manner of men - For outward shape and quality. At Tabor - Whither he understood they fled for shelter, upon the approach of the Midianites, and where he learned that some were slain, which he suspected might be them. Resembled - Not for their garb, or outward splendour, but for the majesty of their looks: by which commendation they thought to ingratiate themselves with their conqueror.

19. I would not slay - For being not Canaanites, he was not obliged to kill them; but they having killed his brethren, and that in cool blood, he was by law the avenger of their blood.

20. Up, and slay - That he might animate him to the use of arms for his God and country, and that he might have a share in the honour of the victory.

21. So is his strength - Thou excellest him, as in age and stature, so in strength; and it is more

honourable to die by the hands of a valiant man.

22. Rule - Not as a judge, for that he was already made by God; but as a king. Thy son's son - Let the kingdom be hereditary to thee, and to thy family. Thou hast delivered us - This miraculous and glorious deliverance by thy hands deserves no less from us.

23. I will not rule - As a king. The Lord shall rule - In a special manner, as he hath hitherto done, by Judges, whom God particularly appointed and directed, even by Urim and Thummim, and assisted upon all occasions; whereas Kings had only a general dependance upon God.

24. Ishmaelites - A mixture of people all called by one general name, Ishmaelites or Arabians, who used to wear ear-rings; but the greatest, and the ruling part of them were Midianites.

27. Thereof - Not of all of it; for then it would have been too heavy for use; but of part of it, the rest being probably employed about other things appertaining to it; which elsewhere are comprehended under the name of the ephod, as chap. xvii, 5. Put it - Not as a monument of the victory, for such monuments were neither proper nor usual; but for religious use, for which alone the ephod was appointed. The case seems to be this; Gideon having by God's command erected an altar in his own city, Ophrah, ch. vi, 24, for an extraordinary time and occasion, thought it might be continued for ordinary use; and therefore as he intended to procure priests, so he designed to make priestly garments, and especially an ephod, which was the chief and most costly; which besides its use in sacred ministrations, was also the instrument by which the mind of God was inquired and discovered, 1 Sam. xxvi, 6, 9, and it might seen necessary for the judge to have this at hand, that he might consult with God upon all occasions. Went a whoring - Committed idolatry with it; or went thither to inquire the will of God; whereby they were drawn from the true ephod, instituted by God for this end, which was to be worn by the high- priest only. A snare - An occasion of sin and ruin to him and his, as the next chapter sheweth. Though Gideon was a good man, and did this with an honest mind, and a desire to set up religion in his own city and family; yet here seem to be many sins in it;

1. Superstition and will-worship, worshipping God by a device of his own, which was expressly forbidden.

2. Presumption, in wearing or causing other priests to wear this kind of ephod, which was peculiar to the high-priest.

3. Transgression of a plain command, of worshipping God ordinarily but at one place, and one altar, Deut. xii, 5, 11, 14.

4. Making a division among the people.

5. Laying a stumbling-block, or an occasion of idolatry before that people, whom he knew to be too prone to it.

28. Lifted up their head - That is, recovered not their former strength or courage, so as to conquer or oppress others. Forty years - To the fortieth year, from the beginning of the Midianitish oppression. The days, &c. - As long as Gideon lived.

29. His own house - Not in his father's house; as he did before; nor yet in a court like a king, as the people desired; but in a middle state, as a judge for the preservation and maintenance of their religion and liberties.

31. Shechem - She dwelt there, and he often came thither, either to execute judgment, or upon other occasions. Abimelech - That is, my father the king; so he called him, probably, to gratify his concubine, who desired it either out of pride, or design.

32. A good old age - His long life being crowned with the continuance of honour, tranquility, and happiness.

33. As soon as, &c. - Whereby we see the temper of this people, who did no longer cleave to God, than they were in a manner constrained to it, by the presence and authority of their Judges. Baalim - This was the general name including all their idols, one of which here follows. Baal-berith - That is, the Lord of the covenant; so called, either from the covenant wherewith the worshippers of this God bound themselves to maintain his worship, or to defend one another therein; or rather, because he was reputed the God and judge of all covenants, and promises, and contracts, to whom it belonged to maintain them, and to punish the violaters of them; and such a God both the Grecians and the Roman had.

IX

Abimelech usurps the government at Shechem, ver. 1-6. Jotham's parable, ver. 7-21. Strife between Abimelech and the Shechemites, ver. 22-41. The slaughter of the Shechemites, ver. 42-49. The death of Abimelech, fulfilling Jotham's curse, ver. 50- 57.

2. Reign - He supposed they would take that government which their father refused; and that the multitude of his sons would occasion divisions, and confusions, which they might avoid by chusing him king; and so they might enjoy the monarchy which they had long desired. Your bone and flesh - Your kinsman, of the same tribe and city with you; which will be no small honour and advantage to you.

3. Brethren - That is, kinsmen. He is our brother - They were easily persuaded to believe what served their own interest.

4. Pieces of silver - Not shekels, which were too small a sum for this purpose; but far larger pieces, the exact worth whereof it is not possible for us now to know. The house of Baal-berith - Out of his sacred treasury; having since Gideon's death built this temple (which he would never have suffered whilst he lived) and endowed it with considerable revenues. Light persons - Unsettled, idle and necessitous persons, the proper instruments of tyranny and cruelty.

5. His brethren -- the only persons who were likely to hinder him in establishing his tyranny. Threescore and ten - Wanting one, who is here expressed. Jotham was left - Whereby he would signify, that this was an act of justice, in cutting them all off in an orderly manner, for some supposed crime, probably, as designing sedition and rebellion.

6. House of Millo - Some eminent and potent family living in Shechem, or near it. King - Over all Israel, ver. 22, which was a strange presumption for the inhabitants of one city; but they had many advantages for it; as the eager, and general, and constant inclination of the Israelites to kingly government; Abimelech's being the son of Gideon, to whom, and to his sons, they offered the kingdom. And though the father could, and did refuse it for himself; yet they might imagine, that he could not give away his sons' right, conveyed to them by the Israelites, in their offer; the universal defection of the Israelites from God to Baal, whose great patron and champion Abimelech pretended to be; the power and prevalency of the tribe of Ephraim, in which Shechem was, whose proud and imperious spirit, would make them readily close with a king of their own brethren; and Abimelech's getting the start of all others, having the crown actually put upon his head, and an army already raised to maintain his tyranny. Of the pillar - Or, by the oak of the pillar, by the oak, where Joshua erected a pillar as a witness of the covenant renewed between God and Israel, Josh. xxiv, 26. This place they chose, to signify that they still owned God, and their covenant with him; and did not worship Baal in opposition to God, but in conjunction with him, or in subordination to him.

7. Mount Gerizim - Which lay near Shechem. The valley between Gerizim and Ebal, was a famous place, employed for the solemn reading of the law, and its blessings and curses: and it is probable it was still used, even by the superstitious and idolatrous Israelites for such occasions, who delighted to use the same places which their ancestors had used. Cried - So that they who stood in the valley might hear him, though not suddenly come at him to take him. Men of Shechem - Who were here met together upon a solemn occasion, as Josephus notes, Abimelech being absent. That God may hearken - When you cry unto him for mercy; so he conjures and persuades them to give him patient audience.

8. The trees, &c. - A parabolical discourse, usual among the ancients, especially in the eastern parts. To anoint - To make a king, which was done among the Israelites, and some others, with the ceremony of anointing. Olive-tree - By which he understands Gideon.

9. honour God - In whose worship oil was used for divers things; as, about the lamps, and offerings, and for anointing sacred persons and things. And man - For oil was used in the constitution of kings, and priests, and prophets, and for a present to great persons, and to anoint the head and face. Promoted - Hebrew. to move hither and thither, to wander to and fro, to exchange my sweet tranquility, for incessant cares and travels.

10. Fig-tree - Gideon refused this honour, both for himself, and for his sons; and the sons of Gideon, whom Abimelech had slain, upon pretense of their affecting the kingdom, were as far from such thoughts as their father.

13. Cheareth God - Wherewith God is well pleased, because it was offered to God.

14. Bramble - Or, thorn, fitly representing Abimelech, the son of a concubine, and a person of small use, and great cruelty.

15. If in truth - If you deal truly and justly in making me king. Then trust - Then you may expect protection under my government. Devour the cedars - In stead of protection, you shall receive destruction by me; especially you cedars, that is, nobles, such as the house of Millo, who have been most forward in this work.

18. Ye have slain - Abimelech's fact is justly charged upon them, as done by their consent, approbation and assistance. Maidservant - His concubine, whom he so calls by way of reproach. Over Shechem - By which limitation of their power, and his kingdom, he reflects contempt upon him, and chargeth them with presumption, that having only power over their own city, they durst impose a king upon all Israel.

20. Devour Abimelech - This is not so much a prediction as an imprecation, which, being grounded upon just cause, had its effect, as others in like case had.

21. And fled - Which he might easily do, having the advantage of the hill, and because the people were not forward to pursue a man whom they knew to have such just cause to speak, and so little power to do them hurt. To Beer - A place remote from Shechem, and out of Abimelech's reach.

22. Over Israel - For though the men of Shechem were the first authors of Abimelech's

advancement, the rest of the people easily consented to that form of government which they so much desired.

23. God sent - God gave the devil commission to work upon their minds.

24. The cruelty - That is, the punishment of the cruelty.

25. For him - To seize his person. Robbed all - Such as favoured or served Abimelech; for to such only their commission reached, though it may be, they went beyond their bounds, and robbed all passengers promiscuously.

26. Gaal - It is not known who he was; but it is evident, he was a man very considerable for wealth, and strength and interest; and ill-pleased with Abimelech's power. Went to Shechem - By his presence and council to animate and assist them against Abimelech.

27. Went out - Which, 'till his coming they durst not do, for fear of Abimelech. Made merry - Both from the custom of rejoicing, and singing songs in vintage time, and for the hopes of their redemption from Abimelech's tyranny. Their goals-Baal-berith, ver. 4, either to beg his help against Abimelech, or to give him thanks for the hopes of recovering their liberty. Eat and drink - To the honour of their idols, and out of the oblations made to them, as they used to do to the honour of Jehovah, and out of his sacrifices. Cursed - Either by reviling him after their manner, or, rather in a more solemn and religious manner, cursing him by their God, as Goliath did David.

28. Who is Abimelech - What is he but a base-born person, a cruel tyrant, and one every way unworthy to govern you? Who is Shechem - That is, Abimelech, named in the foregoing words, and described in those which follow. He is called Shechem for the Shechemite. The sense is, who is this Shechemite? For so he was by the mother's side, born of a woman of your city, and she but his concubine and servant; why should you submit to one so basely descended? Of Jerubbaal - Of Gideon, a person famous only by his fierceness against that Baal which you justly honour and reverence, whose altar he overthrew, and whose worship he endeavoured to abolish. And Zebul - And you are so mean spirited, that you do not only submit to him, but suffer his very servants to bear rule over you; and particularly, this ignoble and hateful Zebul. Serve, &c. - If you love bondage, call in the old master and Lord of the place; chuse not an upstart, as Abimelech is; but rather take one of the old flock, one descended from Hamor, Gen. xxxiv, 2, who did not carry himself like a tyrant, as Abimelech did; but like a father of his city. This he might speak sincerely, as being himself a Canaanite and Shechemite, and possibly came from one of those little ones whom Simeon and Levi spared when they slew all the grown males, Gen. xxxiv, 29. And it may be that he was one of the royal blood, a descendent of Hamor, who hereby sought to insinuate himself into the government, as it follows, ver. 29. Would to God that this people were under my hand; which he might judge the people more likely to chuse both because they were now united with the Canaanites in religion; and because their present distress might oblige them to put themselves under him, a valiant and expert commander.

29. My hand - That is, under my command; I wish you would unanimously submit to me, as your captain and governor; for he found them divided; and some of them hearkening after Abimelech, whom they had lately rejected, according to the levity of the popular humour. I would remove - As you have driven him out of your city, I would drive him out of your country. He said - He sent this message or challenge to him. Increase thine army - I desire not to surprise thee at any disadvantage; strengthen thyself as much as thou canst, and come out into the open field, that thou and I may decide it by our arms.

35. And stood - To put his army in order, and to conduct them against Abimelech, whom he supposed to be at a great distance.

36. To Zebul - Who concealed the anger which he had conceived, ver. 30, and pretended compliance with him in this expedition, that he might draw him forth into the field where Abimelech might have the opportunity of fighting with him, and overthrowing him. The shadow - For in the morning, as this was, and in the evening, the shadows are longest, and move quickest.

38. Where is now, &c. - Now shew thyself a man, and fight valiantly for thyself and people.

40. He fled - Being surprised by the unexpected coming of Abimelech, and probably not fully prepared for the encounter.

41. Dwelt at Arumah - He did not prosecute his victory, but retreated to Arumah, to see whether the Shechemites would not of themselves return to his government, or else, that being hereby grown secure, he might have the greater advantage against them. Thrust out - It seems the same night. Probably the multitude, which is generally light and unstable, were now enraged against Gaal, suspecting him of cowardice or ill-conduct. Zebul's interest was not so considerable with them, that he could prevail with them either to kill Gaal and his brethren, or to yield themselves to Abimelech; and therefore he still complies with the people, and waits for a fairer opportunity.

42. Went out - to their usual employments about their land.

43. Three companies - Whereof he kept one with himself, ver. 44, and put the rest under other commanders.

44. Entering of the gate - To prevent their retreat into the city, and give the other two companies

opportunity to cut them off.

45. With salt - In token of his desire of their utter and irrecoverable destruction.

46. The tower - A strong place belonging to the city of Shechem, made for its defense without the city. Berith - Or, Baal-berith, ver. 4. Hither they fled out of the town belonging to it, fearing the same event with Shechem; and here they thought to be secure; partly by the strength of the place, partly by the religion of it, thinking that either their God would protect them there, or that Abimelech would spare them out of pity to that God.

48. Zalmon - A place so called from its shadiness.

50. Thebez - Another town near to Shechem; and, as it seems, within its territory.

51. And all - All that were not slain in the taking of the town. Top of the tower - Which was flat and plain, after their manner of building.

53. Mill-stone - Such great stones no doubt they carried up with them, whereby they might defend themselves, or offend those who assaulted them. Here the justice of God is remarkable in suiting the punishment to his sin. He slew his brethren upon a stone, ver. 5, and he loseth his own life by a stone.

54. A women - Which was esteemed a matter of disgrace.

56. Wickedness - In rooting out, as far as he could, the name and memory of his father.

57. Render upon their heads - Thus God preserved the honour of his government, and gave warning to all ages, to expect blood for blood.

X

The government of Tola and Jair, ver. 1-5. Israel's sin and trouble, ver. 6-9. Their repentance and reformation, which found acceptance with God, ver. 10-16. Preparation for their deliverance, ver. 17, 18.

1. There arose - Not of himself, but raised by God, as the other Judges were. To defend - Or, to save, which he did not by fighting against, and overthrowing their enemies, but by a prudent and pious government of them, whereby he kept them from sedition, oppression, and idolatry. In Shamir - Which was in the very midst of the land.

3. A Gileadite - Of Gilead beyond Jordan.

4. And he had thirty sons - They were itinerant Judges, who rode from place to place, as their father's deputies to administer justice. Havoth-jair - These villages were called so before this time from another Jair, but the old name was revived and confirmed upon this occasion.

6. Forsook the Lord - They grew worse and worse, and so ripened themselves for ruin. Before they worshipped God and idols together, now they forsake God, and wholly cleave to idols.

7. Philistines, &c. - The one on the west, the other on the east; so they were molested on both sides.

8. That year - Or, that year they had vexed and oppressed the children of Israel eighteen years - This was the eighteenth year from the beginning of that oppression. And these eighteen years are not to be reckoned from Jair's death, because that would enlarge the time of the Judges beyond the just bounds; but from the fourth year of Jair's reign: so that the greatest part of Jair's reign was contemporary with this affliction. The case of Jair and Samson seem to be much alike. For as it is said of Samson, that he judged Israel in the days of the tyranny of the Philistines, twenty years, chap. xv, 20, by which it is evident, that his judicature, and their dominion, were contemporary; the like is to be conceived of Jair, that he began to judge Israel, and endeavoured to reform religion, and purge out all abuses; but being unable to effect this through the backwardness of the, people, God would not enable him to deliver the people, but gave them up to this sad oppression; so that Jair could only determine differences amongst the Israelites, but could not deliver them from their enemies.

10. And served also - Because not contented to add idols to thee, we have preferred them before thee.

11. The Lord said - Either by some prophet whom he raised and sent for this purpose: or by the high-priest, who was consulted in the case. From the Amorites - Both Sihon and Og, and their people, and other kings of the Amorites within Jordan. Of Ammon - Who were confederate with the Moabites, chap. iii, 13, 14.

12. The Zidonians - We do not read of any oppression of Israel, particularly, by the Zidonians. But many things were done, which are not recorded. The Maonites - Either first, those who lived in, or near the wilderness of Maon, in the south of Judah, 1 Sam. xxiii, 25; xxv, 2, whether Edomites or others. Or, secondly, the Mehunims, a people living near the Arabians, of whom, 2 Chron. xxvi, 7. For in the Hebrew, the letters of both names are the same, only the one is the singular, the other the plural number.

13. No more - Except you repent in another manner than you yet have done; which when they performed, God suspended the execution of this threatning.

14. Chosen - You have not been forced to worship those gods by your oppressors; but you have

freely chosen them before me.

15. Do thou unto us - Do not give us up into the hands of these cruel men, but do thou chastise us with thine own hand as much as thou pleasest; if we be not more faithful and constant to thee, than we have hitherto been.

16. They put away - This was an evidence of the sincerity of their sorrow, that they did not only confess their sins, but also forsake them. His soul, &c. - He acted towards them, like one that felt their sufferings; he had pity upon them, quite changed his carriage towards them, and punished their enemies as sorely as if they had grieved and injured his own person.

17. Mizpeh - That Mizpeh which was beyond Jordan.

XI

The birth of Jephthah, rejected by his brethren, ver. 1-3. The Gileadites chuse him for their general, ver. 4-11. His treating with the king of Ammon, ver. 12-28. His war with, and victory over the Ammonites, ver. 29-33. His vow and the performance of it, ver. 34-40.

1. Gileadite - So called, either from his father Gilead, or from the mountain, or city of Gilead, the place of his birth. Son of a harlot - That is, a bastard. And though such were not ordinarily to enter into the congregation of the Lord, Deut. xxiii, 2. Yet God can dispense with his own laws, and hath sometimes done honour to base-born persons, so far, that some of them were admitted to be the progenitors of the Lord Jesus Christ. And Gilead - One of the children of that ancient Gilead, Num. xxxii, 1.

3. Of Tob - The name either of the land, or of the man who was the owner or ruler of it. This place was in, or near Gilead, as appears by the speedy intercourse which here was between Jephthah and the Israelites. Vain men - Idle persons, who desired rather to get their living by spoil and rapine, than by honest labour. These evil persons Jephthah managed well, employing them against the enemies of God, and of Israel, that bordered upon them; and particularly upon parties of the Ammonites, which made the Israelites more forward to chuse him for their chieftain in this war. Went out - When he made excursions and attempts upon the enemy.

4. Made war - The Ammonites had vexed and oppressed them eighteen years, and now the Israelites begin to make opposition, they commence a war against them.

5. Went - By direction from God, who both qualified him for, and called him to the office of a judge, otherwise they might not have chosen a bastard.

7. Expel me - And deprive me of all share in my father's goods, which, though a bastard, was due to me. This expulsion of him was the act of his brethren; but he here ascribes it to the elders of Gilead; either because some of them were among these elders, as is very probable from the dignity of this family; or because this act, though desired by his brethren, was executed by the decree of the elders, to whom the determination of all controversies about inheritance belonged; and therefore it was their faults they did not protect him from the injuries of his brethren.

8. Therefore - Being sensible that we have done thee injury, we come now to make thee full reparation.

9. If, &c. - If you recall me from this place where I am now settled, to the place whence I was expelled. Shall I, &c. - Will you really make good this promise? Jephthah was so solicitous in this case, either from his zeal for the public good, which required that he should be so; or from the law of self-preservation, that he might secure himself from his brethren; whose ill-will he had experienced, and whose injuries he could not prevent, if, after he had served their ends, he had been reduced to his private capacity.

10. The Lord be witness - The Lord be an hearer: so the Hebrew word is. Whatever we speak it concerns us to remember, that God is an hearer!

11. All his words - Or, all his matters, the whole business. Before the Lord - That is, before the public congregation, wherewith God was usually, and then especially present.

12. Messengers - That is, ambassadors, to prevent blood-shed, that so the Israelites might be acquitted before God and men, from all the sad consequences of this war; herein he shewed great prudence, and no less piety. What hast thou, &c. - What reasonable cause hast thou for this invasion? In my land - He speaks this in the name of all the people.

13. My land - That is, this land of Gilead, which was mine, but unjustly taken from me, by Sihon and Og, the kings of the Ammonites; and the injury perpetuated by Israel's detaining it from me. This land, before the conquests of Sihon and Og, belonged partly to the Ammonites, and partly to the Moabites. And indeed, Moab and Ammon did for the most part join their interests and their forces.

16. The Red-sea - Unto which they came three times; once, Exod. xiii, 18, again, a little after their passage over it, and a third time, long after, when they came to Ezion Geber, which was upon the shore of the Red-Sea, from whence they went to Kadesh; of this time he speaks here.

17. *Abode* - Peaceably, and did not revenge their unkindness as they could have done.

19. *My place* - That is, unto the land of Canaan, which God hath given me.

20. *Sihon fought* - So Sihon was the aggressor, and the Israelites were forced to fight in their own defense.

22. *The coasts* - Or, borders; together with all the land included within those borders. *Wilderness* - Namely, the desert of Arabia.

23. *So the Lord* - God, the sovereign Lord of all lands, hath given us this land; this he adds, as a farther and convincing reason; because otherwise it might have been alledged against the former argument, that they could gain no more right to that land from Sihon, than Sihon himself had.

24. *Wilt not thou* - He speaks according to their absurd opinion: the Ammonites and Moabites got their land by conquest of the old inhabitants, whom they cast out; and this success, though given them by the true God, for Lot's sake, Deut. ii, 9, 19, they impiously ascribe to their God Chemosh, whose gift they owned to be a sufficient title.

25. *Than Balak* - Art thou wiser than he? Or hast thou more right than he had? Balak, though he plotted against Israel, in defense of his own land, which he feared they would invade and conquer, yet never contended with them about the restitution of those lands which Sihon took from him or his predecessors.

26. *Three hundred years* - Not precisely, but about that time, either from their coming out of Egypt; or, from their first conquest of those lands. He urges prescription, which is by all men reckoned a just title, and it is fit it should be so for the good of the world, because otherwise the door would be opened both to kings, and to private persons, for infinite contentions and confusions.

27. *I have not* - I have done thee no wrong. *Be judge* - Let him determine this controversy by the success of this day and war.

29. *Spirit came* - Indued him with a more than ordinary courage and resolution. *Manasseh* - That is, Bashan, which the half tribe of Manasseh beyond Jordan inhabited. *Mizpeh of Gilead* - So called to distinguish it from other cities of the same name, having gathered what forces he suddenly could, he came hither to the borders of the Ammonites.

33. *Minnith* - A place not far from Rabbah, the chief city of the Ammonites. *Subdued before Israel* - It does not appear, that he offered to take possession of the country. Tho' the attempt of others to wrong us, will justify us in the defense of our own right, yet it will not authorize us to do them wrong.

34. *His daughter* - In concert with other virgins, as the manner was.

35. *Trouble me* - Before this, I was troubled by my brethren; and since, by the Ammonites; and now most of all, tho' but occasionally, by thee. *Opened my mouth* - That is, I have vowed. *Cannot go back* - That is, not retract my vow; I am indispensably obliged to perform it.

36. *Do to me* - Do not for my sake make thyself a transgressor; I freely give my consent to thy vow.

37. *Mountains* - Which she chose as a solitary place, and therefore fittest for lamentation. *Bewail* - That I shall die childless, which was esteemed both a curse and a disgrace for the Israelites, because such were excluded from that great privilege of increasing the holy seed, and contributing to the birth of the Messiah.

39. *Did with her* - Jephthah's daughter was not sacrificed, but only devoted to perpetual virginity. This appears,

1. From ver. 37, 38, where we read, that she bewailed not her death, which had been the chief cause of lamentation, if that had been vowed, but her virginity:

2. From this ver. 39, where, after he had said, that he did with her according to his vow; he adds, by way of declaration of the matter of that vow, that he knew no man. It is probably conceived, that the Greeks, who used to steal sacred histories, and turn them into fables, had from this history their relation of Iphigenia (which may be put for Jephtigenia) sacrificed by her father Agamemnon, which is described by many of the same circumstances wherewith this is accompanied.

40. *The daughter of Jephthah* - It is really astonishing, that the general stream of commentators, should take it for granted, that Jephthah murdered his daughter! But, says Mr. Henry, "We do not find any law, usage or custom, in all the Old Testament, which doth in the least intimate, that a single life was any branch or article of religion." And do we find any law, usage or custom there, which doth in the least intimate, that cutting the throat of an only child, was any branch or article of religion? If only a dog had met Jephthah, would he have offered up that for a burnt-offering? No: because God had expressly forbidden this. And had he not expressly forbidden murder? But Mr. Poole thinks the story of Agamemnon's offering up Iphigenia took its rise from this. Probably it did. But then let it be observed, Iphigenia was not murdered. Tradition said, that Diana sent an hind in her stead, and took the maid to live in the woods with her.

XII

Jephthah's encounter with, and slaughter of the Ephraimites, ver. 1-6. His death, ver. 7 A short account of three other Judges ver. 8-15.

1. *Northward* - Over Jordan, where Jephthah was, in the northern part of the land beyond Jordan. *And said* - Through pride and envy, contending with him as they did before with Gideon. *Over* - Not over Jordan, for there he was already; but over the borders of the Israelites land beyond Jordan.

2. *When I called* - Hence it appears, that he had craved their assistance, which they had denied; though that be not elsewhere expressed.

3. *Put my life* - That is, I exposed myself to the utmost danger; as a man that carries a brittle and precious thing in his hand, which may easily either fall to the ground, or be snatched from him. *Wherefore* - Why do you thus requite my kindness in running such hazards to preserve you and yours?

4. *Ye Gileadites* - These words are a contemptuous expression of the Ephraimites concerning the Gileadites, whom they call fugitives of Ephraim; the word Ephraim being here taken largely, as it comprehends the other neighbouring tribes, of which Ephraim was the chief; and especially their brethren of Manasseh, who lived next to them, and were descended from the same father, Joseph. By Gileadites here they seem principally to mean the Manassites beyond Jordan, who dwelt in Gilead. And although other Gileadites were joined with them, yet they vent their passion against these; principally, because they envied them most; as having had a chief hand in the victory. These they opprobriously call fugitives, that is, such as had deserted their brethren of Ephraim and Manasseh, planted themselves beyond Jordan, at a distance from their brethren, and were alienated in affection from them.

5. *Said Nay* - To avoid the present danger.

6. *Shibboleth* - Which signifies a stream or river, which they desired to pass over: so it was a word proper for the occasion, and gave them no cause to suspect the design, because they were required only to express their desire to go over the Shibboleth or river. *Sibboleth* - It is well known, that not only divers nations, but divers provinces, or parts of the same nation who use the same language, differ in their manner of pronunciation. *Could not frame* - Or rather, he did not frame to speak right; so as he was required to do it. The Hebrew text doth not say, that he could not do it, but that he did it not, because suspecting not the design he uttered it speedily according to his manner of expression. *There fell* - Not in that place, but in that expedition, being slain either in the battle, or in the pursuit, or at Jordan. See the justice of God! They had gloried, that they were Ephraimites: But how soon are they afraid to own their country? They had called the Gileadites, fugitives: And now they are in good earnest become fugitives themselves. It is the same word, ver. 5, used of the Ephraimites that fled, which they had used in scorn of the Gileadites. He that rolls the stone, or reproach unjustly on another, it may justly return upon himself.

9. *Took in* - That is, took them home for wives to his sons. What a difference between his and his predecessor's family! Ibzan had sixty children, and all married: Jephthah but one, and she dies unmarried. Some are increased, others diminished: all is the Lord's doing.

15. *Mount of the Amalekites* - So called from some remarkable exploit, done by, or upon the Amalekites in that place. It is strange, that in the history of all these Judges, there is not so much as once mention of the high-priest, or of any other priest or Levite, appearing either for council or action in any public affair, from Phinehas to Eli, which may well be computed two hundred and fifty years! Surely this intimates, that the institution was chiefly intended to be typical, and that the benefits which were promised by it, were to be chiefly looked for in its anti-type, the everlasting priesthood of Christ, in comparison of which that priesthood had no glory.

XIII

Samson was an eminent believer, Heb. xi, 13, 32, and a glorious type of him who with his own arm wrought salvation. The occasion of raising him up, ver. 1. His birth foretold by an angel, ver. 2-5. His mother relates this to his father, ver. 6, 7. The angel repeats it to them both, ver. 8-14. Manoah offers to entertain him and asks his name, ver. 15-18. He discovers himself at parting, ver. 19-23. Samson is born, ver. 24, 25.

1. *Did evil* - That is, fell into idolatry, not after the death of Abdon the last judge, but in the days of the former Judges. *Forty years* - To be computed, not from Abdon's death, but before that time. And it is probable that great slaughter of the Ephraimites made by Jephthah, greatly encouraged the Philistines to rise against Israel, when one of their chief bulwarks was so much weakened; and therefore began to domineer over them not long after Jephthah's death. These were a very inconsiderable people. They had but five cities of any note. And yet when God used them as the staff in his hand, they were very oppressive and vexatious.

John Wesley

2. Of the family - That is, of the tribe or people. Bare not - An emphatical repetition of the same thing in other words, which is an usual elegancy both in scripture and other authors.

3. The angel - The Son of God, yet distinguished from the Lord, because he appeared here in the form of a servant, as a messenger sent from God. The great Redeemer did in a particular manner concern himself about this typical redeemer.

4. Beware - Because the child was to be a Nazarite from the womb, ver. 5, and from the conception; and because the mother's pollution extends to the child, she is enjoined from this time to observe the following rules belonging to the Nazarites. Strong drink - Under which are comprehended the other particulars mentioned, Num. vi, 2-4. Nor eat - Any of those meats forbidden, Levit xi, 1-47, which were forbidden to all, but especially to the Nazarites.

5. A Nazarite - A person consecrated to God's service. Begin to deliver - And the deliverance shall be carried on and perfected by others, as it was by Eli, Samuel, and Saul; but especially by David. God chuses to carry on his work gradually and by several hands. One lays the foundation of a good work, another builds, and perhaps a third brings forth the top stone.

6. Man of God - A prophet, or sacred person, sent with a message from God. Terrible - Or, venerable, awful, full of Majesty.

12. Let thy words - Or, thy words shall come to pass: I firmly believe thy promises shall be fulfilled. How - What rules shall we observe about his education?

13. Let her - Whilst the child is in her womb, and after the child is born let him observe the same orders.

15. Made ready - Supposing him to be a man and a prophet, to whom he would in this manner express his respect, as was usual to strangers.

16. Bread - That is, meat, as bread is commonly taken in scripture. To the Lord - Not unto a man, as thou apprehendest me to be; but unto the Lord, as thou wilt by and by perceive me to be.

17. honour - Either by making honourable mention of thee, or by shewing respect to thee, by a present, which they usually gave to prophets.

18. Secret - Hidden from mortal men: or, wonderful, such as thou canst not comprehend: my nature and essence, (which is often signified by name in scripture) is incomprehensible. This shews, that this was the angel of the covenant, the Son of God.

19. Meal-offering - Which were generally joined with the chief sacrifices. A Rock - The angel's presence and command being a sufficient warrant for the offering of sacrifice by a person who was no priest, and in a place otherwise forbidden.

20. The altar - That is, from that part of the rock which served instead of an altar, upon which the sacrifice was laid. Ascended - To manifest his nature and essence to be spiritual. Fell - Partly in reverence to that glorious presence manifested in so wonderful a manner: and partly, out of a religious horror and fear of death; for the prevention thereof they fell down in way of supplication to God.

23. Nor would, &c. - This expression seems to have some emphasis in it, to enhance God's mercy to them, as being afforded them in a time of such grievous calamity; and in a time when the word of the Lord was precious; and there was no open vision.

24. Blessed him - That is, endowed him with all those graces and gifts of mind and body which were necessary for the work he was designed for.

25. To move - That is, to stir him up to heroical designs; to shew forth its power in the frame of his mind, and in the strength of his body, discovered to his neighbours in extraordinary actions; to encline his heart to great attempts for the help and deliverance of God's people, to give some essays of it to his brethren, and to seek all opportunities for it. Of Daniel - A place so called, either from the expedition of the Danites, chap. xviii, 11, 12, which though placed after this history, was done before it: or from some other camp which the Danites had formed there, to give some check to the incursions of the Philistines.

XIV

Samson's marriage with a Philistine, and killing a lion, ver. 1-7. He finds honey in the carcase, ver. 8, 9. His riddle, ver. 10- 14. Unriddled by means of his wife, ver. 15-18. He kills thirty Philistines, and leaves her, ver. 19,

1. Went - After he was come to mature age. Timnath - A place not far from the sea.

2. To wife - Herein he is an example to all children, conformable to the fifth commandment. Children ought not to marry, nor to move toward it without the advice and consent of their parents. They that do, as Bishop Hall speaks, unchild themselves. Parents have a property in their children, as parts of themselves. In marriage this property is transferred. It is therefore not only unkind and ungrateful, but palpably unjust, to alienate this property, without their concurrence. Who so thus robbeth his father or mother, stealing himself from them who is nearer and dearer to them than their goods, and

yet saith, It is no transgression, the same is the companion of a destroyer, Prov. xxviii, 24.

3. *Philistines* - With whom the Israelites were forbidden to marry. For although the Philistines were not Canaanites in their original, yet they were so in their concurrence with them in wickedness, and therefore were liable to the same judgments with them. *Get her* - This action of Samson's, though against common rules, seems to be warranted, by the direction of God, (mentioned in the following words) which was known to Samson, but not to his parents. *Pleaseth me* - Not so much for her beauty, as for the design mentioned in the next verse.

5. *Father and mother* - Who accompanied him, either because they were now acquainted with his design; or, to order the circumstances of that action which they saw he was set upon.

6. *Came mightily* - Increased his courage and bodily strength. *A kid* - As soon and as safely. *Told not, &c.* - Lest by their means it should be publickly known; for he wisely considered, that it was not yet a fit time to awaken the jealousies and fears of the Philistines concerning him, as this would have done.

8. *After a time* - Hebrew. after days; that is, either after some days: or, rather, after a year, as that word often signifies; when the flesh of the lion, (which by its strong smell is offensive to bees) was wholly consumed, and nothing was left but the bones. *Bees* - Settling themselves there, as they have sometimes done in a man's skull, or in a sepulchre.

9. *Came to, &c.* - From whom he had turned aside for a season, ver. 8.

11. *Saw him* - Or, observed him, his stature, and strength, and countenance, and carriage, which were extraordinary. *Brought* - Partly in compliance with the custom of having bride-men; though they were not so numerous; but principally by way of caution, and as a guard put upon him under a pretense of respect and affection.

12. *Seven days* - For so long marriage-feasts lasted. *Sheets* - Fine linen-clothes, which were used for many purposes in those parts. *Changes* - Suits of apparel.

15. *Seventh day* - They had doubtless spoken to her before this time, but with some remissness, supposing that they should find it out; but now their time being nigh slipped, they put her under a necessity of searching it out. *To take that we have* - That is, to strip us of our garments.

17. *The seven days* - That is, on the residue of the seven days; namely, after the third day.

18. *If ye had not &c.* - If you had not employed my wife to find it out, as men plough up the ground with an heifer, thereby discovering its hidden parts; he calls her heifer, because she was joined with him in the same yoke.

19. *The spirit came* - Though he had constant strength and courage; yet that was exceedingly increased upon special occasions, by the extraordinary influences of God's spirit. *To Ashkelon* - Either to the territory; or to the city itself, where he had both strength and courage enough to attempt what follows; and upon the doing hereof they were doubtless struck with such terror, that every one sought only to preserve himself, and none durst pursue him. *His anger was kindled* - For the treachery of his wife and companions. *He went* - Without his wife. It were well for us, if the unkindnesses we meet with from the world, and our disappointments therein has this good effect on us, to oblige us to return by faith and prayer, to our heavenly father's house.

20. *Was given* - By her father. *Whom he had used* - That is, to the chief of the bride-men, to whom he had shewed most respect and kindness.

XV

From the treachery of his wife and her father, Samson takes occasion to burn their corn, ver. 1-5. He smites the Philistines with a great slaughter, ver. 6-8. He slays a thousand of them with the jaw-bone of an ass, ver. 9-17. He is distressed, and supplied with water, ver. 18-20.

1. *Wheat harvest* - Which was the proper season for what follows. *With a kid* - As a token of reconciliation. *Into the chamber* - Into her chamber, which the women had separate from the mens.

2. *Hated her* - Because thou didst desert her: but this was no sufficient cause; for he should have endeavoured a reconciliation, and not have disposed of another man's wife without his consent.

3. *Now shall I, &c.* - Because they have first provoked me by an irreparable injury: but although this may look like an act of private revenge; yet it is plain Samson acted as a judge (for so he was) and as an avenger of the publick injuries of his people.

4. *Foxes* - Of which there were great numbers in Canaan. But it is not said that Samson caught them all, either at one time, or by his own hands; for being so eminent a person, and the judge of Israel, he might require assistance of as many persons as he pleased. And it must be allowed, that the God who made the world, and by his singular providence watched over Israel, and intended them deliverance at this time, could easily dispose things so that they might be taken. He chose to do this not by his brethren, whom he would preserve from the hatred and mischief which it might have occasioned them, but by brute creatures, thereby to add scorn to their calamity, and particularly by foxes; partly, because they were fittest for the purpose, being creatures very fearful of fire; and having such tails as the fire-

brands might most conveniently be tied to; and not going directly forward, but crookedly, whereby the fire would be dispersed in more places. Fire-brands - Made of such matter as would quickly take fire, and keep it for a long time; which was easy to procure. And put, &c. - That the foxes might not make too much haste, nor run into their holes, but one of them might delay another, and so continue longer in the places where they were to do execution.

5. Let them go - Successively at several times; and in divers places, so that they might not hinder one another, nor all run into the same field; but being dispersed in all parts, might spread the plague farther; and withal might be kept at a distance from the fields and vineyards of the Israelites.

6. Burnt her - For the mischief which she had occasioned them; thus she brought upon herself that mischief which she studied to avoid. The Philistines had threatened to burn her and her father's house with fire. To avoid this she betrayed her husband. And now the very thing she feared comes upon her!

8. Hip and thigh - It seems to be a phrase, to express a desperate attack, attended with the utmost hurry and confusion: and perhaps intimates, that they all fled before him. So he smote them in the hinder parts. Rock Etam - A natural fortress, where he waited to see what steps the Philistines would take.

11. Unto us - Thou hast by these actions punished not them only, but us, who are sure to smart for it.

12. Bind thee - Why not rather, to fight under thy banner? Because sin dispirits men, nay, it infatuates them, and hides from their eyes the things that belong to their peace. Swear - Not that he feared them, or could not as easily have conquered them, as he did the host of the Philistines; but because he would be free from all temptation of doing them harm, though it were in his own defense.

13. And they bound him - Thus was he a type of Christ, who yielded himself to be bound, yea and led as a lamb to the slaughter. Never were men so besotted as these men of Judah, except those who thus treated our blessed saviour. The rock - That is, from the cave in the rock, in which he had secured himself, out of which he was first brought up, and then carried down from the rock to the plain.

14. Shouted - Because they had now their enemy, as they supposed, in their hands. Loosed - Hebrew. were melted; that is, were dissolved, as things which are melted in the fire. This typified the resurrection of Christ, by the power of the Spirit of holiness. In this he loosed the bands of death, it being impossible he should be holden of them. And thus he triumphed over the powers of darkness, which had shouted against him.

15. New jaw-bone - And therefore the more tough and strong.

16. Slain a thousand men - What could be too hard for him to do, on whom the Spirit of the Lord came mightily? It was strange the men of Judah did now at least come in to his assistance. But he was to be a type of him, who trod the wine-press alone.

17. Ramath-Lehi - That is, the lifting up of the jaw-bone; by contraction Lehi, ver. 14, as Salem is put for Jerusalem.

18. Sore a thirst - A natural effect of the great pains he had taken. And perhaps there was the hand of God therein, to chastise him for not making mention of God in his song, and to keep him from being proud of his strength. One would have thought that the men of Judah would have met him with bread and wine: but they so little regarded him, that he is fainting for want of a draught of water! Thus are the greatest slights often put upon those that do the greatest services! Shall I die - Wilt thou not finish what thou hast begun? Wilt thou undo what thou hast done.

19. In the Jaw - Either causing the jaw-bone to send forth water, as the rock formerly did, causing a spring to break forth in that Lehi, mentioned ver. 14, for Lehi is both the name of a place, and a jaw-bone. En-hakkore - That is, the fountain of him that cried for thirst; or, that called upon God for deliverance; that is, the fountain which was given in answer to my prayer. In Lehi - According to this translation, Lehi is the name of a place.

20. He judged - That is, he pleaded their cause, and avenged them against the Philistines. Of the Philistines - That is, whilst the Philistines had the power and dominion, from which he was not fully to deliver, but only to begin to deliver them. From this place it is manifest, that in the computation of the times of the Judges, the years of servitude or oppression are not to be separated from the years of the Judges, but added to them, and are comprehended within them; which proposition is of great importance for clearing this difficult part of scripture-chronology.

XVI

Samson is greatly endangered by his intercourse with an harlot, ver. 1-3. Betrayed by Delilah to the Philistines thrice, ver. 4-14. Weakened and effectually betrayed, ver. 15-20. Seized, blinded, bound, imprisoned and made sport of, ver. 21-25. Avenged of the Philistines, ver. 26-31.

1. And saw - Going into an house of publick entertainment to refresh himself. He there saw this harlot accidentally; and by giving way to look upon her, was ensnared, Gen. iii, 6.

2. In the morning - This they chose to do, rather than to seize upon him in his bed by night; either, because they knew not certainly in what house he was; or, because they thought that might cause great terror, and confusion, and mischief among their own people; whereas in the day-time they might more fully discover him, and more certainly use their weapons against him. O that all who indulge any unholy desire, might see themselves thus surrounded, and marked for destruction by their spiritual enemies! The more secure they are, the greater is their danger.

3. Arose - Perhaps warned by God in a dream; or rather by the checks of his own conscience. Went away - The watch-men not expecting him 'till morning, and therefore being now retired into the sides, or upper part of the gate-house, as the manner now is, to get some rest, to fit themselves for their hard service intended in the morning: nor durst they pursue him, whom they now again perceived to have such prodigious strength, and courage; and to be so much above the fear of them, that he did not run away with all speed, but went leisurely. Hebron - Which was above twenty miles from Gaza. And Samson did this not out of vain ostentation, but as an evidence of his great strength, for the encouragement of its people to join with him vigorously; and for the greater terror and contempt of the Philistines. It may seem strange that Samson immediately after so foul a sin should have courage and strength from God, for so great a work. But first, it is probable, that Samson had in some measure repented of his sin, and begged of God pardon and assistance. 2.This singular strength and courage was not in itself a grace, but a gift, and it was such a gift as did not so much depend on the disposition of his mind, but on the right ordering of his body, by the rule given to him, and others of that order.

4. Loved - Probably as an harlot: because the dreadful punishment now inflicted upon Samson for this sin, whom God spared for the first offense, is an intimation, that this sin was not inferior to the former.

5. The lords - The lords of their five principal cities, who were leagued together against him as their common enemy. Afflict - To chastise him for his injuries done to us. They mean to punish him severely, but they express it in mild words, lest it might move her to pity him. Pieces of silver - Shekels, as that phrase is commonly used.

7. Samson said - Samson is guilty both of the sin of lying, and of great folly in encouraging her enquiries, which he should at first have checked: but as he had forsaken God, so God had now forsaken him, otherwise the frequent repetition and vehement urging of this question might easily have raised suspicion in him.

9. With her - That is, in a secret chamber within her call. Nor is it strange that they did not fall upon him in his sleep, because they expected an opportunity for doing their work more certainly, and with less danger.

13. Web - Or, thread which is woven about a weaver's loom: or, with a weaver's beam. If my hair, which is all divided into seven locks, be fastened about a weaver's beam; or interwoven with weaver's threads: then I shall be weak as another man.

15. Not with me - Not open to me.

16. Vexed - Being tormented by two contrary passions, desire to gratify her, and fear of betraying himself. So that he had no pleasure of his life.

17. If I be shaven - Not that his hair was in itself the cause of his strength, but because it was the chief condition of that covenant, whereby God was pleased to ingage himself to fit him for, and assist him in that great work to which he called him: but upon his violation of the condition, God justly withdraws his help. (EFN Isaiah xl, 31 Psalm xxix, 11)

18. And brought money in their hand - See one of the bravest men then in the world bought and sold, as a sheep for the slaughter. How does this instance sully all the glory of man, and forbid the strong man ever to boast of his strength!

19. Sleep - By some sleepy potion. Knees - Resting his head upon her knees. To weaken or hurt, tho' he felt it not.

20. Said - Within himself. Shake myself - That is, put forth my strength. Knew not - Not distinctly feeling the loss of his hair, or not considering what would follow. Many have lost the favourable presence of God, and are not aware of it. They have provoked God to withdraw from them; but are not sensible of their loss.

21. His eyes - Which was done both out of revenge and policy, to disable him from doing them harm, in case he should recover his strength; but not without God's providence, punishing him in that part which had been instrumental to his sinful lusts. Gaza - Because this was a great and strong city, where he would be kept safely; and upon the sea-coast, at sufficient distance from Samson's people; and to repair the honour of that place, upon which he had fastened so great a scorn. God also ordering things thus, that where he first sinned, ver. 1, there he should receive his punishment. Grind - As slaves use to do. He made himself a slave to harlots, and now God suffers men to use him like a slave. Poor Samson, how art thou fallen! How is thine honour laid in the dust! Wo unto him, for he hath sinned! Let all take warning by him, carefully to preserve their purity. For all our glory is gone, when the covenant of our separation to God, as spiritual Nazarites, is profaned.

22. The hair - This circumstance, though in itself inconsiderable, is noted as a sign of the recovery of God's favour, and his former strength, in some degree, upon his repentance, and renewing his vow with God, which was allowed for Nazarites to do.

23. Dagon - An idol, whose upper part was like a man, and whose lower part was like a fish: probably one of the sea-gods of the Heathens.

25. Made sport - Either being made by them the matter of their sport and derision, of bitter scoffs, and other indignities: or, by some proofs of more than ordinary strength yet remaining in him, like the ruins of a great and goodly building: whereby he lulled them asleep, until by this complaisance he prepared the way for that which he designed.

26. Whereon the house standeth-Whether it were a temple, or theatre, or some slight building run up for the purpose.

27. The roof - Which was flat, and had window's through which they might see what was done in the lower parts of the house.

28. Samson called - This prayer was not an act of malice and revenge, but of faith and zeal for God, who was there publickly dishonoured; and justice, in vindicating the whole common- wealth of Israel, which was his duty, as he was judge. And God, who heareth not sinners, and would never use his omnipotence to gratify any man's malice, did manifest by the effect, that he accepted and owned his prayer as the dictate of his own Spirit. And that in this prayer he mentions only his personal injury, and not their indignities to God and his people, must be ascribed to that prudent care which he had, upon former occasions, of deriving the rage of the Philistines upon himself alone, and diverting it from the people. For which end I conceive this prayer was made with an audible voice, though he knew they would entertain it only with scorn and laughter.

30. Two pillars - Instances are not wanting of more capacious buildings than this, that have been supported only by one pillar. Pliny in the 15th chapter of the 36th Book of his Natural History, mentions two theatres built by C. Curio, in Julius Caesar's time; each of which was supported only by one pillar, tho' many thousands of people sat in it together. Let me die - That is, I am content to die, so I can but contribute to the vindication of God's glory, and the deliverance of God's people. This is no encouragement to those who wickedly murder themselves: for Samson did not desire, or procure his own death voluntarily, but by mere necessity; he was by his office obliged to seek the destruction of these enemies and blasphemers of God, and oppressors of his people; which in these circumstances he could not effect without his own death. Moreover, Samson did this by Divine direction, as God's answer to his prayer manifests, and that he might be a type of Christ, who by voluntarily undergoing death, destroyed the enemies of God, and of his people. They died, just when they were insulting over an Israelite, persecuting him whom God had smitten. Nothing fills up the measure of the iniquity of any person or people faster, than mocking or misusing the servants of God, yea, tho' it is by their own folly, that they are brought low. Those know not what they do, nor whom they affront, that make sport with a good man.

31. Buried - While the Philistines were under such grief, and consternation, that they had neither heart nor leisure to hinder them.

XVII

Micah provides an image for his God, ver. 1-6. And a Levite for his priest, ver. 7-13.

1. There was, &c. - The things mentioned here, and in the following chapters, did not happen in the order in which they are put; but much sooner, even presently after the death of the elders that over-lived Joshua, as appears, because Phinehas the son of Eleazar was priest at this time, chap. xx, 28, who must have been about 350 years old, if this had been done after Samson's death.

2. Cursedst - That is, didst curse the person who had taken them away. I took it - The fear of thy curse makes me acknowledge mine offense, and beg thy pardon. Blessed - I willingly consent to, and beg from God the removal of the curse, and a blessing instead of it. Be thou free from my curse, because thou hast so honestly restored it.

3. The Lord - In the Hebrew it is, Jehovah, the incommunicable name of God. Whereby it is apparent, that neither she, nor her son, intended to forsake the true God; as appears from his rejoicing when he had got a priest of the Lord's appointment, but only to worship God by an image; which also both the Israelites, Exod. xxxii, 1, &c. and Jeroboam afterwards, designed to do. For my son - For the benefit of thyself and family; that you need not be continually going to Shiloh to worship, but may do it at home. To thee - To dispose of, as I say.

4. Restored - Though his mother allowed him to keep it, yet he persisted in his resolution to restore it, that she might dispose of it as she pleased. Two hundred - Reserving nine hundred shekels, either for the ephod or teraphim, or for other things relating to this worship.

5. Of gods - That is, an house consecrated for the service of God in this manner. Teraphim - A sort

of images so called. One of his sons - Because the Levites in that corrupt estate of the church, neglected the exercise of their office, and therefore they were neglected by the people, and others put into their employment.

6. No king - No judge to govern and control them. The word king being used largely for a supreme magistrate. God raised up Judges to rule and deliver the people, when he saw fit; and at other times for their sins he suffered them to be without them, and such a time this was; and therefore they ran into that idolatry, from which the Judges usually kept them; as appears by that solemn and oft-repeated passage in this book, that after the death of such or such a judge, the people forsook the Lord, and turned to idols. His own eyes - That is, not what pleased God, but what best suited his own fancy.

7. Bethlehem-judah - So called here, as Matt. ii, 1, 5, to difference it from Bethlehem in Zebulun. There he was born and bred. Of Judah - That is, of or belonging to the tribe of Judah; not by birth, for he was a Levite; but by his habitation and ministration. For the Levites were dispersed among all the tribes; and this man's lot fell into the tribe of Judah. Sojourned - So he expresseth it, because this was not the proper place of his abode, this being no Levitical city.

8. To sojourn - For employment and a livelihood; for the tithes and offerings, which were their maintenance, not being brought into the house of God, the Levites and priests were reduced to straights.

10. A father - That is, a priest, a spiritual father, a teacher or instructor. He pretends reverence and submission to him; and what is wanting in his wages, he pays him in titles.

11. Content - Being infected with the common superstition and idolatry of the times. His sons - That is, treated with the same degree of kindness and affection.

12. Consecrated - To be a priest, for which he thought a consecration necessary, as knowing the Levites were no less excluded from the priest's office than the people. The young man - Instead of his son, whom he had consecrated, but now seems to restrain him from the exercise of that office, and to devolve it wholly upon the Levite, who was nearer akin to it.

13. Do me good - I am assured God will bless me. So blind and grossly partial he was in his judgment, to think that one right circumstance would answer for all his substantial errors, in making and worshipping images against God's express command, in worshipping God in a forbidden place, by a priest illegally appointed.

XVIII

The Danish spies call at Micah's house, ver. 1-6. The report they bring back, ver. 7-10. The Danites send forces, who by the way plunder Micah of his gods, ver. 11-26. They take Laish and set up idolatry there, ver. 27-31.

1. Those days - Not long after Joshua's death. The tribe - A part of that tribe, consisting only of six hundred men of war, with their families, ver. 16, 21. Inheritance - The lot had fallen to them before this time, but not the actual possession, because the Philistines and Amorites opposed them.

2. There - Not in the same house, but near it.

3. Knew - By the acquaintance which some of them formerly had with him.

5. Ask - By thine Ephod, and Teraphim, or images, which they knew he had, ver. 14.

6. Before the Lord - That is, your design is under the eye of God; that is, under his care, protection and direction. This answer he either feigns to gratify their humour; or, did indeed receive from the devil, who transformed himself into an angel of light, and in God's name gave him answers, and those not sometimes very true, which God suffered for the trial of his people. But it is observable, his answer was, as the devil's oracles usually were, ambiguous, and such as might have been interpreted either way.

7. Manner of the Zidonians - Who living in a very strong place, and abounding in wealth, and perceiving that the Israelites never attempted anything against them, were grown secure and careless. Put to shame - Or, that might rebuke or punish any thing, that is, any crime. Putting to shame seems to be used for inflicting civil punishment, because shame is generally the effect of it. Zidonians - Who otherwise could have succored them, and would have been ready to do it. No business-No league or confederacy, nor much converse with other cities, it being in a pleasant and plentiful soil, between the two rivulets of Jor and Daniel, not needing supplies from others, and therefore minding only their own ease and pleasure.

10. Given - This they gather partly from God's promise which they supposed they had from the Levite's mouth; and partly from his providence, which had so disposed them, that they would be an easy prey.

12. Mahaneh-dan - That is, the camp of Daniel.

13. To the house - That is, to the town in which his house was, for they were not yet entered into it.

14. Answered - That is, spake, the word answering being often used in scripture of the first speaker. These houses - That is, in one of these houses. What to do - Whether it be not expedient to take

them for your farther use.

17. Thither - Into the house, and that part of it, where those things were. The gate - Whither they had drawn him forth, that they might without noise or hindrance take them away.

18. These - The five men.

19. Lay thy hand - That is, be silent. A family - Namely, a tribe, that is, a family.

20. Was glad - Being wholly governed by his own interest. The midst - Both for the greater security of such precious things, and that Micah might not be able to come at him, to injure or upbraid him; and, it may be, because that was the place where the ark used to be carried.

21. Before them - For their greater security, if Micah should pursue them.

24. I made - So far was he besotted with superstition and idolatry, that he esteemed those gods, which were man's work. But he could not be so stupid, as to think these were indeed the great Jehovah that made heaven and earth; but only a lower sort of gods, by whom, as mediators, he offered up his worship to the true God, as divers of the Heathen did. What have I - I value nothing I have in comparison of what you have taken away. Which zeal for idolatrous trash may shame multitudes that call themselves Christians, and yet value their worldly conveniences more than all the concerns of their own salvation. Is Micah thus fond of his false gods? And how ought we to be affected toward the true God? Let us reckon our communion with God our greatest gain; and the loss of God the sorest loss. Wo unto us, if He depart! For what have we more.

25. Thy voice - Thy complaints and reproaches. Angry fellows - The soldiers, who are in themselves sharp and fierce, and will soon be enflamed by thy provoking words. Thy Life - Which, not withstanding all thy pretenses, thou dost value more than thy images.

27. Burnt - Not wholly, but in great measure, to make their conquest more easy.

28. And they built a city - That is, rebuilt it.

29. Of Daniel - That it might be manifest, that they belonged to the tribe of Daniel, though they were seated at a great distance from them, in the most northerly part of the land; whereas the lot of their tribe was in the southern part of Canaan.

30. Image - Having succeeded in their expedition according to the prediction which, as they supposed, they had from this image, they had a great veneration for it. The captivity - When the whole land of the ten tribes, whereof Daniel was one, was conquered, and the people carried captive by the Assyrian, 2 Kings xvii, 6, 23, which is called by way of eminency, the captivity. It is not said, that the graven image was there so long, for that is restrained to a shorter date, even to the continuance of the ark in Shiloh, ver. 31, which was removed thence, 1 Sam. iv, 3-5. But only that Jonathan's posterity, (so his name is at last mentioned) were priests to this tribe or family of Daniel, which they might be under all the changes, even 'till the Assyrian captivity, sometimes more openly, sometimes more secretly, sometimes in one way of idolatry, and sometimes in another.

XIX

The adultery of the Levite's concubine, ver. 1, 2. The reconciliation to her, and entertainment at her father's, ver. 3-9. His journey homeward as far as Gibeah, ver. 10-15. An Ephraimite takes him in, ver. 16-21. The men of Gibeah assault the house, ver. 22-24. They force his concubine to death, ver. 25-28. He sends notice of it to all the tribes of Israel, ver. 29, 30

1. A. concubine - Hebrew. a wife, a concubine, that is, such a concubine as was also his wife: called a concubine, only because she was not endowed. Perhaps he had nothing to endow her with, being himself only a sojourner.

2. Against him - That is, against her faith given to him. Went away - Either for fear of punishment; or, because her heart was alienated from him; wherein not only she sinned, but her father by connivance at her sin, and neglect of just endeavours for her reconciliation to her husband.

3. Friendly - To offer her pardon and reconciliation.

12. A stranger - That is, of a strange nation: which the Canaanites possess; for though the city Jerusalem had been taken by Caleb, chap. i, 8, yet the strong fort of Zion was still in their hands, whence it is likely they did much molest, and afterwards by God's permission, drive out the Israelites who dwelt there.

15. To lodge - Though they were soft and effeminate in other respects, yet they were hard-hearted to strangers, and at that time there were no public-houses in that country.

16. Ephraim - Whence also the Levite was, which enclined him to shew the more kindness to his country-man. Benjamites - This was indeed one of the cities belonging to the priests; but the cities which were given to the priests, and whereof they were owners, were not inhabited by the priests or Levites only, especially at this time when they were but few in number, but by many other persons of different professions.

18. House of the Lord - Which was in Shiloh. Thither he went, either because he lived there, for

that was in the tribe of Ephraim; or, rather, because he would there offer prayers and praises, and sacrifices to God, for his mercy in reconciling him and his wife.

20. Let all, &c. - It matters not whether thou wantest nothing or everything, I will take care to supply all thy wants.

21. Washed - As they used to do to travelers in those hot countries.

22. Merry - That is, refreshing themselves with the provisions set before them. Sons of belial - Children of the devil, wicked and licentious men.

23. Into my house - And therefore I am obliged to protect him by the laws of hospitality.

26. Fell down - Namely, dead; killed partly with grief of heart, and partly with excessive abuse. Thus the sin she formerly chose, ver. 2, is now her destruction; and though her husband pardoned her, God would punish her, at least as to this life.

29. Sent - By several messengers, with a relation of the fact.

30. Speak - Let us meet together, and seriously consider, and every one freely speak what is to be done in this case.

XX

The Levite's case heard in a general convention of the tribes, ver. 1-7. They resolve to avenge his quarrel, ver. 8-11. The Benjamites assemble in defense of the criminals, ver. 12-17. The defeat of Israel in the two first battles, ver. 18-25. They humble themselves before God, ver. 26-28. The total rout of the Benjamites, ver. 29-48.

1. All - That is, a great number, and especially the rulers of all the tribes, except Benjamin, ver. 3, 12. One man - That is, with one consent. Daniel, &c. - Daniel was the northern border of the land, near Lebanon; and Beersheba the southern border. Gilead - Beyond Jordan, where Reuben, Gad, and half Manasseh were. To the Lord - As to the Lord's tribunal: for God was not only present in the place where the ark and tabernacle was, but also in the assemblies of the gods, or Judges, Psalm lxxxii, 1, and in all places where God's name is recorded, Exod. xx, 24, and where two or three are met together in his name. Mizpeh - A place on the borders of Judah and Benjamin. This they chose, as a place they used to meet in upon solemn occasions, for its convenient situation for all the tribes within and without Jordan; and the being near the place where the fact was done, that it might be more throughly examined; and not far from Shiloh, where the tabernacle was, whither they might go or send.

2. Four hundred thousand - The number is here set down, to shew their zeal and forwardness in punishing such a villainy; the strange blindness of the Benjamites that durst oppose so great and united a Body; and that the success of battles depends not upon great numbers, seeing this great host was twice defeated by the Benjamites.

3. Heard - Like persons unconcerned and resolved, they neither went nor sent thither: partly for their own pride, and stubbornness; partly because as they were loth to give up any of their brethren to justice, so they presumed the other tribes would never proceed to war against them; and partly, from a Divine infatuation hardening that wicked tribe to their own destruction. Tell us - They speak to the Levite, and his servant, and his host, who doubtless were present upon this occasion.

5. Slain me - Except I would either submit to their unnatural lust, which I was resolved to withstand even unto death: or deliver up my concubine to them, which I was forced to do.

6. Folly - That is, a lewd folly; most ignominious and impudent wickedness.

7. Ye are - The sons of that holy man, who for one filthy action left an eternal brand upon one of his own sons: a people in covenant with the holy God, whose honour you are obliged to vindicate, and who hath expressly commanded you to punish all such notorious enormities.

8. His tent - That is, his habitation, until we have revenged this injury.

10. According, &c. - That we may punish them as such a wickedness deserves. In Israel - This is added as an aggravation, that they should do that in Israel, or among God's peculiar people, which was esteemed abominable even among the Heathen.

12. All the tribe - They take a wise and a just course, in sending to all the parts of the tribe, to separate the innocent from the guilty, and to give them a fair opportunity of preventing their ruin, by doing what their duty, honour, and interest obliged them to; by delivering up those vile malefactors, whom they could not keep without bringing the curse of God upon themselves.

13. Evil - Both the guilt and the punishment, wherein all Israel will be involved, if they do not punish it. Would not hearken - From the pride of their hearts, which made them scorn to submit to their brethren; from a conceit of their own valour; and from God's just judgment.

15. Were numbered - "How does this agree with the following numbers? For all that were slain of Benjamin were twenty-five thousand and one hundred men, ver. 35, and there were only six hundred that survived, ver. 47, which make only twenty-five thousand and seven hundred." The other thousand men were either left in some of their cities, where they were slain, ver. 48, or were cut off in the two

first battles, wherein it is unreasonable to think they had an unbloody victory: and as for these twenty-five thousand and one hundred men, they were all slain in the third battle.

16. Not miss - An hyperbolical expression, signifying, that they could do this with great exactness. And this was very considerable and one ground of the Benjamites confidence.

17. Men of Israel - Such as were here present, for it is probable they had a far greater number of men, being six hundred thousand before their entrance into Canaan.

18. Children of Israel - Some sent in the name of all. House of God - To Shiloh, which was not far from Mizpeh. Which - This was asked to prevent emulations and contentions: but they do not ask whether they should go against them, or no, for that they knew they ought to do by the will of God already revealed: nor yet do they seek to God for his help by prayer, and fasting, and sacrifice, as in all reason they ought to have done; but were confident of success, because of their great numbers, and righteous cause.

21. Destroyed, &c. - Why would God suffer them to have so great a loss in so good a cause? Because they had many and great sins reigning among themselves, and they should not have come to so great a work of God, with polluted hands, but should have pulled the beam out of their own eye, before they attempted to take that out of their brother Benjamin's eye: which because they did not, God doth it for them, bringing them through the fire, that they might be purged from their dross; it being probable that the great God who governs every stroke in battle, did so order things, that their worst members should be cut off, which was a great blessing to the whole common - wealth. And God would hereby shew, that the race is not to the swift, nor the battle to the strong. We must never lay that weight on an arm of flesh, which only the Rock of Ages will bear.

22. Encouraged - Hebrew. strengthened themselves, supporting themselves with the consciousness of the justice of their cause, and putting themselves in better order for defending themselves, and annoying their enemies.

23. Wept - Not so much for their sins, as for their defeat and loss. My brother-They impute their ill success, not to their own sins, but to their taking up arms against their brethren. But still they persist in their former neglect of seeking God's assistance in the way which he had appointed, as they themselves acknowledged presently, by doing those very things which now they neglected.

26. Fasted - Sensible of their not being truly humbled for their sins, which now they discover to be the cause of their ill success. Burnt, &c. - To make atonement to God for their own sins. Peace-offerings - To bless God for sparing so many of them, whereas he might justly have cut off all of them when their brethren were slain: to implore his assistance, yea and to give thanks for the victory, which now they were confident he would give them.

28. Phinehas - This is added to give us light about the time of this history, and to shew it was not done in the order in which it is here placed, after Samson's death, but long before. Stood - That is ministered as high-priest. The Lord said - When they sought God after the due order, and truly humbled themselves for their sins, he gives them a satisfactory answer.

29. Liers in wait - Though they were assured of the success, by a particular promise, yet they do not neglect the use of means; as well knowing that the certainty of God's promises doth not excuse, but rather require man's diligent use of all fit means for the accomplishment of them.

30. The children of Israel - That is, a considerable part of them, who were ordered to give the first onset, and then to counterfeit flight, to draw the Benjamites forth from their strong-hold. See ver. 32.

34. Chosen men - Selected out of the main body, which was at Baal-tamar; and these were to march directly to Gibeah on the one side, whilst the liers in wait stormed it on the other side, and whilst the great body of the army laboured to intercept the Benjamites, who having pursued the Israelites that pretended to flee, now endeavoured to retreat to Gibeah.

37. Drew along - Or, extended themselves; whereas before they lay close and contracted into a narrow compass, now they spread themselves, and marched in rank and file as armies do.

44. There fell - Namely, in the field, of battle.

45. Gleaned - That is, a metaphor from those who gather grapes or corn so clearly and fully, that they leave no relicks for those who come after them.

46. Twenty and five thousand - Besides the odd hundred expressed ver.

35, but here only the great number is mentioned, the less being omitted, as inconsiderable. Here are also a thousand more omitted, because he speaks only of them who fell in that third day of battle.

48. Turned again - Having destroyed those that came to Gibeah, and into the field, now they follow them home to their several habitations. Men - Comprehensively taken, so as to include women and children. If this seem harsh and bloody, either it may be ascribed to military fury; or perhaps it may be partly justified, from that command of God in a parallel case, Deut. xiii, 15, and from that solemn oath by which they had devoted to death all that came not up to Mizpeh, chap. xxi, 5, which none of the Benjamites did.

XXI

The lamentation of Israel over Benjamin, ver. 1-7. They procure wives for the remaining Benjamites of the virgins of Jabesh-Gilead, ver. 8-15. And of the daughters of Shiloh, ver. 16- 25.

1. Had sworn - In the beginning of this war, after the whole tribe had espoused the quarrel of the men of Gibeah. Saying - They do not here swear the utter extirpation of the tribe, which fell out beyond their expectation, but only not to give their daughters to those men who should survive; justly esteeming them for their villainy, to be as bad as Heathens, with whom they were forbidden to marry.

4. An altar - Not for a monument of the victory, but for sacrifices, as the next words shew. There might be in that place more altars than one, when the multitude of sacrifices be required, which was the case, 1 Kings viii, 64, and probably at this time, when all the tribes being met, they had many sacrifices to offer, some in common for all, and some peculiar to every tribe.

5. Great oath - That is a solemn oath joined with some terrible execration against the offenders herein. Put to death - Because by refusing to execute the vengeance due to such malefactors, they were justly presumed guilty of the crime, and therefore liable to the same punishment, as was the case of that city that would not deliver up an Idolater dwelling among them, to justice.

6. Repented - Not for the war, which was just and necessary, but for their immoderate severity in the execution of it. That is no good divinity which swallows up humanity. Even necessary justice is to be done with compassion.

15. The Lord, &c. - The Benjamites were the only authors of the sin, but God was the chief author of the punishment, and the Israelites were but his executioners.

17. An inheritance - The inheritance promised by Jacob and Moses, and given by Joshua to the tribe of Benjamin, doth all of it belong to those few who remain of that tribe, and cannot be possessed by any other tribe; and therefore we are obliged to procure wives for them all, that they may make up this breach, and be capable of possessing and managing all their land: that this tribe, and their inheritance may not be confounded with, or swallowed up by any of the rest.

19. A feast - Probably it was the feast of tabernacles, which they celebrated with more than ordinary joy. And that feast was the only season, at which the Jewish virgins were allowed to dance. But even this was not mixed dancing. No men danced with these daughters of Shiloh. Nor did the married women so forget their gravity, as to join with them. However their dancing thus in public, made them an easy prey: whence Bishop Hall observes, "The ambushes of evil spirits carry away many souls from dancing to a fearful desolation."

21. Daughters of Shiloh - By whom we may understand not those only who were born or settled inhabitants there, but all those who were come thither upon this occasion, and for a time sojourned there: for although only the males were obliged to go up to the three solemn feasts; yet the women had liberty to go, and those who were most devout did usually go. Vineyards - Which were near to the green where they danced. Catch - Take them away by force, which they might the better do, because the women danced by themselves.

23. And took, &c. - That is, each man his wife. By which we may see, they had no very favourable opinion of polygamy, because they did not allow it in this case, when it might seem most necessary for the reparation of a lost tribe. Repaired - By degrees, increasing their buildings as their number increased.

25. Right in his own eyes - What wonder was it then, if all wickedness overflowed the land? Blessed be God for magistracy!

John Wesley

NOTES ON THE BOOK OF RUTH

This short history fitly follows the book of Judges, the events related therein happening in the time of the Judges. It was probably wrote by Samuel. The design of it is,
1. To lead us to Providence, acknowledging God in all our ways;
2. To lead to Christ, who descended from Ruth, and part of whose genealogy concludes the book

I

Naomi removes to Moab, ver. 1, 2. Her husband and sons die, ver. 3-5. Designing to return to Bethlehem, she addresses her daughters-in-law, ver. 6-13. Orpah stays, but Ruth returns with her, ver. 14-18. They came to Bethlehem, ver. 19-22.

1. In the land - Of Canaan. It must be early: for Boaz was born of Rahab. So Christ descended from two Gentile mothers.
2. Ephrathites - Bethlehem was otherwise called Ephratha. Naomi signifies my amiable or pleasant one: Mahlon and Chilon signify sickness and consumption. Probably they were sickly children, and not likely to be long-lived. Such are the products of our pleasant things, weak and infirm, fading and dying.
4. Took wives - Either these were Proselytes when they married them, or they sinned in marrying them, and therefore were punished with short life, and want of issue.
5. Was left of her two sons, and her husband - Loss of children and widowhood are both come upon her. By whom shall she be comforted? It is God alone that is able to comfort those who are thus cast down.
6. Bread - That is, food; so she staid no longer there than necessity forced her.
8. Mother's house - Because daughters used to converse more frequently with their mothers, and to dwell in the same apartments with them, which then were distinct from those parts of the house where the men dwelt. The dead - With my sons, your husbands, while they lived.
11. Your husbands - According to the ancient custom, Gen. xxxviii, 8, and the express law of God, Deut. xxv, 5, which doubtless she had acquainted them with before, among other branches of the Jewish religion.
13. It grieveth me - That you are left without the comfort of husbands or children; that I must part with such affectionate daughters; and that my circumstances are such, that I cannot invite you to go alone with me. For her condition was so mean at this time, that Ruth, when she came to her mother's city, was forced to glean for a living. It is with me, that God has a controversy. This language becomes us, when we are under affliction; tho' many others share in the trouble, yet we are to hear the voice of the rod, as if it spake only to us. But did not she wish to bring them to the worship of the God of Israel? Undoubtedly she did. But she would have them first consider upon what terms, lest having set their hand to the plow, they should look back.
14. Kissed - Departed from her with a kiss. Bade her farewell forever. She loved Naomi, but she did not love her so well, as to quit her country for her sake. Thus many have a value for Christ, and yet come short of salvation by him, because they cannot find in their hearts, to forsake other things for him. They love him, and yet leave him, because they do not love him enough, but love other things better.
15. To her gods - Those that forsake the communion of saints, will certainly break off their communion with God. This she saith, to try Ruth's sincerity and constancy, and that she might intimate to her, that if she went with her, she must embrace the true religion.
17. There will I be buried - Not desiring to have so much as her dead body carried back into the land of Moab: but Naomi and she having joined souls, she desires they may mingle dust, in hopes of rising together, and remaining together forver. 18. Left speaking unto her - See the power of resolution! Those who are half- resolved, are like a door a-jar, which invites a thief. But resolution shuts and bolts he door, and then the devil flees from us.
19. Is this - Is this she that formerly lived in so much plenty and honour? How marvelously is her condition changed?
20. Naomi - Which signifies pleasant, and chearful. Mara - Which signifies bitter or sorrowful.
21. Full - With my husband and sons, and a plentiful estate for our support. Testified - That is,

hath born witness, as it were, in judgment, and given sentence against me.

II

Providence directs Ruth to glean in Boaz's field, ver. 1-3. The favour which Boaz shewed her, ver. 4-16. Her return to Naomi, ver. 17-23.

2. Glean - Which was permitted to the poor, and the stranger, Deut. xxiv, 19, nor was she ashamed to confess her poverty, nor would she eat the bread of idleness. In whose sight - For though it was their duty to permit this, yet she thought it might perhaps be denied her; at least, that it became her modestly and humbly to acknowledge their kindness herein.

3. Her hap - It was a chance in reference to second causes, but ordered by God's providence. God wisely orders small events, even those that seem altogether contingent. Many a great affair is brought about by a little turn, fortuitous as to men, but designed by God.

4. Said,&c. - They expressed their piety, even in their civil conversation, and worldly transactions; which now so many are ashamed of.

7. I pray - She did not boldly intrude herself, but modestly ask leave of us. 'Till now - She is not retired through idleness, for she hath been diligent and constant in her labours. The house - In the little house or tent, which was set up in the fields at these times, and was necessary in those hot countries, where the labourers might retire for a little repose or repast. Being weary with her continued labours, she comes hither to take a little rest.

8. Maidens - Not by the young men, to avoid both occasion of sin, and matter of scandal. Herein he shews his piety and prudence.

9. Touch - So as to offer any incivility or injury to thee.

10. Fell - This was the humblest posture of reverence, either civil when performed to men, or religious, when to God. Take knowledge - That is, shew any respect and kindness to me.

12. Wings - That is, protection and care. An allusion either to hens, which protect and cherish their young ones under their wings; or to the wings of the Cherubim, between which God dwelt.

13. Tho' I be not - I humbly implore the continuance of thy good opinion of me, though I do not deserve it, being a person more mean, necessitous, and, obscure, a stranger, and one born of heathen parents, and not of the holy and honourable people of Israel, as they are.

14. She sat - Not with or among them, but at some little distance from them, as one inferior to them. It is no disparagement to the finest hand, to be reached forth to the needy.

17. An Ephah - About a bushel.

18. Reserved - At dinner, after she had eaten and was sufficed, or satisfied.

19. Where hast thou gleaned today? - It is a good question to ask ourselves in the evening, "Where have I gleaned today?" What improvements have I made in grace or knowledge? What have I learned or done, which will turn to account?

20. To the dead - That is, which he formerly shewed to those who are now dead, my husband and his sons whilst they were living, and now continues to us.

21. Harvest - Both barley-harvest, and wheat-harvest. She tells what kindness Boaz had shewed her; but not, how he had commended her. Humility teaches not only not to praise ourselves, but not to be forward in repeating the praise which others have given us.

22. Other field - Whereby thou wilt both expose thyself to many inconveniences, which thou mayst expect from strangers; and incur his displeasure, as if thou didst despise his kindness.

III

The directions Naomi gives to Ruth, ver. 1-5. Her punctual observance of them, ver. 6, 7. The honourable treatment which Boaz gave her, ver. 8-15. Her return to Naomi, ver. 16-18.

1. Rest - A life of rest, and comfort, and safety, under the care of a good husband.

2. Threshing-floor - Which was in a place covered at the top, but open elsewhere, whither Ruth might easily come. And this work of winnowing corn was usually ended with a feast.

3. Raiment - Thy best raiment. Known - In so familiar a way, as thou mayest do hereafter.

4. Uncover his feet - Remove the clothes that were upon his feet; thereby to awaken him. Will tell thee - What course thou shalt take to obtain that marriage which belongs unto thee.

8. At midnight - He did not discover her sooner.

9. Spread thy Skirt - That is, take me to be thy wife, and perform the duty of an husband to me.

10. Shewed kindness - Both to thy deceased husband, the continuance of whose name and memory thou seekest; and to thy mother-in-law, whose commands thou hast punctually obeyed. Followedst not - To seek thy marriage here, or in thy own country, as thou wouldst have done if thou hadst not preferred

obedience to God's command, before pleasing thyself.

13. Perform, &c. - Take thee to wife, to raise up seed to his brother. Bishop Hall sums up the matter thus. "Boaz, instead of touching her as a wanton, blesseth her as a father, encourages her as a friend, promises her as a kinsman, rewards her as a patron, and sends her away laden with hopes and gifts, no less chast, but more happy than she came. O admirable temperance, worthy the progenitor of him, in whose lips and heart there was no guile!"

14. Let it not, &c. - He takes care to preserve not only his conscience towards God, but his reputation, and hers also, among men.

15. Veil - Or, the apron.

16. Who art thou? - This is not a question of doubting, but of wonder, as if she had said, Art thou in very deed my daughter? I can hardly believe it. How camest thou hither in this manner, and thus early?

IV

The next kinsman refuses to marry Ruth, ver. 1-8. Boaz marries her, ver. 9-12. Their issue, ver. 13-22.

2. Ten men - To be witnesses: for though two or three witnesses were sufficient, yet in weightier matters they used more. And ten was the usual number among the Jews, in causes of matrimony and divorce, and translation of inheritances; who were both Judges of the causes, and witnesses of the fact.

3. Naomi - Both Naomi and Ruth had an interest in this land during their lives, but he mentions only Naomi, because all was done by her direction; lest the mention of Ruth should raise a suspicion of the necessity of his marrying Ruth, before he had given his answer to the first proposition.

5. Buy it - According to the law, Deut. xxv, 5. To raise,&c. - To revive his name, which was buried with his body, by raising up a seed to him, to be called by his name.

6. Mar - Either because having no children of his own, he might have one, and but one son by Ruth, who, though he should carry away his inheritance, yet would not bear his name, but the name of Ruth's husband; and so by preserving another man's name, he should lose his own. Or, because as his inheritance would be but very little increased by this marriage, so it might be much diminished by being divided amongst his many children, which he possibly had already, and might probably have more by Ruth. My right - Which I freely resign to thee.

7. All things - That is, in all alienation of lands. So that it is no wonder if this ceremony differ a little from that, Deut. xxv, 9, because that concerned only one case, but this is more general. Besides, he pleads not the command of God, but only ancient custom, for this practice. Gave it - He who relinquished his right to another, plucked off his own shoe and gave it to him. This was symbolical, and a significant and convenient ceremony, as if he said, take this shoe wherewith I used to go and tread upon my land, and in that shoe do thou enter upon it, and take possession of it. This was a testimony - This was admitted for sufficient evidence in all such cases.

10. From the gate - That is, from among the inhabitants dwelling within the gate of this city, which was Bethlehem-judah.

11. Rachel and Leah - Amiable and fruitful. These two are singled out, because they were of a foreign original, and yet ingrafted into God's people, as Ruth was; and because of that fertility which God vouchsafed unto them above their predecessors, Sarah and Rebecca. Rachel is placed before Leah, because she was his most lawful, and best-beloved wife. Did build - That is, increase the posterity. Ephratah and Bethlehem - Two names of one and the same place.

12. Pharez - As honourable and numerous as his family was; whom, though be also was born of a stranger, God so blessed, that his family was one of the five families to which all the tribe of Judah belonged, and the progenitor of the inhabitants of this city.

13. Took Ruth - Which he might do, though she was a Moabite, because the prohibition against marrying such, is to be restrained to those who continue Heathens; whereas Ruth was a sincere proselyte and convert to the God of Israel. Thus he that forsakes all for Christ, shall find more than all with him.

14. Which hath not, &c. - The words may be rendered, Which hath not made, or suffered thy kinsman to fail thee; that is, to refuse the performances of his duty to thee and thine, as the other kinsman did. Famous - Hebrew. and his name shall be famous in Israel, for this noble and worthy action.

15. Thy life - That is, of the comfort of thy life. Born him - Or, hath born to him; that is, to thy kinsman a son. Better than seven sons - See how God sometimes makes up the want of those relations from whom we expected most comfort, in those from whom we expected least! The bonds of love prove stronger than those of nature.

17. A name - That is, they gave her advice about his name; for otherwise they had no power or right to do so. Obed - A servant, to thee, to nourish, and comfort, and assist thee; which duty children owe to their progenitors.

www.ingramcontent.com/pod-product-compliance
Lightning Source LLC
Chambersburg PA
CBHW020639230426
43665CB00008B/231